ETHIOPIA

A New Political History

Richard Greenfield

PALL MALL PRESS · LONDON

Published by the Pall Mall Press Ltd.
5 Cromwell Place, London, S.W.7

© 1965 RICHARD GREENFIELD

First published 1965
Second Impression, revised, 1967

African paperback edition 1969

SBN 269 16333 6

The author wishes to confirm that where rumours are quoted in the text it is because the circulation of such rumours affected public opinion in Ethiopia, and therefore effectively influenced the development of events. Where the author defines an allegation as a 'rumour' it is because he regards it as unfounded in fact. In the majority of cases this is specifically stated in the text.

Made and printed in Great Britain by
The Garden City Press Limited
Letchworth, Hertfordshire

This book is dedicated to those Ethiopians
my former students and my friends
who led me to love their country

Into their hands there fast devolves
the building of
a new Ethiopia

Contents

Contents

Maps

'Encompassed on all sides by the enemies of their religion, the Ethiopians slept near a thousand years, forgetful of the world by whom they were forgotten'
—GIBBON, *The Decline and Fall of the Roman Empire,* ch. xlvii, London, 1788

'The Ethiopian people have a history of more than three thousand years; but in that long history no progress was made in agriculture, commerce or industry . . . The Ethiopian people manifested great patience, such patience as is unknown in any other nation, and they waited in the hope that betterment would come from day to day. Nevertheless there is no nation which in time would not extirpate ignorance from among its people and not aim at improving the standard of living. While the newly formed independent African nations are making progress, Ethiopia is lagging behind and this fact is now realised.'— *From a radio paraphrase of an Amharic speech read by* CROWN PRINCE ASFA WOSSEN, *December 14, 1960*

Prologue

'Great Prince,' said *Imlak, 'I shall speak the truth.'*—
SAMUEL JOHNSON *Rasselas, The Prince of Abissinia,* London,
1759

*'... this empire hath been shaken in these later ages. We
may justly believe that, like all others, it has suffered its
revolutions . . .'*—FATHER JEROME LOBO, A Voyage to
Abyssinia, Coimbra, 1659 (the original is lost)

Hailé Sellassié I, Conquering Lion of the Tribe of Judah, Elect of
God and King of the Kings of Ethiopia, was in Brazil on a state
visit when many of the leading ministers and dignitaries in his
country were rounded up one Tuesday night in December 1960. On
Wednesday a surprised world heard over the radio that the heir
apparent, Crown Prince Asfa Wossen, had been proclaimed constitutional monarch of Ethiopia and leading figures known for their
progressive views—the Emperor's ageing cousin, Leul-Ras Imru,
and Major-general Mulugeta Bulli—had been appointed to high
office. Hailé Sellassié turned for home. On Thursday it became
obvious that the attempt at a peaceful *coup d'état* was about to
miscarry, fighting broke out and by Friday evening, when the
Emperor landed in Asmara, several leading ministers and dignitaries had been killed, the rebels had been defeated and the Revolution was over. At that time most Ethiopians had scarcely begun
to understand what had occurred.

The ringleaders of the abortive *coup* were Girmamé Neway,
intellectual, American-trained graduate and governor of Ji-Jigga,
and his brother, Brigadier-general Mengistu Neway, Commander of
the Imperial Guard. They led a small group of officers and civilians
conspicuous amongst whom was Lieutenant-colonel Workneh

Gebeyehu, vice chief of staff of the Emperor's private cabinet and head of the security service, and the general commanding the police force.

Revolutions are rarely popular movements, but they are frequently landmarks in the history of nations. In few countries is this suggested more obviously than in Ethiopia, where in conversation and thought the articulate sections of the population have come to refer constantly to the attempted *coup* of December 1960. This book endeavours to explain why this is so. But there is also the point that a revolutionary situation can and frequently does exist both before and after its supporters have found the force with which to express themselves and an atmosphere of internal unrest has certainly typified Ethiopia since 1960. Indeed, before he was hanged on March 20, 1961, the general who had led the attempted *coup* is said by some to have remarked, 'I go to tell the others that the seed we set has taken root'. Far from being discouraged by the aura of secrecy imposed by the traditionalist régime, it seems probable that in Addis Ababa and other Ethiopian towns the memory of the events of December 1960 is already growing into a national myth.

There have been *coups*, revolutions and political assassinations throughout Ethiopia's long history but the abortive Revolution of 1960 was different in one vital respect. Its leaders sought not merely to displace the then national leaders but to reform and remould the whole system and motivation of government. It may be said that in December 1960 Africa's 'wind of change' reached even the remoteness of the Ethiopian High Plateau.

Even if it is too early for the student to assess the full extent of its historical importance, few observers would deny that this attempted revolution marked the awakening of a new political consciousness in Ethiopia. If no more than a beginning to be overshadowed by events to come, nevertheless, it is already a psychological landmark in the political thinking of the growing number of Ethiopians who are aware of Africa and of the outside world. For this reason the author treats it as a turning point around which to discuss the complex politics and hence also the history of Ethiopia.

Ethiopia is an ancient country and no attempt to understand its complicated internal politics and the motivations of the several groups and interests involved could even begin without some examination of their roots which, since Ethiopia was not affected by the colonial era in the same way as the rest of Africa, extend far back into the history and mythology of that land. For this reason the emphases of this book are bound to differ from those adopted in studies of other African nations in the present series.

Young Ethiopia today wants very much to be understood in her struggle to emerge from the dark ages of a particular brand of African feudalism, to move towards a greater degree of social justice and to hasten economic development. Significantly young Ethiopians endeavour to see this as part of what they feel to be, and what indeed may be, the most remarkable renaissance that the world has known—the stirring of the African continent of which Ethiopia, even if her older generation has been reluctant to admit it, is an integral and now committed part. In this sense the holding of the first African Summit Conference in Addis Ababa in 1963, even though it added immensely to the stature of Emperor Hailé Sellassié, was essentially a triumph for the young intellectuals and for the new patterns of thought in Addis Ababa.

For their part, the older conservative generation have their reasons for acting as they do and are sometimes no more guilty of misunderstanding the young than *vice versa*. It is worth remembering that had the Italian fascist invaders not systematically destroyed many of the first fruits of modern education in Ethiopia one quarter of a century ago, the gulf between conservative and radical, between old and young, might not be nearly so marked.

A few commentators have written and many Ethiopians have urged in private that the time has come for sympathetic but critical re-examination of the politics and the present world image of the proud old realm in the wild mountains of north-eastern Africa, more especially in view of recent developments and the changing environment of the great African continent itself. Towards such a re-appraisal the author offers this book.

I

ETHIOPIAN ROOTS

1

Earliest Times

*They tell us this is a table land. If it is, they have turned
the table upside down and we are scrambling up and down
the legs.*—A British soldier on Ethiopian scenery—during
the Napier Expedition, 1867–8

*. . . Men of science today are, with few exceptions, satisfied
that Africa was the birth-place of man himself and that for
many hundreds of centuries thereafter Africa was in the
forefront of all world progress . . .*—Dr LEAKEY, The
Herbert Spencer Lecture at the University of Oxford.
February 10, 1961

THE MOUNTAIN FASTNESS

Ethiopia has been called Africa's Switzerland and she has also been
called Africa's Tibet. Both parallels are to some extent true.
Ethiopia is a land of awe-inspiring mountains, isolated plateaux
and precipitous valleys. Even today mention of this ancient Empire
conjures up mystery and fascination in the minds of men and
sometimes there is almost resentment at Ethiopia's periodic aloof-
ness from the political currents of a wider world. Her scenery, like
her people, has a long and interesting history resulting in variety
and splendour unique in the whole of Africa.

Many scientists believe that the history of Africa began
countless ages ago when there existed an extensive continent in the
southern hemisphere, which they call Gondwanaland. This vast
continent broke up and the separating parts foundered or drifted
away from one another. The largest fragment forms the present
basement or skeleton of the great African continent. Long before
the advent of man on this planet the winds, the beating rain, and

all the forces of weather wore away vast thicknesses of the surface rocks of Africa, sometimes revealing metal ores formerly miles deep in the crust. If especially in the colonial era now drawing to a close, these ores have contributed much to the relative prosperity of great areas of the continent, the manner of their exploitation by man has led to great misery. This is as true of Ethiopia's gold as of South Africa's diamonds or Katanga's copper. The waste surface rock was carried away to the seashore and to the lakes by the rivers and streams of ancient Africa. The seashores themselves changed their position as earth movements caused parts of the continent to rise or fall and as the sea levels changed. The sea frequently encroached across that north-eastern section of Africa which we know today as Ethiopia. On the top of the old basement rocks, muds and shales, red sandstones and white limestones were laid down in those seas and they now lend colour to the scenery of Ethiopia.

The geological history, like the later human history, sometimes erupted into violence. Some thirty million years ago a tremendous series of volcanic eruptions poured hot lava flows over vast areas. Growing volcanoes and great vents in the earth poured forth lava, throwing up large fragments which burst like bombs and scattered their molten contents over the earlier flows and ash or cinder beds which themselves covered the country to great depth. This long spasm of terrestrial convulsion happened at the time of an arching up of the whole of the eastern Horn of Africa. The highlands so formed attracted the rain and having increased the gradients of the rivers, so renewed their energies that they cut their valleys through the grey and black lavas and the bands of red ash into the sandstones and limestones below. Sometimes they even eroded down to the ancient basement rock itself. The highlands of present-day Ethiopia are thus dissected by enormous gorges and canyons thousands of feet deep, the largest and most spectacular of which is the valley of the Abbai (or Blue Nile as it is called in Europe). Except where piles of volcanic lava formed great mountain ranges, the intervening areas were left as flat-topped plateaux, called by the Ethiopians *ambas*. Many are completely isolated one from another or are only joined by the narrowest necks of land between great precipices. Before the days of the helicopter these islands were completely inaccessible, and even the helicopter is none too safe a vehicle since the altitude of the *amba* mountain blocks is often near that aeroplane's safety ceiling and the rotor blades cannot grip the thin but clear and exhilarating air.

The fragmented nature of the highlands of Ethiopia has played a great part in the country's history. Isolated and mountainous plateau massifs have proved, to date, almost insurmountable obstacles to the kings who sought to unify the country, to the invaders who sought to conquer it and to those who have sporadically attempted to develop its economic resources. Isolation, only now beginning to break down, from the contacts and currents of modern Africa, has led to a fierce independence of spirit in many areas where the pattern of life has remained unchanged for hundreds of years and where the central government still has only limited influence.

The roof of the enormous arch in the earth's crust in the region of present-day Ethiopia has subsided to form part of the Great Rift valley, which extends from the Biblical lands through Eastern Africa south almost to the Zambesi river and in passing it divides the highlands of Ethiopia. The Ethiopian sector of the Rift valley is perhaps more interesting and, in places, certainly more spectacular than the others. The purple and blue bastions of its escarpments seem to delimit another world when they appear through the heat haze along the margins of the lowland deserts and rise sheer from the farther bank of the lonely waters of the beautiful Rift valley lakes, the surfaces of which subtly vary in colour due to the different depths, species of microscopic algae and salinity.

The nomads of the hot Danakil deserts and the farmers of the cool mountains of Shewa, Gojjam and Tigré; the fishermen of the coast of Eritrea; the collectors in the coffee forests of Jimma and the hunters in the wet tropical forests farther to the south-west, are as varied in their customs and livelihood as is the scenery itself. But nowhere are the human and scenic contrasts more marked than along the edges of the vast Rift valley escarpments. To the north-east the Rift valley broadens like a funnel to join the Red Sea and part of this region, the Danakil Depression, lies below sea level. There are active volcanoes, glaring saltpans, marshes and deserts of volcanic dust and rubble. The scene is one of violently contrasting blacks, whites and yellows quite removed from the soft greens, browns and mauves of the temperate climate of the plateau, for the Danakil or Afar desert is one of the hottest places on earth. Clear of the Rift valley the Red Sea is itself bordered by massive but eroded fault escarpments, and it separates Ethiopia from similar deserts and mountain terrain in Arabia but, as will be shown, this did not preclude early cultural contact.

All the high mountains of Ethiopia are volcanic in origin— the highest point is probably Bejeda (Ras Dashan), some 15,150 feet high in the Simien mountains. Sometimes the heat-hardened central pipes of old volcanoes, the rest of which have long since

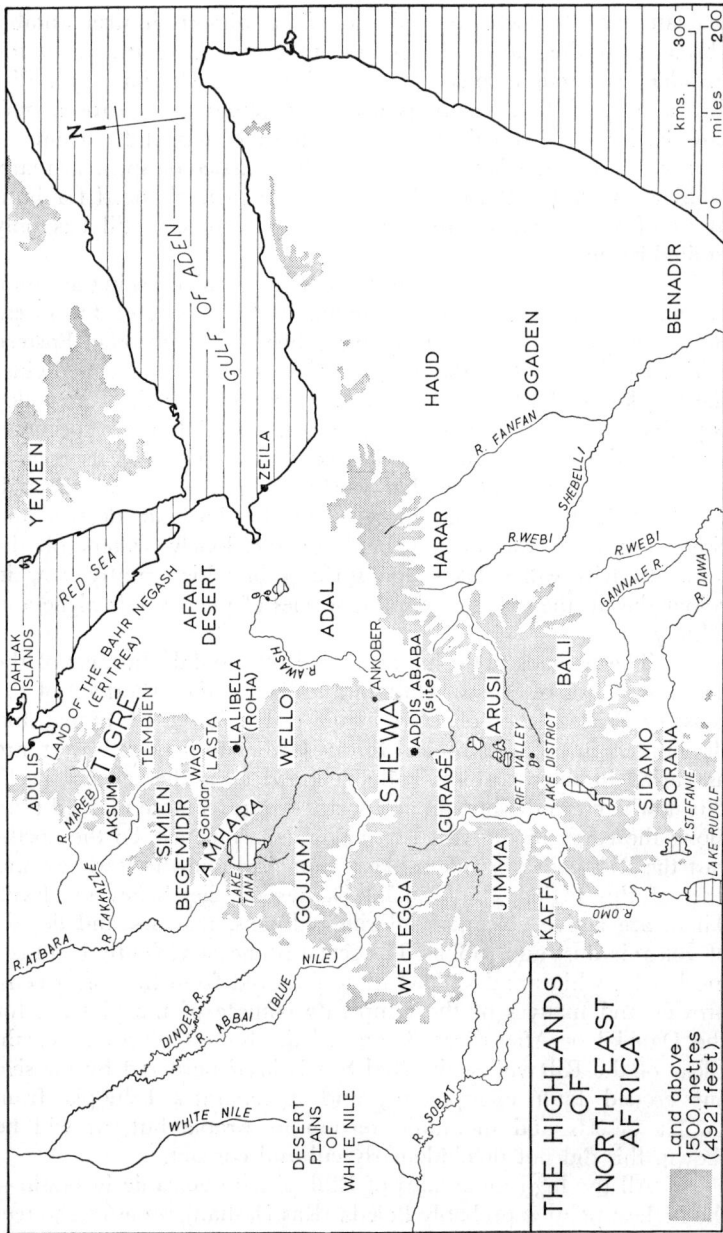

THE HIGHLANDS
OF
NORTH EAST
AFRICA

Land above
1500 metres
(4921 feet)

been eroded away, stand out as great vertical or even overhanging necks of rock, hundreds of feet high, forming mountains of weird and unbelievable shapes. In the Middle Ages the Princes of the Blood were confined to the summit of one of a succession of such features, one being Mount Wehni in the Gondar region, and were removed one at a time in order to avoid disputes over the succession. An Englishman, Thomas Pakenham, recently visited the foot of Mount Wehni but it was left to an intrepid Australian, Barbara Toy, to examine the summit of the mountain prison by the only possible way—a daring jump from a helicopter. The staircase had long since crumbled away. Mountains of such fantastic shape are common in the province of Begemidir, in the Tsellemti mountains (the northern foothills of the Simien mountains), or in the ranges near Adowa. There an Italian army was crushingly defeated in 1896 in a battle which left the flag of independent Africa still flying, by then the only one, in the wild mountain fastness of the Ethiopians.

The plateau to the west of the Rift valley is often described as the Abyssinian plateau because it includes the heartlands of ancient Abyssinia; Tigré and Gondar, and more recently Gojjam and Shewa. The plateau east of the Rift valley is usually referred to by geographers as the Somali plateau, but the actual frontier with the Somali Republic is farther east beyond the Ethiopian province of Harar which includes the Ogaden lowlands. The political empire now includes Eritrea, federated with Ethiopia in 1951 through the good offices of the United Nations, but subsequently completely absorbed and since 1962 regarded as but another province of Ethiopia—and stretches of lower land on all approaches to the plateau. For the whole country the term Ethiopia is usually used and, similarly, the people prefer the term Ethiopian rather than Abyssinian and have in fact always used it when seeking a collective noun to include all the peoples of the empire.

Snow-capped mountains have repeatedly been reported in the literature on Ethiopia, but there are none today. Snow still falls on the Simien and it can lie, especially in the hollows, for many days. Hail also accumulates on ledges on the upper levels of many of the higher mountains, but in the days of the last Ice Age (those of the Pleistocene Period) when ice-caps extended over much of North America, Europe and Asia, and when the existing ice-cap remnants of Africa's great mountains—Kilimanjaro, Mount Kenya and the Ruwenzoris—extended to considerably lower altitudes, there were permanent ice-caps on several of Ethiopia's mountain ranges.

THE PEOPLING OF ETHIOPIA

More significant, however, is the fact that since those glacial times began, a million and a half or more years ago, there have been several periods of heavier rain-fall in eastern Africa—termed 'pluvials' from the Latin word for rain. Today all that remains from these times are lake beds, great flat plains and marshes surrounding shrunken if still existing lakes throughout Kenya, Uganda, Tanganyika and Ethiopia.

The remains of early men or near men have for some time been recognised in limestone caves in the Transvaal. Recently, in long dried out lake beds exposed in the Olduvai Gorge in northern Tanganyika, Dr and Mrs Leakey have discovered what may be the earliest human remains so far found in Africa. The old lake beds of Ethiopia have yet to be explored, but the author has seen bones, stone implements and pottery embedded in them in more than one place. Stone Age rock paintings exist in rock shelters in Ethiopia, as they do in many parts of Africa and even primitive 'paint brushes' have been found. Indeed it may be assumed that the pattern of early human development differed little in the highlands of present-day Tanganyika, Kenya and Ethiopia. Research work has hardly begun in the fields of pre-history, but several sites are known and it is already clear that Ethiopia was a vital area of crucial importance in the understanding of the patterns of the rest of eastern Africa.

Although it is most probable that the human race itself originated in Africa, their beginnings and early migrations are lost in the mists which surround the earliest history of mankind. The bushman and his forerunners and the pygmy peoples were among the earliest inhabitants and in remote refuges in the inhospitable and undeveloped desert and forest areas of Africa their descendants have survived to this day. It is not widely known that there are probably pygmies in the forests of south-west Ethiopia, though this is hardly surprising for those areas are not far removed in terms of African distances from the forests of the basin of the river Congo which one more often associates with African pygmies. There are also traditions and evidences of the previous existence of small people in the forest refuges of nearly all the great East African volcanoes.

Major W. Cornwallis Harris, a British emissary to King Sahlé Sellassié of Shewa, the great-grandfather of Hailé Sellassié I, in a description based on the words of slaves from the south, wrote in 1844 :

Beyond the extensive wilderness which bounds Kaffa on the
south are the Doko, a pygmy and perfectly wild race not ex-
ceeding four feet in height, of a dark olive complexion and in
habits even more closely approximated to 'the beasts that
perish' than the bushmen of Southern Africa. . . . Many
natives of Kaffa and Enarea who have visited these pygmies
in their native wilds, for evil, describe the road from the former
kingdom to pass through forests and mountains for the most
part uninhabited and swarming with wild beasts, elephants
and buffaloes especially. . . . The country inhabited by the
Doko is clothed with a dense forest of bamboo in the depths of
which the people construct their rude wigwams of bent canes
and grass. . . . Both sexes go perfectly naked. . . .

The Doko, also called Dumé, are referred to again by an
American visitor of fifty years later.[1] He states, 'pygmies I believe
inhabited the whole of the country north of Lakes Stefanie and
Rudolf long before any of the other tribes now to be found in
Africa. . . .' He mentions that being not quite pure-blooded they
are somewhat taller and darker than pygmies elsewhere in Africa
and that they used bows with poisoned arrows. He saw them north
of Lake Stefanie.

Within the last few years an engineer supervising the clearing of an airstrip in the remote south-west was surprised to see a
buck fleeing over the new runway pursued at great speed by three
tiny naked men. Mr John Tiffin, formerly the geography specialist
from the General Wingate School, Addis Ababa, led a small party
into the district in 1960, and although he was forbidden by local
officers to penetrate as far as he wished, one district governor
confirmed the existence of 'little men'.

However, the vast number of stone tools and implements
already mentioned which may be found throughout Ethiopia,
although they await proper scientific study, are better evidence that
human beings occupied the area since very early times. Near Dira
Dawa, a railway town in the Rift valley, part of the jaw of a man
who lived ten to fifteen thousand years ago has been discovered, but
there must be older human remains yet to be uncovered. It is not
certain who the earliest inhabitants were but very possibly they
were the forerunners of the bushman remnants of Africa today—
such as those of the Kalahari desert in the south, or the smaller
groups of Kenya and Tanganyika. The word 'bushman' itself may
be a corruption of a word for 'man' and it is certain that bushmen
once lived in areas other than the inhospitable refuges in which
they are to be found today.

Somewhat different from the bushmen are the peoples termed Symbiotic Hunters of whom there are several groups in north-eastern and eastern Africa. In Ethiopia they are represented by the Watta, perhaps related to the Dorobo of Kenya and other peoples. They are survivals of an early stock.[2] Negro peoples are known to have lived in the region of Khartoum for thousands of years before Christ and the 'Shankalla' of western Ethiopia are, in fact, descendants of these peoples.

The history of mankind has been punctuated by several major breakthroughs in skill and technology such as the discovery of how to make and improve bone and stone implements; how to control and create fire; how to cook and make pottery; how to domesticate animals (previously only hunted), and how to cultivate plant life (previously only collected). A more recent illustration—probably from Asia—was the discovery of how to write and modern examples would include the Industrial and the Atomic Revolutions. It is not always remembered, however, that several of the earlier discoveries probably occurred in Africa and were made by Africans.

It is often assumed that the Hamitic-Semitic peoples,* four-fifths of whom are to be found in Africa and which include the Berbers, the ancient Egyptians and the Kushites of Ethiopia, were all invaders, but this is by no means established. The original dispersal, perhaps 8,000 years or more BC, may well have centred from an African heartland even within the boundaries of modern Ethiopia.

In the fourth millennium BC the beginnings of agriculture which may well have developed independently in several places in the world, appear to have been extended to Ethiopia from the western Sudan.[3] It may have been introduced into that area from Egypt or it may have developed there independently in the fifth millennium. At any rate it was quite possibly of north-east African origin. Several valuable crops of today are indigenous to the Horn of Africa.

There is abundant evidence that in Ethiopia, as elsewhere, Stone Age cultures succeeded one after another and one day doubtless they will be recognised and correlated with established successions farther south.† Apart from the Ethiopian lake district already

---

* The first of these peoples have also been called 'Proto-Hamites'. There is considerable disagreement—even confusion—over the terminology best used to describe the peoples and peopling of Africa and several terms— such for example as 'Bantu'—are merely linguistic.

† For instance, the author recently introduced Dr Leakey of the Coryn-don Museum, Nairobi, to stone implements and pottery fragments discovered by Mr C. Webb, who has unfortunately now left Ethiopia, which Dr Leakey was immediately able to correlate with the Wilton A New

mentioned, other areas are rich in worked artefacts, for example the flanks of Wachacha, a vast volcanic mountain near Addis Ababa. Early man often settled on the rims of the volcanic explosion craters which are found in several areas not far south of the capital. Nearly always, but not invariably, he used the beautiful black volcanic glass called obsidian for his tools. These stone industries have lasted until comparatively recent times in many areas and, in fact, well into historical times at Djebel Djinn in the French Somaliland colony. Two years ago an Ethiopian provided the author with fine slivers of obsidian which he was able to use effectively as razors while camping near the Rift valley lakes.

Village farming communities developed in Ethiopia in the Neolithic period. In the south-west, decorated ceramics and even some metal implements have been found in association with the stone tools. It is likely that after 3,000 BC the Negro peoples of the west moved into what is now Wellegga and thence on to the plateau, bringing agriculture with them. The Agau of Ethiopia are an example of an early, now substrate population. They may be found today in the north and central areas of the Abyssinian highland plateau and now they only use their own language amongst themselves and are physically indistinguishable from their neighbours. They were quick to learn and instigate early developments in agriculture. They discovered and developed new strains of plants, some introduced from the west, and they ennobled many of the wild plants of the plateau. They domesticated the donkey and discovered how to breed mules.

The plateau peoples diversified into three main groups which linguistic and other anthropologists refer to as the Central Agau, and the Western and Eastern Cushites. Towards the end of the second millennium what is usually described as a population explosion occurred, doubtless as a result of the use of new techniques to overcome the problems presented by the physical environment, and the most southerly of the Cushitic population expanded and fanned out through Uganda, Kenya, Tanganyika and beyond. This was before the migrations of the Bantu-speaking peoples which were subsequently to affect the southern part of Ethiopia and all the other African countries to the south. It is probable that Cushitic peoples were responsible for the phallic stones of southern Ethiopia (there is one in Addis Ababa on the slopes of the Entotto escarpment) and of the coast of north-east and eastern Africa. Submerged remnants of the Cushitic peoples in east and central Africa are

Stone Age culture of southern and eastern Africa. Dr Leakey then predicted the subsequent discovery of large numbers of microliths in association with the scrapers he was shown.

probably still identifiable in refuges such as highland areas, despite subsequent population movements and developments.*

There are many similarities between the Ethiopian peoples and other Africans farther to the south. It is quite wrong, but a common error, to consider the Ethiopians to be racially a Middle Eastern people just because they draw much of their culture and languages from 'invasions' or migrations from southern Arabia, which occurred subsequent to the period described above. Racially these invasions could have made nothing like the impact on the people of Ethiopia that the great waves of Bantu migration made farther south. It is of course culturally correct for Ethiopian historical and linguistic studies to be dealt with as they have been up to the present time by learned societies and publications dealing with Middle Eastern and Oriental studies. However, Ethiopian studies must also be very definitely included in the new and growing field of African studies—out of right and not merely because the new generation of Ethiopians is more conscious of the rest of Africa than the old.[4]

CULTURAL INFLUENCES FROM ARABIA

In all probability there had long been movement of peoples from Arabia but at the beginning of the first millennium BC, probably still well before the first movements of the Bantu-speakers, there began several centuries of influx of Sabaean peoples from across the Red Sea into northern Ethiopia, nowadays known as Eritrea, bringing new skills in agriculture and trade. There does not appear to have been any great unity amongst their settlements for many years. The remains of old cities and trade routes are scattered throughout Eritrea and northern Tigré—which are culturally synonymous. Research work in this region is in its infancy, yet though so much is conjectural it is already abundantly clear that northern Ethiopia was a very important site of early African civilisation.

Archaeological finds, monuments and some short inscriptions dating from the fifth or sixth century BC have been studied and described and they show that a succession of civilisations existed in northern Ethiopia from even before those times and well before the rise of the now famous Aksumite civilisation. Yeha in northern Tigré is one example. Matara is another and there are many more. Yeha, once the political centre of the north, is one of

* Many who know the Chagga peoples of Kilimanjaro intimately have noticed physical similarities to Ethiopians. Others have said the same of other highland peoples of East Africa.

several important sites where monuments, inscriptions, pottery and bronze tools have been found.

It has until recent years been a characteristic of research workers in Africa to attribute almost every African achievement to one or other 'foreign influence' and Ethiopia has been no exception to this. However, discoveries at Yeha and elsewhere are now seen to demonstrate an extremely inventive and local craftwork. Several fragments of inscriptions exist in a Sabaean type of epigraphy. At the time of its discovery one was seen to be older than any other then known, including those found in Arabia. Others show distinct features of local Ethiopian origin. This is not to say that Africa's early civilisations were not influenced by the neighbours with whom they came into contact—of course they were—but the craftwork of Yeha, like the later stelae of Aksum, the monolithic churches of Lalibela and the castles of Gondar all mentioned below—were the work of local craftsmen. One archaeologist writing about the finds of an expedition he recently led to northern Ethiopia emphasises this. He says of the finds at Yeha that Alexandrian influence, shown by the shape of the jars, 'is probably an aspect of trade' and he stresses southern Arabian influence.[5] To this the author would also attribute the local tradition that Yeha was the Queen of Sheba's capital.

East across the Red Sea, the Yemen supported a civilisation based on elaborate irrigation works. The plateau of Tigré is not unlike the Yemen and immigrants must have easily adjusted themselves. Some appear to have penetrated southwards even to the regions of Harar and Guragé. The local African peoples were led by the immigrants to produce a complete cultural transformation. As well as architecture, art and a more highly developed social organisation, the newcomers brought religions and writing. A French scholar has commented that 'the complete assimilation of these new elements by the people of Tigré and later by those of Amhara was to bring about the development of modern Ethiopia'.[6] And the story of this development teaches much about today.

The Greeks and Egyptians have references in their literature to the Ethiopian region which was important, although towards the fringe of their known world. They referred also to the land of Punt, a semi mythical source of gold and riches somewhere in or near the eastern Horn of Africa. The author has referred elsewhere to stories of the existence of paved roads and tessellated pavements with stone sculptures and graffiti in the unexplored Manya plains in south-east Ethiopia.[7] If they exist, these ruins, though probably of later origin, could conceivably be connected with the kingdom of Punt. However, the region in the upper catchment area of the Webi Shebelli river is very hot and inhospitable. Not only is the bush there very thick, but it is also full of dangerous wild game.

Any examination of the literature, objets d'art and inscriptions of the Middle Eastern countries banishes any doubt of the significance of Ethiopia to her neighbours, which must mean that there was considerable trade right from early times hundreds of years before the Christian era. Recent work[8] shows that there was also considerable trade with Arabia and the kingdoms of the Upper Nile.

THE GLORY OF AKSUM

The rise to prominence of the great centre of Aksum dates from the first two or three centuries of the Christian era. This city state, whose stelae—often miscalled obelisks—are world famous, grew to dominate the whole north. The large stele which still stands reaches sixty feet above its platform base. The style is not found outside Ethiopia but it is repeated in the Lalibela churches (described in Chapter 2) and is clearly of local inspiration. The granite of the stelae is carved to represent cross-beams, floor levels, doors and windows of a style of timber and mud architecture still followed in villages in parts of Tigré. They clearly represent what today are called 'sky-scrapers'. The largest of these lies shattered, and the second was taken by the Italians during the Occupation and has been erected near the arch of Constantine in Rome. It quietly revenges, perhaps, the seizure of Roman ships near Adulis, the port of Aksum, in the reign of that emperor—perhaps by Ella Amida, Emperor of Aksum, after Constantine had attacked the Emperor's allies towards the beginning of the third century AD, or perhaps by pirates or outlaws, but in any case, by Ethiopians.

The significance of the giant stelae is not known but they probably date from the third or fourth centuries AD and may well commemorate great Aksumite kings of the pre-Christian era, such as Endybis, Aphilas, Ousanas and Ouazebas who are known from the coins they caused to be minted.

During the first three hundred years of the Christian era the language of Ge'ez (the word is derived from the Aguezat or Agazian peoples of the north) had developed from Sabaean. This was a new form of Semitic writing; the vowels were incorporated in the consonants as they are in Amharic, the first official language of Ethiopia today (English is the second). Amharic, a more recent language, has also drawn from what may be described as indigenous languages. There are, of course, many languages in use in Ethiopia

today besides the official language. Ge'ez, however, apart from
being the liturgical language of the Church, is no longer used. Its
relation to Amharic and, for example, Tigrinya, is rather like that
of Latin to the Romance languages. Its importance is immense—
for here is one case of a written African history from early times,
far more continuously significant to Ethiopia than the Arabic or
early Portuguese on which scholars are only now beginning to rely
in their study of Africa farther south.

The literature, though it includes the important chronicles
of the king's reigns, is mainly of a religious nature and the manuscripts are often beautifully illuminated. The story of Christianity
in Ethiopia and the role played by her Christian Church, which has
changed considerably throughout history, if the Church itself has
not, will be referred to separately and at greater length below.
Suffice it to say here that cults of worship of the sun, the moon
and the planet Venus which the Sabaean invaders caused to replace
those of trees, waters and a legendary serpent king, were themselves replaced. However, some of the oldest churches in Tigré
today still carry the names of the early sacred sites of pagan Arabia,
and some celebrations, like that of the birth of the Holy Virgin,
still display peculiar features perhaps related to pagan cults.

Some time in the first centuries AD, the *Periplus of the
Erythraean Sea* was written by a Greek sailor, a Roman subject
living in Egypt. It is the log of the journeys of his vessel with
notes on trade and other items of interest. He writes of Aksum's
port of Adulis, as 'a port established by law'. Forerunners of the
present-day *shiftas*, a term used in Ethiopia for armed bandits,
apparently caused some disturbance to shipping, for he writes
'before the harbour lies the so-called Mountain Island, about 200
stadia seawards from the very head of the bay with the shores of
the mainland close to it on both sides. Ships bound for the port now
anchor here because of attacks from the land.' As was stated, it is
possible that the destruction of the Roman fleet referred to above
should be attributed to *shiftas* rather than to royal command!

Excavations are now exposing the foundations of this old port
which have lain covered by sand since soon after some mysterious
catastrophe in the eighth century AD—it is not known for certain
whether Adulis was destroyed by earthquake, flood or enemy
action. Yet even today the inhabitants of nearby villages still refer
to the pillar bases, the piles of stones and the pottery fragments as
the place 'Azuli'.

The author of the *Periplus* continues his description by
stating that Aksum is eight days journey from Adulis. 'These
places', he says, 'are governed by Zoscales, who is miserly in his

ways and always striving for more, but otherwise upright and acquainted with Greek literature.' Zoscales is usually equated with King Za Hakelé of Aksum. The writer of the *Periplus* refers to the considerable imports, mentioning among others sheets of soft copper, small axes, a little wine from Italy, gold and silver plate for the king, made after the fashion of the country, military cloaks, Indian iron, steel, and cotton cloth.

In Aksum the Emperor's present title 'King of the Kings' appears to have been first used. It was probably borrowed from ancient Persia as were the lion symbols and ceremonial umbrellas.[9] At its greatest extent Aksum not only unified the principalities of north Tigré but also, towards the end of the third century AD, from there parts of western Arabia were ruled, shipping in the Red Sea was controlled and the kingdom of Meroé to the west was destroyed in war and, in fact, never did recover from the time when King Ella Amida raised his black basalt stele in the capital city.

Coins were produced by the kings of Aksum in bronze, silver and gold, and even today the urchins of Aksum run after the visitor and attempt to sell early coins they have unearthed. Precious crowns of former Emperors are kept at the Cathedral Church of St Mary of Zion. They, like the gold and painted wooden crosses and the valuable manuscripts in the treasury of the basilica, were nearly all presented by the Emperor Yohannes in the nineteenth century. The church itself was rebuilt in the seventeenth and eighteenth centuries after its predecessor had been destroyed by marauding Muslim warriors in the sixteenth century. It is, however, anchored upon the walls of an Aksumite building.

It is only after seeing the detailed sketches and photographs and, above all, the reconstructions in particular in Littmann,[10] but also in later works, that one can imagine the full glory of the extensive palaces, promenades, stelae, tombs, churches, etc. of the former wonderful city of Aksum.

Near by is the large irrigation reservoir of Mai-Shum, still containing water and locally known as the Queen of Sheba's pool, and the sites of tombs, one of which, to the west of Aksum, is ascribed to the legendary monarch Menelik I—who in Tanganyika is said by some to be buried in a cave on the ice near the summit of Kilimanjaro. Both these stories are doubtless myths, but the Ethiopian story is the older. Menelik I, as will be explained below, is widely believed in Ethiopia to have been half African and half Jew, the illegitimate son of the Queen of Sheba, identified with Queen Makeda of Ethiopia, and King Solomon.

But to wander around Aksum today is a sobering experience. Only recently has any reverence begun to be shown for the fragments of fallen stelae, the bases of stones, tomb covers and other remains. The common people, largely unschooled in the glory of their heritage, use the fragments for house walls, for washing blocks and worse. The poverty, the skin diseases and the flies of Aksum today are all uncontrolled. The visitor with little knowledge of present-day Ethiopia must also be amazed to see one of the several vast new churches which are being built in Ethiopia today, rising directly and immediately over the logical line of the continuation of excavations which were revealing extensive remains of the walls of a large building at a depth of something over 10 feet beneath the surface. In May 1962 a schoolboy sadly commented to the author as concrete was being poured into the wooden frames for the new monster that the Church did not like 'those foreign French people digging in the sacred soil of Aksum'.

A proper knowledge of the city of Aksum and of several others only now being examined, such as Matara near Senafé, which has been described as a little Babylon of the sixth century AD, can give the young educated Ethiopian a basis for his pride in his nation and his dignity. In this context it can have much in common with Zimbabwe and the revival of ancient names like Ghana and Mali. The attitudes of the older generation towards others of non-Christian beliefs, of less significant family, or of darker or more negroid features than they themselves chance to possess, promotes the wrong sort of pride and serves only to perpetuate disunity in the nation. Though doubtless dependent upon slave labour—and the erection of stelae weighing four to five hundred tons implies a high degree of organisation and a large slave-labour force—and early civilisations are as just a basis and as relevant a source from which to draw the inspirations of nationalism as are, for example, the former glories of Iraq, Iran and Egypt. Even the Greek ideas on the organisation of a state seldom reached as far as their own slaves, and their concepts of democracy or the liberty of the individual certainly did not. That would imply more recent conceptions from which, of course, the young African of today can also draw. It is important, particularly in view of the way in which the newer states of Africa seek to uncover the past and the traditions on which to build the myth of nationalism, for the student of Ethiopia to know and understand that a solid historical basis exists for that country's pride. In educational circles in Ethiopia there has recently begun a definite and commendable re-orientation of syllabus and textbook with this in mind.

But following the pattern of all empires, Aksum fell into decline; yet, as with the Roman empire, the Christian Church it had adopted survived the ruin. Contact with the rest of the world in early times through trade and along the trade routes had always been the lifeblood of progress—without the free interchange of ideas, nations stagnated and development stopped. So it was with Aksum, the trade declined with the expansion of the Persian influence on the Red Sea and later, and much more significantly, with the rise of Islam and the *Jehad*, or holy wars, which followed. Ethiopia, as she now is, soon had her energies further distracted by internal strife. Meantime in Egypt the gentle sands had often blown over the tombs and monuments, preserving many for posterity. Not so in Tigré, for the harsher and wetter climate of the Ethiopian plateau and the depredations and civil wars of her subsequent turbulent history have together destroyed most of what remained above ground of one of Africa's great civilisations—of the glory of Aksum.

2

Christianity and Myth

... *The Ethiopian people are ardent believers in their faith and will not be shaken by rumours and by empty words. The Ethiopian people are a faithful and a great people.*— Translated from a leaflet signed by PATRIARCH BASILIOS, December 14, 1960

The queen of the south shall rise up in the judgment with this generation and shall condemn it; for she came from the uttermost parts of the earth to hear the wisdom of Solomon; and, behold, a greater than Solomon is here.—MATT. XII, 42

THE LEGACY OF AKSUM

A year before his death in 337 AD, the Roman emperor Constantine stated that the citizens of Aksum deserved treatment equal to that accorded to citizens of Rome. But by the sixth century, Aksum had passed its zenith. However, the gradual loss of control over her northern seaboard, which she did not fully recover until federation with Eritrea some years after the second World War, though effectively cutting off Ethiopia from the Middle East and from contact with the rest of the civilised world, did not result in her immediate decline. The energies of the Ethiopian state were turned south towards the African interior; into the mountains and plateaux south of the historic Aksumite core of Ethiopia, roughly synonymous with the present-day province of Tigré; over the great chasm of the Takkazzé river to Amhara and beyond Lake Tana to Gojjam; across the even greater Abbai Gorge, a veritable African Grand Canyon several thousand feet deep, to Shewa, which, possessing the recent capital of Addis Ababa is now the centre of Ethiopia, and even beyond. Nor was a disintegration, which the Ethiopian terrain would seem to dictate, into scores of independent kingdoms each in its inaccessible mountain fastness, either immediate or ever quite complete.

Modern reunified Ethiopia is the logical inheritor of the tradition of ancient Aksum. That this is so has, at least up until the beginning of the present century, been due far less to the occupant or even the existence of the imperial throne, than to the Ethiopian Christian Church, dating as it does from the heyday of Aksumite power, and to Ethiopia's long history of national independence.

CONVERSION TO CHRISTIANITY

There are many reasons for believing that the influence of Judaism had long been felt in Ethiopia, not least is the existence to this day of the Falasha, or more popularly the 'Black Jews of Ethiopia'. Perhaps it was immigrants from the Yemen who had first converted a group of northern Cushites to pre-Talmud Judaism. Similarly knowledge of the Christian faith must have reached Ethiopia very early on, as soon, in fact, as it began to spread through the Middle East, though it is unlikely that a Christian Church was founded at that time or many traceable traditions of saints and martyrs would probably still be current. But if we discount certain questionable traditions current among many of the Ethiopian clergy, we are still left with a very colourful story of how the Christian conversion occurred. Unlike the equally colourful story of the origin of the so-called Solomonic line of kings, this one shows much evidence of being historically true.* Two Syrian Christian youths, Frumentius and Aedisius, having survived an act of piracy or a shipwreck on the coast of Ethiopia, were brought to the king of Aksum. The learning of Frumentius, the elder brother, made him a valuable servant first of the king, Ella Amida, and then after his death, of Sofya, who was queen regent during the minority of the young monarch Ezana. Later, Frumentius went to the Bishop of Alexandria, St Athanasius, was consecrated by him, and sent back as first archbishop of Aksum.

The boys' voyage is said to have taken place in AD 330, or not long after'. And after a stay of many years in Ethiopia, Frumentius is said to have been consecrated by St Athanasius shortly after the latter's appointment to the see of Alexandria. That, however, is known to have been in 326, but this discrepancy is a small point. There is one place which should be noted where Ethiopian

---

* See pages 39–44 below. The story of the conversion is to be found in an ecclesiastical history written by Rufinus, a Byzantine monk of the fourth century AD.

tradition differs from the above. The speech of Basilios on January 19, 1951, at the ceremony to mark his investiture as the first Ethiopian national to be archbishop illustrated this. In the course of his address he said : 'During the reigns of the pious kings Abraha and Atzbeha, the torch of the light of Christ was held aloft by St Frumentius. . . . Likewise Abraha and Atzbeha's names were also associated with light, since the light of the gospel penetrated into the country during their reigns.' Mention of these two monarchs rather than of Ezana whose life and times we know of through archaeological sources, was also made on that occasion by Ras-Betwoded Makonnen Endalkatchew, then prime minister, who died in 1963. Many scholars believe this reflects an error which crept into the Arabic and Ethiopian legends and traditions at a later date. Jones and Monroe ascribe this to 'the common tendency of popular history to attach famous events to famous names', and state that these monarchs were champions of the Christian faith, but that they lived two centuries later.[1] Sylvia Pankhurst, on the other hand, draws attention to Shaiazana, brother of Ezana, and resolves the difficulty by suggesting that the christian names of these two were Atzbeha and Abraha respectively.[2] However, the point can still be made here that the Ethiopian Church has of later years lost touch with world scholarship.

CONSERVATIVE TRADITIONS AND OTHER EARLY DEVELOPMENT

The attitude of the Ethiopian Church to archaeological research has already been touched upon. It has similarly resisted the efforts of all, including Hailé Sellassié, to get the priceless old illuminated documents and manuscripts deteriorating in frightening conditions in many churches and monastic centres, stored in a national archive department in Addis Ababa—though even in Addis Ababa, not so long ago, one seven hundred years-old painting was cut to fit a museum wall. The new Institute of Ethiopian Studies will, however, soon obtain the services of a UNESCO expert to make an initial survey for the future collection of manuscripts.* Many documents are so old that they have acquired a mystical and religious significance to their custodians, and scholars have the greatest difficulty even in photographing them. That many are of great beauty is attested by a recent UNESCO book of reproductions drawn from the Lake Tana area.[3] Such attitudes are in part explained by the fact

---

* A catalogue of documents in Addis Ababa churches has now been prepared by this new Hailé Sellassié I University Institute.

that the Ethiopian Christian Church has always been conscious of being the besieged repository of true Ethiopian nationalism and, as will be shown, until recently there has been considerable historical justification for this view. However, today such attitudes are outdated and even tragic and serve well to illustrate the growing gulf between institution and aspiration, between old and young, which is the theme of this book. Instead of the pillar of nationalism the Church is now seen rather as being without a social conscience on the national level.

Beggars may well be fed individually but that is no longer enough. Ethiopian government advisers, whether from the United States or from communist Yugoslavia, say that land reform must be the basis for economic advancement. The Christian Church, however, is herself one of the greatest landowners and is allied with the ultra-conservative feudal landlords. Her attitude to modern education, though not to literacy in the scriptures, is suspect. Even now it may be too late for her to change, for change implies education and the educated, even if sponsored by the Church, almost invariably leave her for government service. The Addis Ababa Theological College had fourteen students in 1962. With few exceptions, though Teophilos, Bishop of Harar, is perhaps one, the Church leaders are complacent in what they believe to be their impregnable position. However, when mass education and literacy campaigns are introduced, as one day they are sure to be, the Ethiopian Christian Church will find she has to espouse social reform.

In the full knowledge that today's Ethiopia contains a large percentage of Muslims, even Abune Teophilos said categorically in April 1962 : 'In Ethiopia the (Christian) Church and state are one'.* Historically this was so, but in a changing Africa, many Ethiopians find it acceptable no longer.

It is significant, however, of the Christian Church that ever since conversion often it alone has spoken out for the Ethiopian nation. Aba Salama Kassati Birhan (Father of Peace and Torch bearer), as St Frumentius is known in Ethiopian tradition, and his successor archbishops, the metropolitans of the Ethiopian Church, had the power to consecrate suffragan bishops but they were themselves consecrated by the Patriarch of Alexandria and were normally Egyptian Copts from that see. This was the main contact with the rest of Christendom. The Arab historian Umari even tried to construct a history from the letters which went to, from or through Egypt. One letter from Constantine, asking in vain that

---

* In conversation with the author.

the Ethiopians depose Frumentius (to make way for one Teophilos since the Imperial court had caused St Athanasius to be expelled from Alexandria and replaced by Patriarch George), incidentally puts the date of Frumentius's consecration at a little before AD 356.

Soon after the establishment of the Ethiopian Church there occurred one of the greater discords that punctuate the history of Christendom. These have often stemmed from attempts by the Church to correlate and evolve a Christian theology relative to the philosophy of the time. Indeed the extent to which any church can claim to teach a 'true' and lively word depends upon its attitude to current philosophical thought. Respect for 'sound learning' largely accounts for the relative strength of the Protestant, Anglican and Roman Catholic churches in European universities compared with the rift between the Ethiopian Church and the school and university students in Addis Ababa today. Only recently, however, has the Ethiopian Christian Church thus lagged behind.

In the fourth century the Christian Church, influenced by the great Middle-Eastern academies, developed two separate schools of thought on the nature of Christ. Controversy came to a head in AD 451 at the General Council of Chalcedon. The Greek and Roman Churches held that the Deity and the human spirit had been brought together but not fused in the person of Christ. Many representatives of the Syrian and Egyptian churches, however, believed in the single (and divine) nature of Christ and their attitude came to be described as Monophysite, Jacobean or Coptic.[4]

The Ethiopian Church is nowhere mentioned in the history of the Great Schism, as the controversy was called, but the Schism has been most important in her subsequent development, particularly with reference to her contact with the Jesuit missionaries, who incidentally sometimes found the learned theological discourse of the Ethiopian monarchs too much for them. Ethiopia followed the lead of the Egyptian see of Alexandria, and to this day is Monophysite.

Although Ethiopia was geographically on the very borders of Christendom, contact remained. In the fifth-century reign of the Aksumite king, Alameda, several monks from the Byzantine empire visited Ethiopia, and many monasteries founded shortly afterwards survive to this day. The monks are now remembered as saints and many traditions of miracles and wonders have grown around their memory, especially that of Pantaleon, who is said to have raised the dead. The Roman emperor Justinian, through Timothy III, patriarch of Alexandria, asked the Ethiopians to invade Arabia. This they did and restored to the throne of Himyar a Christian dynasty which survived until the days of the Prophet. However, the

Ethiopians themselves were finally expelled from Arabia in AD 570 by the Persian rivals of the Byzantine empire, and as has been stated above, Ethiopia later lost her access even to the western shores of the Red Sea—but it is not impossible that the Prophet himself acquired his somewhat imperfect knowledge of Christianity from the oral accounts of Ethiopian slaves living in Mecca and a great respect for Ethiopia is obvious in his writings. A wife of the Prophet is said to have had Ethiopian friends and in 615 some of his followers were given asylum from persecution at the court of Aksum.

In Ethiopia at the same time there appears to have been a period of missionary activity and the Christian faith expanded to the south with somewhat uneven success amongst peoples professing Jewish or pagan beliefs. The Old and New Testaments were translated into Ge'ez and a considerable mythology developed. At village churches today the priests still teach young children that the father of the nation, Ethiops, one of the twelve descendants of Cush the son of Ham, is buried at Aksum. They say also that after the flood the grandson of Noah came from the lower lands to the mountains of Ethiopia.

Ethiopia is a land of Christian churches. Right from early times the armies of the Emperors and *rases* left in their wake churches and monasteries, the latter often on the tops of well-nigh inaccessible *ambas*. Indeed tradition explains that the founder of the ancient and famous monastery of Debra Damo, in Tigré, reached the site via the tail of a magic serpent. When students from Addis Ababa University College visited the famous monastery in 1960 they were hauled up the cliffside in less exotic fashion by a rope, though an iron cage apparatus is said to exist for bishops. The distinctive Christian Church music of Ethiopia also developed during the latter part of the first millennium.

Contact with the Christian kingdoms to the west, and with Nubia in particular, though often not too friendly, was finally broken off by Beja invaders who even moved on to the western parts of the Eritrean plateau. The expansion of Islam did not constitute a threat to Ethiopia for many decades, it is sometimes supposed because of her hospitality to the faithful. However, it should be recalled that throughout the whole of the Middle East it was not unusual for Christian clerks to be employed by Muslim leaders who themselves sometimes stayed in Christian monasteries. Even when, in 642, Egypt passed from the control of the Byzantine empire to that of Arab khalifas who subsequently made Damascus their capital, the relationship between the Alexandrian patriarch and the Ethiopian Church was undisturbed.

The Damascus dynasty was in turn succeeded by the 'Abbasids of Baghdad and the growth of the fanaticism of Islam dates from 847, from the time of Khalif Mutawakkil, but Arab writers of even the tenth century still recorded that the *Jehad* or holy war did not apply to Christian Ethiopia.

THE EXTENT OF THE EMPIRE

In 854 conflicts in Nubia and Egypt led to the Ethiopians being unable to secure a new archbishop for some time. Piracy and war much reduced the commercial importance of the Red Sea; Massawa was lost and Adulis sacked and burnt. In the ninth century the focal point of Ethiopia was moved south, possibly as far as the region of Shewa province where the capital is today. Arab historians mention Kabar—perhaps Ankober, an old settlement on the edge of a vast Rift valley escarpment, long important in Shewan history. There are other possibilities, including earthworks on the flanks of Wachacha, a volcanic mountain mass west of Addis Ababa, the modern capital—which await expert examination. The Christian communities which later built the several monolithic churches cut into the volcanic rocks of Shewa may date from not long after these times—in the early nineteenth century the local king, Sahlé Sellassié, was surprised to find Christian remnants among the Guragé peoples near the site of Addis Ababa, and Christian crusades south and east were a feature of subsequent centuries. For example, there has long been an important monastic settlement beside the holy crater lake at the summit of the spectacular extinct volcano Zikwala, south of Addis Ababa, which will be mentioned again in this book. It must also have been the descendants of converts from this time who much later had to flee to the island refuges of Lake Ziway to escape from Muslim or Galla invaders.

Probably we shall never know for certain how far Ethiopian influence penetrated. East and north-east Africa are mentioned by early geographers and travellers, Greek, Roman, Chinese and particularly Arab. Much confusion, however, still obtains as to the exact meaning of the terms used, such as Zenj, El Habash and Barbara. Particularly confusing is the way in which these writers, especially the Arabs of the tenth century, refer to one or other of these groups as though they included the rest. Roughly speaking the Zenj lay to the south of the Habash, and the Barbara to the east. (The word Somali does not occur until the fifteenth century though individual clans are mentioned earlier.) A sound study of distributions and of the implied overlord or tributary relationships between the nearby peoples and the Habash is well overdue and it may not support, for example, the current Soviet opinion that the Zenj may be absolutely identified with the Bantu and with them alone,[5] or the Somali view that the Ethiopian traditions of the limits of their ancient empire, in particular that it extended to the Indian Ocean, are without foundation despite their also having been recorded by early European visitors.[6] Most histories of Africa now admit the considerable southerly influence of peoples from the Ethiopian Highland kingdom and in 1962 the East African Institute of History and Archaeology started to attempt a broadening of its interests both academically and geographically at least in part because of this.

There remains great scope for historical and archaeological research in north-eastern Africa. There are caves, cairns and many ruins, including some walled settlements built without mortar and therefore somewhat reminiscent of Zimbabwé. There are burial chambers full of mummies, miles of ditches and earthwork defences, and strange deep wells resembling some of those of Arabia, the Northern Frontier District of Kenya and of Masailand in Tanganyika. The construction of a group of these wells at Wachilé in southern Ethiopia is ascribed by the local people to giants, to the supernatural or to peoples resident in the area before their 'own fathers came'. Farther south the Masai, latecomers in their area, say the same. Often one is reminded of the legends of early European history such as those of King Arthur in early English history, and it is clear that much of what might be called the history of the middle ages in Ethiopia, as in most of Africa, is only vaguely known.

Meanwhile to the south, affecting only the extreme southwest of modern Ethiopia, the long disturbance caused by the great migrations of the Bantu-speaking peoples had begun. A series of stone and terrace cultures existed in what is now Kenya and Tanganyika (collectively called Azanian by some authorities), and the ancient cities of Mashonaland came into being. Gold, ivory and slaves were already valuable items of trade, brought from the interior to the east coast of the continent where commerce was controlled by the Persians or more usually the Yemeni Arabs. Then Nilotes moved south from what is now the Sudanese Republic and contacting strong Bantu kingdoms in the regions now known as Uganda, Rwanda and Burundi, moved east before entering the Rift valley in Kenya and Tanganyika.

It is interesting to note in passing that the ruling families of these kingdoms are said by some to have come long ago from 'highlands away to the north east'. When the Emperor Hailé

Sellassié I paid a state visit to Uganda in June 1964 much was made of this. Apart from comment in the Luganda vernacular Press, the *katikiro* (prime minister) of the Kingdom of Buganda, speaking before the *Lukiiko* (Assembly), said, 'I have great honour in welcoming so renowned a ruler of royal blood to this kingdom, led as it is by the Kabaka, a person also of royal blood. Legend maintains there is historic connection between our two countries and when His Highness the Kabaka visited Ethiopia in 1962 he saw for himself the everlasting friendship of the two nations.' Although the Emperor, on the advice of members of his entourage, made no reference to *Buganda*, he did comment that '*Uganda* and Ethiopia have much in common in the spheres of history, geography and state of mind.' Even the old dynasty from the Malagasy Republic which was suppressed by the French in early colonial days long ago is said to have come from the north.

Away to the east of the Ethiopian highlands there were also movements of peoples. One group of peoples migrated from the Somali plateau where there are old cairns yet to be examined, towards the Afar or Danakil desert region. Another, the ancestors of the modern Oromo or Galla peoples, moved to the east and south. Finally a third group, ancestors of the present Somali, apparently possessing a greater cultural maturity, then spread with their herds frorm the coast over the lowlands already peopled by the Galla, the Bantu and their predecessors, by then much interbred. This last expansion has continued to this day. Throughout the whole period immigration continued from Arabia and those with prestige drawn from a superior knowledge of Islam often became, or were adopted as ancestors of lineages that have now become very numerous.

THE PROBLEMS OF ISOLATION

Around the beginning of the current millennium the encirclement of Ethiopia and her frequent cyclic withdrawals, reflecting discord and weakness, to the historic highland core of ancient Abyssinia continued. In many respects this historically repetitive process resembles the story of the Chinese and China, the boundaries of whose effective rule have to this day varied greatly depending on the authority or weakness of the central dynasty or government. On the Red Sea coast an independent Muslim dynasty ruled Dahlak. The port of Zeila (just within Somalia near the borders of the present French colony) was finally lost; the power of the Muslim kingdoms which had sprung up along the coast of what is now the Somali Republic grew from year to year, and Islam extended to Ifat at the very gates of the Shewan highlands. Early writers confirm that some rulers tributary to the 'King of the Kings' were Muslim, but they were not necessarily therefore Somali as is sometimes wrongly assumed.[7]

In contrast with the rising fortunes of Islam, the Christian Church on the highlands had many problems in those times. On the death of one tenth-century monarch there occurred an ecclesiastical scandle when the intervention of Archbishop Petros to settle a dispute amongst the nobles over the succession, was confused by the temporary recognition of a rival archbishop, whose claim was based on papers forged by himself and an Egyptian monk. This impostor was imprisoned as were several archbishops, who were often merely temporarily released to rubber stamp Royal decrees. At times the office was long vacant. During one such period a message was sent, via the King of Nubia, to taunt the Alexandrian patriarch, at that time Philotheos [981–1002], that he obviously cared but little for the spiritual needs of Ethiopians. One, Daniel, was hastily summoned from a desert monastery and sent to Ethiopia. At the end of the eleventh century the Egyptian khalifa, Mustanzir, caused Patriarch Michael IV to send a message to Ethiopia about a paucity of water in the Nile. As a result of this it is said that dams were breached which caused that river to rise ten feet in one day. This seems to have been a period of all round tension since Archbishop George also sent by Michael IV, proved to be an 'avaricious taker of bribes and a withholder of Church funds'. After an outbreak of public indignation, the king made George refund his illgotten gains and packed him back to Egypt, where he was duly imprisoned. One archbishop acting, it is assumed, on behalf of the Vizier of Cairo, went so far as to cause seven mosques to be erected, but he was clapped in jail and they were destroyed by an angry emperor. In recent decades, more properly, it has been the emperor who built an occasional mosque and the Christian Church which frowned. All in all, it seems hardly surprising that there should have been a movement towards ecclesiastical independence from Egypt in 1140. Patriarch Gabriel II received an embassy which had journeyed from Ethiopia to ask for more bishops. The khalifa raised no objection but the patriarch refused, doubtless because he did not ever wish to risk the Ethiopians having enough bishops to elect their own patriarch—a thing which they have been able to do only very recently.

The northern Aksumite region of the Abyssinian Highlands had, according to a letter from the Emperor to the King of Nubia, suffered much from the campaigns of a terrible queen, called Gudit, or sometimes Esat, literally 'the fire', who was probably a Falasha. A veritable Boadicea, she burnt many churches, razed the city of Aksum and pursued the unfortunate Emperor from *amba* to *amba*. Dr Ullendorff suggests that hers was probably a rebellion against the expansion of Christianity to the peoples of the south, and that it spread and got out of control.[8] This seems likely, for Ethiopian tradition has it that the turning point was a resurgence of the Christian faith and the arrival of Archbishop Daniel mentioned above.

THE ZAGWÉ MONARCHS

Eventually, however, the whole ruling line which claimed descent from Solomon was swept away and for nearly a century and a half the Zagwé, kings of a new line who had worked up a rival genealogy based on Moses, ruled from a capital in the wild and rugged fastnesses of the Lasta mountains.* This was, and remains today, a wild and inaccessible area of great black basalt and red sandstone cliffs surrounding remote areas of flat *amba* and mountain, whose windy heights are separated by huge gorges down which, during and after the rains, the rivers hurtle to feed the great Takkazzé, which skirts to the north of Begemidir, the Gondar plateau, and the high Simien.

In 1922 Ras Tafari, now known as Emperor Hailé Sellassié, prepared a list of all the sovereigns of Ethiopia.[9] The semi-legendary nature of the Zagwé dynasty or period is shown by the fact that seven successive monarchs are therein said to have reigned, each for forty years. There were eleven Zagwé monarchs. The significance of their usurped sway does not lie in its territorial extent, for that is uncertain and it is not established that it even included Tigré, Begemidir or Shewa, where indeed the 'true Solomonic line' is said to have taken refuge. It lies rather in the fact that their descendants play their part in the complex feudal picture of present-day Ethiopia, and, more important, both traditional Ethiopian nationalism and the Christian Church can draw inspiration from the wonderful monolithic churches built, or rather cut out of the consolidated layers of bright pink, buff or green volcanic ash called tuff, which is interbedded between the lavas. There are very many such monolithic churches in Ethiopia, but most are in Wello and in this mountainous Wag-Lasta district. By far the most famous group is that at the old Zagwé capital of Roha, which is customarily attributed to the reign of the monarch and saint,

---

* If the history of the churches and monasteries of Egypt, written by Abu Saleh at the beginning of the thirteenth century, is to be believed. This, however, may owe its origin merely to Numbers XII, 1.

Lalibela, whose name today is commonly used rather than 'Roha' for that settlement.

LALIBELA

Roha, or Lalibela, can be reached by a three or four day mule trip and, subject to good dry weather, even by Land-rover from the main Asmara-Addis Ababa road. An occasional charter flight by Ethiopian Airlines to a cleared strip at the foot of Mount Abune (Bishop) Joseph, which need be followed by only a few hours' mule ride, has brought Lalibela almost into the category of a tourist attraction—and justly so, for the rock churches are one of the wonders of African history. One result of the passing of the colonial era has been the popularising of the study of African history throughout the world, but the churches of Lalibela have long attracted the attention of foreign scholars.

One of the first impressions obtained by the visitor to Lalibela, after the awe-inspiring mountain precipices and valleys past which he has journeyed, is of a vast and somewhat scattered African village, with several apparent nuclei or centres near one another on the hillside. The houses are sometimes mud, sometimes stone, and invariably thatched, several possessing an upper storey. The people, especially the children, are ragged but jolly, and there is a distinct atmosphere of friendliness about the place. In the evening the people sing to music from the *masengo*, a type of one-stringed fiddle played with a bow, whose pitch is altered by changing the pressure of the upper palm on the string. Father Alvarez noted them in the early sixteenth century.

The churches themselves are for the most part excavated from the blocks of rock left isolated by deep surrounding trenches, and are reached by subways, bridges and tunnels. There are eleven in all, in three distinct groups, each church differing widely in size, colour of rock and, strangely, in style of architecture. One theme that runs throughout, however, is the shape of the apex of the Aksum stelae. There are other similarities, particularly in the shape of the windows and doors, and imitation beam ends—the timber prototypes of which, for example, may still be found in the famous earlier *amba* monastery of Debra Damo. Authorities on Lalibela, when discussing the styles and technique used in the construction of the churches, differ as widely as do the churches themselves. Buxton suggests that they were deliberate imitations of the several different examples of the Ethiopian architectural styles which had evolved throughout the long history of Aksum and afterwards.[10] Mrs Bidder, who a few years ago produced a gloriously illustrated book about the churches, believes them to be pre-Christian.[11] She describes an inscription in the Hammamat valley, dating from the time of the 11th dynasty [c 2278 BC] which may be considered to refer to Wag and Roha, the district and capital of King Lalibela. She cites what she considers to be pre-Christian themes in decoration, and the frequent walling up of two out of three former sanctuaries constructed in the churches. This she attributes to pre-Christian and perhaps Mosaic times. The priests themselves do sometimes say that some of the churches are older than the times of King Lalibela, but Mrs Bidder's hypotheses are by no means proved. Alvarez, a priest from Europe who visited the area in the 1520s, states that there were much older sites round about.

Similarly, there is a controversy as to why the churches were excavated rather than built—a much more difficult process, for faulty masonry can be removed and replaced, but the excavation of pillars, arches and cornices, once begun, is irrevocable. Whatever their origin, this fact implies a very high measure of organisation in their construction in which, teaches the Ethiopian Church, angels played a considerable part. Some say the sunken sites are for protection and concealment against invaders, but Mrs Bidder, cautiously and perhaps a little fancifully, suggests that for religious reasons 'they had to be One with the Earth, striving up into the Sky, thus connecting Upper- and Lower-World'. It is more likely, however, that some of the more advanced constructional techniques of Aksum, in particular the use of mortar, had been lost and excavation represented the safest way of building on so large a scale. Be that as it may, the churches remain a fascinating field for future African and Ethiopian historians.

The largest church, Medhané Alem, or Saviour of the World, a great reddened structure, some 110 feet × 77 feet × 36 feet high, has small upper windows resembling the tops of the Aksumite stelae, which, lying in shadow behind the four colonnades of oblong pillars, are often missed. The roof, on which the stelae are again suggested, is now protected by corrugated iron, which makes this church very conspicuous from the air.

No comprehensive catalogue has yet been made of the documents and treasures of Lalibela. At the Church of Golgotha, where King Lalibela is buried, one can see the stool, two staves, one surmounted by a cross and the other by a crook or shoulder rest, and a large unmounted cross, all said to have been used by him. Some of the boy deacons assert that Adam lies buried in a nearby tomb. There are many paintings and bas-reliefs in the interior of the churches, awaiting full description and examination. Particularly beautiful are the ceilings and arches of the interior of the

Church of St Mary. They are a glory of green, red and yellow designs, some geometrical and some with representations of animals.

The Church of St George, standing somewhat apart from the rest, is cut in the shape of a cross, and resembles a vast version of King Lalibela's stool. Skeletons in old tombs are visible in the trench walls which surround the church. Also striking is the Church of Emmanuel, with the geometrical sharpness of its red walls, its mock Aksumite architecture, even down to stone representations of wooden cross-beams between storeys, and, of course, its window openings suggesting the stelae.

Any visitor used to the 'museum cathedrals' of England, is struck by the number of pilgrims in Lalibela, and the fact that the churches are perpetually in use, and are a real part of the lives of the villagers, most of whom are in some way connected with them. When the author visited Beit Mariam, the Church of St Mary, in early 1960, a service was being conducted both inside and outside the church, under a great canopy. The priests held a procession past the deep water tanks cut in the rock and led the way around the courtyard of the church to the sound of chanting and drums, their multi-coloured robes and umbrellas making a splendid picture in the bright light of the early morning.

TRADITION AND TODAY

The living quality of the Christian faith, while seen at its best at Roha* or at the great monasteries of Tigré or Shewa is by no means confined to them. It may be observed in any village settlement on the Christian highlands of Ethiopia. It is too easy in Addis Ababa today to overlook the fact that the Christian Church—like the Mosque in other regions, especially the lowland periphery of the plateau—provides the focus for village life. The difference between these, however, is that the political influence of the Ethiopian Christian Church is much greater than that of the Mosque—stemming as it does from a link with the monarchy, and command over the agrarian masses. Nevertheless, its ideas and mores are as remote from the everyday pattern of the classrooms, bars and streets of the cities and towns of Africa as is Lalibela from the main roads of Ethiopia. The impetuous young student may well think of the Church, that the 'writing is on the wall', but as recent history has all too effectively shown, no would-be politician or leader can

---

* After the service, the author spoke to the Chief Priest of the churches, and to the Bishop of Dessie, in the shadow of the Gabré Maskal chapel. The bishop demanded to know whether he did not feel the holiness of Lalibela and the presence of Christ, down to his very bones.

afford to ignore the Christian Church, her patriarchs and bishops, however much he may privately hold her immense conservatism in contempt.

The difference in attitude to the Ethiopian Christian Church as between older generations and peasants on one hand and the new educated class on the other, is fundamental to the understanding of Ethiopia today. The attitudes of the younger groups are not especially modern. An interesting series of comparisons can be made between them and the writings of Ludolph in the seventeenth century or Major Harris in the nineteenth.[12]

Harris refers to the Christian Church as 'that most despotic tyrant' and complains that even Sahlé Sellassié, King of Shewa in the early nineteenth century, sought and accepted the advice of churchmen on all issues and was 'deterred from change of residence or from projected military expeditions by their prophesies and pretended dreams', which, says Harris, 'were modelled according to the bribes that had been received!' This last remark should probably be discounted in their dealings with their monarch. Harris adds that in those days everyone feared the magical power of hermits and monks, and it is interesting to note that much superstition and belief in portents and witchcraft is still current today amongst the older generations even in the city of Addis Ababa, and this fact has been used in the 1960s by anti-government pamphleteers. There are still hermit monks on Mount Menagesha near the Ethiopian capital.

In Harris's view the Christian clergy stood squarely in the path of progress. He wrote of a water-mill which had to cease operations after only three days because 'the intolerant and ignorant priesthood pronounced the revolution of the wheel to be the work of devils and genii.' Parallels to this can be found in the history of many countries in the world, though the Church has not quite so much influence in this age of jet aeroplanes. Nevertheless, despite the changes, the views of many in Ethiopia today very much echo Harris's conclusions on the Church; he wrote: 'Priest-ridden and bigoted to the last degree, the chains of bondage are firmly riveted around the head of the infatuated Abyssinian. The most ridiculous doctrines must be believed and the most severe fasts and penances must be endured according to the pleasure and fiat of the Church. Uncharitable and uncompromising, her anger often blazes forth. . . .'

Before the closing of the residential facilities of the Addis Ababa colleges of the Ethiopian University in July 1962, a reprisal against mild student displays of disaffection with the government, the students had for years shown considerable restlessness against the long periods of rigorous and compulsory fasting, enforced by the college authorities on the orders of the government and the Church.

A very popular Amharic poem written by an Ethiopian university student in 1962 aroused the wrath of the Church of Ethiopia and resulted in the young man's expulsion (later modified to six months rustication). It deals with a voyage of a frustrated youth to the land of the dead to seek answers to the problems which his seemingly hopeless environment presents. A few of its poignant Amharic lines which cannot be properly translated, might be rendered as follows :

> . . . Are there priests, deacons and clergymen in the country
>   of the dead?
> Answer only of that kind which knows not what it talks of!
> What of their number? Overwhelming great?
> And do they sing the same rhyme year after year?
> Do they ever harp on prayer and fasting?
> Two things whose significance they understand not one jot!
> Do they teach the observance of a thousand and one holy
>   days?
> Today is Sunday! Tomorrow is St George, the next Abo,
> Then comes St Gabriel, St Michael and St Mary,
> Then St John, Kidané Mihret, Bishop Taklé Haymanot,
> St Steven and the rest!
> If your people observe all these for their souls' salvation,
> How can they live from day to day?
> And what of those who do not conform and holiday?
> Are they excommunicate—ostracised from society?
> Does your Church use those weapons too?
> What do your priests teach of hell and heaven?
> Is hell said full of worms and no sleep there? and fires that
>   burn without end?
> Are your priests fanatics? How is their ignorance manifested?
> Do they answer Yes! No! Black! White!—No Grey?
> And the educated there, are there any?
> Is theirs too a life of fear and conflict?

Never was this conflict of values more clearly demonstrated than when the chief priest of the Zikwala monastery spoke to a visiting group of schoolboys in 1962. He said that the ministers and dignitaries whom the 1960 rebel leaders had imprisoned as 'empty bags', and finally killed 'that Ethiopia should never be the same again' were 'Saints of the Church'—the boys forgot the respect due to age and position and laughed aloud.[13] The priests can and do say that the rebel leaders were the devil's disciples, murderers with personal and no wider motives and they are listened to in the countryside, but that countryside, like the Ethiopian Christian Church, has also been stagnant and must change, adopt a new approach and accept a new role in Ethiopian society.

Meantime, however, the Christian Church can still make or break a leader and, conceivably, could even try to play the king-maker. True that has not been its historic function. Rather it has tamely consecrated him whose struggles enabled him to seize the throne, but this role of king *confirmer* has been scarcely less impor-tant. Successful contenders for the imperial title invariably took care to produce a genealogy acceptable to the Christian Church which then deliberately went to work throughout the length and breadth of the empire to proclaim them. It does seem, however, that the Christian Church played a major part in the conclusion of the history of the Zagwés as the ruling Ethiopian dynasty in the thirteenth century; and its interests are still closely bound with those of the so-called 'Solomonic line' of monarchs which followed.

THE SOLOMONIC LINE

There are many versions of that change, which was undoubtedly accompanied by considerable strife, and which brought Yekuno Amlak (literally 'Let God be his Help') to the throne. Since many of these versions stemmed from Ethiopian sources of much later date, they must be treated as of dubious accuracy. The later ones suggest that the Church engineered the change, some say through a monk named Yasus-Moa, but most say through the famous saint, Taklé Haymanot.* The most important Ethiopian chronicle, the *Kebra Negast,* or *The Chronicle of the Glory of Kings,* belongs to this period and was written to glorify the newly restored line— though of course, it did draw from older material. The chronicles usually drew from the official records of the King's clerks, and they were written with heavy religious overtones. Naturally, the *Kebra Negast* makes much of the enthronement of Yekuno Amlak, an Amhara prince from the Lake Haik region,† as the restoration of the Solomonic line—which myth is very important, and will be

---

* This saint is frequently but wrongly confused with an earlier ecclesiastic of the same name who is said to have been given wings when the devil tried to destroy him by cutting the rope down which he descended from an *amba* monastery, a scene which is a common subject for church mural paintings. The name Taklé Haymanot (literally 'Tree of the faith') was also much later adopted by the *negus* or king of Gojjam.

† Ignoring the Shewan tradition that he came from Tegulet, north of Debra Berhan.

examined below. Another source states that Yekuno Amlak was the king's groom, and the eighteenth-century *Be'elé Negast*, or *The Riches of Kings*, describes his path to success as stemming from his eating the head of a magical talking cockerel. But the Zagwé were probably not replaced because they had broken the Solomonic succession, as like as not that had been forgotten, but more especially because they were of Hamitic Agau origin, and therefore, as the chroniclers say, 'not Israelites'.

St Taklé Haymanot is represented as being a very canny prelate, for it is claimed that one of the conditions of settlement was that the Church, specifically the famous Shewan monastery of Debra Libanos or, some say, the *Abune* (or Archbishop) himself, should henceforth own one-third of the property of the realm. The monastery also acquired the privileged position of *Echegebeit*, the senior monastic community of Ethiopia. In terms of land, though possibly not of ready money, the Church remains very wealthy to this day. Another condition said to have been agreed upon obviously pre-dates the days of nationalism, and decrees that the Metropolitan should never be an Ethiopian! After announcing the new Solomonic succession and the deposition of the Zagwé monarch, the agreement guaranteed to the latter's successors certain dignities and the fief of Wag-Lasta. To this day, the *Wagshum— shum* or chief of Wag—has special privileges amongst the nobility. Children of his and similar lines are accorded special treatment with reference to education abroad and opportunity within the state.

For an illustration of the tremendous influence of family pride or, as some would put it, snobbery and class prejudice, amongst the older members of the nobility, one should read Thomas Pakenham's *Mountains of Rasselas*, in which he describes how in 1956 a certain *leul-dejazmatch* (a description of feudal titles is to be found in Appendix II) named Asrate Kassa, the surviving son of the late Leul-Ras Kassa, who had at least as good a claim to the Solomonic throne as Hailé Sellassié, looked Thomas up in *Debrett's Peerage* before agreeing to help him organise his fascinating up-country travels.

In Egypt, the good St Taklé Haymanot's name is invoked against the bite of mad dogs, yet another evidence of the contact between early Ethiopia and the outside world. It is the legendary story of one of the earliest of these contacts, the journey of the Ethiopian queen, Makeda, identified with the Queen of Sheba, to Jerusalem to visit the court of Solomon, which gives rise to the following sections from the revised Constitution of Ethiopia published in 1955 :

Article 2 : The Imperial Dignity shall remain perpetually attached to the line of Hailé Sellassié I, the descendant of King Sahlé Sellassié, whose line descends without interruption from the dynasty of Menelik I, son of the Queen of Ethiopia, the Queen of Sheba, and King Solomon of Jerusalem. . . .

and

Article 4 : By virtue of his Imperial blood, as well as by the anointing which he has received, the Person of the Emperor is sacred, His dignity is inviolable and His power indisputable . . .

MAKEDA, QUEEN OF SHEBA

The Queen of Sheba's visit to King Solomon is referred to in the Bible in the first book of *Kings,* x, 1–13, and repeated in the second book of *Chronicles,* IX, 1–12. Ethiopian mythology abounds in differing versions of the legend or, rather legends, since at least three cycles of legends can be discerned grouped together in the present forms of the story. The identification of this queen with Queen Makeda of Ethiopia is best seen in the *Kebra Negast.* It is held in Ethiopia to be a translation of a document found before AD 325 amongst the treasures of St Sophia of Constantinople, but was written in its present form in the fourteenth century in circumstances already described. In Ethiopia today her story is often depicted in coloured paintings which remind one forcibly of strip cartoons.

Other quaint Ethiopian stories about Queen Makeda link her with a dragon and give her ass's feet as a result of stepping in a pool of dragon's blood; with a serpent king whom she is said to have succeeded; with the buildings and stelae of Aksum and even with saints of the Christian Church! Parallels can easily be drawn with the legends of other countries in the Middle East.

Modern scholarship tends to reject the identification of the Queen of Sheba with Ethiopia and she is in any case also claimed by the Arabs, who call her 'Bilkis', and by several other African countries. The Sheba or Saba of the Bible and of inscriptions in Assyria may perhaps have been in northern Arabia. The historic kingdom of Saba, however, was located in the Yemen with its capital at Mari. There was considerable historical contact between this region and Ethiopia and doubtless this accounts for the present distribution of the legend.

The Bible tells how the Queen came to test for herself, by questioning him, the renowned wisdom of King Solomon. She travelled in considerable state, and brought presents of gold, spices and jewels. She was impressed with the houses, the table and the ministers of Solomon, as well as with his wisdom.

The Koran, Chapter 27, describes how a bird from her country told Solomon about her, and how a djinn (demon) helped him to play a trick on her. She bared her legs to cross what she took to be water, only to find that it was a mirror, whereupon, apparently in acknowledgment of his greater wisdom, she admitted to worshipping idols.

The Bible says that before the Queen and her servants returned to her own country, Solomon gave 'all her desires, whatsoever she asked'—and according to the Ethiopian version, a good deal more besides. Solomon is said to have made it a condition that if she wished to sleep alone she should take nothing belonging to him. He then waited for the carefully spiced food with which he had regaled her to take effect. He is shown in Ethiopian paintings feigning sleep. Sure enough, the Queen awakened and went to take a drink of water. Solomon reminded her of her bond, and she, doubtless counting it dishonourable to break her word, slept with him. In Ethiopian paintings the slave who was previously with Solomon sleeps discreetly some distance away, but, judging from the expressions on the monarchs' faces, discernible at one end of the bedclothes, neither liked the other very much.

The *Kebra Negast* chronicler is somewhat extended by his efforts to make the story respectable. He attributes the polygamous habits of Solomon, not to lust, but to his desire to raise sons who would inherit the cities of the heathen, and destroy their idols. If the sons were as good as their mothers were numerous, he must have had some success, for the Bible (I *Kings*, ɪɪ, 6) affirms that 'King Solomon loved many strange women, together with the daughter of Pharaoh, women of the Moabites, Ammonites, Edomites, Zidomans and Hittites . . . and he had 700 wives, princesses and 300 concubines'.

According to Ethiopian tradition, a son, Ebna Hakim (literally 'Son of the Wise') was born to Queen Makeda in what is now Eritrea on her journey home. When the son eventually succeeded to the throne, as is customary in Ethiopia, he was given another name, Menelik I. It is from this son that the Solomonic line, claimed to be one of the oldest, if not the oldest surviving monarchy in the world, is said to have descended. In 1964, the monarch is styled 'Conquering Lion of the Tribe of Judah, Hailé Sellassié I, Elect of God and Emperor of Ethiopia'.

A nineteenth-century Tigréan historian explains the fact that the Bible contains no mention of Menelik I in the following manner : 'Even if the Book makes no reference to it, it is none the less probable that Solomon had relations with the Queen, since everyone knows his inclinations were such.'[14] Indeed, one might be tempted to the conclusion that to be a descendant of Solomon is about as great a distinction as being a descendant of King Charles of England, but the *Chronicle of the Glory of the Kings* describes the special attentions which Solomon bestowed upon the young prince, when later the boy travelled back to Jerusalem to obtain his father's blessing. Solomon had given the Queen, his mother, a ring with the words 'If thou hast a son, give it to him and send him to me'—a story echoed in the Tanganyikan legend, which states that the ring fell from Menelik's dying fingers, and awaits discovery by some Solomonic successor in the famous ice-cap of the Kibo summit of Kilimanjaro. Solomon also sent some twenty sprigs of the Israeli aristocracy to accompany Menelik, and they are said to have stolen the Ark of the Covenant and taken it to Aksum, where it supposedly rests to this day.

THE DYNASTY OF SOLOMON

Including Yekuno Amlak there were fifty-eight 'Solomonic' Emperors from the thirteenth century up to Yohannes III, who, in 1855, was last of the line which had by then become predominately Galla through inter-marriage (see page 56 below). By that time most northern nobles could, with justice, claim some 'Solomonic' blood and when the necessity arose it is even probable that the next three rulers (Tewodros, Taklé Giorgis and Yohannes IV) did so without qualm of conscience. After the death of Yohannes IV— and as a result of power politics not heredity—certain Shewan families provided the Emperors. However, they also have claimed some Solomonic blood. Descended from Sahlé Sellassié, a chieftain who ruled Shewa 1813–47, they suggest that his ancestry can be traced through ten generations back to the Emperor Lebna Dengel 1508–40, or more specifically to the latter's son Yacob who died in 1580. Yacob's grandson by another son became the Emperor Susneyos (1607–32). Several different Shewan genealogies exist.

The importance of this tradition and genealogy lies not in its being believed to be both literally true and theologically significant by the uneducated peasantry, but rather that the whole structure of Ethiopian society—Christian Church and state—is based upon it. It also has legal endorsement since the Emperor Hailé Sellassié first introduced constitutions in the twentieth century.

The fact that the character of the Solomonic succession lies in the realms of myth and tradition rather than history is not tremendously important. All countries have their myths. One has only to examine the mystique of the American marines, or the patriotic songs of England, to detect undercurrents of conceptions long outmoded. For example, British politicians stand and sing lustily at their annual conferences, but their respective parties have travelled far from the respective 'values' of their songs—naked territorial imperialism and bloody revolution! Will the traditional origins and mythology of Ethiopia be similarly allowed to fade naturally into co-existence with the values of today? Only time will tell. But if they are used by the society which they symbolise as an excuse for inflexibility towards a changing world, and hostility towards the pressures of the new Africa, then the whole structure and uneasy cohesion of the Ethiopian state, stemming as it does from these roots, might well be swept violently away, with consequences which, though not necessarily bad, have the one certain and grave disadvantage of being quite unpredictable.

Given a period of enforced order, mass education might conceivably graft the Ethiopian society, along with newly independent societies in Africa, on to a new set of roots, justly drawn, as has been more or less directly suggested in the two chapters above, from a proud and factual national history.

3

Diversity and Struggle

From Menelik King of Shewa and of all the Gallas good
and bad! How are you? By the Grace of God I am well!
Amir Abdullahi would suffer no Christian in his country.
He was another Gran. But by the help of God I fought him,
destroyed him, and he escaped on horseback. I hoisted my
flag in his capital and my troops occupied his city. Gran
died. Abdullahi in our day was his successor. This is not a
Muslim country, as everyone knows!—from a letter from
NEGUS MENELIK II to the British Resident in Aden, 1887

St Mark and Cyril's doctrine have o'ercome
The folly of the Church of Rome . . .
. . . No more the western wolves
Our Ethiopia shall enthrall.

—a popular Ethiopian song from the
time of the Jesuits' fall from influence
in the seventeenth century—LUDOLPH:
A New History of Ethiopia (translation), London, 1682[1]

THE PRESTER JOHN

While the fortunes of the traditional kingdom of the Abyssinian
Highlands thrived for almost two centuries under the restored line
of Solomon, and the literary renaissance typified by the *Kebra
Negast* gained strength, three other, broadly speaking, contempor-
aneous influences began more and more to play their part in the
growth of the Ethiopian state. Each brought violence and death,
and each in its way administered a severe shock, the repercussions
of which, sometimes for better and sometimes for worse, still echo

PEOPLES OF HISTORIC ETHIOPIA

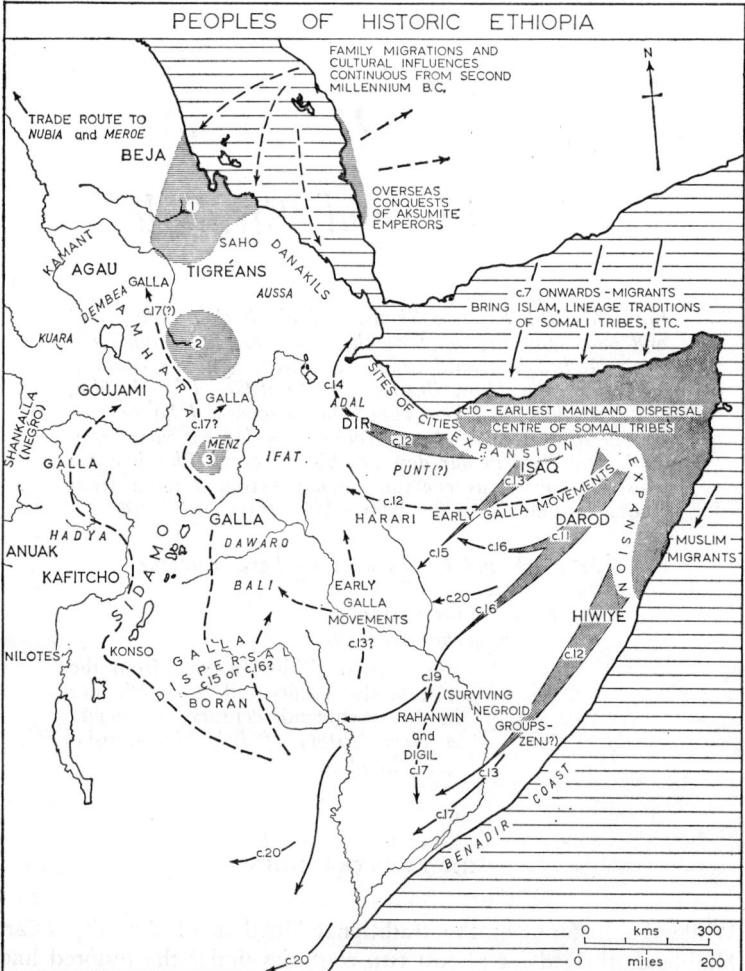

FAMILY MIGRATIONS AND
CULTURAL INFLUENCES
CONTINUOUS FROM SECOND
MILLENNIUM B.C.

N

TRADE ROUTE TO
NUBIA and *MEROE*

BEJA

OVERSEAS
CONQUESTS
OF AKSUMITE
EMPERORS

KAMANT

AGAU

SAHO *DANAKILS*

TIGRÉANS

AUSSA

DEMBEA GALLA
c.17(?)

c.7 ONWARDS – MIGRANTS
BRING ISLAM, LINEAGE TRADITIONS
OF SOMALI TRIBES, ETC.

KUARA

2

GOJJAMI

GALLA
c.17?

SITES OF CITIES

SHANKALLA
(NEGROID)

MENZ
3

IFAT

ADAL
DIR
c.14

c.10 – EARLIEST MAINLAND DISPERSAL
CENTRE OF SOMALI TRIBES
EXPANSION

GALLA

PUNT(?)
c.12

ISAQ
c.13?

EXPANSION

E
X
P
A
N
S
I
O
N

HADYA

GALLA

GALLA
DAWARO

HARARI EARLY GALLA MOVEMENTS
c.12

DAROD
c.16
c.11

MUSLIM
MIGRANTS

ANUAK

KAFITCHO

BALI

c.15

EARLY
GALLA
MOVEMENTS
c.13?

c.20
c.16

HIWIYE
c.12

NILOTES

KONSO

GALLA
DISPERSA
c.15 or c.16?
BORAN

c.19
(SURVIVING
NEGROID
GROUPS—
ZENJ?)

RAHANWIN
and
DIGIL
c.17

c.13

COAST

c.17

BENADIR

c.20

0   kms   300
0   miles   200

c.20

N.B. SULTANATES, EARLY STATES AND DISTRICT NAMES IN *ITALICS*.   c.17 = CENTURY
NUCLEAR AREAS:- I. NORTHERN CITY STATES AND AKSUMITE EMPIRE 2. ZAGWÉ KINGDOM 3. SHEWAN KINGDOM

daily in Addis Ababa. They were the Muslims, the Oromo* and the Roman Catholics, more especially the Jesuits. The process of creating a national atmosphere in which the Oromo (Galla), many of whom are Muslim, and the other non-Christian groups can feel themselves fully integrated, is not yet complete, though great advances have been made especially in the leading Galla families. The considerable, if inadequate advances that have been made are as often overlooked as are the positive contributions made by some of the Jesuits in more recent years.

Influences from and contacts with the lands beyond the traditional highland core of Ethiopia were nothing new, as has been shown. However, in the twelfth century there had grown up a tale in Europe of a powerful Christian emperor who might aid the crusading powers against Islam. The legend of Prester John was to lead several Europeans to observe or play a part in the history of Ethiopia at that time. The presence of Venetians among the many merchant visitors to Ethiopia in the fourteenth and fifteenth centuries led to the availability in Europe of much geographical information, duly plotted on Fra Mauro's map of 1457 and a succession of later works. The papacy tried to establish contact through the Ethiopian monks in Jerusalem and a Spanish king wrote to the Emperor Zara Yakob [1434–68]. There was even the proposal of a dynastic marriage. Zara Yakob's times had parallels with the twentieth-century Ethiopia. He was a fanatical Christian who encouraged the writing of books, the building of churches, the instruction of the public through teaching (sermons), etc. He reorganised the government, suppressed a provincial rebellion and formed an army of spies to seek out those opposed to his convictions. The chronicles record 'there was a great terror and fear in all the people of Ethiopia on account of the severity of his justice and of his authoritarian rule'. The influence of his sway was felt even in the most distant and independent-minded regions of ancient Ethiopia for the chiefs and kings in the south and east were obliged to acknowledge him with tribute.

The kings of Portugal who, from the time of Prince Henry the Navigator, were the monarchs most interested in the discovery of Prester John, soon established diplomatic relations with Ethiopia. Their ambassador, Peros da Covilha, reached Shewa in 1493, but he was never allowed to return. In 1509 the Empress Helena sent an Armenian, Matthew, back to Portugal as her ambassador.

---

* Since it has become the custom to refer to the Oromo peoples as Galla —an unfortunate mistake which stems from an almost meaningless aggressive exclamation—for the sake of clarity the latter term is also used below.

Matthew returned to Ethiopia when a party was put ashore by the Portuguese fleet at Massawa on April 10, 1520. It was led by a noble, Dom Rodrigo de Lima, but what is more important is that it included a chaplain, Father Francisco Alvarez, who subsequently wrote a narrative of the embassy which gives a far better picture of Ethiopia in the period immediately prior to the Muslim and Galla invasions than do earlier itineraries.

Meanwhile, in Rome, a few Ethiopians had spurred on the study of their country and had even seen the printing of their scriptures. Despite some trouble caused by the strange type, the Psalms were printed in 1513, and the New Testament in 1548-9. It was, in fact, the first attempt made in Europe to print in an 'oriental' language.

The interest of the Ethiopian Emperors in Europe stemmed from exactly the same reasons as the interest of the European monarchs in Prester John, namely, the opportunity which friendship might provide for combined operations against Islam. However, at this time there grew up the misconception in Lisbon and Rome that the Ethiopian Church was anxious to accept papal jurisdiction and this led to a disastrous phase in Ethio-European relations which directly contributes to the suspicion with which foreigners and foreign governments are regarded in Ethiopia to this day. As will be seen, this suspicion was later further aroused at the time of the scramble for Africa and was justified by the series of Italian invasions. It arose again at the time of the short period of the British military administration which immediately followed the collapse of the Italian Occupation.

AN AFRICAN FEUDAL SYSTEM

The rulers of sixteenth-century Ethiopia, like the ruling families of Europe and elsewhere, used the marriage arrangements of their sons and daughters as a political weapon, and their successors have continued to do so today. The Empress Helena, for example, was the daughter of the Muslim king of nearby Duara.

The Emperor, or King of the Kings of Ethiopia, as his title suggests, expected and usually received some homage and tribute from the kings of what today are provinces. Hailé Sellassié is the first Emperor not to grant the title of king to deserving princes, *rases* or nobles. Until the time of Menelik II, it was the custom for the Emperor to be crowned and anointed at Aksum and for him to travel round the provinces with a vast train of courtiers, soldiers and servants all equipped with tents and mules. This is a convenient point for a necessary digression on Ethiopian feudalism and, more particularly, the titles boasted by its dignitaries.

The various nobles, the landowning chiefs or *balabat*, the leaders or *shums* (more properly *seyoums*) and the people of Ethiopia all knew their appropriate place and behaviour when at court, or in the highly organised caravans which toured the Empire, or on the field of battle. Most of the noble titles of old have survived and are in use today although some foreign terms have recently also come into use. Very roughly Ethiopian titles and forms of address fall into the following groups : imperial and royal; military and feudal; civil and, lastly, colloquial.

The most important titles with approximate English equivalents are : *negus* (king), *leul* and *leilt* (prince and princess), *tsahafé taezaz* (minister of the pen), *afe negus* (chief judge) and *kantiba* (mayor). Noble titles originally of military origin include : *ras, dejazmatch, kegnazmatch, grazmatch* and *balambaras*. Titles of non-military origin include : *betwoded, negadras, blattenguetta, blatta* and *lij* (a longer description of Ethiopian titles and ranks can be found in Appendix II).

EARLY TRAVELLERS

But, to return to the sixteenth century, it is interesting that some of these titles and terms are to be found in the writings of Father Alvarez. In his picture of sixteenth-century Ethiopia he describes Aksum; the *amba* prison for princes of the blood and the churches of Lalibela and elsewhere. He writes of a man who had fled to a monastery rather than obey the Emperor's command to return to his wife, a daughter of the Emperor who was unfaithful. He was flogged as was the chief justice who had found in his favour, though the latter later resumed his high office nonetheless respected. However, with such traditions the present difficulties met in establishing an independent judiciary remain immense, despite the fact that the ancient *Fetha Negast* (*The Chronicle of the Judgement of the Kings*) has recently been replaced by a new legal code worked out with the assistance of French advisers. It is still believed in Ethiopia, even by young western-trained lawyers, that some judges receive telephone calls from traditional leaders drawing attention to the type of verdict which is acceptable in any particular instance.[2] Influential people can easily quash unfinished legal proceedings.

Alvarez also had many interesting things to say about the Ethiopian Church. It must be remembered that Ethiopia had not yet slipped to the position of a backward country by average European standards of the time. Jones and Monroe in their *History of Ethiopia* point out that Alvarez's own Church was then 'still at a stage of culture not far removed from that of Abyssinia', and that he, therefore, did not suffer from 'the narrow-minded self-righteousness produced by the reformation and the counter reformation'. Certainly there is a greater charity in his attitudes than in those of the Jesuits who were to follow him, or those, for example, of Harris, a protestant visitor in the early nineteenth century, who is quoted on page 37 above. Alvarez records his impressions—that the Ethiopians objected to the practice of spitting in church, that they unashamedly bathed naked at *Timket* (Epiphany)—but his understanding of the practices of the Ethiopian Church, and indeed his own theological knowledge left much to be desired. Jones and Monroe describe how he spent much time with the *abune* and the Emperor, but add 'Alvarez, however, knew nothing about the Council of Nicaea except that it was held under the presidency of Pope Leo and formulated the Nicene Creed—neither of which assertions is true'.

Alvarez describes his visits to Shewa and speaks even of the wonderful bird life in the great gorges, on the edge of one of which stands the important monastery of Debra Libanos. Today one of the old buildings of the monastery has been replaced by a new church. A contractor recently explained to the author how he had been asked by a church dignitary to drill a hole in a stone tomb in order that the saint Taklé Haymanot might watch the Emperor Hailé Sellassié and the bishops inaugurate the new structure!

Alvarez describes meeting an important prisoner—a man of high status, a *betwoded* of the right—who asked his blessing saying, 'What do you think of this, do you thus make prisoners of great men in your country?' Alvarez replied, 'In my country if great lords are arrested for small matters or for the displeasure of the king they give them their own houses for prisons, and it is for very great things that they are quartered in large castles in prison.' However, apart from a few departures in very recent times much the same pattern was, and still is, the custom in Ethiopia. The history of the twentieth century in Ethiopia is full of examples of the confining of eminent noblemen to their houses, to the tops of hills,* to distant provinces or embassies, or more subtly to the impotent

---

* A certain Kegnazmatch Hailé Zelleka, a descendant of Girmamé, a famous *dejazmatch* of Menelik II's reign and a member of the Moja family group implicated in the 1960 rebellion, lived for years confined to a hill near the Imperial Air Force base some thirty-five miles south of Addis Ababa. He has now died of extreme old age, but he received the

Senate, sometimes called 'the garage' in Amharic. (Commoners have always received somewhat sharper treatment.) Alvarez's *betwoded* managed to escape abroad from provincial exile; meanwhile at court proclamations forbade the mention of his name under pain of death.

Alvarez and later writers disapproved of the Church's practice of mass ordination—it is recorded that the archbishop's ordaining breath was sometimes conveyed in a bag—and even today by western standards the number of priests and deacons seems quite astronomic. Since they are uninformed and unproductive economically they are subjected to considerable cynical comment by the educated people. Their numbers have been the subject of recent discussions between the Ethiopian Patriarch and the distinguished Armenian bishop, Paladian who has spent some time in the early 1960s helping to develop a theological college in Addis Ababa.

The Ethiopian monarchs see their realm very much as a besieged island of Christianity set in a hostile, pagan and Muslim sea. This attitude can be readily appreciated for we know from contemporary correspondence that the nearby Christian Church of Nubia was then at the stage of final collapse. Modern scholarship suggests the possibility that Christian influence once extended across the southern Sahara to the gates of West Africa. A medieval Christian sherd or pottery fragment has been found just east of Lake Chad. But Christianity died out in these other regions and the concept of themselves as the besieged bastion of Christendom coloured the attitudes of all Ethiopian Emperors and is very obvious even in the international correspondence of the Emperor Menelik II [1889–1913]. It also reinforced the now outmoded concept of Ethiopians being chosen people, rather different from their neighbours.

The Emperors learnt of wars between the Christian monarchs of Europe with incredulity. In terms of vast disapproval and moral superiority they made it clear that they sought assistance only against Islam! Their campaigns were often of a type that today would be called civil wars, but the concept of linear national boundaries which this implies did not come to Africa until the nineteenth-century scramble. True, Alvarez listed the countries 'on the frontiers of Prester John' but these were as often tributary as

---

author two years ago and asked about such contemporary issues as the space race and racial discrimination in the United States. He joked that he was selling his hill, which was composed of volcanic cinders and ash to the Air Force for runways. The quarries eating into the base of the hill would eventually make its summit untenable, he thought, but he did not live quite long enough to see this become a fact.

foreign. It was among those away to the south-east that the *Jehad* had become infused with new life since the Ottoman Sultan Selem had conquered Egypt and clashes with Ethiopia had become more numerous. The fortunes of war varied greatly but an important new factor was the acquisition by the Emperor's troublesome neighbours of the services of disciplined Turkish troops with efficient firearms. It was because of these that the Emperor Lebna Dengel asked his Portuguese allies for match-locks in 1535.

THE JEHAD OF AHMED GRAN

Before help arrived, however, the green banner of the *Jehad* had swept over the highlands borne aloft by the Muslim, and in part Somali, armies of the Imam Ahmed Ibn Ibrahim al-Ghazi, reputedly a giant of a man whom the Ethiopians nicknamed 'Gran' (literally 'the left handed'). To the religious motive for his expansion might be added the discomfort caused by continued immigration from Arabia into the coastal regions and the consequent population pressures. Gran, whose mother was possibly a Danakil or a Galla, is traditionally said to have been the illegitimate son of a Christian priest who was stoned for this lapse. If so this may in part account for his anathema towards Christianity which, so the stories go, was deliberately fostered by his mother out of a spirit of revenge. Before he embarked on his life ambition of invading the plateau, he had first by deft use of intrigue and dynastic marriage consolidated his power in Adal in the south-east.

After a first skirmish in which he defeated the Ethiopian governor of Bali he strengthened his forces and from 1531 onwards moved successively into Duara, Shewa, Amhara, Lasta and beyond. His nomadic followers proved difficult to control and were activated as much by a lust for loot as by their faith, but in their wake they left a trail of compulsory conversions (the Ethiopian chronicles say that nine out of ten renounced their faith), burning churches and plundered settlements. Gran's Arab biographer describes the vast ecclesiastical buildings, alas no more, and their riches of silver and facings of beaten gold. Gran remarked as he destroyed the mountain-top church of the Holy Trinity in Wello, which stood 130 feet high : 'Was there in the Byzantine empire in India or in any other land, a building such as this containing such figures and works of art?' But although they marched even into such parts as Sidamo and Guragé, the Muslims never completely subdued Tigré in the north.

The defeated Lebna Dengel died almost unattended at Debra Libanos monastery and was succeeded by the Emperor

Galadewos before the 400 Portuguese musketeers requested in earlier years landed at Massawa in 1541. The next year the northern 'King of the Sea,' assisted by the Portuguese, defeated and wounded Gran in the wild mountain country between Amba Alagi and Lake Ashangi, subsequently the scene of other famous battles in Ethiopian history.

After a second battle in which Gran narrowly avoided capture he withdrew to the mountains overlooking the hot and arid Danakil desert region and when he returned he brought as reinforcements 900 Arab, Turkish and Albanian mercenary musketeers, and a number of cannon.

It is difficult today to envisage the colourful spectacle the progress of such armies as his must have made from the now somewhat faded courts of Aussa and Harar. But the story of other battles such as the famous victory in the time of the Emperor Menelik over the Italians, and other great events of African history set against the incomparable scenery of the Rift valley and the mountains of Ethiopia, suggest scenes that must have exceeded the most lavish productions of the modern film industry.

Gran's forces arrived during the rains and defeated the Christians. The Portuguese leader, Dom Christopher da Gama, son of the famous traveller, had previously taken for himself, among the spoils of war, one of Gran's wives. He was captured, tortured and killed. However, Gran overestimated his success and sent his mercenaries back. Meantime, the Emperor Galadewos had come up from the south and united his men with the northern forces. The myth of Gran's invincibility was cracking and in the ensuing clash, near Lake Tana, Gran was shot and his army fled.

Both Christian and Muslim retired to lick their wounds. There followed a series of raids and skirmishes, and after a battle on Good Friday, 1559, the head of Galadewos was taken back to a widow of Gran by his young nephew who also built the wall which stands around the city of Harar. But a third force had entered the field, and soon both Christian and Muslim had to defend themselves against the incursions of the Oromo people, or Galla as they are usually called.

THE GALLA ETHIOPIANS

The Galla are thought to have once lived in the highlands of Bali or more probably in areas now within the borders of the Somali Republic. Some ruins there are ascribed to them by Somali tradition and later movements of the Galla are frequently confirmed, at least in the southern parts of Ethiopia, by the Gallas' own traditions of origin and movement—there is a common belief in a home-land called 'Barigamma', literally 'beyond the sea or dawn'.

Several Ethiopian historians suggest that the Galla movements began in very early times and that the Azebu and Raia Galla moved directly west from the coast of the Gulf of Aden to their present homes long before the coming of Islam.[3] Be that as it may, with one notable exception the usual emphasis of western writers,[4] when describing the Galla, concerns the later effects of Somali expansion south along the Indian Ocean coast and inland, continuous perhaps from the time of the introduction of their faith—although the first mention of the word 'Somali' is much later than that. However, pressure undoubtedly grew stronger in the fourteenth and fifteenth centuries. This pressure was the main factor in causing the Galla peoples to migrate to the south-west, but at times, when the Abyssinian monarchs were strong—and at least partly in consequence of this, the buffer of semifeudatory Muslim states to the west and south of the Highlands was weak—then Abyssinian influence also disquieted the Galla. The effect of these pressures was to cause them to move west and south-west towards the inhospitable saltpans and lava fields and the boulder and sand deserts in the vicinity of Lake Rudolf. The effects of their contact at this time with other African peoples now living in Kenya and Tanganyika are suggested in studies of, for example, the Masai and the Nandi. Another Galla group who migrated in a southerly direction have left descendants along the river Tana in Kenya today. It is often argued that when the ravages of Gran weakened the plateau peoples the Galla rapidly infiltrated northward and settled up on the more fertile plateau. This may well be so but northerly movements began before the incursions of the followers of Ahmed Gran. In these campaigns the Galla used horses and since that time Galla cavalry has become renowned in the literature and oral fables of Ethiopian warfare.

The Galla peoples today form a valuable and significant part of the Ethiopian nation and more will be said of this later when the times of Menelik II and Hailé Sellassié I are discussed. In the sixteenth century, however, most of the plateau peoples feared the Galla as terrible enemies. Of course, like earlier invaders, they did not provide new peoples, only a new strain in peoples already resident in the areas in which they settled. This is especially true in the north where, as pointed out, old men amongst the Azebu and Raia Galla dismiss talk of their being comparative newcomers and consider themselves the inheritors of the traditions of Aksum and even repeat verbal tradition concerning the erection of the giant stelae there.

It would also be quite wrong to consider either the plateau Abyssinians and the other Ethiopians farther south, or the Galla, or the eastern Muslims, or even the Somali, then pushing inland and along the coast, as homogeneous groups, and the relationships between their various component peoples are very complex. There is much difference between the Wellegga Galla, the 'Ittu' Galla of Arusi, and the 'Cottu' Galla of Harar, for the Galla are an assembly of peoples. Similarly if sometimes Galla and eastern Muslim might possess an identity of interests against the plateau Abyssinians, it was no deeper than the co-operation of France and Scotland in their mutual hostility to England in the same period of history.

It was about 1522 when Galla forces entered Bali in the south, and their advances met with no major setback until 1569 when they were attacked by the Emperor Sarsa Denkel. Despite this reverse, they skirted round regions where the local rulers were too powerful, such as Kaffa and Janjero to the west of the river Gojeb in the south-west where Emperor Sarsa Denkel's temporal sway did not extend—though he had managed to introduce Christianity. It must not be forgotten that Galla settlement patterns must also have been conditioned by the fact that as pasturalists they tended to bypass heavily forested regions. Their movements depended also on their social system, new leaders who needed to move into new areas emerged every eight years. The Galla swept over much of the south and in particular occupied the fertile highlands of Arusi just across the Rift valley from Shewa. Most authorities state that by 1570 they were settling in Shewa, and even Amhara farther to the north, but again Ethiopian historians do not always agree with this interpretation. One writer affirms that Gallas were already there because those living at Metcha in Shewa enlisted in the army of the Emperor Amdé Sion and in his reign crossed the Abbai (Blue Nile) to settle in Gojjam near Lake Tana and in the Damot area.[5] Amdé Sion was Emperor in the early years of the fourteenth century! Research is needed into this question and it could well start with a re-examination of the *Chronicles of the Emperors*, the scientific collection of oral tradition, and an examination of place names drawn both from historical sources and the landscape of today.*

Writers tend also to refer to the Galla leaders as kings, and some groups did develop into monarchical states. At base, however, their social systems emphasised the responsibility of the leaders to

---

* The author has heard it claimed that even Mombasa, in Kenya, is a Gallinya name meaning 'place where cattle graze outside the house'.

the people as may be seen, for example, from a study of the traditional cries when leaders were chosen, and in this sense at least their attitudes might almost be said to be 'republican'. Galla 'Gada', or age grades, often take the name of the leader whom the people elect and follow for his eight-year period of office.

Bahrey, an Ethiopian monk whose home in Sidamo in southern Ethiopia was looted by the Galla, wrote a book about them in 1593. He relates how the *luba** Robali 'devastated Shewa and began to make war on Gojjam. The King of Abyssinia gave battle to him at Ziway [the battle of Lake Ziway, 1572], killed his men and captured many of his cattle. Thanks to the booty, many people became rich but Robali killed the *azmatch* [general] Zara Yohannes, chief of the dignitaries—may he rest in peace!' Bahrey lamented the comparative weakness of the 'Abyssinians' which he ascribed to the fact that so many of their social classes, unlike those of the Galla, were unashamedly noncombatant. Doubtless with thoughts of the nevertheless warlike warrior traditions of the Amhara peoples in mind he described in horror how 'one party said an outrageous thing. "Let us not shave our heads when we kill the inhabitants of Shewa and Amhara, for they are but oxen which speak but cannot fight" '.

Meantime Galla also penetrated into the interior of Ethiopia eastwards along the highlands of Harar. By the seventeenth century much of the south and west was under Galla control and the available grazing areas had been occupied and partitioned. This factor was largely responsible for the civil wars and internal anarchy which thereafter were to be typical of Ethiopia for many decades. In Sidamo, states gradually became Galla in the course of time. There were raids into Gojjam and Begemidir and at times confederations of Galla states were formed to attack the forces of the Emperor and his vassals. At the beginning of the eighteenth century the Galla are recorded as having burnt churches and desicrated tombs even in Amhara. They were established in Wello and acquired such power throughout the country that their influence in time extended to the Imperial Court itself. In 1719 Emperor Bakaffa, who had earlier taken refuge with them, introduced Galla to high office and relied on a Galla regiment. Earlier chronicles also record the employment of Galla in the emperor's guard. These events were reflected in the dynastic pattern for his son Yasu II [1730–55] had, like Hailé Sellassié, a Galla wife and such was the predominance of these newer strains that their son Iyoas, who reigned until 1769, spoke only Gallinya.

---

* The *luba* is the Gada in power but it is here applied to its leader.

In the nineteenth century, Galla leaders such as Balambaras Asrate, a colourful character who was once sold into slavery and escaped, were involved in what by that time had become almost a national pattern of intrigue and revolt. There was continual strife and some writers, perhaps impressed by the achievements of the Emperor Menelik II, are apt to over-emphasise the undoubted ability of Ethiopia to absorb diverse peoples and attitudes and forget the almost complete lack of ordered government and national unity in those times.

AMHARAISATION

North of Addis Ababa the Christian Shewan Amhara tended to gather on benches on the walls of the great gorges of the Blue Nile river system and Rift valley fault-escarpments, vacating the plateau which was occupied by the Gallas. However, an inevitable process of mixing ensued and was much accelerated during the next 150 years. It continues today and its present progress can be traced from the establishment of newer Christian churches up on the plateau. Older churches are very numerous, but are largely confined to the gorges.[6]

The language, Gallinya, is understood in most parts of Ethiopia except Tigré, but the Galla *as a whole* are not a potentially separatist group. True, the peasant Galla are proud of their blood. A would-be suitor in Arusi must list eight generations to satisfy a potential father-in-law and, as stated, the Galla peasants are often most surprised at the foreign scholar's assumption that they are a later people with a culture separate from that of the 'Abyssinians'—however accurate that view may have been before provincial amalgams of peoples developed. The author was once warned by an old Shewan Galla of his 'dangerous confusion'. The only *new* blood, he said, was *slave blood* and that was to be found round the former slave-marketing towns. He laughed and displaying typical rural Ethiopian prejudice, asked, 'Have you not seen the thick-lipped people of Ankober?'

What is important is that from the eighteenth and the nineteenth centuries onwards, struggles and rivalry lay between regions, later perhaps provinces, and not between tribal groups. Gojjam and Shewa were at times rivals but many of the peoples in both provinces were of Galla origin. Those in Gojjam were later willing followers of an Amhara ruling house—that of the Negus Taklé Haymanot. Elsewhere there was strong Galla influence in the families who ruled and led Amhara peoples. In Harar today the term Amhara means little more than Christian. Jarso is a Galla name but the people do not speak Gallinya any more. Angolala is an Amharaised area. The people of Marabeté are partly of Galla descent and Galla living in the nearby Shewan fief of Fiché, though many speak only a few words of Amharic, tend increasingly to describe themselves as Shewan and Amhara. This latter word has thus no longer close definition and it is clear that the word 'tribalism' is not suited to Ethiopian studies.

It is true that Galla groups are more homogeneous in Arusi and, for example, along the escarpment of the Rift valley near Kara-Koré, where a large area was placed under military administration because a police column had been annihilated there in the mid-1950s. The writer journeyed round that region in 1958 with a military escort when the governor wanted advice on water supplies for his hill-top camps. The Galla had broken their tree-trunk troughs and filled in their wells. The *mulu asir-alika* (sergeant) of the escort displayed almost 'colonialist' attitudes and boasted, 'The Galla are Amhara's slaves—they do as they are told', and he also remarked, 'Their old men say that where Amhara comes the grass does not grow'. In some areas of Wellegga, also, the local people are liable to despise 'Amhara'—who may well be Shewan Gallas— and may even refuse them water until they get to know them.

But these are largely peasant attitudes and prejudices not unlike those to be found in many ancient countries. They are fading and differ from the attitudes of the educated and of the future which are dealt with in the chapters describing the times of Menelik II and Hailé Sellassié I. Old feelings are, however, real and often stem from the country's history—just as they can be modified by re-teaching it. More will be said about the history of these times, but it might be noted here that the known history of many of the Ethiopian peoples goes back for centuries. Professor Oliver[7] postulates that the origin and the political institutions of the early central and southern African civilisations of Ankolé-Rwanda and Zimbabwé-Monomotapa may be traced back to the kingdoms of southern and western Ethiopia—Damot, Enarya, Kaffa, Janjero, etc. The history of, for example, Kaffa, whose ruler was also a king among kings or emperor (locally *Attio*) is not so widely studied, being based on oral traditions, as is that of traditional Abyssinia drawn from the written chronicles. In Ethiopia the Amhara children who predominate in the schools, do not learn of Kaffa before the time of its incorporation into the modern Ethiopia by Menelik II at the end of the nineteenth century. At his trial Brigadier-general Mengistu, the surviving leader of the 1960 Revolution, was to register a protest about the unbalanced history taught in Ethiopia today. He clearly thought that if

Ethiopians are to overcome their differences and understand the common glory of the national heritage, the emphasis of history teaching should be on the contribution made by all the peoples of Ethiopia. There are, however, other reasons for the unbalanced nature of the studies. The sources for the study of national history must draw also from archives and records of the foreign powers which influenced that history, and these tend to concentrate on 'highland Abyssinia' and the east. But even so the Brigadier-general had put his finger on one of the several fundamental differences between the needs of modern Ethiopia, irrevocably part of the new Africa, and the instinctive conservative and parochial attitudes of her feudal leaders.

THE JESUITS

One significant foreign influence which broke through into the closeted and inverted confines of medieval Ethiopian history, and one about which we have considerable information, was that of the Jesuits. Before the death of Gran, when the Emperor Galadewos was still dependent upon his Portuguese allies, he had to acknowledge a bogus but cunning deceit on the part of a Portuguese chaplain who claimed to be the legal metropolitan bishop of Ethiopia. A new metropolitan was sent for from Egypt, but there was some friction.

St Ignatius Loyola, when in Rome on business for the newly formed Society of Jesus, asked the Pope to send him to Ethiopia and although his request was refused, the Jesuits were entrusted with the anticipated reconversion of the realm of Prester John from the Monophysite 'error'. Bishop de Oviedo arrived in Ethiopia in 1557 and although he remained a staunch upholder of the national faith until the time of his death, Galadewos greatly enjoyed his theological arguments with Oviedo. Galadewos was succeeded by his brother whom Portuguese records describe as 'cruel and hard of heart and utterly insensible to the beauteous mysteries of the Catholic Faith'. The Emperors whom the Ethiopians most like to remember are the great warriors and when, some few years later, Sarsa Denkel came to the throne he proved to be such a figure. He put down a rebellion by the 'King of the Sea' and defeated both the Turks and the King of Adal; he fought the unruly Falasha and the Galla; he forcibly converted Kaffa and Enarya—and despite their unpopularity with the Ethiopian Church he allowed the Roman Catholics to preach and their influence greatly increased.

In 1603 a Spaniard named Father Pedro Paez who proved to be a man of charm, subtlety and skill in languages and architecture came to the Jesuit mission which had been built at Fremona near Aksum. He started a school for the sons of the nobility and taught the Catholic Catechism in Ge'ez. He was called to the court and succeeded in converting the Emperor Za Dengel. The Emperor sought military help from Spain, to be sealed as usual by a dynastic marriage, but the nobles took an historic step to be repeated in the twentieth century, in obtaining release from their oath of allegiance to the Emperor at the hands of the archbishop. The excommunicated Emperor was killed in battle.

After a period of confused intrigue one Susneyos* became Emperor and under him the Roman Catholic interpretations were again widely taught and eventually he also adopted the new persuasion. At this time the Ethiopian Church and its dignitaries were discredited through abuses and immorality, and this is of great importance in interpreting the times. Similar abuses in Europe helped to bring about the Reformation and the ensuing Counter-Reformation. Impressed, doubtless, by the obvious morality of Paez and his followers the Emperor issued a proclamation condemning the corruption in the national Church. At this point Paez died and was succeeded by Alfonso Mendes who arrived with the title of patriarch and perhaps because of this adopted the authoritarian manner which contributed to his downfall. This Jesuit was of a different make-up from his predecessor's. His arrogance, his haste and the savage methods he used to alter the religious customs of the people led to resentment and rebellion. In view of the modern vogue in pamphlets (1961 and 1962) it is interesting to note that pamphlets were prepared describing the Jesuits as 'kin of Pilate'.

After a battle in which 8,000 people were slain, the Emperor's son remarked. 'The men you see strewn upon the earth were neither pagans nor Muslims. . . . They were your own subjects, your compatriots, some of them your kinsmen. . . . This is no victory that we have gained.' At the time of the army pay crisis in 1961 almost identical words were to be used in pamphlets directed at the army soldiers who had fought their compatriots in the Imperial Guard a few months before.

The Emperor, horrified at the carnage Roman Catholicism had brought, issued a proclamation in 1632 restoring the traditional religion :

> Hear ye ! Hear ye ! We first gave you this faith believing that it was good. But innumerable people have been slain. . . . For which reason we restore to you the faith of your forefathers. Let the former clergy return to the churches, let them set up their altars, let them say their own liturgy. And do ye rejoice.

---

* Sometimes written Susenyos. His coronation name was Melek Seged III.

And so they did. Ludolph quotes their song :

> At length the Sheep of Ethiopia free'd
> From the bold lions of the west
> Securely in their pastures feed.
> St Mark and Cyril's doctrine have o'ercome
> The Folly of the Church of Rome.
> Rejoice! Rejoice! Sing Hallelujahs all!
> No more the western wolves
> Our Ethiopia shall enthrall!

As the people rejoiced, the Emperor abdicated in favour of his son Fasiladas who ordered that the Jesuits be confined first in Gojjam and then to their home at Fremona. Several were given asylum by nobles, and Mendes and others fled to the 'King of the Sea', who at that time was in rebellion, and he passed them on to the Pasha of Suakim who ransomed them to the Spanish government. Meantime Emperor Fasiladas, who went to live permanently at the new capital, Gondar, and whose desiccated but well-preserved body may be seen today in a tomb on an island in Lake Tana, led a violent purge of the Roman faith throughout his realm. Many priests and converts, including the Emperor's brother, Ras Se'ala Krestos, Governor General of Gojjam, were executed.

Assessments of the Jesuit episode vary. Ludolph, writing in Germany in the seventeenth century, having discussed the matter with his Ethiopian companion stated that it was 'a thing almost impossible to be believed, with what an universal joy this edict was received among the people'. Bruce, who left Ethiopia in 1772, records the bitterness of all towards their memory. Captain Harris who visited Shewa in 1842, in a section which draws heavily on Ludolph's earlier account, recalls this episode :

> The rosaries and the chaplets of the Jesuits were tossed out of the door and burned in a heap. Men and women danced for joy . . . thus perished the hopes of a mission that for craft and cruelty has seldom been equalled in the annals of time. Whilst Rome must indeed have been prompted by no ordinary motive to persevere so pertinaciously . . . the dauntless but unsuccessful agents employed in the enterprise have left an indelible stain upon the page of her history.

The attitudes of Bruce, Harris and others were doubtless coloured by their own religious opinions, but it is obvious that the Emperors and feudal leaders, often motivated by the possibility of military alliances with Europe, underestimated the religious nationalism of their people, who, according to the Jesuit Father Jerome Lobo, were 'possessed with a strange notion' that they were 'the only true Christians in the world'.

Clearly at this time the Ethiopian Christian Church was the true repository of Ethiopian nationalism—a position which its ignorance, conservatism and landed wealth, not to mention the vast numbers of the Emperor's Muslim subjects, prevent it from properly claiming today.

After the expulsion Rome sent an unsuccessful Capuchin mission to try to regain influence, but missionaries endeavouring to enter Ethiopia were usually expelled or killed. Later the Jesuits persuaded Louis XIV to send emissaries to Ethiopia to soften the way for their re-entry but their journeys met with no success. Expulsions were not confined to Roman Catholics. For example, Protestants were expelled from Tigré in 1838 and the protestant missionary Krapf was expelled in 1842—in which year the Roman Catholics sought to divide their missionary interests in Ethiopia into two Apostolic Vicarates. The Lazarist fathers were allotted traditional Abyssinia and the Capuchins, Eritrea and the 'Galla lands'. Only under Hailé Sellassié did the Jesuits again for a time attain a position of influence in the state.

AN AFRICAN PARALLEL

Because of the recently more marked 'African' orientation of Ethiopia, as illustrated in the 1963 Conference of African Heads of States in Addis Ababa, and the state visits in 1964 to the countries of East Africa, it is interesting to compare the early times with the history of the realm of the Mutapa (Monomotapa)—very broadly speaking another feudal 'king of the kings' farther south in Africa where the Jesuits were also involved.

There a Father Gonçalo da Silveira, who penetrated into central Africa some 300 years before Livingstone, seems from the outset to have been inspired by the possibility of martyrdom and almost to have sought it.*

Gonçalo, like the fathers in Ethiopia, sought to convert the ruler and in fact declined to baptise any chiefs or people until he had first converted the Mutapa himself. Father Godignus, a contemporary historian, stated :

> The emperor of this region holds sway over many villages and kings who pay him tribute, as do also the Mongazes who have

---

* He was not, as is sometimes stated, the first martyr of the Society of Jesus, for Father Antonio Criminale had already been killed on the east coast of India.

independent villages without kings, and the Fumas who are governors of villages and are elected by the inhabitants who have no kings. [A superficial parallel with the Galla is clear and there exists also another with the 'King of the Sea'.] Formerly the king of Sofala was subject to the emperor but he is now free owing to his friendship with the Portuguese. [Godignus continues] . . . The emperor is very rich and powerful and in time of war he can put 100,000 warriors in the field with great ease. He has a personal guard of 30,000 chosen men who all live in neighbouring villages in continual readiness. These men are under the orders of the prefect of the gates of the kingdom, who is called Mocomorgo or Zono. When Father Gonçalo came to the region the holder of this office was Caiado, a great protégé of the king. . . .

Within the upper circles of this African feudalism, Gonçalo, like his fellows in Ethiopia, was received with honour and was regarded as a representative of Portugal. The Mutapa hoped, as did the Ethiopian Emperors, for military alliance—in this case against his half-brother Tsheput, who was in rebellion. Eventually, however, the chiefs and nobles of the court turned their ruler against Gonçalo and he was strangled in March 1561 on the fourth Sunday in Lent.

There followed much trouble within the realm and many leaders died, including the Mutapa's own mother and most of those involved in the Jesuit's death, but the subsequent history of central Africa would seem to justify the fears and suspicions held farther north by the Ethiopian Christian Church. A few years later the king of Portugal sent an expedition under Francisco Barreto with instructions not only to avenge Gonçalo but also to acquire the mineral wealth of the region. It is significant that the twentieth century, at the time of writing, has not yet seen the passing in Mozambique of the Portuguese rule which ensued.

It is hardly surprising that even in Addis Ababa, let alone in the Ethiopian countryside, there remains a deep suspicion of Jesuit intrigue and a fear, not in every case justified, of the designs of members of the society.

Thus it was that the several political factors which were to interact in and around the traditional Abyssinian highlands in more recent times were formulated by the end of the seventeenth century. But to this complex pattern of internal politics, characteristic of the story of the re-emergence and world recognition of the Ethiopian state by the end of the nineteenth century, must now be added the pressures of the era of imperialism and even more pertinently the Ethiopian responses to them.

II

ETHIOPIA EMERGENT

4

Out of Chaos

'Perhaps one should not delve too deeply into the period between Susenyos and the advent of Theodore II . . .'— J. DORESSE, *Ethiopia,* London, 1956

'It was reported that the King of England was coming as no one not royal was likely to be called Theodore.'—THEODORE BENT, *The Sacred City of the Ethiopians,* London, 1896

THE GONDAR COURT

The Ethiopian court at Gondar gave itself up to pleasure and intrigue. Ethiopian and European sources alike provide a picture of decadence where political assassinations, more than once of monarchs by their own sons, were commonplace. Great care and skill was bestowed on the building of castles, churches and baths, and there was an artistic and literary revival. However, the relative power of the Emperors declined in favour of the great provincial *rases* and the Galla leaders. During the eighteenth and the first half of the nineteenth centuries the Empire of Ethiopia disintegrated into a series of almost independent feudatories whose main link was not the monarchy but the Christian Church.

There was a serious earthquake in the Gondar region in 1704 and at least one castle tower, that of Jan Tekel, collapsed. There were civil wars in which, not for the last time, great mirrors in the palaces were smashed. Later, in 1868, the Emperor Tewodros II (Theodore) sacked the town of Gondar and some years afterwards it was burnt by the dervishes, warriors of the Mahdi of the Sudan. Lastly during the liberation from the Italians it was bombarded as Patriot and British forces closed for the final reckoning with the already shattered Italian armies in 1941. The gaudy splendours of the Gondar court are thus difficult to recapture. Only the impressive shells of the castles remain, though even they quite dominate the town. The oldest, that of Fasiladas, is at the southern end of the group and the creations of later Emperors lie in chronological succession to the north. In recent years a progressive *kantiba* (mayor) has thrown open the gates of the historic curtain walls and visitors may wander in the quiet of the well-kept gardens and examine the towers and churches without the tiring necessity, so common in Ethiopia, of first having to obtain a pass from one or other government department. Gondar town is kept very clean and is deservedly proving a tourist centre. There are some wonderful vistas in the mountains north of the town and to the south lies Lake Tana and its famous island monasteries.

The castles are often described as Portuguese, but they are not, for in many ways they reflect traditional architectural developments. They were, in fact, all built after the final expulsion of the Jesuits even if there remained many descendants of the Portuguese soldiery. The Italians restored the floors of the oldest and largest of the castles—that of Fasiladas—and there is a wonderful view from the high battlements. The writings of Poncet, a doctor sent by Louis XIV of France, or Bruce, a Scotsman who was better received because he brought letters from Mark VII of Cairo (whom he mistakenly believed to be the relevant patriarch), bring to life the material splendour and intrigue which typifies the courts of Gondar.

Powerful and dominating figures stand out, either relatives of the monarch, such as the Queen Mother, or great *rases*, like the silver-haired and cloaked figure of Mikael Sohul of Tigré, whose power resulted from the firearms imported into that province and from the disaffection of the nobles towards the Galla-dominated monarchy. Ras Mikael, angered one day by an attempt to shoot him as he rested on the verandah of his house in Gondar, caused the Emperor to be strangled that same evening. Mikael and his descendants ruled a united Tigré for many decades, the position of *Bahr Negash* (King of the Sea) having virtually disappeared. Even so, the Tigréan rulers had to wait until 1872 before a representative of their ruling houses—Yohannes IV—was to seize the imperial throne itself.

It is interesting to recall that Bruce describes having attended a trial in one of the castles after which a notable ecclesiast who had been party to a rebellion, and who was accused of treason, was hanged while still wearing his robes of office.[1]

Bruce, whose stories of Ethiopia, in common with Poncet's,[2] were not at first believed, unintentionally makes a point that is often missed. He records the manners and polite solicitations of the Emperor and members of his court as to the welfare of all in their circle, their charm and the unobtrusive ways in which they rewarded with gifts of money or land all those loyal to them, a practice still current in Addis Ababa and also recorded in British history. But Bruce also notes the ruthlessness, the murders and the great cruelties and tortures which were practised and which were evidently the cause of his eventually writing, 'Nothing occupied my thoughts but how to escape from this bloody country.' These two contrasting pictures are not incongruous.

In the 1960s the nobility remain as courteous as ever, and visitors to Ethiopia who move only in their circles—and that means most, especially from Britain—are very likely to receive a misleading impression. Their circle is the Ethiopian 'establishment' and to be accepted in it is very different from the lot of the vast majority of the Ethiopian people. This was not politically significant in Bruce's time, even if the cruelties horrified him and he wished to leave, but it is today. Those cruelties were born of contempt—and that contempt remains in the attitudes of some of the Ethiopian 'establishment' towards the common people. The times of Bruce have gone and on the fringe of the traditional 'establishment' there is a class of educated people, far from the majority of whom are drawn from significant families, and even those that are, are often introduced to new attitudes.

All around Ethiopia are countries which have become independent, the leaders of which came to prominence in struggles against the 'establishment'—that is to say, in their case, against the colonial governments. That the new leaders themselves became *ipso facto* the new significant families and the new 'establishment' does not alter the fact that their roots are in the masses, with the people. Their democratic attitudes are vastly different from those of ancient aristocracies anywhere in the world. More will be said below of the effect of contact between these African leaders, and young students from their countries, on the students and younger government officials in Ethiopia, especially in Addis Ababa. Outside Africa care should be taken to enquire into the extent of the circle in which would-be rapporteurs of the Ethiopian scene have moved, especially if their visits were brief.

THE TIME OF THE JUDGES

The Ethiopian historians refer to these confused and decadent times from 1769 to the reign of Tewodros II, which began in 1855, as the 'time of the judges'. They refer to the last verse of the book of Judges in the Old Testament which reads : 'In those days there was no King in Israel : every man did that which was right in his own eyes.' A contemporary Ethiopian chronicler wrote deploring the 'ignorance, debauchery, witchcraft and drunken orgies' even of the clergy.

In the mid-nineteenth century, the Emperor was but a puppet, real power being divided amongst the nobles, the chief of whom were the rulers of Begemidir, of Gojjam and of Simien. Civil warfare was rife. In addition the Ras of Tigré and the ruler of the more southerly Shewa were to all intents and purposes independent. Indeed, according to Bruce, the Shewans had deliberately allowed the Galla to occupy Wellegga, thus increasing their independence from the Gondar court. It is, however, doubtful if they could have prevented these incursions.

The history of the ruling house of Shewa which, in view of the later importance of Shewa and the leading Shewan families, is relevant to the problems of the 1960s, has usually, but quite inadequately, been represented as a long succession of military campaigns against alien 'Galla' peoples in order to regain or retain the Shewan frontiers. But like the Gondar Emperors the Shewan rulers sometimes married into leading Galla families for political reasons. Sahlé Sellassié, ruler of Shewa in the early nineteenth century is an example. He fought many campaigns and, in fact, received a serious leg-wound in a battle with Galla forces near Mojo, a settlement some fifty miles south of present-day Addis Ababa—but he also married the daughter of a Galla chieftain. Likewise the whole Shewan population has long been enriched by Galla blood.

For centuries the somewhat peripheral position of Shewa in relation to the heartlands of the Ethiopian empire which lay farther north had led to its being neglected as rather unimportant by the Emperors. In the *Chronicles* the daughters of the ruling houses are never recorded as having been given in marriage to the rulers of Shewa. In the late nineteenth and early twentieth centuries much has been made of the existence of a branch of the 'Solomonic' family tree in Shewa—to the point where all other Ethiopian families with any claim to 'Solomonic' blood have tended to be ignored. It is, however, an open though academic question whether the Shewan ancestors of Sahlé Sellassié either styled themselves *negus* or cared much for the 'Solomonic succession'. Gebré Sellassié, the chronicler of Sahlé Sellassié's famous grandson who became the Emperor Menelik II was one of those chiefly responsible for this distortion by omission, but later historians outside Ethiopia have not been guiltless.

Sahlé Sellassié, Negus of Shewa from 1813, was only twelve years old when he succeeded to his throne after the assassination of his father, Wossen Seged. Sahlé Sellassié whose name means 'Clemency of the Trinity' was the great grandfather of Hailé Sellassié—'Power of the Trinity'. Sahlé held courts at Angolala, then a fortress agair.st the Galla, at Ankober, now only a small village in wild and beautiful scenery on the end of the Rift valley and at Debra Berhan, which name means 'hill of light', since a great cross is said to have once appeared in the sky overhead. Debra Berhan is a cold, wind-swept spot up on the plateau through which the main road from Addis Ababa northward to Asmara now runs. The King of Shewa had several visitors including Rochet d'Héricourt on behalf of King Louis Philippe of France, and Major C. W. Harris on behalf of the British government.[3] There survives some interesting, if over-critical, commentary on his times.

For example, an interesting parallel with today, as will be shown later, is that even in the days of Sahlé Sellassié a careful eye was kept on the opinion of the world. Harris records the releasing from prison of seven of the *negus's* relatives—all in wretched and half blind condition. The king remarked : 'My children you will write all that you have now seen to your country and will say to the British Queen that although far behind the nations of the white men from whom Ethiopia first received her religion, there yet remains a spark of Christian love in the breast of the King of Shewa.' (Incidentally, despite the king's remark, his ancestors had been Christian for longer than had Major Harris's.)

As has already been mentioned, Harris had little time for the Ethiopian Christian Church—but he was very biased. His English pride had been greatly offended when he had been refused permission to visit the tomb of King Sahlé's forefather, King Asfa Wossen.* That king's tomb is in the Church of the Archangel Michael at Ankober, and the grounds for the refusal were that Harris and his companions drank coffee and smoked tobacco—both of which habits were then regarded as 'Muhammadan abominations'. He was, however, received after he had sent as presents a rich altar cloth and some money.

King Sahlé Sellassié told Harris many fascinating stories of his life and times. Once when returning from a campaign against the Galla he had collapsed, 'I felt suddenly unwell and giddy. The

---

* That monarch's stormy reign had seen three rebellions including one led by his son Wossen Seged, the heir apparent, who was wounded in battle and imprisoned.

earth became blue and I fell from my mule.' This seemed to be a
signal for general confusion. He told how the enemy attacked his
disordered army and how a governor rebelled and tried to secure
the throne for his own son. However, the people dashed cold water
over their king, he recovered and restored order, the rebellious
governor being confined to the dungeons of Goncho for life. Serious
trouble was thus averted but this illustration still serves to show
how disorder and fragmentation are always possible on the death
or even in the declining years of an absolute monarch. Not surprisingly, in the early 1960s there has been debate in Addis Ababa
as to whether or not the heir apparent, the Crown Prince, Asfa
Wossen, would be allowed to succeed Hailé Sellassié.

Such situations have been especially typical of Ethiopian
history, in part because the terrain favours regionalism. In such
confused times power may be seized by the first strong man who
can organise himself, but the country benefits little from the energies dissipated in the subsequent re-unification struggle which all
this necessarily involves.

THE RISE OF KASSA

In the sorrily disunited state of nineteenth-century Ethiopia such a
strong man arose. He was a rebellious chief named Kassa and his
climb to the throne of the King of the Kings, which he occupied
with the coronation name of Tewodros (Theodore), is a strange
story.

Kassa was born at Kuara in the west of Ethiopia, into a
period of strife so confused that it is difficult to describe. Ras
Walda Sellassié, who had ruled Tigré since the death of the sons
of old Ras Mikael, and who had spent his time in constant strife
both with Ras Gugsa, representative of the ruling dynasty of
Yejjow Gallas at Gondar, and with Dejazmatch Sabagadis, had
recently died. Then Sabagadis made his bid for supreme
power, and at that time young Kassa was sent to a monastery near
Lake Tana. However, Ras Mariyé, the son of Ras Gugsa, formed a
league with Dejazmatch Wubie of Simien against Sabagadis,
who in his turn was defeated in battle and killed. Then followed
a time when Galla influence was in the ascendancy, but it was a
time of much lawlessness. Young Kassa had to flee from the
monastery when it was sacked by Dejazmatch Maru, another
defeated rebel, and he took shelter with his uncle, Dejazmatch
Kanfu, who was a governor of some local importance.

There were several Europeans at the courts of the period—
and they were usually well informed since the *rases* hoped through

them to obtain foreign alliances and firearms. When one of their number, Arnauld d'Abbadie,[4] met young Kassa, he wrote of him that although then unknown 'he will one day become *ras* over the whole of Abyssinia' which proved a remarkable prophecy.

The whole of the region of present-day Ethiopia continued in this state of great turmoil and disunity—so much so that most foreign travellers failed to recognise any thread that could lead to unity again and therefore wrote of the kingdoms as quite separate entities. Foreign governments dealt separately with provincial kings and *rases*, but Ras Ali, a minor and a nephew of Ras Mariyé still nominally ruled from the settlement of Debra Tabor up in the northern mountains and his mother, the Empress Menen, was the regent even if their joint influence was often only very local indeed. Meantime, in Tigré, Dejazmatch Wubie finally overcame the sons of Sabagadis and consolidated his power. Further south Dejazmatch Goshu ruled in Gojjam and Sahlé Sellassié was *negus*, or king, of Shewa.

Then Dejazmatch Kanfu, Kassa's guardian died. His sons squabbled and were driven from their father's lands by Dejazmatch Goshu. Kassa's mother looked after her son and it is likely that unconsciously or even consciously she implanted an ambition for power in his mind—as, by tradition, had the mother of Gran many years before. Kassa's father, Hailu Weleda Giorgis, was dead and his mother was very poor. She never lost her pride but was driven to the lengths of becoming a seller of *Kosso,* a drug derived from the flower of a tree and used as a medicine against tape-worm (a common parasitic infection owing to the Ethiopian taste for raw meat). At one time young Kassa had to hide in a peasant's hut and if later, when he had risen to supreme power, he rewarded the peasant, at the time his life was that of a brigand—though among such men he was soon recognised as a courageous and imaginative leader.

In those times brigandage was the only 'honourable' course open to a son for whom there was little to inherit, or who wished to put his qualities and ambitions to a greater test than his inheritance and social position allowed. Although he was a bandit, Kassa was also a patriot as far as the outside world was concerned, for when the Egyptians menaced Ethiopia he marched to great victories against the peoples of the western bank of the Nile near Metemma. The number of his followers grew with his fame, and too late the Empress Menen saw the danger and sent forces against him. He defeated them and she was obliged to give him the governorate of Dembea. Since she felt it was clearly necessary to recognise such a powerful upstart, in the usual manner, she begrudgingly arranged that Kassa should journey under safe conduct to Ras Ali's capital and be given the latter's daughter Tawabatch for wife.

The troublesome Egyptian attempts at expansion under Muhammad Ali were checked by the diplomatic intervention of France and Britain at the instigation of Dejazmatch Wubie, but not before the Ethiopian leaders had been forced to fight in the Gallabat region. This time Kassa was defeated and wounded and the gleeful Empress, still smarting from her earlier defeats, sent him a joint of beef with the comment that men of his rank and quality were not entitled to a whole cow.

Kassa was furious and as soon as he had recovered he declared himself independent of her sway. A certain Dejazmatch Wonderad boasted that he would bring 'the *Kosso* vendor's son, dead or alive, to the foot of the throne', but Kassa defeated him, made him eat a meal and with it drink a large *Kosso* instead of the traditional *tej* or honey-mead. The empress herself rallied her forces and marched against Kassa, but she too was defeated and captured and after an interval Ras Ali met the same fate. Then it was the turn of Dejazmatch Goshu Birru of Gojjam,* from whom Kassa had demanded homage. The proud *dejazmatch* was angry and, considering himself insulted, took the field near Gorgora on the shore of Lake Tana, but was captured. In order to humiliate him further, Kassa sent word to his wife, who was still holding out on an *amba* top, that he would return her spouse if she surrendered. She, however, sent back word, 'Let Kassa take the *amba*, but let him not give me back my husband!' Ethiopian history, right up to the Patriot fights against the Italians, is rich in such tales of proud warrior women. Nor is this spirit dead today.

After this series of battles, Kassa marched north into the Simien mountains. When he reached the camp of his last main rival, Dejazmatch Wubie, his troops were weary and did not wish to attack until Kassa addressed them : ' . . . and now after all our numerous conquests does yonder rheumatic dotard check your prowess? . . . Follow me and tomorrow by this time my name will be no more Kassa—but Tewodros, for God has given me the Kingdom.' Dejazmatch Wubie was captured, his army defeated and his treasures located and looted from the caves in the cold, high peaks of the Simien mountains.

It is significant that Kassa chose the name Tewodros for a prophecy had been current in Ethiopia for a few hundred years that a king of that name would restore the greatness of Ethiopia.

---

* Goshu, Wobie and Sabagadis have often been wrongly termed *ras*.

In the 1950s and '60s the descendants of the great families of Ethiopia still regarded Kassa or Tewodros as an upstart, despite the fact that he revived the great chronicles and claimed the Solomonic blood. There have been attempts on the part of members of the aristocracy to defame his memory. One such attempt, for example, is in an Amharic historical novel about a Gondari woman, named Taitu, related to Tewodros by marriage, whose husband was a *dejazmatch* and one of the Emperor's soldiers. In general it discredits Tewodros and without historical foundation accuses him of sexual promiscuity. 'Why does he want to speak to me?' Taitu is made to cry out, when the Emperor calls while her husband is away, 'I am the wife of his honest servant!' However, this work aroused considerable resentment, for Tewodros is highly thought of by very many Ethiopians and particularly by younger folk of more progressive outlook. His importance to younger Ethiopians is not unconnected with the fact that in his attempts to re-unify and modernise Ethiopia he did not rely either on the Solomonic myth or the Ethiopian Christian Church.

In 1961, a university student praised Tewodros in a public oratorical contest. Conservative elements in the government obliged the president of the University College to send home a student leader as being responsible. He was actually accused of inviting the Emperor to the contest in a casual manner in that the invitation was not in an envelope and was left on an ADC's office desk, but more relevant was a previous refusal to submit the speeches for censorship. Forewarned, Hailé Sellassié did not attend the debate but a member of the Imperial family who sought to intervene on the student's behalf reported that when the Emperor heard the several speeches on a tape made by the security police his anger made him quite unapproachable on the subject for several days. In 1963 the unabashed students staged a play on the life of Tewodros, which was popularly acclaimed in Addis Ababa.

EMPEROR TEWODROS AND REFORM

Tewodros as an Emperor took severe action against anyone who criticised his mother or himself. He had the missionary Henry Stern flogged and imprisoned when he published a work containing some slightly disparaging remarks—though as it were to prove the might of the pen, Stern wrote a much more violent work after the death of the Emperor. However, Tewodros may also have considered his harsh actions necessary in view of the new dignity he sought to lend to the imperial throne, and there remains some doubt as to how seriously he personally took his claim to Solomonic blood. In a letter to a party of Europeans who were casting him a mortar, he said :

> . . . In Europe I am insulted, and it is said that I am not the true inheritor of the throne but only the son of poor peasants : my legal origin and my right to the throne can be seen from Abraham to David and Solomon, from there to Fasil[adas], and from Fasil to me. . . . I say this not for my own sake but for yours, that you should not be ashamed as though you had taken a rebel for a king. Further, I well know that God will raise whom He will and will cast down whom He will.

Doubtless because of his dubious origins, Archbishop Salama who was captured with Dejazmatch Wubie was at first reluctant to crown Kassa. There is evidence that Kassa was instead prepared to make a deal with a certain Roman Catholic, Monsignor de Jacobis, and this probably decided matters. On February 5, 1855, the day after the end of the battle, Kassa left the little church of Mariam Deresse crowned as the Emperor Tewodros II and proceeded to Gondar, the traditional centre. The nature of the countryside dictated, however, that he had always to be on the move.

Soon afterwards he set off again, this time against the Gallas. He defeated them, killed their leader Adara Billé and caused the *afe negus* to see to it that Amba Magdela in their country was fortified whilst he marched on to end the independence of Shewa. The king, Hailé Malakot, son of King Sahlé Sellassié died of dysentery during the campaign and his son, the young Prince Sahlé Mariam, much later to attain fame with the coronation name of Emperor Menelik II, surrendered. Before his death his father had given him a necklace cord and locket which Tewodros took and opened to find a parchment containing many of the secrets of the Shewan royal line. In a sense it was a will telling the young prince where secret *caches* of arms and riches were located. Tewodros did not harm the boy and left him captive, companion for his own son, on Amba Magdela. He appointed an administrator named Bezebé to govern Shewa and returned to Gondar. In a very short time he had restored to one rule the ancient heartlands of Ethiopia, and the 'time of the princes' seemed passed.

But Emperor Tewodros's ambition did not stop at reunification of the country, for he also sought to change and develop it. Ethiopian historians count him as their first 'modern monarch'. They seldom agree with the usual foreign image of Tewodros—that he was talented but mad—and in many ways they are right

for that is superficial. He has been described as an African Napo-
leon, but Alan Moorehead draws attention to the striking resem-
blance between the Tsar Ivan IV, called the Terrible[6] and Tewodros, whom he also describes as 'the raging reformer who finds his
reforms rejected and wants to pull the whole world down in ruins
to appease himself for his failure'. There is much in this. Moorehead also puts his finger on the virtue so much respected by
Ethiopians—the courage of Tewodros.

Another most interesting comparison—an African one—can
be made with the Buganda kingdom of modern Uganda. Writing
of the nineteenth century, Fallers states :

> It took many campaigns and constant journeys for the reign-
> ing Kabaka to quell rebellion and to keep the kingdom to-
> gether, but the Bakabaka (monarchs) continued to strengthen
> Buganda by rewarding loyalty with favours, ordering execu-
> tions, transferring subordinate chiefs, dividing districts and
> contracting marriages of convenience.[7]

Tewodros became attached to two Britons, John Bell and
Walter Plowden.* The former fought and died at Tewodros's side
as a '*liquamaquas*'† and the latter was killed by the grandson of
Wubie of Simien, Dejazmatch Negussié, who was supported by
France as a pretender to the throne. Tewodros avenged him in
1861 when he captured Negussié, had him tortured to death and
killed many of his followers. Nevertheless, Tewodros's odd friendly
relationships with British officers, and, in spite of this, war with
Britain, contributed to his eventual collapse and that paradox is
not unique. Tewodros was also a keen Christian yet he quarrelled
with the Christian Church. He once said, 'Let God give victory
to my arms and peace to my Empire and the cross shall not lack
support in this country.' He never understood how Britain could
tolerate idolatry in India, let alone support Islam in Egypt and
Turkey, and considered that Britain as a Christian country was
therefore morally bound to support him—a view not shared by the
British government. When Patriarch Cyril IV of Alexandria visited
Ethiopia in 1856 Tewodros scorned him as the ambassador of the
Muslim ruler of Egypt, Said Pasha. The patriarch's sharp retort
cost him five days in prison in the company of the archbishop.

The close relationship between the monarchy and the
Christian Church has continued, with but few shifts in emphasis
relating to the character of the monarch and his bishops, right up

---

* Walter Chichele Plowden, author of *Travels in Abyssinia and the Galla
Country*, ed. Trevor Chichele Plowden, London, 1868.
† See Appendix II.

to the early 1960s. No Emperor since Tewodros has so forcefully tackled the reformation of the Christian Church, perhaps warned by his failure. Tewodros sought to extend the control of the monarch, that is to say the civil government, over the administration of the church lands and wealth. In return the state would support the clergy. There were to be two priests and three deacons to each church. There was considerable outcry at this suggestion which was shelved until 1860 at the suggestion of Wagshum Tafari, a supporter of the archbishop and the spokesman of the Emperor's counsellors. After 1860 the country rapidly deteriorated into chaos and reforms such as Tewodros's, or something like them, remain to be undertaken, preferably but not very probably by the Church herself. There was nothing unchristian in Tewodros's intentions, indeed it is said that Tewodros was only dissuaded from a campaign forcibly to convert the Kamants, an unassimilated Agau people who live to the north of Gondar, by the argument that they might 'become proud' and cease to carry essential fuel from the hills to Gondar.

Tewodros attempted to introduce administrative reforms and to subdue and control the great feudal nobles. In his reign works were composed in Amharic as well as ancient Ge'ez. Plowden stated that he attempted to abolish slavery and at first paid his soldiery and discouraged their living off the land. He initiated road building and quickly saw how Ethiopia would need modern firearms and artillery, preferably as Brigadier-general Mengistu remarked at his trial in 1961, of their own manufacture.* Tewodros caused a vast mortar to be cast and dragged to his fortress capital at Amba Magdela. A recent article, specifically on firearms in Ethiopia, has referred to Tewodros's efforts as an 'attempted Industrial Revolution'.[8]

TEWODROS AND BRITAIN

In foreign policy also Tewodros was very shrewd. He was quite aware of the expansionist ambitions of Europe and Egypt that were to cause such difficulties for his successors. Lejean, a French consul, quotes him as remarking :

---

* Brigadier-general Mengistu said, 'While I was in exile during the five years of the [Italian] Occupation, I ruminated over how the Ethiopian armed forces had been so easily broken by the forces of the enemy. I realised that it was fundamentally because of our overall backwardness. In this case it was because of having to buy the munitions of war—for a country that fights with ammunition which it does not itself manufacture is scarcely in a strong position.'

I know the tactics of European governments when they desire
to acquire an eastern state. First they send out missionaries,
then consuls to support the missionaries, then battalions to
support the consuls. I am not a Rajah of Hindustan to be
made a mock of in that way. I prefer to have to deal with the
battalions straight away!

Tewodros also more than held his own against the Galla and
the Muslims. Baker, the explorer, describes how furious he found
Musa Pasha at Khartoum over one of Tewodros's letters claiming
much of the Sudan and demanding the surrender even of Shendy
and Khartoum itself.[9] In the famous letter to Queen Victoria,
which the British Foreign Office mislaid and left unanswered with
disastrous consequences, he stated :

My fathers, the Emperors, having forgotten the Creator, He
handed over their kingdom to the Gallas and the Turks. But
God created me, lifted me out of the dust, and restored this
Empire to my rule. He endowed me with power and enabled
me to stand in the place of my fathers. By this power I drove
away the Gallas. As for the Turks I have told them to leave
the land of my ancestors. They refuse. I am now going to
wrestle with them.

And he went on to ask for support from the British queen.

When no answer came and when Tewodros learned that
the British consul, Cameron, was visiting his enemies in the Sudan,
he had him and many other Europeans put in chains. He had
taken this type of action before, for example over the French
consul, Lejean, quoted above. The latter committed several grave
breaches of etiquette : he rode up to the Emperor on a donkey; he
treated him, as Tewodros remarked, 'like a shopkeeper' when he
tried to barter silks with him direct, but he overstepped a gener-
ous limit when, although asked to wait, he demanded an immediate audience because he was wearing the uniform of the King of
France. In Tewodros's words, 'I said who is his father? Seize him!
And I put him in chains in the very dress of his king.' The English
translation of the Amharic expression 'who is his father' leaves
much to be desired, but indicates the great personal and family
pride of the Ethiopians. This consul was later released and expelled.

Not so Cameron, and there followed a series of emissaries
and diplomatic notes from Britain successively sterner in tone.
Queen Victoria explained to Tewodros 'how nations assuming to be
civilised' held the persons of ambassadors as sacred and asked him

to prove that 'he rightly understood his position among sovereigns'. Today this seems a patronising if motherly note and is rather reminiscent of another occasion when the good queen presented a pair of woollen combinations to a Scotswoman in whose draughty cottage she once had tea.

THE NAPIER EXPEDITION

Her diplomacy was of no avail and eventually the British government resolved on force. Thus the expensive Napier expedition, so superbly redescribed by Alan Moorehead in *The Blue Nile*, was born. In the meantime Tewodros's behaviour became more and more inconsistent and violent, and thousands of his people died at his hand or command. The deterioration of his character followed upon the death of his first wife, but some say it was the result of a priest's attempt to poison him. He did marry again, this time to Dejazmatch Wubie's daughter, whom he discovered hiding from him in a tomb, but except perhaps in his last hours he had little time for her. Rassam, Britain's last major emissary before General Napier, claims that Tewodros said to him one night: 'I used to hear that I was called a madman for my acts.... Now I have come to the conclusion that I am really so. But as Christians we ought always to be ready to forgive each other.' Despite his imprisonment of the British messengers Tewodros was often quite tender towards them and even charged Rassam to see that he was properly buried if he died in battle. Rassam remembered his promise. The relationship between these two was decidedly unusual and reflects Tewodros's love-hate relationship with Britain. It is often quoted how he chided his soldiers that they had no chance against the weapons and discipline of Napier's approaching army, a fantastic expedition complete with elephants, a brass band and a delicate young cavalry officer wearing a green veil. Tewodros awaited the arrival of the European column with morbid enthusiasm.

What is not always made clear is that this was because Tewodros had tried to drag his country into the modern age but had failed. That is perhaps what unhinged him. To the last he demanded skilled artisans from Queen Victoria and he did not imprison his German workers. In an ironic way, by defeating his army and destroying his mountain citadel at Magdela, Napier was to prove to the Ethiopian chiefs that their Emperor had been right all along in demanding that Ethiopia keep up with the rest of the world in techniques and warfare. Thus it is perhaps not so strange that Tewodros almost wanted the defeat to happen. He is recorded as having given voice to his disillusion with his 'wicked' subjects whose rebellious behaviour he said had made him decide to 'give them war'.

Napier fought no one along the route. On the contrary, his preposterous column was fed and helped all the way. All he did was give the final dramatic touch to the collapse of Tewodros who had burnt Gondar and Debra Tabor and carried his treasure to the Amba Magdela. The Emperor who had 'intended if God had so decreed to conquer the whole world' remarked of the *amba* : 'I have lost all Abyssinia but this rock.' So he had, for Gojjam was in revolt and Wagshum Gobazé, after raising the standard of rebellion in Lasta, had marched on Tigré and defeated the Emperor's army. Then in his turn Balambaras Kassa, self-styled *dejazmatch,* whom Gobazé had left in charge had declared Tigré completely independent of both of them.

Meantime, significant events had occurred in the *amba* fortress of Magdela. Ahmadé Beshir, a Galla leader had been killed leading a rebellion and his younger nephew Imam had been proclaimed the successor by his mother, Woizero Worqet. Imam, however, in company with twenty-four of his leaders had gone over to Tewodros. When Woizero Worqet again rebelled, Tewodros's commander-in-chief, Ras Engeda, blamed Imam's party and imprisoned them all. An important figure for the future then known as Sahlé Mariam, the heir apparent of Shewa who had previously surrendered to Tewodros, had lived on the Amba Magdela, and had married one of the Emperor's daughters, deserted her one night and managed to flee the rock with a few of his followers. They crept silently through the valleys which were full of Tewodros's soldiers and by dawn reached the high table land of the Wello Gallas. Looking through a telescope, Tewodros saw Sahlé Mariam meet Woizero Worqet and in a fit of rage he had her son Imam and his followers murdered. Sahlé Mariam was accompanied by his uncle Seifu and his friend and adviser, Girmamé, whom he later created *dejazmatch.** The European prisoners on the *amba* had hopes that Sahlé Mariam might march on Magdela but he was to make his bid much later and in the meantime the kingdom of Shewa once again became almost independent. The chaos of the 'time of the princes' had returned.

In course of time both Kassa of Tigré and Sahlé Mariam of Shewa were to wear the imperial crown, for Tewodros was doomed. His army led by Dejazmatch Gebriyé put up a great fight beneath the towering rock face of Amba Magdela, but it consisted of about 3,000 men armed with matchlocks and percussion

---

* An ancestor of the 1960 rebel brothers Girmamé and Mengistu Neway.

guns, not rockets and Snider breech-loading rifles. The result was
a massacre. Gebriyé was killed and Tewodros's great mortar burst
on its first firing.

THE SUICIDE OF THE EMPEROR

There remains some mystery about what ensued. Tewodros released
his prisoners and sent his herds of cows and sheep to Napier, but
Napier refused them, thus indicating that he did not wish to come
to terms, despite the fact that his proclamations had repeatedly
stressed that the release of the prisoners was his only aim. Tewodros
had been puzzled by Napier's message, 'I guarantee honourable
treatment for yourself and all the members of your majesty's
family', and had dryly remarked : 'Has he counted the number of
my wives and children?' Tewodros was asked to 'submit to the
Queen of England' but that did not make it clear whether or not
he would be made a prisoner. Strangely there still lingered in the
Emperor's mind the hope that Britain would help him to modernise
his country. The missionary, Stern, absurdly wrote that Tewodros
'had to learn that a British general is as true to his word as he is
faithful to his sword'—but the truth is that escape from his
dilemma was impossible through Galla country, and Tewodros, believing himself betrayed and hourly deserted by more and more of
his followers chose, like Saul on Mount Gilboa, not to surrender
but rather to fight and to die.

Napier's troops bombarded and stormed the citadel of Amba
Magdela. Tewodros and some soldiers were carrying stones to block
the first gateway when a shell burst, killing Ras Engeda. The little
party withdrew up the hill and Tewodros discarded his colourful
uniform. As the British rockets killed a horse just behind him he
remarked to his servant : 'What a terrible weapon, who can fight
against it?' He stood behind his shield and watched the battle
until the outer gate fell, then he shouted to his soldiers, 'Flee, I release you from your allegiance. As for me I shall never fall into
the hands of the enemy.' He drew his pistol—a gift from Queen
Victoria—he put it into his mouth and he fired. . . . It was April 13,
1868.

Recently, near a bridge on an Addis Ababa street behind
the Prince of Paradise Palace Lieutenant-colonel Workneh, head
of the Ethiopian Secret Service and a Gondari, emptied the
last magazine of his carbine at the army soldiers who pursued him
and threw it down. The attempted *coup d'état* had failed and a
dream of building a new Ethiopia lay shattered. He had seen the
American Ambassador to safety, but his polite request for sanctuary

was refused, as of course it had to be. He had not left for the hills with the others. Cornered, he stood up and shouted to his assailants, 'Tewodros has taught me something'. He put his pistol into his mouth and he fired.... It was December 16, 1960.

The body of Tewodros was not difficult to recognise and was found on the pathway up to the top of the Amba Magdela. The fallen Emperor's soldiers had fled to hide in the hillside caves. They were terrified of the Galla peoples who lived all round the *amba* and whose memories of many recent harsh campaigns were all too vivid. The valleys rang with Galla taunts, 'Come, my beloved! Come!', but on the next day the soldiers chose rather to give themselves up to the British when they found that prisoners were not to be killed. Rassam, as good as his word, had the body of Tewodros delivered to the Ethiopian Christian Church and it was reverently buried. 'Even in death,' writes Rassam, 'Tewodros had not wholly lost the affection of at least some of his subjects.' Indeed his death became the subject of a ballad :

> From the heart of Magdela comes a lament
> For he is dead whom woman never bore.
> In the heart of Magdela, hast thou seen the lion die?
> Death were dishonour at the hand of man.

In January 1961, a ballad entitled *The Death of the Lion* was a popular tune in the *tejbeits*, or drinking houses, of Addis Ababa until the tapes were impounded and it was suppressed by the police.

After the fall of Magdela the breeches of the guns were blown, the citadel was burnt and Napier's column turned to leave Ethiopia again, together with the captives whom Tewodros had released. The late Emperor's wife died on the march but his son Alamayu, whom Tewodros had always wanted to send to England, was taken there. It appears that the British government made Dr Jex-Blake, the headmaster of Rugby School, guardian of the young prince. After two years he entered Rugby School. The entry in the School Register reads :

ALAMAYU, SIMYEN, only legitimate son of the late Theodore, King of Abyssinia and Teruwark, Princess of Simyen, Queen of Abyssinia : since March 4, 1872 ward under the British government of Dr Jex-Blake, School House, Rugby. Aged 13 April 23rd, 1874. Came to Rugby in September 1874 and entered Mr Elsee's House.* Left Rugby December 1877.

* This is now known as 'Kilbracken House'. The writer is indebted to Mr N. C. Kittermaster, Librarian, Rugby School, for the above information.

Sandhurst 1878. Died at Headingley near Leeds, November 14th, 1879 and was buried in St George's Chapel, Windsor, November 21st, 1879. The coffin bore the following inscription :

PRINCE ALAMAYU

OF ABYSSINIA

BORN APRIL 23RD, 1861

DIED NOVEMBER 14TH, 1879.

A memorial Tablet was placed in Rugby School Chapel in 1880.

Thus like the Red Indian princess, Pocahontas from Virginia, this African prince died young far from his homeland, perhaps like her also, a victim of the British weather.

The column paid for all its supplies *en route* but took over 500 precious documents and riches, most of them from the Church of Medhané Alem (Saviour of the World) at Magdela—in fact there was a representative of the British Museum in attendance. All that can be said, apart from the fact that looting was a worldwide practice, is that the precious documents have been the subject of great care and much study whilst in Britain. One, however, was returned to the next Emperor, Yohannes. It was the famous *Kebra Negast*, the *Chronicle of the Glory of the Kings*, and Yohannes had said his subjects would not obey him without it. King George V returned Tewodros's crown in 1925 when Hailé Sellassié, then regent, visited Britain.*

The vitally significant political consequence of General Napier's campaign and of the battle of Amba Magdela was that it led the major European powers, and in particular Italy, to underestimate the military power of Ethiopia. It was not the British and General Napier who defeated Emperor Tewodros but rather it was Ethiopia herself. Like some vast and terrible version of Thomas Hardy's Egdon Heath, his own untamed country destroyed him. Tewodros had the will but not the means to build up his country anew. Not so Hailé Sellassié, who achieved much more. But if, much to his fury, young Ethiopia still talked of Tewodros, it was perhaps because in these latter years Hailé Sellassié who had the means, seemed to them to lack the will.

---

* At the Woolwich Royal Academy Officers' Mess there was, in 1961, a large and splendid Coptic Cross in soft silver brought from Magdela and now amongst the Mess silver. It is well cared for but perhaps it too will one day be returned.

5

Tigré Versus Shewa

As a Tigréan his enthronement greatly stimulated the pride
of the northern province and left it unready to accept
the Shewan rule that was to follow.—SIR GERALD PORTAL,
My Mission to Abyssinia, London, 1892

John is the greater warrior but Menelik the abler politi-
cian.—G. F. H. BERKLEY in *The Nineteenth Century and*
After, London, January 1903

DEJAZMATCH KASSA OF TIGRÉ

After the death of Emperor Tewodros, two Wello Galla 'queens'
were proclaimed but like the immediate predecessors of their
line had only local influence. In the midst of the ensuing chaos,
the senior chieftain took the field and seized the Imperial
throne. He was Wagshum Gobazé, ruler of Lasta and heir to the
Zagwé tradition. He marched through the Lake Tana region. But
power was soon concentrated in the hands of two men, Sahlé
Mariam of Shewa and Kassa of Tigré. Sahlé Mariam, who was
crowned as the Negus Menelik of Shewa—a famous name—sent a
delegation led by his chief lieutenant Gobena to submit to the *Wag-*
shum. Kassa was later crowned as Emperor Yohannes. The relatives
and the descendants of their royal houses continue to play a great
part in the contemporary Ethiopian scene. Beneath the surface
Ethiopian politics are a mass of family and faction alliances and
rivalries—to such an extent that some Ethiopians now favour a
clean sweep and a new start—a new attitude of vital significance.

Of these two Kassa was first to reach the throne of the
King of the Kings. He was a nobleman, the son of Dejazmatch
Mercha of the Tembien region. His mother was the daughter of

Dejazmatch Dimtsu of Enderta region whose capital was at Makellé. This Dejazmatch Dimtsu was a brother-in-law of Dejazmatch Sabagadis of Agamé region whose capital was Addigrat, and who before the rise of Tewodros had held power in all Tigré, the great northern province of the Ethiopia of today. Because of these important family relationships Kassa could command a feudal following from much of the north, but another telling factor in his rise to power was his friendship with General Napier.

It will be recalled that Kassa had declared himself independent in 1867. Napier had passed through his Tigréan domains on the tortuous route to Amba Magdela. Napier had stated to Tewodros, and had reiterated on many occasions : 'My sovereign has no desire to deprive you of any part of your dominions nor to subvert your authority, although it is obvious that such would in all probability be the result of hostilities.' That last fact especially was clear to Kassa. Further, Napier's declaration 'To the Governors, the Chiefs, the Religious Orders and the People of Abyssinia' contained the words :

> When the time shall arrive for the march of a British Army through your country, bear in mind, people of Abyssinia, that the Queen of England has no unfriendly feeling towards you, and no design against your country or your liberty. Your religious establishments, your persons and your property shall be carefully protected.... There is no intention to occupy permanently any portion of the Abyssinian territory, or to interfere with the government of the country.

If Kassa saw no reason to doubt these sentiments, then it was natural that he should ally himself to Napier. His army met Napier's column in February 1868, near Antalo. Under the shade of a large red umbrella, and wearing a lion skin over his silk clothes, Kassa left his tent astride his white mule and was received with full military honours by Napier mounted on an elephant. There was an escort of more elephants and red-coats. A salute was fired and the brass band played. The gifts, the displays of military might—it is recorded that the British column proceeded towards Magdela somewhat less confident than before having seen the bearing and arms of Kassa's soldiery—and the hospitality lavished by both sides have all been described, but one is left to wonder whether Napier gave Kassa any undertaking with regard to the fate of Tewodros and the citadel of Magdela. If he did it would explain a lot. On the other hand, Napier did offer the conquered citadel to Wagshum Gobazé who refused it, adding that he had been wise enough to keep away from it while Tewodros lived and would not change now. On its route back to the coast, Napier's column, sped by sniping warriors out for plunder, met Kassa again at Senafé. Napier left him a considerable quantity of guns, ammunition and military supplies, and with these he set out to make himself King of the Kings of Ethiopia.

Alan Moorehead criticises Napier for leaving Ethiopia and not establishing a garrison 'to tide the country over the next few years of political disorder', but there can be few supporters of this view. Winning a battle is a vastly different matter from the pacification of so wild a country. No invader from Gran to Graziani has ever succeeded in subduing the Ethiopian peoples.

In 1871 Kassa was nearly surprised by Wagshum Gobazé's army at Adowa but, assisted by a former sergeant from General Napier's force, he rapidly deployed his troops and saved the day. The sergeant became a general and eventually died under Egyptian arrest at Massawa. Many nobles and chieftains rallied to help Kassa, among them Ras Alula, later to become one of Africa's greatest soldiers. Wagshum Gobazé, who had proclaimed himself Emperor with the name Taklé Giorgis II, taunted Kassa. To emphasise the numbers of his own army he sent Kassa a present of grain. Kassa returned it—cooked!* Weapons and tactics, not numbers, did decide the eventual battle. Sixty thousand troops commanded by Taklé Giorgis were defeated by 12,000 led by Dejazmatch Kassa. Taklé Giorgis was taken prisoner and Kassa marched on the Wello Galla. By 1872 he had so built up his position that he was crowned at Aksum as the Emperor Yohannes IV† after the writer of the Book of Revelation.

Yohannes was described by Sir Gerald Portal as taller than most, 'of very dark skin, though not by any means black', with a thin intelligent looking face and keen bright eyes. His forehead was prominent and his nose thin and aquiline. Yohannes was a fervent Christian; he obliged the Muslim Galla leader Muhammad Ali to adopt the Christian title of Ras Mikael; he expelled Roman Catholic missionaries and even published an edict demanding that all Muslims should adopt his faith or leave the country. This, however, could not be applied and it was followed three years later by a more tolerant pronouncement. Emperor Yohannes once rebuked Lij Mertcha, a young noble, for having taken snuff in his presence. Many of the older generation in Ethiopia have remained fond of snuff—in 1962 Hailé Sellassié sometimes carried a

---

* Versions of the story of the cooked grain (*teff*) exist in Shewa where the cooking is ascribed to Menelik II.
† Outside Ethiopia 'Yohannes' is sometimes written as 'John'. In Tigré he was called 'the red' since to Ethiopians he appeared light skinned.

4—E * *

box with him. Yohannes' dislike of tobacco has frequently been commented upon, but there is little evidence to support accusations made at the time in Europe that he punished all smokers by causing them to be disfigured, although he may have so punished second offenders who ignored his warnings. On the whole his subjects thought him just and he himself once boasted that even a child could travel in safety throughout his kingdom. Of paramount importance, moreover, was the fact that he fulfilled better than most the Ethiopian image of the greatness of warrior monarchs which is to some extent still current.

It is fashionable to describe the Solomonic descent in terms of Shewa (see pages 43 and 70–71 above) and to portray Emperors Yohannes and Tewodros as usurpers.* That view was one reason which encouraged Menelik of Shewa also to style himself King of the Kings. The warrior Yohannes never bothered to discuss genealogy, but resolved to come to terms with Menelik in his own way, in due course. Meantime, however, other enemies demanded his attention. It was typical of Ethiopia's history that once again she should awake from preoccupation with internal difficulties to find that Islam prospered on her boundaries.

THE WARRIOR EMPEROR

A revival of Egypt under Khedive Ismail led to the territorial expansion of that power in the wake of the declining Ottoman Empire—an aspect of Ismail's reign not always emphasised by historians. The opening of the Suez Canal had brought a new significance to the Red Sea and by 1872 Egypt was in control of its western coast and had occupied the highland town of Keren on what is now called the Eritrean plateau. By 1875 Egypt had encircled the highlands of Ethiopia and was in possession of the important sultanate of Harar to the south-east. Egyptian armies, often with European and American officers, were defeated and practically annihilated by Ethiopian forces led by the Emperor Yohannes on several occasions. Munzinger, a Swiss who governed Massawa on behalf of the khedive, was killed in the lowlands of the Rift valley and an expedition which he commanded was destroyed. Then a further defeat of the Egyptians at Gundet near Adowa so infuriated the Khedive Ismail that he promoted yet another invasion from Massawa but that also was defeated at Gura in 1876. After that battle Yohannes returned Egyptian prisoners with the grim

---

* Despite the connection with the Solomonic dynasty recently described by J. Tubiana in his 'Quatre généalogies royales Ethiopiennes'. *Cahier d'études Africaines*, Vol. 2, 3, Paris, 1963. See chart, page 127.

message, 'Here are your soldiers Ismail! If you want any more eunuchs for your harems drive me up the rest of your army.' The Egyptians evacuated the highlands and Yohannes marched south to settle his own internal problems.

The rulers of more southerly parts of Ethiopia were daily consolidating their own positions and *ipso facto* the relative independence of their provinces. Ras Adal of Debra Tabor who had first been placed as ruler in Gojjam by Wagshum Gobazé was firmly established in that province. He had assumed the title of *Negus* (or king) with the coronation name of Taklé Haymanot, thereby founding a royal line of considerable subsequent importance. Although he acknowledged Yohannes as King of the Kings he was to all intents and purposes independent and from this time may be dated the rise of Gojjam as a political factor of cardinal significance. However, secretly supported by Yohannes, who lent him soldiers, the Negus Taklé Haymanot pushed his boundaries farther to the south-east. There was a period when this brought him into armed conflict with Menelik of Shewa who had similar ambitions of expansion into these regions, for from them came valuable items of trade : coffee, civet, gold, ivory—and slaves.

RIVALRY WITH MENELIK

Menelik even claimed the title of King of the Kings for himself. On his escape from Amba Magdela and the captivity imposed on him by Emperor Tewodros, Menelik—or Dejazmatch Sahlé Mariam as he was then—had sheltered with Woizero Worqet, leader of the Wello Galla of that region. She had refused to return him to Tewodros who in turn had murdered her son Imam whom he held in captivity. Sahlé Mariam, like many Shewans, had some Galla blood and Woizero Worqet respecting this fact had sent him back to Shewa. Indeed her advisers had persuaded her that as he was also a direct descendant of the Shewan *negus* (or king) Sahlé Sellassié—and therefore a representative of the supposed Solomonic line, a branch of which was believed to have taken refuge in Shewa during the time of the Zagwé dynasty— he was in every way a desirable pretender to the Shewan throne. Not everyone in Shewa shared this view and as soon as Sahlé Mariam reached the Wello frontier with Shewa, at a place called Waqi Dibo, he was arrested and for a time detained. His capters were messengers of a faction which opposed his reappearance. Any history of the monarchies of Ethiopia would demonstrate clearly that a good family claim to the throne has never been enough to gain the crown. Up to this day strong men have rarely hesitated to conspire—almost as a matter of tradition—to contest the succession. Eventually, however, in 1865, Sahlé Mariam managed to outwit his enemies. He was crowned Negus of Shewa but not before his cousin, Bezu Aba Dika, who opposed him, had on his order been tied up in wax-soaked bandages and burnt alive. Since his coronation the new monarch had been occupied in consolidating his control of the Shewan plateau and in extending his rule southwards over the Galla.

In 1873 certain rebels from Shewa had taken refuge with Emperor Yohannes and they proved a useful pretext for him to intervene and assert his own supremacy over Menelik. After a short and decisive campaign, the foot of the Emperor Yohannes was guided by the stooping Menelik on to the back of his own neck. This traditional sign of homage, performed in 1878, marked the success of Yohannes in reconsolidating the empire of Tewodros. However, Yohannes unlike Tewodros was prepared to acknowledge the local feudal rights of tributary kings provided they accepted his senior status. It is possible that this attitude was dictated by expediency but, nevertheless, during his reign the feudalism, which had contributed much to the weakness of Ethiopia before the times of Tewodros, revived.

An interesting tale is told in Ethiopia about the preliminary negotiations between Menelik and Yohannes. Menelik paid a young man—or some say three genuine hermits—to journey to the mobile court of Yohannes in the guise of a priest. Yohannes is said to have asked the imposter whether God would permit him to destroy Shewa. 'Yes,' was the reply, 'you may conquer Shewa but if you destroy it also you will not go to heaven.' This warning is said to have made a deep impression on the religious Emperor and he came to an agreement with the Negus Menelik of Shewa. Inevitably Yohannes and Menelik arranged a dynastic seal to this settlement of their rivalry. Ras Aria Sellassié, the only legitimate son of Yohannes, was to marry Zauditu, Menelik's daughter from an early Galla liaison—both Aria and Zauditu were young children.

FIRST IMPACT OF THE SCRAMBLE

Much farther to the south in Africa, but about this time, another ruler engaged in local wars, and concerned over mounting foreign pressure, followed a similar course. Lobengula, ruler of the Ndebele married the daughter of Mzila, ruler of the Shangala, a related people away to his east. It is not the main purpose of the present book either to make comparisons or to recount in detail the resistance of Ethiopia to the religious and imperialist pressures of the late nineteenth century which had so great an impact on the rest of Africa—except in so far as they have affected the development of the present situation in Ethiopia. General parallels in nineteenth-century African history are, however, common enough and 'Menelik of Shewa' has been described elsewhere as 'not essentially different from Mutesa of Buganda, Kabarega of Bunyoro, or Msiri of Katanga'.[2] There was, however, at least one essential difference in that the Ethiopian *rases,* the Negus Sahlé Sellassié of Shewa and the emperors Tewodros, Yohannes, and Menelik, unlike Lobengula, did not rely on *assegais* to combat European and other encroachment. They all imported firearms in quantity.[3]

In the reign of Emperor Yohannes, the Ethiopian tradition of separatist and rebellious feudal chieftains was further maintained by Ras Woldé Mikael from his lands towards the western frontiers. However, it was from beyond those boundaries that a serious new development occurred. The passing of the power and personality of both the Khedive Ismail and of General Gordon had left a vacuum. Long weary of oppression, poverty, and the corruption of Egyptian officials, the people of the Sudan were able at last to rise in rebellion in 1883. Their inspiration moreover was drawn from a great revival of Islam under Muhammad Ahmad Ibn Abd Allah —the mahdi, or 'guided one'—who claimed descent from the Prophet and who proclaimed again the *Jehad* or holy war. Ethiopia was not the only power to be alarmed by this development. The political and economic implications of the mahdi's movement were in direct conflict with the imperial ambitions of France and Britain in the whole region of the Upper Nile. Those two powers therefore looked on with anxiety, particularly since Egypt, unable to control events, tottered towards revolution. When that occurred Britain intervened, and there began her 'temporary' occupation of Egypt which lasted well into the present century. But soon herself in ever graver difficulties against the mahdi, Britain realised for the second time the value of an agreement with Kassa of Tigré, now the Emperor Yohannes IV.

Rear Admiral Hewitt visited the King of the Kings and two treaties were signed at Aksum on June 3, 1884; one concerned the suppression of the slave trade and the other was an alliance against the 'dervish' warriors of the mahdi.* Yohannes was to recover for Ethiopia, the north-western and present-day Eritrean

* The Persian term 'dervish' accurately applies to the several religious orders of Muslims who follow mystical systems of devotion. The mahdi did not use it—but it has been popularly coined to describe his followers.

province of Bogos previously ruled by Egypt, and in return Ras
Alula was to relieve several Egyptian garrisons—these proved the
only garrisons to be successfully relieved in the chaotic withdrawal
from the Sudan during which General Gordon and others lost their
lives. The arms, munitions and military stores of the relieved garrisons were handed over to the Ethiopians. Augustus Wylde who
accompanied the British delegation described Queen Victoria's
letter to Emperor Yohannes as a 'most gorgeous document, however in very good taste and the envelope was of velvet worked with
gold thread'. Wylde also noted, with some disapproval, that 'a
Greek consul is always hanging about the King's house'. The era
of diplomatic missions and intrigue so typical of the ensuing reign
was beginning. Significantly also, Yohannes was the first Ethiopian
Emperor to have a consulate in London.

Even at the time of the Napier expedition the European
view that the promotion of trade was best served by policies which
avoided political interference was beginning to fade. The era of
territorial imperialism which, despite a few decaying vestiges of
empires, may now be considered to be over in Africa, is usually
dated from the Berlin Conference of 1884–5. Certainly Italian
attempts to expand inland from the coast where they had already
settled, date from this period. Egyptian power collapsed in the
Sudan and therefore in the Horn of Africa, but ports in the latter
region were occupied by the French, the British and the Italians.
Assab and the best port, Massawa, a fine natural harbour, were
acquired by the Italians. British approval of this is hard to reconcile
with their agreement with the Emperor Yohannes, and there can be
no doubt that Britain encouraged the ambitions of the weaker Italy
in north-eastern Africa from fear of French expansion in the Nile
Valley. However, Ras Alula, the governor of the northern marches
of Ethiopia, proved more than a match for the early phases of
Italian expansionist ambition.

Ethiopia alone in the whole continent was not overwhelmed
in the scramble for Africa. This must be attributed as much to the
military skill of her generals—in particular Ras Alula—as to the
diplomatic skill of the Emperors. Other factors included the difficult mountainous terrain of Ethiopia and her imports of firearms. Further, despite the intrigues of nearly every feudal leader,
each prepared to trade parts of provinces in order to further his
own advancement through alliances with one or other of the
European powers—a tradition which died hard as will be shown
—Ethiopian nationalism, nevertheless managed to rally itself at
each real moment of crisis and present a united front.

Ras Alula was soon disturbed by Italian penetration inland

but was first distracted by more serious threats from dervish advances. He marched to defeat them at Kufit, overwhelming them by personally leading a last desperate charge with the cry : 'This time we will conquer or die.'

Italian diplomatic intrigues against Yohannes were meantime given an ear at Negus Menelik's Shewan court, but on his return from the west the faithful Alula met subterfuge with force. He imprisoned members of what he considered to be a bogus expedition actually engaged in espionage and then, undeterred by failure to take the settlement of Sa'ati which the Italians had occupied, he caused their withdrawal by the simple expedient of wiping out a reinforcement and supply column at Dogali. The British, who needed Ethiopian support against the dervishes but who were on good terms with Italy, grew alarmed at the increasing tension between the two powers and sent an expedition to Yohannes under Sir Gerald Portal. This mission was received near Lake Ashangi by Emperor Yohannes but its attempted mediation served little useful purpose.

Sir Gerald, who was much more important in the subsequent history of Uganda, was, however, considerably affected by his visit to Yohannes despite his occasional proud intolerance of other people's names and customs. It is perhaps because Yohannes would not see him on a Sunday that he later sent his curt message to Kabaka Mwanga in Kampala that they could not meet since he was going to church! He was typical of his generation of British empire builders,* but he cut no ice with Ras Alula, who deliberately delayed his party *en route*. Portal's argument that it was in Ethiopia's own interest to cede areas to Italy infuriated the patriotic Alula who retorted that as far as he was concerned Ethiopia's natural frontier was the sea and Italian advances would be permitted only when he 'could go as Governor to Rome'. The mission served only to infuriate the Italians and puzzle Emperor Yohannes.

How can you say that I shall hand over to them the country which Jesus Christ gave to me? [wrote Yohannes to Queen Victoria] That command to me would be unjust on your part. If your wish were to make peace between us it should be when they are in their country and I in mine. But now on both sides the horses are bridled and the swords are drawn; my soldiers in numbers like the sand are ready with their spears. The

---

* Lord Cromer wrote praising Portal, shortly after the latter's death, as 'one of the best specimens of that class of Englishman, pre-eminently healthy in mind and body, who to the great benefit of their country issue forth year by year from our public schools. . . . He may be said to have passed through his short but honourable career singing "*floreat Etona*".'

Italians desire war, but the strength is in Jesus Christ. Let
them do as they will, as long as I live I will not hide myself
from them in a hole.'

Yohannes tried to rouse the whole nation against Italy, but
the Negus Taklé Haymanot of Gojjam was involved in a war with
the dervish leader Hamdan Abu Anja whose armies had swept over
most of his provincial kingdom. Menelik of Shewa had recently
signed a friendly agreement with the Italians and had received a
large consignment of rifles from them. He therefore preferred to
remain an observer. Angered but undeterred, Yohannes nevertheless turned and marched to the north but he wisely refused to allow
his troops to smash themselves to pieces against the strong Italian
coastal forts when the latter would not take the field.

THE DEATH OF YOHANNES

Meantime on the western front the armies of Gojjam were defeated
to the north of Lake Tana and several of the king's relatives were
captured. The dervishes marched on to burn Gondar. The Negus
Taklé Haymanot, who in turn had hoped for help from his Emperor
against the dervishes, was very angry and encouraged by Menelik he
raised a rebellion. The prestige of Yohannes suffered and although
he managed to subdue the Gojjam revolt, he was not strong enough
to proceed beyond the great gorge of the Blue Nile to deal also with
Shewa. Menelik's army was encamped on the southern side of the
gorge and he spun out negotiations with Yohannes for three months,
meantime despatching his cousin Ras Makonnen, father of Hailé
Sellassié, who had arrived in Shewa with a supporting army from
Harar, on a diplomatic mission to Rome.

Yohannes had sent a deputation to the khalifa perhaps to
arrange peace, perhaps to estimate his strength, but a sarcastic
reply urging him to embrace Islam decided him and he turned yet
again to meet the dervish threat. Apart from Shewa, all Ethiopia
rallied to his banner. Clearly he hoped for a final victory in the
west which would leave him free to deal with the Italians and
Menelik, for he sent a message ahead to warn the khalifa of his
approach, 'so that as many as possible might be got together at
Gallabat to receive the punishment they deserve'. Ras Mangasha,
the illegitimate son of Yohannes by his brother's wife, and Ras
Alula commanded one wing, Ras Mikael and the Negus Taklé
Haymanot the other, and Emperor Yohannes took the centre.

The dervish fortifications at Gallabat were very strong but
prolonged assault broke the outer wall and the battle was won

before Yohannes was wounded in the arm and stomach. It was some time before the seriousness of the wound was realised, even by Yohannes, who carried on giving orders.

As the news spread, the triumphant Ethiopian army faltered, instead of destroying the inner fortress they withdrew with their loot. Sometime earlier, Yohannes's son, Ras Aria, had died of poisoning and the *rases'* thoughts turned to the certainty of yet another troubled succession.

So completely did the Ethiopian army disintegrate that the few survivors from the dervish camp were able to overtake the handful of retainers withdrawing towards their mountain home bearing the body of the Emperor. It had been cut in halves for ease of transport. His aged uncle, a *ras* of nearly eighty years, stood over the caskets and fought with sword and shield when all his ammunition was expended. He fell, speared from behind, and the Emperor's body and his sword were carried to the khalifa, some small consolation for the loss of his army.

To the generals around his death bed in 1889, Yohannes had acknowledged Ras Mangasha as his son, but the imperial title of King of the Kings was not to remain in Tigré. On Yohannes' death, Menelik of Shewa proclaimed himself Emperor. However, rivalry between the royal houses and between the peoples of these kingdoms—now provinces—has not yet abated.

6

Rebuilding the Empire

I shall endeavour if God gives me life and strength to re-establish the ancient frontiers [tributaries] of Ethiopia. From a letter of MENELIK II to the powers of Europe, 1891

Modern Ethiopia dates from the reign of the Emperor Menelik II.—S. PANKHURST, in *Ethiopia—a Cultural History*, London, 1955

THE SHEWAN GALLA CONFEDERATION

In its extent, its government and its problems, present-day Ethiopia is largely the creation of the Emperor Menelik II. The process dating from long before his assumption of the imperial crown, began as the expansion of the southerly kingdom, now province, of Shewa, of which he was *negus*.

Since Menelik's time Shewa has continued to grow from its small heartland in the Menz area and now it dominates Ethiopia. Interpretations of Menelik's expansionist policy vary widely. Not only are they made something of a political issue, for the Somali Republic views Menelik II as a *participator* in the 'Scramble for Africa', but scholars also disagree.[1] The author inclines to the view that Menelik was motivated in part by a desire to occupy as many areas as possible before they were seized by the imperialist powers of Europe and his actions were, therefore, to some extent a *response* to the 'Scramble for Africa'. Undoubtedly Menelik also saw his campaigns as the re-occupation of provinces long previously subject to Ethiopian suzerainty. However, the fact remains that between 1872 and 1896 the territory which Menelik ruled was more than doubled in area.

The escape of the young Menelik from captivity during the

reign of Tewodros and how the Wello Galla helped him has been described. Menelik had been born at Angolala in Galla country and had lived his first twelve years with the Shewan Galla with whom he thus had much in common. After his return to Shewa from Magdela he had sheltered at first with the Buta family of the Ada Galla, from south of the town of Bishaftu—or Debra Zeyt as it is now called.* When the young heir came to power in Shewa, though a descendant of King Sahlé Sellassié and an heir to the supposed Solomonic succession, he already knew Shewa well enough to see that in order to rule effectively and to further the boundaries of his domains he would need to cultivate his Galla connections. In particular he grew to depend upon Gobena, a Galla who had lived at court as a youth and who grew to be a great soldier. Subsequently he was created *ras*. Some traditions state that Gobena, whose personal influence was soon very considerable, was a deprived son of the great Galla leader Danci of Tulama and that his successful jousting brought him to the notice of Menelik. It is, however, more likely that he held his position as of right. His wife was the daughter—some say sister—of the leader of the Salalé Galla, Biru Nagawo, who was later killed fighting with the Chabo group—Salalé is a settlement just to the west of Addis Ababa, which was not then in existence. Gobena was the architect of the Shewan Galla Confederation which sought to unite all these groups and which Menelik used to further extend the areas under his control.

This aspect of Menelik's policy had the full approval of the Emperor Yohannes while he lived and was assisted by the advice of diplomatic representatives at the Shewan court and other Europeans in the service of the Emperor. More significant, however, was the Emperor's own skilful diplomacy which secured an overwhelming superiority in both the quantity and the quality of the firearms of his army. These forces were used first to subdue the several Galla groups in Wello to the north, whose settlement had, since the sixteenth and seventeenth centuries, tended to isolate Shewa from the ancient centres of Amhara and Tigré. Some say the Shewans had previously encouraged these incursions for this very reason, but it is doubtful if they could have prevented them. After returning from Wello, the Shewan armies turned their attention to the south.

Many Galla leaders, through the influence of Gobena, had thrown in their lot with Menelik and indeed their followers formed

---

* Bishaftu, or 'place of water', is Gallinya, but it is Ethiopian government policy to use Amharic as first of the two official languages, the second being English. Debra Zeyt or 'place of olives', is a biblical name. Adama is thus now Nazret, Ambo is now Hagera Hiwot, Walliso, a Guragé word, becomes Ghion, etc.

the basis for the expansion of Shewa which Menelik and Gobena planned. Obviously it is wrong to describe this period as an extension of 'Amhara' influence and control, though this mistake is often made. One of the first to join was Biratu Golé, leader of the Meta Galla from beyond Wachacha, the vast volcano immediately west of Addis Ababa. He had been decorated by Gobena but, hesitant, he still sought and secured an agreement with Menelik that the Galla leaders would never be mistreated. Then Tufamuna, the Galla leader from Gulelé, a village now almost a suburb of Addis Ababa, refused to join the Shewan Galla Confederation. His people, who were more widely scattered before Addis Ababa was built on their land, were nevertheless between the pro-confederation Abichu and Meta groups. Tufamuna was killed in battle and the confederation was then strong enough to take on and defeat the Abu Galla of the Mount Zikwala region and the Jillé Galla of near Lake Ziway, and afterwards to advance farther to the south and west, where the leader of the Ambo Galla was killed in battle.

Many of the details of these events, drawn here from oral tradition, are also described in a collection of Galla songs made by Cerulli, though, as one would expect, there are contradictions and problems which future research should help to solve, if the Ethiopian government allows examination of what it regards as a thorny issue rather close to the problem of feudal land ownership. One song compares Gobena—a Galla who lived as an Amhara—with a gun made half of iron and half of wood. It is said that Gobena very seldom spoke Gallinya, preferring Amharic the language of his adoption. Another interesting tale is that when Ras Gobena eventually died, it was a week after being cursed by a sorcerer whom he had ordered to be put to death. The *ras* is said to have fallen dead from his horse and to have been the second posthumous victim of the witch-doctor.*

GALLA AND GURAGÉ CAMPAIGNS

South-west of these above mentioned extensions to Menelik's power lies the region of Guragé, west of Lakes Ziway and Shala, beyond the western escarpment of the Rift valley. That this region has had many connections with the historic Abyssinian core of Ethiopia is suggested by the existence of a few ruined rock churches and by isolated pockets of peoples, such as those speaking a semitic language on the islands of Wonchi—a remote crater lake set high

---

* Such people may still be seen. In 1961 the author met a Galla sorcerer in Arusi whom he mistook for a fairly prosperous landowner—which of course he might also have been.

in the mountains whose crest has collapsed to form a beautiful series of volcanic calderas farther to the west near Ambo. Much research remains to be done, but it seems that the Guragé people are probably of Sidamo stock influenced considerably from Tigré and perhaps Harar. Their ruling dynasty, claiming descent from an Ethiopian general named Sebat, had been earlier overthrown by the Negus Sahlé Sellassié of Shewa and Guragé was permanently conquered by Menelik in 1875. He offered the area to Dejazmatch Girmamé as a feudal fief but the latter refused it and Menelik then divided it into five districts of *negarit* or military (literally 'drum') administration—one small area remaining independent under Omar Baksa, a Muslim chieftain who entered the region and expelled Menelik's nominee.

In 1881 Menelik and his uncle Ras Dargé, a son of the Negus Sahlé Sellassié, met with indifferent success against the Galla of Arusi, south-eastward across the Rift valley, and therefore concentrated on the south-west. As mentioned, these excursions eventually brought them into conflict with the Negus Taklé Haymanot of Gojjam, who was also bent on expansion. Ras Gobena had the best of the initial exchanges, but it was at this point that the Emperor Yohannes intervened, took over the administration of the Wello Gallas, baptised their chieftain Muhammad—subsequently known as Ras Mikael—who was to become a very important figure in the early years of the twentieth century. It appears from an old Ethiopian manuscript that Yohannes had first encouraged Taklé Haymanot, even providing him with soldiers, in order to counterbalance Menelik's growing power but he later took over land from them both. He did, however, inspire Menelik to renew his efforts towards the occupation of the sultanate of Harar to the south-east.

THE CONQUEST OF HARAR

British officers acting on behalf of the Khedive Tewfik had carried out the Egyptian evacuation of Harar in 1884–5, but they had left the Emir Abdulla, son of the last emir prior to the Egyptian interlude, and a fanatical Muslim, in control. The sultanate of Harar had been regarded with the greatest hostility by the Ethiopian emperors ever since the days of Gran, but Menelik was the first emperor to possess the power to occupy it permanently. He wrote to the emir that Harar had been an Ethiopian province for 400 years and that the Ethiopian government must now be resumed and annual land tax be paid. The emir retorted that he knew no master save the Ottoman sultan and on receipt of a second order to submit he sent Menelik a muslim dress, turban and prayer carpet with the message, 'When you are a Muslim I will consider you my master.' Menelik replied, 'I will come to Harar and replace the mosque by a Christian church—Await me!'[2] An added incentive for him to do this was the obvious interest which the European powers were taking ostensibly in the trade of the region. In 1887 an army was sent out on the pretext of punishing the emir for attacking a commercial expedition belonging to Menelik's Italian allies and the walled city was taken.

Ethiopians claim that their columns then pushed on to the coast of the Indian Ocean and only stopped short of the sultanate of Mogadishu because its ruler pledged them tribute. Menelik took the advice of his general Ras Tasamma and allowed his troops to withdraw. Within a few years the Italians were to establish themselves on that same coast and initiate a pattern of events which culminated in the emergence, much later in 1960, of a new nation, the Somali Republic, on the coastal periphery of the Ethiopian Highlands.

After the conquest of Harar there was considerable discussion as to who should be left in charge of the lengthy pacification of the Harar province. Ras Dargé had refused to journey there but many of the Shewan nobility and Menelik himself were in Harar. There was a meeting and it was decided to recommend to the Emperor the candidature of a Shewan noble who had previously been somewhat troublesome in the southern provinces. However, Dejazmatch Girmamé heard of this and having great influence with Menelik visited him late that same night and persuaded him not to trust a potential rebel with a governorate which would give him access to supplies of firearms from Europe. Instead he proposed one of Menelik's many relatives, Balambaras Makonnen, for this important position. Menelik agreed and the surprised nobility only heard of the Emperor's change of mind when the proclamation was made the next morning when Makonnen was also created *dejazmatch*.

As a fourteen-year-old Makonnen had been taken to court and pledged to the service of Menelik by his father, Dejazmatch Woldé Mikael, the lord of the Shewan fiefs of Doba and Menz. His mother, Tenagne Worq, was, like Negus Hailé Malakot, Menelik's father, a child of the Shewan *negus* Sahlé Sellassié, but despite his family Makonnen was always conscious of his debt to Dejazmatch Girmamé and sent him rich presents obtained from the coast and from Europe—indeed in this way Girmamé first tasted champagne! The appointment of Makonnen was important because his province was to see British and Ethiopian troops combine to put down the *Jehad* of the Somali Muhammad Abdille Hassan, sometimes known as the 'Mad Mullah'—though he was neither mad nor a mullah; because there the thorny problem of the Ogaden frontier with the Somali colonies first arose and more especially because Makonnen's fortunes never waned and by result one of his sons, Tafari, was later in a position to seize the Regency and eventually to become the Emperor Hailé Sellassié. The descendants of Dejazmatch Girmamé have also made a place for themselves in the subsequent history of Ethiopia.

WELLEGGA AND JIMMA

Meantime to the south, Kumsa, Galla ruler of Wellegga (where pockets of the pre-Galla inhabitants such as the Gunza tribe still survive) came to an agreement with Menelik II. Earlier it had seemed that Wellegga would fall under the influence of Gojjam rather than Shewa, but Moreda, Kumsa's shrewd old father had deliberately not allowed the young Kumsa to be baptised a Christian at that time but had left him for Menelik to baptise. Long afterwards Ras Gobena had approached Kumsa with regard to the Galla Confederation and it was agreed that land ownership would not be altered, no one would be appointed over Kumsa in Wellegga and he, in return, would send tribute in gold to Menelik. Neither Kumsa, who was thereafter called Dejazmatch Gebré Egziabher, nor Gobena are highly thought of by the Wellegga people, who feel they betrayed them to the 'Amhara' (Shewans). Kumsa's descendants have since ruled Wellegga as a western province of Ethiopia and have been styled 'governors general' rather than elected 'kings' (or more properly leading *balabat*).* Later the land of the *balabat* was largely confiscated and the iniquitous *gabar* system was imposed upon the people of Wellegga, but by that time it was too late for the rulers of Wellegga to complain effectively or

---

* The word 'king' is an oversimplification. There was a considerable degree of popular selection and democratic responsibility in the governments headed by these leading *balabat*. Bakaré, 'king' of Wellegga was succeeded by Moreda who had two sons, Kumsa who became Dejazmatch Gebré Egziabher, and Amanté, who was later killed by an elephant. (As in other areas of Ethiopia bright young boys were 'adopted' by the great houses and treated almost as sons—some say Amanté was adopted. He is an ancestor of Yilma Deressa. See footnote, page 231.

Kumsa (Gebré Egziabher) was succeeded years later as governor-general by his son Dejazmatch Habté Mariam, murdered by the Italians during the Occupation, and he by his son Fikré Sellassié who retired in 1963 to the senate. Fikré Sellassié was then succeeded by a Shewan *fitwrary* with the rank of deputy governor, but Fikré Sellassié's uncle Fitwrary Yemané Gebré Egziabher was made assistant-deputy governor.

renounce their relationship with Shewa. (The *gabar* system involved the allotment of land by the Emperor to soldier-settlers from Shewa. The local residents were thereafter obliged to undertake a form of forced labour as part payment to these new landlords who had been imposed upon them.)

Ras Gobena made an agreement with Abba Jiffa II, the last king or sultan of Jimma, a Muslim state in the west of considerable antiquity. Through the agreement the passage of Shewan troops was to be allowed, tribute was to be paid to Menelik, military co-operation against the kingdom of Kaffa was agreed upon, and in return Menelik undertook neither to invade nor to build Christian churches in Jimma. To this day descendants of the sultan live in Jiran, in the hills above the modern town of Jimma. Tutors sent by the sultans of Zanzibar have seen to it that the sons were educated to read in Arabic—many Arabic treasures have been reported at Jiran including a three-volume history of the Galla—and some have attended Ethiopian government schools and colleges. During the Occupation 1936–41, the Italians sent the sultan via Mecca to Italy. There he was a guest of King Victor Emmanuel and on his return to Ethiopia the Italians used him as their governor of Jimma.*

ADDIS ABABA AND THE CITY LANDS

About the time of the incorporation of these areas, Addis Ababa (which means 'new flower') was founded. The site was chosen by the Empress Taitu, Menelik's wife, but a strong influence was Menelik's wish to found a capital on the site of that of the early Emperor Lebna Dengel. The chronicler of the reign of Menelik,[3] states that Menelik quoted his grandfather the Negus Sahlé Sel-lassié : 'O land today you are full of Gallas but one day my grandson will build here a house and make of you a city.' About 1886 large areas of land on the site were distributed; the recipients among others were the Empress, Ras Mikael, Ras Dargé, Afe Negus Nasibu, the *Echegé*, Dejazmatch Girmamé, Balambaras Makonnen, etc.—and areas were set aside such as that for the quarters of the palace guard. Dejazmatch Girmamé, having previously refused the overlordship of Guragé was given land in the Bishaftu and

---

* In 1961 Jimma became the seat of a Shewan *dejazmatch* with the rank of deputy-governor but the sultan's surviving son Dejazmatch Abba Jebel is district governor of Jimma. Such government appointments in Wellegga, Jimma and other areas, including Tigré, are often quoted to illustrate the resilience of the Ethiopian feudal system and thus a shallowness in Ethiopia's modern façade. (1964.)

Adama regions south of Addis Ababa. Unlike the monarchs who succeeded him, Menelik himself never owned land—perhaps contenting himself with the claim that all Ethiopia belonged to him.

Up to the 1960s, however, the Ethiopian Emperor has given out land as a reward for faithful service, usually a small area in the city and a larger area in one of the provinces conquered by Menelik. Many, but not all, Ethiopians are unashamed to go and beg land from their Emperor for it is the custom. The recipients normally build houses on the areas within the city and often let them to foreign residents. Very considerable profit is obtained from technical assistance organisations, particularly those associated with the United Nations or the government of the United States. These seem able to pay enormous rents which repay the cost of the construction of the buildings within a very few months. It is certain that capital investment in these directions could better serve the national interest if the government sought to divert it to other spheres. However, although in the undoubted interests of the governed, such a measure does not seem to be acceptable to the present governing clique. The ministers are themselves landowners and the government is not even allowed to participate in the profitable activity above described. This is but one of the many instances where the tight hold of the landowning families makes all the outward semblances of a modern state seem quite ineffective—and where foreign aid further secures the *status quo*.

Recently published maps of the city of Addis Ababa, beautifully produced from Hunting's aerial photographic surveys have been suppressed, allegedly for strategic reasons, with the effect of still confining this land speculation to the present twenty or so privileged families. Even the Imperial Ministry of Education has been hard put to it to retain their one copy used for planning school zoning and development. A Guards' captain called in March 1962 with orders to remove it. A junior minister, one of the Board of Governors of the University, joked with the author at about the same time that the University must not expand towards the northeast for he was engaged in land speculation in that direction. Landtaxes are minute and income from land is not always subject to taxation. Many educated Ethiopians who do not belong to the tight little clique of land-owning families deplore this system which has developed since the time of Menelik's campaigns.

THE FALL OF THE SOUTHERN KINGDOMS

The state of Wellamo in the south-west was a tributary of Kaffa in 1893 when Menelik conquered it. Its last king, named Tona, was the fourteenth monarch of its third dynasty. Ancient defence works built to repel the Arusi Galla may still be seen in the Wellamo of today, which also includes several smaller states and tribal areas overcome by Menelik's armies. Kanta of Kullo region and the last king of Konto also surrendered to Menelik. Kamma of Gofa was conquered in 1883; Abba Boka of Gomma in 1886, and a similar fate overtook many a lesser chieftain. In 1891 Enarya was conquered; the last king, Abba Gomboli, submitted to Menelik, and his son, after baptism, was known as Fitwrary Gebré Sellassié. In 1894 the kingdom of Janjero was conquered for Menelik by Ras Woldé Giorgis and the same pattern ensued. Abba Bagibo, the last monarch of the Mwa dynasty then in power, fled to Guragé but eventually went to Addis Ababa and submitted. The Christian names of his son who served in the new administration of the region were Gebré Madhen.

In 1897, Gaki Seroco, 'divine' king of Kaffa, through whom the god Heko spoke, and last of a dynasty of nineteen generations which claimed descent from Solomon and the Queen of Sheba, was deposed and the kingdom was occupied. This king had ruled only seven years and was unable to resist the combined forces of Ras Woldé Giorgis, Ras Damissé and Abba Jiffa, Sultan of Jimma, although he had repulsed previous campaigns led by Ras Gobena and others. The trenches and fortifications of the Kaffa kingdom, which is said to have once stretched from the Sudanese lowlands to the Rift valley lakes, may still be seen in places.[4] The soldiers had no rifles, only spears, but even so the final campaign lasted eight months before the last Kafitcho emperor, who had previously entertained Menelik as a guest, was sent as a prisoner in golden chains to Ankober and thence to Dessie, where he lived in poverty in the house of Ras Mikael. The tale is told that on the way, as he rode behind Ras Woldé Giorgis over a bridge across the Gojeb river, he hurled his royal ring into the water with the words, 'The empire of Kaffa has come to an end! There will never be another emperor of Kaffa! The emperor's ring shall rest in the bed of the river.'

Later, the young Emperor Eyasu was to allow Gaki Seroco to come to Addis Ababa, where he died in 1919. His authority over his subjects was religious and pagan and for this reason Menelik is said not to have been prepared to use him as governor general or indirect ruler.[5] His gilt and plumed head-dress and the wooden coronation stool inlaid with silver were brought to Addis Ababa. Like the stone of Scone, however, these were stolen from the capital by a band of intrepid young warriors from Kaffa who took them home. Menelik seized them again and this time sent them to

Switzerland, from which country they were subsequently repurchased by Hailé Sellassié. The crown has recently been placed on display in the museum of the Institute of Ethiopian Studies in Addis Ababa.

Meantime, Kaffa was ruled by Ras Woldé Giorgis on Emperor Menelik's behalf. The *ras* set up his capital at Anderacha and it is only in recent decades that Bonga, the site of the former royal capital, burnt together with the palace after the conquest, has been re-occupied. Some semblance of the old social structure of the kingdom exists even to this day, but descendants of Menelik's soldiers form a new class for whom some of the peasants have been obliged to work.

Menelik had remained aloof from the struggles farther north and he had thus been able to embark on this series of conquests to the south and west of Shewa. His armies were far better equipped than those of both his predecessors and his adversaries and thus he was able not to raid and withdraw as had been the previous pattern, but to establish garrisons in the lands over which he extended his sway in much the same manner as did colonialists from Europe in other parts of Africa. Indeed many of the old leaders in Ethiopia have not unnaturally inherited attitudes towards these conquered provinces and their peoples and thus to the nature of the Ethiopian state as a whole, which the young Ethiopians of today—young Africans—cannot possibly support and indeed make little attempt to understand.

One foreign visitor to the far south, travelling in the region north of Lake Rudolf records how the people at first fled, fearing that his column was *'Habash'*,* but later begged him to 'lay before King Menelik an account of their real condition because they knew him to be a good and just man and were sure that he was not aware of the behaviour of his own people in those regions'—an attitude paralleled in the early 1960s by that of the peoples of south-western Ethiopia towards the local police on the one hand and the Emperor Hailé Sellassié I on the other. This visitor,[6] whose account is typical of many, goes on to state of these unfortunate Ethiopian subjects that 'although they themselves were anxious to arrive at a friendly understanding with the Abyssinians, and were prepared to pay whatever taxes were right, still they were never allowed a chance of doing so . . . were shot down . . . etc.' In the 1960s it is pointless to deny that in many southern regions descendants of the early garrison settlements, government officials and

---

* *Habash* is a general term used for the Christian highlanders.

even Christian clergy not infrequently adopt the worst possible type of 'colonial' approach towards their fellow countrymen of slightly different ethnic groupings.

If late nineteenth-century Ethiopia provided an environment which nurtured the family pride of those who considered themselves 'born to rule' it was by no means unique. As is true of all such families in those times, the sons included many who were popular and accepted by their subjects. The best were indeed dedicated, but the worst were feared as tyrants and none was free from condescension.

Woldé Giorgis himself, the Shewan overlord who was sent to rule Kaffa, serves well as a prototype. Not only is his career typical but complicated family relationships such as his have to a considerable extent continued to govern most higher appointments in Ethiopia right up until the 1960s. His mother, Ayahilush, was the daughter of the Negus Sahlé Sellassié, King of Shewa, who was grandfather both of the Emperor Menelik and—through a daughter—of Ras Makonnen, governor of Harar and father of Hailé Sellassié. But Woldé Giorgis was not only Menelik's cousin, he was also his brother-in-law, for he had married Shimabet, a sister of Menelik's fourth wife, the Empress Taitu.

As a young man, Woldé Giorgis served in the Galla campaigns under Ras Gobena, and was created *fitwrary* and governor of Limu. He then held several successful commands in the southern wars and acquired the governorships of several regions as feudal fiefs which he governed with the title of *dejazmatch*. He led the conquest of Wellamo. In the Italian war we find him fighting the Danakils. Later he was back in the south-west at the fall of Kaffa, which, with the title of *ras*, he ruled for thirteen years until he assumed the senior governorship of Amhara, Simien and Begemidir. He was granted the title of *negus* or king, now no longer conferred, and before his death at Gondar in 1918 he played a prominent part in the conspiracy of Shewan nobles which led to the deposition of the 'unsatisfactory' Emperor Eyasu and the eventual rise of Hailé Sellassié. Few would say that such families as his have no cause for some pride. To this day they jealously guard their dominating position in Ethiopian politics.

Woldé Giorgis governed Kaffa responsibly but his successor, Dejazmatch Birru and those who followed him pillaged it. Commerce declined, crops failed and farmers were ruined by harsh feudal levies. Slavery was rife and many starved. According to contemporary accounts the population of the whole south-west de-

within Ethiopia have not been unknown to use privately the term 'colonialism' when discussing Menelik's expansionist achievements. The Ethiopian government, however, points out that Menelik II believed that his predecessors of much earlier times had ruled these conquered regions or at least had received tribute from them—and that, although not easy to prove, was almost certainly the case. Certainly the early Jesuit visitors thought so.[7]

Nor were Menelik's personal attitudes at all the same as those of European colonialists. Those who claim they were, usually cite the visit of the wealthy Haitian Negro, Mr Benito Sylvain, to Menelik's court, 'in order to secure his Majesty's adhesion to a program for the general amelioration of the negro race'. Sylvain, we are told,[8] had considered it 'especially appropriate that the greatest blackman in the world should become the honorary president of his projected society' but the Emperor had remarked, 'In coming to me for the leadership, you are knocking at the wrong door, so to speak. You know, I am not a Negro at all; I am a Caucasian.' It is not suggested that Menelik's ideas were at all akin to the currently projected 'African Image'.[9] They were not. But even if the above account of Sylvain's visit is accepted as true, it still admits that Menelik was exercising a characteristic 'fine dry humour'. Menelik's own features were dark and negroid and he may well have derived amusement from the fact that many of the Ethiopian courtiers considered him, therefore, to be ugly. It is unfortunately not so often quoted that Menelik is also said to have remarked to Sylvain, 'The Negro should be uplifted. I applaud your theory, and I wish you the greatest possible success.'

On another occasion he set out a feast for the leading men of Shewa and deliberately neglected to provide knives in order to point the foolishness of traditional prejudices which held blacksmiths in contempt, as a despised class. Indeed most Ethiopian memories of Menelik II show that in his other attitudes also he was a wise and, for his time, enlightened person. His time, however, was that of the 'Scramble for Africa'! Not by any means all, but at least several of his campaigns of conquest were initiated in order to frustrate the colonial ambitions of one or other European power. It is difficult to see what other courses were open to him and even the Somali government indirectly admits this when it states:

> During the nineteenth-century 'Scramble for Africa', Abyssinia had every right to safeguard her integrity, and the skill with which she conducted her external affairs, surrounded as she was by European colonial powers, is to be admired.[10]

Thus if Mogadishu in the 1960s talks of Menelik II

as a 'black Imperialist' it is because of what he did, not what he was, and in Addis Ababa that argument is held to be scarcely more relevant today than the facts that Duke William of Normandy once ruled England or that Red Indian chiefs once ruled America : what really matters is that Ethiopia today does govern and will probably continue to govern all these regions. Even if the present status of these territories, or rather of their inhabitants, is admitted to be ambiguous, emotionally loaded terms are well avoided.

Very few inhabitants and few leaders of Ethiopia would really wish the southern,* the predominantly Galla, the Eritrean, or the Somali regions to achieve self-government in the colonial pattern, although there is considerable feeling against government from Addis Ababa in at least the last two of these regions. Fragmentation is, however, foolish economics and alien to the declared pattern for Africa. Today, dissatisfaction begins to stem from the nature rather than the location of the central government. It is quite untrue to speak, as newspapers often do, of 'Amhara' or 'Abyssinian' domination of the Ethiopian Empire as if that constitutes the only problem. The problem is rather one of social injustice manifested in a multitude of ways. It is true that the system of taxation, the siting and distribution of new roads, industries and schools and the recruitment of students and government employees leaves much to be desired : it is true that different provinces are treated differently and that corrupt governors can and do end up owning vast areas of their provinces—nevertheless, there are downtrodden peasants or herdsmen enough in every religious and racial grouping and in every province.

Of course, there is no permanent reason why all the peoples of Ethiopia should not learn to live happily together, joking perhaps about each other's origins—a process which has begun in the university. Race prejudice is, however, a serious problem in Ethiopia and, as everywhere else in the world, it dies hard. A fair skin is often admired but discrimination is based much less on

---

* South-western Ethiopia although in some ways in a similar position to the Bahr-el-Ghazal, Upper Nile and Equatoria provinces of the Sudanese Republic, has not demonstrated similar disquiet and there is certainly no sign of a secessionist movement such as exists in the southern Sudan (1963-4). The difference is due to the fewer educational facilities in the Ethiopian region and the much smaller influence of Christian missionaries from abroad. Also the Ethiopian rulers are not of Arabic extraction and culture and there is no apparent policy of promoting Islam which is therefore not seen as an alien or imposed religion and is no more important than Orthodox Christianity among these largely pagan and very backward tribes which are divided by the Ethio-Sudanese frontier.

colour or even provincialism, than on features and hair texture. School children have to be discouraged from jibing at those of their fellows who possess more markedly negroid features and what in this context is called 'slave hair'.* The terms *'Shankalla'* and *'Baria'* are used in a derogatory sense and are much resented because of their historic association with slavery. But divisions are at once forgotten if an outsider criticises Ethiopia. At the university in 1960 and again in 1964 incidents caused tension between Ethiopians and other African students but the influence of the latter, nevertheless, helps to bring home the understanding that it is less significant that Gallas, Harari, Somali, Eritreans, Tigréans and Amharas may all be counted in the higher circles of government, than that the beggars who today crowd the streets of Addis Ababa, capital of Shewa, are Amharas—as Shewan as any of their rulers—and as Ethiopian.

Especially since 1960 educated Ethiopians often feel that there is not time to worry about how their country came into existence—it exists. What must matter in the future is what 'being an Ethiopian' means, and even that is not the widest of horizons. It has been remarked that Ethiopia's leaders have not been thrown up from the people like those of the new African countries, and though they may have greater experience and skill at diplomacy they lack a feeling of responsibility to, and identity with, the ordinary people. When they try to suppress modern ideas in the vigorous and growing educated class, they, not alone amongst present-day governments in Africa, would appear to be attempting the impossible. If an underlying revolutionary situation exists in Ethiopia today it is because the whole basis of conservative government thought seems to the young to be as dead as the Emperor Menelik II who inspired it. Nor, as will be shown below, has the latter day paternalism of Hailé Sellassié I been a universally accepted substitute.

Hence even the content of much formal education has been seen to be almost completely lacking in inspiration and attempts

---

* An Ethiopian university lecturer recently quipped,

> If you're white—'s all right
> If you're brown—stick around
> If you're black—go back!

but a very dark skin is itself no disadvantage in obtaining employment in Ethiopia. Galla and 'Amhara' get along well as do 'Amharas' and Tigréans. Sometimes Tigréans are thought clannish and rather too excitable (and their girls not sufficiently exciting) by Amhara youth and there is occasional tension between Ethiopian Somali students in Addis Ababa and their fellows.

are made, not invariably with success, to change this. Significantly also the oath 'May Menelik die if . . .', and subsequently, 'May Hailé Sellassié die if . . .', may still be heard in Ethiopia, but in 1961 it was not unknown to hear the oath sworn in the name of Girmamé or Mengistu, leaders of the December Revolution. Although that attempted *coup d'état* failed, and perhaps in part because of that fact, it has provided an idealism for educated youth which can only expand in the barren vacuum which has existed since. The subsequent 'martyrdom' of Brigadier-general Mengistu (he was hanged on Thursday, March 30, 1961)—an enormous if unusual political mistake on the part of Hailé Sellassié —has assured beyond any doubt that December 1960 will be seen to be a major turning point in Ethiopian history.

Amharic, because of its epigrammatic syntax and polish, loses much in translation, but it is worth quoting the general's analysis of what he saw as a completely moribund situation. At his trial in early 1961 he said :

> The reason for all my actions lies simply in the fact that when Jesus Christ created Adam in his image, he meant to give him dignity. When Jesus Christ gave his life for the children of Adam [it was for this] he sacrificed himself. We Christians believe this. Ruling régimes have been changed many times in the history of [the rest of] the world, and now the [rest of the] world is even divided over matters of education and concepts of government. But when we turn to examine Ethiopia in particular, what do we find but the history of a long succession of monarchs? Now I have no wish to blame the dead [chroniclers] who must have had problems of their own, but were not all our fore-fathers upright men with history? True history has been deliberately stifled in order to praise only Emperors !

A necessary new approach in Ethiopia has been ably described by Father Savard, a Jesuit lecturer at the University College, in a recent article.[11] The history and culture of all the peoples can and must play a part in developing the nation now that its frontiers have attained some measure of stability. He points out that the Amhara have been outstanding in giving status to their women; that the Somali *shir* or council embodies a democratic ideal of service to the community as does the general assembly of the Guragé; that the Galla systems show the value of training and education and illustrate that after a period in control, it may be desirable to replace a group of rulers. The Sidamo, he says, have a very egalitarian social system very different from the caste and class structure of old Kaffa society.

The younger educated generation firmly rejects Menelik's feudal practice—still current—of maintaining stability through the calculated balance of disunities. The creation of national unity, they feel, must be a positive process. It must depend upon literacy and education, both of which the older generation openly fears. It must depend upon a new solidarity of the Ethiopian people and not the loyalty of the chiefs. The old attitudes were well illustrated in an Amharic booklet published in Addis Ababa in 1962, in memory of one of the dignitaries killed in the *coup*. This seeks to point out his greatness by quoting from his advice to Emperor Hailé Sellassié on methods of ruling what he is clearly seen to have regarded as different subject peoples within the empire.

The recommendations of communist Yugoslav economic advisors and of Americans from 'Point Four', agree that economic development waits upon land reform. Such reform, however, would strike not only at the roots of economic stagnation but also at the landowning classes themselves who owe much of their power to Menelik's system of rewards. True, nowhere else does land reform present such complex issues but, true also, the present government, although it pays lip service to the five-year plan even so, appears to lack the will to see these as a challenge to be accepted.

Thus Menelik—nevertheless a great Emperor—did mould the very past that impatient would-be reformers of today wish to renounce in order to create new attitudes and a new Ethiopia. This fact is not invariably acknowledged but nor is the fact that Hailé Sellassié, at least in his early days, was such a reformer. He was to further extend the effective rule of Menelik's central government, dominated as it then had to be by Shewans at the expense of local rulers and peoples who were at that time semi- or completely independent. Present disagreement over the methods to be used to complete and extend this process lies at the heart of the internal problems of contemporary Ethiopia, for Menelik's empire is not yet a nation.

PRESSURES ON ETHIOPIA DURING THE SCRAMBLE FOR AFRICA

IN THE LATE NINETEENTH CENTURY

ITALIAN ° BRITISH
EGYPTIAN FRENCH
× Battle Site ▲ Amba

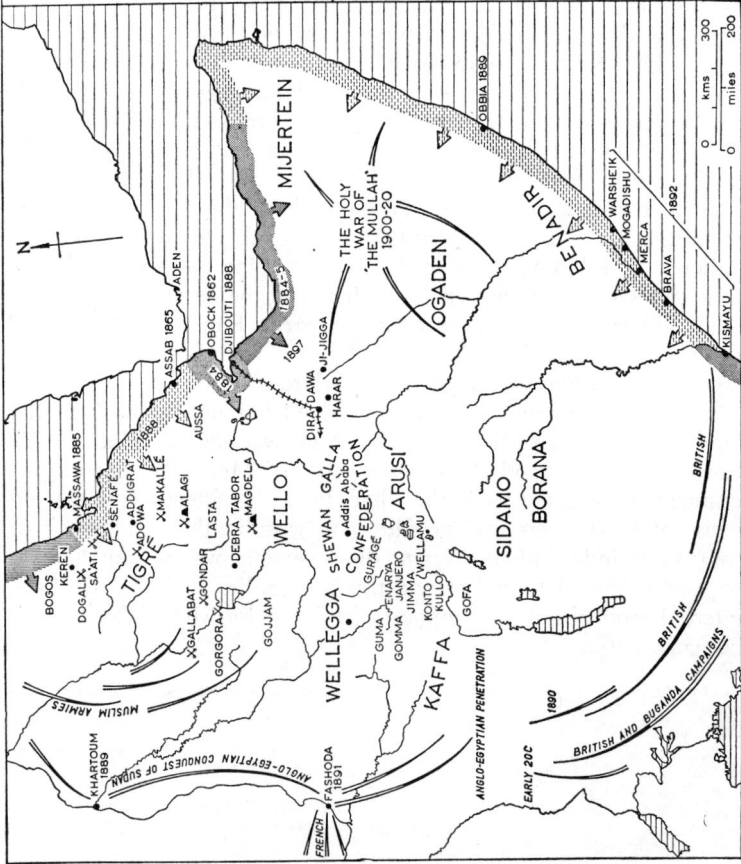

The *Jehad* of Muhammad Abdille Hassan (called the 'mad mullah') was aimed first at the Somalis of the Qadariyah sect but later involved British, Italian and Ethiopian forces as well as other Somalis. See R. Hess, 'The Mad Mullah and Northern Somalia', *Journal of African History*, Vol. V, No. 3, London, 1964.

MIJERTEIN

THE HOLY WAR OF 'THE MULLAH' 1900-20

OGADEN

BENADIR

OBBIA 1889

WARSHEIK
MOGADISHU
1892
MERCA
BRAVA

KISMAYU

ADEN

ASSAB 1865
OBOCK 1862
DJIBOUTI 1888

1894-5

1897

1884

MASSAWA 1885
KEREN
BOGOS
DOGALI ×
SAATI ×
× SENAFÉ
ADDIGRAT
ADOWA
× MAKALLÉ
▲ ALAGI
LASTA
× GONDAR
GALLABAT
GORGORA ×
GOJJAM

DIRA DAWA
HARAR
JI-JIGGA

AUSSA

DEBRA TABOR
▲ MAGDELA

WELLO

SHEWAN GALLA
CONFEDERATION
Addis Ababa
GURAGE
ARUSI

SIDAMO

BORANA

WELLEGA
GUMA ENARFA
GOMMA JANJERO
JIMMA
KONTO WELLAMU
KULLO
GOFA
KAFFA

TIGRÉ

MUSLIM ARMIES

KHARTOUM 1889
FASHODA 1891

ANGLO-EGYPTIAN CONQUEST OF SUDAN

ANGLO-EGYPTIAN PENETRATION

EARLY 20C

BRITISH

1890

BRITISH AND BUGANDA CAMPAIGNS

FRENCH

N

kms 0 300
miles 0 200

7

The Scramble Halted

Crispi had been mistaken in thinking that Menelik was one of those African monarchs with a passion for abdicating in favour of a European state.—L. WOOLF, *Empire and Commerce in Africa*, London, 1920

Why don't they just say they will buy Abyssinia!—Remark by the EMPEROR MENELIK when studying the terms of a suggested 'concession' in 1902

THE DIPLOMACY OF MENELIK II

Menelik is described by those who remember him as being of very dark complexion. He had fine white teeth but the smallpox had left its marks on his face. He stood over six feet in height and was very courteous. As a diplomat he made a great impression on the many foreign emissaries who came to treat at his court. With their help he steadily imported firearms to further his plans for the expansion of Shewa. Through diplomacy rather than personal military leadership, when, at the age of forty-five the time came for him to succeed Yohannes, he fulfilled the Ethiopian image of a conquering warrior king even though his personal inclination was to avoid conflict whenever possible.

In the anarchy which followed the death of Yohannes, the Italians also made a bid for the spoils of the apparently disintegrating empire. They moved their capital from Massawa to Asmara, but despite the fact that the Ethiopian centre of gravity had itself moved away from Tigré to the more southerly Shewa, Menelik was the first to realise that the usefulness of his Italian alliance had passed. Even so, for some time he allowed the friendship to persist and meanwhile took stock of the internal position in Ethiopia.

The important political figures of whom Menelik had to be wary were Ras Mangasha of Tigré, the only surviving son of Yohannes; Ras Alula, Governor of Hamasien, the able general who had risen from peasant stock; Ras Hagos, Ras Hailu Mariam; Wagshum Gabru, Governor of Begemidir; Dejazmatch Tasamma and the Negus Taklé Haymanot of Gojjam. Some of the bishops of Gojjam and Shewa had long recognised Menelik as King of the Kings and his only real ecclesiastical opponent, Teophilos, who was the *Echegé* (or Chief Monk—the administrative head of the Church), was not very influential. Two other nobles from whom he felt more certain of support were Dejazmatch Makonnen of Harar and Ras Mikael of Wello.

After signing the famous treaty of Wuchali with the Italians—largely negotiated by Makonnen and which led to his being made *ras*—Menelik marched north and with their help defeated Ras Mangasha his only significant rival for the throne. For the Tigréan, however, defeat merely meant submission. In order to have more control over him, Menelik forced Mangasha to divorce his wife and marry the daughter of Ras Wolie who was the brother of the Empress Taitu—another and not the last attempt to link the royal families of Shewa and Tigré in dynastic marriage. Neither Mangasha's son, Seyoum, who was killed in the 1960 Revolution, nor the latter's sons —one of whom, named Mangasha, succeeded him as governor-general of Tigré—have, as will be shown, a completely clean record of loyalty to the house of Shewa or to Hailé Sellassié who later became its representative.

The Italians were to interpret Article XVII of the Treaty of Wuchali, signed in 1889 by Count Antonelli (on behalf of King Umberto I) and Emperor Menelik II, as giving them a protectorate over Ethiopia. Menelik knew that the Amharic version of the subsequently disputed Article merely stated that 'it shall be *possible* to communicate with the kings of Europe with the assistance of the Italian government', and did not imply that he *had* to use that channel if he chose to enter into agreements with the other powers. In fact the very day he signed the treaty he wrote direct to Queen Victoria and there is some evidence that Menelik was deliberately deceived.[1] Another agreement later in the year arranged the advance of four million lira against the customs of Harar as security. It is quite inconceivable that Menelik would have agreed to his historic country becoming a protectorate. When he learned of the Italian interpretation, which was gaining some acceptance in Europe, he at once denied it and in 1895 he renounced the whole treaty and repaid the loan. By being in a position to do this he was more fortunate than many other African monarchs and chieftains whom Europeans claimed to have signed away their heritages.

An amusing tale is told of this diplomatic incident. It appears that the Italian emissary, Count Antonelli, left in a huff after finding himself unable to convince the Emperor and Empress Taitu, who played a considerable part in the discussions, that Ethiopia was unwise in repudiating the treaty. Menelik, not wishing the international quarrel to become personal, sent word that the count be given a mule and not left to walk to his Legation. Antonelli furiously gave 100 thalers to the servant who brought the animal remarking that he wished to owe nothing to the Emperor of Ethiopia. When the servant reported this and offered Menelik the money, Ras Makonnon, who was with Menelik, remarked, 'As a tip it is too much! But as the price of an Imperial mule it is really too little!' Menelik laughed, 'It is a tip,' he told the servant, 'keep it.'[2]

The treaty had confirmed Italian possession of the port of Massawa, the lowlands occupied during Yohannes's reign and parts of the highlands including Asmara. In Tigré today people still state that Menelik sold Eritrea to the Italians and since he was not crowned King of the Kings at Aksum,* and did not take another name when he succeeded Yohannes, many of the northerners at the time acknowledged him only with the greatest reluctance. They also attributed the famine of 1889, the year in which Yohannes died, to divine concern over this matter.

Menelik soon realised that the Italian imperialist appetite had been merely whetted by the treaty and by the later convention signed at Naples which had stated that 'a rectification of the two territories shall be made, taking as a basis the actual state of possession'. It was only when Menelik firmly objected to continued Italian territorial advances that the latter began at last to see what General Baratieri, Governor of Eritrea, had long stressed even to the point of resignation—namely, that to be effective their policy of 'divide and rule' in Ethiopia should be changed to oppose and not assist the dominance of Menelik II and of Shewa. The Tigré of Yohannes had lost its predominance.

Before his death the Emperor Yohannes had already recognised the new and growing danger of European territorial imperialism, and had tried therefore to limit religious strife with Islam. He had written to the khalifa, the successor of the mahdi of the Sudan, 'Let us not kill the poor and harmless to no purpose, but let us both unite against our common enemies the Europeans. If these conquer me,

---

* He had been crowned *negus* at Ankober, Shewa and then Emperor at Entotto near Addis Ababa, a departure from tradition. He had decided against Aksum because of the local opposition there after the defeat of Ras Mangasha Yohannes.

they will not spare you. . . . It is therefore our common interest to agree to fight and destroy them.'³

Menelik II caused similar messages to be sent in 1889 and 1895 but with little result. Meantime he had also sent a very significant letter to the European powers (see Appendix III) which, as well as defining Ethiopia's frontiers, described his intentions in the following words :

> 'While tracing today the actual boundaries of my Empire, I shall endeavour, if God gives me life and strength, to re-establish the ancient frontiers [tributaries] of Ethiopia up to Khartoum, and as far as Lake Nyanza with all the Gallas.'

Further it continued on a note of caution to his brother monarchs in Europe,

> 'Ethiopia has been for fourteen centuries a Christian island in a sea of pagans. If powers at a distance come forward to partition Africa between them, I do not intend to be an indifferent spectator !'

SHEWA, TIGRÉ AND ITALY

An archaeologist at that time in northern Ethiopia reported a temporary rivalry between Ras Alula and Ras Mangasha and commented that the support of local governors depended upon that all important factor in feudal Ethiopia—family connections.⁴ Adowa was for Mangasha, Aksum for Alula. However, these differences appear to have faded somewhat in the face of the Italian threat to Tigré. Doubtless swayed by local feeling in that northern province the archaeologist also remarked that 'the Emperor Menelik lives in Shewa, powerless and inert'. The Italians knew however, if only because of the weapons they themselves had supplied, that the Shewan emperor was anything but powerless, and they, therefore, sought an alliance with Ras Mangasha of Tigré. Their proud old enemy Ras Alula modified the oath of friendship proposed by the heir of Yohannes saying only, 'I am the faithful slave of Mangasha and therefore I swear to be the friend of his friends.' Yet strangely, even at this stage, the Italian policy had not gone over completely to the new line. To the consternation of their allies, Ras Mangasha and also the Sultan of Aussa, the Italians presented the Emperor Menelik with two million cartridges. At this time Ras Sabat and Ras Alula did in fact raise a small rebellion but it failed. Ras Sabat was imprisoned on Amba Alagi but Alula was pardoned.

Then the dervish forces of the Sudan once again remustered and launched an invasion of the north. They were defeated by the

Italians but meantime Ras Mangasha journeyed to Menelik's court in the hope of becoming *negus* of Tigré, if he changed his allegiance. He was not received too well in Shewa, partly because it was felt he should not barter his loyalty in this case, but also because the Empress Taitu had promised the crown of Tigré to her brother Ras Wolie. Menelik gave Mangasha to understand that the prize he sought might be won in battle against the Italians. If it should come to an open clash with Italy there seemed no doubt at the court of the loyalty of Alula, who had accompanied Mangasha, and he was received with open arms by the *fitwraries* and *dejazmatches* who, rather than *rases*, were influential at Menelik's court.

Menelik's main problem was to present the Italian threat to all the provincial rulers as something so serious that they had to combine against it and not seek to exploit it to their own ends. Uncharacteristically it was some time before even the Ethiopian Christian Church became a positive influence for national solidarity. Its attitudes showed a tragic lack of grasp of current realities—as they do today. While understanding crusades and the *Jehad*, the bishops quite failed to comprehend the nature of nineteenth-century imperialism. Keen enough to unite the country against the dervishes, they hesitated over the Italians who were Christians. Also the monks of Tigré were very much opposed to any action that might lead to a further rise in the political influence of the Shewan monasteries. Menelik understood how outmoded these attitudes were. Indeed from his reign may be dated the beginning of the implementation of the dream of Tewodros that the central government rather than the Christian Church should become the symbol of national unity— a process naturally in the interests of non-Christian Ethiopians, and a process furthered considerably, though few would say sufficiently, in the reign of Hailé Sellassié.

But the masses and lesser leaders recognised the Italian threat as a challenge to all Ethiopia, and their anger steadily mounted as it did years later, again against the Italians, in 1935, and against the Somali Republic in early 1964. For example, at the end of 1894 one northern chieftain seized an Italian officer and replied to his taunt of 'God will punish you, Italy is great', with the remark 'And Ethiopia is greater still!' The Italian troop build-up and minor military actions steadily aroused the nationalism of Ethiopia and the chances of exploiting her feudalism and dividing her nobles was correspondingly diminished.

A WAR OF INTRIGUE

The Italians took the initiative when General Baratieri ordered the occupation of Aksum, a curious step which he should have realised would further stir the latent patriotism of the Ethiopian leaders. Then the Italian forces tried to surprise the Tigréan army but two days of indecisive fighting at Coatit resulted. Baratieri, who like the Emperor Fasiladas before him, had expelled Roman Catholics—the French Lazarist fathers—for intrigue, was, nevertheless, himself heavily involved. But it is a cunning man who can outwit the Ethiopians at what they sometimes joke to be a national pastime.*

Baratieri hoped to subvert the loyalty not only of Menelik's recent rival, Mangasha, but also of his old rival the Negus Taklé Haymanot, ruler of Gojjam, of Ras Mikael of Wello, who was actually in negotiation with Italy, and of Ras Makonnen of Harar. This last *ras* had even written to Baratieri that if there was war he would rebel against the Emperor Menelik. Indeed all the chiefs except Ras Alula were in secret communication with Italy who aimed to create alliances across all Ethiopia north of Shewa. It has been written that perhaps these leaders informed Menelik of their intrigues with the Italians and very possibly this is so.[5]† However, that in itself is no guarantee that they felt committed to support him. There seems an Ethiopian tradition right up to and including the 1960 Revolution and its aftermath not so much to avoid taking sides as to appear until the actual moment of conflict to be on both! Such 'insurance' can have its limitations and often its absurdities. When Menelik ordered Ras Mikael to attack the Sultan of Aussa, an ally of the Italians, the *ras* was gravely embarrassed and compromised by sending a letter to the sultan warning him of his attack! Ras Mangasha in a letter purporting friendship forwarded by General Baratieri to Rome, attributed his earlier armed clash with Italy to the intervention of the Devil—for which word, commented Baratieri, read Menelik. Certainly the Emperor grew impatient over these intrigues; he had sent out a proclamation warning against the menace which Italian imperialism constituted to the nation and when he caught Wagshum Burru of Lasta redhanded he imprisoned him for treachery.

---

* This is perhaps not unrelated to the polished epigrams and *'double entendre'* of Amharic verse. Today, however, many an Ethiopian recognises that the tradition of personal advancement through intrigue has outlived its usefulness and that the national interest demands co-operation rather than conspiracy.

† It is interesting that the *Ethiopian Herald* of March 1, 1964, an edition to mark the anniversary of the battle of Adowa, explained that Hailé Sellassié's father, Ras Makonnen, was 'in charge of negotiations with the enemy'. But such articles are read less and less by Ethiopian intellectuals who claim that their history is daily distorted for political reasons. One such remarked to the writer, 'Our opiate is our ability to be endlessly pompous over Adowa and our independence'.

Meantime the Italians occupied Addigrat and Adowa, but General Baratieri—characteristic of later members of his profession —moved far ahead of the home government which had to pay for his operations. He went home and by force of personality rather than wisdom—again characteristic—he managed to carry the people and government of Italy along with his grand designs. He had some military success against Ras Mangasha and succeeded in annexing Tigré and occupying its present capital of Makallé where the Emperor Yohannes had built a new palace.* But his triumph was short lived. Menelik was on the march, gathering an army as his predecessor had said 'in numbers like the sand' from the consistently under-estimated millions of Ethiopia. An historian of the campaign has written, 'Never probably in the history of the world has there been so curious an instance of a commander successfully concealing the number of his army and making his advance behind a complete network of insinuation, false information and circumstantial deceptions.'⁶

Ras Makonnen, who was governor-general of Harar, had already marched north at Menelik's command. His troops had reached the wild and precipitous mountains north of Lake Ashangi. These mountains and the slopes of those which rise from the rolling lime-stone country extending north to the town of Makallé, capital of Tigré, have been the scene of many crucial battles in Ethiopian history. On this occasion an Italian administrative confusion led to the decimation of a small Italian force led by Major Toselli on the cold and windy heights of Amba Alagi. Theirs was a hopeless and needless defence against Ras Makonnen's overwhelming numbers. The *ras*, who had negotiated to the last minute, then pushed on into Tigré, and news of his victory rallied Menelik's chieftains. The pro-Italian group in Lasta was overthrown and the Negus of Gojjam joined his Emperor. The Italians withdrew to the north leaving a garrison at Makallé and meantime, the Shewans took the opportunity of raiding the lowland sultanate of Aussa in the Danakil country and burning its capital. Ras Makonnen subsequently wrote to General Baratieri and apologised for his part in the battle of Amba Alagi. He stressed that he had been pressed forward by the Emperor's troops and that his men had attacked without orders. The *ras* had been to Italy and doubtless knew the resources and power

---

* From early 1961, Leul-Dejazmatch Mangasha Seyoum, the energetic great grandson of Yohannes has ruled from there as governor general of Tigré province. By 1965 his vigour and willingness to strip off his shirt and work on development projects alongside the common folk had greatly added to his stature in the eyes of the Ethiopian intelligent-sia.

which lay behind a European army, and did not expect Ethiopians to win.

However, eventually Makonnen cast in his lot with Menelik, writing to Baratieri, 'Where the Emperor bids me there will I heroically shed my blood'. His forces then made repeated attempts to carry the town of Makallé by storm and their failure drew a withering remark from Empress Taitu when she arrived with the Emperor Menelik. 'Is this a banquet you have prepared for us as a reception?' she asked. 'Shame on you that one simple Italian colonel should cause you so much trouble.' Ras Makonnen was greatly incensed and personally led attack after attack with such recklessness that Alula and another *ras* had to drag him away. Despite astounding displays of courage and determination on the part of the common Ethiopian peasant soldiery—one man, having fought his way to the fortress walls, was killed trying to undermine them with only a hoe—the Italians had to be permitted to march out with military honours. They fell back on the town of Addigrat.

With Makallé in his hands Menelik wrote to the Italian monarch suggesting peace, and the garrison of the fort of Enda Jesus on the heights above Makalle was allowed to return to the main Italian forces. It is not clear why this happened, and Gamerra's memoir goes so far as to say that the other *rases* hated Makonnen because he accepted huge sums of money from Italy.[7] Major Gamerra was an Italian commander subsequently taken prisoner and later released by Menelik's order. Ras Mangasha also looked to his own interests. Styling himself 'Son of King John, King of the Kings', he wrote an innocent letter to Queen Victoria asking for help against the Italians. However, his messenger was told to state that Mangasha had never recognised the Shewan Emperor and that with the support of the Negus Taklé Haymanot of Gojjam he would soon make a claim for the title of King of the Kings. Even Menelik himself, the oral message went, recognised Mangasha's special status and remained standing before him. Empress Taitu however demonstrated a wider loyalty. She was especially opposed to the concession of any Ethiopian land to Italy. She remarked to the chiefs : 'Yield nothing ! What you give away today will be a future ladder against your fortress and tomorrow the Italians will come up it into your domains. If you must lose lands, lose them at least with your strong right arms.' Later history proved her right.

THE BATTLE OF ADOWA

Before Mangasha could receive a reply from Britain his and other intrigues paled into insignificance for, reacting to political pressure from Italy, General Baratieri advanced; but his army was crushingly defeated in one of the greatest battles in the history of Africa, the battle of Adowa on March 1, 1896. Makonnen was not, as is sometimes stated, the genius of victory, nor were Mangasha or Menelik the architects of the Italian rout. They were defeated by the master plan of that hoary old patriot, Ras Alula. Amidst all the intrigue the only person to whom he felt he could confide his plan was in fact the Empress Taitu. Indeed, as was shown in the later war of 1935–42, the women of Ethiopia are to be noted for their patriotism and bravery. Ras Alula lured the Italians to believe that on St Mary's Day the whole Ethiopian army would be weakened by a mass pilgrimage to the holy city of Aksum—thus forcing the attack at the time of his choosing. The inaccurate maps used by the Italian columns contributed to their disorder, but Ethiopian tradition also records that a patriot named Awalom acting as a guide, deliberately misled them according to a prior Ethiopian plan—and indignantly refused payment for so doing.

Once the three Italian columns, led by Major Generals Albertone, Arimonde and Dabormida (all of whom lost their lives) were separated, the greater numbers of the Ethiopian forces carried the day. Their total firepower, thanks to the foresight of the emperor and others, was not noticeably inferior to that of the Italians and in strategy they were far ahead. The Ethiopian minister of war at the time of Adowa was Fitwrary Gebeyehu. The armies were led by Ras Mikael, Ras Mangasha, Ras Alula, Ras Wolie, Ras Makonnen, the Negus Taklé Haymanot, Wagshum Gangul, the Emperor Menelik and even the Empress Taitu who had claimed it to be 'her war' and insisted on an active role. Other names which are still recalled with pride in Ethiopia are Fitwrary Habta Giorgis, Fitwrary Damtew, Ras Abaté and Dejazmatch Balcha who stepped into leadership when Abaté was killed. The peasant troops also fought ruthlessly and well.

The Italian humiliation, which they long remembered, would have been even greater had the Ethiopians followed up the few demoralised stragglers who retreated from the carnage, but they did not—except that Ras Alula sent out one party in the hope of seizing his old enemy General Baratieri. Indeed a strange factor about Adowa is also that the military advantage was not followed up politically. A settlement did cancel the Treaty of Wuchali and acknowledge the full sovereignty and independence of Ethiopia, but the Italians were allowed to retain Eritrea. For his part Menelik, who never really wanted a battle and would have preferred to negotiate, still considered his main territorial interests lay farther south and he feared to overstrain his resources.

The victory at Adowa proved of vital significance. However, it is disturbing but not perhaps surprising that the young men of Ethiopia who in the 1960s so frequently speak of it with understandable pride do not seem to be aware of the attitude of the few aged survivors of the battle. Those old men recall only their horror at what they had done and at the death of 'so many Christian men'. The usual feasts that mark victories were curtailed.

AFTER ADOWA

Sir Gerald Portal, in a dispatch from Cairo before the battle, had noted, 'although Menelik's army is so large, neither he himself nor his forces appear to be thought very highly of by the soldiers of Tigré and Amhara'. This traditional rivalry exacerbated by the sacking of villages led to many skirmishes as Menelik's Shewan army turned south again. They culminated in a severe defeat inflicted by the Azebu Galla; in all, more men were lost on the return journey than on the field of Adowa! As under Tewodros, so under Menelik the attitudes of the people as well as the terrain at first militated against the creation of a centralised type of state framework. Indeed, no sooner had Menelik reached Addis Ababa than he and his army had to set off again for the south-west.

It is often said that Adowa put Ethiopia on the map of the modern world—though, as Margery Perham has pointed out,[8] the conflict arose rather as the result of Europe putting herself upon the map of Africa—and the times of Menelik II are remembered largely because Ethiopia managed to preserve her independence from the scrambling powers of Europe.

After Adowa, Menelik's Ethiopia was at once accepted by the European powers as a very real political force. But if the crushing defeat of a European army greatly enhanced Menelik's international reputation, the host of foreign advisers, ambassadors, emissaries and even pure adventurers who followed this event brought problems as well as opportunities. Each fought to promote the influence and advantage of his own government and there was competition in the production of impressive but not always economically sound military and commercial schemes. Menelik, like Tewodros, was concerned to modernise his realm and he listened frequently to the advice of foreigners—French influence being perhaps paramount—and used Europeans if at any time he thought their experience more pertinent than that of his own subjects. He must have been a shrewd judge of their vanities, since he rewarded some quite cheaply with high sounding orders and titles. His measures, such as the creation of ministries, the beginning of modern education, the construction of telephone and telegraph systems and the railway, the introduction of vaccination, etc., have all helped set the pattern for today and are also important in the assessment of Menelik's reign.

THE PATTERN OF CONCESSIONS

Again like Tewodros, Menelik was interested in industrial development. One traveller recalls his question 'What progress does industrial development make in China? Do they make guns?' Later the rapid industrialisation of the empire of Japan was to have a marked influence on the thought of the Reforming Party of the early 1930s. Perhaps the most important project which Menelik II permitted on the advice of his foreign experts was the building of a railway inland from the port of Djibouti, in the French Somaliland colony on the coast of the Gulf of Aden. As with any development project in Ethiopia there was, as there is today, considerable conservative opposition to be overcome. Indeed to some extent objections to the railway presented by the Empress Taitu and for some time also, by Ras Makonnen and others, were valid, and Menelik was torn between his conviction of the probable economic benefits, in particular to the considerable trade in low-price commodities such as coffee, skins and wax, which constituted the bulk of Ethiopian exports,[7] and the obvious dangers, which he had not been the first Emperor to see, presented by the imperialist ambitions of the European powers by whom he was surrounded.

The railway was at first seen by the French as a political weapon to assist them to thwart the British ambition to control a broad strip of Africa from Egypt to the Cape. However, although the concession was originally given by Menelik to M. Ilg, a Swiss engineer, and to a French company before the battle of Adowa, construction did not actually begin until the famous Fashoda incident had frustrated the French plans and had led to the firm establishment of British influence on the Upper Nile. Moreover a treaty negotiated by Colonel Harrington on behalf of Britain with the Emperor Menelik, defined Ethiopia's western frontiers, and formed part of a series of agreements by which Menelik, between 1897 and 1908, successfully obtained international recognition of Ethiopia's frontiers, leaving only that with the former Italian Somaliland in any real doubt. Britain on behalf of her interests in Egypt and the Sudan had come to terms over any future use of the Nile waters.

Menelik, in turn, hoped that he had defined and thereby confined the disquieting advances of European territorial imperialism inland from the coasts of the Horn of Africa and from Eritrea. Thus in 1897 when the railway was begun in French Somaliland it was purely a commercial venture. Costs were high and there was considerable sabotage from the local people and soon the French company ran short of funds. During the next few years London financiers managed, through a group of companies, to almost establish control over the whole scheme. France was nearing a general election and a press campaign against 'foreign control' obliged the French government to agree to buy out most of the British influence. Incidentally this involved the French state in a degree of control over the company, and it was even provided that the Ministry of the Colonies would eventually acquire the line. The British plan, which had hinged upon enough control to build a branch line to a port in the former British Somaliland, thus fell through. Harrington, by then Sir John and British Representative in Addis Ababa, answered this by informing Menelik in 1902 that control over the railway was about to pass from a private company to the French state. It was then the turn of the Emperor, with more justice, to cry 'foreign control'.

Menelik was considerably angered by what he regarded as an attempt to compromise the political independence of his country by economic means—in the jargon of today he saw these intrigues as an example of neo-colonialism. The building of the railway stopped. In fact, it did not reach Addis Ababa until 1918, by which time a plan for internationalising both the line and the port of Djibouti had fallen through, the original French company had gone into liquidation and a new concession given by Menelik to his doctor who hailed from Guadeloupe had brought another company into operation.

It will be appreciated that Menelik was quite adept at commercial dealings—in fact he even financed several entrepreneurs himself—but he always saw to it that the independence of Ethiopia was not compromised. There can be no doubt that such was not infrequently the aim of the powers of Europe. Thus Menelik was angered, but not surprised when France, Britain and Italy notified him of a treaty they had made in 1906 acknowledging Ethiopian independence but significantly adding that 'in the event of rivalry or internal changes in Ethiopia they recognised their mutual right to take action to protect their nationals'. Although they affirmed they did not intend to interfere in the internal affairs of Ethiopia, there were ominous discussions on spheres of influence.

The Emperor was getting old, but he replied after an interval: 'We have received the arrangement made by the three powers. We thank them for their communication and their desire to keep and maintain the independence of our government. But let it be under-

SOME SOLOMONIC CLAIMS

A simplified diagram

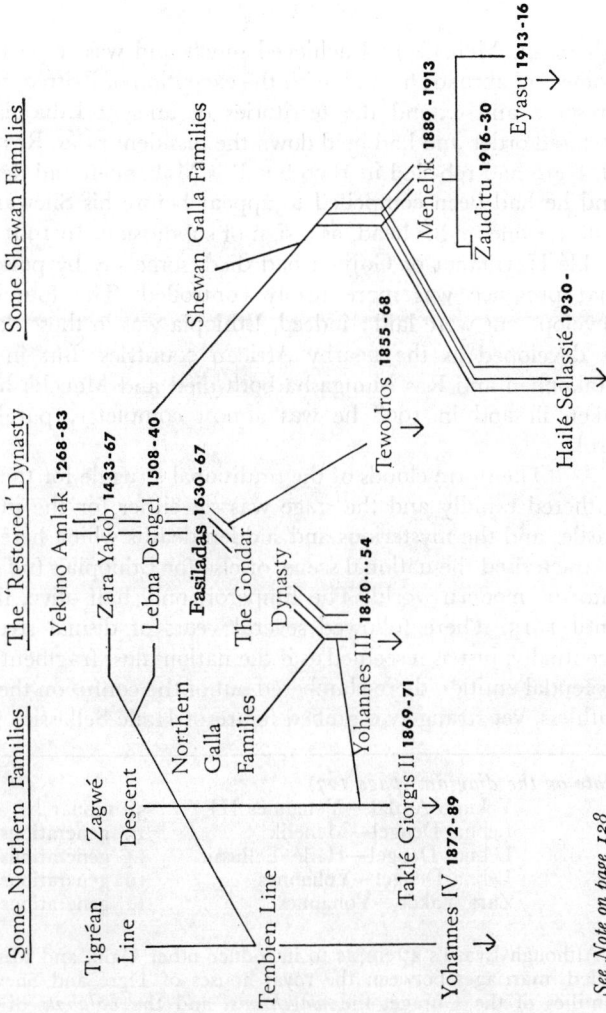

Some Northern Families

The 'Restored' Dynasty

Some Shewan Families

Tigréan Line

Zagwé Descent

Yekuno Amlak **1268-83**

Zara Yakob **1433-67**

Lebna Dengel **1508-40**

Northern Galla Families

Fasiladas **1630-67**

The Gondar Dynasty

Shewan Galla Families

Tembien Line

Yohannes III **1840···54**

Tewodros **1855-68**

Menelik **1889-1913**

Eyasu **1913-16**

Taklé Giorgis II **1869-71**

Zauditu **1916-30**

Yohannes IV **1872-89** →

Hailé Sellassié **1930-** →

See Note on page 128

stood that this arrangement in no way limits what we consider our sovereign rights.'

NEARING THE END

All in all, Menelik had achieved much and was respected both at home and abroad; he had, with the exception of Eritrea, managed to preserve and extend the territories of ancient Ethiopia. He had restored order and had held down the dissident *rases*. Ras Mangasha of Tigré had rebelled in 1899 but Ras Makonnen had defeated him and he had been compelled to appear before his Shewan Emperor with a stone on his head, as a sign of submission. In 1901 the Negus Taklé Haymanot of Gojjam had died, some say by poisoning, and that province was more firmly controlled. The foundations for development were laid : indeed, Ethiopia was in those days at least as developed as the nearby African countries. But in 1906 Ras Makonnen and Ras Mangasha both died and Menelik himself was taken ill and in 1908 he was almost completely paralysed by a stroke.

The storm clouds of the traditional struggle for the succession gathered rapidly and the stage was set either for the intrigue, the battles and the mysterious and sudden deaths which heretofore had characterised the national scene, or else for Ethiopia's full emergence into the modern world. The Emperor, only half alive, lingered on until 1913. There followed several years of dismal struggle until eventually, just as it seemed as if the nation must fragment again into its feudal entities, there clambered out of the confusion the small and ruthless, yet strangely dignified figure of Hailé Sellassié.

Note on the diagram (page 127)

Yekuno Amlak—Yohannes III	58 monarchs
Lebna Dengel—Menelik	13 generations
Lebna Dengel—Hailé Sellassié	14 generations
Lebna Dengel—Yohannes	10 generations
Zara Yakob—Yohannes	12 generations

Although Eyasu's attempts to introduce other Galla and Muslim strains failed, marriages between the royal houses of Tigré and Shewa and the families of the Guragé, the *wagshums,* and the *balabats* of Wello and Wellegga occurred. But increasingly Ethiopians began to say 'his mother was *Addisgé*' or 'his father was *Moja*' (Shewan families), etc., for since the 1930s intermarriage has made it increasingly difficult to ascribe new generations in the leading families to one particular region. There has emerged a highland, Christian, aristocracy involving such families as those of Leul-Ras Seyoum, Leul-Ras Kassa, Ras-Betwoded Makonnen, Princess Tenagne Worq, etc.

III

TAFARI MAKONNEN

8

The Shewan Coup d'État

Lij Yasu had himself no cut-and-dried plan for keeping the holy throne of Menelik. But he wanted to break away from the domination of the Church and he took the Mohammedans into his confidence.—L. Farago, *Abyssinia on the Eve*, London, 1935

The King of Abyssinia wades in blood to his Throne—a proverb from southern Ethiopia quoted by H. Darley, *Slaves and Ivory*, London, 1926

DYNASTIC SCANDAL AND THE SUCCESSION

Towards the end of 1907, the ailing Menelik had summoned a Council of Ministers to ease the burden of government. In mid 1908 he called to him the leaders of the Christian Church and the nobility and pronounced that his grandson Lij Eyasu, a boy of twelve years, was to be his successor. This act initiated a long period of renewed political intrigue which greatly hindered the development of the Ethiopian nation.

Throughout the long history of the Ethiopian throne there occur many alleged scandals and rumours about the succession, and the families of Menelik II, Ras Makonnen and Hailé Sellassié I himself are not exempt from them. It is not suggested that they are all true, more often they are not, but they are the stuff of which feudal court life and politics are made anywhere in the world. The historian is driven to looking into them because the truth is always hard to discover beneath the network of intrigue, deceit and secrecy which has typified Ethiopia for so long. However, these stories also have a political significance and are relevant to the understanding of contemporary Ethiopia because their repetition has been recognised, especially since 1961, as an important factor in swaying the opinion of a largely uneducated general public.

The leaders of the 1960 Revolution thought in terms of a bloodless change of government and were taken aback by the degree of popular support the traditionalists were able to rally. They were thus quite unprepared for an actual battle with army forces. In retrospect those who survived admit that one weakness of their attempted coup (which in the author's opinion was, from the outset, certain to be a failure for other reasons discussed below) was that it failed to use the radio and other propaganda to the best effect. The public statements of the revolutionaries concerned only social injustice and their language was that of African nationalism rather than Ethiopian feudalism. It thus tended to appeal only to the converted. This error, as will be shown later in this book, was probably Girmamé Neway's, and it was quickly seen by the Addis Ababa underground movement of 1961 and 1962. Their pamphlets were full of dynastic and other scandal which the uninvolved intelligentsia rejected as irrelevant nonsense. But it was not designed for their consumption. Thus a study of the political patterns and the history of the first part of this century is incomplete if it confines itself to what is known to have happened, quite apart from the fact that little is known for sure. What Ethiopians believe to have happened is also vitally relevant.

The Empress Taitu had borne the Emperor Menelik no children and he was reluctant to acknowledge a girl, Zauditu, whose mother was the daughter of a Galla *balabat* from Wello, as his daughter. He is said by some to have consulted priests as to his failure to produce an heir. The priests are said to have advised him to enquire into his early liaisons lest unknown to him an heir might exist. This he did, and there was 'recognised' another daughter, Shoa Rega, said to have been a child bride in Harar. Be that as it may— and it is almost certainly apocryphal and an attempt to discredit the heir—Lij Eyasu was the son of this daughter and Ras Mikael of Wello, her second husband. The *ras*, formerly Muhammad, had, it will be recalled, been forcibly converted to Christianity by the Emperor Yohannes.

Later the same year, 1908, Menelik was paralysed, losing even the power of speech, and he indicated that the young prince should be committed to the care of the bishops and *rases* and that his former general, Tasamma, should become Regent. The latter took over the government, his seal reading 'Ras-Betwoded Tasamma, Regent Plenipotentiary of the Ethiopian Realm'. The struggle for power continued to obscure all else and even to undo much of what

Menelik II had achieved. One noble, Ras Abaté, even tried to seize the person of the young prince but was unsuccessful.

THE INTRIGUES OF THE EMPRESS TAITU

Taitu had been born in Gondar in 1844 but she was from Yejjo, Galla country to the north of Shewa. Her family had connections with the Gondar line of emperors and was powerful throughout the whole north. Needless to say she was not at all popular with the Shewan nobility.* Taitu's first husband, before he was poisoned, had been a commander in the army of the Emperor Tewodros. Her second had been Dejazmatch Taklé Giorgis but she had left him to marry a richer and more powerful noble whom she had persuaded to revolt against Emperor Yohannes. This intrigue was discovered and she had been forced to marry a simple soldier whom she had followed on foot and whose grain she had dutifully ground for some time before she had left him for a non-commissioned officer in Menelik's army, and him for Fitwrary Zekagachew, the brother of Menelik's wife Befana. However, later she left the *fitwrary* for Ras Woldé and him for Menelik, while Befana took refuge in a convent in 1883.[1]

Doubtless because she had borne Menelik no children, the Empress tried to keep complete control over the country through promoting members of her own family, most of whom lived in northern Ethiopia, and she had built up a powerful court party through matrimonial alliances and friendships. She was supported by Ras Wolie her brother and his son Ras Gugsa Wolie who had married Zauditu, Taitu's own step-daughter; by most of the lords of Tigré; by Leul-Ras Hailu Taklé Haymanot of Gojjam, whose marriage to the widow of Dejazmatch Yilma she had engineered; by Dejazmatch Ayelu, the commander of her guard; by Dejazmatch Kebede and others.

Very conservative and religious in her old age, the proud and autocratic Empress was heartily disliked by Lij Eyasu. Taitu, incidentally a very large woman, was, however, a formidable opponent for any group to challenge. She was possessed of a very masculine personality,[2] and had long taken an active part in affairs of state. Once she rose to her feet as a portrait of Queen Victoria was presented to her, in order to honour another Empress. In so doing she surprised those present to the extent that they scarcely knew how to

---

* Taitu was not a Tigréan as several historians in Europe have claimed but her great-grandfather was Ras Gabré of Simien, her grandfather Dejazmatch Hailé Mariam and her father Dejazmatch Boutol (the brother of Dejazmatch Wubie who had been defeated by Tewodros).

answer her close but kind enquiries into the private life of that British monarch.

Taitu's aim had at first been to be recognised as regent. She would have abdicated in favour of her nephew Ras Gugsa, thus restoring the Gondar line. The capital would have been transferred to Gondar and Shewa might well have become semi-independent. However, that was not to be and it appears that later she favoured Menelik's daughter Zauditu (her step-daughter and Gugsa's wife), and tried to secure the succession for her.

Taitu's constant intrigues brought crisis after crisis until the Shewan nobles intervened in 1910 and with a show of force and the Archbishop's help reasserted the position of Ras-Betwoded Tasamma, the Regent. But this solution was short-lived because in 1911 the Regent was taken ill very suddenly and he died. The Council then declared that Eyasu was old enough to act for himself under, of course, their guidance, while the Emperor lived—but since on occasions Menelik rallied just sufficiently to inspire caution in those about him, the impasse continued.

THE POLITICAL AMBITIONS OF LIJ EYASU

Menelik's incorporation of Harar, Jimma and the several kingdoms and states of southern Ethiopia within a new and more exactly defined polity presented a much enlarged pattern of internal political forces to be united (or, failing that, balanced) by the King of the Kings if he was to rule successfully. Tewodros had tried to weld a much smaller Ethiopian state into one unit and had failed. His successor Yohannes had not even attempted this, probably only in part because he was distracted by dervish, Italian and other pressures. Instead he had come to terms with the rulers of the different parts of the empire. Even Menelik as often as not had appointed or confirmed the hereditary rulers of incorporated lands, or their sons, as his governors—a practice still to some extent current in the early 1960s. Even so, Menelik's conquests had inevitably altered the whole internal balance of Ethiopia. The empire had expanded to include effectively an enormous number of Galla and Muslim subjects, many of them influential.

Eyasu's own father, Ras Mikael, had the allegiance of other Galla groups besides his own Wellos. He had also the friendship of the northern *rases* of Begimidir and Tigré and at least the respect of Hailu of Gojjam, son and heir of the Negus Taklé Haymanot. Thus Eyasu could hardly be a symbol of the continued ascendancy of Shewa. In fact the Shewan *rases*, whose patience had already been sorely tried by the intrigues of the northern Empress Taitu gave ready ear when several of their number stressed that they themselves had a good claim at least to Menelik's Shewan throne. One of their party, though not their leader, was the young Dejazmatch Tafari, son of Ras Makonnen of Harar and later to become Emperor Hailé Sellassié, who was related, though through the female line, with the allegedly 'Solomonic' succession of the Negus Sahlé Sellassié of Shewa. The Ethiopian Christian Church also feared Eyasu and regarded his father Ras Mikael, despite his conversion to Christianity, as at best an unknown quantity and it was widely rumoured that the young heir's relatives has influenced his religious upbringing. Nor did it escape the notice of the Church leaders that the Shewan *rases,* like the Gondar *rases* before them, were suspicious of the northern Galla families.

Of the foreign powers, French commercial influence remained paramount but German influence had been allowed to increase at Taitu's court. Eyasu, for example, had had a German governess. Significantly, Germany before the first World War was on good terms with Muslim Turkey. On Ethiopia's frontiers the situation seemed far from secure. The proximity of restless provincial rulers and covetous Colonial governors, not only in Eritrea but also in the Somaliland 'Protectorates' to the east, might well prove very dangerous indeed.

At first, however, although Eyasu was theoretically in power, in actual fact he had none—a situation enjoyed by many with liberal tendencies in Addis Ababa in the 1950s and early 1960s. Real influence remained with the Empress Taitu. With her step-daughter she kept a close guard over the dying Menelik. On one occasion Lij Eyasu did attempt to interfere with the palace appointments, and a skirmish resulted in the palace grounds, during which Taitu succeeded in having Menelik carried to safety in a cellar and the deadlock was unresolved. It is not clear when or how the paralysed Emperor finally did die, but it is known that, as with the Emperor Bakaffa centuries before, his death was kept secret for a long period and he was even impersonated. Earlier in Ethiopian history there had been created special officers within the feudal hierarchy whose task it was to impersonate the Emperor.*

---

* Many important dignitaries were captured and imprisoned during the 1960 Revolution because they assumed that the death of royalty would not be publicly announced until councils of leaders had met in secret. When called they came, all unsuspecting, to the headquarters of the Imperial Guard or to the palace. Also strangely reminiscent of this was a mysterious impersonation of Hailé Sellassié, then still very much alive, late one night in the dying hours of the *coup d'état* in Addis Ababa in December 1960. See p. 423.

The official date of the Emperor Menelik's death is given as December 12, 1913. Lij Eyasu, who expected to be crowned as His Imperial Majesty Eyasu V, and his young companions are reported to have paid scant respect to the strict court and national mourning occasioned by his grandfather's death, and this very likely added to the increasing suspicion with which the young monarch was regarded by the Ethiopian Christian Church.

In Ethiopia, historians are as yet silent over Eyasu. A visiting writer in 1931 wrote, 'People do not readily speak of him, for the whole country is policed with spies', and this has been even more the case ever since Eyasu's somewhat mysterious death in 1935. His name is mentioned only in whispers even in the 1960s. European historians not infrequently dismiss Eyasu out of hand. That he was young and impulsive cannot be denied; that he was inclined to be a playboy may also have been true—though in this direction his character deteriorated sharply, even absolutely, after his deposition —but he must be given credit for a certain political shrewdness, even if he showed little sign of being what is sometimes called 'a modern monarch', a term which some might feel is in any case scarcely applicable to Ethiopia.

Eyasu was well aware that the title King of the Kings had passed from the Gondar-Galla line, via Tigré, to the ruling house of Shewa but recently. He saw that on these grounds alone he might rally the whole north, but, moreover, if it could be created, a union of the muslim and Galla peoples of the empire would give a force equal to anything Shewa could put in the field. On the international front he believed that through shrewd alliances he might even be able to expand the frontiers of Ethiopian rule still farther. The first World War was on the horizon. Germany occupied no land on the periphery of Ethiopia, and if she was intending to fight Britain then might it not be perfectly possible for him in alliance with General Von Lettow Vorbeck in German East Africa (now Tanganyika) to secure further extensions of Ethiopia at the expense of British, Italian and French occupied Africa? This ambition perhaps more than anything else was the cause of Eyasu's subsequent misfortune. Von Lettow Vorbeck's memoirs and other works on his campaigns contain no suggestion that such an alliance was actually proposed, but several writers on Ethiopia mention it.[3]

THE CONSPIRACY OF THE SHEWAN NOBILITY

Eyasu decided to use his powerful Galla father to the full. In 1914 he conferred upon Ras Mikael the title of *negus* of Wello and Tigré. Dejazmatch Seyoum, whose family (he was the son of Ras Mangasha and the grandson of the Emperor Yohannes) had little reason to support the Shewan party, was made *ras* and governor general of Tigré where, under Menelik, he already held six governorships. In 1915 Eyasu added Begemidir and Gojjam to the crown of the Negus Mikael. Mikael had for some time been preparing to invade and recover Eritrea from the Italians. They and equally their French and British allies viewed his promotion with some alarm and linked it with their suspicion of all the foreign ambitions and friendships of the German Kaiser or the Turkish Sublime Porte. Very possibly inspired by diplomatic intrigue, the Shewan *rases* had made the position of one German adviser appointed by Taitu quite impossible so that he had had to resign. To the allied powers it seemed clear that Eyasu's attitudes were dangerous. His religious leanings were towards Islam, and therefore Turkey, and his political ones towards Germany. A new *Jehad* in north eastern Africa could conceivably have tremendous repercussions in the Middle East and India and completely change the world balance of power in favour of the central powers.

The Italians explored the possibilities of alliances with some of the Tigréan nobles, and the whole of that northern province was in more than customary turmoil. The Shewans' restlessness increased and by 1916 Eyasu appears to have come to a decision to press ahead with his plans for control as a matter of urgency. He built mosques and made a series of matrimonial alliances with the daughters of influential Muslim leaders. Previously he had married Sable Wangel, Leul-Ras Hailu's daughter, but there had been no male issue—though Cheesman in his book *Lake Tana and the Blue Nile,* refers to a daughter of this union. He had then wed the daughter of an important Galla from Wellegga.* Eyasu's Muslim wives included a daughter or a niece of the Sultan of Jimma, and some of Eyasu's descendants live in Jimma today. He made approaches to the Mahdi of the Sudan with a view to an alliance with his daughter, but at this time his favourite was a Danakil princess, the daughter of Sultan Abu Baka. Some say she was successful in making Eyasu's political leanings to Islam, religious also. It is certain that he was very attached to this girl by whom he had a son—Menelik. Eyasu clearly sought to breed a new aristocracy dependent upon himself—and indeed his several children were not infrequently the source of trouble to Hailé Sellassié long after the latter had seized the throne.

---

* This girl subsequently married Fitwrary Sharew, father of the Ethiopian Ambassador in Sweden who was dismissed after the 1960 Revolution and then Dejazmatch Woldé Mariam, the Galla father of Lij Kassa, appointed President of the Ethiopian University in 1962. Lij Kassa is the husband of Hailé Sellassié's granddaughter Immabet Sable Desta.

Eyasu is said to have had constructed a genealogy tracing his father back to the prophet, to have declared Ethiopia subject to the religious authority of Turkey and to have presented the consul-general of that land and other people with Ethiopian flags carrying a crescent and the words, 'There is no God but Allah'. In 1916, after visiting Dira Dawa and French Somaliland, he started to raise an army at Ji-Jigga, a desert town beyond Harar, much later to be governed by the 1960 revolutionary leader Girmamé Neway. Earlier in the year he had had Dejazmatch Tafari, son of Makonnen, recalled to Addis Ababa from the provincial governship of Harar in order to transfer him to Kaffa, thus leaving very few in the south-east to oppose him. Following protests from foreign legations in Addis Ababa a deputation of priests and notables journeyed to remonstate with him without effect.

Some writers go so far as to suggest that then the famous Colonel T. E. Lawrence came secretly to Ethiopia and was involved in the production of propaganda against Eyasu at the instigation of the British government.[4] This cannot be proved, but it is interesting. Pamphlets depicting a befezzed Emperor Eyasu amidst a group of Muslim sheiks were produced, according to the story, in Khartoum. However, there were also printing presses in Ethiopia at this time. Another account asserts that there were several different photographs and leaflets, some obscene, and that the pictures, faked by an Armenian named Leon, all bore the Amharic caption 'The Anti-Christ'. Certainly, the repercussions of Eyasu's actions were also domestic for the Ethiopian Christian Church and the Shewan nobility genuinely shared the alarm of the legations and it would be difficult in the circumstances to believe that they were not encouraged by foreign diplomats. Indeed the lively interest which the British government took in the intrigues for the throne and many aspects of Britain's support for the Shewans, in particular Dejazmatch Tafari, are well described by Leonard Mosley who has been able to consult and quote the diplomatic dispatches of Wilfred Thesiger, the British minister, and to draw from conversations with surviving members of Tafari's party and family[5]. From his accounts it appears likely that the diplomatic records of Italy, Germany and Turkey might also contain much of relevance.

Worried nobles and churchmen conspired together in Addis Ababa and elsewhere throughout August and September and troops were dispatched from Addis Ababa to Harar province. Tafari arranged that his wife and son be smuggled out from Harar and left his money with the British minister. Several plots came to naught. Much hinged on the attitude of the Archbishop Abune Mattheos who greatly feared the military power of Negus Mikael. On September 27, 1916, the Council of State met, having called their forces together. Prominent among the leaders were Leul-Ras Kassa Hailu, Ras Woldé Giorgis, Bejirond Takla Hawariat, Kantiba Gabru and Nagradas Gabré-Hiwot Baykedagn, the last having been concerned also in the unseating of the Empress Taitu when she sought to take over more power than the Shewan leaders felt desirable. The conspirators approached Abune Mattheos, 'We will never submit to Islam! We do not wish our country to be delivered to the foreigner through the malice of Lij Eyasu, who is leading our kingdom to ruin!' they said. After some hesitation he confirmed their proclamation, making Menelik II's supposed daughter Zauditu, whom Eyasu had confined to her Addis Ababa residence, the new empress, and Tafari, son of Makonnen, Regent with the title of *ras*. The Archbishop's announcement stated that all who failed in this their new allegiance would 'incur the wrath of the Father, the Son and the Holy Ghost, of the Twelve Apostles and of the Three Hundred and Eighteen Fathers of the Council of Nicaea, the curse of Arius and the reprobation of Judas.' For good measure he added 'with my humble breath I excommunicate Lij Eyasu.' It was not many years before the wrath of the Ethiopian Christian Church was again invoked and as recently as December 1960 it was brought to bear against all those participating in the abortive *coup d'état*.

Eyasu grew alarmed at the presence of Shewan troops in the vicinity of Harar. He was also aware of the part which the British minister in Addis Ababa was playing against him and he chose to contact the British consul in Harar. That officer reported that the Emperor asked for British protection for Ethiopia and hence himself. If this is true, it represented nothing more than an attempt to confuse the British Foreign Office in order both to gain time and to frustrate any intention Britain might have entertained of supporting her diplomatic involvement with military force or supplies.

On September 28, 1916, a telegram signed by Ras Tafari ordering the 'Governor of Harar' to seize and enchain Eyasu was given to that deposed Emperor by the Head of the Harar post office. Eyasu immediately swore before the bishop and priests of Harar that he was still a true Christian and a faithful Ethiopian. He created three *fitwraries dejazmatch* and imprisoned the Emperor's second cousin Kegnazmatch Imru, whom Tafari sent to arrest him. Some say that Eyasu had long tapped the telephone conversations between Tafari and Imru and was not surprised when the latter bravely set off for the palace with his small guard. Imru, like Tafari, is a small man and Eyasu was very tall and well proportioned. He is said to have hurled Imru to the ground shouting, 'What do you want with me? Liar! Slave! Bastard of a dog! Would you lay hands on the master who has nurtured you, on the heir of those who made your fathers what they were?' Had courtiers not restrained him, Eyasu might well have killed the *kegnazmatch* there and then, but Imru survived imprisonment to play a significant part in many later events.

Shewan forces attacked the city and Eyasu sent troops to meet them, but he was not fully prepared. He called the Danakil and Ethiopian Somali chieftains to him and ordered them to leave for their home areas, there to raise forces and await his call. He himself left the city on horseback carrying only his lance as if he was out to enjoy a little exercise. The guards prostrated themselves at the gate of the walled city as he passed. Some hundred or so followers joined him. The small party passed by a large Shewan force whose soldiers also prostrated themselves before Menelik's giant grandson, but a few hours after his departure Dejazmatch Balcha led his troops into Harar and many Muslims were put to the sword.

THE NEGUS MIKAEL SUPPORTS HIS SON

Meantime, Eyasu was acclaimed in the railway town of Dira Dawa at the foot of the Rift valley escarpment and he set off northward across the desert to join his father the Negus Mikael. The *negus* had learnt earlier over the telephone of the disquiet which existed in the governing circles in Addis Ababa. He had in fact been contacted by Shewan leaders who had stressed the dangers of Eyasu's policies. They requested Mikael to bring pressure on his son to abdicate, they stressed the dangerous international implications of the present trends and claimed their actions to be in the best interests of the empire. Indeed, it appears that Mikael was expected to agree with them and his angry indignation took them by surprise. Mikael confided in his *tsahafé taezaz* (Privy Seal) but the only reconstruction which made any sense to him was his secret fear that his son was dead—murdered by the Shewans.

The puzzled and angry old King called his horsemen together. He over-rode the judgement of his more cautious chiefs who argued that the Shewans had modern guns and it would be wise to wait and call up Ras Seyoum's Tigréan infantry and the Italian equipped forces of Leul-Ras Hailu of Gojjam. The *negus*, however, despised Tafari as a soldier—the Wello soldiers jokingly called him 'the feared one'—and Mikael and his chiefs set off for Shewa with a large force.'

Back in Addis Ababa, Tafari and the junta of Shewan nobles grew alarmed. They had visions of a rising in the north and of a Muslim horde led by Eyasu, who could so easily personify the age old concept of the warrior Emperor, sweeping like the hordes of Ahmed Gran over the country. Menelik's ageing Minister of War,

Fitwrary Habta Giorgis, appealed to the French Legation and received the promise of a shipment of machine-guns—but delivery would take a little time. Meanwhile, the Empress Taitu thought of a plan. In her body she was old and senile, but her shrewd political mind was as active as it had been at Adowa years before. She ordered that a message be sent to the Negus Mikael to inform him that his son was in prison in Addis Ababa. Taitu hoped thus to provoke Mikael to action before his Wello forces were joined by Eyasu's followers and before the whole north had been raised.

In the meantime a small force was sent out from the capital. Some say that Ras Lul Seged, its commander, offered to ride north with Taitu's message. Certainly he had cause to hate Eyasu. That Emperor had forcibly abducted Lul Seged's wife—Menen, a beautiful grand-daughter of the Negus Mikael—and had obliged Tafari to leave his own wife and marry her. Ras Lul Seged did not blame Tafari. When Eyasu had sent the latter away from his post as governor general of Harar province, Menen—and Eyasu—had stayed there. However, it is difficult to reconcile this story with the fact that Ras Lul Seged was under detention at Debra Berhan to the north of Addis Ababa. It is more likely that Tafari ordered that Ras Lul Seged be set free and invited him to prove his loyalty to Shewa, for the old man mustered what few troops he could—some 3,000—and dutifully marched towards Mikael's forces. The old *negus* swept this feeble force aside on the plains north of Addis Ababa, not far from Ankober, and continued his advance. Ras Lul Seged and many of his followers, including Liquamaquas Abebe Atnaf Seged (the father of Lieutenant-General Abiye Abebe, an important son-in-law of Hailé Sellassié) were killed. The foreign legations in Addis Ababa began to make hasty plans for the anticipated fall of the city. Meantime messages reached the Negus Mikael to the effect that his son was very much alive and was engaged in raising an army. Eyasu, moreover, sent urging his father to wait for him and the advancing Wello forces were halted.

The French machine-gun consignment reached the port of Djibouti but a delay of two weeks was anticipated before it could be brought by rail and mule to the encamped Shewan forces which the Minister of War, Fitwrary Habta Giorgis, had led out from the capital. The *fitwrary*, therefore, indulged in a typical piece of Shewan intrigue. He dispatched small parties in a methodical encircling movement but he also sent a message from his headquarters at Debra Berhan addressed to the Negus Mikael. It read :

I address this letter so that it shall reach my dear master and friend the Negus Mikael wherever he is. Know that by the

Grace of God I am well . . . I announce to you my loyalty to
our Emperor Eyasu, your son—grandson of our venerated master the Emperor Menelik. Two valiant soldiers such as we two
should never be at enmity over the defence of the traditions
which are the very soul of our country. I pretended to lend
myself to the black designs of the son of Makonnen, and of the
officers who have supported his treason, in order to keep the
army in my own hands thus to turn it against him with the help
of your horsemen. However, a large consignment of arms from
Europe is at this moment in Addis Ababa and I have ordered
that it be sent here so as to prevent its falling into the hands of
the usurper, which would inevitably happen if we marched
against him at this moment. So we must not reveal our alliance.
If you have any confidence in our old friendship stay for a few
days in your present position and rest your horses and men so
that they will be ready for the signal. . . .

The *fitwrary* also arranged that others should write insulting letters
to increase any favourable impact his own might receive.

Mikael, who knew of rivalry between the conservative war
minister and the more progressive Tafari, was deceived. He replied
that his son Eyasu should be restored to the throne, but conceded
that Tafari should retain the title of *ras* and the province of Kaffa.
The *fitwrary* stated that as there was no telephonic communication
he had to use a horseman and this would involve delay in answering
but in the meantime during the lull he dispatched a token gift of
ammunition to the *negus*. After nearly a fortnight the machine-guns
were distributed and Tafari's army moved north from Addis Ababa,
which he left in the charge of Dejazmatch Balcha, who had returned
from Harar, and negotiations were then ended by a second letter
from the *fitwrary* to the Negus Mikael. The *fitwrary's* secret intentions may never be known, but with the arrival of the machine-guns
he became convinced that the Shewans held the initiative. He wrote :

. . . I have reflected since my last letter and urge you to do
likewise. Your son is to blame ! I range myself on the side of his
enemies and urge you to follow suit. Come and make known
your loyalty to Tafari, the son of Makonnen ! If you do not—
then in spite of my stated affection for you, I shall have no
choice but to be your enemy. I tell you this loyally. I have no
wish to deceive you and profit from your trust by attacking you
unexpectedly. I await a reply.

At the time of receiving this missive Mikael also learnt of the
encircling troop movements. The furious old *negus* dispatched some
of his forces on a flanking movement under cover of darkness but

they wandered into swampy ground. Mikael at once ordered his Galla horsemen to charge the Shewan lines at full gallop across the plains of Segalé. But the mistake of delaying when time was not on his side was already made and it was too late. The Shewan machine-guns opened fire, and there was great confusion as the lines of rushing cavalry wilted and collapsed on entering the beaten zone of the fire of those weapons. Urged on by their trumpets and unaware because of the dust of the fate of the first waves, the Wello horsemen continued to brandish their lances and rush into the fray.

The fighting was fierce and it was a very near thing for the Shewan forces, for it was not until a body of Leul-Ras Kassa's levies arrived that the issue was decided. The proud and brave old *negus* could have escaped but instead he dispatched the Danakil Princess and her son, Eyasu's heir, in the care of her eunuch, to a secret hiding place and then, calling his own guards around him, he galloped into the midst of the battle where he, his chief commander Ras Ali and his *tsahafé taezaz* were eventually captured and taken chained to Addis Alem to the west of Addis Ababa.

Eyasu had delayed too long on the plain of the River Awash down in the Rift valley. There he had received messages not only from the Muslim leaders of the east of Ethiopia but also from Arabia. He had, however, reached the precipitous Ankober escarp-ment in time to dispatch a message to warn his father, the *negus*, even to withdraw but not to engage the Shewan forces in any cir-cumstances until support arrived from the east and north, Eyasu's messenger, however, was attacked by a swarm of bees and collapsed badly stung. When he eventually arrived the battle of Sagalé had been lost.

Eyasu heard of the disaster and set off to the north accom-panied by his few followers, for the Shewans made no attempt to follow up their victory. At Aksum he sheltered in the house of Leul-Ras Seyoum until the latter found his presence an embarrass-ment and asked him to leave. Eyasu retired to wander in the north and in the desert lowlands for several years.

Meantime in Addis Ababa it had been agreed between the diplomats that the Italian minister should ride out and ask the *negus*, whom everyone still expected to have won, to respect the sanctity of the legations. However, it was a victorious Shewan army which marched back to Addis Ababa on November 2, 1916, and a great victory parade was held at the site of the present Imperial Racing Club course at the north of the city, whose streets were festooned with makeshift gallows. Dejazmatch Balcha had shown that he believed in speedily and ruthlessly restoring order in that frightened city. It is recorded that then, as after the suppression of the 1960 *coup*, foreigners travelled into town to photograph the gibbets and their ghastly exhibits.

Some say that for a time there was tension between Woizero Menen who not unnaturally sided with her new husband, Ras Tafari, and her mother Woizero Sehen who was a daughter of the Negus Mikael. Not long afterwards, however, Woizero Sehen was suddenly taken ill and died. Dr Grabedian, her physician, was expelled from Ethiopia shortly afterwards and never spoke of her death, fearing his motives would be thought suspect.[6]

At the parade the victorious troops marched past Ras Tafari, notables and invited guests. The soldiers were followed by the fettered but proud figure of the Negus Mikael. It is typical perhaps of the feudal attitudes and relationships between the leaders of Ethiopia that the *negus* paused and bowed slightly outside the main tent. Escorted by Kegnazmatch Imru, he was uncertain whether or not he would be allowed in, but he was waved on. One of the diplomats present, although a supporter of Tafari, wrote : 'It was horrid and made us all feel a bit sick. The Bishop Petros, who had been captured too, had been brought into the tent and embraced by his triumphant brother-in-God, but the Negus who had fought so well for his worthless son, was sent away.' The Wello generals were in chains and they supported great stones on their shoulders—the customary sign of submission. There were also the shattered remnants of the late Ras Lul Seged's force, followed by one of his sons in a sheepskin for mourning. Leul-Ras Kassa Hailu, the architect of victory, himself brought up the rear.

Few in Ethiopia know where the Negus Mikael was imprisoned or how he died. There is a strange story that as he left the palace, captive in a car, he threw out a bag of money which was caught by a Danakil standing by the roadside who promptly disappeared. Some say the money went to spirit Eyasu's wife and young son to Tajura where they took refuge with the French authorities. In fact, Mikael was imprisoned on an island in Lake Ziway, one of the largest of the beautiful groups of lakes in the Rift valley, 150 miles or so south of the capital. Fitwrary Habta Giorgis was responsible for him and he stayed on the island for some years. Later he was brought, very sick, to Holeta, much nearer the capital. There he died in 1918, paralysed and without the power of speech, in the arms of his faithful *tsahafé taezaz*. Some time after Tafari had been crowned Emperor a delegation of the *shums* or leaders of Wello were permitted to come from their provincial capital at Dessie to Addis Ababa to take away the mortal remains of their *negus* for safe keeping. His grand-daughter, the Empress Menen, retired for a period of ritual mourning at Addis Alem.

A REVOLT IN TIGRÉ

A headstrong young son of Ras Seyoum Mangasha, named Dejaz-match Kassa, who was governor of Aksum, Adowa and Shiré, openly refused to acknowledge Ras Tafari. Kassa was perhaps motivated more by his personal friendship and admiration for Eyasu than consciousness of his own descent from Emperor Yohannes, and Tafari, therefore, required Kassa's father, Seyoum, to use his good offices in the quarrel. Seyoum had been governor-general of all Tigré since he had been appointed *ras* in 1914, and he called his son to his court—in the palace of the Emperor Yohannes at Makallé. Dejazmatch Kassa, however, refused to go. The order was the usurper's, he claimed, and not really his father's. Reluctantly Ras Seyoum marched to Adowa at the head of 1,000 soldiers. Kassa was warned and had left Adowa before Seyoum's forces caught him up. His followers were defeated but the young *dejazmatch* fled into the Simien mountains.

After some time word reached him that he would be forgiven if he returned to Adowa and acknowledged his father and the Regent. He did this, bearing a stone on his back and with a knife tied around his throat—the traditional signs of submission and repentance. However, on arrival, he was thrown naked to the ground and given forty lashes with a hippo-hide whip. He did not once cry out and afterwards was carried to a near-by hut. At first he was not expected to live but later recovered and was taken to Shewa and confined near Addis Ababa, in the houses first of Ras Birru and then of Ras Getachew. Fellow Tigréans made several attempts to free him and one day he managed to crawl through a window and escape on a horse. A 'phone call to the capital alerted the government and the young *dejazmatch*, doubtless on his way towards Tigré, was inter-cepted by a group of Galla *zabanias* (watchmen) north-west of the capital. His horse was shot from under him. Sheltering behind its body Kassa returned the fire until he was killed by a bullet in the temple.

THE EMPRESS ZAUDITU

Zauditu was unable to command the loyalty especially of the northern areas of Ethiopia and great havoc was wrought by rival armies particularly in Wello. Not long after the battle of Sagalé, the old Empress Taitu also made her last unsuccessful bid for power.

---

* This whole incident was applauded in an unsigned threatening letter received by University College students after the unsuccessful *coup d'état* in 1960. The letter purported to come from relatives of dignitaries who had been killed.

However, she was arrested by Dejazmatch Gabré Sellassié.* She consented to the loss of all her rights, and acknowledged the proclamation naming Zauditu as Empress and Tafari as Regent. Taitu was in turn confined to a house on Entotto hills, a beautiful ridge rising some two thousand feet to the north of Addis Ababa city and now covered by eucalyptus trees. There she died in 1918.

Zauditu had been the child bride of the son and heir of the Emperor Yohannes—young Ras Aria Sellassié, who had died in 1888. Her second husband had also died and she had then married Dejazmatch Wubie but after three years they had separated and she had married Ras Gugsa Wolie, Taitu's nephew, in 1901. His ambitions were obvious and dangerous and by the new settlement the Shewan *rases*, who disliked the powerful northern barons, insisted on another separation. Ras Gugsa's children were to have no claim on the succession and he himself was ordered to live away from Addis Ababa in the north where he was given a governorship. It is hardly surprising that Zuaditu, sick of dynastic politics, turned more and more towards the comforts she derived from the Ethiopian Christian Church.

On February 11, 1917, Zauditu was crowned Empress at St George's Cathedral in Addis Ababa. The German and Turkish delegations, for whom this represented a diplomatic defeat, were not represented. They feared they would be asked to sit in positions which did not accord with protocol—a fear which was almost certainly groundless, for the Ethiopian has a high sense of protocol and courtesy. They probably over-estimated the influence of their gleeful enemies, the diplomatic representatives of Britain, France, Russia and Italy. On the following day old Ras Woldé Giorgis was created *negus*, since the Regent, Ras Tafari, was only twenty-five years old. However, the path of the latter, destined to become the Emperor Hailé Sellassié I, was becoming much clearer, and on that day he was invested with the insignia of the Grand Cordon of the Order of Solomon.

---

* Dejazmatch Gabré Sellassié was the father of Dejazmatch Zewdé Gabré Sellassié (see page 166, note).

9

Ras Tafari's Path to Power

*A few years ago Tafari Makonnen sat his throne, as one
resident of Addis put it, with his feet under him, ready for
a quick move.*—J. BAUM, *Savage Abyssinia*, London, 1928

*Every labourer is a father, his labour is his child. Choose
your project carefully and achieve it worthily.*—HAILE
SELLASSIE in a broadcast, September 18, 1959.

THE CHILDHOOD OF TAFARI

Tafari Makonnen was born on July 23, 1892. At his baptism some
days later, according to custom, he was also given a 'Christian name'
—Hailé Sellassié—which he would use in church, for example at
confession. His father, Ras Makonnen, was the younger son of
Tenagne Worq, a daughter of the Shewan Negus Hailé Malakot,
son and successor of the Negus Sahlé Selassié, who claimed the
Solomonic Succession. Tenagne Worq had married Dejazmatch
Walda Mikael, son of a noble, Walda Malakot, who was famous at
Sahlé Sellassié's court for his road building. Ras Makonnen, then, was
of a noble Shewan family and his wife Woizero Yeshimabet, whom
he married in 1875, was the daughter of a Galla *balabat* and a former
slave girl named Waleté Giorgis, whose previous liaisons had been
with Ras Dargé and a lesser chieftain who had been hanged for
rebelling against Menelik. This girl, Tafari's maternal grandmother,
was of Guragé descent. The Guragé hail from an area south-west of
Addis Ababa and though very industrious are often looked down
upon. To this day Hailé Sellassié is apt to remark with a smile that
he is a Guragé and after the liberation he ordered that the market cry
'Guragé!', to attract a casual labourer or porter, be replaced by

'Coolie!' There were ten children but only Tafari and his half-brother survived childhood. His mother died in childbirth when Tafari was only two years old—or at least so say Hailé Sellassié's biographers. (Some Ethiopians, on the other hand, maintain that she died at his delivery.)

As with Lij Eyasu and with Tafari's son the present Crown Prince Asfa Wossen, certain scandalous stories about Tafari's birth are still current in Ethiopia. It is whispered that he was born ten months after Ras Makonnen had left for a visit to Europe and that the Church proclaimed the 'miracle of delay' to enable Tafari's illustrious father to be present at his birth. These old tales are only important in that they have been used in the early 1960s by pamphleteers seeking to discredit Hailé Sellassié. They even hint that his early nickname 'the Indian' denotes a blood-kinship with a certain merchant Muhammed Ali. Suggested origins of this gossip are both the interest which the Imperial court took in his birth, for the Empress Taitu is said by some to have summoned his mother (assuming her to be still living) to Addis Ababa as soon as she was able to travel, and the mystery which surrounds the apparently unhindered export of capital abroad by this merchant—but that if true could be explained in a multitude of ways.[1] The tale was in any case spread by supporters of Lij Eyasu who had every reason to discredit Tafari.

The young noble received his first lessons from a priest, Aba Walda Kidan, but Ras Makonnen was anxious that he should learn French. Makonnen had been to Europe more than once—he represented Menelik at the coronation of Edward VII of Britain, for example—and he arranged that a doctor whom he had invited to Harar to start a hospital should control his son's lessons. It was decided that the French speaking Aba Samuel should act as a young companion to the boy and he received educational instruction from Catholic priests. Since the second World War the second official language of Ethiopia has been English rather than French, but the Emperor still prefers to speak French and often hints that the University should use it as well as English as a language of instruction. He addressed the Addis Ababa Conference of Heads of African States in May 1963 in Amharic, but in conversation used French and this was well received. Many of the older generation speak French and even Brigadier-general Mengistu Neway preferred that language and spoke very little English. The young Tafari's other companions of early times were his second cousin Imru Hailé Sellassié and Tafari Belau.

In 1903, Tafari was taken to Addis Ababa to be presented at court and three years later, on another journey to Addis Ababa, his father Ras Makonnen was taken ill and died. Before his death Makonnen had made the boy a district governor and had granted him the title of *dejazmatch*. The Emperor Menelik confirmed this title and appointed the young Dejazmatch Tafari as nominal governor of Salalé, while the elder half-brother, Dejazmatch Yilma, succeeded his father as governor general of Harar.

In accordance with Ethiopian tradition, Tafari, like all children in any way connected with the royal family, lived at court. They had often to serve their elders and always to know their place. They were taught riding, shooting and hunting and introduced to all aspects of Ethiopian life so that they might grow up to understand the thought-patterns of those whom they would rule. At this time Tafari was often in the company of Lij Eyasu who was a little older than he. The two not infrequently quarrelled. Palace servants remember how one young noble called his horse 'Endurance', how Lij Eyasu called his 'Father of Peace', but grew angry and insisted on a change of mount when young Tafari announced the name of his horse— 'Ruler of All'. (This story loses a little point in the translation of the names from Amharic and it should also be remembered that Ethiopian wits frequently make interplay between the names of famous men and their horses.) At court Tafari learnt much in the hard school of feudal intrigue; more perhaps than Lij Eyasu.

Tafari Makonnen had always been small, with delicate hands and striking eyes. His skin was very light even for an Ethiopian and his appearance almost middle-eastern.*

In 1907 the young Tafari was made governor of Ba'Aso and was sent, at its foundation, to Menelik II School, Addis Ababa. That year his half-brother Yilma fell ill and died, and Dejazmatch Balcha subsequently took over the province of Harar. When Tafari was seventeen years old he left school and became governor general of Sidamo. He was quite a reformer and tried to register the land for the purposes of efficient taxation. In 1911 Dejazmatch Balcha was transferred to Sidamo and Dejazmatch Tafari took over his father's province of Harar.

In July that same year the Emperor Eyasu caused Ras Lul-Seged to be detained at the palace while horsemen took his wife Woizero Menen and her household away to the railhead and thence

---

* Some Ethiopians are quite as dark skinned as any Africans, yet others are very pale indeed. A good example of a dark-skinned Ethiopian is the aristocratic governor general of Eritrea, Leul-Dejazmatch Asrate Kassa, youngest but only surviving son of Leul-Ras Kassa Hailu. He could be a Ghanaian, though his nephew, Dejazmatch Amaha Aberra, ambassador to Western Germany (1965–), could be mistaken for a European.

to Harar to marry Dejazmatch Tafari—her third husband. Tafari was already married and had a daughter, Romanaworq who was to marry Dejazmatch Beyenna Merid who was later murdered by the Italians. Their sons, Merid and Samson, though barely recognised at court, have been prominent in Addis Ababa's social set, but Lij Samson died in a car crash in July 1963. Woizero Menen, who had also had children, was the daughter of Woizero Sehin, eldest child of the Negus Mikael of Wello and Jantirar Asfaw. She it was who was destined to become Empress of Ethiopia. A masterful and proud Galla, she was very close to the Ethiopian Christian Church, many of whose monasteries and churches she enriched. She was Lij Eyasu's niece and in her youth a woman of striking beauty. She owned considerable areas of Addis Ababa and was very wealthy in her own right—many say more so than Tafari. About a year older than her husband, she died but recently on February 15, 1962, in Addis Ababa after a long illness. Their oldest child Princess Tenagne Worq was born in 1913.

The governor generalship of Harar was a prize in which the young Dejazmatch Tafari delighted. He was very progressive in his attitude to the usual despoiling plunder and slavery which were rife in Menelik's captured provinces. He tried to apply the principles he had learnt in his semi-western education and again sought to register the land, set up an administrative service and in general to create a basis for economic development. In fact his few years in Harar gave him the experience on which some time later he based his 'model provinces program'.

In the 1950s Girmamé Neway, whose social conscience lay behind the Revolution of 1960, returned from studies in America and after some time in Addis Ababa tried to apply his principles to government in the provinces in much the same way as had the Emperor in his youth. When discussing the tensions of the country with His Majesty early in 1962, the author suggested the parallel. For the Emperor had failed to back Girmamé against the landowners, whose feudal interests were threatened by that progressive young governor, and had in fact transferred him to a desert province in which the frustrated young man had planned the revolt. His Majesty smiled but made no comment.

In 1915 there occurred a tragic accident on Lake Alemaya, a few miles north of Harar. A boat overturned and Dejazmatch Tafari was one of the few survivors. He lost his childhood companion, Aba Samuel, who was probably the last person he ever completely trusted. Afterwards he kept his own counsel and often sat thinking for hours deep into the night. In 1916 Emperor Eyasu, as has been described above, recalled Tafari to Addis Ababa and endeavoured to send him to Kaffa, with results that ended instead in the latter becoming the Regent of Ethiopia. In that year also a son, Asfa Wossen the present Crown Prince, was born to Woizero Menen in Harar, for she had not accompanied Tafari to Addis Ababa. Probably because of this fact, and because the Emperor Eyasu was in Harar, mischievous minds suggested a likeness between the child and his great uncle the Emperor. This story, reproduced in subversive leaflets in the early 1960s, is held by some to account for the antipathy between Hailé Sellassié and the Crown Prince but it might well have been forgotten had not Hailé Sellassié later so obviously favoured his younger son Makonnen, the late Duke of Harar. Despite these long standing rumours the author favours the view that Asfa Wossen is Tafari's son—certainly childhood photographs of the three princes, Asfa Wossen, Makonnen and Sahlé are almost indistinguishable, whereas Eyasu's sons have all been six-footers.

THE CONSERVATISM OF HABTA GIORGIS

Even after his *coup d'état* and the subsequent defeat of the Negus Mikael, the Regent Tafari was not by any means the undisputed power in the land. For some time Leul-Ras Seyoum of Tigré was confined to Addis Ababa, since he was a possible rival. True, the feeble old Negus Woldé Giorgis counted for little and retired back to Gondar to his death, but there remained the intensely conservative and religious Empress Zauditu, and Menelik's former Minister of War, the aged Fitwrary Habta Giorgis.

Habta Giorgis had once been made *dejazmatch*, but it had long been traditional for a Minister of War to be styled *fitwrary* (see Appendix II) and in fact there was a joke in Ethiopia amongst the ruling classes that Galla peasantry expressed surprise at his reverting to that title. 'What! Does he go back again?' they are said to have asked in a pun which is difficult to translate. The *fitwrary* was a great patriot. Once an Italian visitor quietly attempted to assess his loyalty to the Regent whom he was known to distrust, by guiding the conversation towards the discussion of past internal strife in Ethiopia and mentioning the *fitwrary's* defeat of the Negus Mikael at the battle of Sagalé. 'Don't talk about that hockey game,' was the *fitwrary's* sharp rejoinder. 'Let us talk of Adowa!' The remark brought the conversation to a fairly rapid close.

An American traveller, James Baum, had occasion to call on the old man to obtain permission to travel through Arusi. He wrote : 'No one could leave his presence without being impressed with the intangible spirit of power and straight-shooting honesty that seemed to radiate from the man. He was by far the strongest personality we

6—E • •

met.' But he also called him : 'The backbone of the Queen's party, the anti-foreign, reactionary group, he was the spirit of darkest Abyssinia incarnate.'[2] A British consul was less complimentary, writing that he quickly learnt to respect the *fitwrary's* 'staunch conservatism which was proof against all modern ideas and innovations'. He added, 'If ever he visits England he will find congenial company on the benches of the House of Lords, or should this historic institution no longer be in existence, among the heads of colleges at Oxford and Cambridge.'[3] The *fitwrary* was opposed to Ras Tafari obtaining too much influence and he suspected him of being a secret Roman Catholic. In an attempt to frustrate Tafari he once went so far as to make a vital journey in an automobile after having vowed never to use such a satanic device. His attitude to trains was also significant. He is recorded as having boasted never to have seen one, let alone travelled on one. He thought of planes as 'childish toys, or an affront to the Almighty by endeavouring to extend the powers of man beyond those granted him . . . or a devilish device of the foreigner to spy out the land from abroad and so facilitate ultimate foreign conquest'.[4] Tortured with rheumatism in his old age, Fitwrary Habta Giorgis led the formidable group of nobles whose vested interests dictated their opposition to reform. He had himself received from the hand of the Emperor Menelik enormous tracts of land, 40,000 *gashas* at a time.*

THE IMPRISONMENT OF EYASU

Eyasu, whom many considered to be still the rightful Emperor although he was never crowned, remained at large and commanded a considerable following. The whole north was in a state of continual strife and the danger of a large scale Muslim rising was ever present. The deposed Emperor was reported at several places including Magdela, the citadel of Tewodros. The Regent asked the British for aeroplanes with which to bomb him out but the request was not granted. It is said that Eyasu communicated secretly with the Empress Zauditu urging her to recognise him as co-ruler and to banish Tafari. Fitwrary Habta Giorgis and Leul-Ras Kassa unsuccessfully laid siege to Magdela in mid 1917 and later that year Eyasu's army was defeated but Menelik's elusive grandson again escaped.

However, in 1921, Ras Gugsa Aria, a northern noble, arranged the capture of Eyasu who was at that time in Gugsa's Tigréan fief, and handed him over to Zauditu. The Shewan *rases* were bound by a law of the late Emperor Menelik that princes of the blood should

---

* A *gasha* is an Ethiopian land measurement of approximately 90 acres.

not be put to death. They petitioned Zauditu not to entrust Eyasu to the Regent who was at that time away in Harar. Several nobles asked that they might guard Eyasu before Zauditu delivered him to Leul-Ras Kassa Hailu bound in golden chains. These chains had been made in Kaffa and had been intended by the ruler of that state for Menelik, should he have fallen into his hands. As it was, Menelik had used them on the divine King of Kaffa himself. Enchained, Eyasu was taken first to Ambo and then to Fiché, some seventy-five miles north of Addis Ababa on the track to the great gorge of the Blue Nile, and to the province of Gojjam.

At Fiché in the early 1960s, the grandson of Leul-Ras Kassa, Fitwrary Amdé Aberra, who is the governor of that region, has a fine house overlooking the deep and beautiful gorge of a Blue Nile tributary below the famous Shewan monastery of Debra Libanos. The *fitwrary* was himself educated at Sandhurst Military Academy in England, but his grandfather thus chosen to be warder to the deposed Emperor, though of considerable military experience, was by nature a churchman. However, feudal leaders had to be soldiers of a sort. Although there was only the merest beginning of a national army in that Russian (Tsarist) officers were engaged in 1916 to train a palace guard and Tafari formed his own guard in 1917 (later to become the Imperial Guard), the head of every peasant household in highland Ethiopia owned a firearm. But it was Leul-Ras Kassa's family more than his nature which made him a fit person to guard Menelik's heir. His father had been Hailu of Lasta. His mother, Woizero Tisamé, was the daughter of Ras Dargé, a son of the Negus Sahlé Sellassié. His claim to the throne was thus at least as good as the Regent's, but Kassa was unambitious and for this reason also and because he was trusted both by the progressive Regent Tafari and the conservative bishops, he was singled out to guard the deposed Emperor in his banishment. Eyasu was treated well, and allowed, with a certain amount of contempt, to indulge his appetites as he wished. The imprisonment raised Tafari's prestige considerably and for a period quietened the unrest which had typified the Danakil regions and Tigré for several years.

THE PROGRESSIVE PARTY

Ras Tafari sought to adapt the provincial administration towards his concept of a salaried civil service responsible to the central government, rather than allow an unpaid feudal hierarchy to continue to live off the country as the price of keeping some form of order and collecting and forwarding certain tribute to the central coffers. This feudalism varied from province to province, but was especially

pernicious in the predominantly Galla and negroid provinces where
the Governors and their officers as often as not looked on their
provinces as conquered fiefs which they would only hold for a
temporary period and from which they ought, therefore, to squeeze
as much personal spoil as they could, as quickly as possible. This
frequently involved slave traffic which the Regent knew to be
dangerous, for it roused indignation in Europe and indirectly
encouraged those seeking to advance European territorial imperialism. However, save in his own province of Harar, where for example
he caught and hanged slave-traders, the Regent was unable to make
much progress, because of the conservative opposition which centred
round the aged Minister of War.

But apart from building up his military power, Ras Tafari had
slowly been gathering more and more supporters around him. He
could count on several of his relatives such as Leul-Ras Kassa and
Kegnazmatch Imru, but he sought also self-made men who would
owe everything to him. Many such men have come to prominence,
faded, and even returned, but no one has been consistently trusted
by Tafari.

Strangely, one of his early supporters was an adversary of his
father Ras Makonnen. This was Yigezu, son of Negadras Behabté, a
slave in Menelik's mother's household. Noticed at court, Yigezu had
been placed in charge of the Harar customs after the conquest of that
province and in the typical feudal manner still extant, had been
played off against the governor general, Ras Makonnen, who sought
to conserve all levies and dues within his own province. After his
successful *coup*, Tafari called Yigezu to Addis Ababa. In 1918 he
was made Minister of Commerce and *kantiba* or mayor of Addis
Ababa with the title of *dejazmatch*. He was given the daughter of
Leul-Ras Hailu, previously married to Lij Eyasu, as wife but within
a few years a pigment disease from which he suffered obliged him
to retire to Arusi. Some say he had leprosy and that he sought to stem
its ravages with sorcery.[5] Certainly he came into violent collision with
Roman Catholic missionaries working with the Arusi Galla and at
one stage an old tutor and friend of Tafari's, Monsignor Jarosseau,
who had lived long in Harar, came to the capital and urged the
Regent to intervene. Thirty years later Tafari was to extend great
trust also to a grandson of Dejazmatch Yigezu for Lieutenant-colonel
Tamrat Yigezu was chairman of the secret Commission of Enquiry
into the events—though not the causes—of the 1960 December
Revolution.*

---

* The Lieutenant-colonel is not, as is often stated, the son of the dejazmatch, but he uses his name instead of his father's, who still lives.

Other early allies of Tafari Makonnen included Negadras Gabré-Hiwot Baykedagn, a Tigréan from Adowa. He had sided with Tafari against Lij Eyasu and Tafari visited him almost daily. It is said today that the *negadras* remarked at the time that he was playing 'a long term danger to the country against an immediate one', although this may be apocryphal. Gabré-Hiwot had been educated in Germany and was a gifted linguist, at one stage interpreting for the German Embassy. When private secretary and interpreter to Menelik he fell foul of the Empress Taitu, who had him posted to the frontiers in charge of customs, but he returned to Addis to intrigue against Taitu and to write an Amharic pamphlet, *The Emperor Menelik and Ethiopia*, in which he railed against the reactionary attitudes of his fellow countrymen and the lack of opportunity for Ethiopians to receive modern education. He warned that other ancient nations such as China and particularly Japan were indulging in necessary innovation far faster than was Ethiopia. He condemned the attitudes of his country's traditional leaders and wrote '. . . up to now they regard the land they are appointed to govern as their own land bought by their own money. They do whatsoever they like with the taxes collected. . . . When, O People of Ethiopia, when will you wake up from your sleep? When will you open your eyes and see what things are being done in the world?' In 1923 he published another pamphlet entitled *Political Economy*. He was a great wit, as by the nature of the languages are most Ethiopian scholars. A protestant or perhaps even an atheist, he once feared he was dying and sent Kegnazmatch Imru to fetch priests. The *kegnazmatch* returned with the news that the orthodox priests refused to come but the Roman Catholics were willing—it was only when Gabré-Hiwot shouted, 'If the butchers disagree does that mean I am not to get my meat? Bring the Catholics !' that Imru is said to have formed the opinion that if the *negadras* could joke like that, as like as not he was not dying at all. Unfortunately, when he did die, some time after the Regent came to the throne, poisoning was suspected. His son later became ambassador in Cairo and Minister of Pensions.

Blattenguetta Hiroy Woldé Sellassié, sometime editor of the progressives' newspaper, *Light and Peace*, was another important man. For a time in charge of the Addis Ababa municipality, he became Foreign Minister in the years immediately preceding the Italian invasion.

A third distant relation of Hiroy, was Lij Takelé Woldé Hawariat. Lij Takelé came to prominence in the same municipality under the patronage of Lij Eyasu and Negadras Gabré-Hiwot, but he sided with Tafari against Lij Eyasu. The two were close friends sleeping in the same room and discussing the palace politics together. Lij Takelé was typical of those most interesting, even brilliant men who, for the early part of their lives, are so ahead of their time that they never themselves achieve real prominence, yet to a large and usually unacknowledged extent are, nevertheless, responsible for the initial thought which moulds events. Takelé was, however, never content with position in the second rank. His intelligence and his intrigues dictated for him a very chequered life as often as not in disgrace, or even in detention, yet never far from the strands of the nation's life. Takelé eventually rose to the heights of *dejazmatch* and *afe negus* (Lord Chief Justice), but suffered confinement, more often than not without trial, both before and afterwards.

Takelé first brought the Habtewold family to the attention of the Regent. Three brothers Habtewold were to become ministers, although it was some time later that Tafari first met Makonnen Habtewold, who, even though his brother Aklilu actually became Prime Minister, was by far the most influential of the three.

Makonnen's birth-place was Bishaftu and he had attended a priest's school on the slopes of Zikwala volcano to the south of Addis Ababa. His good singing voice had attracted attention and after being taken to court he had read holy works to the ailing Menelik. In his spare time he had studied French and in 1913 had left the Church and joined the government. He rose from the position of a humble clerk and attached himself to the Regent's party.

Not unnaturally the Regent's party included a disproportionate number of men from Harar, some of whom survived in power for many years although several were killed in the attempted *coup d'état* in 1960. One of Tafari's early followers who still clung to power in 1964 was Tefera Worq Kidani Wold, the rather unpopular Minister of the Imperial Palace.

In order to ensure the growth of a class of modern educated young men from whose numbers he could draw his supporters in the years ahead, Ras Tafari took considerable trouble to extend government schooling. He enlarged Menelik's School for the sons of nobles and founded the Tafari Makonnen School in 1925. He also encouraged other leading Ethiopians to found and finance schools and three promised to do so. But it was not only at home that Tafari sought and secured allies.

THE REGENT AND THE OUTSIDE WORLD

In 1923 Ras Tafari went to visit Aden and members of his entourage are reported to have wept and torn at their clothes when he insisted on being flown in an aeroplane. It was the first time he had seen one, but they were very soon to be introduced to Addis Ababa and to be of considerable assistance in his struggles.

Also in 1923, Ras Tafari achieved a diplomatic success of some significance when he had his country accepted as a member of the League of Nations. Ethiopia was accepted unanimously but only after long discussion, largely on the issue of slavery. Britain for example was one of those critical owing to her experience of the lawlessness of the peripheries of the Ethiopian Empire which abutted on her dependencies to the west and south. However, to many admission seemed a good way of ensuring that the Ethiopian Regent would comply with the international 'conscience' regarding traffic in slaves and arms.

On his part, Tafari—tragically as it turned out—thought that membership of the League of Nations with its high sounding principles would ensure his country a period in peace in which to develop free from the danger of the colonial ambitions of other powers. He might have read a warning in 1925 when Britain and Italy circularised an agreement which contained among other provisions recognition of each others 'spheres of economic interest' within the Ethiopian boundaries. Using his League membership, Tafari, in a strong parallel with the Emperor Menelik in 1906, succeeded in obtaining a statement that such agreement in no way limited Ethiopia's sovereignty. He made those two powers (and France, who had complained at being out of the agreement) look rather ridiculous by his dignified insistence that the League 'Treaty Series' publish his protest together with the offending agreement However, even if the writing was on the wall, Ras Tafari was soon afterwards too absorbed with internal difficulties to be able to concern himself much more with it.

In 1924, Tafari did, however, undertake an extensive foreign tour which took him to Palestine, Egypt, France, Belgium, Holland, Sweden, Italy, Britain, Switzerland and Greece. Woizero Menen, Tafari's wife, also travelled as far as Egypt and Jerusalem. Tafari's modern outlook created a lasting impression everywhere he went and it was this trip which laid the foundation for the myths which grew in subsequent years around his personality. Its significance has even been compared with the visit of Peter the Great to western Europe 200 years previously.[6] There can be little doubt that his experiences confirmed his conviction that Ethiopia was in need of innovation and development, but it is not too clear, even in those days, quite what it was that impelled Tafari to believe this. Many writers have assumed that he was motivated by a belief in social reform but the author would question this. Tafari is recorded about this time to have remarked to a woman visitor to Ethiopia, 'We need

European progress only because we are surrounded by it.' He added that such progress was 'at once a benefit and a misfortune. It will expedite our development but we are afraid of being swamped.'[7]

LEUL-RAS HAILU OF GOJJAM

In those days, as for safety's sake he has always done since, the Regent ordered the most influential of Ethiopia's leaders to accompany him abroad. His entourage of ten notables included Leul-Ras Kassa Hailu, the jailer of Eyasu, Ras Seyoum Mangasha, grandson of Yohannes, and Leul-Ras Hailu Taklé Haymanot, governor general of Gojjam. The latter, Leul-Ras Hailu, was perhaps the most significant and certainly the most written about. He was the son of the late Negus Taklé Haymanot of Gojjam. Despite his travels Hailu remained a convinced provincial-feudalist, although whilst in Europe he did become fascinated by machines of all kinds which he delighted in personally dismantling. He had a car re-assembled at his Gojjam capital of Debra Markos and he drove round and round the town at twenty-five miles an hour past his terrified and prostrate subjects. It is even said that he tried to bring a dismantled tug-boat to Lake Tana and that the engine is to this day stranded on some *amba* summit.

When he met King George V of Britain, that monarch is said to have asked him, through an interpreter, 'Can you speak English?' When the Prince of Gojjam replied in the negative the King asked, 'French? Arabic?', but received the same reply. Exasperated he asked, 'Well, what do you speak?' Leul-Ras Hailu retorted, 'Can you speak Amharic? Gallinya? Guragé?' When George V admitted he could not, Hailu commented 'I am glad to see that we are both equally ignorant!' It seems that George V laughed so much that Queen Mary came over to speak to him.[8]

Many foreign visitors, some fortunately writers, were intrigued by this noble who was to play the important role in the Ethiopian politics of the next twenty years which is described below. It would, however, be very revealing if someone, preferably an Ethiopian, were to compile his complete biography before too much oral evidence is lost.

RAS TAFARI TAKES OVER THE GOVERNMENT

Tafari had led Zauditu to reaffirm Menelik's edicts against the slave-trade and he made it clear that he wished to co-operate with other League powers against the traffic. It was not so easy for him to convince his own southern governors that they should implement his international agreements, however. But time was on his side, and in 1926 two leading reactionary leaders died within months of each other. The first was the old warlord Fitwrary Habta Giorgis. Tafari immediately rushed troops to Addis Ababa from Harar and personally took over the vacant command of the army. He placed his own supporters in the *fitwrary's* governorships. The second was the old Egyptian Archbishop Mattheos. The *Echegé*, or chief monk, an avowed enemy of Tafari, was thus left unsupported and Tafari banished him. The balance of power had changed drastically.

Empress Zauditu, who had previously dismissed the Council of Ministers called by the ailing Menelik, saw all influence slipping from her grasp and she appealed to Leul-Ras Kassa to support her in arms. He mustered some troops but it was a half-hearted gesture for he soon saw that Tafari was already too strong to challenge openly and he resigned himself to a period of life under honourable surveillance in Addis Ababa. Other nobles watched uneasily and Tafari decided to press his initiative. In early 1928 he summoned Dejazmatch Balcha to Addis Ababa from his governor generalship in Sidamo in the south. Dejazmatch Balcha, one of Menelik's generals, was a governor of the old school. He paid no taxes to the central government. He saw no reason to outlaw slavery and his rule was one of exploitation based on fear. It never occurred to him to seek the development of the provinces as parts of the nation, for that concept was foreign to him. Even if he did understand, as a soldier, what allegiance meant, he felt no respect for Tafari. One writer records Dejazmatch Balcha's remark to a British Colonial Service officer, named A. T. Miles, that Tafari was 'half man, half snake'.[9] When cautioned about such an indiscretion in front of the horde of slaves in attendance, the *dejazmatch* explained that all their tongues had been cut out as a foresight in this respect. Certainly, the proud old governor was capable of such cruelty and this was perhaps not unconnected with the fact that Dejazmatch Balcha was a eunuch. When a young Galla youth, he had been picked up by the Emperor Menelik who saw him lying on a battlefield in this condition and with other wounds. Menelik had given orders that the boy be nursed back to health and sent to court.

Dejazmatch Balcha ignored Tafari's summons, but received a second somewhat more terse command. It is not quite clear why this time he chose to obey it but the writer quoted above,[10] states that Zauditu sent him her ring as a secret signal that he should come to Addis Ababa and help her overthrow the Regent. He marched to Addis Ababa at the head of 10,000 men. Undeterred, Tafari asked him to a banquet which he attended with 600 personal guards, but while the *dejazmatch* was in Addis Ababa, Tafari's emissaries, led by Leul-Ras Kassa paid the soldiers $10 each and sent them home. Tafari tried to reason with Balcha, but he, almost certainly encouraged by Zauditu, openly stated his disagreement with Tafari's attitude towards the government of the country. He hinted darkly at the possibility of his own armed intervention before he haughtily left the banquet with his guards, only to find that his camp was almost deserted and surrounded by the Regent's soldiery. Dejazmatch Balcha, who could find no ally other than the *Echegé*, took refuge in a church and claimed sanctuary, but he gave himself up when Tafari, who had caused machine-guns to be set up outside, gave him a twenty-four-hour ultimatum to surrender. The dejazmatch was imprisoned for two years, but then having signed an admission of the error of his ways he was permitted by Tafari to retire to a monastery from which he only emerged eight years later to die bravely as a Patriot fighting the Italian Fascist invaders.

Tafari has never allowed a monument to be erected to the old warrior Fitwrary Habta Giorgis but there is a hospital named after Dejazmatch Balcha in Addis Ababa. Built from money raised from his property, and opened in 1948, it has since been enlarged and is one of several hospitals being run largely by foreigners.*

In the treatment of Dejazmatch Balcha, the conservative nobles saw clearly the manner of their own end. Actually they conspired together and found it easy to persuade Zauditu that Tafari intended to take all power from her, because this had a firm foundation in fact. The accounts of non-Ethiopian writers usually describe how one September morning in 1928, Ras Tafari went up the hill to the old *ghibbi* which dominates the lower south-eastern parts of Addis Ababa city. (This great palace was built by the Emperor Menelik and was being restored in 1964.) Tafari's intention is said to have been to attend to the normal business of government but on arrival he was called before the Empress. As he walked unaccompanied into the great hall Dejazmatch Abawukow, commander of the Imperial Guard, is said to have staged a *coup* at the instigation of the Shewan nobles. If this is so, he was neither the first nor the last holder of that office to use his powerful position in such a way. However, Tafari, those accounts continue, saw the machine-guns on the roofs of the great mausoleum where Menelik II lies and realised he had to act quickly. Without staying to discuss Zauditu's allegations that he sought to displace her, he turned on his heel and walked alone to the main gates with the guns trained on him and ordered that they be thrown open. Meanwhile, news had

---

* Dejazmatch Balcha Hospital is staffed by Soviet doctors and nurses. Much unfounded nonsense has been written in Kenya and other places about its being a centre for continent-wide sabotage and subversion.

reached his home and Woizero Menen, his wife, had armed his Harari retainers as best she could and dispatched them in haste to the great palace. As the gates were opened Tafari's men rushed in and overcame the guardsmen who all surrendered. Tafari rode home. However, many Ethiopians recount in private that this 'official story' is not the truth. They say that the Regent's party and his soldiers from Harar themselves staged a successful *coup d'état*, seizing control of the palace, which was the centre of government, and overcoming Zauditu's guard.

In either event the nation's leaders met directly afterwards and had no alternative other than to endorse the Regent's actions. He demanded the title of *negus*, withheld at the coronation, and a proclamation to this effect, which also confirmed that the Regent should henceforth have complete charge of public affairs, was issued by the humbled Empress

On October 7, 1928, a hurried ceremony took place near the Trinity Church. A new cathedral has since been raised next to the old church beside which a tent was set up for the ceremony. In the presence of the archbishop, bishops and clergy, the nobility, the *corps diplomatique* and neighbouring colonial governors, Zauditu placed the crown upon Tafari's head as the curtains around the two were raised. Gold medals issued for the occasion were distributed and then the Negus Tafari Makonnen rode in an open carriage back to his palace.

Empress Zauditu, left almost alone, must then have decided that she had either to seek allies and overthrow Tafari fairly soon, or else resign herself to the total eclipse of her already almost nominal powers as Queen of the Kings of Ethiopia.

RAS GUGSA WOLIE LEADS THE CHALLENGE

The following year the Ogaden was in disorder. There was a rising of the Azebu Galla in the north. In fact every part of the country hummed with intrigue. The Regent concentrated on his program of reforms and consolidated his power in preparation for the future. He arranged for a Belgian mission to come and train the Imperial Guard. He made new arrangements for the import of arms, for the foundation of a state bank, etc. With the Church he was more cautious. He obtained a new archbishop from Egypt—Querillos or Cyril—and five Ethiopian bishops were consecrated. This was the beginning of his program to establish the Ethiopian Christian Church as a national church, but he proved to be no Henry VIII. The Church's immense landed wealth was undisturbed and she continued to draw large sums from the government and the peasantry. However, soon afterwards, and not for the last time, the Regent was to be glad of the Church's support. In many areas feudal governors and their huge retinues still lived off the countryside and it was from this direction that the challenge, doubtless stimulated by Zauditu, eventually materialised.

Ras Gugsa Wolie had long disliked the Negus Tafari. He was the estranged husband of Zauditu, and a nephew of the late Empress Taitu and thus commanded the support of the north where he held the governor generalship of Gondar and Begemidir. Encouraged by continual disturbances amongst the Azebu Galla since the previous year, in March 1930 he raised his standard : his feudal retainers who owed him military service flocked to him. The governor general of Tigré's royal rank, as grandson of the Emperor Yohannes, had recently been recognised and Seyoum Mangasha, then created *leul-ras,* was not easily drawn to join Ras Gugsa, who nevertheless marched on Shewa and Addis Ababa. Leul-Ras Kassa watched these dramatic events but did not commit himself either way, neither did Leul-Ras Hailu of Gojjam, although he probably hoped for a breakdown of the increasing central authority which might present him with a chance to become an independent *negus* as his father Taklé Haymanot had been.

Stating that he merely intended to make his submission to the new *negus,* Ras Gugsa edged his 10,000 men supported by ten machine-guns and two field-guns nearer and nearer to Shewa. Unwilling to leave Addis Ababa, the Negus Tafari sent Dejazmatch Mulugeta north to Dessie, capital of Wello. Mulugeta had succeeded the late Fitwrary Habta Giorgis and a certain Fitwrary Birru Walda Gabriel as Minister of War. He led a somewhat larger force than Ras Gugsa's and had thirty machine-guns and five field-pieces in support. Also aeroplanes purchased by Tafari only six months previously buzzed to and fro carrying messages between Addis Ababa and Dessie. The two French pilots, M. Maillet and M. Corriger, brought the Minister of War reconnaissance news of the disposition of Ras Gugsa's army and Mulugeta used this to great advantage. He ordered a rapid and successful outflanking march. Bombs were hurled from the planes after leaflets, signed by the recently arrived Archbishop Cyril, had been dropped, testifying that Tafari was supported by the Christian Church—an effective move, employed again in 1960. The battle took place at Ankim on March 31, 1930, and lasted from early morning almost to midday, when Ras Gugsa received a sword wound on the forehead. He fell and was cut to pieces. In the resultant confusion his army disintegrated.

THE DEATH OF EMPRESS ZAUDITU

Meantime in Addis Ababa a thirteen-gun salute announced the victory, and looting which had broken out in the market place was quickly put down. On the next day the Empress Zauditu suddenly died. The cause of her death is uncertain. Hailé Sellassié's biographers, Christine Sandford and Leonard Moseley, state respectively that she succumbed to 'severe mental stress' and that ' it could be said that she died there and then of a broken heart'.[11] *The Times* (London), in common with other papers commented, '. . . the emotion which the Empress felt at hearing of the violent death of her former husband . . . [was a] . . . contributory cause of her death', and a few days later stated that she was also suffering from para-typhoid. Other accounts assert that she was weak from her strict adherence to the Lent fast and that she died in her curtained enclosure in church. Alternatively, yet others state that she was shocked by immersion in cold 'holy water' after a heart attack, a miscalculation for which her priests are said to be responsible. Isaacs, on the other hand, in a school text-book entitled *Modern Ethiopia* and published in Addis Ababa, says that Zauditu was diabetic and adds the conservative comment that she died of heart failure. Dutton's book suggests that she was strangled.[12]

The Empress, who was fifty-four years old, died at 2 p.m. and was buried in the tomb of the Emperor Menelik II by 8 p.m. the same evening. It has been stated that the funeral was 'quiet and with almost indecent haste',[13] but it should be remembered that it is the custom in Ethiopia to bury the dead far sooner than in Europe and America. Even so, at the time there must have been an outburst of that scandalous gossip which abounds in feudal society for, shortly afterwards, in 1935 the Swedish general who served as military adviser in Ethiopia took some pains to refute it.[14] He wrote :

> Some have tried to hint that hers was not a natural death, and that Negus Tafari was implicated in it. These malicious reports are without foundation. That the Empress died of a disease [diabetes] from which she had long suffered is fully testified by the doctors, among them Dr Hanner [the Swedish consul] who attended her and were present at her deathbed. . . . In the fight for power he has shown humanity and nobility of character. Apart from those enemies of his who fell in battle, their weapons in their hands, he had never taken anyone's life. The former Emperor Eyasu still lives. . . .

On the next morning a meeting of all the bishops was interrupted by the arrival of the Negus Tafari and the Archbishop announced that he was to be the new King of the Kings and led him to the throne. Tafari moved into Zauditu's palace. The Archbishop then publicly proclaimed the death of the Empress and his recognition of Tafari, who from that time used the name Hailé Sellassié, which means 'Power of the Trinity', as Emperor. Ras Gugsa's governorships were given to Leul-Ras Kassa Hailu, whose father's family, it will be recalled, was descended from the *wagshums* of the north and who was therefore acceptable to those unruly subjects. Arrangements were set in motion for a great coronation ceremony to follow the mourning period of Zauditu's death, and Hailé Sellassié issued his first proclamation dated April 3, 1930 :

> In accordance with the Proclamation which our Creator abiding in His People, and electing us, did cause to be made, we have lived without breach of his Covenant as mother and son. Now, in that by the law and commandment of God, none that is human may avoid return to earth, Her Majesty the Empress, after a few days of sickness, has departed this life. The passing of Her Majesty the Empress is grievous for myself and for the whole of the Empire. Since it is the long-standing custom that when a King, the Shepherd of his people, shall die, a King replaces him, I being upon the seat of David to which I was betrothed, will by God's charity, watch over you. Trader, trade ! Farmer, plough ! I shall govern you by the law and ordinance that has come handed down from my fathers.

Thus it was that after more than a quarter of a century of dispute the throne of Tewodros, Yohannes and Menelik II was seized by yet another strong man and the country again began to drag itself into the modern world. Seen from 1964, when Hailé Sellassié's ageing grip is in its turn relaxing and the power groups are again assembling, although it is clear that much has been achieved, it is also true that compared with several other African states a lead has in many respects been almost hopelessly lost. The reasons for this lie in the story of Hailé Sellassié's character and reign, and in particular in the fact that great as his intentions once were, and considerable as his achievements have been, his techniques of close personal control, if at first necessary, soon became obsolete.

10

A Radical Paternalism

*As a father should bequeath not only wealth to his children,
but also provide them with proper education ... so should it
be the duty of those for whom much has been done to
show gratitude.*—THE EMPEROR HAILE SELLASSIE in a broadcast, August 1959

*Individuals have made invaluable contributions to the pro-
gress of society ... but if they operate as individuals they
will be the sowers of a harvest of misery.*—GIRMAME NEWAY,
Ethiopian Student News, New York, March 1952

THE CORONATION

There was much comment in the press of Europe when the state
coach of imperial Germany was purchased for Hailé Sellassié's coronation. Twenty coronets were made by a firm in Regent Street,
London. The velvet was royal blue for the Crown Prince and for
the Princesses, and crimson for the nobility. The Lion of Judah,
King Solomon's seal and the star of the east were incorporated
in the motif. The British monarch presented sceptres in similar
vein and there were other splendid gifts. Many accounts exist of the
coronation of 1930, which was postponed until November, it is said
because of a government financial crisis, and it was clearly an
impressive occasion. The Ethiopians have a talent for ceremonial.

Addis Ababa then, as recently in 1963 for the Conference
of African Heads of States, became the scene of great activity. High
fences were constructed to hide views of the poorer parts of the
city, a practice still current today at all state visits, for such parts
of the city have not benefited from the building programs of the
last thirty years. The living conditions of the vast majority of the

people have changed little though splendid boulevards now co-exist with the appalling poverty and squalor of the backways. In the 1950s all two- or more-storeyed buildings were required to be built close to the roads to impress the visitors and this has resulted in many an almost useless façade. For example, the class-rooms of the Commercial College on the road which carries the traffic to Jimma are often so noisy that teachers cannot be heard by the pupils. Ironically one of the first public engagements of Emperor Hailé Sellassié in Dar-es-Salaam in 1964, on his state visit to the United Republic of Tanganyika and Zanzibar (Tanzania) was to lay a commemorative stone for a slum clearance pro-gram—a ceremony he had never performed at home.*

Before the coronation an equestrian statue of the Emperor Menelik, one of the finest of its type in the world, standing 30 feet above the ground, was erected outside the Cathedral of St. George ready to be unveiled by the new Emperor. It was on the site of the famous hangman's tree—the square was then supposedly disused for this purpose, but was made functional again in 1960. To mark the coronation, prisoners were freed and special postage stamps were issued.

---

* In 1960 the author conducted some visiting African Nationalists on a tour of the city of Addis Ababa, and was embarrassed by a comment from one of the French-speaking visitors. 'Yes, the Palaces, they are magnificent. So also is the Mausoleum. But where are the sewage works?' A smooth young government officer came to the rescue, 'Addis Ababa is on a slope', he said. 'May I be forgiven for thinking "Thank God for the French!"' was the retort.

Dejazmatch Zewdé Gabré Sellassié, a recent *kantiba* (mayor) of Addis Ababa tried to alter this situation. He even caused the traffic flow to be measured on the roads he wished to develop and compared the density of traffic there with that past the Jubilee Palace and Africa Hall where great dual carriageway projects were to be initiated. Those projects are now completed. Dejazmatch Zewdé is no longer in office. Had he not been a noble he could not have ventured even as far as he did.

His father was Dejazmatch Gabré Sellassié, formerly a governor in Tigré. His mother, Woizero Walata Israel was a daughter of Leul Ras Seyoum Mangasha. She subsequently married Crown Prince Asfa Wossen, when the latter was sixteen: but he divorced her during the war years as they had no son and heir and in April 1945 he married the present Crown Prince, Woizero Medferiashworq Abebe.

Dejazmatch Zewdé was later appointed Ambassador to the Somali Republic. In 1961, after the abortive *coup d'état,* but before the execution of Brigadier-general Mengistu Neway he was appointed to the unenvi-able position of Minister of Justice. His handling of the enquiries sub-sequent to the *coup* was bitterly criticised in conservative circles. He later left his ministry and in 1964 was reportedly back at Oxford University of which he is a graduate.

Official guests, newspapermen and others crowded the city. The Italian Prince of Savoy arrived, and Marshal Franchet d'Espérey of France. Germany, Belgium, Sweden, the Netherlands Japan, Egypt and Greece were all represented. There was present a deputy of the Patriarch of Alexandria. A special ambassador, Mr Murray Jacob, arrived from the United States and the Duke of Gloucester represented Britain. The latter, attended by Leul-Ras Kassa Hailu, brought a Naval brass band with him, thereby following, though doubtless unconsciously, a precedent set by a very different mission of some sixty years before—that of General Napier to the citadel of Tewodros. There was even a satiric novelist in the person of Mr Evelyn Waugh.

Tarmac or hardtop roads were constructed and the police were given uniforms. Electric light, lately introduced by Negus Tafari, made Menelik's rambling old *ghibbi* on the hill look for all the world, said the *Manchester Guardian,* 'like a modern liner at sea at night'. *The Times* (London) reported that beggars were cleared from the streets, lepers expelled and caravans were forbidden to enter Addis Ababa.* Triumphal arches were erected.

There was a service lasting all night although some of the priests had been in continual session for two weeks. They danced, chanted, beat their drums and clapped their hands continuously. The costumes were brilliant and magnificent. Amidst the glitter of coronets, jewelled swords and gold braid, the traditional lion manes lent a truly African touch to the splendour. *The Times* took it all to its heart and adopted that superior and quite humourless approach, which, in common with certain radio announcers, it takes to serious state ceremonial occasions in Britain. It commented, 'The unofficial Europeans were dressed some in morning and some in evening clothes' (the function was all night, so that was presumably correct), and added with awful disapproval, 'An interesting note was struck by an American woman who wore a tweed suit and toque decorated with a small star-spangled banner. Few European women were present. They wore heavy cloaks and large veiled hats.'

Tafari and Woizero Menen had spent that night at the cathedral but they did not appear to the congregation until just before 8 am. Even in the 1960s the Emperor frequently attended services of prodigious length, a considerable physical achievement for a man over seventy. The robes of state were brought out and don-

---

* In 1962, the June 1 issue of *Time* magazine was banned in Ethiopia for reporting similar measures prior to a conference of African leaders and even more recently that journal incurred a ban of somewhat longer duration on similar grounds through its cover of the Conference of African Heads of States held in Addis Ababa in May 1963.

ned by Tafari. During the next hour he received all the ceremonial insignia of his office : lances, orb, spurs, sword, etc., and finally the archbishop placed the great golden crown studded with precious emeralds and rubies, on Tafari's head. There was a roar of acclamation which spread to the population outside. A salute of guns thundered over the city and the band of HMS *Effingham* played the Ethiopian national anthem.

The Negus Tafari had become His Imperial Majesty, Hailé Sellassié I, Conquering Lion of the Tribe of Judah, Elect of God and King of the Kings of Ethiopia. The Crown Prince, Merid Azmatch Asfa Wossen, had signified his fealty, Woizero Menen had been crowned Empress, and the Archbishop had pledged the loyalty of himself and the Ethiopian Christian Church. Yet it is worth noting that even then, father and son were not as close as might have been expected. As the years passed, the gulf between them grew.

The *rases* and the ministers had all paid their homage, and after more ceremony the Imperial couple drove to the palace. Festivities continued on the morrow, the Emperor visiting several other churches, taking the salute at a march past and attending a race meeting—the sport of kings—where it is reported he presented gold coins to several European children. Hailé Sellassié has ever since maintained this custom, although children have not always been the recipients—Sir Harry Luke used to show such a memento. Eventually, however, the foreign visitors all departed. The exchange rate for the then national currency, the silver Maria Theresa dollar, depreciated to a more usual level. The beggars returned to the city and normal life resumed.

THE 1931 CONSTITUTION

As Emperor, Hailé Sellassié continued to push forward reforms aimed at modernising the country and breaking the power of the feudal barons through the development of the authority of the central government or bureaucracy. There are those who see this as his greatest achievement. In 1962 the Ethiopian bureaucracy was described as 'a unique social class which performs the function of a transformer'.[1] There is no reason to doubt that the adoption of such a role was, at least until 1935, the aim of the Emperor. This writer, an Ethiopian academic, argued that since it controls every aspect of the national life and has even become 'the custodian of the national culture', the bureaucracy may still come to operate effectively and 'thus avert the need for violence amongst people whose minds have been stirred by [what this writer terms] the desire for vast and fast progress'. But violence occurred in 1960 and in retrospect an ever increasing number of Ethiopians argue that Hailé Sellassié's 'transformation' of Ethiopia has been far too slow.

One of Hailé Sellassié's first actions in 1931 was to 'grant' the people their first constitution. Although even in form, let alone practice, its limits on his absolute powers were infinitesimal, it was an interesting development. The Emperor's decree announcing the granting of a constitution 'unasked and of Our own free will' stipulated that a senate and a chamber of deputies would be established. The Emperor was to appoint members of the senate 'from among the nobility who have for a long time served his empire as princes or ministers, judges or high military officers'. Not all the places were immediately filled but Leul-Ras Hailu, Leul-Ras Seyoum, Ras Desta and a few others were named soon afterwards. The chamber of deputies was also to be nominated but 'by the nobility and the local *shums* . . . until the people are in a position to elect'. The Parliament's function was to discuss those matters placed before it by the Emperor. His permission could technically be sought to discuss other issues, but that did not in practice occur. Indeed one writer, a few years later, stated that the Emperor was 'the only speaker of this unique parliament; he makes no replies and there are no debates. The members' duty is simply to listen to their ruler and take note.'[2] Members of the chamber of deputies retained their seats for only three months.

Ministers, who were not then drawn from Parliament, and still were not in 1964, could not attend its meetings without 'having obtained the consent of His Majesty'. The Emperor convened and dissolved Parliament, appointed ministers and had full power to issue decrees taking the place of laws when the chambers were not sitting. In practice he issued decrees at any time. Laws and decrees were signed by the Emperor and then notified to the ministers concerned by the *tsahafé taezaz*. The constitution did not make specific provision for the Council of Ministers although a council of the nation's leaders had met before.* The constitution did state, however, that ministers should write to the Emperor with 'their opinions regarding the affairs of their respective departments' and that they were responsible for such opinions. They could not have enjoyed much control over their ministries, however, for

---

* Menelik II's concept of a council of ministers had not effectively taken root. In 1911, Thesiger, a British Foreign Office official had described it as 'a novel institution'. He wrote 'Its members have only a vague idea of their duties or of their powers, while as a body they have the confidence neither of the country nor of the principal *rases* who are to all intents semi-independent'.

Article 11 of the constitution read, 'the Emperor shall lay down the organisation and the regulations of all administrative departments. It is his right also to appoint and dismiss the officers of the army, as well as civil officials and to decide as to their respective charges and salaries'. The Emperor also retained the right to 'confer the title of prince and other honorific titles, to establish personal estates', 'to pardon, to commute penalties, and to reinstate', 'to negotiate and to sign all kinds of treaties', 'to declare war', to determine the armed forces necessary both in times of peace and war', etc.

It was stated that judges should be 'selected from among men having experience in judicial affairs' and that the 'receipts of the government treasury . . . should only be expended in conformity with the annual budget'. The constitution also confirmed the Emperor Hailé Sellassié's line as the only legitimate line, descended 'without interruption from the dynasty of Menelik I, son of King Solomon of Jerusalem and of the Queen of Ethiopia known as the Queen of Sheba' and went on to affirm that the Emperor's person was 'sacred, his dignity inviolable and his power indisputable'. It is interesting that this 1931 constitution did not define the order of succession too closely as did the later revised constitution of 1955—when Hailé Sellassié felt himself to be in a much stronger position *vis-à-vis* his feudal rivals.*

In a speech to Parliament the Emperor stated that the backwardness of the Ethiopian people had previously 'justified their sovereigns in ruling over them as a good father guides his children' but that the 'moment had come for them to collaborate in the heavy task which up to the present their sovereigns have accomplished alone'. The Minister of Finance replied stating that the constitution was not a translation of the laws of one of the civilised countries but a unique gift (in actual fact it was modelled on the 1889 constitution of the Empire of Japan). 'For 3,000 years,' he continued, the Ethiopian nation 'had been waiting patiently with arms outstretched to Heaven for some great gift'. Similar speeches referring to the constitutions were still being made in the early 1960s. Indeed, since the second World War so much has been written in Ethiopia and abroad about the magnanimity of his gestures that Emperor Hailé Sellassié might even be excused for not understanding why all his people have not been eternally grateful.

---

* Article 4, 1931 merely stated that the 'throne and crown of the Empire shall be transmitted to the descendants of the Emperor pursuant of the laws of the Imperial House'.
Article 5, 1955 read 'the order of succession shall be lineal and only male, born in lawful wedlock, may succeed male; the nearest line shall pass before the more remote and the elder in the line before the younger'

In Europe in the 1930s, however, comment on these developments all too frequently followed the bias of Italian writers. Perhaps the kindest observations were those of General Virgin who lived in Ethiopia 1934–5. Having described the Ethiopian community as being ordered on the 'same principle as that of European countries during the middle ages. Power is distributed from above according to a carefully graded and uniform scale. At the top of the hierarchy sits the Emperor, autocrat, Commander in Chief of the army, Chief Justice and leader of the whole administrative and social life of the country', he wrote of the 1931 constitution that, although it left 'the power in the Emperor's hands, it is remarkable from many points of view. By it the Monarch sets up the law as the highest standard to which he too must conform and at the same time renounces the right to make that law. Then also the constitution determines the freedom and privileges of the citizens and affirms the right of all who are deserving and competent to serve the state. All these are principles which we take as a matter of course, but in a feudal state like that of Abyssinia, where noble birth has hitherto been almost the only consideration, they represent a revolution in social ideas.'[3]

But the Ethiopian Parliament met very irregularly and often there was not time to assemble the delegates before decisions had to be taken. By the time of the Italian invasion, although fine new premises had been constructed Parliament itself was almost defunct.

Since this first constitution was 'granted' the Ethiopian government has described itself as a Constitutional Monarchy. Even considering the 1955 revised constitution for the empire, it would be more accurate to talk of a Monarchical Constitution. By itself, however, that is not necessarily a criticism. It would be as unrealistic to expect Ethiopia slavishly to copy the organisation and rituals of the surviving monarchies of Europe as it has been to expect exact replicas of the 'Westminster pattern' to take root after independence in Britain's former African dependencies. Ethiopia needs a strong central government and will continue to do so. The issue in the 1960s is one of motivation. The most pertinent criticism is one that few Ethiopians dare write about. It is that the actions of the Ethiopian central government are seldom dictated by the 'bureaucracy' (which, as the university scholar above quoted recognises in his Amharic publications, is in consequence very frustrated), but rather by a group of aristocrats and reactionaries who put self interest before the national interest. Preoccupied by this problem, it is not surprising that many Ethiopians have not given Hailé Sellassié the credit which he deserved for his leadership in the early days when he applied the same calculating ruthlessness against all that seemed to him to stand in the way of national progress that he had applied in his personal struggle for the throne.

ECONOMIC AND SOCIAL DEVELOPMENT

Progress was, however, quite positive in the fields of customs administration, organisation of the police force and the military (through French, Belgian and Swedish missions), public works and roads, public health and education. Cars and taxis were imported and radio telegraphy was introduced. Model provinces were set up where the administration was controlled by western-educated men on the basis of responsibility to the Ministry of the Interior in Addis Ababa. One such area, detached from Harar in 1934, was Chercher, the mountainous tract on the Rift valley edge west of Harar city. A new town, Asbe Teferi, was constructed there and some rudimentary land measurement and reform was introduced. It was governed by Takla Hawariat, later the last Ethiopian representative to the League of Nations, and by Dr Workneh Martin. Taxes were raised in cash, local salaries were paid and the surplus, rather than a haphazard tribute, was remitted to Addis Ababa.

Apart from the missions, foreign advisers were appointed to ministries. They were drawn from different nations : for example General Virgin, the Swede, was technically in the Ministry of Foreign Affairs, Mr Colson, an American, in the Ministry of Finance, M. Auberson, a Swiss, in the legal department and an Englishman, Mr de Halpert, advised on the suppression of slavery and was attached to the Ministry of the Interior, and there were others. In 1932 the Anti-Slavery and Aborigines Protection Society sent a delegation headed by Lord Noel Buxton to discuss the problem with Hailé Sellassié. They were frankly disappointed at the little notice apparently taken of the several edicts against slavery which had been published from time to time since the reign of Yohannes. However, Hailé Sellassié promised to abolish this offensive institution completely by 1952 and he undoubtedly meant this.

In the 1930s the main problem remained the traditional attitudes of the older provincial rulers and of 'Amhara' soldier-settlers in the conquered provinces. In supposed imitation of Menelik I, Menelik II had divided the conquered provinces one-third for the local peoples, another for the Christian Church and the last for the soldiery. As explained above, these men considered themselves entitled to services from the conquered as a payment for their exile from their highland homes. Only governors of the new school paid their soldiers properly, the others instead turned a blind eye towards often blatant oppression and abuse. Typical of the old school was Dejazmatch Balcha whose humbling has been described, but the Sultan of Jimma also condoned the slave-trade and Maji in Kaffa was for a time a sizeable market for slaves.

However, by 1934 Hailé Sellassié had established sixty-two local bureaux to control slavery and after 1936 Italian attempts to justify their colonial adventures included an effective campaign against slavery in Ethiopia. If in 1964 the status of some servants in certain houses, even in towns, is somewhat ambiguous, the days of the slave-trade and slave markets may be generally regarded as over.

In the 1930s Hailé Sellassié initiated legislation aimed at progressively abolishing the traditional feudal dues payable by the farmers and peasants, usually in the form of food and produce levies, in favour of controlled taxation. He also decided that another custom only slightly adapted from days of great antiquity should gradually cease. This was payments made to government officials, on transfer, on their promotion or decoration, and even on family occasions such as the birth of their children.

The ideas behind the model province program were beginning to take root and spread. Later, in 1933, when Imru, by then *ras,* was transferred from the governor-generalship of Harar to take over Gojjam, he left his entire provincial administration behind him in order to start again. He is honoured in the early 1960s for many things, and his early understanding of the necessity for an efficient civil service, loyal not just to the governor-general but to the central government he represented, is one of them.

Hailé Sellassié maintained the concern for the armed forces which his realism has always dictated. Long before the coronation he had sent several promising young soldiers to the French military academy at St Cyr. His own guard at Harar had grown from a cadre of Ethiopians who had been NCOs in the King's African Rifles (the forerunner of the Kenya Rifles) and a few from the Italian colonial forces in Tripoli. From 1930 until 1935, a Belgian mission trained the Imperial Guardsmen and in 1934 a small military college was opened at Holeta* in a converted palace. On the advice of General Virgin five highly qualified Swedish officers were engaged to supervise training there. Even after the outbreak of hostilities with Italy these officers chose rather to resign their Swedish commissions than to abandon Ethiopia. By 1935, of the 200,000 to 300,000 men who were mobilised, some 7,000 had received some form of modern military training.

---

* Later known by the Amharic name 'Guenet'.

The Educational Department had been made a ministry in 1930 and between the coronation and the outbreak of war ten new government primary schools were opened in the provinces. Some of these schools used French and some English along with the vernacular language. A school for girls was opened in 1931. Several Ethiopian teachers had been sent abroad for short spells and the government figure of forty Ethiopian students engaged in advanced studies abroad when the Italian invasion began could be considerably increased by the inclusion of private students. By 1936 there were in all some 200 foreign-educated Ethiopians at home and abroad.

In 1934, a school for the sons of the *balabat* of the conquered provinces was opened in Addis Ababa. It is still locally known as the *balabat* school but is officially called 'Medhané Alem' (Saviour of the World). Because of the habit of looking down on the peoples from the conquered provinces to the south as 'slaves', it is often said that this school was opened for freed slaves, but even though it today maintains a tradition of emphasising social responsibility, that was not in fact the case.

Several printing presses were established in the capital and there was considerable writing. The Amharic newspapers were weekly and lively and an acrimonious exchange of views between Blatta Kidané Mariam, attacking the Ministry of the Interior, and the official reply from Lij Takelé Woldé Hawariat demonstrated a considerably wider measure of freedom of the Press than existed especially in the 1940s and '50s, but also in the early 1960s.*

In the 1930s and subsequently, there were many frustrations; for example, complaints that the Emperor's insistence on the personal supervision of reforms, such as those in the Addis Ababa prison administration, delayed vital changes, and that old ministers and young directors-general could not work as a progressive team. One observer wrote that the 'older men of rank, who still wore baggy white jodhpurs with bandages round their heads and

---

* The national press and radio suffered rigid control. The greatest freedom from control and censorship since 1958 was wrested from the authorities by the university students, spurred on at first by Pan-African scholars. However a *Policy Statement on Student Affairs approved by the President on October 18, 1962* and signed by a Jesuit Dean states categorically in a section entitled 'Student publications'—'there should not be any article or editorial criticising the national government or derogatory to any particular religion.' It further insists on 'an official faculty adviser' to help the students abide by what are curiously referred to as these 'rules of academic freedom'. There was a student strike over the suspension of a student editor for disobeying a censorship order in mid-1964.

straggly beards round their chins' disliked the civil service and the young directors and 'to keep them in their place they made these young men with moustaches and European clothes bow down to the ground in the presence of age; and if the young whipper-snappers still wore *shemmas,* they had to tie them across their chests out of respect for the old men's blood and rank. Meanwhile, the old men would sit heavily in their chairs exchanging words of primeval wisdom, supporting their policy by proverbs, and pretending not to notice the callow youth around them. . . .'[4]

Also there was occasional friction within the more modern group who supported reforms. The Emperor's influential cousin, Imru, had opposed the inclusion of an article in the Constitution, stipulating that the Imperial succession should henceforth be governed by what he considered to be the alien European custom of primogeniture. Lij Takelé Woldé Hawariat also disagreed with his monarch on several occasions. His rise to influence had at first been rapid. He had become secretary-general in the Ministry of the Interior and then director-general in the Ministries of Public Works and Transport and then of Agriculture, where he was in charge since there was no minister. Before this he had served some time as deputy governor of Kaffa and as a judge on the anti-slavery courts. However, his outspoken nature and his habit of putting forward ideas on all sorts of issues, especially laws, in audience with the Emperor, though it won him the title of *blatta,* eventually led to trouble. 'Why do you meddle in things which you do not quite understand?' asked a somewhat irritated Hailé Sellassié one day, and shortly afterwards, perhaps also because of his predilection for intrigue, Takelé found himself out of favour—as he has often been since. However, in general, opposition in those days took the form of a ginger group for few doubted the good intentions and steady achievements of the Emperor and his government.

The Bank of Ethiopia, founded in 1931 issued new currency which gradually became accepted, although the silver Maria Theresa dollar is preferred to this day in certain remote areas. The Ministry of Commerce managed also to establish a basic receipt system for customs revenues, and although local corruption remained rife, this represented a considerable advance. The central government, using 'Amhara' soldiers, police and officials, established a far firmer hold over Jimma as the sultan's power declined, and there and elsewhere some slave-traders were caught and punished, and lawlessness generally decreased.

As will be shown there were troubles in the provinces, in Gojjam, Tigré and the south-west, but the years 1930–5 were nevertheless a great period in the consolidation and development of the empire. Also beyond the boundaries of Ethiopia, the world powers, not then so afraid of Russia and China as to distrust forthright programs of social reform as being perhaps 'communistic', looked on with unrestrained approval. Even Mussolini wrote of 'the young, resolute and intelligent man who has the supreme power in his hand in Ethiopia now'.[5]

The period of growth following his coronation, perhaps Hailé Sellassié's finest hour, was to be interrupted by the ambitions of certain provincial nobles, the greed of Italy and the inactivity and, in some cases, indifference of foreign powers—many of whom Hailé Sellassié had regarded as friends. From that time Hailé Sellassié's confidence in his reforming mission appears to have begun to wane.

THE EMPEROR AND THE PROVINCIAL NOBILITY

In the north, Hailé Sellassié sought to play off the two main feudal leaders, Leul-Ras Seyoum and that prince's relative and rival, Dejazmatch Hailé Sellassié Gugsa. Like Seyoum, Hailé Sellassié Gugsa was also of the royal Tigréan line. His father Leul-Ras Gugsa Aria, was a legitimate grandson of Yohannes and before he died in 1932 he had shared the rule of Tigré with Seyoum, and had always been friendly with the Italians.

Hailé Sellassié hoped to frustrate the emergence of a united and separatist Tigré. After the coronation, at which Seyoum enjoyed some prominence as a prince, Dejazmatch Hailé Sellassié Gugsa's special position was also recognised. At the same time as the Crown Prince married Leul-Ras Seyoum's daughter, Hailé Sellassié Gugsa married the Emperor's second daughter, Zanabe Worq. She, however, died soon afterwards and the Emperor at once began again to favour Seyoum. Hailé Sellassié Gugsa later journeyed to Addis Ababa to ask for the extension of his Tigréan fief and for his father's title of *ras*, but without success. Like Ras Mangasha, neither he nor Leul-Ras Seyoum had really begun to see their lands as part of the Ethiopian nation. Hailé Sellassié Gugsa was greatly irked by the treatment he received at the hands of the Shewan Emperor and this doubtless contributed to later events.

Nor did Leul-Ras Hailu of Gojjam concern himself too deeply over instructions from Addis Ababa. A prince in his own right, he still hoped to extract his father's title of *negus* from the Emperor, but Hailé Sellassié allowed that title to fall into abeyance. Earlier, Emperor Menelik II had hoped to break up Gojjam, renowned, like Tigré, for local nationalism, but even he had had to appoint Hailu governor of the eastern part of his father's dominion. For a period Hailé Sellassié cautiously refrained from too much interference in Gojjam where the people were more attached to their feudal lords than to the young Shewan Emperor, despite the fact that the *rases* of Gojjam paid scant respect to the liberties and rights, such as they were, of their subjects. Indeed, many writers tell awful tales of the courts of the Gojjam *rases*.*

Some years previously a woman traveller had visited Debra Markos, Leul-Ras Hailu's capital, and had been received by Hailu whom she describes as a 'semi-independent hereditary prince'. She wrote, 'Debra Markos consists of some hundreds of huts plastered over a slope and dominated by the large walled domain of Ras Hailu on whom the life of the town depends. . . . It is the most feudal town in Abyssinia for Ras Hailu has complete control over every man, woman and child within its borders. He is a very rich man, even judged by European standards, and is said to be able to muster a fighting force of 40,000, but, like all these Ethiopian lords, he has nothing on which to spend his money. . . .'[6]

EYASU ESCAPES FROM CAPTIVITY

However, in May 1932, Leul-Ras Hailu was involved in the escape of the deposed Emperor, Eyasu, from his captivity at Fiché. Accounts vary as to exactly what happened, except that they appear to agree that the six-foot deposed Emperor was smuggled out in women's clothing while Leul-Ras Kassa, his custodian, was in Addis Ababa attending the two royal weddings—that of Crown Prince Asfa Wossen and of Dejazmatch Hailé Sellassié Gugsa.

Leul-Ras Hailu had had secret dealings with Italy, who saw that her interests lay in opposing the decline of the provincial barons and in thus obstructing the growing influence of Hailé Sellassié's central government. Hailu was therefore not short of money or of weapons. He made tentative approaches to Leul-Ras

---

* In the 1930s de Prorok claims to have come across an unfortunate youth who had been made a eunuch and had escaped from great depravity and torture in the house of a Gojjam *ras*. (*Dead Men do Tell Tales*, New York, 1942; London, 1943) Hartlmaier (*Golden Lion*, London, 1956) accuses Hailu himself of burning a *shum* (chief) alive, by wrapping him in honey-soaked muslin and having him ignited. This incident is also described by a French ethnological expedition who claim to have witnessed it in 1929 (Griaule, *Abyssinian Journey*, London, 1935). Nor was this apparently the only incident of arbitrary cruel execution. A version of the burning is also included by de Montfried (*Le Masque d'Or*, Paris, 1936), but the author suspects that this was an attempt to discredit Hailé Sellassié in the eyes of world opinion at that critical time.

Kassa and to other influential leaders in Addis Ababa but discovered that all feared the undoubted loyalty to Hailé Sellassié of the new military forces, even though they knew that there was considerable affection amongst the peasants for Menelik's legitimate heir. Hailu therefore arranged that he should receive the following missive from the former prisoner. 'May this letter come to Leul-Ras Hailu Taklé Haymanot! By the Grace of the God of my Fathers I have escaped peacefully. Come and join me for I want no more of our brothers' blood to be spilt!' Hailu then showed this letter to Hailé Sellassié and requested personal command of the military in order, he argued, that he could apprehend the pretender. But Hailé Sellassié hesitated.

Dejazmatch Yigezu, though technically governor of Dorani, was usually at hand in Addis Ababa and his advice was highly respected at court. But because of his disease he was at the time bathing in the hot springs at Ambo, now called Hagera Hiwot. The *dejazmatch* had married one of the deposed Emperor's former wives, but Eyasu was not a man to indulge in personal revenge. He looked down on lesser leaders whom he often half affectionately, half contemptuously, referred to as 'Sheep of my [grand] father' and certainly considered a quarrel with Dejazmatch Yigezu beneath him. Nevertheless, a Galla peasant took some delight in informing the *dejazmatch* of Eyasu's escape and suggesting that Eyasu was approaching Ambo. An alarmed Yigezu fled naked into the night.

Meantime in Addis Ababa a message, carried by a mounted *fitwrary*, and addressed to Leul-Ras Hailu, informing that prince of Eyasu's growing impatience at the delay, fell into Hailé Sellassié's hands. The Emperor's picture was then complete but he was uncertain of the balance of power and still he hesitated. A decision was immediately taken, however, on the arrival of a car bearing a shivering *dejazmatch*, clad only in his muslin *shemma*. Leul-Ras Kassa had cunningly written to Hailu hinting that he would support him. A clandestine meeting was arranged to enable Kassa to march north with a guard and secretly take Hailu prisoner. Eyasu's party meantime endeavoured to raise a rebellion but after three days their revolt was put down and Eyasu, deserted by his followers, was caught, after a chase, in a cave.

Twenty revolutionaries were executed and their bodies were hanged from trees beside the roads out of Addis Ababa. Leul-Ras Hailu was tried for treason and was sentenced to death, but the Emperor decided instead to fine him 300,000 Maria Theresa dollars and to banish him. The Addis Ababa newspapers of July 11, 1933, carried this item. 'Deportation. Ras Hailu took the train last Sunday, in a carriage reserved for him, to be taken to the province of Arusi where he will serve life imprisonment.' Hailu was to reappear, but in the interim he lived on an island on one of the Rift valley lakes south of Addis Ababa. Much of his property, with the exception of his Swiss bank account which could not be touched, appears to have been confiscated and Ras Imru was nominated to take over the administration of the province of Gojjam.

Hailu's son Alem Seged, a youth of eighteen years, tried to arouse the people of Gojjam to revolt, but Hailé Sellassié sent Dejazmatch Wodajo and a bishop to Debra Markos. The boy was made to swear fealty before the sacred Tabot or Ark of the Covenant and was brought to the capital. There was a solemn reunion and Alem Seged went to live with Ras Desta. However, he was later rumoured to have been transported to the ancient Shewan settlement of Ankober where Ras Mangasha had died, and there to have met with an accident which necessitated the amputation of his legs. De Montfried claims that wounds caused by the instruments of his confinement became infected with gangrene and that the operation was conducted by Dr Hanner.[7] Certainly Dr Hanner was running the Imperial Hospital at the time and was, in fact, also Swedish consul in Ethiopia from 1926–36, but the writer has found no independent confirmation of de Montfried's story. Indeed, in 1937 a London evening newspaper which published a very garbled version of it, later withdrew it when challenged.

THE FATE OF EMPEROR EYASU

Eyasu himself was sent south again in chains to the province of Harar. This time the chains were iron.

There are persistent stories of his being kept in a vast cage at Garamulata in the hills not far from Dira Dawa. De Prorok claims that he visited the cage with an Armenian who drove supplies to the camp for a Greek merchant. Eyasu, according to de Prorok's most sensational account, lived on a second floor in the cage, high for all to see. The cage, he says, was located near a monastery. De Prorok describes the many guards detailed to prevent anyone—in particular Muslim or Italian agents—from communicating with the deposed Emperor. He claims to have bribed these guards in order to witness an unparalleled orgy of which he gives a lurid account. Really wild parties do take place to this day in Ethiopia, as the author has witnessed, but the Imperial family, quite unlike de Prorok's picture of Eyasu in his later years, in no way condones them.

A later traveller, D. Buxton, denies the existence of the

cage.[8] General Virgin mentions it but did not see it. Perhaps the story is exaggerated from the conveyance used to take the chained Prince to his prison—a structure such as those sometimes used to carry corpses in Ethiopia. Buxton writes of a stone prison, resembling a church, crowning a hill over the village. It had three concentric walls and heavily barred gates. There were two very high rooms, he writes, with small windows near the top of the walls perhaps 18 feet from the ground. He suggests that one was a bathroom off the royal chamber, and concludes 'the place was certainly impregnable and well designed for its purpose'. The general tone of Buxton's writings commends him as an honest and meticulous observer.

De Prorok shrewdly points out how manageable a puppet monarch the deposed and by then debauched Emperor might have made for the Italians after their invasion of Ethiopia.[9] But Eyasu did not live, and his death is a deeper mystery. It has been observed that often nothing is more difficult to establish than the truth, amidst the rumours and intrigue of Ethiopian feudalism.

Subsequent to de Prorok's account, a sixteen-roomed sumptuously appointed palace is said to have been built within the monastery enclosure. The imperial prisoner was transferred there, most accounts agree, under the overall guardianship of the Bishop of Harar, a man whom Farago describes as 'the great political priest of Abyssinia' . . . [an] unconditional supporter of the Emperor [and one who] tries to win the rebel princes of the Church to Hailé Sellassié's side'.

The Emperor kept in touch with the bishop and his prisoner through a secret messenger. The man he selected for this task was a certain Aba Gebré Hanna Jimma. Hanna, as he was normally called, was himself from Harar, but at the age of eleven he had joined Menelik's court as a junior butler. In 1916 he and a certain Lij Desta Damtew—a young man being brought up at court because his father, Fitwrary Damtew, a Shewan of the Addisgé family, had died at the battle of Adowa—decided to run away to-gether and become monks. Desta, later an important *ras*, returned to the court, but Hanna spent twelve years at Debra Libanos monastery. However, in 1928, he returned to Addis Ababa to become Hailé Sellassié's special treasurer, a position of great trust.

Eyasu, it seems, was, at least for some time, reasonably comfortable in restriction. Once when he was ill Hailé Sellassié sent two doctors from Addis Ababa to treat him. Farago does report, however, that the custodian bishop had once to journey from his monastery into the city of Harar to deny rumours that Eyasu had died of poisoning. It does seem that the population expected Eyasu to die, but despite the many mentions of Eyasu by the several travellers who wrote about Ethiopia prior to the Italian wars, none describes his death. Indeed, apart from de Prorok and the bald statement that Eyasu died, conveyed in a footnote in General Virgin's book, the literature of the period appears to contain very few references to Eyasu's timely death—and this curious omission has been noted by reviewers.

De Prorok recounts how Italian agents are said to have come to Harar with bribes intended for government officials including the aged Dejazmatch Gabré Mariam, the provincial governor general. They also brought money to raise a revolt among the Danakil peoples of the desert. This alleged plan to kidnap Eyasu was frustrated by the bishop, whom informers had told of the secret mountain rendezvous of the conspirators, all of whom were killed or captured. Farago gives a very similar account of the incident except that he adds that the monastery was actually *attacked* by the Danakil. At the time that these rumours swept Harar, the governor general was suddenly nowhere to be found—a habit of Ethiopians when dangerous decisions are needed. The bishop had been on very bad terms with the governor for years and his report of the crisis, in all probability carried back to Addis Ababa by Aba Hanna, was doubtless responsible for the removal of the old man who was in any case no friend of Hailé Sellassié. Another factor was that a younger governor general would be needed to lead the armies against the Italians, if the storm clouds already gathering were to lead to war.

The man chosen to succeed the *dejazmatch* was a former mayor of Addis Ababa, Dejazmatch Nasibu Zamanuel. He had worked with the Belgian mission there training the Imperial Guard, and at the time held a governorship in the south of Ethiopia. Hailé Sellassié came to Harar for his installation. He left Addis Ababa by the Imperial train, but was delayed *en route*. It is said he took the opportunity of a little hunting at Awash station in the Rift valley. (There are buck and lion in the bush thereabouts and years later the King of Greece is reported to have burst into a fury on discovering that a lion which he had shot had been released from a cage by a frightened court official who had orders to see that the visiting monarch enjoyed himself.) Hailé Sellassié himself is a good shot. On this trip, over which he took his time, he drove from Dira Dawa up to Harar to attend Dejazmatch Nasibu's 'shum-shir' or 'change of appointment' feast. It is also said he held secret conferences with provincial leaders on the threats to Ethiopia's internal security and national integrity presented by the warlike preparations of the Italians in Eritrea and Italian Somaliland.

Meanwhile at Garamulata, Eyasu was fully aware of the relevance of international politics to his own personal safety. Some say minstrels sang the news in Danakil beneath the prison walls. It is doubtful whether after the years of imprisonment and depravity Eyasu wished for anything but to be left in peace—but he feared he would not be allowed to live lest he be used by the enemies of the state. The following story is told of his last hours by a former slave, now very old, who claims to have been in Eyasu's service.

His Highness was very nervous and paced the cell into which, within the palace, he had been confined since the troubles. One night I remember a car arriving and His Highness called and asked me if it was a certain man he feared. I said it was not. The next night I told him it was only Aba Hanna; but later a second car came and the two occupants, one of them a *fitwrary*, waited until dark. They crept up to the cell room. There were holes in the door and His Highness must have seen their guns poking through them for he spat at the peep holes. He could spit well! He gripped the window bars as they shot him. He was a great powerful man and he shook the whole building until I thought it would fall and then I heard him slide to the floor. The two assassins seemed to dance over the body in accordance, I think, with certain witchcrafts before it was carried out at night and sent by train to Addis Ababa.

There it is said to have been received by a certain high official still alive in 1964, but who delivered it to a police officer, Abebe Aragai, subsequently *ras*, and only he knew where it was buried.

Ras Abebe Aragai, Minister of Defence, received shoulder wounds in the Green Salon of the Prince's Paradise Palace in December 1960. He bled to death before the doctors in the adjacent Hailé Sellassié Hospital had a chance to aid him. If the former slave's story is true—and that is by no means established—then the secret died there, for Aba Hanna was also in that room but it is difficult to see any reason why Eyasu's body should have been brought to Addis Ababa at all, except perhaps as evidence of his death.

De Prorok claims to have carried the news of the death of Eyasu to the Danakil princess's son who was living under French captivity or protection in their Somaliland colony. The young man's followers are said to have acknowledged him as Emperor Menelik III as he spoke condemning Hailé Sellassié not only as a usurper but also as a dangerous progressive! A plot to abduct the young prince had failed in July 1934 but he appears to have disappeared during the war years—at all events the author has been unable to confirm rumours that he still lives.* He was in any case but one of Eyasu's sons. The deposed Emperor's eldest son Lij Girma Eyasu was imprisoned in southern Ethiopia. During the Italian war he escaped to Kenya and refugees at Isiolo wanted to proclaim him their leader. However, he was arrested by the British when on his way to Moyale and later both he and his three-year-old daughter died of food-poisoning at Taveta, Kenya.

The historian must conclude that the cause of Eyasu's un-announced but timely death (probably in July 1935 though it was not widely known about in Ethiopia until November) is not estab-lished. It could have been typhoid fever which is said to have been rampant in the hills near Harar at that time, and if it was it is likely that stories and malicious rumours of his death would have soon developed. Leonard Mosley in his recent biography of Hailé Sellassié states of Eyasu—whom he incidentally paints in the worst possible colours and about whom he has nothing good to say, even to the extent of warning the reader against any who one day might have—that 'on November 22, 1935, he died at the age of thirty-seven from general paralysis of the insane.'[10] Many in Ethiopia who recollect the early years of this century, and not only the many who followed Eyasu, do not believe any of this. Even so the only reason why the slave's story is included here is on account of its political rather than historical significance. In 1961 and '62 subversive pamphlets in Addis Ababa alleged that Eyasu was mur-dered and referred to acts of witchcraft. Also an Amharic booklet produced in Cairo in 1961, and written by Getachew Garedew, who describes himself as 'Founder Member of the People's Govern-ment of Ethiopia', accused Aba Hanna and a certain ras—not Nasibu—of responsibility for the death of Eyasu, acting it is asserted on orders. Significantly the ras is not the same noble whom

* A noble prisoner detained in great secrecy in Addis Ababa—and defin-itely alive as recently as 1959—was whispered to be he. In his book *Remote People*, London, 1931. Evelyn Waugh comments of Lij Eyasu 'People do not readily speak of him, for the whole country is policed with spies'. The same may be said with respect to Eyasu's descendants today. In 1962 there was a son of Lij Eyasu confined at Jimma and an-other detained in great poverty in Sidamo.

In this general context but unconnected with Lij Eyasu the author ob-served a small room with heavy double-barred windows in a corner of the uppermost floor of the Palace of the Prince of Paradise next to the Emperor's former wardrobe room. In 1962, the author was checking all floors (except the basement) of the vacated palace for possible university use. Old palace servants were either unaware, or would not be drawn, on the previous use of the little room. It may just have been a strongroom.

the Addis Ababa underground normally castigates in this context.*

It was the evils of a feudal system which were responsible for the imprisonment of Eyasu and for these rumours, for they are no more than that, of his death. And if Hailé Sellassié was himself a product of that system he was also one of its first effective critics. It is difficult to predict how far he could or would have carried out his program of reform and it may not be fair to judge him on his recent failures—for example, in the vital area of land reform—because the calculating confidence of the young, ruthless revolutionary, Tafari Makonnen, was as shaken as was his proud old country by the aggressive onslaught of organised Fascism.

---

* Getachew had twice suffered periods of political imprisonment at the hands of Lieutenant-colonel Workneh. He was arrested after the failure of the 1960 *coup*, but released since he had not been involved. However, he subsequently fled to Ji-jigga and over the border. In 1964 Getachew Garedew lived in the Somali Republic and broadcast for Radio Mogadishu. The author visited Mogadishu in July 1964 in an unsuccessful attempt to meet Getachew.

IV

WAR WITH ITALY

11

Hailé Sellassié
—Conscience of the World

*In the minds of those long-sighted people who can see far
ahead into history—and they are very few—was formed the
idea of a direct intervention in the internal affairs of
Ethiopia*—MARSHAL DE BONO, *Anno XIIII*, Rome, 1937

*The world was not yet ripe for that all-important idea of
collective security . . . consequently the world was unable
to ward off the mass destruction which threatened it.*—
BRIGADIER-GENERAL MULUGETA BULLI, commander of the
Imperial Guard, Korea, May 1955

ITALIAN AMBITIONS AND INTERNATIONAL REPERCUSSIONS

There is evidence that at one time or another all the imperialist
powers, including even Belgium, Russia and Egypt, cast envious
eyes on the green Ethiopian highlands. It is fortunate for Ethiopia
that they often disagreed amongst themselves and contented themselves with making treaties, the one with another, defining their
covetous ambitions against the day when they might act—or, at
other times, signing pious agreements confirming each others'
usually insincere resolve not to act at all. But if these agreements
meant little, even more meaningless was Italy's twenty-year Treaty
of Friendship, signed in 1928 with the Empire of Ethiopia.

Italy was a late participant in the Scramble for Africa and
had managed to secure only a few areas of desert or semi-desert.
Significant amongst these was perhaps her best area, Eritrea, in
that it consisted of the natural littoral and the peripheral foothills
of the Ethiopian Highlands. The Italians had been disappointed in

the 1919 Treaty of Versailles which had apparently overlooked their desire for a 'place in the sun' but their new fascist régime led by Benito Mussolini promised great things in the sphere of imperialist expansion. From their capital at Asmara, Eritrea, Italy's colonial administrators had long coveted the last uncowed fragment of ancient Africa with its cool stimulating climate and often thick volcanic soils far surpassing those of even the former so-called 'White Highlands' of Kenya in their agricultural potential—but the bitter experiences of history had taught them caution. It was precisely because the Ethiopian Emperors and *rases*, secure in their mountain stronghold, had so long frustrated Italian colonial ambition that Mussolini showed such interest in Ethiopia. It seemed to him to be necessary, as veteran Gabriele d'Annunzio put it to a young soldier, to wipe out as a matter of honour 'the scar, yes, the shameful scar, of Adowa', that rout of 1896.

The Ethiopian crisis when it developed was of immediate international significance because it proved the second, and in the event the mortal, blow to the League of Nations—the first being the desertion of that body by the United States. Most of the literature on the Ethiopian crisis is written from the point of view of its significance in terms of the interplay of international diplomacy;[1] of how it is generally supposed to have helped drive Italy into the arms of Germany in the crucial years before the second World War. Actually there is much to be said for the Ethiopian contention that the second World War should be dated from 1935 and not 1939 or later when other powers became involved.

That there was a moral issue in the world conflict is as seldom disputed as it is defined, but for his part Hailé Sellassié saw it as the principle of collective security against that of aggression. Some of his nobles saw his faith in the League of Nations as naïve idealism. Some European diplomats were irritated that he should labour what seemed to them to be an unrealistic grasp of the nature of international diplomacy. But to the people of the world it was not only expedient for Hailé Sellassié to stand up for that principle of collective security, it was also demonstrably right. Because of this, and because the aggression of a great power against a small one was almost poetically reflected in the lonely dignity of the Emperor's small cloaked figure addressing the General Assembly of the League or in pathetic exile in Britain, Hailé Sellassié came to induce an emotional response from the peoples of the world. This arose not out of his innate virtue but out of their guilt, but Hailé Sellassié nevertheless seemed to personify the violated conscience of the world and since 1935 and in particular since 1942, he has cleverly made little attempt to play this down.

A particularly significant part of the world-wide sympathy which developed for Ethiopia, the Ethiopians and the Emperor Hailé Sellassié was that felt by black Africans throughout the continent. It was reflected in political agitation in the capitals of Europe at the time, in verse and in the biographies of their politicians. Later it was to help enable the Ethiopian government to identify with those new African nations who saw a common bond in having emerged into an era of independence from one of territorial imperialism—despite the fact that the *mores* of the African revolution had not much affected conditions within the Ethiopia⌐ empire. Identification with Ethiopia was particularly common als⌐ in the West Indies—and not only amongst members of the Ras Tafarian religious sect in Jamaica—and in the negro communities in the United States. The writings of several leading negro Americans, for example, James Baldwin,[2] show that they had no illusions about the attitudes of some Ethiopians to black skins and slave origins, but this made no difference.

One marked exception to this climate of world sympathy for Ethiopia was, however, the attitude of the Roman Catholic Church.

THE WAL-WAL INCIDENT

Ethiopia had long been regarded in Europe as the 'bad neighbour' *par excellence*, mainly because of the boundaries of Menelik's empire were not effectively controlled from Addis Ababa. However, it is equally true that Britain did not maintain sufficient forces adequately to control the frontiers either in her former Somaliland Protectorate or along the desert frontier of northern Kenya, or in the eastern provinces of the former Anglo-Egyptian Sudan. It is perhaps significant that little was heard of frontier trouble between the Sudanese Republic and Ethiopia between 1956 and 1962. However, in the 1930s, it was easy for the Italians to prepare accusations against Ethiopia based on frontier incidents, especially along the desert boundary of former Italian Somaliland and the province of Harar which had not been adequately defined and across which nomadic Somalis travelled in the process of transhumance. The movements and even the raids of nomadic peoples with no frontier concepts could not, however, be ascribed with any real justice to the machinations of a government miles away in Addis Ababa, whatever its responsibility in international law—especially since the European powers by agreement had in effect limited the quantities of firearms entering Ethiopia, thus making police action on the part of the Ethiopian government most difficult.

In November 1934, feelings in Ethiopia against the already

obvious designs of the Italians exploded when some Ethiopians attacked some employees of the Italian consulate in Gondar. Hailé Sellassié immediately paid the compensation demanded but shortly afterwards there occurred a much more serious incident at Wal-Wal, near the frontier of what was then the Italian-ruled portion of the present Somali Republic. It seems clear that the settlement, around some desert wells, was well within Ethiopia, but unbeknown to the governor general of Harar it had been garrisoned for some years by the Italians.

During Hailé Sellassié's Regency and before his coronation, Ethiopian troops had not penetrated more than 100 miles or so beyond Ji-Jigga, a little town which lies below the long pass up to the city of Harar. In 1931 Dejazmatch Gabré Mariam and Fitwrary Shiferaw led troops from Harar and Ji-Jigga down into the Ogaden. The Ethiopian columns tentatively probed into the lands which Menelik II's diplomacy and armed forces had secured. The columns certainly found that Italians had encroached into what they considered to be their territory, but they did not go on to Wal-Wal. Technically that area was under the governor of Ji-Jigga and his director, Grazmatch Afeworq, but they were not fully aware of the dangerous situation that had developed.*

Towards the end of 1934, a joint Anglo-Ethiopian Boundary Commission examining the limits of the grazing areas of the nomadic Somali peoples not only came across an Italian garrison of colonial troops at Wal-Wal, but saw also that the recently appointed Italian 'commandatore' had caused a fort to be built from the crumbling old stone defence-works of Muhammad Abdille (called the 'Mad Mullah'). The commission's Ethiopian escort, commanded by Fitwrary Alemayu Goshu, was angered by this discovery. Their anger is more understandable when it is remembered that they believed that in ancient times this area and indeed the whole of the Somali coast, which they called the Benadir, had paid tribute to the highland Emperors and thus, prior to the colonial era, was part of historic Ethiopia, a claim reiterated by the Ethiopian Prime Minister at the Addis Ababa Summit Conference in 1963.

General Virgin records that the Italians would not allow

---

* It is this frontier region which has flared into open war on several occasions in recent years, notably in December 1960 and again in 1964. On the latter occasion it took on a wider significance, somewhat reminiscent of the 1930s, since military or supply agreements involved several of the major participants in the cold war, and because the fighting was also thought to hinder progress towards inter-African co-operation and unity. A cease-fire was arranged through the OAU.

the commission to proceed. It withdrew to Ada, a near-by settlement where there was, however, insufficient water for the escort, which remained drawn up a few yards from the Italian positions. A central government order to the Ethiopian escort to behave with circumspection was too late and fighting ensued on December 5, 1934. The Italians used an armoured car and planes. Alemayu died bravely early in the battle and since his deputy had rushed away to Ji-Jigga, a Muslim Ethiopian, Ali Nur, subsequently made *balambaras*, took command. They had no other means, so he led his soldiers in repeated charges against the armoured car in attempts to overturn it with the bare hands. Well might the Prophet have said that it has fallen to the Ethiopians to receive nine-tenths of the courage of mankind! Eventually, however, the Ethiopians suffered the heavier casualties and were obliged to withdraw. They took splinters from the bombs to Ji-Jigga and with an eye on the morale of his men, Grazmatch Afeworq made a knife from one of them with which to cut his meat.

Hailé Sellassié, on learning of the incident, asked that the Italian government submit the quarrel to arbitration, but the latter refused and instead made completely unacceptable demands on Ethiopia. That their rejection was intended—even desired—by the Italian government is clear from the wording which included the 'Governor of Harar province to proceed in person to Wal-Wal to offer ceremonial apology', the 'arrest, dismissal and punishment of those guilty, after they shall have honoured the remains of their victims in accordance with Somali custom . . .' and the 'Payment of 200,000 Ethiopian dollars indemnity'.[3] Thus it was that in January 1935 Ethiopia lodged a formal complaint with the League of Nations.

ETHIOPIAN TRUST IN THE LEAGUE

The League procrastinated and meantime the Italians moved troops to East Africa in increasing numbers. Further Ethiopian appeals to the League were met with the barren suggestion that the dispute should be settled under the Ethio-Italian Treaty of Friendship. The British government made some attempt at mediation but obtained little support and no results. The United States took refuge in isolationism and the French, terrified of driving Italy into the arms of Germany and upsetting the balance of European power, favoured territorial adjustments in favour of Italy at Ethiopia's expense. Moreover, the published memoirs of British political figures of the period—Anthony Eden apart—show that they too shared the fears and views of the French government rather than the emotional indignation of British public opinion. They definitely considered that colonial wars such as Britain had fought in the nineteenth century were in rather bad taste in the current century, but it was only the British people and sections of the press who saw Italy's military bid for 'a place in the sun' as being morally indefensible.

In conversation with Mussolini on June 25, 1935, Eden put forward the views of the British public and it is interesting that the *Duce* soon afterwards turned the conversation to the Italian defeat at Adowa in 1896. There followed much discussion in high places in Europe over whether Ethiopia might not be persuaded to accept Italian 'protection' or how it might be partitioned to Italy's advantage. Few of the statesmen of Europe, it seems, were really aware of the spirit of the Ethiopian leaders and people, although Eden recalls remarking to Laval and Leger that he was informed that one of the *rases* had already sent a telegram to Hailé Sellassié reading 'What are you waiting for? Are we women?' Mussolini was perhaps another exception, for he had remarked, 'The Abyssinian people will not work and are only of value as soldiers'. However, he also knew that the military potential of Ethiopia was much impaired by the failure of the European powers to provide her with the modern arms she had long requested. Thus Ethiopia was to find it impossible to repeat the triumph of Adowa.

However moral the Emperor's trust in the League, it was a political mistake and there were many Ethiopians who frankly told Hailé Sellassié so at the time. The Italians had been allowed to increase their strength undisturbed and had even been permitted to run some forty consulates in Ethiopia. There had been some difficulty in landing war materials in Italian Somaliland but Graziani gives statistics which show the impressive build up of personnel, mules and camels, vehicles, planes, guns and armour from the time of the initial mobilisation, through the opening of operations and the battle of the Gannale river to the offensive which led to the occupation of the Ogaden and the fall of the city of Harar in eastern Ethiopia.[4] Likewise de Bono tells the same tale of the mobilisation of Eritrea in the north.[5] It was too late when the Ethiopian minister in London, Dr Workneh Martin, in a fiery speech condemning those whom his countrymen had trusted in vain to help them, pointed out that the Ethiopians could have attacked earlier and 'secured a victory'.

ETHIOPIA'S FEUDALISM EXPLOITED

But the Italian preparations were not confined to war materials. Their intelligence had done a good job in exploring the ground, noting water supplies, etc., and particularly in playing on the feudal disunities inherent in the Ethiopian nation. De Bono describes how the Italians had counter-balanced Leul-Ras Seyoum Mangasha by supporting Leul-Ras Gugsa Aria until the latter's death in 1932 and how his son, the Dejazmatch Hailé Sellassié Gugsa, who was the Emperor's son-in-law, had nevertheless remained pro-Italian. He recounts that expeditions sought to befriend the Danakil sultans of Aussa and Biru and adds that similar preparatory work was done almost everywhere. Among examples of its special success he quotes the regions of Begemidir, Dongola, Simien, Gojjam, Wello and the lands of the Azebu Galla. He estimates that the Ethiopians were deprived of at least 200,000 men and affirms that the results of this disintegrating political action were obvious from the outset. There is no doubt this was so, for then as today the forces of feudalism militated against unity and the national interest.

Of the same Leul-Ras Seyoum, de Bono writes, he 'declared his loyalty to the Emperor but he was not really sincere, and was always undecided in his ideas. In his character he was a precise reflection of his father' (Ras Mangasha, the surviving son and disappointed heir of the Emperor Yohannes). 'Unknown to the central government', de Bono continues, 'we were still exchanging greetings in February and March [1935], and he had accepted a present which I made to his little boy.' A war correspondent with the Italians wrote 'Ras Seyoum was nibbling at the Political Bureau bribes',[6] and Seyoum himself claimed after the occupation that the Italians had offered him the Ethiopian throne if he would fight against Shewa.[7] Doubtless their thought had been nothing more than to create him a puppet monarch as they might have made Eyasu had he lived. Probably they just encouraged Seyoum's personal ambitions as they did those of Leul-Ras Hailu of Gojjam. The Italians had long been observant students of the internecine rivalries which arose out of Ethiopia's sorry feudal state and her resistance to the consequently rather ineffective government program of unity. On a number of occasions they were able to turn this knowledge to their own advantage with no great difficulty. Before the invasion, one observer wrote of the damage being done to Ethiopia's national interests by local chiefs who had accepted Italian bribes. 'They are hopelessly irreconcilable and say quite plainly "rather Italy than Hailé Sellassié". The Emperor has many enemies who will make war and help the Italians to hunt him down.'[8]

It is very difficult to see why the Ethiopian government allowed this situation to develop. At least one foreign adviser had drawn attention to it. In 1935 General Virgin wrote 'During recent years Italy had installed in Abyssinia a crowd of consuls and *agents commerciaux* in places where there was not a single Italian or any good reason for their presence. These people who had many agents working under them carried on intensive pro-Italian propaganda, distributed arms and bribes and tried to stir up feeling in the different districts against the central government, while at the same time striving with all their might to provoke dissensions among local authorities—dissensions which gave the Italian government a pretext for interference and for attacks on Abyssinia in the fascist press.'

Italian writers admit that they used their consular staff, medical missionaries and others to sow disaffection against the Shewans and the 'Shewan Emperor', as they called him, amongst the peoples of the other provinces, but to the last the Wello Galla remained an unknown quantity. Neither side seemed to realise that they had every justification for looking on both Shewans and Italians as would-be oppressors. De Bono feared their cavalry and though he 'advised the mounted officers not to bring their chargers out with them' because of the climate, he tried to buy up horses locally and even in the Sudan, in the Yemen where he was unsuccessful, and in Libya. In the south of Ethiopia the corrupting power of Italian bribery and intrigue is confirmed by a later remark of an Ethiopian major,[9] who was trying to join the Patriot Ras Desta in Sidamo : 'Almost all the Balis were against us. This *coup* had been subtly prepared by the Italians. They had bribed our compatriots. Of the men from the Bali province only four or five chiefs and about two hundred warriors remained faithful to our cause.' However, he adds that they 'fought [together] with us to the bitter end and we have nothing but admiration for them.' It might be noted that on the Ethiopian side de Bono admits like skill at espionage and intrigue, in particular on the part of Hailé Sellassié's consul in Asmara, Eritrea.

THE CRISIS MOUNTS

The Ethiopian armed forces consisted of the feudal levies of the governors and *shums*, the troops of the central government and Hailé Sellassié's own standing army. According to General Virgin only this last was 'trained and armed in the modern manner.' The others, he wrote, consisted of 'men who lack all training other than that afforded by their natural aptitude for warfare and their traditions'. In everything except overall numbers, the Ethiopians were far worse equipped than the fascists and their colonial troops.

For example, de Bono remarks of air power, that telling feature of the second World War, that he never once saw any of Ethiopia's thirteen aeroplanes airborne. Moreover the Italian general staff was well aware that the Emperor was unlikely to attack them and the Italian government assured them that the League would not have the resolution to act effectively, if the offensive could be mounted speedily. 'The Negus Neghest' (King of the Kings), wrote de Bono in one of his despatches, 'is ordering too many prayers and fasts to give us reason to think that he wishes to attack us. . . .' Mussolini wrote back to him, 'In case the Negus should have no intention of attacking us we ourselves must take the initiative. This is not possible unless by the end of September you have at your disposal, besides the blacks, at least 100,000 white soldiers who will have to be rapidly increased to 200,000. . . .' De Bono, who was in Eritrea at the time of Adowa, watched the arrival of these arrogant young men with some emotion, and profiting from his memories of that battle, set up a large branch of the Florence Geographical Institute at Asmara, to make maps for the coming invasion of Ethiopia.

Meantime within Ethiopia there was discord. The Emperor had withdrawn all forces at least 30 kilometres from his frontiers to avoid provocation and to point to the aggressor, for he still hoped that the League would act. He did not order a general mobilisation to take place until late September 1935 but others acted independently. The old Minister of War, Ras Mulugeta, ordered Leul-Ras Seyoum to mobilise western Tigré. Warriors mustered at Adowa, only to be dismissed when the difficulty of controlling and provisioning them was realised. Others rallied to the Crown Prince at Dessie, to Dejazmatch Hailu Kebeda at Makallé, to Leul-Ras Kassa Hailu, to Dejazmatch Ayelu Birru, and also to Dejazmatch Nasibu and Grazmatch Afeworq in Harar province away to the south-east which faced the second threat—that from General Graziani in Italian Somaliland. Ras Imru, governor general of Gojjam issued a warning order.

The Italians obtained regular information on the plans discussed for the northern front and knew that all except the Tigréans, seemed to favour a tactical retreat from that province and then engagement involving some kind of encircling action once the Italian supply lines were drawn out. Leul-Ras Seyoum of Tigré, however, did not relish the advent of Shewan troops in his fief. 'They do more damage than locusts and the earthquake,' he commented. Unknown to him or to Hailé Sellassié, all this time the other leading Tigréan noble, Dejazmatch Hailé Sellassié Gugsa, was negotiating with de Bono to betray the centre of the Ethiopian line by leading his forces over to the Italians.

WAR AND THE FAILURE OF THE LEAGUE

In September 1935, at the very time that the League took the cynically expedient step of exonerating both parties to the Wal-Wal incident, an increasing number of Italian air reconnaissance flights from Eritrea caused a false alarm and the drums were beaten and the warning pyres lighted throughout Tigré. Warriors rushed to Leul-Ras Seyoum, who was typically uncertain of what to do. His wife brought him his sword and shield and urged him to lead his men—but it was decided that the crisis was past and the feast of Mascal commemorating the discovery of the True Cross which follows the New Year in Ethiopia was celebrated in peace. It is a time of colour and great beauty, for the hills are clothed with lovely daisies. About this time Mussolini telegraphed to General de Bono to attack Ethiopia from Eritrea and Somalia on October 3, 1935, without any such formality as a declaration of war.

On that day aeroplanes dropped leaflets in Amharic warning the Ethiopians of their impending 'liberation' and ending with the phrase, 'I shall be pitiless', and the signature of de Bono. A second Arabic leaflet was prepared for Graziani's front, but there the Italian forces had anticipated the order and had already entered the torrid Danakil desert region near the great volcano of Musa Ali, and the leaflets were a little late. On that day the main Italian ground forces crossed the Mareb river into Tigré and on that day also, as an almost necessary symbol, Adowa was bombed from the air.

On October 7, the League of Nations, unanimous but for Italy, declared that power the aggressor, and settled to discussing what to do next. It was the League's last testing time and it failed. Half-hearted sanctions excluding the vital commodity—oil—were begun in November and the United States government also called on American industry for a voluntary 'moral embargo' which was equally ineffective. Only Britain had moved armaments and ships which caused Mussolini to sneer at the League decisions. 'Forty nations led by one', he said. The French were still determined to prevent war with Italy at all costs and the possibility of territorial exchanges was again discussed. The British government associated itself with partition proposals but when the governments of her Allies and indeed some Commonwealth Dominions, and even more pertinently the British general public saw that Italy, the aggressor, stood to gain vast areas of Ethiopia and that part of the British Somali Protectorate was involved, there followed such an outcry that the government had to withdraw and Sir Samuel Hoare, the Foreign Minister, resigned. He was replaced by the Minister to the

League, Anthony Eden, of whom it might be said that his popularity and indeed his whole career was made, as it was broken, by his attitude to north-eastern Africa.

But it was all too late. Frequent appeals by the League to both belligerents went unheard. The Ethiopian forces, after a resistance that none (but themselves) had thought possible, began to give ground. No nation moved to their defence. In Geneva debate continued until two subsequent events caused general despair. Attention turned from Africa when in March 1936, Germany recognised the continued weakness of the League, and Adolf Hitler's troops goose-stepped into the Rhineland. Then in May, the Emperor Hailé Sellassié fled a few days before the occupation of his capital and all hope that an independent Ethiopia could survive was abandoned in the outside world.

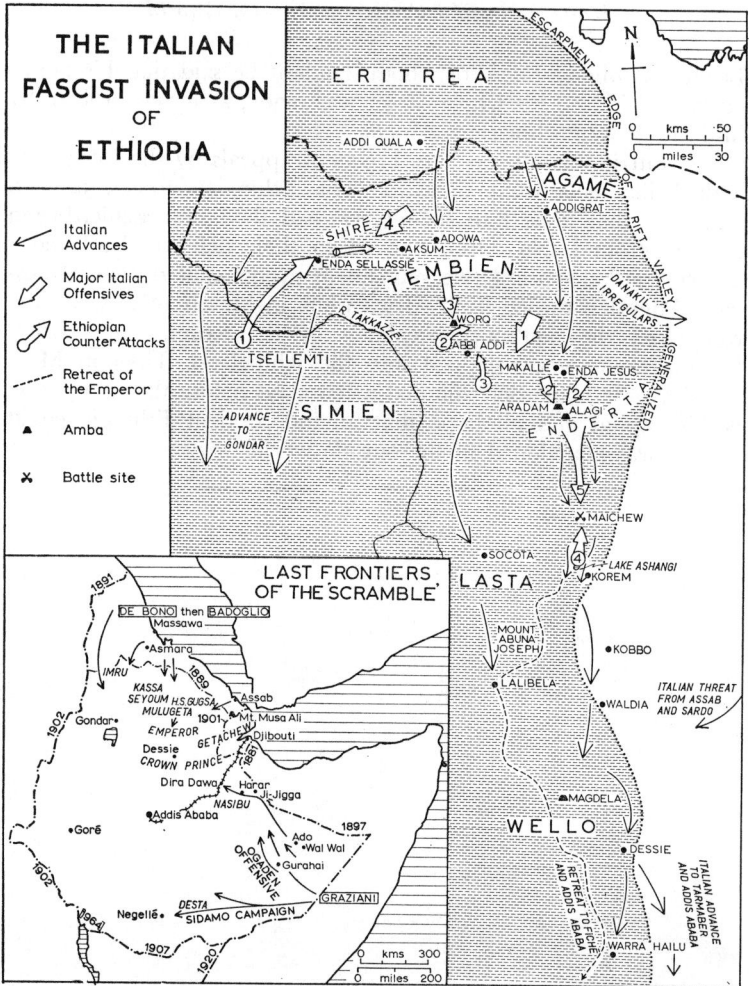

Major Italian Offensives:

1. First Battle of Tembien—defeat of Leul-Ras Kassa.
2. Battle of Enderta—defeat of Ras Mulugeta, Minister of War.
3. Second Battle of Tembien—defeat of Leul-Ras Kassa and Leul-Ras Seyoum.
4. Battle of Shiré—defeat of Ras Imru.
5. Battle of Maichew and Lake Ashangi—defeat of the Emperor.

Ethiopian Counter Attacks:

1. Ras Imru.
2. Wagshum Hailu Kebede.

3. Dejazmatch Gabré Hiwot.
4. Emperor Hailé Sellassié.

12

Defeat and Departure

*The war which lasted from October 3rd to May 5th, may
with full justice be termed a 'fascist' war, because it was
waged and won in the very spirit of fascism*—Mussolini,
in his foreword to Pietro Badoglio, *The War in Abyssinia*,
London, 1937.

*I ruminated over why the Ethiopian armed forces were so
easily broken by the forces of the enemy and I realised that
it was fundamentally because of our backwardness.*—
Brigadier-general Mengistu Neway at his trial in March
1961

MOBILISATION OF THE FEUDAL ARMIES

The advancing Italians at first met with little resistance, and within
a few days Addigrat was taken and the columns moved on towards
Adowa. What Ethiopian resistance there was, was concentrated on
ambas, but it was isolated and local. De Bono writes of 'enormous
numbers of killed and wounded on the field' before the fall of
Adowa, but the Ethiopians were in the main following the
Emperor's tactical plan of withdrawal into the mountains to the
south of Tigré. He knew that he could not defeat the Italian forces
with their immense superiority in equipment and provisions.
Retreat emphasised that Italy was the aggressor and Hailé Sellassié
still hoped for outside help. If none came at least the Italian
extended supply lines might become vulnerable.

 The Emperor had relied much on the advice of General
Virgin and Mr Colson, an American. Both these men worked
loyally for him but both in turn strained their hearts and had to
leave. Hailé Sellassié urged his followers to adopt the use of khaki-

drill rather than the traditional white *shemmas* so conspicuous from the air; he recommended guerrilla warfare, and he called Europe's bluff by asking for financial assistance if there existed so much concern over the backwardness of his country. He urged his soldiers not to despair when a brave leader fell. He spoke to a gathering of notables at the recently innovated Parliament. Ras Mulugeta, the Minister of War, the old conservative who had fought at Adowa, was there, as were the court officials, the Archbishop, who is reported to have slept through the address, and the *Echegé*. Hailé Sellassié said '. . . and I your Emperor who address you will be in your midst, not hesitating to pour out my life blood for the independence of Ethiopia'. These words were expected of him, but in one of his rare moments of complete frankness, he remarked at the British Legation, 'Je ne suis pas un soldat!'

Plans of defence were discussed and sections of the defensive lines and positions in reserve were allotted to the feudal leaders. Leul-Ras Seyoum and Dejazmatch Sebat of Agamé were to flank a line whose crucial centre was entrusted to Dejazmatch Hailé Sellassié Gugsa and his forces. Dejazmatch Ayelu Birru was also to operate on the western flank and even enter Eritrea across the Takkazzé river should that prove feasible. Behind the line, Leul-Ras Kassa Hailu and Ras Mulugeta were to march up with the Wello Galla forces. Ras Imru of Gojjam was to organise the provisioning of the western section of the front before joining the battle. Dejazmatch Nasibu was to control the Harar front, but lest the Italians should make a sudden westward push across the Danakil desert from Assab, Ras Getachew from the governorate of Kaffa was to guard the eastern flank of the northern armies from a position to the south-east of the Dessie escarpment. He was a Wello from that region and was noted for his family—he was related to the Empress Menen—rather than his ability.

Foreign observers, while reporting the high morale of the Ethiopians, were nevertheless unanimous on the certainty of their defeat. To most the feudal system took on a pathetic grandeur for it was the old Ethiopia which girded its loins, blindly sure of its ability to defend the empire against any foreigner; to the correspondents there seemed an element of high tragedy in the magnificent futility of the *rases* and their brave but grossly inadequately armed soldiery. But the Ethiopian officer who looks back on those times from today sees but little to admire and his anger does not necessarily abate when he sees like arrogance and ignorance in high circles in his government today.

At the Mascal celebrations in 1935, the cavalcade of *dejazmatches* traditionally shouted advice to the Emperor, and called

'Do not meddle further in the affairs of the outside world, but look after your country!' The same *non sequitur* is heard sometimes even in the 1960s in certain quarters in Ethiopia when the question of national development and the training of young men abroad is raised. Only when the Ethiopian delegation at Geneva had cabled that war was inevitable, had the Emperor issued a proclamation of mobilisation :

> Italy prepares a second time to violate our territory. The hour is grave . . . soldiers gather round your chiefs, obey them with a single heart and thrust back the invader. You shall have lands in Eritrea and Somaliland. . . .

The war drums were beaten outside Menelik's old palace and they recalled the ambitions of Menelik's soldiers for the acquisition of large areas of conquered provinces and the service of subject peoples. There existed little national unity in the modern sense. Later Marshal Badoglio was to compare

> . . . the *rases* with no qualities at all as commanders looking askance at each other, interested above all things in keeping and strengthening their own positions, absolutely incapable of appreciating a situation or thinking out a manoeuvre and above all of translating it into action . . . [with the Ethiopian fighting men and] the exceptional courage of individuals and their capacity to try to take advantage of particular situations in the minor field of tactics. . . .'[1]

Once when the Emperor urged guerrilla warfare, in view of the local knowledge and greater mobility but inferior equipment of the Ethiopians, Leul-Ras Seyoum, before leading his army to destruction, had retorted, 'A descendant of the Negus Yohannes makes war, but cannot carry on guerrilla warfare like a brigand chief!'

DE BONO AND HAILÉ SELLASSIÉ GUGSA

The Italians hastily built roads and with an eye on world opinion issued a proclamation announcing the suppression of slavery in Tigré, only to be besieged by hordes of angry Ethiopian 'household servants' demanding to know who was then to feed them. Adowa had been occupied by Italian forces on October 6, 1935, and two days later Dejazmatch Hailé Sellassié Gugsa offered to betray to the Italians the centre of the Ethiopian line. The resentment which the *dejazmatch* felt over the way he had been denied the title of *ras* and had been played off against Leul-Ras Seyoum has been touched upon. He preferred to lead his men against Hailu Kebede, formerly Hailé Sellassié's diplomatic and consular representative at Asmara, who had been sent to report on the Tigréan nobles only a few months previously, or against his rival, Leul-Ras Seyoum, should that wily noble actually take the field. He hoped still to obtain feudal precedence but at the hand of the Italians. Such rewards meant more to him than any vague nationalism.

The Italian bombers had demonstrated the high command's interest in Makallé—witness the ruined shell of Dejazmatch Abraha's castle which to this day stands sentinel on a hill beside the town. However, de Bono did not wish to seize the capital of Tigré immediately as Dejazmatch Hailé Sellassié Gugsa suggested. Nevertheless the Italian commander entertained the *dejazmatch* to lunch when, his forces considerably depleted since his intentions had become known, he marched to join the Italians at Addigrat.

De Bono then received the submission of the clergy and people of Aksum. The cathedral chapter was headed by a senior monk, for the real head had left with the Archbishop and the withdrawing Ethiopian forces. On his return to his headquarters de Bono found that Mussolini had telegraphed that Dejazmatch Hailé Sellassié Gugsa should be appointed puppet governor general of Tigré, and in deference to the expressed anxiety of certain European powers and the United States as to the safety of their subjects, de Bono was to refrain from air attacks on the cities of Addis Ababa and Dira Dawa.

About this time the Italian high command grew dissatisfied. They considered de Bono's careful campaigns to be unadventurous, and feared that the League's sanctions, whilst not an immediate deterrent, might become one if the war dragged on. The Secretary of State for the Colonies and the Chief of Staff, Marshal Badoglio, an Adowa veteran, made a ten-day visit to Eritrea, and the use of poison gas must have been discussed. At all events to his credit, de Bono declined to use it.

LEVIES LEAVE FOR THE NORTHERN FRONT

On November 8, 1935, Makallé, the Tigréan capital of the Emperor Yohannes was occupied and his great-grandson Dejazmatch Hailé Sellassié Gugsa (who became an Italian *'ras'*), was left to garrison it. Meantime, Leul-Ras Kassa Hailu's forces approached the front via the sacred Christian shrine of Lalibela from across the wild mountains of Lasta. In Addis Ababa, over 300 miles farther south, where the decision not to defend Makallé had been taken, the provincial governors and their levies had begun to arrive in answer to the mobilisation orders. Those awaiting orders included Betwoded Makonnen Demissie, progressive and respected governor of Wellegga, who despite a period in prison for supporting Empress Zauditu, was widely regarded as a friend of Hailé Sellassié, Dejazmatch Moshesha Woldé of Kembata and Dejazmatch Abebe Damtew of Gemu Gofa, the brother of Ras Desta. Dejazmatch Makonnen Endalkatchew of Goré was expected daily. A tall and proud figure, Makonnen was the leading representative of the important Addisgé family group from Tegulet, Shewa. He held a remote governorship because he had been a close associate of Eyasu and had incurred disfavour following his elopement and marriage to Yashash Worq, daughter of Yilma, Hailé Sellassié's half-brother. She was previously married first to Leul-Ras Gugsa Aria of Tigré and then to Betwoded Makonnen Demissie. Dejazmatch Mangasha Yilma, her brother, who was a director in the Ministry of War, was sent north to organise the camps on the route to Dessie.

Meantime, the Minister of War, Ras Mulugeta, never very popular amongst the Shewans, grew steadily more arrogant and difficult. He frequently demanded the expulsion of all foreigners from Ethiopia and he felt his hand strengthened by the release of some of Menelik's conservative soldiery. These included Dejazmatch Balcha and Fitwrary Birru Walda Gabriel—the latter had preceded Mulugeta as Minister of War but had then been sent to a provincial governorship and later detained, quite why is not clear, but probably because he was thought to be an illegitimate son of the Emperor Menelik and thus a possible pretender to the throne. Such feudal feuds and family rivalries were not forgotten. They were merely made subservient to the national interest, for a period, and were never far beneath the surface.*

---

* This was one reason why many educated Ethiopians began in the 1950s to favour a completely new start. The leaders named in the above paragraphs and their children retained much power in Ethiopia as of right and serve as an example of the importance attached to birth in Ethiopia.

In 1964 Dejazmatch Hailé Sellassié Gugsa was still serving life imprisonment for treason—he would have been hanged had he not been a noble. Leul-Ras Kassa's important family is mentioned in the note on page 239. One of Betwoded Makonnen's sons was a general. Ras-Betwoded Makonnen Endalkatchew, a former President of the Senate died in 1963 and his son Lij Endalkatchew Makonnen, formerly Vice Minister of Education then ambassador to the United Kingdom, was Minister of Commerce and Industry. Dejazmatch Abebe's daughter was Crown Princess Medfariashworq Abebe. Ras Desta married Emperor Hailé

When on October 17, 1935, Hailé Sellassié reviewed the provincial troops, the march past lasted four hours and Ras Mulugeta called to him as he passed, 'Send all the foreigners packing. I swear perfect loyalty to you.' He meant it. This old man, who was well over seventy, was as proud an Ethiopian as was the great Ras Alula before him, but unfortunately he was nowhere near as competent a soldier. The soldiers from Gemu Gofa were so unruly that Addis Ababa had to be put out of bounds to them, and the Emperor was relieved when the assembled forces marched off north. Ras Mulugeta himself left on October 21 and once outside the influence of the Emperor he began to assert himself even more. For example, he had a director of the Ministry of Finance chained as being party to the obstruction of his earlier attempts at mobilisation. Young government officers and tax collectors often explain that they would get the same treatment from some proud and rich old nobles if they dared to regard them as subject to the laws of Ethiopia. Near Debra Berhan a quarrel developed between the well equipped, organised and uniformed Imperial Guard and the army levies. The latter were jealous since they had to provide their own rifles and generally look after themselves. They jeered at the guards and fighting broke out. There were wounded on both sides before the difference was smoothed over. Ras Mulugeta's troops lived off the country, while he himself drank heavily, as was his custom. He even attempted, though without success, to counter-

---

Sellassié's eldest child, Princess Tenagne Worq, in 1924 when she was eleven years old. Of their six children Lij Amaha died when he was sixteen but another son Lij Iskander was commander of the Imperial Navy —and in some ways, like a great imperial namesake of the middle ages, quite progressive in his outlook, although uncritical of his grandfather. He was unmarried. Of the four daughters, Princess Aida was married to Leul-Dejazmatch Mangasha Seyoum, great grandson of Emperor Yohannes and governor general of Tigré; Immabet Hiruta (Ruth) was a headmistress and was unmarried; Immabet Sable was married to Lij Kassa Woldé Mariam, President of the Hailé Sellassié I University and Immabet Sophia was widowed in the 1960 Revolution. Her husband Captain Dereji was second in command, and senior Ethiopian officer at the Imperial Military Academy at Harar. Princess Tenagne Worq married Andargatchew Messai in 1944. Andargatchew was Representative in Eritrea (1952–9), *ras* and governor general of Sidamo 1961–5), but he retired after a serious car accident in 1964. Ras Desta's children, although not very popular, have always seemed to the author to possess a sense of personal service and responsibility which some of their detractors might do well to copy. (Unfortunately but perhaps inevitably, their critics generalise from the example presented by other perhaps more typical children of the leading families.)

mand the Emperor's orders to Dejazmatch Abebe Damtew, ordering him to march north and to ignore the other Italian threat down on the south-eastern front in the Ogaden.

THE SOUTH-EASTERN FRONT

There, the sandy bush had afforded little cover against the attacks from the ground and air which followed the temporary stay to Graziani's operations during the October rains. Grazmatch Afeworq attempted to breed a contempt in his men for the aeroplanes and his view was confirmed by the futility of some initial bombing sorties. However, the Italian pilots, completely unopposed, soon improved their aim and on November 2, 1935, they commenced an intensive bombardment of the garrison at Gurahai, a position they coveted for a landing strip. Grazmatch Afeworq was wounded at his Oerlikon anti-aircraft gun and fearful of the effect on his men, ignored his wounds. Unable to move from the gun turret, he remained firing at the enemy planes until two days later, when he collapsed as gangrene spread from his wounds.

Against orders, Fitwrary Simu had Afeworq placed in a lorry and ordered the evacuation of the position. One hundred and fifty miles away was a Red Cross post, but Afeworq died before it was reached. Hailé Sellassié had been right to warn his men not to panic and give up when a leader was killed or wounded. He remembered the disaster which followed the fall of the Emperor Yohannes at Gallabat. Grazmatch Afeworq was posthumously created *dejazmatch* of the Ogaden. Ali Nur, hero of Wal-Wal, became *kegnazmatch*, but Dejazmatch Nasibu ordered that Fitwrary Simu be executed for cowardice. The Emperor later commuted the sentence and Simu was deprived of his property, given thirty lashes and stabbed twice in the back with a bayonet. A second *fitwrary* in the group was also deprived and flogged.

A column commanded by Fitwrary Gongol, marching in the hope of relieving Gurahai, successfully defeated an Italian armoured force. The Ethiopians in ambush shot the crews of the three light tanks as they successively and foolishly left their vehicles. The Somali colonial soldiers fled and Fitwrary Gongol, who was wounded, was taken back to base. So ended a phase in the battle for Harar province, for Graziani halted, to assess the reported threat presented by the movement of Ras Desta Damtew's forces from Sidamo and the west.

Hailé Sellassié took this opportunity to fly to visit the Ogaden forces while he waited for troops to reach Addis Ababa from the south and for the road to Dessie, on the route to the northern front, to dry out. At this time also General de Bono was recalled and promoted to the rank of marshal. Marshal Badoglio, his successor, had orders to push on more speedily with the war and if necessary to use poison gas against the Ethiopians.

MULUGETA ALIENATES THE WELLO GALLA

The city of Dessie, capital of Wello and half way between Addis Ababa and the northern front, was the seat of the governorate of the young Crown Prince acting under the advice of Dejazmatch Wodajo Ali. Although of vital significance because of the hostilities, this is far from the reason for this appointment. There had been a violent quarrel between father and son in Addis Ababa and despite the Empress Menen taking the part of her son, the Emperor had sent him off to Dessie and the youthful Leul Makonnen, his younger brother, had come to prominence in Addis Ababa. The Crown Prince's house was full of spies, as indeed it has been since the restoration and it was rumoured they even included his priestly confessor. When the mobilisation order arrived, the Crown Prince and Dejazmatch Wodajo found it very difficult to raise troops from amongst the Wello Galla in the face of Italian bribery and a continuing loyalty to Eyasu, Menelik's grandson, of whose mysterious death the countrymen were unaware, rather than to Hailé Sellassié. When Ras Mulugeta arrived, as might be expected, he applied his own logic to the situation. He ordered floggings and marched on the village of Kobbo, a main centre of the Azebu Galla on the Rift valley floor well south of the Lake Ashangi basin, and practically destroyed it. The fact that Ras Mulugeta rarely paid his men doubtless contributed to the looting. Then to all able bodied survivors the *ras* gave the choice of death or military service.

Leaving a garrison behind, Mulugeta pushed on north to Amba Alagi, which Leul-Ras Kassa Hailu had already reached. The *amba* was forthwith garrisoned by Ras Kebeda, and Betwoded Makonnen of Wellegga also camped there before advancing. Ras Mulugeta prepared to continue his march northward again into Tigré. Now, however, he was in the region of aerial reconnaissance and runners from his forces and from Leul-Ras Kassa's complained of the difficulty of movement in these circumstances. 'They chain us down like prisoners', they said.

HAILÉ SELLASSIÉ LEAVES FOR THE NORTH

However, at the end of November the Emperor set off from the capital to drive to Dessie. He left the Foreign Minister, Blatten-guetta Hiroy and Mr Colson, the American adviser in Addis Ababa, to deal with international communications. Also in Addis Ababa, were several of the younger group of men whom the Emperor had drawn from poor and humble origins—one for example was a hard-working, thin and, even then, ill-looking man named Makonnen Habtewold, who, as Director of Commerce, had been responsible for the breaking down of the feudal governors' internal tolls in Ethiopia.

The drive to Dessie which in those days took three days can now be covered in one. Scenically it is magnificent and is bettered only by the country still farther north along the same route along the edge of the Ethiopian plateau which rises for thousands of feet along the west of the Great East African Rift valley.

With the Emperor there travelled his favourite son, the young Leul Makonnen, Duke of Harar; Dejazmatch Hailé Sellassié Abaneh; the former prisoner Fitwrary Birru Walda Gabriel, who was Minister of War before Ras Mulugeta; Dejazmatch Wandirad and Dejazmatch Adafrisau, commander of the Imperial Guard. Hailé Sellassié set up court at Dessie in some style and pausing only to send a telegram of condolence on hearing of the death of George V of Britain, he began a vigorous program of inspections and negotiations for the loyalty of the local chieftains who had been much affected by Italian leaflets and money.

RAS IMRU TAKES THE INITIATIVE

Ras Mulugeta had moved forward to the great *amba* of Aradam, twelve miles south of Makallé and was busy establishing his men on its windy precipices. He was angry because the Emperor announced that Leul-Ras Kassa Hailu was to be in charge of the front. Was he not himself Minister of War—and Kassa a quiet religious man and not a soldier? He need not have worried, for the Emperor had also informed each commander to take no offensive action without his own direct authorisation which would be brought by aeroplane (but these planes were still in Addis Ababa).* There was some further friction between the Imperial Guard and the army on the way to the front but it was smoothed over.

Ras Imru had moved north, but not only was there immedi-

---

* The devolution of authority is still not understood in Ethiopia. Senior government officers feel that it detracts from their position not to be taking all the decisions—and in certain cases there is the additional motive that the man who decides is the one in position to accept (or refuse) bribes.

ate trouble back in Gojjam, but some of his officers, led by Dejaz-match Gassasa Balau deserted and returned home. Not everyone understood the urgency of the national plight. Major G. Burgoyne, a British officer serving with the Ethiopian Red Cross, wrote to his wife,* 'Along the road to Korem, the British ambulance unit found several thousand soldiers sent there to build the road but not work-ing because there were four Church feast days together. . . .'

Nevertheless, despite all these problems, the front held for some months. Marshal Badoglio was of course preparing his offen-sive, but in the meantime some Ethiopian commanders took the initiative. Seyoum remained entrenched on the margins of the Tembien mountains, in order to keep in contact with the Tigréan guerrilla forces behind the Italian lines. Mulugeta remained pre-occupied with the task of smuggling 30,000 or so troops, a vast cannon captured at Adowa and his mule-loads of Maria Theresa dollars past the Italians and into the supposedly impregnable caves of Amba Aradam. Meantime to the Wello Galla he gave only supply responsibilities, for he distrusted and despised them as fighters. So precipitous are some of the Ethiopian valleys that Leul-Ras Kassa was able to lure the Italian planes into one defile in which he had set up a red tent surrounded by others, all of them empty, and then to ambush them. Years before, Italian artillery had narrowly missed killing Ras Mangasha when they had fired on his red tent and Kassa counted on their mistaking his decoy for the headquarters of Mangasha's son—Leul-Ras Seyoum.[2] The crossfire of the Ethiopian soldiers damaged several planes and killed a gunner.

Meantime Ras Imru and Dejazmatch Ayelu, the latter tem-porarily redeeming himself for earlier secret negotiations through his son with Marshal de Bono, decided on a surprise attack. (Ayelu had fought against Ras Gugsa Wolie in 1930 and thought he had never been properly rewarded after the suppression of that revolt.) Their forces crossed the Takkazzé river gorge and, sweeping small defensive posts aside, marched on to capture the town of Enda Sellassié. Ras Imru decided to by-pass the heavily defended sacred city of Aksum and to march on the Italian supply depôt at Addi Quala. However, he left a large enough force in position to

* Mrs Clarissa Burgoyne—personal communication. The major's letter was marked Waldia, Wednesday, January 22, 1936. The major was killed a month later by an Italian bomb. In the early 1960s, his wife, though over seventy, travelled widely and fearlessly in remote parts gathering mater-ial to supplement her husband's last letters. It is to be hoped that the manuscripts she has so kindly allowed the author to examine will soon be published.

tie down the Aksum and Addigrat garrisons. Taunted by the Emperor's telegram, 'Why do you not do likewise?', Seyoum and Kassa sent a force under Dejazmatch Hailu Kebede which took Abbi Addi, capital of the Tembien.

THE ITALIANS USE POISON GAS

The Italians knew of only one way to stop Imru's flanking movement and they showered his columns with gas bombs. Later, canisters having been found to affect only a limited area, the Italians sprayed mustard gas from the wings of their planes. Soon they were using it along the entire front. Villagers and their animals, soldiers, women and children were indiscriminately choked, blistered and burnt. The pleas of the International Red Cross went completely unheard. For example, Dr John Melly wrote in a letter :

> This isn't war, it isn't even slaughter—it is the torture of tens of thousands of defenceless men, women and children with bombs and poison gas. They are using it incessantly and we have treated hundreds of cases, including infants in arms—and the world looks on—and passes on the other side.

The Geneva Convention of 1925 had gone by the board and the world had discovered a new horror—afterwards called 'total war'.

Yet in all this even Marshal Badoglio wrote, 'against the organised fire of our defending troops, [the Ethiopian] soldiers, many of them armed only with cold steel, attacked again and again in compact phalanxes pushing right up to our wire entanglements which they tried to beat down with their curved scimitars'. In the long run, however, the bravery of individual Ethiopians could be no answer. The older leaders slowly began to appreciate this— which the Emperor and the foreign advisers had long realised. The chief of the Belgian military mission, although only in his forties, had gone completely grey whilst in Ethiopia. Colonel Konovaloff, a White-Russian adviser attached to Leul-Ras Seyoum's staff had little confidence in the nobility as military commanders.[3] Amongst the other foreign advisers was a Texas-educated ex-revolutionary from Cuba named Captain Delvalle. He was a member of the entourage of the Minister of War. Nor has the custom of employing advisers ended even in military circles; witness the role of Brigadier-general de Gavre of the United States Military Aid Group and some of his officers, when Major-generals Merid Mangasha and Kebede Gebré attacked and recaptured Addis Ababa in December 1960.

The Ethiopians began to mass near the Italian lines. Still

Badoglio contented himself with bombing these concentrations and their bases—the Emperor had to order the daily evacuation of Dessie and Gondar—but all the time Italian aerial photography revealed the extent of the Ethiopian positions. There were some daring raids such as those led by Dejazmatch Gabré Hiwot for Leul-Ras Seyoum whose forces occupied the southern Tembien, but on the whole the stagnant situation continued into 1936.

GRAZIANI DEFEATS RAS DESTA

In the south Graziani, at first confused by the apparent disappearance of the forces of Ras Desta of Sidamo and his chiefs such as Dejazmatch Beyenna Merid of Bali, tempted them to show themselves from the cover of the gallery of vegetation along the river sides by ordering his planes to fly low to attract fire. Ras Desta had warned his men against this tactic, but it succeeded and, once located, bomb and gas attacks followed. One of the former destroyed a Swedish Red Cross unit. In early 1936 Graziani's columns advanced. On this front as elsewhere the Ethiopians fought well and it was said that Graziani himself had saluted in tribute at the burial of Balambaras Abba Bullo, a brave soldier. Nevertheless Ras Desta's forces were driven back to their hilly refuge in southern Sidamo. The government in Addis Ababa ordered Dejazmatch Makonnen Wossen of Wellamo into Sidamo in support and the aged Dejazmatch Gabré Mariam, formerly governor general of Harar, was dispatched with troop reinforcements from Dessie. The Emperor, who had just received news that one of three girls in Tigré who had been sexually assaulted by the Italian soldiery— recruitment circulars in Italy sported a bare bosomed Ethiopian maiden as part of the spoils of war[4]—had killed her assailant with his own bayonet, sent a cable to Ras Desta demanding to know why he could not do more on his front, when in Tigré even the spirit of women could triumph. However, after taking Negellé, the local capital, Graziani decided not to push home his advantage but to concentrate on preparations for an attack on the more important city of Harar on his right flank.

BADOGLIO TAKES THE TEMBIEN

On the main northern front, meantime, the battle of Tembien opened in earnest. High explosive and gas bombs rained on the supply routes. Pamphlets declared that the Emperor was dead and others, counting on the clergy's influence, and in an attempt to subvert them, promised that the Italians would rebuild all damaged churches. Large bodies of Gallas roved unchecked throughout northern Wello and the 'Amhara' administration of the whole region broke down. Leul-Ras Kassa sent demands for reinforcements. Ras Mulugeta also requested supplies and instructions from his Emperor and was furious when the latter ordered Dejazmatch Moshesha Woldé of Kembata to leave him and join Kassa. To a man, the Ethiopian forces, after some recent successes, were over confident and realised too late the magnitude of Marshal Badoglio's offensive when at last it broke upon them.

First to meet it was Dejazmatch Wodajo, governor of Dessie and his Wellos. Wounded and defeated, he just managed to reach Mulugeta to warn him. As it was, deeply shocked by his first realisation of the awful power of a modern army, it is extremely doubtful whether he was really able to convey to the Minister of War actualities well outside that old man's experience. The *ras* telephoned Hailé Sellassié who ordered forward Betwoded Makonnen Demissie and his Welleggas. Arriving on the flanks of Amba Aradam, Makonnen barely had time to urge Mulugeta to withdraw immediately from the hilltop before he and Dejazmatch Moshesha Woldé, whose forces were moving along the front on earlier orders, found themselves faced by hitherto unprecedented masses of Italian and colonial troops. Since Leul-Ras Kassa remained immobile, they gave battle, but the odds were hopeless.

Betwoded Makonnen was wounded when he led his men in the storming of four machine-gun nests. Some aged *balabat* had insisted on accompanying the attacking party. Unlike the others he had to be mounted on a mule which brayed and surprise was lost. Soon afterwards Makonnen died and both his and Moshesha Woldé's forces were routed and withdrew in disorder. However, their defence gave Mulugeta some little time to try and get some of his men off Amba Aradam, which by then was afire having suffered a tremendous and concentrated aerial and artillery bombardment, the like of which, though typical of the second World War, was then new, not only to Ethiopia, but to the whole world. Even so, some Ethiopian soldiers bluntly refused to obey the *ras's* orders to abandon the *amba,* saying it was better to die than to retreat before the enemy was physically upon them. That was not long delayed for crack Alpini troops scaled what the old *ras* thought were the impregnable cliff-faces of the *amba,* and there was soon a danger of complete encirclement.

In the final stages of the battle, mustard gas was employed to drive the Ethiopians from trenches they were hastily constructing farther to the rear on Amba Alagi and it was but a pathetic few survivors harassed by the Azebu Galla who finally reached

Korem near Lake Ashangi. The old Minister of War was not among them and some mystery surrounds his death. Italian and Ethiopian writers state that the Galla, who had good reason to hate him, fell on him when they heard he was in retreat but it is more likely that the *ras* was killed by Italian bombs. That indeed is also suggested by G. Steer, the London *Times* correspondent, who described the death of that brave but outdated warrior as follows :

> A messenger with torn clothes came up. 'Master, your son has been murdered and mutilated by the Galla on the edge of the mountain.' In his last black rage the old *ras* turned round to avenge his son. The Galla surrounded him, and planes, recognising the khaki in the middle of their allies, flew low to bomb. Mulugeta fell near his son : his bodyguard carried him off the field, over the rocks and short grass which concealed their enemies. So died the last of Menelik's high officers, the man who had stopped more lead in his rhino-skin shield and killed more men with the sword than any in Ethiopia.[5]

His failure was but a measure of the failure of the feudal Ethiopian army. His brave and picturesque generation belonged to a system hopelessly at sea in the brutal realities of the twentieth century. Nor is it forgotten by many young Ethiopians today that most of the blood which such as he shed so profusely was Ethiopian and they do not listen when old men extol the virtues of his generation as examples.

Defeat followed defeat, for the forces of Leul-Ras Kassa Hailu, of Leul-Ras Seyoum Mangasha and even of Ras Imru fared no better. Similar tactics were used against Kassa and Seyoum who were not fully aware of the disaster which had overtaken Mulugeta. Superior forces raced to encircle them. Alpini troops scaled the precipices of Amba Worq and took that position by surprise assault. Six times Kassa ordered counter-attacks on the *amba,* and six times the Ethiopians failed to retake it. Meantime, air attacks on their supply lines resulted in a desperate shortage of munitions and food. In the nick of time Kassa withdrew from the encircling Italians. The second battle of the Tembien was lost and many of the survivors of Kassa's Gondari soldiers went home. With only the levies from his Shewan fief of Fiché and in the company of Seyoum and the remnants of his Tigréan army, Kassa retired to Socota, the ancient market centre and capital of Wag, where his ancestors lay in the mausoleum cut from the rock, and from thence he journeyed to join the Emperor, who was by this time ensconced in a cave at Korem.

Ras Imru likewise was unaware of the defeat of the Minister of War. His campaigns on the north-western flank of the Italian armies had met with considerable successes, but when he boldly attacked the whole 2nd Army Corps just south-west of Aksum his men ran short of ammunition and were defeated. Initiative on the last hopeful Ethiopian sector thus passed to the Italians, who pushed forward over the Simien escarpment and on towards Gondar, the ancient capital.

With the towering mountain barriers of Amba Alagi and the Simien both breached, the Italians knew that the routes to Gojjam and Shewa were open. One more battle should win them Dessie and, they resolved, a speedy offensive could make the capture of that town a gateway into Addis Ababa itself.

THE EMPEROR JOINS THE FRONT

Today the enclosed plain which surrounds the shining blue Lake of Ashangi is a peaceful place. Villages are clustered on the mountain spurs that run down to the lake basin and the lines of the ancient basalt lava-flows in the hill sides stand out starkly against the greens and mauves of the mountains. It is difficult to conceive this scene of breathtaking and almost timeless beauty as a backcloth to the events of early 1936. The shattered remnants of the northern armies gathered there and the glorious valleys and hills were every day systematically inundated with the deadly burning Yperite or mustard gas. Italian leaflets were scattered over the surrounding countryside urging the 'People of Wello' to 'rise against the people of Shewa who stole your fine horses in the time of Lij Eyasu'.

Hailé Sellassié was anxious to attack the Italian columns, for the reinforcements which daily climbed the pass of Amba Alagi and entered the mountains made every moment of delay more dangerous. He had previously urged his commanders not to give battle on a broad front but he now saw that this was the only tactic which might hold the disintegrating Ethiopian feudal armies together. Also the historic concept of the Warrior Emperor demanded that he lead a battle. In his heart he knew it was foolish but there seemed no alternative. Badoglio was relieved when he learnt of the Ethiopian preparations for battle. He wrote :

> I had in fact been afraid that the *Negus*, alarmed by the general collapse of the armies of the various *rases* might withdraw his army to Dessie or even farther south, thus compelling me to organise a large-scale battle hundreds of miles from our bases . . . but the *Negus* was falling into the same error into which, in spite of repeated warnings, the *rases* had fallen. I

therefore telegraphed to the head of [the Italian] government that, whether the *Negus* attacked or whether he awaited my attack, his fate was now decided, he would be completely defeated.

The Empress from Addis Ababa and the chiefs all urged the Emperor to lead a great battle in person, but when he finally decided to attack, the feudal army commanders delayed him for eleven days, during which time one or more of their number betrayed every detail of the battle plan to the Italians. The many subversive pamphlets in Addis Ababa in the early 1960s did not mention this, but with little justice they accused Hailé Sellassié of cowardice. For example, on his birthday in 1961, a widely distributed tract entitled *Birthday of Destruction* and signed 'The new Government of Ethiopia' contained an Amharic statement: 'Yohannes fell at Metemma [Gallabat], Tewodros shot himself at Magdela, Menelik won his great victory at Adowa, but you—you are the dirt of history—you ran away from Maichew.' Whatever charges may be justly laid against the Emperor Hailé Sellassié —and this and other pamphlets make many accusations—cowardice is not one of them. Even Brigadier-general Mengistu admitted this at his trial, but in 1961 anger and frustration mounted to the point where many attempts were made to discredit Hailé Sellassié because he was the government, despite the fact that general discontent in Addis Ababa had not reached that point at the time of the 1960 Revolution.

Since the departure of the Emperor to the northern front, the Empress Menen had telegraphed repeatedly for news until Hailé Sellassié's headquarters had sent her the message: 'His silence is caused by the numerous visits of the *balabat* (notables) which leave him no spare time.' But towards the end of March, Hailé Sellassié was able to radio a message which was picked up and recorded by the Italians. In it he gave the Empress the numbers of his troops and his estimate of the enemy and said:

> We are drawn up opposite the enemy and observing each other through field glasses . . . since our trust is in God our Creator and in the hope of His help and as we have decided to advance and enter the fortifications and since God is our only help, confide this decision of ours in secret to the Archbishop, to the ministers and dignitaries, and offer up to God your fervent prayers.

ANALYSIS OF DEFEAT

Uncertain of the fate of his cousin, Ras Imru, Hailé Sellassié wrote

him a pen picture of the tragic situation as he saw it on the eve of
the battle of Maichew and Lake Ashangi. Earlier, the Ethiopian
armies, he wrote,

> . . . went to pieces without having suffered serious losses and
> without any attempt whatever at resistance. This is a grievous
> matter! Our army, famous throughout Europe for its valour,
> has lost its name, brought to ruin by a few traitors! [He wrote
> of] the brave deaths of Dejazmatch Moshesha Woldé, Dejaz-
> match Beyenne and of Betwoded Makonnen, [and added] those
> who were first to betray Us and those who afterwards followed
> their example, namely the chiefs of the forces of Wello such
> as Ras Gebret, Dejazmatch Amedieh Ali and others of the
> army of the Shewan Dejazmatch Auraris and Dejazmatch
> Belaineh, have all been arrested. . . . Ras Kassa and Ras
> Seyoum are with us, but have not a single armed man with
> them. For yourself, if you think that with your troops and with
> such of the local inhabitants as you can collect together you
> can do anything where you are, do it. If on the other hand
> your position is difficult and you are convinced of the impossi-
> bility of fighting, having lost all hope on your front, and if
> you think it is better to come here and die with Us, let us know
> of your decision by telephone from Debat. . . . From the
> League we have so far derived no hope and no benefit!

But Ras Imru was in no position to march even a remnant
towards Lake Ashangi. He telegraphed to Addis Ababa,

> The greater part of the Gojjam troops have deserted and refuse
> to fight except in their own district . . . even our own personal
> soldiers . . . we have not been able to carry out our plan. All
> the local tribes have not only deserted but have shown little
> respect for their chief, the Dejazmatch Ayelu.

The Dejazmatch was shot at.

These messages were, in Marshal Badoglio's sardonic phrase,
'of remarkable interest'. He adds of 'the *Negus* and the *rases*' that
'although their defeat was mainly attributable to their own incom-
petence, they blamed with impunity their troops whose courage
on the contrary had proved itself in all circumstances to be of the
highest order'. While representing a sound general comment on
the attitudes of Ethiopian feudal leaders in this context it was of
course only in part true, for the technical superiority of the
Italian armies and the demoralising use of gas were more important factors. A few years later the patriot guerrilla forces of the
Ethiopian people, who never admitted defeat, were to see even

8—E * *

greater ineptitude in the sphere of military leadership, demonstrated by the Italians themselves.

The Emperor was aware of the weakness of the Ethiopian high command. He called Colonel Konovaloff, the military adviser, and bluntly demanded an explanation of Leul-Ras Kassa's failure to hold the Tembien. In his memoir Konovaloff writes :

It was difficult to answer the question. I thought again of how Ras Kassa had retired; with an absence on his own part as on the part of his chiefs of the slightest initiative or any display of forethought or decision. They knew nothing about modern warfare, nothing at all. [But, he adds] . . . I did not want to sadden the spirit of the Emperor with the revealing details . . . the total ineptitude of the chiefs, the complete disorganisation and demoralisation of their forces. . . .

On the next day it was significantly three Ethiopian officers who had trained at St Cyr Military Academy whom Hailé Sellassié sent out with the colonel to make the detailed plan for an attack on Maichew.

Meantime the Italians began to move up forces which Konovaloff realised could repeat the earlier encircling tactics. The Emperor with Seyoum and Kassa seated with him held a traditional feast and raw meat was served to the soldiers as is still the custom today. Attacks by Italian planes were becoming much more frequent in the region of the Emperor's cave by the time the reluctant leaders eventually declared their forces ready for the attack. It was planned that the army should advance in three columns, led by Leul-Ras Kassa, by Leul-Ras Seyoum and by Ras Getachew. 'Why by them and not by others of greater energy and capacity?' asked Konovaloff rhetorically in his memoir. His answer is echoed repeatedly today and the very echo a quarter of a century later reveals the lack of change in Ethiopia which so dismays that country's youth. Konovaloff answered : 'Because the sovereign had to reckon with his feudal seigneurs of the empire although they had proved their ineptitude already. . . . He had better men but he could not use them.'

THE BATTLE OF MAICHEW

The battle which began on March 31, 1936, was to last several days. The Ethiopians broke through the outer defences of the Italian lines but the delay had allowed time for those defences to be constructed in depth and the offensive soon began to slow down. Hailé Sellassié was with the armies on the plain before Maichew firing a machine-gun. He sent a telegram to the Empress :

From five in the morning until seven in the evening our troops attacked the enemy's strong positions fighting without pause. We also took part in the action and by the Grace of God remained unharmed. Our chief and trusted soldiers are dead and wounded. Although our losses are heavy the enemy too has been injured. The Guard fought magnificently and deserve every praise. The Amhara troops also did their best. Our troops, even though they were not adapted for fighting of the European type, were able to bear comparison throughout the day with Italian troops. . . .

One wonders what the proud Empress Menen, granddaughter of the Negus Mikael, last king of the Wello Galla, made of the final sentence of this message, for Hailé Sellassié concluded, '. . . The Galla helped us only with shouts, not with their strong right arm.'

In the battle the Minister of the Court was killed. Dejazmatch Mangasha Yilma, director of the War Ministry, the close relative of the Emperor who had worked under old Ras Mulugeta also gave his life, as did the *balabat* of Maichew, Dejazmatch Abera Tadla, Ras Kebeda, old Dejazmatch Wandirad who had been wounded at Adowa so many years before, and many many more. Leul-Ras Seyoum Mangasha slipped away from the field to march back into his fief of Tigré, they said at the time to raise guerrilla war while it was still possible.

News arrived of the fall of Gondar away to the west. The Ethiopian forces began to disintegrate into almost complete chaos. Hailé Sellassié gave away his belongings and left for Korem. Planes swooped to bomb and machine-gun the broken columns retiring towards Lake Ashangi, and the Azebu Galla, who had been bribed by both sides, only now descended from the hillsides. They knew no wider nationalism, how could they? But they understood loot. The Emperor tried in vain to organise a counter-attack but the last vestiges of his control were slipping away. Soldiers fired into the air and rushed leaderless over the countryside. Horrified, a director general of the Ministry of the Pen named Woldé Giorgis, one of the Emperor's two secretaries and later to become a great power in the land, said to Colonel Konovaloff : 'I hate the sight of these swine in tatters! Had I the power I would have the whole lot shot!' On April 2, 1936, the Imperial Foreign Office sent a despairing telegram to their Legation in Paris : 'The military situation will become impossible . . . impossible to find reinforcements . . . the Emperor will remain where he is until death. Then, collapse of the Empire!'

THE FALL OF DESSIE

At Dessie the young Crown Prince, Asfa Wossen, aged only eighteen, had struggled desperately to retain the loyalty of the Galla chiefs. Defeated troops, formerly commanded by the governor, the wounded Dejazmatch Wodajo Ali, had bypassed the main Ethiopian forces when they had fled from the Italian offensive against Amba Aradam. They arrived near Dessie and camped outside the city, planning sedition. The Crown Prince tricked their leader into coming to a feast. Then he sent instructions to the soldiers that they should join his forces and receive free pardon and an issue of ammunition or else disband and return home to their farms. The ruse, very reminiscent of Hailé Sellassié's dealings with Dejazmatch Balcha in 1928, was successful, for as the first son of the Galla Empress, Asfa Wossen had some following. The leaders were arrested and flown to Addis Ababa. (It was to them that the Emperor referred in his letter to Ras Imru.)

However, as the situation at the front worsened, so Asfa Wossen's position deteriorated. He learnt of the previously feared advance of another Italian force across the torrid volcanic wastes of the Danakil desert to occupy Sardo, the capital of the sultan of Aussa who along with several sons of the 'Mad Mullah' had gone over to the Italians. During the battle of Maichew the Crown Prince telegraphed to the Emperor that this force so lately in the coastal Assab region was now only seven days' march from Dessie. The Emperor could only reply that this news was a 'source of great anxiety' and advised him to put the question before the Council of Ministers in Addis Ababa. Events, however, overtook the expression of this dilemma. The Crown Prince learnt of a plan of the Wello chiefs to capture him and he was obliged to slip quietly out of the town to join his men at a large village to the south-west, Warra Hailu, the birthplace of the Empress Zauditu. For a day the city of Dessie lapsed into a state of complete disorder and gunfire spread throughout the town before, on April 15, the Italian forces entered and raised the standard of the House of Savoy over the palace of the Negus Mikael.

RETREAT TO ADDIS ABABA

The Emperor had made his way through the confusion back to the cave at Korem. Dejazmatch Wodajo, earlier abandoned wounded when his men fled towards Dessie, acted as governor of Korem and there several notables rested. Ras Getachew set off south via the Rift valley floor but near Kobbo he was obliged to fight several

large scale engagements with the Raia and Azebu Galla, out for
revenge for the treatment they had earlier received at the hands
of Ras Mulugeta.

Hailé Sellassié still talked of counter-attacking. The position,
however, was hopeless and Colonel Konovaloff, his White Russian
Military Adviser, records his tired master's comments : 'My chiefs
will do nothing. My brain no longer works!' and later, of the
Italians : 'It is beyond our power to hold them back.' In the
company of Leul-Ras Kassa and his sons, the colonel and several
dejazmatch, the defeated Emperor set off over the difficult mountain country to the north-west of the city of Dessie. They marched
at night to avoid the aeroplanes. It was Lent, and meat and milk
were unobtainable, although other foods and *tej* (mead) were
offered by the people as was the custom, for Leul-Ras Kassa was
the governor general, and was he not in the company of the King
of the Kings? They crossed a tributary of the Takkazzé river and
spent Easter at the camp of Fitwrary Belai, governor of Lasta. Here
Hailé Sellassié changed the route towards the historic Christian
shrine of Lalibela, a group of thousand-year-old rock-hewn
churches. Then the weary group moved on past the house where
Emperor Tewodros II once asked, 'To whom do those tents belong?' and first learnt of General Napier's British expedition of
1867–8 which led to his defeat and suicide. In a cave Hailé
Sellassié learnt that the Wello leaders Dejazmatch Abauko and
Dejazmatch Belai Kebede had betrayed him, but that the people of
Waldia district had taken to the hills to continue the fight against
the invaders as guerrillas. Crossing a Blue Nile tributary the column
pushed on to Amba Magdela, last citadel of Tewodros, harassed
as was his fleeing army in 1869, by the local Galla. Tired of being
sniped at, Hailé Sellassié sent the remnant of the Imperial Guard
up Tewodros's Magdela citadel and once against its houses were
fired.

Dejazmatch Aberra, son of Leul-Ras Kassa Hailu, went
ahead and cleared a way. Hailé Sellassié made for the village of
Warra Hailu, but the Italians got there first. Since his followers
declined to attack them, the Emperor turned west again towards
Leul-Ras Kassa's fief of Fiché in Shewa province, near the northern
road out of Addis Ababa. It was a weary leader who eventually
climbed into a car and sped south to his capital. He arrived on
Thursday, April 30, 1936.

GUERRILLA TRAINING IN THE CAPITAL

When Hailé Sellassié had left Addis Ababa for Dessie, his faithful lieutenant Dejazmatch Yigezu, who was influential though a sick man, had been appointed Deputy for Overall Home Affairs, a position almost tantamount to Regent. Though under his broad responsibility, the city of Addis Ababa had been specifically left in the capable hands of Hailé Sellassié's liberal friend of very early times, Blatta Takelé Woldé Hawariat, who had afterwards been out of favour. However, at the time of national crisis in 1935, Hailé Sellassié had to forget his personal differences with useful men. When state prisoners such as the Emperor Menelik's eunuch general Dejazmatch Balcha had been freed, the Emperor had examined a list of twenty names submitted to him before his journey to the northern front and from them had chosen Takelé to be director general of the Addis Ababa municipality. The two were to some extent reconciled and Takelé had typically taken the opportunity to stress his own theories, this time on the virtues of guerrilla warfare against a modern army. In fact to use his reported words, 'knowing the Emperor's weakness for whites', he had also sent Europeans to urge this military tactic.

After Hailé Sellassié had left for Dessie *en route* to the northern front, Blatta Takelé had formed the Patriotic Association which later became more associated with Makonnen Habtewold, much later a powerful minister who was killed in the 1960 Revolution. Dejazmatch Yigezu had encouraged Takelé to start a training camp on some land the latter had inherited from his father at Sabata near Addis Ababa. There a Canadian taught the rudiments of guerrilla warfare to many young Shewans. When news of the position on the northern front suggested a rapid deterioration and near chaos, Takelé decided not to send all the rifles that arrived by rail to the front but kept some, dividing them between this new guerrilla force and the followers of two other Shewan leaders. The first was the popular and fearless Dejazmatch Fikré Mariam Aba Techan.* Fikré Mariam had received some of his education in French, but he remained a typical warrior Ethiopian. Some of his achievements in the campaigns against the Italians were to become almost legendary. The second was Balambaras Abebe Aragai, one of the two chiefs of the Addis Ababa police force. Abebe's father was Afe Negus Aragai but he was the more respected because his mother was the daughter of Emperor Menelik's great Galla general, Ras Gobena.

THE DILEMMA—GORÉ OR GENEVA

On the return of the defeated Emperor, Takelé urged that the

---

* A member of the wealthy and powerful Moja family group, several of whom were implicated in the 1960 Revolution.

government retire to Goré in the south-west of Ethiopia. The rains, he said, would immobilise the Italian ground and air forces and give a respite in which effective guerrilla forces might be organised on a larger scale. He even predicted that world conflict coupled with internal disorder—for Gojjam was already in open revolt and the Italians were never effectively to rule there—might make reconquest possible. If the Italians were held and supplies could be arranged through the Sudan and Kenya, the empire might still be saved, he postulated. Dejazmatch Habté Mariam, the Galla ruler of Wellegga province in the south-west of Ethiopia was then considered to be loyal to the Emperor and this also was an important factor.

At this time the railway to the coast of the Gulf of Aden, which terminated at Djibouti in French Somaliland, was still operating and in the south-east Dejazmatch Nasibu's forces were still in possession of Ji-Jigga and Harar, but the Italian columns were hourly approaching Addis Ababa from the north. Remnants of the broken northern armies straggled into the capital in a state of complete disorganisation. All that could be mustered to defend the last natural bastion, the mountain escarpment of Tarmaber, were officer-cadets from the Holeta Military College. Even the local Shewan troops, except for those under Dejazmatch Aberra Kassa, were rapidly disintegrating into unco-ordinated bands.

This was the position presented to the Council of Ministers at the Great Palace on that Thursday when Hailé Sellassie, Ras Getachew, wearing golden pince-nez, but no longer commanding any troops, and Leul-Ras Kassa arrived from the north. Hailé Sellassié, tired and dispirited, automatically approved of the plan to move the capital to Goré, presented by Lorenzo Taezaz, his secretary, and received foreign diplomats. Together with Leul-Ras Kassa and others he heard Blatta Takelé urge that the war be continued, but the Empress encouraged by the priests tried secretly to persuade him to accompany her to Jerusalem. A special train and a British warship HMS *Enterprise,* were standing by. It is doubtful whether the Emperor was swayed by her determination to invoke the aid of Heaven, but his mind turned once more to the League of Nations at Geneva.

Not surprisingly enthusiasm to continue the war was more obvious amongst those who had not themselves experienced gas attacks and the disillusionment of the northern defeats, nor witnessed the apparent disintegration of the nation. Some of these considered Leul-Ras Kassa's openly stated fear of the southern Galla peoples, who lived along the suggested line of retreat, to amount to an obsession. There was much discussion. Dejazmatch Fikré

Mariam was for staying : so at first was the director general of the Ministry of Commerce, Makonnen Habtewold, who had worked day and night, sleeping in his car, in order to get the few provisions which were available to the fighting fronts (so impossible a task that it is hardly surprising that when the young officer-cadets learnt how few supplies were available for the defence of the capital they blamed Makonnen and threatened to hang him). Blattenguetta Hiroy Woldé Sellassié, the Foreign Minister and Dejazmatch Yigezu, Deputy for Home Affairs, supported Blatta Takelé's pleas for a continued struggle. Then to the horror of these men, some of whom were to become great Patriot leaders, Leul-Ras Kassa supported by Ras Getachew and Fitwrary Birru, a former minister of war, spoke in favour of the Emperor's flight to Europe.

Meantime, Friday saw the Italians at Debra Berhan one hundred miles to the north, with nothing but flat plateau between them and the city. Takelé informed the foreign legations that he would maintain order until the Italians were near, but would not surrender. With whatever troops he could muster and with the police, he would retire along the Addis Alem road to the west. He called the citizens to a great meeting near the new palace of the Prince of Paradise. It was held on the site of the present Imperial Racing Club now called Janhoy Meda. The false tradition has grown up that its name derives from the shout of welcome raised then to Janhoy ('Majesty'), but it was earlier known by this name. 'They are prepared to die for you', remarked Blatta Takelé, director general of the municipality. The Emperor was not impressed. 'They shout like this with your machine-guns behind them, but none would fight for us. The masses would betray Us', he remarked. Woldé Giorgis, a director in the Ministry of Interior, and even Makonnen Habtewold appeared to support him and the hot patriotic blood of Dejazmatch Fikré Mariam boiled over and he was heard to say : 'If the Emperor of Ethiopia should flee—our honour demands that we ambush the train at Akaki and that he die at our own hands.'

THE DEPARTURE OF THE EMPEROR

That afternoon the Council of Ministers voted 21 to 3 (Blattenguetta Hiroy Woldé Sellassié, Dejazmatch Yigezu and Blatta Takelé) that Hailé Sellassié should accompany his family and leave for Djibouti. The image painted by radical and 'subversive' pamphleteers of Addis Ababa's underground movements in 1961 and '62, of the Emperor hastening at once to save himself is not accurate. He ordered the drums to be beaten and tried to call out armies to defend the city or at least to cover a westward retreat. The soldiers cheered but the great chiefs refused to lead them. It was only then that the Emperor gave way to Leul-Ras Kassa. Woldé Giorgis was sent to inform the British Embassy that he would board their vessel. The Addis Ababa station-master was alerted. Four royal cars and much baggage was loaded and at 4.20 a.m. on Saturday, May 2, 1936, the royal train moved quietly off down to the Rift valley and on towards Djibouti in French Somaliland and the safety of a British warship. Hailé Sellassié saw the main party off but he, Leul-Ras Kassa and Ras Getachew themselves later boarded the same train at a pre-arranged stop at Akaki lower down the line.

One by one, the leaders and the people of the city of Addis Ababa and beyond heard the news. It fell to Blatta Kidané Mariam to take the news to Dejazmatch Fikré Mariam and Blatta Takelé. Incredulous, they drove down the bumpy 'murrum' road to the Akaki railway station and learnt that it was true. Takelé, hot and dusty in his white dress, fell in a fit. 'My country there is no one to defend your cause', he cried as they took him to the car. The *shums* (leaders) and priests of the villages despaired; never in their proud history had such a thing happened : that the 'Elect of God' should leave the chosen Ethiopian people for asylum in some foreign place.

At Debra Markos, capital of strife-riven Gojjam, a telephone call from Addis Ababa informed an uncowed but war-weary noble of this news, and also that he, Ras Imru, had become Viceroy. It was not the last time that he was to be called upon in a desperate national crisis for he was nominated Prime Minister during the short-lived *coup* of December 1960.

Not so many days later, on June 28, 1936, at the General Assembly of the League of Nations in Geneva, Hailé Sellassié was to say : 'I was defending the cause of all small peoples who are threatened by aggression. What have become of the promises that were made to me? . . . God and History will remember your judgement!' The world conscience was stunned by his words. The hearts of the peoples of the world, though not immediately of their governments, warmed towards the little Emperor. But back in the mountains of Ethiopia, enthusiasm for their King of the Kings was not so marked.

13

The Patriots

Les Anglais ont évacué l'Abyssinie aussitôt conquise. S'il avait été possible de la coloniser ils y seraient restés.—Remark of BISMARCK—quoted by A. D'ABBADIE *in Douze Ans dans la Haute Ethiopie,* Paris, 1868

Our thoughts and actions were thus continually refreshed by a sense of proportion born of the contemplation of a struggle of transitory mortals against the background of the 'timeless hills'.—J. AMERY, *Sons of the Eagle,* London, 1948

THE RISE OF NEW LEADERS

The usual emphasis in the discussion of the years 1936–41 has been on the very considerable material achievements of the Italian colonialists. Little has so far been written on the reaction of the proud and independent Ethiopian people to this brief period of colonialism and on their contribution through a long guerrilla war of attrition to the speedy collapse of Italian power once foreign armies entered the field.[1]

The traditional feudal rulers of Ethiopia had failed in the battles of the Tembien and at Maichew and there arose a new group of leaders drawn chiefly from the local country *balabats*. Their ranks included several members of the noble families, but more significantly including several with at least a rudimentary knowledge of modern warfare and moreover the conviction that feudal organisation was quite inadequate. They frequently discussed amongst themselves how the political system of their country might be overhauled in the event of an Italian defeat and withdrawal.

Several were graduates of the new Holeta Military College

and a few had attended courses at St Cyr in France. In the *mores* of this group may be detected very much that is traditional —the respect and affection for strong men and the careless disregard of even life itself if the stake were personal honour or national pride. But there emerged also the merest beginnings of a questioning of the whole basis of a national life which could allow so proud a nation to collapse before the armies of the despised *'ferenge'*.* In the 1950s those Patriot leaders who had acquitted themselves well and who survived were to become a political force in Ethiopia. Admittedly, they differed from the young radical groups of the 1960s in that their discontent had little consistency or basis in economics or political ideology and was, moreover, not influenced by the wider African scene. But they commanded a greater measure of popular sympathy and support than the would-be revolutionaries of the early 1960s.

THE FALL OF HARAR

In 1936 the invading Italian armies from Eritrea had been the first to achieve major victories. On the south-eastern front few engagements had broken the stalemate in the Ethiopian war. African colonial troops, known as *'bandas'*, had mounted an offensive for Italy under the Sultan of Shiaveli and had been defeated by Dejazmatch Beyenna Merid, but Graziani had made no move. With Dejazmatch Nasibu, governor general of Harar province were the forces of Dejazmatch Amdé Mikael from Arusi, Dejazmatch Abebe Damtew from Gemu Gofa, Dejazmatch Makonnen Endalkatchew and Habté Mariam. Steer comments on this last commander that he was 'a rich army contractor who had made enough to tip his ceremonial spear with gold' and adds that he 'enjoyed less control over his troops than over their pay'. Many of his men understandably deserted and he himself later went over to the Italians.

When Ras Desta had been defeated in Sidamo and the southern route to Addis Ababa had seemed to be open, Hailé Sellassié had ordered Nasibu to mount an offensive to distract Graziani. Initially it had been successful. The *dejazmatch* had three experienced foreign officers on his staff : Tarik Bey, a Sudanese who had fought the Italians in Tripoli; Major Faruk, formerly Turkish military attaché in Athens; and Wahib Pasha who had commanded a machine-gun corps at Gallipoli in 1915. The lightning attacks which they had advised had demoralised the Italian

---

* *Ferenge*—a foreigner with a 'white', or as the Ethiopians would say, 'red', skin.

forces, but the latter had retaliated with gas attacks from the air. The Ethiopian forces, running short of ammunition, had eventually attacked in mass. Heroism is no match for machine-guns, and the initiative had been lost. Then Graziani had counter-attacked. Dejazmatch Nasibu recalled his forces towards Harar. One group especially had fought well, that led by Fitwrary Million, whom some say was a son of an illegitimate son of the Emperor Tewodros.

The retreat was not orderly, but Graziani hesitated and missed an opportunity to encircle the Ethiopians and to seize Harar. Both armies prepared again for battle, but on May 2, 1936, a train was reported to have reached Dira Dawa carrying the Emperor and his entourage to Djibouti. Completely unnerved, the four *dejazmatch*—Nasibu, Abebe, Makonnen and Amdé—promptly abandoned their forces and followed suit. Fitwrary Million remained but was obliged to withdraw with little more than an irregular band to the mountains of Garamulata west of Harar, where Tafari Makonnen had been governor and where Eyasu had been incarcerated. Graziani's forces entered Ji-Jigga and Harar on May 7 and 8 respectively, but at a feast of raw meat in the hills, the local people proclaimed the tall and handsome grandson of the warrior Emperor Tewodros as their leader. He was subsequently to disappoint them for he went over to the Italians and accepted their title of *dejazmatch*. But throughout the length and breadth of Ethiopia many leaders emerged of sterner stuff than he.

A LAST CHALLENGE

On the way to Djibouti the train carrying Hailé Sellassié was stopped near Chercher by Bejirond Takla Hawariat, who had helped him to the throne and helped prepare the first Ethiopian constitution. Takla Hawariat—father of the 1964 Minister of Press and Information, Blatta Germatchew, who is also a playwright and novelist—was typical of many who saw the departure of an Emperor abroad as a disaster of great and almost mystical dimensions. Yet he was an educated and a travelled man. He had in fact been to school in Russia before the Revolution and had lived in Aden. On his return he had worked in the Ministry of Finance. There he had lost favour through opposing a large vote (said by some to have been a million Ethiopian dollars) towards the enlargement of the palace called Prince's Paradise which had been built by Ras Makonnen. Takla Hawariat had been posted to Chercher as a governor and had not seen his master for some time. With his rifle in his hand, he greeted Hailé Sellassié and bluntly asked that his Emperor journey with him into the hills and raise a Patriot force.

Hailé Sellassié was willing but the *rases* advised against it and the train moved on.

Some time later Takla Hawariat himself was to go to Djibouti to help the consul, a certain Lij Andargatchew Messai, organise relief for the many Ethiopian refugees. But when pressed by newspapermen about his differences with Hailé Sellassié, all Takla Hawariat would say was: 'Our differences are personal— where the country is concerned we are one.' This attitude, typical of that of many older Ethiopians, has contributed to a mistaken impression in the outside world that Hailé Sellassié is an Emperor of undisputed popularity and accepted ancient lineage.*

CONFUSION IN THE CAPITAL

Meantime in Addis Ababa Blatta Takelé suggested that the city be fired. Blatta Kidané Mariam asked: 'Are you mad?' but Takelé replied that besides defying the Italians, it would drive out the people who would then become guerrillas. 'The world will say that Tafari was the only stabilising force', remarked Kidané Mariam, but Takelé blazed back that he cared nothing for the outside world. They need not have argued. Since the lorries had carried the State Bank holdings to the railway station and the Emperor had left, no shops had opened, no *zabanias* (watchmen) had reported for duty and the rabble that once was the armies of the north soon began to shoot and loot. The great palace of the Emperor Menelik II, and the new palace named the Prince's Paradise were open and unguarded, and in vain Balambaras Abebe Aragai tried to save them and to restore order.

Lorenzo Taezaz, the Emperor's secretary, had not known of the sudden arrangements for the departure of the Imperial train. Early in his life he had grown frustrated by the lack of opportunity offered to him, an Eritrean, in the administration of his homeland which was an Italian colony, and he had fled to Aden. There his ability had been recognised by Hailé Sellassié whose service he had joined. Lorenzo again packed to follow his master. He and many who had not left at 4 a.m. crowded into the second train at 10 a.m. In the city, perhaps because the proprietor was an Italian national (he came from the Dodecanese Islands), the wealthy Ganotakis grocery was raided. Shop after shop was then broken into and an attempt was made to break the Bank. Foreigners and some leading Ethiopian dignitaries and Churchmen fled

---

* Germatchew was created *dejazmatch* and a provincial governor in 1965. His father returned to Ethiopia from Madagascar (now the Malagasy Republic) in 1955. He lived in Hirna in Harar in voluntary exile before failing health brought him to Addis Ababa.

to the foreign legations. Balambaras Abebe Aragai gave up, and in the developing chaos he joined Takelé and on horseback these two rode wildly through the streets firing the city. As the French Legation contacted Marshal Badoglio and informed him that the city was open, so hundreds flocked to join the guerrilla forces. Chaos was complete. A Sikh contingent from the British Legation had to raise local sieges at the request of other diplomats, such as those of the United States, besieged in smaller compounds. Abebe contacted an official of the French Legation and Takelé, fearing that he wished to surrender to the Italians, threatened to machine-gun him unless he left the city immediately for Jiru, in eastern Shewa, where he was a *balabat*. This he did, to rank among the most renowned of the Patriot leaders.

BADOGLIO ENTERS ADDIS ABABA

On the evening of May 4, 1936, the Italian advance guard, drawn from the first Eritrean brigade, reached the outskirts of Addis Ababa. On the following day, a Tuesday, Marshal Badoglio and his forces took possession of the city. 'Addis Ababa', he wrote, 'was a very sad spectacle. Almost all the dwelling houses and shops, especially the European ones, had been sacked and burnt, the public buildings had been destroyed; even the Imperial *Ghibbi* (palace) was in ruins, and the very lions, symbol of the now fallen Empire, had been killed . . .' This scene, the Marshal stated, must dispel any remaining doubts as to the 'barbarism of the people' and to illustrate this his book[3] includes photographs of bodies on the roadways in the front of looted shops. The Marshal does not comment on the ropes round the feet of the bodies; doubtless they were dragged from picture to picture by the 'civilised' Italian soldiery. The flag of Savoy was raised and the death penalty for looting or the possession of arms was introduced, and at least 1,500 citizens were shot in the ensuing search conducted by the *carabinieri*. Leaflets urging the citizens to return to their houses were distributed—but many chose to stay in the hills. A battalion was sent by rail to link up with Graziani's forces in the south-east. To all intents and purposes the war appeared won. On May 9, 1936, Mussolini announced that the territory and peoples of Ethiopia were now annexed to 'the full and entire sovereignty of the realm of Italy' and that the title of Emperor of Ethiopia was assumed by Victor Emmanuel III 'for himself and his successors'. On the next day Marshal Badoglio was appointed governor general and Italian Viceroy. But before many weeks had passed he was recalled for duty elsewhere and was succeeded by Marshal Graziani.

The Italian propaganda machine started at once to try to influence governments, newspapers and public opinion abroad. Typical of this was Mussolini's statement . . . 'with the population of Abyssinia peace is already an accomplished fact. The manifold races of the former Empire of the Lion of Judah have shown by clear signs that they wish to live and work tranquilly under the Italian tricolour. The chiefs and the *rases,* defeated fugitives, no longer count and no power on earth can make them count. . . .'[4] But the truth was that as Badoglio had arrived at the east of the city, so many Patriots who were to ignore these decrees had left from the western suburbs and dispersed throughout Shewa. Blatta Takelé went to Sabata. Dejazmatch Fikré Mariam went to the districts of Menz and Tegulet and others went to Tefeké near the Awash river. Yohannes Semerjibashan who started the underground paper *Pillar of Light of Ethiopia* and who was assassinated in Addis Ababa after the war, and Blatta Kidané Mariam, however, chose to stay in Addis Ababa. This latter courageous leader organised the Ethiopian Youth Movement and a women's movement, and was not finally apprehended until he had planned several acts of sabotage. Many other Patriots were arrested and disappeared. The story was that they had been sent to Rome, but it is most probable that they were thrown to their deaths from an aeroplane.[5] In July 1936, a Church leader, Bishop Petros, was shot in an Addis Ababa square, where his statue stands today. He had refused to broadcast against the Patriot fighters and the bravery of such as he inspired the Ethiopian resistance—even the Italians reported that his death 'made a deep impression on the native mind'.

THE PATRIOTS RALLY

Near Addis Ababa, irregular bands attacked the railway station at Akaki. This and other engagements demonstrated the great problem which the lack of overall leadership was to present to the Ethiopian Patriots. Throughout highland Ethiopia many individual commanders remained in the field. In the provinces south of the capital several like Ras Desta Damtew in Sidamo, Bejirond Fikré Sellassié in Arusi, Dejazmatch Beyenna Merid in Bali, remained for a long period in almost complete control of their fiefs or governorates. The same may be said of Dejazmatch Aberra Kassa in Salalé, just north of Addis Ababa. In eastern and northern Shewa respectively, Patriot bands flocked to join Balambaras Abebe Aragai and a Galla leader named Gimma Sembeté. Away to the south-east resistance continued around Harar under Fitwrary Baidé and others. There was resistance too in the north and in most other areas. In Wello for example, Patriot forces momentarily recaptured the city of Dessie after the fall of Addis Ababa but had to retire in the face of an Italian counter-attack with air support.

Blatta Takelé's guerrilla forces at Sabata just west of the capital rallied to their commander, who produced sixty Czechoslovak machine-guns from his *cache* in the altar of the church in which his father had been buried. Some fifteen of those he sent to Fitwrary Geressu Duké, another leader, and with the remainder he equipped his men and set off to join the battle being waged in the south-west by the Viceroy. Ras Imru had retreated from the Tembien to Gojjam and thence to Goré. Leaflets were dropped by the Italians urging the 'liberated' Galla to kill Blatta Takelé and other leaders, for, said this propaganda, they were the Emperor's men and represented 'Amhara tyranny'. Yet Blatta Takelé's wife was a Galla! The Italians appear not to have understood that leading families were as often Galla as Amhara, or were a mixture of both, and constituted a class, not an ethnic group.

DIVIDE AND RULE

In their attempt to consolidate their rule, the Italians sought always to play on divisions, real and otherwise, amongst the Ethiopian peoples. They deliberately favoured the predominantly Galla rather than the Amhara provinces and the muslims rather than the Christians; for instance they built mosques and encouraged pilgrimages to Mecca. They divided Ethiopia (including Eritrea and Italian Somaliland) into six provinces and called it Italian East Africa. These were 'Eritrea', which included much of Tigré and was centred on Asmara; 'Amhara' centred on Gondar; 'Shewa', centred on Addis Ababa; 'Galla-Sidamo' centred on Jimma; 'Harar' centred on that city; and 'Somalia' which included much of the Ethiopian Harar province. All were directed from Addis Ababa, seat of their Viceroy. Locally real power was concentrated in the hands of the Italian army, the officials and the Fascist Party—the last in many ways dominating the others. The machinery of government did not always work too well. There were, for example, five different police forces in Addis Ababa—the *carabinieri*, the colonial police, the police of the army, the Blackshirts and the secret police of the party (the ovra). Considerable misunderstandings occurred between them. Corruption in high circles was also rife. However, the obstinate antagonism of the vast majority of the Ethiopian people remained their main concern.

THE BLACK LIONS

The Emperor's Viceroy, Ras Imru, had at first considered withdrawing from Goré to the Sudan with the remnants of his forces, but he was approached by a newly formed Patriot group, who called themselves 'The Black Lions' and who asked him to become their leader. This group is interesting because its very composition as well as its approach to Ras Imru reflects not only the disillusionment which the newer educated group felt at the failure of the feudal armies, but also the beginnings of a more modern and democratic concept of organisation and particularly leadership. The group was formed largely of graduates of the Holeta Military College under the chairmanship of Dr Alemeworq, but there were also others such as the sons of Dr Workneh Martin, the Ethiopian Minister in Britain, Yilma Deressa (Minister of Finance in 1964) and several educated young Ethiopians most of whom later lost their lives in the Graziani massacres.*

A good short description of the activities, tactics and organisation of the Black Lions has been published by Tedessa Metcha, one of their number.[6] Article 2 of their constitution stated that their ultimate authority was a committee and that even though its president was also military commander in chief, 'unless the committee decide, no one can dictate'. A new approach to the nation at war, in marked contrast to that of Ras Mulugeta, the Minister of War who had been killed on the northern front, and others, was expressed in Article 4 which forbade 'the disturbing of any peasant or any robbery'. Patriotism was asserted in Article 3 in that 'no one, either Ethiopian or foreigner, could be recognised as replacing the Emperor, even if he was in exile . . . any one attempting to replace him or claim his sovereignty must be opposed', but their attitude to exile was more clearly expressed in Article 7 'that no one might leave Ethiopia for exile abroad without the express approval of the committee'. An Ethiopian warrior tradition dating from long before the time of Tewodros and one still extant as the

---

* Dr Alemeworq was a great Patriot. His right arm was blown off by a bomb in an assassination attempt after the war and he has since died. Dr Workneh Martin was a descendant of a prisoner taken to Britain by the Napier expedition after the defeat of Emperor Tewodros in 1868. Yilma Deressa is a Galla of *balabat* extraction from Wellegga. His father, Blatta Deressa, was descended from Amanté (see footnote page 101). Picked out and sent to graduate at the London School of Economics, Yilma, Minister of Finance since the killing of Makonnen Habtewold in the 1960 Revolution, is nevertheless regarded as a diehard conservative. With the death of the Empress Menen in 1962, he became perhaps the most influential Galla in Ethiopia.

events of the 1960 Revolution clearly demonstrate was that, '. . . members were obliged to go to the aid of anyone in trouble [i.e. wounded]. In order that they should not fall into the hands of their enemy those unable to travel and "run with the group" must be offered weapons with which to kill themselves.' This Article, number Ɛ, also made it clear that if they were unable to commit suicide the responsibility for the administration of the *coup de grâce* rested on the senior man present. It is interesting to note that years later no Ethiopians fighting for the United Nations in Korea were taken prisoner. A delegation of two men from the Black Lions committee and twenty-five soldiers called on the Ethiopian Viceroy and on Abune (bishop) Mikael of Goré who blessed their enterprise. Imru sent his daughter to Khartoum and took over command of these Patriots. In his book, Tedessa Metcha describes how 'their spirits soared at the news' for no one had forgotten how the *ras* had fought on the northern front and how 'ignoring the exhaustion of his soldiers he was always fresh'.

At first the new combined group was an efficient and manageable force. Tedessa says the soldiers which Ras Imru brought with him were experienced and brave even if they had no modern training. They were equipped with captured Italian rifles and machine-guns and a few high powered Belgian rifles. Imru, he says, depended willingly on his under commanders who included two *kegnazmatch* and a *balambaras*. Their first plan was to move to Ambo and thence to attempt the liberation of Addis Ababa, but on reaching the province of Wellegga the Patriots found that many local villagers and their governor, a *dejazmatch*, were opposed to the force crossing their country. Ras Imru sent a major to explain his purposes to them before pushing on himself. Meantime his advance guard ran into an Italian ambush at Abo. Three officers were killed before the Patriots, using fixed bayonets and knives, were able to clear a route ahead. Imru gave the funeral oration himself, saying the gallant dead continued with them in spirit, and morale remained high as is evident from the story of a Major Belehu, who returned from guilty exile in the Sudan to join the group. He remarked 'I will die one day, happy or not. I was not happy taking pleasures in Khartoum so have returned to be happy and to die in my own country! Even if I die and the birds eat my flesh—are they not Ethiopian birds and does not my body even so return to Ethiopian soil?'

THE PROBLEM OF REFUGEES

As they had progressed other villagers including women and

children had trailed along with them in increasing and hampering numbers. Ras Imru was also concerned at growing evidence of the build-up of Italian forces and according to Tedessa was angered when he was told that Dejazmatch Habté Mariam of Wellegga had opened his capital of Lekkemt to the Italians. It is, however, stated in Lekkemt that it was not Habté Mariam himself but other Wellegga *balabats* who were responsible for this. Their aim was to overthrow Habté Mariam and they were encouraged by the Italians. Despite his knowledge that Imru did not like him, Habté Mariam is said to have tried to join the Viceroy. Be that as it may, Ras Imru ordered camp to be struck, so that a check of men and equipment could be made and he called the committee together. Future plans were discussed and it was decided by a majority to abandon the march on Ambo and Addis Ababa and proceed instead towards Kaffa. It was hoped to join up with other forces under Betwoded Woldé Tsadik, Negadras Woldé Semait and the *kantiba* (mayor) of Jimma.

One important Wellegga leader who was prevented by Italian troop concentrations from joining up with Ras Imru was Blatta Deressa, a former follower of Eyasu. He eventually made his way to the Sudan. There was a meeting at which the several Patriot leaders who, like Blatta Takelé, had managed to join the Viceroy, all conferred on a plan. Takelé once again urged guerrilla tactics and suggested that the Viceroy reduce his army, which with followers had come to number nearly 30,000, to 3,000 men. He was opposed by Dejazmatch Tayé Gullilat, who as a direct descendant of King Sahlé Sellassié was a very influential figure.* Ras Imru, however, decided not to reduce his forces and the somewhat head-strong Takelé predicted his death or capture within fifteen days. He then invited the *ras*'s officers to join his forces and, when they nearly all refused, he blew his trumpet and left with his own guerrilla band.

The progress of Ras Imru's Black Lions was marked by engagement after engagement with Italian forces and his company swelled to almost unmanageable proportions through the addition of the wives and children of Amhara officials and retired soldiers long settled in the Jimma region. They had been obliged to flee

---

* Dejazmatch Tayé, directly descended by a male line from King Sahlé Sellassié, and a cousin of Leul-Ras Kassa, was a leading pretender in the royal house of Shewa. Probably partly because of this, but also because he protected slave-traders while a governor in the southern provinces, he was not in favour with Hailé Sellassié—and nor has he been since the Restoration. He lived, in 1964, in a large richly furnished house surrounded by pastures and cattle on the Asmara road, near Addis Ababa.

from Jimma because the sultan, encouraged by the Italians had
put a price on 'Amhara' heads. In his use of this term, the sultan
meant 'Christian'. Ras Imru planned several successful sorties but
in retrospect Tedessa is nevertheless constrained to imply some
over-confidence and a failure on the part of the committee to
appreciate the full significance of the mounting number of contacts
with Italian forces. In a section entitled 'How we fell into the
hands of the enemy' in which he describes their march from Gojib
to Bonga, he quotes the proverb, 'If the poor did not eat butter in
their dreams they would notice skin irritation'. When the irrita-
tions were appreciated it was too late.

THE CAPTURE OF RAS IMRU

Some thirteen days after the departure of Blatta Takelé, one evening in December 1936, guards were detailed as usual for the night.
But nearly all the sentries and patrolling scouts silently disappeared
without trace almost as soon as they left the main camp. When the
sun rose Italian troop movements were apparent on all sides and
some were obviously preparing to attack. Surrounded, his soldiers
desperately hungry and weary from fatigue, the Viceroy again
called the committee to assemble near his tent. The meeting was
interrupted by the arrival of a Galla *kegnazmatch* from Jimma. He
was not a follower of Ras Imru and probably sought to secure his
own safety in all eventualities by acting as negotiator. He was
accompanied by two Italian officers bemedalled and resplendent
with golden epaulets. They saluted and invited Ras Imru to negotiate. Imru sent three of his officers with them to speak to the
Italian commandant but they could make little progress, for the
latter merely demanded unconditional Ethiopian surrender. Imru
then stated that civilians must be evacuated from the fighting zone
before he would discuss any terms. The Italians agreed and the
Ethiopian women, children and aged were fed through the lines
into Italian custody. Unlike some of the feudal lords the peasants
had no doubt with whom their loyalty lay and many were loth to
leave. After their departure even Imru was amazed at the apparent
meagreness of his fighting force, but he still hesitated to agree to
surrender. The Italians then threatened to use mortars, bombs and
poison gas and added, 'We are not fools! Did you think you could
go on after handing your burden over to us! We shall be brutal
and kill the civilian hostages if you do not surrender!'

It is reported that the Viceroy's first reaction to this was to
state blandly, 'That would be their wedding day!'—a typical
affirmation of his belief in the willingness of all Ethiopians to die

for their leader and their independence. But he turned to the committee. 'We have come a long way together—what are we to do now?' he asked, and stressed the bad effect capitulation would have on the morale of Patriot forces elsewhere in Ethiopia. When some Holeta-trained officers, fully realising the hopelessness of the military situation and fearful for his safety, urged surrender, Imru could only say, 'I will think about it'. The Italian commander sent a message, 'Hurry up!' and then, 'I have received a telegraphed order from Graziani to destroy the hostages and gas your camp unless you offer surrender within a few hours.'

Imru again addressed the committee. 'What of our loyal Eritreans?' he asked, for he knew well the treatment the Italians meted out to soldiers from their colony who preferred to fight for Ethiopia, 'What will happen to them? As for me, I can surrender, but give them rifles.' Everyone was called together and under cover of an apparent disarming parade the Eritreans were given the best equipment and ordered to attempt to burst or filter out of the encirclement and make their way to the south. In fact they succeeded to a man and joined the forces of Dejazmatch Woldé Mariam in Gemu Gofa and fought alongside the Patriots there up until the time when that group was obliged to leave the southerly provinces of Ethiopia and seek refuge in Kenya.

Ras Imru ordered all remaining weapons to be destroyed or dumped in streams and after discarding a pistol that Hailé Sellassié had sent him, he mounted a mule, unarmed, and led his brave remnant towards the Italian lines.

Behind him there rode one of his commanders, Kegnazmatch Dejené who purposely wore the uniform of a senior Italian officer. Tedessa comments on the impression aroused by the sight of its gorgeous decoration, 'To us it was nothing, but to them it came as a shock'. 'Where did you get this?' the *kegnazmatch* was asked. 'In battle' he replied. Again a question, 'How?' 'I captured it while fighting for my master, Ras Imru,' was the reply. 'Where is the owner?' the *kegnazmatch* was asked, rather tactlessly. His proud retorts eventually cost him his life. 'If I captured him do you think he could be alive? I killed him of course!' he said. The prisoners were led into a stockade and the *kegnazmatch* was manacled and closely guarded. Greatly amused he teased his warders. 'We were unarmed and you took us as women might. Now you guard us like lions with machine-guns. Will you look after me thus for the rest of my days? I am then your king!'

The capture of the Viceroy was proclaimed throughout Ethiopia. His followers were told, 'The great Italian government graciously pardons you and will repatriate you to your provinces', but the *ras* they took to Italy as they did many other feudal leaders and their families. Yilma Deressa was one among their number. There the Italians screened them and those who were thought more likely to collaborate were returned first. Some of these have nevertheless attained high positions since the war, a matter of rather bitter comment and grist for family rivalries. Ras Imru was not allowed to return. The Italians found him impossible to screen and in Ethiopia a legend has grown up that for years he refused even to speak to them. This was not quite so—for example, one relative of the Duke of Aosta was quite intimate with him—but he certainly did not co-operate with Italian officialdom and in view of the post-war growth of a myth around Ras Imru's character such stories are not without interest.

Blatta Takelé's guerrilla band was later also surrounded and after three weeks his force, depleted by desertions, numbered only 130. The battle turned, however, when one Patriot arrived at Takelé's field headquarters with the head of the Italian commander, a colonel who was posthumously made a brigadier-general. Takelé retired to Jimma and stayed there for a brief period, during which he was at first mistaken for their absent Emperor by the people, and then he left for the hills and made plans to contact the other resistance leaders.

THE COLLABORATORS

Leul-Ras Kassa Hailu had accompanied Hailé Sellassié into exile and thus only a few of the leading traditional figures remained. One was the heir of the royal line of Negus Taklé Haymanot of Gojjam, Leul-Ras Hailu who had long since been deposed from the governorship of that province and detained. Hailé Sellassié had released him before he had left and had tried to take him into exile with him, but the wily Hailu had slipped away. His apparent aim during the Italian occupation, as before, was to become *negus* (king) of Gojjam. It is not impossible that he also dreamed of the Imperial throne itself, likening himself perhaps to Dejazmatch Kassa of Tigré who had profited from an earlier *'ferenge'* invasion and the subsequent fall of Tewodros, and had become the Emperor Yohannes. But it could be an oversimplification to call Leul-Ras Hailu a traitor, as Ethiopians often do, for he may well not have accepted the premises on which the judgement is based i.e., that Ethiopia was a nation state and that as such it demanded his first loyalty. Certainly he held no brief for colonialism. Some twelve years before he had remarked to an English woman 'You have done a great deal for Egypt, but you have not taught her to do anything for herself. It is not good for a country to be milk-fed by strangers!'[7] Leul-Ras Hailu's actions were dictated by what he thought to be the best interests of his own dynasty and these he would probably have identified with the best interests of Gojjam. Some lesser parallel to his ambition existed in the nature of Leul-Ras Seyoum of Tigré, grandson of the Emperor Yohannes, who also accepted Italian rule in order to retain his fief and who was accorded second place to Hailu in the Italian hierarchy. Dejazmatch Hailé Sellassié Gugsa who had sought to displace him by going over to the Italians early in the war came only third. Dejazmatch Habté Mariam, descendant of Kumsa, King of Wellegga, never finally decided where his best interests lay but early on he appeared to have thrown in his lot with Italy. These three understood, even if they did not belong to, an era in which nationalism had overtaken feudalism. Ras Getachew, after a disagreement with Hailé Sellassié in Jerusalem, also returned and collaborated with the Italians and another, later to be tried for treason, was the great Amharic writer Professor Afeworq, who died in exile in 1964.

ECONOMIC DEVELOPMENT

After the capture of Ras Imru, the Italians occupied Gambela and declared 'all Ethiopia' to be under their control. This was an extravagant claim, for their rule as often as not was confined to their forts, to the towns, and, in daylight, to the periphery of the great new roads which their engineers and huge bands of forced Ethiopian labour were hastily constructing. The Italians appropriated Ethiopia's gold reserves and production but even so there is no parallel in the history of colonial Africa for the amount of money spent on capital development by a colonising power. The new all-weather roads with their tunnels, bridges and escarpment buttresses were especial marvels of innovation and engineering, but hospitals, schools, municipal buildings, etc. (all for Italians) were also constructed. Works commenced before the war as propaganda projects such as the Hailé Sellassié I hospital which according to one writer had always excluded Ethiopians,[8] were improved and many Italian structures remain in use today. On the side of the roads there still stand monuments to those Italians who lost their lives during their construction.*

---

* Of course, all this economic development is no justification of Italian rule. The African's indictment of colonialism is essentially human rather than economic (though it is sometimes both)—and, for example, the apology written for British readers, a book by F. Quaranta, *Ethiopia—an Empire in the Making*, London, 1939, contains all the offensive patronage

REPRISALS

Amongst Italy's unwilling subjects 'lawlessness' continually increased and the desperate Graziani felt driven to extremes of appalling violence. One of the most daring of all operations in the Patriot struggle was an attack, by the Shewan Patriots, on Addis Ababa itself. Dejazmatch Aberra Kassa entered the city from the north, and from the south-west there came the forces of the Adowa hero, the cruel eunuch Dejazmatch Balcha, Grazmatch Zaudi Asfaw and the great leader, Dejazmatch Fikré Mariam. At one stage in the assault, some of Fikré Mariam's officers, disturbed by the build-up of Italian forces, once the element of surprise had passed, urged their leader to retire perhaps to renew the attack on the morrow. Fikré Mariam retorted, 'That is how we lost at Maichew! Come! This night is our wedding night!' and with these words, personally led a lightning sortie which nearly succeeded in seizing the great palace in the very heart of the city.

Towards the end of 1936, Menelik's aged general Dejazmatch Balcha took sick and was cornered near Jimma. He demanded that senior Italian officers come to accept the surrender of such as he. A captain dutifully fetched a chaplain-major—who had previously been a missionary and who therefore spoke Amharic —and only then did the eunuch *dejazmatch* suddenly produce his Belgian carbine from beneath his cloak. Many died before they shot the old tyrant laughing from his bier.

A son of Leul-Ras Kassa who had been governor of Gondar had chosen to die at the fall of that city but his two brothers fought on in Shewa. Eventually, however, they gave themselves up when the Italians threatened to exterminate the whole population of their Salalé fief if they would not accept an offer of safe conduct. Leul-Ras Hailu was the go-between, but the pledge he gave the two young nobles was not honoured and they were executed and their bodies displayed at Fiché. On hearing of the murders, the infuriated peasants from the untamed Kassa fief of Marabeté marched to Salalé to kill all those who rejoiced in the betrayal and death of Leul-Ras Kassa's sons. The death of the Patriot brothers did not prove the awful deterrent which the Italians had intended. Rather, their selfless courage served as an immediate example to other Patriots, their names became a legend and they were written about as soon as that was possible.[9] Leul-Ras Kassa and his youngest son lived in exile in Britain and the powerful Kassa family survived

---

and justification of discrimination which typify the official publications of the southern parts of Africa in the 1950s and '60s.

these tragedies and remained an important factor in Ethiopian court politics in the post-war decades.*

Ras Desta Damtew, Hailé Sellassié's son-in-law, had also stayed on when Hailé Sellassié had sent a plane from Addis Ababa before the fall of the capital, though the *ras*'s family had left on it for Addis Ababa and had afterwards journeyed to England. He had at first tried to raise a rebellion in Guragé, but he was not popular there and the people would not listen to him. At this time Ras Desta derived much resolution and strength from his friendship with Tademe Zelleka a great Patriot hailing from Menz. The two had then gone to Sidamo and Tademe eventually went on to Kenya. The situation in Sidamo meantime became critical. Ras Desta Damtew's forces ran short of ammunition and he was obliged to venture from the comparative safety of the Sidamo hills and the main body of his forces, and move towards the river Awash. There he was captured. Despite wounds he was tied to a tree by the Italian soldiery, and shot. Earlier, Graziani had dropped leaflets offering Dejazmatch Gabré Mariam the province of Sidamo (from which Hailé Sellassié had once displaced him in order to promote his son-in-law Ras Desta) if he would abandon that *ras*. But Gabré Mariam was a Patriot and had haughtily replied that in any case he already ruled the area. However, in one of a series of engagements in the vicinity of the Rift valley lakes, both Dejazmatch Gabré Mariam and Dejazmatch Beyenna Merid (who had married Romanaworq, a daughter of Hailé Sellassié by the latter's first marriage) were ambushed and killed. Fitwrary Shimelis, another leader, also lost his life in these battles, but the Italian forces suffered considerable losses. An additional hazard for them was that

---

* The Kassa family, or at least some of its members—consider with some justice that they have good claim to the throne. They can point out that the late Leul-Ras Kassa stood down in favour of Tafari Makonnen when the legitimate monarch, Eyasu, was displaced. Leul-Dejazmatch Asrate Kassa became the most powerful and conservative member of their house. Asrate, younger brother of the three Patriots, was taken to England during the Occupation. He succeeded Ras-Betwoded Makonnen Endalkatchew as President of the Senate in 1961 but in early 1964 was sent to govern Eritrea. The eldest son of the eldest son, Fitwrary Messai Wondwossen, recently governor of Lasta for a short period, had been taken as a child with his mother to Italy. Perhaps the most progressive, he is quiet and unassuming. Others of this family are the ambitious and conservative Dejazmatch Amaha Aberra who sometimes uses the Amharic plural (the royal 'we') in conversation; Amaha has held several important governorships and ambassadorial posts and his younger brother Fitwrary Amdé Aberra, the soldier governor of Salalé and Marabeté. There exists an extensive network of relatives but these are not all necessarily on good terms with the leading figures in the family.

their wounded were normally enshipped at Djibouti which involved a train journey down the line from Addis Ababa which was a favourite target for Patriot attacks. The Ethiopians, often on the advice of their priests who were angered by the growing influence of the Roman Catholic Church, ignored warning notices posted by the colonial government referring to the death of these Patriot leaders as 'the justice of God'.

THE GRAZIANI MASSACRE

As Italian Viceroy, Marshal Graziani's telegrams show that he recognised that many of the Ethiopian leaders were quite prepared to face death rather than submit and that they would all have to be killed if the country was ever to be effectively 'pacified'. However, in February 1937 he made a strange and almost fatal miscalculation of the pride of the Ethiopian people. He announced that he would distribute gifts to the poor after the manner of the Emperors, outside the palace. Grazmatch Letibellu Gebré, who was later killed in the 1960 Revolution, provided grenades and two young men, Abraha Deboch and Mogas Asgadom, hurled them at the Italian Viceroy. He and others were wounded and the Italian troops present opened fire on the crowd. The aged and lame who came for alms as well as state dignitaries were killed. Then the Blackshirts were let loose in the city and for three days a reign of terror ensued, not only in Addis Ababa but in other towns also. Very many thousands died and homes and buildings were fired. The windows of St George's Catheral, built in the reign of Menelik II, were smashed and the interior decorations were destroyed.

Ethiopia has not yet recovered from this cruel blow. Two to three hundred educated young Ethiopians, mainly those captured with the Viceroy, Ras Imru, perished with the thousands of ordinary folk who were murdered. Today amongst the educated there is to some extent a missing generation. Had they lived these men might well have communicated between those now under thirty-five or so and the proud and powerful older ruling generation which so much misunderstands them. Thus might have been averted even the revolutionary situation of the 1950s and '60s—although it is an open question whether communication alone would have changed the attitudes of the large-scale land-owners.

THE ETHIOPIAN CHRISTIAN CHURCH

Another sufferer was the Ethiopian Christian Church. The murder of Abune (bishop) Petros was followed by that of Abune Mikael who was also accused of encouraging the Patriots. Many priests and deacons died for their country and their faith. The Egyptian Archbishop, however, collaborated to some extent. He was wounded in the attempt on the Viceroy's life and since the Italians wished to separate the Ethiopian Christian Church from the see of Alexandria, they afterwards took him to Italy. Nevertheless, he would never consent to the changes in the status of the Church that were suggested to him and retired to Egypt. Back in Ethiopia the Italians encouraged the Muslim faith and raided several Christian monasteries including that on Mount Zikwala, but the worst atrocity took place farther from the capital. The Italian forces discovered guns at the ancient Shewan monastery of Debra Libanos and 350 monks were killed. Their bodies were thrown over the edge of the near-by gorge. At the end of 1937 Abune Abraham was declared by the Italians to be the new Archbishop of the Ethiopian Christian Church. This was achieved by playing on the Church's own desire (since achieved) to be independent. Abune Abraham, a very feeble and old man blinded by poison gas, was one of the only two surviving bishops in Ethiopia. The other was Abune Isaac whom the Italians had been obliged to keep in prison for some time before he would agree to collaborate. Before he died in 1939 Abune Abraham was led to consecrate twelve bishops. The Holy Synod promptly met in Egypt and under the presidency of the Alexandrian Patriarch Yohannes XIV, Abraham and all those consecrated, or to be consecrated, by him were solemnly excommunicated. Nor was he supported by all the Ethiopian Church for he endeavoured to excommunicate the Patriot fighters. The clergy of Gojjam would not even attend his local synods and the Italians burnt many churches in that unruly province. Meanwhile the Ark of the Covenant was smuggled out from Addis Ababa's St George's Cathedral to Balambaras Abebe Aragai, Patriot leader of eastern Shewa, for safekeeping and for the encouragement of his men. Church treasures were stored in ancient excavated caves near Debra Berhan.

There were many Italian punitive expeditions to the Ankober area and large tracts of land were depopulated. The house where Abebe usually slept may still be seen on a ridge in that precipitous region and old men yet speak of those times when they and their friends fought on uncowed. As far back as September 1896, an observer wrote that the Italians even then doubted whether this and other areas could be permanently colonised because that would mean that 'they would have to maintain perpetual warfare in the Shewan mountains for the inhabitants of this district being a warlike race would never submit'.[10]

Balambaras Abebe had begun to style himself *ras*—a title later confirmed by Hailé Sellassié after the Restoration. At this time, however, it had been granted by Leul Tsahai Eyasu, a son of the deposed Emperor Eyasu, who doubtless hoped that Abebe might later help him to secure the throne, for he claimed to be the legitimate Emperor. However, he died of fever during the Patriot campaigns before his plans could be brought to fruition.

INCIDENT IN ROME

Patriot resistance to the Italians further increased after the Graziani massacres and the unbroken spirit of the Ethiopian peoples was evident even in Italy itself where in 1937 an imperial ceremony was held to commemorate the first anniversary of the occupation of Addis Ababa. An Eritrean youth aged twenty-one named Zerai Deress was sent to Rome to present some captured Ethiopian trophies, including a sword, to certain high officials at a function attended by both Mussolini and the King of Italy. Zerai did not know that he would have to present these in a public place where he could become an object of ridicule. In the middle of the parade his eyes lighted on the captured gold Lion of Judah which the Italians had removed from its stand near the Addis Ababa railway station. Identifying himself with Ethiopia's shame he knelt to pray. Two policemen tried to move him, but he turned furiously upon them, drew the ceremonial sword and killed five fascist officials before he in his turn was brought down by gunfire. Seriously wounded he was taken to hospital and some years later he died in an Italian island prison.[11] A statue and an Amharic booklet published after the war commemorate his patriotism. The first vessel of the new Imperial Ethiopian navy was called after him.

THE COMMITTEE OF UNION

Back in Ethiopia a secret meeting of the Patriot leaders was arranged to take place in Shewa province. Some of the arrangements for the meeting were made by a young major who had fought in the attack on Addis Ababa, a certain Mesfin Sileshi. This man was later to become an enormously rich deputy governor general of Shewa, a *ras* and a nominal lieutenant-general.

An Amharic account of the meetings and plans to co-ordinate the Patriot resistance—through the creation of a Committee of Union and Collaboration—was written from his own diaries by a second major. It was published years later but unfortunately by that time some of the chief participants—notably

Blatta Takelé—were in disfavour, and the account accordingly suffered in passing through the hands of the Ministry of the Pen.

Dejazmatch Fikré Mariam, Abebe Aragai, Blatta Takelé, and others met near Ambo. No sooner had the unpacking of the mules begun than Leul-Ras Hailu and a force of Eritrean troops commanded by Italian officers appeared on the scene. However, they retired after a short battle, and the meeting was resumed. 'Ras' Abebe's wife was pregnant and Dejazmatch Aberra Kassa's wife was nursing a very small child. Blatta Takelé told them the rumour circulating among the soldiers that he was a magician was correct. Doubtless he did this to give them courage, but one is led to wonder whether he sometimes believed it himself, for certainly he used witchcraft as well as the usual intrigue in his post-war feud against Woldé Giorgis Woldé Yohannes, who had by then become an all-powerful Minister of the Pen.

An aged *dejazmatch* of the Emperor Menelik took the chair and appointments were made. Abebe Aragai became chief of staff. Grazmatch Zaudi Asfaw, a great-grandson of the Negus Sahlé Sellassié and a cousin of Leul-Ras Kassa, together with Esayas, an Eritrean, later to become a lieutenant-general, were put in charge of Galla affairs and Blatta Takelé became political secretary. He put himself forward with the words, 'For this job you cannot find a better man than myself.' It was agreed that Takelé should go with one major to Wellegga, thence to Gojjam and Begemidir and finally to Khartoum to consolidate resistance efforts. Abebe Aragai glanced at those who should remain. Talking in a group were Grazmatch Zaudi, Mesfin Sileshi and Dejazmatch Hailé Mariam Mammo. 'How am I going to control these savages?' Abebe was heard to mutter.

It might be noted that in the background at this meeting were two young men of respected families—Lij Merid Mangasha and Lij Abiye Abebe, later to become generals and to oppose the 1960 Revolution and secure the return of Hailé Sellassié. Dejazmatch Hailé Mariam was the father of Captain Dereji, the Emperor's grandson-in-law, who was killed entering the rebel-held Prince's Paradise Palace in that same revolution. Both father and son were brave and reckless men and the manner of Dereji's death recalled to many the abandon with which his Patriot father gave his life against the Italians—for such was the latter's fame that a play was later written about him.[12]

UNREST THROUGHOUT THE EMPIRE

By November 1937 the Italian policy of repression was recognised as a failure. Marshal Graziani, already a broken man, was replaced by the six-foot-eight royal Duke of Aosta. Concentration camps such as that at Denané were closed, and there began a period of economic development, the settlement of Italian peasant families and a general policy of appeasement and ingratiation. But this failed to win over the Patriots to a belief in the benefits or necessary permanency of colonialism, and the fighting continued.

There was continuous rebellion in Gojjam, led by Dejazmatch Negash Bezebé, Dejazmatch Mangasha Jambari (both formerly of the new provincial civil service) and by Lij Belai Zelleka, perhaps the most daring Patriot of them all.

Belai once rebuked his followers who had begun to call him *ras.* 'The name my mother gave me was Belai—it is enough,' he said. The joke is not obvious in translation, but 'Belai' means 'above all'.

In Begemidir and Tigré, Ras Wubeneh Tesemma, Dejazmatch Asfa Wogara, Fitwrary Mesfin Redda, the brothers Lij Desta and Lij Yohannes Maru and Dejazmatch Hailu Wondé fought on.

In the Tembien, Dejazmatch Hailu Kebede led the Patriots. He was the son of Wagshum Kebede, the son of the *wagshum* of the time of Emperor Yohannes. That old man frequently chuckled over his son's scorn of the enemy whom he never managed to identify clearly in his mind, for he was almost in his dotage. 'Tell the dervishes he does not joke', he instructed those about him when news of his son's threats against the Italians was brought to him. Fitwrary Hailu Kibret, the son of Dejazmatch Kibret, a close friend of Dejazmatch Hailu, became the latter's first lieutenant as soon as he had recovered from the wounds he had received at Maichew. This young man, also travelled to Khartoum with messages from the Patriots, more than once. But eventually, Dejazmatch Hailu was killed. His head was mounted on a stake and the Italians brought his body to his aged father. 'He thought he could fight the great Italians', they jibed. The old man paused before asking defiantly, 'And how many of you Turks did he kill?' The honest reply, Fitwrary Hailu recalled, was more than a thousand. The *fitwrary* soon became more prominent. By nature he was something of a fanatic and remained so all his life. He carried the absent Emperor's photograph wrapped in the green-yellow-red tricolour flag of Ethiopia and made soldiers kneel before it.* However, such loyalty was by no means universal. One Patriot leader jibed at him, 'Youth is a wonderful thing, is it not, *fitwrary*? One

---

* The Ethiopian flag is green-yellow-red. The Ethiopian colours are green-gold-red.

is able to believe anything!' About this time the young Crown Prince caused a new revolver to be sent to the *fitwrary* from Jerusalem. In 1962, Fitwrary Hailu Kibret and his nephew were hanged for intrigue in the year following the abortive *coup d'état*.

Dejazmatch Gabré Hiwot led a revolt in north-eastern Tigré. Down in Harar, Fitwrary Million surrendered and several other leaders including Fitwrary Baidé, who later died in Jerusalem, were forced to withdraw into British Somaliland, but to the east in Arusi Dejazmatch Abaye and Kegnazmatch Selebe Aga fought on. In Sidamo and Borana the mantle of Ras Desta fell on the three *kegnazmatch*, Bayenna, Goudeta and Bekelé.

In Shewa, Dejazmatch Fikré Mariam and Gimma Sembeté were killed but 'ras' Abebe maintained his independence in the region near the ancient centre of Ankober. Strangely, the body of Dejazmatch Fikré Mariam was never found so it is not impossible that this great Patriot, knowing himself to be dying and keen not to damage the morale of his followers, buried himself or crawled away to a cave. At all events his spirit lived on and his name became a myth.

The vacillating Dejazmatch Habté Mariam of Wellegga was murdered by the Italians but resistance even there continued. In the predominantly Galla lands in the south there was a very formidable leader in the person of the giant Fitwrary Geressu Duké, whose followers dubbed him 'ras'. One writer states that he kept a written record of some of his exploits but on one occasion he had to bury it and the author has been unable to discover whether or not it existed and survives.[13] Geressu's fortunes fluctuated. Once in a battle on the volcanic Mount Zikwala to the south of the capital, famous for subsequent engagements, he was wounded and surrounded but managed to shoot his way out. Leaving his would-be captors firing at each other, he made his way south to Soddu. The Italian propaganda said 'Geressu who was like a lion, has now become a hare, so you must chase and catch him'. But it was not long before the countrymen were whispering 'Geressu has become a lion again' for the Galla flocked to him and he quickly remarshalled his forces. Even after British entry into the war, he never obtained the assistance of parachuted Commonwealth officers as did many of his fellows farther north—nor did he need them. During the liberation campaigns he combined with foreign columns most effectively in the mopping-up operations on the Omo river.

Fitwrary Hailé Abamersa from Arusi died fighting in Gemu Gofa in the far south and other leaders in those parts included Dejazmatch Woldé Mariam, Fitwrary Tademe Zelleka and Zaudi

Ayelu, many of whose followers eventually journeyed to Kenya as refugees.

Among the Ethiopian Patriot leaders were numbered several women such as Woizero Balainesh in Arusi, Woizero Ayalech, Woizero Likelesh Beyan, Woizero Abedech Cherkose and Woizero Kebedech, Leul-Ras Seyoum's daughter (whose husband Dejazmatch Aberra Kassa had been murdered with his brother in breach of their safe conduct), but perhaps the greatest was Woizero Shoaregad Gedlé. She joined the Patriots after having given most of her money to the Red Cross at the time of the invasion but was taken prisoner and sent to a Mediterranean prison island after the attempt on Graziani's life. Returning two years later she narrowly escaped death in reprisals for the killing of an Italian officer in Addis Alem. She rejoined the Patriots but was captured. Her adopted son was murdered before her eyes and she was tied to a tree and publicly flogged. However, she recovered, escaped and fought on to the end of the Occupation in the Debra Berhan region of central Shewa but died later, some say, in quite mysterious circumstances in 1946.

Prices were put on the heads of several Patriot leaders and one who continued to be much sought after by the Italians was Blatta Takelé. On one occasion he was trapped in the basement of a building and seventeen of his guerrillas were killed before he and his son-in-law managed through a ruse to escape. His Patriot wife died from bullet wounds after another action and he himself moved to Gojjam, thus avoiding a clash of personalities with his former subordinate in the Addis Ababa municipality, Abebe Aragai.

Takelé went to visit Khartoum, where there was much talk amongst the Ethiopian exiles of setting up a republican government. Letters were actually written to this effect by an Ethiopian personality, who became prominent in the 1960s, to the French authorities, that country being a republic, requesting assistance and guidance in the matter. The letters were also secretly copied and sent by Major Mesfin Sileshi to Hailé Sellassié, in his exile in Bath, England. It was quite natural for Ethiopian leaders at that time to look to France for inspiration and friendship. Many of the more Ethiopian people, who never admitted defeat, were to see even collapse of her armies and those of the British Expeditionary Force before the German onslaught. Several Ethiopian officers had been trained in France and they had considered her the world's premier military power. However, stimulated by these events Italy began to consider entering the European war on the side of Germany and the Patriot leaders at once took heart. They had been disappointed that Italy had kept out of the war for so many months after it had spread to western Europe in 1939.

Similarly in London, Italy's moves were a signal for far greater activity on the part of the Ethiopian colony there and their families all of whom had remained staunchly monarchist. Hailé Sellassié became more than just one of the growing number of London's exiled monarchs. He had patiently waited for an opportunity such as this, as had several exiles in Jerusalem where affairs were looked after by Dejazmatch Makonnen Endalkatchew. Hailé Sellassié soon became a political factor of world importance and before long plans for his return to Ethiopia were being discussed. In London that great warrior and propagandist Miss Sylvia Pankhurst had long edited the *New Times* and the *Ethiopian News* —which also ran to some Amharic editions for circulation in Italian-occupied Ethiopia. Nor had she allowed the British public to forget the plight of the Ethiopians, and British government recognition of the Italian occupation was soon to be withdrawn. However, some groups of Ethiopians elsewhere made approaches to the British authorities to try to prevent the return of the Emperor.

These negotiations were going on when Blatta Takelé left Khartoum, ostensibly to visit a cotton plantation, but actually in order to slip back over the border into the Ethiopian hills. Once there he was met by the elder brother of Fitwrary Hailu Kibret, and was taken to Gondar. He had to settle a dispute between certain leaders, and to dissuade others from proclaiming Lij Yohannes, a son of the dead Emperor Eyasu, as their leader. In 1963 Lij Yohannes lived in exile in Jimma as did Betwoded Negash (previously *dejazmatch*), a great Gojjam Patriot leader. At a meeting of Patriot commanders a document was prepared for the League of Nations and others 'whom it might concern', setting out the wishes of some 900 Patriot leaders, touching on the form which future government of their country might take.

News of this also reached Hailé Sellassié and a secret communication, signed by the secretary Woldé Giorgis and purporting to have been written on the Emperor's instructions, was soon afterwards received by Dejazmatch Wobneh, whom Ethiopians nickname 'Amoraw' ('the Eagle'). The new trend, read the missive, was contrary to the traditions and wishes of the Ethiopian masses. Should a man seek the throne, it suggested, if it were the will of God that he succeed, the Emperor would not mind for that would be in conformity with the long-standing traditions of the country; but republicanism was an alien concept, one that would endanger Ethiopian advance to freedom (independence).

The letter also contained secret instructions, but when the *dejazmatch* tried to put them into effect they resulted in dissension and fighting amongst the Patriots. The home of Hagos, the 'Eagle's' brother, was burnt. Blatta Takelé restored some semblance of unity by confining the operations of some leaders to certain geographical limits and by pointing out that only the Italians rejoiced at internal divisions amongst the Patriots themselves.

AN ALLY AT LAST

Meanwhile, far away at the headquarters of the League of Nations, Ethiopia had not been quite forgotten. Hailé Sellassié's representative had protested when sanctions against Italy had been lifted and had taken every opportunity of publicising his country's plight. He produced details of Italian oppression, the obstinate resistance of the Patriots and indeed any communication from Ethiopia, always providing it gave evidence of continued support for his master.

However, that international body was to all intents and purposes already dead and in the summer of 1939 the representative Lorenzo Taezaz had made a different and much more significant contribution to his country's struggle. Assisted by the British government in the Sudan and in the company of a French officer, he had secretly crossed the Ethiopian border and travelled as inconspicuously as possible throughout the province of Gojjam, which at that time was in a state of fairly typical turmoil and revolt. On his return he was able to describe the 'Committee of Union and Collaboration', the Patriot leaders and the extent of their support, the underground newspaper, the poor morale of the Italians, etc. His report was of inestimable value for soon afterwards Italy declared war on Britain and the Patriots gained a prestigious, if not at the time a very powerful ally. It was not long before supplies, propaganda and even Commonwealth officers on attachment to Patriot forces entered Ethiopia from the Sudan and Kenya. But more important, though not at the time so universally acclaimed, the support of the British people for Ethiopia came to be expressed as the official support of the British government for Hailé Sellassié, the Emperor in exile in Bath.

14

Victory and Restoration

One would think the Emperor would be the best judge of
when to risk his life for his throne.—SIR WINSTON CHURCHILL
in a memo to his Foreign Secretary, December 31, 1940

The asylum afforded us by the British Nation during long
and bitter years, the stand of non-recognition by the United
States of America, China, the Soviet Union and others, the
devoted and selfless efforts of Patriots, foreign as well as
Ethiopian . . . have been of inestimable value to Our cause.
—THE EMPEROR HAILE SELLASSIE on the fifth anniversary
of his 1941 re-entry into Addis Ababa

THE ACHIEVEMENT OF THE PATRIOTS

'The assassination of our officers from April 1939 until today has
become a normal phenomenon . . . in the whole empire rebellion is
latent and will have a tragic end when, in case of war, hostilities
begin. If from any of our frontiers a single British or French unit
marches resolutely into our territory with its flag flying, it will not
need armed men because the greater part of the Abyssinian people
will join it and fight against us'. So wrote General Bonacorsi,
Inspector General of the Blackshirt forces in Italian East Africa a
short time before Italy declared war on Britain and France.[1] Nor did
he overestimate the patriot contribution for the official British War
Office publication on the Abyssinian campaigns states . . . 'when the
Italians needed every man in the firing lines at Keren and Harar
(and when they did indeed transfer the equivalent of seventy-five
battalions to these fronts) the existence or the danger of an Abyssinian rising tied down the equivalent of fifty-six battalions in the

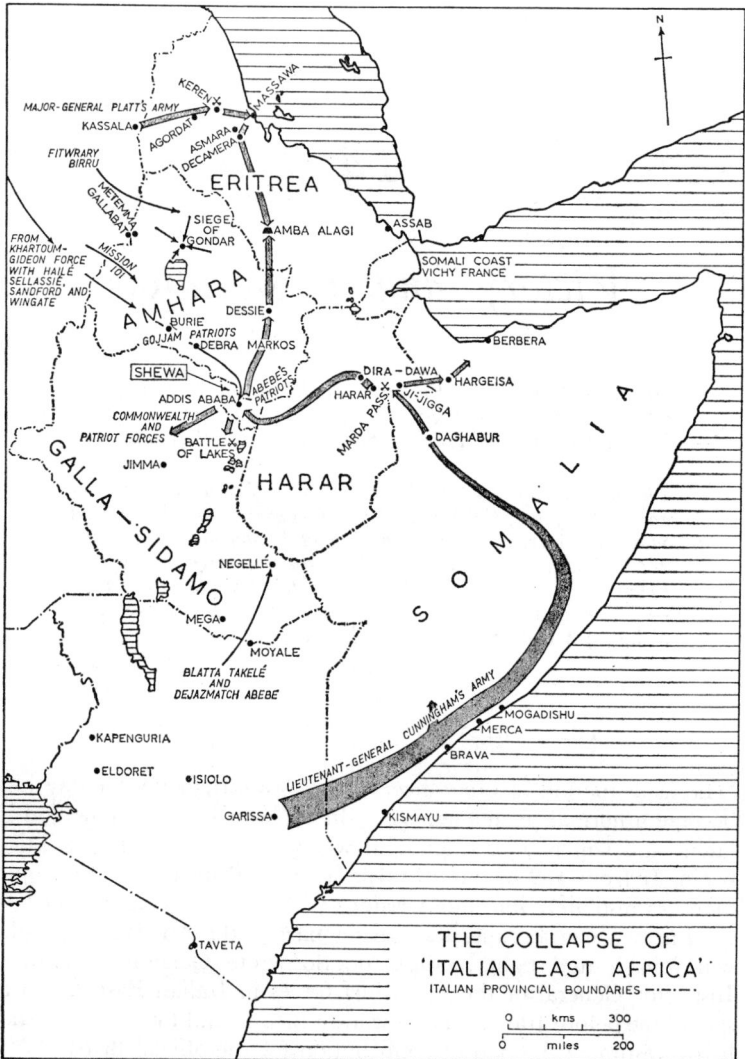

N

MAJOR-GENERAL PLATT'S ARMY
KASSALA●
AGORDAT●
KEREN ✕
MASSAWA

FITWRARY BIRRU

ERITREA

ASMARA
DECAMERA

ASSAB

SOMALI COAST
VICHY FRANCE

METEMMA
GALLABAT

FROM KHARTOUM-
GIDEON FORCE
WITH HAILÉ
SELLASSIE,
SANDFORD AND
WINGATE

SIEGE
OF
GONDAR

AMBA ALAGI

MISSION 101

AMHARA

DESSIE●

BURIE●
GOJJAM *PATRIOTS*
●DEBRA MARKOS

SHEWA

ADDIS ABABA●
ABEBE'S PATRIOTS

DIRA-DAWA
HARAR ✕
DIRE-JIGGA
MARDA PASS ✕

BERBERA

HARGEISA

COMMONWEALTH
AND
PATRIOT FORCES

BATTLE ✕
OF LAKES

DAGHABUR

JIMMA●

HARAR

G A L L A – S I D A M O

S O M A L I A

NEGELLE●

MEGA●

MOYALE●

*BLATTA TAKELÉ
AND
DEJAZMATCH ABEBE*

●KAPENGURIA

●ELDORET
●ISIOLO

LIEUTENANT-GENERAL CUNNINGHAM'S ARMY

MOGADISHU
MERCA

BRAVA

GARISSA●

KISMAYU

●TAVETA

THE COLLAPSE OF
'ITALIAN EAST AFRICA'
ITALIAN PROVINCIAL BOUNDARIES —·—·—

0   kms   300
0   miles   200

Amhara and Walkait areas . . .' and adds also that the Italians could never be certain of the loyalty of their levies.[2] The Italian and colonial troops numbered 170,000. The entire forces from Britain, Nigeria, Ghana (then the Gold Coast), the Sudan, Southern Africa, the Indian sub-continent, Belgium and Free France numbered only 20,000 men. There is no record of the number of Ethiopian 'irregulars' who fought alongside these armies and whose efforts over the years had brought vastly superior Italian forces to the verge of collapse, but they knew what they had done.

Clearly an Emperor who sought to establish absolute control over Patriot leaders and forces who had made and were making such a vital contribution to the liberation of their country would need much more than powerful friends. The skill which Hailé Sellassié displayed in restoring his damaged personal image and in attaining an even stronger control than ever before cannot be overstated. This is especially true since he had defied the national tradition to stand, fight and if necessary die for every inch of Ethiopian soil. There is little doubt that had he done so he would have been captured and then killed or used. It is also very likely that had he not become the living symbol of Ethiopia's outraged independence and of her unity, the ancient empire would at least have been mandated and very probably partitioned after the war. Hailé Sellassié's decision to go into exile may have been hasty but it proved politically correct. Understandably, however, it was not its wisdom which was remarked upon by those Patriot leaders who had fought on and who survived the occupation period and their antagonisms and jealousies were to have considerable repercussions on post-war Ethiopia.

HAILÉ SELLASSIÉ RETURNS TO AFRICA

It was not long after Italy's entry into the war that Hailé Sellassié left England secretly by flying boat. He dined in the Italian club at Malta—all pictures of Mussolini having been hurriedly removed and stored in the lavatory—before proceeding to Egypt and thence eventually to Khartoum. But it was some time before any quantity of arms and supplies could be scraped together, for France was collapsing and Britain, all unprepared, was herself in mortal danger. The delays disappointed and occasionally dispirited Hailé Sellassié, who was ever anxious to re-enter his country—and it must be pointed out that at this time as at the battle of Maichew, he was not lacking in courage. It was more than a nice sense of history, which led him to ask that if there should be a battle over Gallabat on the Sudanese border, he be allowed to be present with some Ethiopian troops. He was conscious of the need to restore his warrior-image and he recalled the victory there of his imperial predecessor, the Emperor Yohannes, which cost that monarch his life. However it was not to be. Gallabat and Kassala together with the whole of British Somaliland on the other frontier away to the east fell to the Italian forces. Ethiopian Patriots who had taken refuge in Somaliland were evacuated by sea to Kenya.

The exiled Emperor broadcast to Ethiopia from the Sudan that relief was at hand and leaflets dropped from the air caused many desertions from the Italian forces. A column led by Major Mesfin Sileshi which journeyed to the Sudan in order to collect supplies for the Patriot forces of Dejazmatch Mangasha Jambari of Gojjam took back news that they had seen the Emperor and the Italian propaganda that he had died in exile was then known to be false.

SANDFORD'S MISSION

In September 1940 Major Sandford entered Ethiopia with a small force to help co-ordinate Patriot and British actions. With him were Ajaz Kebede Tesemma, later a key witness at the trial of Brigadier-general Mengistu, Getahun Tesemma, later to become an ambassador and minister, Gabré Maskal, Lij Merid Mangasha, the Emperor's personal ADC, and others. It was decided that Gojjam rather than Gondar should be the route to be taken by Hailé Sellassié, in part because it was felt more likely that the Patriot leaders there would accept him. Some leaders near Gondar had said openly that the country 'belonged to those who had shed their blood'. However Sandford never wavered in his opinion that the anointed King of the Kings was more likely to prove a unifying factor for the Ethiopian people than another. His wife has written two books which attest to their continued faith in the Emperor whom they supported,[3] and several of their children have settled in the country.

Sandford drew up an agreement between Dejazmatch Mangasha Jambari and Dejazmatch Negash by which these two Gojjam leaders pledged to sink any differences and to regard Hailé Sellassié as their leader and if necessary arbiter. Thus the British sought to co-ordinate all effort against the Italians, but right up until Hailé Sellassié's triumphal re-entry into Addis Ababa a deep pattern of intrigue involved all the various parties and power groups, the Emperor not least. The full story of his struggle has not yet been told and cannot be recounted here, save to remark that it survived as a factor in the pattern of opposition which was to develop in the 1950s against Hailé Sellassié.

FEUDAL GOJJAM

In November, Major Orde Wingate—who was later to become a major-general and achieve great fame before his death in Burma in 1944—flew to join the expedition. Patriot morale rose with the news that the Emperor was soon to enter the province. Italian morale suffered great reverses and in a subtle bid to retain his crumbling control of Gojjam, the Duke of Aosta raised the salaries of his soldiers and played his trump card. He appointed Leul-Ras Hailu Taklé Haymanot, heir to the former ruling house of Gojjam, as governor general and in all likelihood promised him the eventual title of *negus* he so much desired.

The old prince had lived in Addis Ababa, exempt from Italian colour-bar regulations, recognised as the first noble in the land. Some account of him is given in the memoirs of an Italian nobleman who was also a doctor, but who served in the Italian Administration.[4] He tells of the dignified old man who dyed his hair, moustache and goatee beard and who sought rejuvenating medicines because 'his desires outran his performance'. The doctor notes also his dazzling false teeth and the way in which his attitudes changed instantaneously and completely in accordance with his assessment of the status of those about him. Amongst his possessions he counted a number of female attendants, his own confessor and photographs of the King of Italy, of Mussolini and of Miss Marlene Dietrich.

The Prince of Gojjam set about his task in the only way he knew; he played on the family ties and the feudal loyalties of the leaders. He sent out many letters and was supported in like vein by an official proclamation of the Italian government. Many of the Patriots found themselves in two minds, and their dilemma is clearly seen from a letter written by Belai Zelleka, whom several writers at the time adjudged the most able military commander amongst the Gojjam Patriots. He wrote to his prince respectfully hoping that 'the Saviour of the World' would grant His Highness health and only then voiced his disapproval :

> Your Highness! Gojjam has been destroyed chiefly by those who were once of your following . . . it would have been a good thing if the Italians had at least brought you in the first days when they aggressively invaded the country. It seems to me that having up to now acted as guide in the countries of Shewa and the Gallas, and after having seen the destruction of the people and provinces of Ethiopia, you have perhaps come here now to show the way and have your own country destroyed. . . .

Lij Belai's confusion between the values of patriotism and provincial feudalism, however, went deep, for the Patriot leader continued:

> Your Highness! The country and I are yours! But . . . if you
> have come with the intention of driving us one against the other
> with deception, I shall abandon your country and retire to the
> desert to resist like a man with my warriors for the independence
> and the honour of my country and I shall so bear myself that
> my history shall be written in Europe. . . .[5]

Lij Belai was from a poor family and had always had *shifta* (bandit)
inclinations. He was not in fact officially *lij*—that was a wartime
sign of respect which stuck and after the war his lack of *balabat* background weighed against him. Leul-Ras Hailu Taklé Haymanot
therefore dangled before him the lure of a marriage into his own
powerful house. He also appointed his son Dejazmatch Mammo to
an important local command. The alliance between the two powerful
Patriot leaders, Dejazmatch Negash, a relative of Leul-Ras Hailu
and Dejazmatch Mangasha Jambari appeared successful. It was
to this that Hailu then turned his attention. Leaflets were prepared
by the Italians, carrying a fake of Hailé Sellassié's seal and the forged
signature of Woldé Giorgis Woldé Yohannes. They declared that
for his services Mangasha was to become Negus of Gojjam. With
this simple stroke the Duke of Aosta and the Prince of Gojjam
sought to rally all the many members of the proud house of Taklé
Haymanot including Negash, against Mangasha Jambari in jealous
indignation. Leul-Ras Hailu then let it be widely known that only
he could prevent the use of poison gas in his province. However, these
tactics did not have time to bear fruit for Sandford, Wingate and
the Patriot commanders succeeded in bluffing their enemy into
rapid withdrawal. Much of Gojjam, never really controlled, was
quickly abandoned by the Italians.

THE ETHIOPIAN EXILES

Back in the Sudan there were some delays and frustrations. Hailé
Sellassié was anxious to collect together exiled Ethiopians and form
an army. Many of the refugees who had gone to Djibouti, British
Somaliland and even Jerusalem had ended up in Kenya and two
columns had marched there direct from Ethiopia. One—including
the Eritreans from Ras Imru's group and led by Dejazmatch Woldé
Mariam and Fitwrary Tademe Zelleka (later *dejazmatch*)—had
passed south along the Omo river and into Kenya to the east of
Lake Rudolf. At one stage they had had to depend for food on fish
from the River Omo. An echo of earlier attitudes is reflected in their

pressing boys and youths from the southern provinces into service as porters when all their mules had died. They expressed some surprise when these youths were treated no differently from any other Ethiopian refugees once the column arrived in Kenya. A second column, led by Afe Negus Zaudi Ayelu had made its way past Kapenguria to Eldoret but all were accommodated at a camp at Isiolo until incursions into northern Kenya by the Italians caused their transfer to Taveta.

Zaudi Ayelu took charge of the refugees but significant amongst them was the tall, fair and fine looking prince, Girma, eldest son of Eyasu. He had escaped from confinement in southern Ethiopia and many Kenyan exiles regarded him as lawful heir to the monarchy. News of this was sent to Hailé Sellassié then in England. Once Leul Girma tried to plan a march from Isiolo back to Ethiopia but it was frustrated by the British authorities. Later, however, he did set off with a small group but was turned back in the Northern Frontier desert district of Kenya for reasons not yet revealed. Leul Girma and his small daughter both died of food poisoning in Taveta before the liberation of Ethiopia was effected.

Hailé Sellassié had kept in touch with the situation in Kenya through Afe Negus Zaudi Ayelu, but it had needed a visit from Major-general Dejazmatch Abebe Desta and Lorenzo Taezaz at the instigation of Hailé Sellassié, before the keenness of the exiles in Kenya to join the struggle was generally acknowledged and they were formed into battalions to march with the Commonwealth troops in the impending invasion of Ethiopia.

Among those in exile in Kenya were Dejazmatch Shifferaw Balcha, a Galla Patriot leader who had come via Djibouti and Berbera; Kiflé Dadi (later *dejazmatch*) of the Moja family group of Shewa and several children. Ketema Yifru, acting Foreign Minister in 1964 and others grew up there as boys. An important Patriot leader who came south to Kenya at this time was Blatta Takelé Woldé Hawariat. Although not in charge, Blatta Takelé's personality and speeches bolstered the spirits of the exiles in the Kenyan refugee camps to the extent that the British authorities began to fear his growing influence and ambition and ordered him not to talk politics. He was, however, allowed to teach religion. Thereafter while the British thought he was merely teaching the scriptures, he was, in fact, preaching a great 'Exodus'. Such was the enthusiasm created that he was eventually allowed to select and train troops. As chief of staff he chose a thirty-three-year old Sidamo Galla named Mulugeta Bulli. Mulugeta had learnt French, had graduated from the Holeta Military College, had been gazetted *shambel* (captain) and was chief instructor at the College before he went north to fight in the battle of Maichew. Years later he was to become a very important major-general.

Several of the refugees from more significant families were transferred to the Sudan and underwent some officer training at the Sobar Academy in Khartoum, but Takelé was inexplicably detained by the British in East Africa. Mulugeta Bulli, however, joined this group which also included Asrate Kassa, surviving son of Leul-Ras Kassa and several future generals—Merid Mangasha, Assefa Demissie, Aman Andom, Mengistu Neway, who had also left Ethiopia via Djibouti, and others. Leul-Ras Kassa, Fitwrary Birru and Dejazmatch Makonnen Endalkatchew were called to Khartoum from their exile in the Holy Land.

HAILÉ SELLASSIÉ ASSERTS HIS CLAIMS

The Kaid, as the Commander in Chief of the Sudan was called, was at that time General Platt. He was openly opposed even to Hailé Sellassié's presence in Khartoum and tension mounted between his staff and even the British officers serving with Hailé Sellassié. A serious quarrel developed when Sirak Hiroy, son of the former foreign minister, reported to Hailé Sellassié that some local British officials were about to allow another of their countrymen named Courteney Brocklehurst into southern Ethiopia with a promise to the Galla people that if they rose against the Italians they would be protected from future 'Amhara overlordship' as well. The Emperor sent a telegram to Mr Churchill which contained the statement that his 'reluctance to admit the mission did not in the least alter his intention to institute a reasonable degree of local autonomy'. For better or for worse he has not done so, and it is doubtful if he had any intention of doing so, but this incident illustrates his awakened suspicions of British intentions. Possibly he need not have feared, for both Churchill and Eden were his staunch supporters. Mr Eden had publicly and categorically stated that 'His Majesty's (i.e., the British) Government would welcome the reappearance of an independent Ethiopian state and will recognise the claims of the Emperor Hailé Sellassié to the throne'.

Eventually the last of a series of delays was cleared away. Eden and Smuts both visited the Middle East and the former confirmed that it was the policy of his government that Hailé Sellassié should be assisted to recover his throne forthwith. Even so the Emperor was to owe much to certain Britons in whom he inspired faith and loyalty. He was to be grateful for the individualism and skill of Wingate and the thoughtful planning of Sandford for the British government did not attach him to either of the two sizeable invading armies. Indeed, not all the British Commonwealth generals then in Africa approved of his return at all, but as one of them remarked to a disgruntled Patriot leader, that was a political matter and he was content to be a soldier.

On January 20, 1941, a simple ceremony held on the western banks of the dry course of the Dinder river marked the departure of Hailé Sellassié from the Sudan. Among those with him as he crossed into Ethiopia were his eldest son, Asfa Wossen, the Crown Prince, Leul-Ras Kassa Hailu, Gabré Giorgis, the Echegé, his favourite son Makonnen, Duke of Harar, Dejazmatch Makonnen Endalkatchew, Dejazmatch Adafrisau, Kegnazmatch Mokria, formerly commander of the Imperial Guard, Lorenzo Taezaz and Woldé Giorgis. Sir Douglas Newbold, Chief Political Officer in the Sudan recorded in a letter, 'I hope he doesn't get blotted, I've come rather to like him'.[6]

THE CAMPAIGNS OPEN

A printing press and Amharic type had been acquired and a propaganda campaign under the charge of George Steer was to play a vital part in the campaign. A paper, *Banderachin,* was produced and pamphlets were dropped from the air to great effect on the Italian colonial troops, many of whom deserted. The famous Ethiopian scholar Professor Tamrat, later in voluntary exile in Jerusalem, and Sirak Hiroy worked on the propaganda. The theme of the pamphlets announcing the presence of the King of Kings on Ethiopian soil was the expedient one of forgiveness of his enemies. It is interesting to note that the phrase 'Ethiopia stretches her hands towards God' was in frequent use and was also selected as the password to show that the Emperor had returned to Gojjam. This biblical phrase was used by the Emperor Menelik on September 27, 1890, when he rejected the suggestion of Italian protection. 'Ethiopia does not require the protection of anyone; Ethiopia stretches out her hands to God !' he had stated.

About the same time as the re-entry of the Emperor, British Commonwealth troops invaded Eritrea from Kassala and soon afterwards the armies from Kenya in the south were also committed.

As the pathetically small camel caravan of what Wingate dubbed 'Gideon Force' pushed from the Sudan up into the Ethiopian Highlands, the Patriots throughout Gojjam rose in revolt. While Hailé Sellassié once more held court in a cave the Italians strove in vain to persuade Leul-Ras Hailu to attack their enemies, but he chose to wait with his not inconsiderable force of feudal levies about him. When Gideon Force arrived nearby, Wingate sent the old prince a messenger calling upon him to come and acknowledge the King of the Kings, but he politely declined and withdrew to his capital of Debra Markos. He was playing for the stakes he understood—his own position in what he regarded as his provincial fief.

Meanwhile, however, the invading forces in the north, led by Major-general Platt, received the surrender of the Eritrean town of Keren after a bitter siege lasting fifty-three days. The gateway to Asmara and Tigré province was open. Similarly in the south, Lieutenant-general Cunningham's force met with rapid success. Italian Somaliland colony was occupied and the southern settlements of Ethiopia were soon abandoned by the Italians. The British Somaliland colony was encircled, the Ogaden occupied; Nigerian troops forced the Marda pass and Ji-Jigga and Harar were quickly taken.

THE PATRIOTS, THE BRITISH, AND THE NOBILITY

British Commonwealth military historians do not always give credit to the work of the Patriot forces. The Italian collapse can only be explained if the long guerrilla war of attrition they had endured is remembered. For instance one account quite incidentally records that the southern armies were amazed at the ability of some Patriots to throw grenades as if they were cricket balls and it is only from asides such as this that the casual reader can learn of the presence of Patriot forces. On the other hand, the younger generation in Addis Ababa prefers to talk as if the Patriots alone defeated the Italians, whom incidentally they freely forgive. They forget that only invading armies and a more organized warfare was actually able to effect their liberation.

Dejazmatch Makonnen Desta, who was to become Minister of Education, and Azaj Kebede Tesemma were prominent in the Sudanese and Patriot attacks on the outer forts of Debra Markos in Gojjam. It is interesting to record also that at this time a company of the recently formed 2nd Ethiopian Battalion was serving as the Imperial Guard for the Emperor. (The Amharic is often translated as 'Bodyguard'.)

When the news of the surrender of Keren and Harar reached the Italians they withdrew from Debra Markos and Leul-Ras Hailu promptly responded by sending his Alfa-Romeo car complete with uniformed chauffeur to bring the British commander into the city (actually a small town, but in Ethiopia the English word city is used rather freely in translation of the several Amharic terms). The offer was refused. On April 4, 1941, Leul-Ras Hailu decided to surrender Debra Markos and, dressed in Italian general's uniform, he received the commander of the British Commonwealth forces in his citadel.

Irritating difficulties had already arisen between the Ethiopians and the British in Khartoum and these developed when it was announced that an 'Occupied Enemy Territory Administration' had been set up. Hailé Sellassié, indignant at not being consulted over this move, could scarcely have been pleased to hear that a colonial governor, Sir Philip Mitchell, had been placed in charge as 'Chief Political Officer'. In his memoirs, Sir Philip regrets not having been able at the time to meet the absolute monarch whom he was going to 'provide with the means of re-establishing his government' ![7]

The differences between the Ethiopian and the British concepts of government soon became very apparent. When Leul-Ras Hailu was required to move from the citadel of Debra Markos to his town house, Dejazmatch Negash, his relative, announced that the Emperor had appointed him the new governor general of Gojjam and for this reason the citadel and in particular its stores should be handed over to him. Colonel Bousted, who commanded the Commonwealth troops, refused, saying that as Negash was an officer of the Emperor he took his military order from the Commander of Ethio-British forces and not from the Emperor personally. The *dejazmatch* was required to wait in the forts outside the town. For two days there followed what the British described as 'anarchy' and the Ethiopians as 'celebrations' and then the Emperor arrived.

Leul-Ras Hailu came to pay homage—twenty minutes late—and the Emperor received him very coldly. Hailu suggested to the Emperor that he had secretly been rather loyal, but Hailé Sellassié did not laugh until he afterwards talked to a group of Ethiopian and British officers, for Hailu remained for some time a power to be respected and he even continued to be officially responsible for 'law and order'. He refused, for example, to hand over the Italian *residente* on the grounds that it was a breach of etiquette for a noble to surrender his guest on demand.

Leul-Ras Hailu had instructed Lij Belai Zelleka to allow the retreating Italian forces to cross the great gorge of the Blue Nile out of Gojjam into Shewa, without risking a fight. The Patriot leader did so and Wingate, who regarded this as a traitorous act, was baffled and hostile when Lij Belai had the seeming effrontery to arrive in person to pay his respects to Hailé Sellassié. Wingate dramatically had Lij Belai's every movement covered by machine-guns to emphasise his displeasure, but the Patriot probably saw his first loyalty as being to the ruler of Gojjam and to that province, and only then to a King of the Kings who had not even gained control over his own province of Shewa. To call his action 'treachery' as most British military historians do is nonsense for his record of patriotic and daring guerrilla warfare is unsurpassed. When he greeted the Emperor he meant what little he said, 'I don't know how to make speeches but I am a loyal Ethiopian'. Years later he was condemned to death as indeed was Leul-Ras Hailu himself. Being a noble, the latter was reprieved and that not for the first time. Hailu lived under house arrest in his palace in Addis Ababa, opposite the Secondary School of the Saviour of the World, until he died.

Leul-Ras Hailu was not so successful at 'tacking to the wind' as that other great provincial prince, Leul-Ras Seyoum Mangasha of Tigré. After Maichew, Seyoum had been taken to Italy and on his return had co-operated with the Italians. A letter of his to a friend dated as late as December 19, 1940, contained the phrase, 'May our powerful Italian government keep you in peace'. In January 1941 an Italian official in a letter to the Director of Political Affairs suggested him for office in Gondar with 'titles and authority equal to those of Ras Hailu'. Less than four months later, in April 1941, he wrote to Leul-Ras Kassa, 'I have recently returned from a visit to the British government authorities at Asmara. You will know that no man will be happier than I when the flag of Ethiopia, the sign of our fathers and grandfathers, has been planted again in this country.—*Seyoum*'. The grandfather he had in mind was the Emperor Yohannes, an ally of the British. On the same day he wrote in like vein to the Emperor, acknowledging him but signing himself in full Seyoum Mangasha Yohannes.[8] Yet in May 1941 he was to offer his services to mediate between the Commonwealth commanders and the royal Duke of Aosta. It is hardly surprising that although he subsequently had to be confirmed as governor general of Tigré, Seyoum was later called to Addis Ababa by his Emperor and not permitted to leave for several years.

The able Italian General Nasi had proclaimed Dejazmatch Ayelu Birru as governor of Gondar, but the *dejazmatch* recalled his former loyalty. He was the feudal heir of Simien and had fought alongside Ras Imru before the latter's retreat to Goré and eventual capture. Dejazmatch Ayelu and his forces rejoined the Patriot armies and later joined in the attack on Gondar. In the south-east, once it was certain that alien rule was collapsing, Fitwrary Million of Harar who had defected to the Italians for their title of *dejazmatch*, chose to kill himself sooner than face public shame. Ras Getachew, son of Ras Abaté one of Menelik's generals and a relative of the Empress, was arrested for his support of the Italians. The Emperor is said to have later remarked, 'I pardon you, but I don't know if God will', a remark worth thinking about, and Getachew was forced to live in provincial exile.

Hailé Sellassié watched the behaviour and attitudes of all the Patriot leaders with an astute eye, for it was not at first at all certain that leaders such as the six-foot-three Galla Fitwrary Geressu Duké or Balambaras Abebe Aragai, both of whose followers termed them *ras,* would take kindly to the re-imposition of imperial authority. Ras Imru was in Italy but another great Patriot leader whom Hailé Sellassié had thought to be safely detained in Kenya was allowed across the frontier into Ethiopia by General Cunningham. That was Blatta Takelé Woldé Hawariat. In the company of Dejazmatch Abebe Damtew, and a British colonel, Takelé had entered Borana in the south, but after considerable success in the region of Negellé he was wounded and taken prisoner by the Italians. Hailé Sellassié also had the problem to consider of the lesser commanders, like Mesfin Sileshi and Zaudi Ayelu all of whom would expect their rewards. For this reason the Emperor was most anxious to re-establish himself in Addis Ababa with minimum delay. However, from the military point of view, General Platt's force pushing south from Asmara and General Cunningham's troops from Kenya were much more powerful and significant than was Gideon Force and these generals seemed to ignore the Emperor's presence.

THE RECAPTURE OF ADDIS ABABA

Hailé Sellassié feared that Cunningham especially had learnt too much from the many exiles in Kenya about the potential divisions of Ethiopia, the situation in the southern provinces and the impact which his flight to Europe had made upon the local leaders and their people. It was therefore with certain personal reservations that he learnt that Addis Ababa had fallen on April 6, 1941, the same day that he had entered Debra Markos.

After receiving the surrender of Harar from the Italian governor and the bishop, Cunningham's troops had paused to repair the escarpment road which had been dynamited by their retreating enemy, and had then pushed on to Dira Dawa, the railway town on the floor of the Rift valley. Paradoxically they had been urged to hurry by the Italian police commandant from Dira Dawa. The main Italian force had left, but one of their colonial battalions had mutinied and was engaged in looting the town. From there on there was no real resistance to Cunningham's forces either along the Chercher mountains or on the Rift floor until the Awash river gorge was reached. Vehicles were manhauled over the gorge and new bridges were slid across the basalt flows which formed the banks of the river Awash. The armies halted at Akaki, just south of Addis Ababa and the city was entered the following day after one of the fastest advances in military history. In many ways the fine Italian designed roads of Ethiopia were vital factors in the campaign.

The flag of Savoy was lowered at the 'little *Ghibbi'* (the palace called Prince's Paradise), and the military commander's Union Jack was raised. More important, in the afternoon the Emperor's standard was raised on the 'big *Ghibbi'*—the rambling old palace of the Emperor Menelik II. General Weatherall, the senior British Commonwealth officer present, received a special cheer when the translator rendered his 'This is a proud day for me—to have come and reconquered Addis Ababa for you' in terms which denied any suspicion of a new colonialism. A proclamation from Hailé Sellassié was then read out, to the same effect. The different spheres of responsibility had however still to be delineated in detail, and this was at a time when officers with legal experience were difficult to find. Victory in Ethiopia was in marked contrast to the world scene. Two days later, for example, Germany attacked Greece and Yugoslavia.

Cunningham sent forces in pursuit of the Italians to the north and south. From Debra Markos Hailé Sellassié ordered Abebe Aragi to send a Patriot force of 500 to join the attack on the city of Dessie and ordered other leaders to harass the Italians in all theatres. He conferred with Brigadier Lush, the deputy to Sir Philip Mitchell who flew up from Addis Ababa, about the division of authority between himself and the British in the interim period during which the Italian forces in the south and north would be overcome and the Emperor's government re-established. Then he prepared to leave for Addis Ababa. Cunningham opposed this on the grounds of security but Hailé Sellassié, suspicious of Cunningham and the British government, but encouraged by the British officers with Gideon Force, especially Sandford, by then his personal political adviser, and Wingate, was not to be refused. He sent a party including Dejazmatch Makonnen Endalkatchew and Mulugeta Bulli on by air to make all the necessary arrangements and he then set off southwards across the Blue Nile chasm to Shewa. He was careful to require Leul-Ras Hailu as well as Leul-Ras Kassa to accompany him when he left Gojjam.

There was a feast at the monastery of Debra Libanos, and the Emperor and Leul-Ras Kassa prayed by the Patriot graves of the two of the latter's sons who had been murdered by the Italians. On May 5, 1941, five years to the day since Marshal Badoglio's troops had entered the city, Hailé Sellassié drove down the old road from Entotto ridge, pausing at the Church of St Mary, and into the city. Wingate on a white horse led Gideon Force, and 15,000 of Abebe Aragai's unbeaten Patriots lined the route. In the loudspeaker car, Yilma Deressa, who had returned from Italy and who had recently joined the British propaganda unit, shouted excitedly into the microphone. There was a salute of twenty-one guns. South African tanks flanked the gates of Menelik's old palace, and General Sir Alan Cunningham met the Emperor on the steps of the audience hall. There were speeches. Hailé Sellassié expressed a determination to re-establish Christian ethics in government, liberty of conscience and democratic institutions throughout Ethiopia. This was the first of many extravagant and widely reported speeches—speeches which have borne little relation to contemporary Ethiopia. 'Today,' said the Emperor, 'is the beginning of a new era in the history of Ethiopia'—and perhaps it was, for there could be no lasting return to the old ways. The second World War was even then nurturing seeds which would change the whole world, Africa not least.

Hailé Sellassié moved into the Prince's Paradise Palace and a few days later there was held a traditional review. Abebe's Patriots graphically re-enacted deeds of valour and shrieked out the names of witnesses who loudly called their confirmation—all this before the throne in the time honoured manner. This proud ritual is not really boasting but it is not approved of by many British writers— the same who would be most offended if their own understatements were to be missed! However, the Ethiopian knows how to take his fellows. The Crown Prince led up Abebe's shy little son Daniel, much later to govern Arusi, to be presented since he had ridden to the review at the head of his father's troops.

To end the proceedings, priests of the Ethiopian Church conducted a service. One of them cried out : 'Now the hour of lying and intrigue has ended because before so great an Emperor no man can lie and intrigue. Now is the time for the winnowing of grain; the hour of truth, of justice and of right. . . .' Abebe Aragai spoke to the Emperor : 'I am your loyal subject', he said, 'I never submitted to the enemy. I never hoped to see you alive again and I am grateful to God. . . .' The Emperor responded recognising his title : 'Ras Abebe Aragai, in due course you will be rewarded.' And so he was. He became chairman of the Council of Ministers, but because he was thought to have regarded high office merely as a reward, and not also as a responsibility, he was to pay an awful price in that same palace years later in December 1960, at the hands of members of a new generation who saw themselves as 'Patriots' no less than he.

MOPPING UP

Meanwhile the Italian armies had moved away from the city of Addis Ababa to the south; harassed by the Patriots and pursued by British Commonwealth armies. After the battles of the Lakes, the Italians retreated beyond the Omo Gorge. Fitwrary Geressu Duké, mounted on horseback, led his large forces across the Omo;* they played a considerable part in the engagements before and after the fall of Jimma in June when the Italian remnants were driven towards Dembidollo. There they surrendered to a Belgian force from the Sudan. The Patriot commanders present and those at the capture of Goré and Gimbi were Azaj Kebede Tesemma and Mesfin Sileshi. Similarly to the north, Leul-Ras Kassa's levies from Fiché entered Gojjam and greatly assisted the clearing up of the isolated Italian pockets there. Ras Abebe's forces had ambushed six Italian trucks containing Maria Theresa dollars on the Dessie Road and had pushed on north, to the Tarmaber escarpment. The battle continued along the floor of the Rift valley and Dessie surrendered after a short bombardment. Amongst abandoned equipment there were found forty-four trunks of uniforms and personal effects belonging to the Italian viceroy.

After taking his turn at watching superior air power from a cave, the royal Duke of Aosta surrendered at Amba Alagi on May 18, 1941, and the forces of the Northern and Southern armies were united with the Tigréan troops led by Leul-Ras Seyoum who played an active role in the last phases of the re-occupation. The Duke of Aosta inspected a guard of honour, declined accommodation in an Asmara palace, and was taken to Kenya. He later died in a prisoner-of-war camp there. The Italians at Debra Tabor surrendered to Fitwrary Birru Walda Gabriel, and only the forces at Gondar remained. Fitwrary Birru, the former Minister of War, had spent the occupation period in Jerusalem before rejoining Hailé Sellassié in Khartoum. When Hailé Sellassié had re-entered Gojjam, Birru had led a mission to the Patriots of Begemidir. Crown Prince Asfa Wossen and 10,000 Patriots were involved in the siege of Gondar before that historic city finally surrendered after the rains in November 1941.

Ethiopia immediately committed herself to continuing the war as an ally of Britain and soon afterwards of the Soviet Union when that country was invaded. At the end of 1941, after Pearl Harbour, the United States also entered the war, but as early as the capture of Massawa, President Roosevelt had announced that the Red Sea was no longer a war zone and military supplies for the defence of north-eastern Africa and the Middle East against the Axis powers might be carried by American ships. Ethiopian troops fought in North Africa and elsewhere but back in Ethiopia, apart from the

---

* Unlike the Blue Nile, it is the gorge rather than the river Omo or Ghibbi which divides the country. Although impassable in flood the Omo can be forded in places. The author negotiated it on foot about the same time of the year in 1962 about twenty miles above the road bridge, after ensuring that there were no crocodiles in the vicinity.

clearing of a few isolated pockets, the fighting war against the Italians was over.

Problems persisted in plenty and it remained to be seen whether Hailé Sellassié and the Patriot leaders would be able to solve them and to build the nation anew. One thing should have been obvious from the start—that the task was enormous and it would not be resolved if narrow personal and provincial struggles were again to dominate the national scene. Some leaders like Ras Imru understood this but many did not.

It would be easy to overestimate the overall impact which the experiences of war made on traditional Ethiopia. The abstract concept of the monarchy itself remained almost unshaken. The feudal leaders were somewhat discredited in their capacities as military commanders but the real cement of traditional highland Ethiopia— the Christian Church—emerged unscathed. True, many of her bishops and priests had collaborated, but many had not. She had hidden arms and had provided martyrs. It was left to modern education in the post-war era to begin to undermine the influence of this most conservative of Ethiopia's institutions and even in the 1960s, that process, though clearly discernible in the city of Addis Ababa had scarcely begun in the countryside.

The spirit of her Patriots had served Ethiopia well in war. They were impelled, as their title implies, by patriotism and by the firm repudiation of the human humiliation which any form of colonialism entails. It is, however, not enough to know what men are against; more important is what they are for. A key to the thought of the Patriots may be found in a letter written by a Lasta *dejazmatch* to another Patriot leader (a *kegnazmatch*) in the Simien mountains. The following paragraph occurs :

> I for my part, being convinced that the Italians have invaded our country for the sole purpose of destroying the great men of Ethiopia and their children, to dishonour and expropriate us from our properties; to destroy the Christianity of our ancestors and supplant it with their own; being convinced of all these things, have up to now successfully fought against them.[9]

Great as was the contribution of the Patriots to the glory of their historic country; within a few years their principles along with the despotism and paternalism of the Ethiopian government began to be rejected as inadequate even by some of their own sons. After the second World War new generations all over the world have seen more to fight for than aristocracy, property and sectarian Christianity, and some might add, especially in Africa, even nationalism. Yet those were the values of the noble *dejazmatch* as shown in his letter. In the 1960s the educated among the younger generation of Ethiopians, that is those under about forty, would dismiss out of hand the old man's pride as arrogance and his horizons as inadequate.

They are not entirely right but can hardly be expected to show much sympathy now that their eyes are opening to what appears to them to be the unnecessary poverty and backwardness of their fellow countrymen, more especially since rich former Patriot and feudal leaders appear to look on unconcerned; since their government, attacked in 1960 as being riddled with corruption and nepotism, is hostile to even mild expressions of criticism; and since the triumphantly unreformed Ethiopian Christian Church daily asserts its ignorance and dubs their discontent and their idealism as 'wickedness'. All this will change and is changing. Future historians will undoubtedly attribute this change to the influence of the 'African Revolution' upon the new generation of Ethiopians and will cite more recent re-orientations of foreign policy (witness towards Portugal, Ethiopia's historic ally) as a manifestation of this. But despite their narrower horizons, the early struggle of the Ethiopian Patriots against the territorial imperialism of Italy would seem to merit a chapter in the history of the 'New Africa'.

V

REVOLUTION

15

Two Decades of Intrigue

These can open the way for and facilitate victory; but after-wards if you wish to keep possession, infinite difficulties arise, both from those who have aided you and from those you have oppressed.—MACHIAVELLI, *The Prince*

Rumour was rife in Addis Ababa; the Emperor was to have been murdered the very next week; the conspiracy had been discovered only in the nick of time. . . .—BUCHOLZER, *The Land of Burnt Faces,* London, 1955

CONCORD WITH BRITAIN

The difficulties facing Hailé Sellassié when he reassumed the throne were truly immense. It was necessary first to establish a police force and some form of internal administration. This itself was a task of formidable proportions since lawlessness and obedience only to local war leaders or strongmen had been encouraged for years and was in any case traditional. It was necessary to obtain financial and technical assistance, and the obvious source at that time was Britain. On the other hand, it was equally necessary to treat that great power with caution and even suspicion because of her imperial traditions and more especially because the military campaigns had left her very popular with the people and in an all-pervasive position throughout the empire. It is probable that right from the earliest moment Hailé Sellassié saw that the presence of the British would later become an embarrassment but at the time he was most concerned for his own position. He needed help but had no wish to become a foreign puppet —or in fact a puppet at all, for it soon became clear from his attitude to suggested administrative reforms and methods of accounting for financial assistance, that he was not interested in recommendations for greater efficiency if at the same time they tended to weaken his personal control. Throughout his life Hailé Sellassié's most significant quality, apart perhaps from his patience, has been a complete grasp of the elements of power.

Then, quite apart from reasserting the traditional independence of the country and the traditional autocracy of the crown, there was the vital question of the future of the former Italian colonies. Eritrea to the north was to become a considerable problem. It was racially culturally and even economically a part of the historic Empire of Ethiopia and for the most part inseparable from Tigré province, but the period of Italian colonialism had, nevertheless, lent Eritrea some sense of separate political existence. Also there was Italian Somaliland, called by the Ethiopians the Benadir Coast. To these territories Hailé Sellassié laid immediate claim. In Addis Ababa the *Ethiopia-Eritrea Unity Association,* under the presidency of a judge, and the *Ethiopia-Somalia Unity Association,* led by Haji Omar, were formed.

The attitudes of Ethiopia's ally in arms were somewhat different. In the first place Britain was not at all certain that the reoccupation of Ethiopia was permanent. There remained Italian pockets in parts of the country and the situation in North Africa was far from secure. Rommel's offensive against Egypt was yet to come and these facts demanded that the Ethiopian situation be seen against a world view of the conflict with Germany and Italy. The cardinal facts that seemed to emerge were that Ethiopia formed a vital link in the defence of the Middle East and was an important overland supply route for the Sudan and Egypt since the Mediterranean was to all intents and purposes closed. Military convoys from southern Africa led to the pioneering of land routes via northern Kenya and it is significant that a small team of British troops were sent to re-open the railway even before the new bridge had been completed over the gorge of the river Awash and while the port of Djibouti, although blockaded, remained in the hands of the Vichy French who were collaborating with the Axis powers.

Similarly, Britain saw herself as being responsible under international law for Italian lives and property in Ethiopia, and up until the signing of any peace treaty, for the administration of the occupied Italian colonies. Not at all unnaturally the Ethiopians, themselves the victims of Italy's total disregard of the same international law and not recognising even the existence of any Italian property especially within Ethiopia, were not quick to understand the British view. Differences over Italian property were to a large extent resolved by compromises. Since much of the Italian public and private property was the direct or indirect result of theft, a joint

Anglo-Ethiopian commission was set up to settle the ownership of immovable property.

Contrary to the usual assertions, there had been some little friction between the Italians and their former subjects, but it soon passed. The Red Cross and the military authorities set up camps and soup-kitchens and deported large numbers of military prisoners, civilians and refugees. However, quite a proportion of the Italian population, particularly artisans, remained in Ethiopia—some even hiding from the British in Ethiopian houses in order to do so. Once forgetful of the myths of fascism the Italian has no racial attitudes, nor does he demand a higher standard of living than his individual industry and skill can earn him. Significantly, Italians were accepted, even popular in Ethiopia in post-war years.

BRITISH MILITARY ADMINISTRATION

The speedy collapse of the Italians had caught the British unawares. As stated above, Sir Philip Mitchell had been appointed Chief Political Officer under the general control of the military commander, then General Wavell, with Brigadier Lush as deputy. Colonel Rodd, subsequently Major-general Lord Rennell of Rodd, became controller of finance and accounts. It was he who wrote up the semi-official history of the military administration.[1] The British had little idea of how to set about this administration for, as Rodd complains in his book, 'It was not a subject dealt with at Staff College.'

Sir Philip Mitchell had signed a thirty-three-point directive before moving his headquarters from Cairo to Nairobi—General Rommel having at the time relieved him of the necessity of administering much of North Africa. These directives included the following statements :

> . . . any part of Ethiopia which is wholly cleared of the enemy comes *ipso facto* and at once under the rule of the Emperor who will be present in person to claim it and give it effective administration. It may also be claimed that a part at least of the country was never conquered at all by the Italians . . . but [they went on] . . . in practice it will be necessary to act from the start on the assumption that the country is under British military guidance and control until it is formally handed over . . . the situation is difficult and delicate. On the other hand the Emperor himself is probably alive to the facts that it is in his own interest that there should be a preliminary period of

military control by British forces and that his own administration will take a considerable time to organise.

The Emperor was aware of this and aware also of the fact that not all Ethiopians welcomed the advent of a central administration of any kind.

It had been agreed that the Emperor should have the sole right to make *awaj* or 'proclamations' and the British would issue public notices. Temporary agreement was also reached on arrangements for legal procedures regarding foreigners, and the British successfully restored confidence in the currency by providing lorry-loads of silver Maria Theresa dollars. These coins had long been popular in Arabia and Ethiopia and were still in use in remote areas of Ethiopia in the early 1960s. The Ethiopian people had shown conservative attachment to the plump profile of the Austrian Empress, and Menelik II's attempts to replace these coins with similar pieces struck with his own effigy had not been fully successful. Even the date on the dies was never changed. These dollars and the East African currency in the possession of the Commonwealth troops were interchangeable and were quickly accepted. Branches of Barclays Bank followed the military administration teams into the provinces.

Hailé Sellassié soon decided to make a firm gesture to assert his independence. In May 1941, without consulting the British, he appointed seven cabinet ministers and made Ras Abebe Aragai governor of Addis Ababa. It caused a stir but was a shrewd move. Since he had neither the money to pay them nor the organisation through which to raise taxes it was agreed that for the time being they be regarded merely as advisers to the British military administration. But the appointments nevertheless served to emphasise the Emperor's anxiety to take over the administration of the country which the military had set up, and negotiations began.

In the meantime there was, in fact, considerable initial disorder. In the south-west a son of Eyasu rose in revolt. Several of the Emperor Eyasu's sons have already been mentioned as have the facts that Eyasu had, in the true Solomonic tradition, deliberately set out to raise sons from the families of as many chieftains as possible and had perhaps sought to establish a new aristocracy to replace the members of the traditional ruling families especially those of Shewa. The particular son of Eyasu in question had claimed the title of *ras* and the historic name of Tewodros. He raised his standard at Gambela. A political officer named Dallas was sent from the capital with Belgian troops to put the rebellion down.

Not long after the news of the fall of the last major Italian garrison, in the northern city of Gondar, Hailé Sellassié asked that some of the Commonwealth troops no longer deployed there be sent to pacify the Raia and Azebu Galla in eastern Tigré. This request was, however, refused on the grounds that the troops were needed for the defence of Egypt against the Germans.

There was trouble also to the south. For example in Adola an important Galla leader, Grazmatch Sera, was murdered. He was known to have spoken out for some measure of local autonomy as against 'Shewan control', and since he was killed near the camp of the British political officer he might have been suspected of trying to negotiate this. Indeed considerable suspicion of the intentions of the British had developed throughout Ethiopia following their decision to administer northern Tigré from Asmara in Eritrea, and more especially since it was known that that former Italian colony was to remain under British administration until the peace treaty.

In view of these slight but growing tensions, Hailé Sellassié reconsidered the appointment held by Ras Abebe Aragai, whose popularity with the Shewan masses and whose earlier association with one of Eyasu's sons he still resented. Nor did the Emperor consider Abebe Aragai as able an administrator as he was a warrior and in fact was never from this time onwards quite confident that Abebe Aragai might not be too pliable in dealing with foreign powers and interests—in this case the British military administration. He therefore replaced him by bringing forward Blatta Takelé Woldé Hawariat, by then *dejazmatch*, another Patriot leader. Dejazmatch Takelé, Hailé Sellassié knew, was one of his critics but one who always put his country before other considerations. Hailé Sellassié felt, moreover, that Takelé, who had always shown considerable political acumen, was more likely to be a match for the subtle designs which the Emperor always anticipated from his British allies. Takelé was made *kantiba* of Addis Ababa and governor general of Shewa—the only one since the Restoration, for his successors have been deputy-governors.

Hailé Sellassié had re-entered Addis Ababa in May 1941 and by the end of the same year it became known that the few months of British military administration were to end with the signing of an Anglo-Ethiopian agreement in January 1942. The speed with which these negotiations were completed was only equalled by the popular acclaim their signing was to receive from the Ethiopians. If there was a sharp increase in retail prices just before the Emperor's nominees took over the government, nevertheless all were happy at the rapid re-establishment of Ethiopia's traditional independence. The negotiations which preceded the signing of the agreement and military convention were not however without interest.

BRITISH FINANCIAL ASSISTANCE

Hailé Sellassié informed Sir Philip Mitchell that he would like financial assistance both for the development of Ethiopia and for the formation of a standing army. He asked for British advisers especially for himself on general political matters and for the Ministries of Finance and Justice. He considered it time that provincial administration was taken over by Ethiopians and that a draft treaty with Britain be prepared for discussion. Lastly, if he was considered to owe anything for the liberation campaign he wished to be told.

The only part of the Italian fiscal arrangements still operable were the customs revenue. These were levied at the pre-occupation rates but the revenue produced was quite insufficient to run the country. The Italians had always subsidised their administration and development programs and it soon became clear that revenues would not allow, for example, even for the upkeep of all the existing roads, let alone the development of necessary services for the Ethiopian people, rather than the colonists—services which the Italians had so neglected. During the period of British military administration the costs of government over and above revenues were met directly by the British government and small grants-in-aid were also paid for road repair and police costs. In addition two non-recurrent grants were made to Hailé Sellassié, who had asked for them to enable him to recoup expenses incurred personally in hiring administrative staff and in order to make payments to some of the more important notables.[2] He still received personal payments from the British civil list, but these would soon terminate.

The question of financial assistance for the new government was therefore urgent once the revenues and responsibility for expenditure were handed over to them, or rather to the person of the Emperor. The first draft agreement suggested by the British cabinet aimed to endow Britain with such sweeping control that Ethiopian independence would have become a complete farce. There was an exchange of notes between the Emperor and the British Political Officer and it seems clear that Sandford did his duty in warning the Emperor, for Sir Philip Mitchell records that he sometimes wondered whether Sandford 'in his devotion to the Emperor's interests was really going to break off relations with Great Britain'.[3] However, despite the dearth of trained and experienced Ethiopian administrators and the seriousness of the international situation in 1941, today it seems scarcely conceivable that the British cabinet could have expected Hailé Sellassié to have agreed to the first of five points which Sir Philip Mitchell put to him—namely that 'the Emperor agree to abide in all matters touching the government of Ethiopia by the advice of His Majesty's Government'—even if this was followed by a promise on their part to 'use their best endeavours to re-establish the Ethiopian government'. This was reminiscent of the treaty of Wuchali. Clearly the British cabinet was then still obsessed with the concept of colonialism as a civilising mission of benefit to backward peoples and this illustrates how rapidly London adjust-ments to 'the wind of change' have subsequently developed. Small wonder with such premises for discussion with a monarchy which was heir to centuries of independence that Sir Philip was driven frankly to admit his frequent exasperation. One suspects that his past dealings with the monarchs of Uganda were scarcely preparation for such negotiations. He was further irritated by the insistence of Hailé Sellassié that they conduct negotiations over every detail in person, interpreters being used.

The British War Office let it be known that they completely disapproved of negotiations at this early stage. Doubtless they were concerned about their supply routes and the imminence of British military collapse in North Africa. Perhaps it was this which led them to put up the preposterous claim that Ethiopia was still a conquered Italian territory. Britain had, however, long since withdrawn her temporary and unfortunate recognition of Italian rule in Ethiopia and this view was not accepted. More interesting is the view of the military administrators. It is too simple to say that the measure of control over expenditure they envisaged was due only to their know-ledge of colonial custom and their failure to comprehend the fierce independent spirit of the Ethiopians. They were also schooled in the concept of responsibility to the tax payer, British or Ethiopian, for the expenditure of public funds and did not comprehend that this is the very anathema of feudalism.

Rodd admits that he incorrectly anticipated the result of the negotiations. He was well aware that the inadequate machinery with which the Emperor proposed to run the country was fraught with the danger of corruption, so he set up central and provincial treasuries and accounting systems. It is clear from his book that he was, therefore, not a little amazed to learn that finally the British government not only waived any degree of budgetary control over the expenditure of her assistance but that she proposed not even to channel it through her financial controller (and thence to the ministries and departments of the Ethiopian government) but rather direct to the Emperor. Thus it was that in 1942 Hailé Sellassié received quarterly and in advance one and a half million pounds sterling and in 1943 a further million. The agreement did not con-tinue but provision was also made for smaller payments in 1944 and 1945 should it have done so.

In addition another million pounds sterling was left to be allocated by the British Diplomatic Representative whose appointment replaced that of the Political Officer (military administration). The sum was earmarked for non-recurrent items, including the settlement of Patriots on farm land, etc. Other items in the agreement included the provision but not the payment of advisers, police officers and judges; the guarantee of free use of immovable property required by British forces for war purposes; prior agreement over any possible use of Ethiopian forces beyond her frontiers; future assistance in obtaining the return of art treasures and other loot from Italy; the administration of justice, etc. No charge was made for the liberation campaigns and a separate military agreement covered the provision of a British military mission to create and supervise the development of an Ethiopian national army. The British government had agreed with Hailé Sellassié that a sizeable modern army was essential to maintain the authority of the central government. It was, however, also clear that it could not be paid for out of revenue for many years and for this reason it was made the subject of a separate agreement.

The agreements recognised the positions both of the British government and of Ethiopia, or rather Hailé Sellassié since they were made with him personally. They began :

> Whereas His Majesty the Emperor, true to his coronation pledges not to surrender his sovereignty or the independence of his people, but conscious of the needs of his country, has intimated to the Government of the United Kingdom . . . that he is eager to receive advice and financial assistance in the difficult task of reconstruction and reform, and whereas the Government of the United Kingdom recognise that Ethiopia is now a free and independent state and His Majesty Hailé Sellassié I is its lawful ruler, and the reconquest of Ethiopia now being complete, shall help His Majesty the Emperor to re-establish his government and to assist in providing for the immediate needs of the country . . .

The agreements were signed on January 31, 1942, in the council room of the palace, with considerable pomp and ceremony. That afternoon the Emperor, the Crown Prince, Leul Makonnen, Duke of Harar and Princess Tsahai, the Emperor's youngest daughter, came to tea with Sir Philip Mitchell. There were receptions and balls and it was even hinted to Sir Philip before he left for Nairobi that it would be nice if Leul Makonnen—who during the war had been to school at Wellington, England, though he had not reached the higher forms (grades)—could go up to Oxford.

HAILÉ SELLASSIÉ'S DIPLOMACY AND THE FIRST CHALLENGES

Then with more confidence and power, Hailé Sellassié turned his full attention once more to the internal scene, from which the British military administration was already rapidly withdrawing. He set out to use what support he had as best he could. There was pressure on him to reward powerful Patriot leaders but he also knew that it might be safer to appoint to high office those who had been in exile with him, for their future more obviously depended upon the stability of his throne. In practice he did both. Ras Abebe's title had been recognised. Hailé Sellassié also elevated Hailu Belau (a Gojjam Patriot and a grandson of the Negus Taklé Haymanot) and the former exiles Fitwrary Birru and Dejazmatch Adafrisau to the rank of *ras*. Hailu was appointed governor general of Gojjam, Adafrisau of Sidamo, and Birru, who was also encouraged to marry into Hailé Sellassié's house, was given Kaffa and Jimma. Birru Walda Gabriel, one of Ethiopia's richest landowners, was, as has been mentioned, suspected by many of not actually being the grandson of Walda Gabriel but rather an illegitimate son of Emperor Menelik II. His title of *fitwrary* was an example of the special case where this normally comparatively junior title was very senior because it was associated with the office of Minister of War.

Fitwrary Geressu Duké, the Galla Patriot leader, was made *dejazmatch* and a governor in Goré in the far south. Subsequently he became the jailer of the collaborator Dejazmatch Hailé Sellassié Gugsa. An 'Italian' *ras*, Gugsa had been captured originally by the British and taken abroad. However, he was returned and stood trial in Addis Ababa and was sentenced to death. The Emperor did not confirm his sentence, perhaps because the *dejazmatch* had married his daughter before the war or perhaps because the Emperor knew that part cause of his defection was the way he had been repeatedly played off against Leul-Ras Seyoum over the matter of governorships in Tigré, as part of Hailé Sellassié's pre-war policy of frustrating the emergence of a united and separatist Tigré. One example from the exiles is Dejazmatch Makonnen Endalkatchew, the noble who had administered the refugees in Jerusalem on the Emperor's behalf; he rose to great influence at court from this time.

Except in a few blatant cases, Hailé Sellassié announced his recognition of preferments given by the Italians since he could not risk a large number of deprived and aggrieved *shums* taking to brigandage. After a search conducted by the British, Ras Imru had been discovered in a small village in Tuscany, Italy, and had been flown back to Ethiopia in November 1943. He was appointed governor general of Begemidir. The Crown Prince and Leul Makonnen had their governorships of Wello and Harar respectively restored to them. Asfa Wossen went to live at Dessie, but Makonnen Duke of Harar, on the other hand, was more frequently in Addis Ababa near the Emperor, with whom he grew in favour. But of the leading nobles, Hailé Sellassié trusted Leul-Ras Kassa more than the other princes.

The powerful Italian collaborator Leul-Ras Hailu of Gojjam was watched and confined to Addis Ababa where he was soon joined by Leul-Ras Seyoum, to whose Tigréan subjects the Italians mischievously gave some 4,000 rifles before their final surrender. This caution on the part of the Emperor did not prevent subsequent trouble in either Gojjam or Tigré but it greatly reduced the chance of any unmanageable resurgence of the feudal separatism of those former kingdoms.

Sometimes Hailé Sellassié is criticised for not making a clean sweep of the old leaders while he was secure under British military protection. This, however, is unrealistic. There were very few educated Ethiopians available, particularly since many had died fighting or in the massacres and rightly or wrongly, but understandably at that time in Africa, the Emperor feared British power and designs as much as those of his reactionary fellow countrymen. Also Hailé Sellassié was himself much older than the Ras Tafari of the reforming zeal of old. He seemed no longer prepared to crusade and confined himself to the balancing of all the factors which together went to make up the Ethiopian scene. He played one off against the other with considerable skill. For example he frequently suggested that Dejazmatch Takelé was very anti-British and difficult for him to control when it was actually he himself who did not wish to fall in with certain British advice and suggestions. Subsequent events, however, indicate that the British were not completely taken in by this stratagem.

However, serious challenges to Hailé Sellassié's rule did develop. For example, the Patriot Belai Zelleka, who had been made a governor in Gojjam with the rank of *dejazmatch,* had to be removed after a short period because of his growing unwillingness to serve under an Emperor whom he began openly to say had deserted the country in its hour of need. Belai had, however, been outstanding among the Patriot commanders and partly because of this, but partly on account of his popular support, he was merely required to live in Addis Ababa. However, he was soon involved in a plot with seven other *dejazmatch*, notably Mammo, the son of Leul-Ras Hailu. The conspirators were imprisoned but managed to escape though several people were killed in the process. Fifty guardsmen, including some

officers, were reputedly hanged for complicity in the revolt. Belai
Zelleka and Mammo Hailu were sentenced and hanged—the latter's
father, Leul-Ras Hailu, being forced to sit as one of the judges.
Sometimes this revolt is dismissed as Gojjam provincialism, but it
was not so. Doubtless some conspirators merely hoped to release
Leul-Ras Hailu and so gain local preferment in Gojjam. Others had
little more imagination than many other would-be *shiftas* in
Ethiopian history. But to its leaders it was an attempt to take over
the central government itself. Belai Zelleka's father was a poor
Gojjami farmer from Dejjen but his mother was a Shewan Galla from
Deneber and many of the conspirators were Shewan. The harshness
of the punishments and particularly the hangings on Janhoy Meda
aroused considerable public reaction against Hailé Sellassié at the
time.

One Patriot who had hoped for high position was Fitwrary
Hailu Kibret. He was to be almost immediately disappointed. The
fitwrary had fought on until the defeat of the Gondar garrison and
then had returned to Addis Ababa where the Crown Prince had sent
him to the Emperor. In audience, however, he lacked the respect by
then normally accorded to Hailé Sellassié and from his own account
claims to have sat down and opened his briefcase for some notes
while remarking, 'You should have waited for advice from someone
who was here. Instead you appear to have appointed a bunch of
collaborators ! By the Good Lord those old days are past and we want
a New Ethiopia !' He very soon found himself in a minor governorship under the Crown Prince in Wello.

Several former Patriot leaders lost influence in these early
years. Not surprisingly one of the first to be replaced in this phase
of the Emperor's delicate system of *shum-shir* (appoint-demote) was
the governor general of Shewa, Dejazmatch Takelé. He had learnt
of the Emperor's habit of blaming him if events did not please the
British. At this time Takelé suggested the calling of a parliament. It
is said that he was inclined in 1961 to boast of this, but it is doubtful
if democratic instincts alone were his immediate motivation. He
wanted institutions to counteract the personal element in the
Ethiopian government. It is likely that he also saw that if the
Emperor were to say to the British advisers, 'Parliament does not
agree', not only would they be more impressed but he, Dejazmatch
Takelé, would not make enemies needlessly. However, at the time
he was suspected of having designs to use a parliament to put
forward his own ideas of change. Takelé had been closely associated
with the *Ethiopian National Patriotic Association* and was respected
by the members of the *Ethiopian Patriots' Association*. However,
these associations had never come to voice progressive opinion or to

agitate for much beyond the self-interest of their members. More pertinent perhaps was Takelé's influence with the growing army. The Emperor certainly did not consider the time yet propitious for calling a parliament. Therefore he discussed the problem of Dejazmatch Takelé with a man of growing importance—the Minister of the Pen, Tsahafé Taezaz Woldé Giorgis Woldé Yohannes.

A program had been started for training soldiers for the reconstituted Imperial Guard. The new material was largely drawn from unemployed in the streets of Addis Ababa and Dejazmatch Takelé was interested in the scheme. At this time Takelé was offered the chance to revenge himself upon a former fellow Patriot (a *dejazmatch* and in 1964 a senator) who had spied upon him at the time of the Patriot opposition in the Gondar region to the return of Hailé Sellassié. Perhaps because he suspected the offer as a plot, Takelé ignored it, but, warned of his mounting unpopularity with the inner court clique, he appears to have decided secretly to divert 500 of the military trainees into becoming a personal guard for himself whilst still providing 1,000 for the Imperial Guard. It will be remembered that Takelé had trained guerrilla forces outside Addis Ababa in 1935.

The Emperor soon learned that something was afoot. He knew that Nega Hailé Sellassié, one of the training officers, was particularly popular and capable (he later became a brigadier-general) and Hailé Sellassié sent a captain to watch him. Woldé Giorgis, however, chose to put Takelé under observation, and soon afterwards either he or the Eritrean director general of the municipality, Dawit Okbagzy, whom the author found a very genial man, but whose enemies, nevertheless, insist had a reputation for spying on everyone for everyone else (or both he and Woldé Giorgis, if they were in league, as is likely) informed Hailé Sellassié that the plans were the brainchild of Dejazmatch Takelé. Some British military officers who were inclined to feel bitter at the rather sudden departure of their administration were played upon in the hope of securing their support for the arrest of Takelé, but this failed. Nevertheless he was arrested and to all intents and purposes disappeared. Actually from March 1942 onwards he was imprisoned for two and a half years in the Prince's Paradise Palace. His room was dark and his eyesight was affected.* Takelé was already respected as a Patriot and a nationalist but from this time on, many also regarded him as a committed enemy of the régime.

---

* These intrigues are as described by Lieutenant-Colonel Workneh Gebeyehu, later chief of security.

Ras Abebe Aragai was made Minister of War (later re-termed Minister of Defence). His power was limited, however, by the presence of the British military mission. They staffed and trained half the army until 1947 and for three more years the senior British officer acted as the minister's adviser and other British officers remained as advisers and instructors. Moreover the Imperial Guard remained under the direct command of the Emperor.

Dejazmatch Makonnen Endalkatchew was made Minister of the Interior. Lorenzo Taezaz, formerly Hailé Sellassié's secretary and then Ethiopian representative at the League of Nations (by then *blattenguetta*), was Foreign Minister. When he died on a tour abroad in 1947, all his private papers were seized and disappeared, probably because of his knowledge of the war-time correspondence between Hailé Sellassié and the Patriot leaders.

A significant name in the list of Ministers was Makonnen Habtewold who had been a follower of Hailé Sellassié since the early days of the latter's struggle for the throne. Makonnen was made Minister of Agriculture. Often unnoticed in the shadow of the ruthless and all powerful Tsahafé Taezaz Woldé Giorgis, he and his brothers climbed steadily to a position of great influence and power.

The former Patriot, Mesfin Sileshi, also acquired prominence. He became a *dejazmatch* and held governorships and ministerial appointments. Although he only took a leading place in the government on occasions, the great wealth he began to amass, largely through land speculation, brought him very considerable power. He had easy access to the Emperor and became a significant conservative influence behind the scenes. Mesfin's actions and attitudes were not untypical of those of many who considered that a Patriot or family background entitled its holder to be heard and obeyed in every sphere of the government and national life.

Yilma Deressa, one of the former progressive group, also demonstrated some skill in his land dealings. He came to exert considerable influence, partly because of his Galla *balabat* background and his training in economics. However, he subsequently spent a period abroad as an ambassador, some say because the expansion of his rich coffee-holdings clashed with the interests of Dejazmatch Mesfin. But even from abroad Yilma continued to develop his holdings through his wife.

The year 1942 saw many publications of the *Negarit Gazeta,* proclaiming laws and appointments. A Council of Ministers was formed and in September the office of Prime Minister was created, Dejazmatch Makonnen Endalkatchew being the first to be appointed. Proclamations dealt with all the spheres of life of a modern state. There were regulations for the police, for justice, for public health, etc., and like the publications of more recent date they were very impressive to read, but bore little relationship to the real state of affairs. These modern institutions and regulations could not function because the feudal society on which they were super-imposed allowed them no roots. The feudal and landowning classes considered laws to be irrelevant to themselves and only important in so far as they were useful to further their own aims. The Emperor took the same attitude to parliament which he re-established in 1942, and of which his ministers were not members.

An important development was the final closing of the Bank of Italy and the opening in the same premises of the State Bank of Ethiopia which started well and remained one of the islands of comparative efficiency in Ethiopia—except for customers in a hurry to take out money. The British banks withdrew and all that remained of British influence was the railway administration; the administration of Eritrea and of the Ogaden and the 'Reserved Area' (referred to below); the British Council (also later to be closed for some years), an Ethio-British Club, a few advisers, the military mission and, of course, normal diplomatic representation. The flirtation with Britain was thus almost at an end but it had served to secure Hailé Sellassié once again as Emperor of Ethiopia.

THE TROUBLED PERIPHERY OF THE HIGHLANDS

The authority of the central government which the Emperor dominated was not, however, felt far from Addis Ababa in the early 1940s. The disturbed situation in the north attracted the attention of the British governments in both Eritrea and the Sudan. The people of Ethiopia also recall the unrest of these times. The most alarming disorders occurred in Tigré where there had been *shifta* trouble ever since an attack on Alamata village and a British military convoy in 1941. Alamata controlled the spectacular and vital road pass up the Rift valley wall and over the dissected plateau to the north.* The unrest increased until it represented a serious challenge to Hailé Sellassié's government. Discontent had long simmered in part over the continued confinement of the Tigréan prince Leul-Ras Seyoum to Addis Ababa. There had been frustrated plots to assassinate both the Emperor and the Crown Prince. These had led to arrests in Addis Ababa and in the Tigréan town of Addigrat. The Ethiopian authorities had asked the British to arrest a certain

---

* Together with the Simien escarpment road and Tarmaber, the Alamata pass ranks among the finest of the engineering feats of the Occupation period. For a description of this route see the author's 'Some Routes in Northern Ethiopia', *Ethiopia Observer*, Vol. VI, No. 4, London, 1963.

Fitwrary Tesemma in this connection. Other rebels were Yekuno Amlak Tesfae, a nephew of the collaborator Dejazmatch Hailé Sellassié Gugsa and, more important, Blatta Hailé Mariam. Hailé Mariam was a provincialist. He claimed he could rebuild Tigré and recapture the glory of the times of Emperor Yohannes. He was little interested in either religion or the British but he found it convenient propaganda to claim that Shewa was opposed to the Alexandrian connection of the Ethiopian Christian Church and that the British one-time allies of Yohannes would support an independent Tigré.

Meantime to the north, events in Eritrea were moving only slowly towards a resolution of the future of that seemingly impoverished land.

Even under the Italians the ports of Eritrea had been merely *dhow* harbours and communications with the plateau had been confined to the somewhat inefficient railway right until it was decided to invade Ethiopia. Those preparations led to the construction of spectacular roads and the growth of towns, but the criterion was always strategic, not economic. The collapse of the Italian orientated colonial economy, the loss of individual savings, the inability and in any case unwillingness of the British to subsidise the territory, the consequent calamitous rise in taxation and in the cost of living, etc., all caused severe economic distress to the whole population. The Eritrean economy reverted to pre-fascist—but not pre-Italian—levels. There was competition for employment and inevitably, therefore, friction between the small Eritrean and the Italian working classes; there was resentment against the continued alienation of land, against the arrogance of the Sudanese military and other employees of the British and a growing suspicion of the goodwill of the latter. The atmosphere of repression induced by the former fascist government was to some extent alleviated, and this together with modest increases in educational opportunity had led to the dissatisfaction and disaffection of both town and country areas coming to express itself more and more in political awareness and activity.

It is not surprising that Ethiopia's agents and political representatives in Eritrea took advantage of the mounting unrest as best they could. Nor were they alone in this. British interest was obvious but Italy also displayed great interest and disbursed considerable sums of money in the Eritrean political arena. Like most of the lowland periphery of the ancient Abyssinian highland core, Eritrea had a large population of Muslims—later in 1952 the British Administration estimated some 514,000 out of a total population of 1,031,000. These numbers also encouraged the Muslim powers, not always well disposed towards Christian Addis Ababa, to seek to involve themselves in the destiny of the former colony.

Brigadier Longrigg, a British chief administrator of Eritrea, has written that he considered 'racially and culturally the Eritrean highlands are Ethiopian' but that 'once off the coptic highlands it is certain that no considerable element whatsoever of the population desires a close connection with the Ethiopian Empire'.[5] Those areas were largely Muslim and they did express considerable separatism through political organisations. Divisions were not, however, as simple as that and several British writers, with the notable exception of Sylvia and Richard Pankhurst, tended to ignore the sizeable Muslim membership of unionist organisations. Also the movement of Christian Eritreans into Ethiopia had been significant since 1935.

Unionist sentiments were apparent from 1941 and the first pro-union political movement—the *Mahiber Fekri Hager**—emerged in 1942 and it soon had pamphlets and propaganda in circulation. It was the forerunner of the Unionist Party which worked closely with the Ethiopian Christian Church in Eritrea. The Church under the leadership of Abune Markos was actively committed to the struggle for union with Ethiopia. British reports suggested that this was because the Ethiopian government was thought far more likely than the British to return the estates of which the Church had been dispossessed by the Italians, who had leased them to the poverty-stricken villagers and settlers. True the Christian Church was a great landowner in Tigré to the south but, far more important, the Ethiopian Christian Church was basic to the philosophy of the Ethiopian state. Attempts by British officers to persuade church dignitaries, including Abune Markos, that the Church should not interfere with politics were frequent. The clerics listened courteously but ignored such advice which in its way was a typical product of the insularity and mental inflexibility demonstrated by some Britons in Africa. Later the Unionist movement received quite overt financial assistance from representatives of the Ethiopian government, but their measure of control over party policies has been much exaggerated. Indeed their lack of it was to lead to a protracted struggle after the British left.

There was some sympathy for the view that Eritrea should be independent from Shewa, as well as from Italy and Britain, united perhaps with Tigré under the possible but unsolicited leadership of Leul-Ras Seyoum Mangasha. This was argued by Fitwrary Tesemma Asberom (who was considered pro-Italian and whom

---

* 'The party with love of the country'—or, the patriotic party.

the Ethiopians wished to apprehend) and his son Abraha. These two were later made respectively *ras* and *dejazmatch* by the British who may well have hoped to retain both an interest in any Tigré-Eritrea state which might emerge and the transfer of certain Muslim parts of western Eritrea to the Sudan which at that time they also ruled. The *Eritrean Weekly News*, a government paper published in Tigrinya, was accused of bias on this issue, for in one article it claimed that 'Ethiopia could not manage Eritrea in a spiritual way because she herself was twisted inside'.[6] It was edited at first by a British army officer but later by his assistant Woldeab Woldé Mariam. A third member of staff was a young linguist named Edward Ullendorff, who later became professor of Ethiopian studies at London University.

From Asmara, Tesemma's supporters observed with some approval the growing tension in Tigré to the south. That province was restless under its Shewan governors, Dejazmatch Bezebeh Sileshi and then Ras Abebe Aragai, afterwards Minister of War as already stated. In Addis Ababa, Hailé Sellassié, who received reports of the conversations of British officers and knew he had cause to be suspicious of British overall intentions, grew alarmed. He decided in August 1943 to order Ethiopian army forces (and their British as well as Ethiopian officers) to move north into Tigré province in support of the governor general.

In September a company of the 5th Ethiopian battalion and three armoured vehicles under a British commander were caught in an ambush in a valley near Amba Alagi—scene of earlier conflicts. The dead included Ethiopian and British officers. In October another British commanded force was attacked to the north of the *amba* but it fought through to occupy the key towns of Makallé, seat of the Tigréan Emperor Yohannes, and Quiha on the Great North Road which together with Addigrat had been taken by the rebels. In the last engagement Hailé Mariam was estimated to have led 6,000 men.

Having manoeuvered British troops into engagements to thwart what he secretly suspected to be a British supported separatist movement, Hailé Sellassié blandly asked the British to send troops on stand-by and ammunition from the Sudan Defence Force. Ammunition was brought as far as the international border but the use of the troops was refused by the Sudan government. The Emperor then requested Aden for an air strike.* The British

---

* It has been asserted that with the personal approval of the British Minister in Addis Ababa he acted over the head of General Sir William Platt, the C.-in-C., in Nairobi, who had opposed him years before. See L. Mosley, *op. cit.*

adjudged the rebellion to be a threat to their military communications because of the Great North Road and accordingly Blenheim fighter-bombers from Aden attacked the rebels. Hailé Sellassié's troops then put down what remained of the rebellion. Dejazmatch Mangasha, son of Leul-Ras Seyoum, who had been with the rebels, was subsequently imprisoned in the palace at Makallé. He did not take an active part but many claim that he sympathised with the rising. However, he was quite young and may have been used by the rebels.

Away in the south of Ethiopia there were particularly serious tribal clashes in the area of the frontier with Kenya in April 1942 —though troubles there are the rule rather than the exception (1963, the year of Kenya's independence, and 1964 have been no different). Violent clashes also occurred in the south-east in May 1943 in the hills between Harar and Ji-Jigga between Ethiopian Somalis and irregular troops supporting Christian settlers. In 1943 another tribal raid across the Kenya frontier involving the destruction of twenty-two Durreh villages led to talks in London in which the possibility of sending British troops into Ethiopian Borana was considered. In June 1944 the struggling government in Addis Ababa was further disturbed by news of a large raid by the Arusi Galla across the river Webbi Shebelli (the Leopard river) involving the destruction of some twenty-five villages in the Ogaden.

The Italians had ruled their adjacent Somaliland colony, the former British Somaliland and the areas of Ethiopia occupied by Somali peoples, all as one unit from Mogadishu. They had regarded it all, moreover, as part of Italian East Africa centred upon Addis Ababa. The frontier between Italian Somaliland and the Ethiopian province of Harar had never been properly defined either on maps or on the ground. Although the excuse for the 1935 invasion, demarcation was actually rather meaningless for the nomadic Somali peoples moved regularly across it in the process of transhumance as they still do in the 1960s. Except for the Arusi Galla in the north west and a few Christian highlanders in the villages in the foothills of the Harar Plateau most of the population of the Ethiopian Ogaden is Somali. It seemed simpler in 1941, and the Emperor agreed, that this area should continue to be administered along with the British and Italian colonies from Mogadishu. At that time no Ethiopian administrators were available and land communications with the Ethiopian Highlands were very poor indeed.

However, by 1944 Hailé Sellassié had found strength enough to exert himself in the east. The Danakil Sultan of Aussa, Muhammad Yayu, who flew his own red flag like the former sultan of Zanzibar and who had previously been presented by the British with an engraved revolver in recognition of his part in the war-time blockade of Vichy Djibouti, was arrested when an Ethiopian military column reached his capital. He was taken to Addis Ababa, where he died in captivity, and was succeeded in office by a 'co-operative' relative.

Also in 1944 negotiations for a new agreement between the Ethiopian and British governments began, following the Ethiopian notice of termination of the 1942 agreements. Earl de la Warr headed the British team of negotiators and the new agreement was signed in December 1944. The Ogaden and certain other areas defined on their strategic or military importance—such as the border of French Somaliland, the railway route, etc.—and termed 'The Reserved Area', remained 'temporarily' under British admin-istration, but to further confirm Ethiopian sovereignty her flag was to be flown beside the Union Jack. It was agreed that Ethiopia should take over management of the railway although she did not choose to do so until 1946. Arrangements for the recruitment of British advisers, should the Emperor ask for them, were set out, the military mission was continued and diplomatic relations with Britain were normalised. That year a United States economic mission visited Ethiopia—sign of a new flirtation.

In 1948 there was some agitation in Harar for the regional independence of the whole province and minority discontent in the south east led several times to violence, for example, in 1951. On at least one occasion rebel leaders were hanged.[7]

The 1944 agreement with Britain was superseded after a further ten years by another agreement which arranged that the Ethiopian government should 'reassume jurisdiction and administra-tion of, in and over' the Ogaden and the 'Reserved Area' in 1955. One account describes how the reserve of the British and Ethiopian army officers engaged in the actual handover was overcome by toasts to their respective monarchs drunk in whisky thoughtfully allocated for the purpose by the British military authorities.[8] Not long afterwards, in 1955, the seizure by government troops of water holes near Dira Dawa, in an attempt to bring rebellious Issa tribesmen to heel, led to another series of engagements. Never-theless the control of the Addis Ababa government continued to make advances.

There is considerable evidence that all the Indian Ocean coastal lands, now occupied by Somali tribesmen, were once part of the Empire of the Prester John.* It has been argued that the

---

* See, for example, the log kept by Vasco da Gama. Ethiopians sometimes state that the words 'Somali', 'Mogadishu' and even 'Mombasa' are of Ethiopian origin. See also pp. 29–30, 51–3, 109–10 and 270 above.

Ethiopian emperors never *ruled* these regions, in the modern sense of the word, but nevertheless when they were able they exacted tribute from muslim rulers east of the plateau and confirmed them in office. That was the traditional way in Africa and elsewhere of ruling until the last hundred years. Moreover, there has never been a Somali 'nation' in the history of the Horn of Africa. In the author's opinion this fact is overlooked by sympathisers of the Greater Somaliland concept. When it is realised that no Somali state as such existed to be 'divided' during the nineteenth century Scramble for Africa, then the Ethiopian view that that concept represents nothing more than territorial aggrandisement based on tribalism is easily understandable. The invasions and westward expansion of Somali peoples, inland from the Horn of Africa, are facts of history.[9]

The Somali herdsmen are very proud peoples and in recent years they have responded to a political call for unity despite traditional rivalries and feuds among themselves.[10] Quite when their pan-Somali nationalism began is an academic point. Some publications maintain that there were beginnings even before the Horn of Africa was partitioned during the Scramble.[11] Others claim that the Italians, or the British, or even Mr Ernest Bevin in person, subsequently originated it.[12] The author subscribes to none of these views. If colonial powers were so skilled at educating subject peoples to hold convenient alien ideas they would have taught them to like colonialism! It is perhaps not irrelevant that those colonial powers are often criticised in the next breath, and certainly with more justice, for not developing modern Somali education to any significant degree! Pan-Somaliism is of Somali origin, if recent, but it was easier for it to develop—and that development was far from discouraged—whilst the three of the five areas inhabited by Somalis were ruled as one. The others are the Northern Frontier Region of Kenya and French Somaliland, and in neither are the Somalis the only inhabitants.

THE DISPOSAL OF ITALY'S FORMER COLONIES

The attitudes of both the Somalis and the Eritreans towards the government in Addis Ababa were to become vital factors in the politics of the Horn of Africa, but before the issue of the post-colonial status of the former Italian colonies could be decided on its merits the question of their future became one of many pawns in what were beginning to be known as the politics of the 'Cold War'. Much hinged not only on the attitudes of the United States, France, the Soviet Union and Britain (who in the interim administered both territories) but also of the United Nations General Assembly, for the great powers could not agree. Nor indeed were their individual attitudes at all consistent because they regarded Italy's former colonies as mere pawns in a wider diplomacy. The Soviet Union, for example, at first supported the return of her former colonies to Italy, but after the defeat of the Communist Party in the Italian General Election of April 1948 she completely reversed her attitude, and was not alone in such 'adjustments'.* Political pressures on the British government were many and varied, for example, the *Catholic Herald* urged the return of her former colonies to Italy while Miss Sylvia Pankhurst, through *New Times and Ethiopia News,* Mr Jomo Kenyatta and others fought to keep Ethiopia's claims before the British public.

The international struggles which preceded the eventual granting to Italy in 1949 of a ten-year United Nations Trusteeship over her former Somaliland colony, in the face of spirited Ethiopian objection, were protracted and complex—as also were those which led later to the 1952 Federation of Eritrea with Ethiopia.

Despite United Nations mediation the Italian and Ethiopian governments failed thereafter to agree on the delineation of the Somali frontier. Throughout the 1950s incidents continued and if major disturbances were held off for some years the new Somali Republic, formed in 1960 by the amalgamation of the British and Italian territories, inherited the problem. In fact it made it worse by repudiating the 1897 agreement between Britain and Ethiopia which had defined the part of the frontier which lay between the former British Somali colony and Ethiopia. It had even been demarcated on the ground. Significantly a map on which Menelik II had marked his eastern frontiers with the encroaching Italians, although acknowledged by the Italian Foreign Office on September 3, 1897, was later 'lost'—as it more or less had to be prior to 1935 —and had not been 'found' by 1964.

In the 1950s Ethiopia largely dropped her own territorial claims to other Somali lands and instead supported the progress of the Trust Territories towards independence—though in this context it is significant that the future of the French colony containing the vital rail terminus and port of Djibouti, was seldom discussed. But

---

* The communist bloc did not see their *volte-face* as being inconsistent. The Ukraine delegate said his government 'had hoped the former Italian colonies might be placed under the administration of a democratic Italy freed from fascism. The present government of Italy, however, had 'delivered that country bound hand and foot into the hands of the capitalists.' His government had, therefore, 'realised the impossibility of allowing Italy to administer any of its former colonies'.

the new Somali Republic has itself made claims and has shewn no enthusiasm for the proper demarcation of the common frontier, strangely echoing the Italian Foreign Minister Tittoni's comment to his Chamber of Deputies in the early years of this century : 'I do not see the urgency and necessity of such delineation. Between the Benadir proper and Ethiopia there is a very vast region which belongs no one knows exactly to whom . . . let us leave, therefore, to time the solution of problems such as this'. The thought-patterns of territorial imperialism are, of course, not confined to Europe and although Italian and United Nations efforts during the ten-year trust period failed to forestall this problem, it must also be remembered that its roots go back to the sixteenth century, to the Imam Ahmed Ibn Ibrahim al-Ghazi (Gran) and beyond.

CONFLICTS AT COURT

It is often thought in Ethiopia that Earl de la Warr suggested to the Emperor that the time might be propitious for the release of Dejazmatch Takelé Woldé Hawariat. Whether or not this is so, Takelé was freed in 1945, created *blattenguetta* and appointed deputy *Afe negus*. The then *Afe negus*, roughly Lord Chief Justice, was Zaudi Ayelu who had been rewarded, at least in part, for his loyalty to the Emperor while a wartime refugee in Kenya. Afe Negus Zaudi retired from the political forefront and Takelé was once again prominent. It was not long, however, before his old rivalry with Woldé Giorgis, the Minister of the Pen, who soon afterwards took to himself also the Ministry of the Interior, led to another intense period of involved court intrigue.

Everything revolved round the court and the person of the Emperor, rather as it had done in Europe in bygone days. Several foreign visitors who did not understand this have recorded the exasperation which they experienced when calling at the offices of the various ministries of the Imperial Government. Polite young officials would apologise that no decisions could be made that day because the minister, the ministers of state, the vice-ministers and the assistant ministers—and sometimes even the director general and directors—were not in their offices. They had gone to the palace. They went for the monarch's decision on even petty points, for the Emperor was head of the government and of the judiciary and also combined in his person the functions both of chief legislator and chief executive. He did, in fact, both reign and rule.

However, as often as not courtiers merely stood around and bowed when the Emperor arrived to attend to affairs of state. It was important for all to be seen at court because the tradition of attendance on the monarch was a form of the constant expression and renewal of loyalty. Hailé Sellassié played a central role in encouraging this 'showing' of people and, therefore, even those who wanted nothing could not afford not to go to court for fear of his displeasure. But most reasoned that their Emperor would know of their loyalty and remember their faces when he decided to bestow titles and position, or gifts of land or money. In such an atmosphere nepotism and patronage, the courting of other courtiers and the intrigues of rival cliques, factions and families could only thrive. As the great men of the empire waited about, they carefully noted the glances and muttered asides of their fellows, and behind their superb manners, their kisses, smiles and bows, the whole energy of their minds was often consumed by suspicion, hatred, narrow ambitions and conspiracy. Few indeed developed any detachment or comprehension of wider issues.

THE PLOT OF THE PARLIAMENTARY REFORMERS

A group of former Patriot leaders planned to oblige Hailé Sellassié to relinquish much of his personal control and become more of a constitutional monarch. Although impelled by a growing awareness of the comparatively slow rate of economic development in postwar Ethiopia these men feared that a frontal challenge to the monarchy might even lead to British intervention. However, they thought that the new authoritarian measures which they envisaged while retaining the symbolism of monarchy would not only avoid foreign interference but might also give the necessary initial boost for renewed economic and social progress. Their master plan, they decided, would need to be directed by people removed from the rival family and provincial interests which enmeshed the throne.

Blattenguetta Takelé Woldé Hawariat seems to have been immediately suspected of involvement. He was demoted and posted to Borana as a governor under the authority of the governor general of Sidamo. Another man, posted as deputy to the *blattenguetta,* was Gebré Medhin Hailé Mariam. Gebré Medhin, a great man of liberal tendencies and high principles, was judge in a case involving a concession and the Ministry of Agriculture. He is said to have ignored telephoned advice concerning his verdict. Some say he was even called before his Emperor and questioned over his loyalty. He is said to have replied to the enquiry '. . . and who made you what you are?' with the words 'The Great Lord made me'. He was arrested in Goré and detained for years without charge. Only in the 1960s was he re-appointed to a post in the governorate general of Illubabor but, a sick man, he was obliged to come to live in Addis Ababa.

Ras Abebe Aragai was largely responsible for the government's part in uncovering the plot. He confided what information he had to Colonel Mulugeta Bulli, commander of the Imperial Guard, Colonel Makonnen Deneke then deputy commissioner of police and Tafari Sharaw an influential businessman who kept himself informed of most intrigues and who much later came to prominence in Sweden when he was dismissed as ambassador for speaking out in favour of the attempted *coup d'état* of 1960. The full story of this episode cannot yet be recounted but among other things it led to the assassination of Yohannes Semerjibashan, the former Patriot, who was shot down early one evening as he entered his house near the Nazret School in Addis Ababa. Meantime in Borana there developed an atmosphere of not inconsiderable disaffection towards the central government. Once again certain influential conservatives sought to lay the blame on the progressive and ambitious Blattenguetta Takelé who was arrested. Abiye Abebe, later an important general, and others were sent as his judges but found nothing on which to accuse him and a foreign judge in the service of the Ethiopian government shortly afterwards ordered his release. It is a significant guide to the patterns of thought of the several conservative leaders, including one bishop, that they admit today to having written to Takelé and to having asked him what it was 'he wanted for himself'.

Meantime the potential revolt reached no more serious proportions. Some several hundred soldiers under the command of Major Tsigué Dibou, who died with the rebels in the 1960 attempted *coup*, were on the verge of revolt and a large force commanded by Colonel Tesfai Desta, was suspected of complicity. This very able officer had written two Amharic books on military tactics and had been a much respected training officer at Holeta College. Not for the last time Hailé Sellassié raised his soldiers' pay to retain their loyalty and offered free education to the sons of serving soldiers. Colonel Tesfai decided for the second time in his career, the first being after the battle of Maichew, to leave for Djibouti. He took all his papers with him. Later he arrived in Cairo but refused to broadcast against his country on the grounds that it was the régime, and not his country and people, that he opposed. The Ethiopians believe that it was as a result of a disagreement with Nasser that he left Egypt to live in Germany where he still lived in 1964.

It is true that a plan to march on Addis Ababa had been considered but it had been abandoned. Also Blattenguetta Takelé had been cleared of the charge of 'fomenting tribal war'. However, in the capital the tirade against him turned in new directions. Dejaz-match Mesfin Sileshi, the former Patriot major, and Woldé Giorgis harked back to the discussions of 1940 when certain Patriot leaders sought to proclaim a republic. The elder statesman Leul-Ras Kassa Hailu knew well that Takelé had served his country better than most in those dark days and it is said that this trend in the accusations disturbed him. One day in audience with the Emperor, he heard Woldé Giorgis, who ran an efficient spy ring, state that he strongly suspected that Takelé still visited foreign embassies at night with sinister schemes in his mind. This was too much for the normally quiet and religious old prince and he lifted his stick to Woldé Giorgis and thundered 'What! Will such as you betray this great man again?' and with that he turned on his heel and strode from the room. For some time afterwards he did not speak even to Hailé Sellassié. While conservative opposition to the powerful 'upstart' Woldé Giorgis increased, Blattenguetta Takelé was to ask, 'Who are my judges? With what am I charged?' but the Emperor when told is said to have uttered an Amharic proverb (literally 'above the head is air') to the effect that he had to safeguard his own interests before those of any other, and to have added 'We are the judge of such things'. He obliged Takelé to sign a document 'to err is human but to forgive is the role of Emperors' and consigned both Takelé and his son-in-law back to prison.

THE PLOT OF THE BETWODED NEGASH

There had been a minor revolt in Gojjam led by Dejazmatch Aberra against the paying of personal tax but after two months fighting the trouble had been subdued by the Imperial Guard. However, in the early 1950s there developed a much more serious challenge led by a Gojjam Patriot leader, Betwoded Negash Bezebé, a descendant of the royal house of the Negus Taklé Haymanot. Betwoded Negash had been a vice minister in the Prime Minister's office and then president of the Senate. There is no doubt that he was motivated to a con-siderable extent by personal ambition, but once again the conspiracy was national and not confined to Gojjam.

An Eritrean, Yohannes Rama, was deeply involved as, in all probability, was a distinguished Shewan who spent subsequent years abroad as a foreign service officer. The plot was to assassinate Hailé Sellassié in favour of Betwoded Negash. Some conspirators hoped that they might subsequently proclaim a republic under the leader-ship of Hailé Sellassié's relative Ras Imru, but he was not involved in the plan. As stated, Ras Imru had been appointed to Gondar as governor general of Begemidir. However, Hailé Sellassié resented the considerable popularity of the former Regent. Ras Imru had been a progressive governor before the war and was remembered for his justice—many a proverbial good judgement is attributed to him. All admired his fight to the end against the Italians and he retained the respect and affection of the army officers, particularly those trained at Holeta Military College. Ras Imru used the familiar mood when talking to Hailé Sellassié and voiced his disagreement with some of Hailé Sellassié's policies on successive occasions. For example, although he himself speaks little of the language, he urged the Emperor to choose English rather than French as second official language to Amharic after the war. Partly to restrain his critic but also perhaps to neutralise a potential rival, Hailé Sellassié appointed (Ethiopians say 'exiled') the *ras* to embassies abroad. At the time of the Betwoded Negash conspiracy, Ras Imru was ambassador in the United States, where incidentally the proud old noble was much irritated by first-hand experience of racial discrimination.

Machiavelli wrote that 'there are many who think that a wise prince ought when he has the chance to foment astutely some enmity so that by suppressing it he will augment his greatness'.[13] One serious student of Ethiopian affairs has suggested that the Betwoded Negash conspiracy might fit this category and that Hailé Sellassié conceived the plot in order to claim western assistance as a bulwark against communist conspiracy.[14] The author doubts this and considers that as an interpretation it probably derives from the masterly way in which the Emperor held his hand. The conspirators approached many government officials, several of whom proved sympathetic and the officer cadets of the second Imperial Guard Training Course were also in the secret. Much of the tactical planning is said to have been effected by Bekelé Antanateos, a discharged officer who had been trained at Holeta Military College before the Italian war and who had fought at Maichew. Considered with some justice to be something of a trouble-maker he had not been promoted and had become disgruntled. The main mistake which the conspirators made was to attempt to enlist the support of the famous Galla Patriot Dejazmatch Geressu Duké.

Geressu was a governor in the south and had fallen foul of certain influential court officials in Addis Ababa. A Shewan Amhara had been sent to Goré as a director and being appointed by the Emperor had arrogantly ignored the Galla *dejazmatch* and acted independently of him within his governorate. Dejazmatch Geressu promptly had him flogged and this action resulted soon afterwards in his recall to Addis Ababa at the instigation of the proud and horrified relatives. Hailé Sellassié received him and he admitted that he may have been in the wrong, but when the conspirators attempted to play upon a grudge they subsequently assumed him to bear they failed properly to assess the simplicity of his character and his abiding loyalty to the throne. He duly reported their approaches and with Hailé Sellassié's approval and guidance he played a double game until more was known. Then a certain young and up-and-coming colonel of the Imperial Guard named Mengistu Neway was entrusted with the apprehension of the conspirators. Betwoded Negash and many others were arrested at bayonet point at a clandestine meeting in Dejazmatch Geressu's house in the market area of Addis Ababa.

The chief conspirators were tried at the Emperor's special court. Those present recall how one poor clerk—a priest—endeavoured to obtain mercy by pleading a Ge'ez proverb before the Emperor. 'Your Majesty, who knows when someone commits a sin?' he asked. But the next prisoner, Major Bekele, was angered by such submissiveness and defied Hailé Sellassié with the words, 'Who are you? You have blood on your hands! Torture and kill me as you will....' The Emperor, already on his feet, without comment swept his cloak over his shoulder and left the court. The major was subsequently flogged and imprisoned and his property was confiscated.

In Ethiopia, if a man is hard on his own children over small matters, but pardons someone unrelated to him who has really tried to harm him, people aclaim him as 'great' and 'just'. There were rumours that Hailé Sellassié was hard on his favourite son Leul Makonnen, who gave himself increasingly to rather wild ways. Although Betwoded Negash and the conspirators appealed to Parliament, the ministers and nobles urged that this be ignored and that they should hang, but Hailé Sellassié, mindful also of the resentment caused by the manner of the deaths of Dejazmatch Belai Zelleka, Dejazmatch Mammo Hailu and the others, ordered imprisonment. In mid 1964 Betwoded Negash was still living under restriction in Jimma.

THE FALL OF WOLDÉ GIORGIS

Hailé Sellassié has never allowed any Ethiopian to remain in high office long enough to build up too sizeable a following and become a threat to his own position. Soon it was the turn of Woldé Giorgis Woldé Yohannes to be discarded. He had contributed much. Under him the central government had been stabilised and a very firm control established over the capital and the provinces. He had lasted longer and had acquired more power than any other of Hailé

Sellassié's ministers before or since. Because he used his power he was greatly feared.

Like so many of the men whom Hailé Sellassié relied heavily upon, Woldé Giorgis, the son of an Amhara leather tanner or saddlemaker from Bulga, Shewa, was of the humblest origins. He had worked as a dispenser and interpreter in Addis Ababa's Menelik II Hospital and then as a clerk before being taken to court. He became one of Hailé Sellassié's lieutenants in his early days when the Emperor sought to break the power of the great conservative barons. Before the Italian war he became a director in the Ministry of the Pen and he often acted as Hailé Sellassié's secretary. In 1934 he is recorded as having remarked of his fellows—the young followers of the reformer Emperor—'. . . the men who take it upon themselves to make a European country out of this backward African empire will be the first martyrs in the revolution, for the conservatives rule the country and conservative here means backward and pitiless. We of the younger generation are the friends of progress and humanism while they are its enemies!'[15] He never lost his antagonism towards the leading representatives of the feudal families, for it is they he meant by 'conservative', and their unrelenting opposition to him meant that in the last resort his power depended solely upon the Emperor—a not uncommon relationship for those who have been most trusted by Hailé Sellassié.

When the war came, he accompanied his master to the northern front and into exile in Britain and was also with him when he re-entered the empire from the Sudan. A skilled administrator he soon became Minister of the Pen and later also Minister of the Interior and accompanied Hailé Sellassié on the latter's state visits to Europe and the United States. People called him the 'uncrowned Emperor'. Some say that Hailé Sellassié took exception to the fact that while in France Woldé Giorgis was decorated before Makonnen, Duke of Harar, and was described by a publication there as 'the real ruler of Ethiopia'. Certainly hostile tongues at the Ethiopian court whispered that he had been heard to claim that he could secure the return of anyone banished to the provinces by the Emperor but that his own banishments were irrevocable. Indeed, the Emperor seldom overruled him.

Some argue, though the author considers it unlikely, that Woldé Giorgis planned a *coup d'état* to make himself dictator. They quote a story that arms were later discovered in the cellars underneath his fine house on Entotto ridge above Addis Ababa. Still others declare that his only mistake was to confuse power with station : they claim that he tried to marry into the tight clique of leading Ethopian families who both despised and feared him.

Hailé Selassié's eldest child, Princess Tenagne Worq, had been widowed when the Italians had murdered Ras Desta. Whilst in exile in England she had become attached to another Ethiopian named Abebe Retta—the Minister of Health in 1964. Abebe had been educated by the Ethiopian Christian Church to become quite a scholar in classical Ge'ez, but was of humble Tigréan origin. Whilst in England he had joined Hailé Sellassié's household and at times had driven the exiled Emperor's car. However, despite issue, a marriage between the princess and one of Abebe's lower station could not be considered.

It was some time after the return of the exiles that whispers again began over a proposed match for the widowed princess and this time the name of Woldé Giorgis was mentioned. It was said that he had asked Hailé Sellassié for Tenagne Worq's hand and that the Emperor, who admired Woldé Giorgis's shrewd mind, had agreed. Some even affirm that cards were printed. But Tenagne Worq's mother, the Empress Menen, proud grand-daughter of the Negus Mikael, intervened. She is said to have been supported, as she usually was, by the priests; by her son, the heir-apparent Asfa Wossen, who feared that Woldé Giorgis would intrigue to secure the succession for himself or for any offspring; by Makonnen Endalkatchew, spokesman of the Addisgé families and by representatives of another proud and important Shewan family group, the Mojas. This may well be, for certainly there was no love lost between Woldé Giorgis and the *balabat* and feudal classes. Although the political influence exercised by the Empress over Hailé Sellassié was in no way remarkable, she was, nevertheless, a dangerous enemy. She was satisfied to get her way, but her relatives and members of her party at court gloated and waited for Woldé Giorgis—whom they despised as 'the cobbler's son'—to make another miscalculation.

Woldé Giorgis had always made enemies. Before the war he had clashed with the important Swedish adviser, General Virgin, who was indignant at having to approach the Emperor through Woldé Giorgis. Indeed many foreigners half resented and half feared the Emperor's cunning and informed private secretary, and out of earshot of the court they referred to him as the 'Eminence Grise'. But being unpopular with the foreign community is no disgrace in Ethiopia and more important was the fact that many Ethiopians resented his ruthlessness and also his business connections and those of his relatives with certain wealthy Italians. Eventually opposition to Woldé Giorgis came to centre around another of the Emperor's humble protégés, Makonnen Habtewold. In his rivalry for the Emperor's ear Makonnen sought and secured the alliance of his brothers Aklilu and Akalaworq, of Ras Abebe Aragai and of

Blattenguetta Takelé Woldé Hawariat and the struggle soon became intense. Blattenguetta Takelé had once again been called to prominence by Hailé Sellassié as a counter balance to Woldé Giorgis, for the Emperor knew well and even approved of the mutual animosity between these two. Takelé was later made Vice-Minister of the Interior.

Intrigue flared into open hostility soon after Makonnen had used his position 'behind the curtain' of the throne to help one of his relatives Sahlu Defaye to become governor of Nazret. A follower of Woldé Giorgis on the other hand had been appointed chief of that municipality and a quarrel between these two spread to their patrons when the governor suspended the chief of the municipality from work. Makonnen who was a master at intrigue got several other ministers involved by attributing certain national evils and corruptions for which the government was being increasingly blamed, to the influence of Woldé Giorgis. Further, he gambled with his own position by personally attempting to convince Hailé Sellassié in 1955, that Woldé Giorgis had antagonised not only the people but most of the ministers through wielding powers belonging more properly in the hands of the monarch. The Emperor hesitated but stated that should the ministers agree, and he be not asked to carry the responsibility alone, he would send Woldé Giorgis to a provincial governorship. Makonnen then sought the help of Major-general Mulugeta Bulli, the first post-war commander of the Imperial Guard who had his own reasons for disliking Woldé Giorgis. Several of Mulugeta's officers had urged him to initiate a military *coup* but he knew that such an action was impossible while Woldé Giorgis was in power, because of the latter's well-developed security service and because of the universal fear he inspired. These two and the heads of the important families, convinced the ministers privately to oppose Woldé Giorgis and the Emperor eventually appears to have been relieved to have the chance of getting rid of a person whom he had begun to feel might be a danger to his throne, and who had, therefore, outlived his usefulness. By letter he appointed a new Minister of the Pen and Woldé Giorgis, who for once was not appraised of events in time to act, was called and appointed governor general of Arusi. He bowed low and made no comment, for he knew he would have been arrested if he had.

ERITREA IS FEDERATED WITH ETHIOPIA

Meantime in the north, as noted on page 289 above, the United Nations decided upon the future of Eritrea. After eleven years of British administration and mounting political pressure both inside and outside Eritrea, the General Assembly of the United Nations resolved on December 2, 1950, that Eritrea should be federated with Ethiopia.

The resolution, which was passed by 46 votes to 10, recommended that Eritrea should 'constitute an autonomous unit federated with Ethiopia under the sovereignty of the Ethiopian crown'. The Federal government was to control 'defence, foreign affairs, currency and finance, foreign and interstate commerce and external and interstate communications including ports'. There was to be common citizenship and an Imperial Federal Council with Eritrean and Ethiopian representation. The Eritrean government was to have 'legislative, executive and judicial powers in the field of domestic affairs', and to be responsible for 'all matters not vested in the Federal government, including the power to maintain the internal police, to levy taxes to meet the expenses of domestic functions and services and to adopt its own budget'.

The United Nations required that an Eritrean administration be organised and a representative assembly be elected during a transition period to last at the latest until September 15, 1952. Señor Matienzo of Bolivia was appointed United Nations commissioner with the responsibility of drafting an Eritrean constitution to be 'based on the principles of democratic government', to be approved by the Eritrean General Assembly and to be ratified by the Emperor of Ethiopia.

Several political parties had been formed. The *El Rabita* with a largely Muslim membership was against union and some suspected that it had British backing. The *Pro-Italia* party, whose support included Eritrean half-castes and those who had received titles or preferment from Italians, was similarly suspected of receiving Italian money. British writers point out, doubtless correctly, that the Ethiopian government supported the Unionists—the largest party.

Considering the obvious contrast between the economic, educational and political development of Eritrea and neighbouring Ethiopian Tigré, the Ethiopian government needed to conduct its propaganda and negotiations with great skill. Outstanding were Colonel Nega Hailé Sellassié, appointed Ethiopian liaison officer in Asmara in 1946, and the Foreign Minister, Aklilu Habtewold. The Ethiopian role was, however, mainly diplomatic in the United Nations and it is also quite certain they would have met with no success there if the majority of the Eritrean population, honestly desiring closer links with Ethiopia, had not organised themselves through the Unionist Party—a point which does not always emerge too clearly from the writings ot former officers of the British administration.

One event had been particularly significant. On August 28, 1946, a bloody clash had occurred in Asmara between Sudanese troops who were subsequently withdrawn, and Christian Eritreans. Hailé Sellassié had immediately donated £2,000 to a committee set up to assist the victims, and the incident, partly because of the historical and religious animosity between the Sudanese and the Christian highlanders, had made a deep impression and had assisted the propagation of the Unionist cause. Tedla Bairu the son of Bairu Ogbit, a prominent Eritrean long associated with unionist ideals, had resigned from his post of assistant civil affairs officer of the British administration to become secretary-general of the Unionist Party. He had been replaced in the administration by 'Dejazmatch' Abraha. Woldeab Woldé Mariam, the former British appointed editor, also became a political leader, but of the separatists. Attempts were made to poison, shoot and bomb him—in fact he survived at least seven assassination bids. Abd el-Kadir Kebiré, president of the *El Rabita* Party, was less fortunate. He was shot down in an Asmara street in March 1949 by unknown assassins. In 1950 Vittorio Lunghi, a half-caste advocate of independence, long active in sabotaging the Unionist Party, was also assassinated.

The Emperor had entertained Abune Markos and the Catholic bishop of the Ethiopian rite in Eritrea, Monsignor Kidanimariam, on visits to Addis Ababa and in 1947 he had appointed Leul-Ras Seyoum Mangasha, grandson of the northern Emperor Yohannes who fell fighting the Sudanese, as governor general of Tigré. It proved a nominal position since real power was vested in a Shewan deputy, Fitwrary Yemani Hassan of the Moja family, but the appointment made a favourable impression throughout the north. Several Eritreans in Ethiopian employment—notably Dawit Okbagzy and Ephrem Tewoldé Medhin—had visited Eritrea for barely disguised political purposes. Blatta Ephrem had been minister in London at the time of the 1946 Paris Conference which had discussed the drafts of the Italian peace treaty, and had attended the conference. Although led by Aklilu Habtewold, the Ethiopian delegation had included another Eritrean, Blattenguetta Lorenzo Taezaz, then ambassador in Moscow, and two Ogaden Somalis, Haji Omar and Haji Farah. Certain Ethiopians, including Wagshum Wossen and Betwoded Andargatchew Messai, had also visited Eritrea.

Andargatchew came from Salalé in Shewa where his father had been in the employment of Leul-Ras Kassa. He had been consul-general at Djibouti in French Somaliland, at the time of the Italian invasion of Ethiopia. After the Restoration, Andargatchew had risen to become deputy governor general of Harar with the title of *afe mesfin*—(voice of the prince)—for Makonnen, Duke of Harar and second son of Emperor Hailé Sellassié, was the nominal governor there. Andargatchew had survived a subsequent period of disfavour and, some say, house arrest, had become quite wealthy as agent for a British commercial company and had been recalled to the government service in Addis Ababa as Minister of Justice. He it was who finally married the Emperor's widowed daughter, Princess Tenagne Worq. (Meanwhile his first wife appealed to the Church, was offered land by the Empress and eventually went abroad to Jerusalem and thence to exile in Birmingham, Britain.) With the title of *betwoded*, Andargatchew governed Gondar and he and his wife, the Imperial Princess, had toured Eritrea in 1947 'for health reasons'.

United Nations staff also travelled around Eritrea sounding out opinions of the several political parties which had grown up during the period of the British administration and the views of the Eritrean peoples. Trevaskis, who was political secretary of the British administration, claimed that since union was not to be, the Unionists and the Ethiopian government considered that a federation should . . . 'in practice leave full control in the Emperor's hands'; but that opinion in 'the Western Province, though still divided, was anxious that the [to them] unwelcome link with Ethiopia should be no more than a tenuous formality'.[16]

It is interesting that Longrigg wondered whether Eritrea would in future 'disappear, as a political unit, completely from the map' and that Trevaskis wrote in 1960 that union rather than federation was the only 'practical solution to the problem. Ethiopia needed Eritrea's ports and industrial installations for her own development. She had the resources to finance Eritrean development and the land to absorb Eritrea's surplus population and livestock. Eritrea was the economic complement to Ethiopia, and economically the union of the two countries was logical and rational; it offered Eritrea the only alternative to parasitism or bankruptcy. . . .' The main difficulty, Trevaskis admitted, was some Muslim opposition to such a union, but after full consideration he saw no alternative course that would be both practical and durable.[17]

Federation was among the alternatives Trevaskis considered and rejected. He argued : 'Ethiopia's empire had been preserved by the concentration of power and authority in its central government. To admit the principle of federation in the case of Eritrea might well spark off secessionist movements in other provinces where the direct control of the central government was unwelcome.' Ethiopia would not favour federation, Trevaskis argued, and therefore it could not survive. In the conclusion to his book, he urged the

Ethiopian government to try to make federation work, but in the end he proved to be quite right.

Despite the pledges of the various political parties to co-operate and respect United Nations decisions on the new constitution, the grave differences between them were very difficult to surmount. Ethiopia was represented at the discussions by Aklilu Habtewold. Here also difficulties at once arose, for he demanded that the Emperor be empowered to appoint not only a governor general but all executive officials and to approve or reject all legislation; that there be no Eritrean flag and that Amharic be the sole official language even if Tigrinya and Arabic were also used. Matienzo ruled that the Ethiopian government should itself be the Federal government and that the Emperor should be represented by a governor general, but that the latter should not control the executive since the United Nations had decided that Eritrea was to be 'an autonomous unit' and have 'the widest possible measure of self government'. He thought Eritrea should have a separate flag if it wished and should itself decide on its official languages.

Whilst Matienzo sought advice from leading constitutional lawyers, the British administration divided Eritrea into sixty-eight constituencies each with a population of approximately 15,000, and an election was held based on male suffrage. In Massawa and Asmara elections were direct but elsewhere village and family groups elected regional electoral colleges and they chose the regional representatives. The result of the election reflected regional differences. There was an even division between Muslim and Christian and an uneasy alliance led by the Unionists (thirty-two seats) resulted. However, the assembly approved Matienzo's proposals for a constitution with only minor amendments.

The single legislative assembly was to elect both its own president and the chief executive. The latter in turn would appoint judges on the president's recommendation and the secretaries or heads of government departments. Other government appointments were to be the responsibility of a civil service commission and the supreme and subordinate courts were to be independent of both the legislature and the executive. The Emperor's governor general or representative was to promulgate Eritrean legislation and read the speech from the throne. He was, in fact, meant to be merely a constitutional figure, except that he could refer back to the legislature any legislation which he considered to encroach on the jurisdiction of the Federal government (the Ethiopian government) or to involve 'international responsibility'. Eritrea was also to fly her own flag and Tigrinya and Arabic were to be recognised as her official languages.

The transfer of power from the British administration to

Eritreans was speedily and fairly smoothly effected. The Eritrean constitution, approved by the Eritrean Assembly in July 1952, was ratified by Hailé Sellassié in August. A fortnight later the Unionist leader Tedla Bairu was elected chief executive of Eritrea and he appointed a cabinet. Then in September Hailé Sellassié ratified the Act of Federation and nominated his son-in-law Betwoded Andargatchew Messai as his representative. Together with Princess Tenagne Worq, Andargatchew took up residence in the palace at Asmara. Tedla Bairu became *dejazmatch* and on September 16, 1952, Sir Duncan Cumming, the last British administrator of Eritrea, signed the formal proclamation handing over Eritrea from Britain to Ethiopia.

AUTOCRACY AND DEMOCRACY IN ERITREA

Trevaskis, in his subsequent book on Eritrea, has pleaded that the British 'caretaker' administration be not measured by its meagre economic achievements, compared with those in other administered areas during the same decade, but by the fact that 'a subservient population accustomed to hear and obey the orders of an alien colonial government' became [Trevaskis writes 'were converted into'] 'a people who were learning to think and act for themselves'. This, however, was not a quality which endeared them to the government in Addis Ababa.

On December 2, 1950, Aklilu Habtewold had remarked in the General Assembly of the United Nations that 'Ethiopia wanted outright annexation but accepted federation in a spirit of compromise.' That spirit, however, proved transient. Not long after Eritrea attained her internal self government, conflict between the Eritrean and the Ethiopian (i.e., the Federal) government developed. This is hardly surprising for the Eritrean constitution, reflecting as it did the democratic concepts of the United Nations Charter, was in basic contradiction to the authoritarian tradition of Ethiopia. One wag described the constitution as a 'Bolivian concept of a Swiss federation adapted to an African absolute monarchy',[18] but, in fact, it was not adapted at all and could not be. Therefore it was increasingly ignored. Matienzo had seen power as being delegated upwards from the people but the power of the Emperor of Ethiopia, on the other hand, came theoretically from heaven and, where it was delegated at all, it was delegated downwards to the governors and leaders of the people. And the Federal Constitution notwithstanding, that is precisely how Betwoded Andargatchew Messai saw his own appointment.

Discussion and criticism of the Eritrean and Ethiopian

governments continued for some time in the press, but before long the Emperor's Representative attacked one of the more outspoken newspapers, a Tigrinya paper entitled *All the News of Eritrea*. An editor, Eyasu Teklu was arrested and throughout Eritrea political comment subsided. There were unexplained arrests—for example of Omar Kadir, a former representative in the Federal Council, and Sheikh Ibrahim, the Secretary of the Eritrean State Property Administration—and several politicians fled abroad. One, a Muslim, returned on what he thought was a safe conduct but was jailed. Others, like Woldeab Woldé Mariam, who went to Egypt, have stayed abroad. For some years Woldeab broadcast against the Addis Ababa government from Cairo.

There was continued friction between the Eritrean government and Andargatchew, particularly when he began to tour Eritrea making political speeches which the Eritrean government considered unconstitutional. However, in Addis Ababa it was represented that certain members of the Eritrean government were endeavouring to prevent Andargatchew from bringing greetings from the Emperor to his Eritrean people. On March 22, 1955, in a speech delivered at the commencement of a session of the Eritrean Assembly, Betwoded Andargatchew openly reaffirmed his stand stating that 'there are no internal or external affairs as far as the office of His Imperial Majesty's Representative is concerned and there will be none in the future. The affairs of Eritrea concern Ethiopia as a whole—and the Emperor.'

Four months later Dejazmatch Tedla Bairu resigned. His action followed months of intrigue and was the culmination of a personal struggle with the *betwoded*. There had been attempts to displace the chairman of the Eritrean Assembly—at this time he also resigned—and it is likely that the Ethiopian government hoped to advance a number of more 'co-operative' assembly members and officials. Hailé Sellassié appears to have feared the repercussions of Dejazmatch Tedla's action for he urged him to stay his hand, but without success. It was announced that he resigned 'for health reasons' and he was replaced by Dejazmatch Asfaha Woldé Mikael, who some years before had been prominent in the Addis Ababa branch of the Unionist Party. The Emperor posted Dejazmatch Tedla Bairu to Sweden as ambassador for a period of years before he was recalled to Addis Ababa and later retired into the senate.

By 1955, opinion in the Unionist Party had veered away from closer connection with Ethiopia. There is no doubt that because of this fact many considered that the *dejazmatch* had grown too powerful. However, public opinion was increasingly ignored and the vital question was never asked—namely, how was it that what seemed to be one of the strongest nationalist parties in Africa could so shift in its fundamental emphasis, with the subsequent encouragement of separatism, to a degree which was later seriously to embarrass the Ethiopian government. Many Ethiopians think that the Eritreans' actual experience of the techniques of Ethiopian government was responsible for this and that solution to their problems lay in reform of the Ethiopian government rather than divorce from it—but it is no longer easy to convince every young Eritrean of this. Responsibility for the deterioration in the spirit of Ethiopian nationalism in Eritrea may not ultimately be laid at the door of a few militant separatists.

In 1956 new elections were held in Eritrea on the same basis as those held during the period of British administration. There were, however, no political parties. It was explained by a journal then edited by Sylvia Pankhurst that the contest was rather one of personalities, individual candidates formulating their own slogans and policies. The Emperor made frequent visits to Eritrea, although Ethiopia, like Britain, was powerless to prevent a certain rundown of the economy compared with Italian times when political factors had fixed it at a false level. Indeed, Eritrea was given far greater consideration than any Ethiopian province save Shewa, although some suggest that rumours of corruption deterred investment. Elementary-school statistics were already ahead of Ethiopia but secondary schools were established. There was some economic development, more particularly in the ports of Assab and Massawa (which compare favourably with Mogadishu) than in Asmara, where the cableway became derelict and nearby satellite settlements like Decamera degenerated almost into ghost towns. Several Eritreans obtained leading posts in Addis Ababa.

After a pattern well developed in Ethiopia, considerable publicity was given to the beneficence of the Imperial family. Princess Tenagne Worq gave thousands of presents to school children and in February 1958 the Emperor gave Eth.$28,000 to those Massawa dockers who lost employment through the closure of the Suez Canal. At this time also Hailé Sellassié accused outside influence—the Egyptians, whose military attaché he had expelled some two months previously—of fomenting trouble amongst Ethiopia's Muslim communities. But December of that year saw another development pointing the future trend. After a period of marked political activity, it was announced that the Eritrean Assembly had voted 'unanimously' to discard the Eritrean flag and fly only the Federal (the Ethiopian) flag.

In 1958-9 severe famines in Tigré affecting Eritrea followed in the wake of droughts and locust swarms. In January 1959 the

Emperor declared a tax amnesty but much food landed by the United States government and private American organisations did not reach the people but deteriorated at the coast since no one authorised its transport up country. The people were still recovering when in August the chief executive, the President and vice president of the Eritrean Assembly all came to Addis Ababa for discussions, the content of which has not been revealed. In September the Eritrean Assembly voted—again unanimously—to replace their own laws and accept the Ethiopian penal code.

In addition to his post in Eritrea, Andargatchew Messai had been appointed Ethiopian Minister of the Interior with the title of *ras*. However, in December 1959, Brigadier-general Abiye Abebe, another son-in-law, took over as Representative in Eritrea. He had married Princess Tsahai, a London-trained nurse who died at Lekkemt in 1942. Under Abiye's guidance, in May 1960 the Eritrean Assembly voted 'unanimously' to change the name 'Eritrean Government' to 'Eritrean Administration', the chief executive became chief of administration, the insignia of the Imperial Lion was adopted for administrative purposes and the Eritrean seal was altered to read 'Eritrean Administration under Hailé Sellassié I, Emperor of Ethiopia'.

In Addis Ababa the *Ethiopian Herald* commented that 'Eritreans have grown to recognise that a closer union was essential and necessary' and, referring to the United Nations establishment of the Federation in 1952, concluded that 'the Eritrean people were even then solidly in favour of unconditional union'.[19] The Federation continued to exist in name for two more years, during which time the number of disorders and strikes increased, though not all of them were politically motivated. But after these developments its total abolition was merely a matter of time. On November 14, 1962, the chief of administration announced it to a surprised and angered Eritrean Assembly as a *fait accompli*.

THE 1955 CONSTITUTION

The negative history of how federation with Eritrea became a dead letter is not, however, the whole story. A professor of law has pointed out that the United Nations commissioner in Eritrea indirectly prompted the Emperor of Ethiopia to announce a second and revised constitution in 1955 because the anomalous situation arose in which the Eritrean Assembly was elected while the Ethiopian Senate and Chamber of Deputies were still both appointed—a situation which he described as 'paradoxical'.[20] In one way, however, it was very logical. Hailé Sellassié's speeches have always revealed a basic

assumption that society was ordained by God and that God pur-
posefully guides the Ethiopian people through the Emperor and to
some extent through the Christian Church—in other words that
power devolves from above. It is difficult to argue the need for an
elective assembly if that assembly is not intended to govern in the
name of the electors—in other words, to exercise power delegated
from below. In his speech to Parliament from the throne in November 1948, Hailé Sellassié commented on the role of the monarch and
Parliament. He said, 'Nor have We failed to bring before you what
We have accomplished to secure Ethiopia's prosperity and the well-
being of Our people : and also We have pointed out what Parliament has contributed and where your efforts have been needed.'

The Ethiopian Parliament played no part in the drawing up
of the revised constitution. Its preamble notwithstanding, the two
houses were called upon for no effort other than mechanical endorsement. The preamble referred to the earlier constitution :

> . . . granted to Our faithful subjects . . .[and continued]
> WHEREAS ALMIGHTY GOD, THE SOURCE OF ALL BENEFITS has
> strengthened and inspired Us to lead Our beloved People.
> . . . We have prepared a Revised Constitution for Our Empire
> after many years of searching study and reflection; and
> WHEREAS Our Parliament, after due examination and delib-
> eration has submitted to Us its approval of this Revised Con-
> stitution; Now THEREFORE WE, HAILÉ SELLASSIÉ I, EMPEROR
> OF ETHIOPIA, do, on the occasion of the Twenty-fifth anniv-
> ersary of Our Coronation, hereby proclaim and place into
> force and effect as from today the Revised Constitution of the
> Empire of Ethiopia, for the benefit, welfare and progress of
> Our beloved People . . .

The Revised Constitution was a longer document than its
forerunner of the 1930s. It was divided into eight sections entitled
'The Ethiopian Empire and the Succession to the Throne', 'The
Powers and Prerogatives of the Emperor', 'The Rights and Duties
of the People', 'The Ministers of the Empire', 'The Legislative
Chambers', 'The Judicial Power', 'Finance' and 'General Provisions'.

The Senate remained appointive. Its members had to be aged
thirty-five but candidature was technically no longer confined to the
nobility and *shums*. The Emperor was sole interpreter of the qualify-
ing phrases 'generally esteemed', 'served . . . with distinction' and
'secured the confidence and esteem of the people', and his first
eighteen appointments were made on October 26, 1957. Betwoded
Makonnen Endalkatchew, the Prime Minister, became President of
the Senate with the rank of *ras-betwoded*. Asrate Kassa, sole sur-

viving son of Leul-Ras Kassa, was made vice president with the rank of *leul-dejazmatch*. Other appointments included Abune Basilios and five bishops, the *wagshum*, four *dejazmatch*, a *fitwrary* and a *grazmatch*. Two days later they were joined by seventeen others including Blatta Deressa, Dejazmatch Bezebeh Sileshi (the brother of Dejazmatch Mesfin Sileshi and a Shewan governor of Tigré prior to the re-appointment of Leul-Ras Seyoum), a *ras*, four other *dejazmatch* and four more *fitwraries*. Amongst younger folk the Senate was referred to in Amharic as 'the garage'.

The Chamber of Deputies, however, became at least nominally elective. Electors had to be over twenty-one and 'habitually present' in their electoral districts. Candidates had to be over twenty-five, *bona fide* residents in their constituency and the owners of property. Two deputies were to be returned from each rural constituency of approximately 200,000 inhabitants and one from each town of 30,000 inhabitants. Larger towns were allotted extra deputies, one for each additional 50,000 inhabitants. A Chamber of Deputies Law set out in detail how these elections were supposed to be conducted every few years and established a National Board of Registration for the electorate which was placed under the charge of another member of the Kassa family, Dejazmatch Amaha Aberra. Since there had never been a population census and maps were not available, the division of the Empire into constituencies was difficult. It has been claimed that more than three million voters registered and made their choice from 366 candidates in an election held in September 1957.[21] There were places where the candidates were fairly representative. Considerable interest was displayed by the citizens of the Tigréan town of Adowa, for example. However, the progressive views of the three candidates returned were feared, they were not allowed to take their seats and were said to be 'communists'. Neither parliament nor elections were explained in terms the people could understand—they could have been compared with the selection of *chika-shums* (local chiefs) for instance—and in most places neither election campaigning nor contesting candidature nor voting in the sense understood elsewhere in Africa did in fact take place. Moreover, owing to the barely significant development of even elementary education, few potential voters understood what a parliament or an election was. Foreign observers have recorded that in the countryside people were ignorant of the existence even of the constitution itself.[22] Little or no attempt was made to rectify this and any basic issue which the new constitution might otherwise have been expected to raise lay masked for some years. Nevertheless the offices of several of Ethiopia's diplomatic representatives abroad issued statements on mounting election excitement in the Empire. However, a follow-up by newspaper reporters in Nairobi, Kenya, failed to reveal even one visitor from Addis Ababa who knew that an election was taking place. In fact, the majority of the deputies continued to be appointed.

Of course political history in Africa and elsewhere clearly demonstrates that it is not possible to adopt a system of government based on universal suffrage overnight, but it is difficult to resist the conclusion that the establishment of an elected assembly in Ethiopia was largely a propaganda sop to forestall criticism from Eritrea, from the emergent countries of the world and from even farther abroad. Following the departure of the last few vestiges of the formerly pervasive British presence, Ethiopia had come increasingly to depend upon foreign aid from the United States. American senators and representatives were known to be touchy about monarchy and especially about absolute monarchy. However, Hailé Sellassié's paradoxical character cannot be completely ignored and perhaps, as in pre-occupation days, there was some genuine desire to initiate reform. Parliament did discuss bills on occasions. For the first time there did exist machinery for the representation of the views of provincial folk at the centre and for some time provincial members' speeches were even reported in the government-controlled press in Addis Ababa, but coverage given to some mildly critical comments brought that to an end. The Emperor clearly intended to control parliament and took no risks.

Even in theory, let alone practice, the Ethiopian Emperor retained sweeping powers to 'convoke', 'postpone', 'suspend', 'extend' or 'dissolve' parliament. The revised constitution stated that a session could be postponed for thirty days and if the parliament were dissolved a freshly elected house had to meet within four months. As well as the Emperor, ten members of either house could technically initiate legislation. Proposals from both chambers were to be forwarded for signature and '*in the event* that such law shall receive the approval and signature of the Emperor . . . it shall be published in the *Negarit Gazeta*',* which was issued by the Ministry of the Pen.

The Emperor's power to appoint government officers, declare war, confer titles, to pardon and commute legal penalties etc. remained substantially the same as in 1931 and Article 36 described his 'duty to take all measures that may be necessary to ensure, at all times, the defence and integrity of the Empire, the safety and welfare of its inhabitants' etc. The succession was defined very closely, the Regency of the Crown Prince or the heir presumptive, the constitu-

---

* Article 88, author's italics.

tion of a council of Regency and all foreseeable eventualities were provided for.

The position of the Council of Ministers and of the ministers themselves was given some definition. They gained 'the right to attend' sessions of Parliament and to speak on any 'question concerning the conduct of their ministries'. The Prime Minister was to be a sort of messenger. He would 'present to Parliament proposals of legislation made by the Council of Ministers and approved by the Emperor . . . and . . . also present to the Emperor the proposals of legislation approved by the Parliament and the decrees proposed by the Council of Ministers'. In actual fact the Emperor continued to propose legislation and the office of prime minister, after Ras-Betwoded Makonnen Endalkatchew's elevation to the Senate, remained vacant until March 1961. Only a small proportion of the new laws passed through Parliament. As well as the Council of Ministers, the revised constitution provided for a Crown Council to include the Archbishop, the President of the Senate and such 'Princes, Ministers and Dignitaries' as the Emperor may designate, to be called by the Emperor 'in such instances as He deems appropriate'. It did not, however, mention either the Ministry of the Imperial Court (or the Palace) which is not a ministry with representation on the Council of Ministers, or the Emperor's own appointed 'Private Cabinet' but, because of their proximity to the ruler, both were subsequently very important in Ethiopian politics and government.

The influence of the Ethiopian Christian Church was more obvious in 1955. Where previously it was merely implied that the monarch would be a member, the revised constitution guaranteed it and excluded those who were not from recognition as members even of the Imperial family. It also defined the coronation oath whereby the Emperor swore, 'We profess and will defend the Holy Orthodox Faith based on the doctrines of St Mark of Alexandria.' The Crown Prince or Heir Presumptive's similar oath was likewise defined. A special general article (Article 126) declared that the Ethiopian Christian Church was 'the Established Church of the Empire and is, as such, supported by the state'. It further stipulated, perhaps by way of return, that 'the name of the Emperor shall be mentioned in all religious services'.

The chapter on the rights and duties of the people, although impressive to read, was perhaps the least relevant to Ethiopian realities in the 1950s. Freedom of assembly, of movement, of speech and of the press, freedom from the censorship of correspondence etc., were all guaranteed. Article 43 stated that 'no one within the Empire may be deprived of life, liberty or property without due process of law'. Yet the police forbade public meetings and all publications continued to be subject to rigid censorship. Newspapers were forbidden to discuss anything 'political' and no person, no government department or policy was ever criticised. Neither peaceful demonstrations—unless government instigated—nor political parties, nor trade unions were allowed. It is a moot point how much such an Emperor is bound by his own creature, but the stipulations of the revised constitution did not prevent the *Afe negus* (president of the Supreme Court) from being himself arrested in 1961 and detained for years without charge or trial.

It has often been argued that the Ethiopian people were not sufficiently politically conscious for even a limited document like the 1955 Constitution to represent more than an ideal for the élite. This was so but it need not have been. Moreover it was also true that in a changing world a gap of twenty-four years between the successive stages of serious political development must seem inordinately long. Hailé Sellassié was well aware that the Constitution by itself was innocuous. In his speech from the throne on November 4, 1955, he remarked, 'No single document however profound and comprehensive can of itself bring about far reaching and fundamental constitutional progress.'

The Emperor also stated that 'no constitutional progress can take effect unless it is rooted in the fundamental traditions, customs, habits and predilections, as well as the legal customs of the society on which it is based'. Yet the theory of government which the revised Constitution went some little way towards propounding (and which in a speech in November 1957 before the assembled senators and deputies Hailé Sellassié called the 'solemn pledge so often reiterated by Us that our beloved people are to share in the responsibility for the public affairs of Our Government'), was definitely not rooted in the Ethiopian tradition to which he referred. Although not necessarily alien to the individual traditions of the various composite groups of Ethiopia (see page 112 above) it was quite alien to the national tradition as created by the Emperors Tewodros, Yohannes and particularly Menelik II. It was in fact a quite revolutionary concept. The key to 'far reaching and fundamental' change lay therefore in the mass political education of those to whom power was to be transferred. This was not attempted.

It has also been pointed out—again correctly—that Hailé Sellassié's own political awareness was far superior not only to that of the vast majority of his subjects but also of his ministers and all those about him, and that they were suspicious and frightened even of the very little modern education that had been introduced. But the selection of those men, like the political backwardness of the masses, was a factor over which Hailé Sellassié could, by the 1950s, have exercised some larger measure of control. Neither the peoples of Eritrea nor any other peoples have greater *natural* political aptitude than the Ethiopian masses and even Machiavelli said the 'impression that one gets of a ruler and of his brains is from seeing the men that he has about him'.

THE 1940S AND '50S

Thus the two decades which followed the Restoration in Ethiopia saw Hailé Sellassié's personal power much enhanced but they will probably be remembered more for what did not happen than for what did. The plots which developed in such quick succession had not unnaturally been centred on personalities with some popular appeal. These had usually been provincial or Patriot leaders to whom had gravitated the discontented, the frustrated, many who resented the Shewan hegemony and even some who felt the lack of an inspiring national idea and direction. But the political machinations above described were nevertheless superficial and far removed from the needs of the Ethiopian peasants. They had absolutely no positive effect upon the economic problems of Ethiopia or upon the social and political framework under which conditions in the countryside had remained unchanged for so long. Nor is it by any means certain that their success would have made much difference. Moreover neither the federation of the politically more mature territory of Eritrea, nor the revised Constitution of the Empire which that federation had provoked, made any deep or lasting impression on the nature and framework of Ethiopian government. Within that aged framework new rivalries developed and new struggles occurred. Hailé Sellassié sought to be informed of them all. He encouraged and used them with consummate skill. And so it went on into the 1960s.

Meanwhile a new force had reached manhood—the educated élite of a new Ethiopian generation—an élite whose travels and studies, particularly in the spheres of economics and political science, had made them intensely embarrassed for their historic but backward country. Small groups in Addis Ababa and abroad began to discuss amongst themselves how Ethiopia's economic and political introversion could be ended. Their country, they argued, could afford to 'sleep no longer'—nor did they fail to recognise that all about them Africa was astir.

16

Three Thousand Years

Le Congrès danse. Il ne marche pas.—TALLEYRAND

While social and political conditions remain as backward as they are, a ready supply of capital alone can do little to initiate a cumulative economic advance.—E. LUTHER, *Ethiopia Today* (New York, 1958)

THE EMERGENCE OF A NEW ÉLITE

After the Italian war a very small but slowly increasing proportion of Ethiopians—mainly urban dwellers—who had received any education other than in the priests' schools began to display their growing awareness of, and interest in, the outside world. This in turn led to definite dissatisfaction over the state of their own country.

There seems little doubt that these feelings would have emerged more positively rather earlier had Ethiopia been less isolated. Professor Afeworq, who published an Amharic-French phrase book and guide in Rome in 1908, serves as an example.[1] Once abroad, his indignation reached the point where it intruded even into his translation texts. A section entitled 'The peasants of Ethiopia' included the following passage :

From the moment that the fruit of their sweat is taken for the maintenance of soldiers; when the finest stock they have so carefully raised goes to fatten feudal nobles; when the mules and horses which they have kept in order to barter for pedigree cows or oxen are selected for confiscation by the local authorities; from the moment when they find they cannot rest, for on returning home weary from work in the fields they come

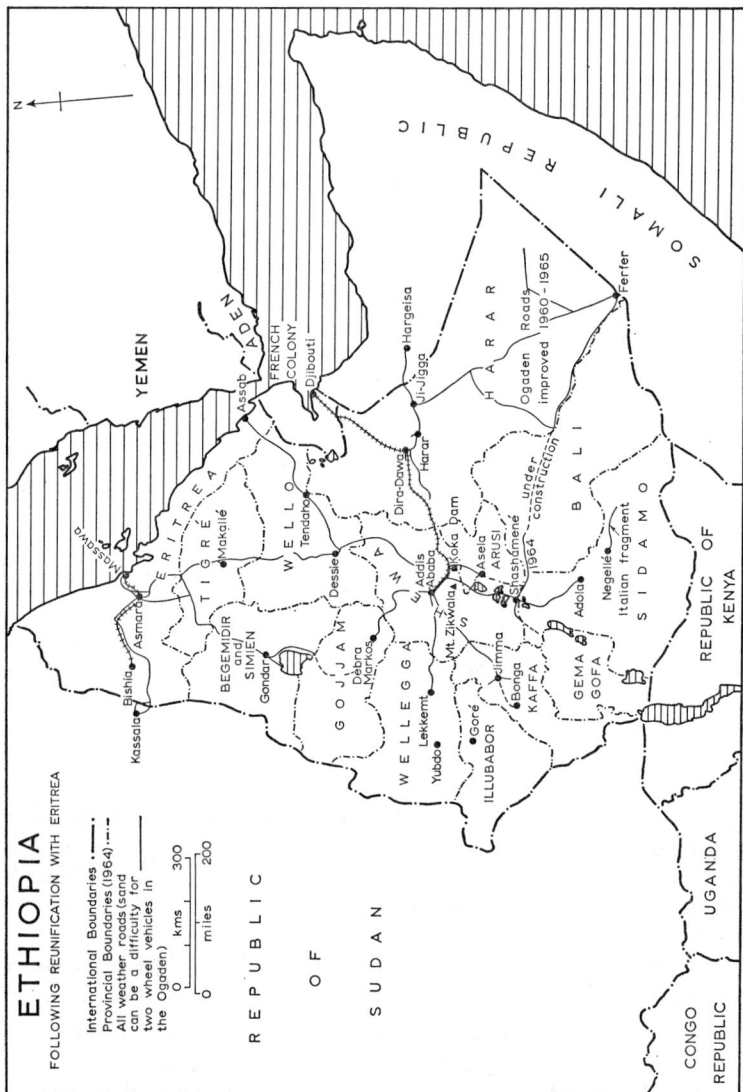

ETHIOPIA
FOLLOWING REUNIFICATION WITH ERITREA

International Boundaries ......
Provincial Boundaries (1964) ----
All weather roads (sand
can be a difficulty for
two wheel vehicles in
the Ogaden)

upon their dwellings taken over by soldier-oppressors who behave as masters, from that time on what use can they see in regular work?

Even in Addis Ababa, ever since the first decades of the twentieth century, an occasional pamphlet and Amharic verse drawing inspiration particularly from the young Turks and the Japanese has urged vigorous programs of economic and to some extent political modernisation. Some members of Tafari's progressive group of the 1920s have been mentioned,* in particular Negadras Gabré-Hiwot Baykedagn, whose Amharic pamphlets criticised the traditional leaders of Ethiopia and urged her people to 'wake up from sleep'.

In the 1930s, before the war with Italy, there had been attempts on the part of members of the first foreign-educated élite to organise themselves into a political pressure group. From the first this group included those with military as well as university or college training. A group known as the *Jeunesse d'Éthiopie*, most of whom had been educated to speak French, congregated in a tin-roofed building in Addis Ababa and discussed the central government's attempts at reform and published a newspaper. The way in which they regarded themselves is illustrated by a remark made by one of their number, Yilma Deressa, a young London-trained foreign office official—son of the Wellegga Galla *balabat* and Patriot, Blatta Deressa. Yilma said, 'We young Abyssinians are in duty bound to our country, we are the bridge that the Emperor has thrown across to European culture. . . . We have to pay for our studies out of our own pocket and then work for the state for nothing.' Speaking of the future, Yilma explained that the Emperor was 'educating a number of clever young Abyssinians in Europe at his own cost . . . to complete the civilisation of our country'. It is significant that the young progressives felt quite powerless without the Emperor. On the same occasion Yilma explained an administrative delay with the words 'His Majesty . . . lies in bed with a chill, until he authorises us we can undertake nothing'.[2] Also interesting is the fact that at least one observer felt them to be almost ludicrously out of touch with the Ethiopian countryside.[3]

Of those who had returned from abroad, most were from France but some were from Britain, Egypt, the United States, Belgium, Germany and even Italy. At the time of the invasion in 1935, about 200 Ethiopians had received or were receiving training abroad. Most of them were landowners' sons, or children brought up in the leading households. It has often been stated that

---

* See pages 153–6 above.

the majority of this early élite perished during the campaigns and the Italian Occupation. That this is not, in fact, quite true has been demonstrated by a recent study,[4] which reveals that those educated in the United States and Britain suffered a decimation greater than those who had pursued their studies in France—perhaps because in Italian eyes the latter seemed more orientated towards the Roman Catholic Church.

However, if not the majority, a very significant proportion of the young men was killed, especially in the slaughter which followed the bomb attempt on the life of the Italian viceroy, Marshal Graziani. From the Holeta Military College, for example, Lieutenant Mammo Gabru, Lieutenant Kiflé Nasibu and many others who were captured with the viceroy, including an aviation captain named Bahru Kaba, trained at St Cyr, died in the massacre. So also did George Hiroy, eldest son of the 1936 Foreign Minister; and Joseph and Benjamin Workneh, two sons of the Ethiopian Minister in Britain. The list is very long. A few like the senior Ethiopian instructor at the Holeta Military College, Captain Mulugeta Bulli, and Yilma Deressa, survived. Of the fifty who were alive in 1964, thirty held high government positions—assistant minister, vice minister, minister of state, minister or ambassador— but their number and influence, not to speak of their family background, was quite insufficient to have much effect upon the traditional views of the majority of Ethiopia's leaders. Also their own involvement in the processes of Ethiopian government and their consequent disillusionment has led in most cases to their being themselves classified by younger men as traditionalists or conservatives.

Nor did the associations of wartime Patriots or their publications become significant meeting points or a focus for the debate of new ideas. This was partly the result of the influence of conservatives like Makonnen Habtewold but also because the Patriot leaders who survived were, with few exceptions, either imprisoned or, as landowners, integrated as a new strain in the nobility and the existing pattern of traditional life—the framework of which was then still big enough to contain their aspirations and intrigues.

Thus the rise of a new élite was delayed. When eventually it began to seek expression it recognised itself as being drawn mainly from the post-war generation. Its *mores* were radical and almost incomprehensible to the old men of Ethiopia and indeed had little in common even with the remnant of the *Jeunesse d'Éthiopie* which survived the campaigns and the fascist Occupation, only to be termed 'the bankrupt élite' by younger men.

In the immediate post-liberation period Menelik II School, Medhané Alem and Tafari Makonnen Secondary Schools (the last run by French-Canadian Jesuits) were reopened in Addis Ababa, and the Itegue Menen School, founded by the Empress in 1932 but used by the Italians as a hospital, again pioneered modern education for girls. More important, however, was the establishment but a few miles from the city centre of two secondary boarding schools run at first on what are usually described as 'British lines' by largely foreign staffs. These were the Hailé Sellassié I Secondary School founded in 1943 and the General Wingate School founded in 1946.

In its context, the education traditionally offered by the Ethiopian Christian Church on the highlands should not be ignored. Advanced instruction in religion, in the composition of subtle and refined verse and the comprehension of church music had produced many wise men the like of whom had served Ethiopia well during the reign of many kings. They understood their country and their countrymen and were often the shrewdest of negotiators, but they had little comprehension of a wider world. To a lesser extent the same may be said of the product of the Koranic schools in Muslim areas. The impact of the new government schools was significant because they were orientated to what have come to be known as 'western' philosophies and thought-patterns and were not, like Menelik II's school had to be, largely staffed by Egyptian Copts as a sop to the Ethiopian Christian Church.

The conscious and unconscious democratic attitudes of the foreign teachers could not but be transmitted to the children and the process at first received the full encouragement of the Emperor. For instance, he sent his youngest son, Leul Sahlé to Hailé Sellassié I Secondary School and when visiting the school one day was very angry with him when he found that he was eating apart from the other boys. Clearly he then believed that this new generation, like his progressive party of the 1930s, would lend strength to his rule.

For a short time the majority of the students were children from court or important households or were relatives of outstanding Patriots, although the Emperor sometimes brought back poor children from his tours of different provinces of the empire. But before long the schools began to recruit from a much wider social *milieu* than heretofore. The more conservative of the *rases* and of the nobility soon began to ask Hailé Sellassié whether he was sure that the education of 'young nobodies' was a good thing—would they not turn against him in time? The attitudes of Leul-Ras Kassa and Leul-Ras Seyoum while not as reactionary as that of the minister who is reported to have remarked before the war 'What

do you want with schools, Janhoy? [Your Majesty] I did not go
to school, but in spite of that I have become a minister',[5] nevertheless demonstrated their distrust of education—a distrust shared by
most of the nobility with the notable exception of Ras Imru.
Although educational development, compared with that in many
other African countries, was far from startling, its effect, they
agreed, could be revolutionary. They were right.

COMPARISONS

Every day saw instances of the collision between the values
of the teachers and the taught and culture-shock was a normal
experience of pupil and teacher alike. A new boy, one of Ras
Abebe's relatives, brought his servants to the Wingate School. The
headmaster told them to go but they camped in a tent on a lawn
for some days before they would leave. The flippant and casual
remarks of teachers such as 'You're all equal here you know', were
actually revolutionary—and popular. The author once heard a
teacher joke to an outspoken natural leader amongst the boys:
'Be quiet you! We'll have a vote! Who do you think you are
anyway, a *dejazmatch*?' The children laughed but none would
have known how to recount the incident before their fathers. Even
in the 1960s older Ethiopian teachers bow to students from noted
families. When one such was expelled from the Wingate School,
the headmaster was surprised to be called on by a very important
dejazmatch. A statement to the effect that the boy could not be
readmitted was met for a moment with a look of blank incredulity.
Then the *dejazmatch* smiled and explained to the foreigner, 'You
do not seem to understand. I am a man with the power of life and
death in this country and I have come here and am asking you to
take back this child.'

Conservative courtiers and the Ethiopian Christian Church
demanded that religion, morals and Ethiopian traditions be given
great emphasis in all instruction but all the textbooks were foreign
orientated. Ethiopian priests, who were accustomed to teaching by
rote, refused point blank to be questioned or to discuss anything
with the students. It is no exaggeration to say that many considered the earth to be flat and were extremely suspicious of all
foreign teaching, particularly that of the Jesuits at Tafari Makonnen School which, ironically, was probably the most innocuous.
Foreign teachers in turn took few pains to disguise the fact that
the recruited Ethiopian teachers of 'morals' seemed to them
medieval in their approach and quite 'unprofessional' in their
ignorance of the wider world. The students were quick to detect

this and ultimately the presence of Ethiopian Church teachers served only to emphasise the apparent backwardness of Ethiopia's own traditions and beliefs.

In short, young Ethiopians began to expand their intellectual and geographical horizons and to question and evaluate their immediate environment. Of their superiority over Europe's African colonies, and indeed over all other Africans, they had at first no doubt, and they compared themselves—albeit unfavourably—with Sweden, Britain, France and the United States. However, it was not long before their enquiries led them farther afield. By the time that Ghana emerged as an independent nation, on March 6, 1957, although their elders shrugged their shoulders, many young Ethiopians approved, and the more aware displayed emotions akin even to pride. Kwame Nkrumah in due course was invited to Addis Ababa and photographed—some steps below the throne, but nevertheless seated, and talking with the Emperor.

However, while the inspiration which the symbol of Ethiopia's independent statehood had provided for the struggle against colonial governments was readily admitted, neither the Ghanaians nor any of the new political figures from the emergent African nations seemed much disposed to consider Ethiopia as their natural leader. The earnest young men in the entourages of the growing number of visiting African personalities talked of Padmore and Marx not of Menelik, and this further spurred the few educated Ethiopians—those whose upper age limit at the time of writing (1964) is perhaps forty or a little more—to new thought in the fields of economics, education and political development and to comparisons which their elders thought quite beneath them. They avidly talked and read about new nations and in particular the emergent states of black Africa. And they were profoundly shocked by what they learned.

THE ETHIOPIAN ECONOMY

Since the régime allowed no criticism, discussion was furtive. Even the library shelves of the University College carried neither the works of even moderately left-wing writers nor any post-liberation work critical of Ethiopia—although the Jesuit authorities had these for their own use on the shelves of the special library in their residence.* In the 1950s Ethiopian students, who included quite

---

* In 1960 the author heard the College Librarian refuse to issue a visiting professor of economics with Luther's *Ethiopia Today* (New York, 1958), a critical and useful study by an American economist formerly employed by the State Bank. The book was kept off the shelves and issued only to

senior government and military officers in evening classes, complained that works on Ethiopia were either 'boring or banned'. As a result teachers were plied with probing questions which, as government employees, many hesitated to answer—and evening classes were known to include a sprinkling of informers. Trusted teachers were often urged to return from home leave bearing 'true books'.

This small but growing number of Ethiopians began to regard government press statements, such as those to the effect that Ethiopia was 'assisting the backward countries of the world', with suspicion. By 1960 many educated or semi-educated town dwellers realised that all was not well. It was a mere handful, however, who had access to and fully comprehended the picture which United Nations and other specialised statistical publications had begun to reveal to the outside world.

Books which deal with the post-occupation economics and social aspects of post-liberation Ethiopia fall into two markedly dissimilar groups. Most are unrestrained in praise of Emperor Hailé Sellassié for the lead he has given in these spheres and content themselves thereafter with listing the undoubted achievements. Others stand openly appalled at the contrasts between palaces and hovels, the lives of nobles and serfs, conditions in Addis Ababa and in Menelik II's 'conquered' provinces, etc. They dwell on the bottlenecks caused by the refusal to delegate authority, the various antiquated systems of land tenure, the corruption, inefficiency and self satisfaction of officials and the difficulty in defining a boundary between the property of the state and that of the Imperial family. They criticise the rigid censorship of all publications and mock at the new democratic institutions of the capital as a shallow façade. If these writers evoke any response from the régime's apologists it is defence that the monarch in his wisdom makes haste slowly so as not to disrupt undefined 'traditional values'—an argument which finds few sympathisers in the helter-skelter of modern Africa. Strangely there is truth in both eulogy and condemnation. This is because neither invoke any standard of comparison when discussing the Ethiopian economy and the actual but modest achievements of the post-Occupation period.

Measurements of production, trade and the economic material consumed in the processes of living do not answer all the questions which must arise about a people or a nation. Also—and

---

certain staff members. The author lent the professor his own copy but this was subsequently stolen and the embarrassed professor arranged for a new copy to be sent to Addis Ababa through the United States diplomatic bag!

not only in an economically retarded country like Ethiopia—
statistics need to be treated with caution and a considerable margin
of error must be assumed. Nevertheless, statistics are in many
respects a guide to some aspects of a nation's development if they
are used comparatively. United Nations statistics give the 1957 *per
capita* income of Ethiopia as US$30, assuming a population of 20
million, and thus suggest that at the time under discussion she
lagged behind nearly every African country. Comparisons with
some other countries as they then existed are : Tanganyika $48;
Uganda $57; Nigeria $69; Congo $76; Kenya $78; Egypt (UAR)
$109; French West Africa $133; Tunisia $177; Ghana $194; and
South Africa $346.[6]

AGRICULTURE IN ETHIOPIA

Agriculture has always been and will continue in the foreseeable
future to be the mainstay of the Ethiopian economy. For several
centuries, almost without exception, travellers in Ethiopia have
confessed themselves staggered by the agricultural possibilities of
the country. Trained scientific observers of the 1950s and '60s are
no different. In the many books and pamphlets written on Ethiopia the phrase 'granary of the Middle East' occurs with mono-
tonous regularity, as a description of the country's agricultural
potential. But a 'potential' it has, however, remained.

Agriculture is the dominant activity in Ethiopia and must
account for well over 75 per cent of the gross national product, but
the subsistence proportion is absolutely preponderant; the greater
part of the cultivable land is idle yet soil erosion is serious; local
and foreign markets are inadequately developed; exports and
imports run at a minimum; agricultural implements and farming
methods have hardly changed since biblical times; there is great
poverty and serious famines occur—at least 100,000 people died
in Tigré and Wello in 1958-9.

The mountainous terrain of most of Ethiopia has made
communication difficult and expensive. Historically it aided the
struggle of the Ethiopian people to preserve their independence
in all but the coastal periphery, but it has also meant that national
unity was more difficult to achieve. Ethiopian history has, therefore, been dominated by warriors and campaigns. Not only have
warring armies repeatedly ravaged the countryside but the barons
who maintained them have demonstrated nothing deeper than an
acquisitive interest in agricultural production surplus to the immediate need of the peasants. The economic and social climate which

the production of such a surplus demands has scarcely ever been considered.

A recent study of typical 'Amhara' peasantry has described them as profoundly unconscious of historical change, and this is perhaps why few rural Ethiopians are recorded as having asked why their agricultural industry is as moribund as it is.[7] The question is, however, asked repeatedly in the towns and sometimes by Guragé farmers near Addis Ababa. A significant development of government primary education and a weakening of the influence of the Christian clergy could end rural stagnation, as it is ending elsewhere in Africa. Without commensurate social change education would doubtless also lead in time to a peasant movement against what Marx once called 'the idiocy of rural life'—and that is what the landowning families greatly fear. However, in the 1950s and early 1960s the basic conservatism of the peasant remained little affected by progressive opinion in Addis Ababa.

No comprehensive soil survey has been undertaken in Ethiopia but certain conclusions were inescapable. For example, an overall phosphorus deficiency existed which could be at least partly remedied by the use of chemical fertilisers. Modern research also suggested ways of minimising problems due to shrinkage and cracking in the darker soils. Since the Restoration, the Ethiopian government has not lacked expert agricultural advice both from Americans, under the general Point-4 agreement signed on June 11, 1951, and from United Nations agencies. However, as one FAO* publication pointed out in explanation of why recommendations by its experts were not published, 'it is the right of the Imperial Ethiopian government to accept or to reject them'. This, of course, is indisputable but unfortunately resistance to change and development was not a peasant monopoly.

Land measurement was urged by Menelik II and he was by no means the first Ethiopian Emperor to do so, but what little was done was inadequate and very inaccurate. The writer of FAO's *Agriculture in Ethiopia* wryly comments 'later checking showed numerous errors [and] the actual area was always greater than the area shown in the official figures'. Even by the 1960s land in

---

* Food and Agriculture Organization of the United Nations. United Nations publications—and H. P. Huffnagel's *Agriculture in Ethiopia*, Rome, 1961, quoted above is a case in point—cannot for obvious reasons interpret facts and situations to the extent which one might dearly wish, bearing in mind the qualifications and experience of the writers. Nevertheless, Huffnagel's work, especially the section on land tenure, is valuable and interesting despite his assertion being quite untrue that 'famine or a severe food shortage is unknown'.

Ethiopia had been properly measured only in a few areas. There had been neither population census, except in Addis Ababa, nor ordnance survey—though later in the 1960s, the Mapping and Geography Institute and United States Technical Assistance Personnel made certain basic moves towards adequate mapping.

In 1958, Luther commented that for largely historical reasons 'the distinction between land owned by the state as such, and by the Imperial family, is not clear'.[8] Land is also owned by other leading families, by the Church, by persons 'rewarded' by the monarch and by kinship and tribal groups. Ethiopian land-tenure systems are so many and varied that some ten years ago Gebrewold Engeda Worq, a minister of state in the Ministry of the Pen who was killed in the Green Salon in December 1960, wrote in the introduction to a revised edition of his Amharic book *Systems of Land Tenure and Taxation in Ethiopia* that his purpose was 'to enable every Ethiopian to learn the land tenure and taxation system of the rest of the regions of Ethiopia other than his own'.[9] His book illustrates just how complex and deep rooted these systems are, but even so, for many years there has been public admission, by the Emperor and others, of the dire need of reform. Nor is this impracticable, for in legal theory all land belongs to the Emperor. But up to the middle 1960s despite much discussion and some minor resettlement on Hailé Sellassié's personal estates, significant steps have yet to be taken.

In brief, the land system which gives rise to endless litigation, can be summarised as follows. *Rist* land, although often collectively held, can technically be disposed of and inherited. *Gult* land, of which *madarya* is the most common form, is land dispensed by the Emperor which entitles the recipient to the peasants' taxes. It is not inherited and can be withdrawn. The recipients have usually received it by grant and the income therefrom as a form of payment. *Rist-gult* is *gult* land held by a family or the Church, which is hereditary subject to the payment of a small fee on transfer. When rent is paid in kind the maximum proportion of a peasant's crop, up to half, that can be taken by the landlord is technically fixed by law (Article 20991). This law entitles the Church to a larger proportion than other landlords. In highland Ethiopia, north of the capital, most of the land is owned by the Church or by kinship groups. To the south and west, pastoral areas apart, the traditional *balabats* have been largely, though not completely, dispossessed in favour of small-scale settlers and large-scale absentee landlords. Few indeed have any real security of tenure or can predict the amount of the taxes which they will be called upon to pay at any time.

Taxes on the peasantry are heavy. Few men object to paying taxes provided they are given opportunity to increase their
own wealth. But in Ethiopia only massive reform can create the
conditions necessary for this and only education and firm and dedicated government can rid the rural administration of grafters who
have changed little from the seventeenth-century governor Takla
Giorgis, who remarked that peasants were like camels—when the
taxes were increased they groaned with the load but in the end
they carried it. Many local officials after issuing tax receipts (which
they not infrequently neglect to do) remark in Amharic that the
villager must 'now pay for the table'.

There exist few reliable figures on Ethiopian agricultural
production in the 1950s. Coffee, which is said to be indigenous in
Ethiopia, has, in some areas, had to overcome the opposition of the
Christian clergy who for centuries have regarded it, together with
tobacco, as a 'muslim abomination'. It was the major cash crop
in the 1950s and quite dominated the export trade. An Ethiopian
economist has stated of the peasants, who collected rather than
cultivated it, that 'being numerous and unorganised, and individually less wealthy than the merchants, [the peasants] are compelled
to sell their produce at prices lower than actually warranted by
market conditions'.[10] He also commented on the high rate of usury,
the profit accruing to middlemen and the need for market co-
operatives. By contrast African coffee growers in Kenya, for
example, were obliged to belong to co-operatives of which in 1961
there were 126, operating 160 coffee factories and 245 seedling
nurseries. Quality was high, growing and marketing were arranged
and, through licences, the government controlled production.[11]

In Ethiopia a coffee board has existed since 1957 but
Ethiopian coffee has yet to gain much reputation for quality—as
distinct from flavour—and strong government measures could
improve this to the general increase of returns. Moreover it must
be remembered that world surplus stocks are high and current
production is more than sufficient to glut the market. Therefore
world export agreements are unlikely to allow Ethiopia any significant increases in the quantity she places on the market. Diversification is thus also essential. With the important proviso that it is
largely self sufficient on a subsistence level, the Ethiopian economy
is like that of many African states in that it depends far too much
for economic health on one commodity. Ethiopia provides perhaps
2 per cent of world coffee sales and is completely vulnerable to fluctuations in world prices, as a glance at the changing state of her
foreign capital reserves indicates. The United States purchases
more than half her crop. In 1959 she exported 42,000 metric tons

of coffee compared with 105,000 tons from the Ivory Coast, 89,000 tons from Angola, 93,000 tons from the Congo-Ruanda-Urundi, 136,000 tons from East Africa, etc.[12]

It is recognised by trained Ethiopians as well as foreign experts who visited the country in the 1950s that the figures for cereals, pulses, oilseeds, ch'at, hides and skins, etc., which made up the rest of the export trade statistics (see Table 1), could all have been improved. The state of the world market in tea, sisal and pyrethrum has been healthier than coffee. These crops and rubber, tobacco, cotton and other fibres, groundnuts, vegetables, grapes and other fruit could all have been produced on a large scale. It was observed how gifts of mechanical equipment from abroad were used to advantage on large farm-estates owned, but not managed, by members of the Imperial family and the nobility. A few foreigners, including Brigadier Sandford and Marshal Tito, farmed tracts of land and several made a good living. It was obvious to all that the formation of rural co-operatives for the provision of tested seeds, for advice, equipment and marketing, for the construction of earth dams and access roads, etc., could have revolutionised peasant production, if, as Luther commented in 1958, the government had not been 'seemingly apathetic about co-operative farming, possibly because it feared the possible political consequences of the idea of associations of peasants'.[13]

There is also a recognised future in Ethiopia for a greatly expanded dairying and livestock industry once a firm campaign against disease—which was neither understood nor, partly in consequence, effectively controlled—could be mounted. Inland fishery industries such as contribute substantially to the economy of Uganda, and poultry farming could have been introduced.

Considering the national importance of the agricultural industry to the economy, the Ministry of Agriculture can hardly be said to have received an adequate proportion of the national budget—approximately 1 per cent in the 1950s. Some investment had been made in agricultural schools and a college. If the curricula of these and the attitude of the students left much to be desired, it must also be admitted that little opportunity existed for agricultural graduates to do direct and productive work. Many grew frustrated, especially the majority who were employed by the government. In the Ministry of Agriculture as elsewhere, even petty issues were decided at ministerial level. Nor was frustration confined to Ethiopians, the advice of foreign experts from both sides of the 'iron curtain' urging extensive agricultural reform was politely disregarded. Individual officers of the various aid organisations of the United States, who were the most involved, not infrequently finished a tour in Ethiopia greatly disillusioned by what they considered ingratitude and a waste of their country's money.

The United Nations and the Economic Research Service of the United States Department of Agriculture have published figures —not quite identical—but which both show that slight increases in the indices for Ethiopia's agricultural and food production over the period 1957–61 compared with 1952–5, whether measured absolutely or *per capita*, are not to be compared with figures for Ghana, the Sudanese Republic, the Rhodesias and Nyasaland, Kenya or Tanganyika.[14] Yet Ethiopia is potentially richer agriculturally than any of these countries and very possibly than all of them together.

MINING IN ETHIOPIA

Despite the fact that the mineral resources of Ethiopia are to a considerable extent unknown, for a geological survey has yet to be established, the history of mineral exploitation is a very long one. Expeditions sent into Punt by the Egyptian ruler Sahure in the middle of the third millennium BC returned with silver and gold alloy. The interest of Aksumite kings in gold mines was commented upon by several early writers, and examples of their gold coinage have been recovered. In the fifth century AD, for example, Cosmas described how 'the King of Aksum, through the intermediary of his prefects at Agau sent men for the gold trade'. Cosmas described the weather encountered and the barter trade conducted on the six-month journey to the south which was quite possibly to the gold-bearing region in the province of Sidamo which is still important today.* An ambassador of Emperor Justinian to the Aksumites in the sixth century AD reported that Aksum and Adulis were chief centres of trade in gold dust, etc. Later Almeida mentioned that gold was used to pay for imports and Baratti, another missionary, wrote that it was worked by labour made captive during military campaigns. Poncet recorded that gold was kept in the Imperial treasury and used to pay soldiers and defray court expenses. Bruce mentioned that gold was brought from the lands south of the Blue Nile and there are many other references.

---

* Considering the terrain crossed and the descriptions given, particularly of *kremt*, Ethiopia's cool, wet rainy season from July to September, this identification made, for example, in R. Pankhurst's *An Introduction to the Economic History of Ethiopia*, London, 1961, is justified. The author is aware that a more southerly destination was once suggested, in passing, by E. Burke, in a valuable paper entitled 'Some Aspects of Arab Contact with South East Africa', *Proceedings of the Leverhulme History Conference 1960*, Salisbury, 1962. However, in subsequent conversation with the author, Mr Burke agreed with the 'Ethiopian' interpretation.

Gold has been mined in Eritrea and occurs in several other Ethiopian provinces where the basement rocks, or material eroded from them, are not completely masked by more recent sedimentaries and volcanics. Some is produced at Akobo in the south-west but some three-quarters of the total production is believed to come from placer deposits, reportedly 980 to 995 fine,[15] in the vicinity of the town of Kebra Mengist, better known by its local name Adola, some 300 miles south of Addis Ababa, in Sidamo province.

The twentieth century has been a period of transition, the traditional connection between the nation's gold production and the Emperor's personal treasury being replaced by a system of state ownership. Even in the 1960s much secrecy still obscures detail of mining methods, production and marketing. One foreigner, a former overseer at Adola, informed the author that in the 1940s the labourers were paid Eth. $2 (us $0.80) for each Maria Theresa ounce of gold which they washed, and from this sum they bought their food. The majority of Ethiopians prefer not to discuss Adola and indeed know little about it. However, a combination of ignorance and natural suspicion, engendered in part perhaps by the atmosphere of secrecy and mystery which has surrounded this and other matters, leads them sometimes to confess that they suspect that the mines are worked by political prisoners. The author does not believe this, although in the 1950s employees in Addis Ababa did often request written documents with which to frustrate any attempt by the police to forcibly transport them as vagrants to the mines.

A geologist working for the United States Foreign Economic Administration estimated gold production between 1889 and 1945 as 621,100 troy ounces (worth us$350,000 a year),[16] but production has been higher than that since the Restoration, partly perhaps because of closer control and imported machinery paid for from a 1946 Export-Import Bank Credit. Until 1958, when it became subject to a newly constituted Ministry of Mines and State Domains, mining was dealt with by a department of the Ministry of Finance. In 1958 Luther asserted that mechanisation was prevented from becoming really effective by 'certain highly placed Ethiopian officials with a direct interest in preserving the loosely controlled system of placer mining . . . [that] organisational troubles arose . . . [and that] the American chief mining engineer received little or no co-operation from the minister of finance and other officials'. The minister was Makonnen Habtewold. In 1953 he was made head of a mining board which dissolved itself in its frustration less than two years after its establishment—'as a result', claims Luther, of Makonnen's 'indifference and obstructionism'.[17]

The author has yet to meet an Ethiopian who can justify the contention, invariably made on the few occasions when the issue is discussed, that government statistics would never represent the total gold production of the nation's mines. Nevertheless this suspicion was a not unimportant factor in the political discontent which grew up in Ethiopia in the late 1950s.

Gold is flown from Adola partly by civil aircraft and partly by military flights. This, and the fact that the flights are not scheduled, forbids calculation of the total weight of gold transported. Several writers and official publications of the Ethiopian government have stated in recent years that mechanical mining of proven placer deposits near Adola must greatly increase the production. A book by a Ministry of Information official, published in Tokyo in 1960, stated of Adola that 'a new vein [?] of gold has been discovered in recent years, and according to estimates, the production of gold has been trebled or quadrupled from a value of $1.5 million to about $5 million', [presumably us$].[18] This statement is not fully reflected in government figures for the late 1950s (see Table II).

The photographs and captions in one of the very few articles on mining in Ethiopia—by an academic geologist—do, however, suggest increases in production.[19] One photograph illustrates a Banka hand-drill taking six-metre cores, twenty-five metres apart on traverses crossing the Shanka valley at every hundred metres distance. The hand-washed samples are stated to contain an average of 0.5 grams of gold per cubic metre. A gold dredge of a type made by a San Francisco firm is also shown working placer gold at Chakiso on the Shanka valley, some twelve miles from Adola, handling 200 cubic yards an hour and recovering 448–504 grams of gold a day. This suggests that the content of the gravel being worked is lower than that being explored, where a ten-hour day might, at the same rate of operation, be expected to produce 850 grams of gold a day. Moreover, the annual production of this one dredger, if it could be kept working for 300 days a year, even at the lowest production rate, and in the lower grade gravels would amount to 134 kilograms of gold worth over us$151,000.

However, gold production from the whole of the Shanka valley was 97 kilograms in 1960 and 49 kilograms in 1961, worth us$109,000 and us$55,400 respectively. Deposits in the Laga Dembi and Boré valleys are also extensive and could be developed mechanically. Dredging of the latter, which is richer than the Shanka valley, could produce the equivalent of the whole Adola production, certainly for eight years, most probably for twenty and perhaps for even longer. Gold-bearing gravels also exist at least in hand-washable quantity in the Aflata, Ujuma Burjuji and Gambela valleys in the Adola region.[20]

Therefore although Ethiopia's relatively small gold production has not become a significant factor in her economy, it is not impossible that future development might lead to export figures which could lessen her dependence on coffee. Rather perhaps as Ghana's gold exports, worth over US$30 million in 1959, constituted more than 10 per cent of her total exports and lessened her dependence on cocoa. Ethiopian gold production in the 1950s was insignificant compared with that of South Africa, Southern Rhodesia and the Congo, and was much lower than that of Ghana and Tanganyika (see Table 3). During the 1950s the gold reserves of the Ethiopian State Bank fell from US$4.3 million to US$3.2 million (though her foreign exchange holdings increased considerably) and were well below the reserves of the UAR, for example, which stood at US$174 million. Nor was there significant local craft work in gold, as there was in silver usually obtained from melted Maria Theresa dollars.

About 5 kilograms of platinum was hand-washed annually at Yubdo in Wellegga in the 1950s and local workings elsewhere have produced sodium, potassium and magnesium salts and some sulphur. Surveys for oil in the Ogaden region have so far met with no commercial success. The geological succession there is not greatly different from that of the oil-rich areas of Arabia, but the geological structure as distinct from the composition of the beds may not have favoured oil traps. Exploration was, however, hopefully continuing in 1964. No other large mineral deposits have been reported. Small but commercially workable deposits often of high grade ore have been noted from time to time. These include copper, iron, manganese, gemstones, glass, asbestos, lignite and graphite.

The picture was, however, nowhere one of significant development of a mining industry. This was because, despite the stalwart work of certain individuals, in the basic needs of geological survey Ethiopia was far behind the rest of Africa. It could be argued also that development awaited a proper national plan. True, Yugoslav experts had helped prepare a Five-Year Plan for the period 1957–61, but, like many other schemes and plans, its existence was utilised for propaganda, but it was not implemented. Until 1959 it was, in fact, subject to the Ethiopian mania for secrecy and when it was finally published it was out of date. Its authors described the exploitation of the nation's mineral resources as 'meagre' but remarked also that 'in so vast and so insignificantly explored a country as Ethiopia, unforeseen prospects for the further development of mining may open up at any time'.

POWER AND MANUFACTURING INDUSTRY IN ETHIOPIA[21]

With her agricultural industry only one stage removed from subsistence and mining not significantly developed, power production
was understandably small in Ethiopia in the 1950s. Her *per capita*
production of public power was the lowest in Africa, apart from
Nyasaland and Togoland. Figures in the 1963 Ethiopian Statistical
Abstract specifically excluded 'the capacity and production of
electrified energy by the industrial firms'. However, their total
contribution, according to United Nations statisticians who saw
figures from the viewpoint of continent-wide comparison, was
'negligible'. Consumption of energy in 1961 measured *per capita* in
kilograms of coal or its equivalent, was Ethiopia 9, Nigeria 47,
Kenya, Tanganyika and Uganda 69, Ghana 92 and UAR 297.

For years after the Restoration the production of electricity
in Ethiopia was largely limited to expensive thermal methods. But
the Ethiopian terrain and in particular the Awash and the Blue
Nile river systems presented a very considerable potential for the
production of hydro-electricity. Under an Italian war reparations
agreement a dam was built in the late 1950s on the Awash river at
Koka. Opened by the Emperor in May 1960, its production of 53
million kilowatt hours was half its 1963 scheduled maximum.
Moreover, from the beginning this dam was planned with the aim
of making the construction of additional hydro-electric stations
downstream an economic feasibility. Visiting dignitaries were
assiduously shown the dam and a small palace was built overlooking the gorge and reservoir. Much, with justice, was written about
the contribution which cheap electricity—there was no capital out-
lay to be recovered—could make to the national economy. Production, however, was to be a feature of the 1960s rather than the
1950s. Much the same may be said of the valuable but unspectacu-
lar United States government assistance program which began
in 1956 to survey the Blue Nile basin for overall development to
include a large dam. Thus, although Italian and American co-
operation were utilised by the Ethiopian government in the 1950s
to take certain basic steps towards the realisation of part of the
nation's hydro-electricity potential, the actual industrial situation
throughout the 1950s was but little affected. Several of the provincial capitals had no electricity at all for most of the 1950s and
only a fraction of 1 per cent of the nation's population used it in
their houses.

Similarly the development of communications in the 1950s
was less impressive than the record of the early 1960s. The cost of

maintaining Italian roads after the Restoration had proved impossible and they had greatly deteriorated. However, statistics issued by the Imperial Highway Authority, despite such items, for example, as a slight decrease in the total asphalted surface between 1959 and 1961 (1,182 kilometres compared with 1,094) showed an overall picture of considerable improvement by the late 1950s. The fact that the communications infra-structure for economic development was not adequately developed was recognised but improvements were nevertheless reflected in lower overall freight charges and in the number of registered vehicles, just under 16,000 in 1961. (Compared with 30,000 in Uganda, 36,000 in Tanganyika, 44,000 in Ghana, 74,000 in Kenya, and 93,000 in the UAR.) Both the World Bank and the United States government recognised that the development of the Ethiopian highway system was a cardinal prerequisite for overall progress and they involved themselves in assistance schemes.

By 1962 there were 23,370 kilometres of road in Ethiopia, including 4,580 kilometres of all-weather gravel or hardtop surface. The all-weather road was, however, mainly to be found in Shewa and Eritrea, 1,250 and 890 kilometres respectively. Figures for Wello and Tigré, 1,680 and 440 kilometres, were considerable because of the road from Addis Ababa to Asmara, but Sidamo, Gojjam, Begemidir and Kaffa had only 260, 210, 290 and 140 kilometres respectively. In the predominantly Galla provinces of Wellegga and Arusi there were only 90 and 70 kilometres and there was no all-weather road at all in either Bali, Gemu Gofa or Illubabor in the south.

Between 1953 and 1960 traffic on the only major non-government enterprise, the Franco-Ethiopian railway from Djibouti to Addis Ababa showed some slight decline, but American technical and managerial help enabled Ethiopian Airlines to develop internal and international services to compete with the growing number of companies which, elsewhere in Africa, were associated with the airline companies of the European metropolitan powers.

However, despite isolated achievements such as the airlines, an adequate basis for the significant development of manufacturing and construction industry hardly existed. Thus very little developed. Although Ethiopian cement production more than doubled in the 1950s it remained much lower than that of the Sudan, Nigeria or Kenya. In 1960 Ethiopia produced 28,000 metric tons compared with 2,047,000 metric tons in Nasser's Egypt. The low comparative position of Ethiopia in Africa was further reflected in building permit statistics, employment figures and salaries in the construction industry, etc. Despite Menelik II's early beginnings, post office telephone and telegraph statistics also illustrated the slow rate of Ethiopian economic growth *vis-à-vis* the developing countries of Africa.

The United Nations and the Ethiopian government have separately published figures of the state of industrial development and employment in Ethiopia but it is difficult to see how accurate figures could have been assembled. Labour was often casual, there was neither a ministry of labour nor trade unions—and Ethiopia, incidentally, had not ratified the United Nations Convention Concerning the Abolition of Forced Labour (No. 105 of 1957) which called for the suppression of forced labour in the sense of 'a system of forced or corrective labour which is employed as a means of political coercion or punishment for holding or expressing political views and which is on such a scale as to constitute an important element in the economy of a given country'.[22]

In 1957 the gross value of industrial production was less than US$25 millions in Ethiopia proper and US$9 millions in the proportionally more industrialised Eritrea. Well over half these figures were accounted for by the production of food and drink although textiles, long a cottage industry, were also just significant. United Nations sources state that by 1960 there were 150 firms employing five or more workers (total 26,000 employees). Ninety per cent of such manufacturing industry as existed was in the immediate vicinity of Addis Ababa or Asmara. There were also a few factories at Jimma and in the Dira Dawa and Harar area, and a tomato-canning plant, worked partly by child labour, at Shashamené. Except for small salt, brick, cement and printing works, all manufacturing involved the slight basic processing of but a fraction of the national agricultural produce.

ETHIOPIAN TRADE

Extensive smuggling, particularly of coffee, make the published figures of Ethiopian trade somewhat unreliable but they, nevertheless, indicate that by the end of the 1950s her international trade was about half that of the Sudanese Republic, about a quarter of that of Ghana, the East African common market or Morocco, and a seventh of the United Arab Republic (see Table 4).

Since 1957 Ethiopian imports have exceeded her exports and her trade has remained completely western orientated with the United States her major customer. By the beginning of the 1960s trade had developed but little with the other countries of Africa and while there was trade with Yugoslavia and the Soviet Union it was not of major importance (see Table 5). To a greater or lesser degree these facts had some influence on the international policies pursued by the Ethiopian government.

INTERNAL REVENUE AND EXPENDITURE

Even by the end of the 1950s the economy of Ethiopia provided no great scope for the raising of government revenue. Not only was the nation barely on the threshold of modern development but the government was by its nature sensitive to political and social factors which severely limited the sources of revenue and even curtailed economic growth–for revenue was exacted from commercial transactions rather than from real estate and non-productive capital. Budget figures, although they do not represent any significant degree of planning, for the government operated by 'budgetary decision', have nevertheless been published since the Restoration. (More exactly to cover the period from 1935 EC or September 1941 onwards.)

An analysis of the sources of Ethiopian government revenue in the 1940s and '50s (see Table 6) clearly demonstrates an overall dependence upon export and more particularly import duties. The purpose of these customs duties has been solely to raise revenue. Apart from a sugar plantation established in the 1950s there has been little infant industry which might require protection. Moreover, Ethiopia was not party to the General Agreement on Tariffs and Trade (GATT), and could therefore impose duties as she saw fit. Contributions to the national exchequer through the various taxes on land, although they raised half as much as the customs duties, were not uniform, were avoided by certain landowners, notably the Christian Church, and like the whole land system were in recognised need of reform. Income tax became increasingly important as the Ethiopian bureaucracy developed but business profit assessments were often arbitrary and were the subject of disputes and wearying negotiations, accounts of which served only to discourage would-be investors.

No outline of the fiscal realities in Ethiopia would be complete without some reference to corruption. The author's personal observation in Ethiopia in the late 1950s and early 1960s led him to believe it was widespread. Writing in 1962, Lipsky commented that public funds were often 'handled in an arbitrary manner' by heads of departments, used for private loans and 'occasionally even deposited in ... private bank accounts'. Many commentators on under-developed countries (or developing countries as they prefer. with varying degrees of justice, to be called) excuse bribery and graft on sociological grounds. But whatever the tradition of a country, corruption within a modern fiscal system cannot be ignored economically. It constitutes an additional and often excessive extra form of taxation, retarding economic growth. When it occurs in the upper levels of society it may not even lead to investment but rather to expenditure on luxury consumer goods, to hoarding and export, and thus become a drain on the balance of payments. Although the Ethiopian government in the 1950s was less corrupt than Egypt or Liberia, the problem was, nevertheless, real.[23] The *entrepreneur* class in Ethiopia is largely of foreign origin. Not only does it therefore have an interest in by-passing exchange control regulations, but being interposed between the feudal classes (often sleeping partners) and the workers and peasants, it makes for social immobility.

Defence and internal administration, including the police, were not unnaturally the main item of budgetary expenditure in the two decades following the Restoration. However, expenditure on those ministries basic to the national economy—agriculture and industry—was low. For example, a fifth and a tenth respectively of the vote variously described as 'Civil List' or 'Imperial Palace'. Expenditure on public health has not been spectacular, just over half the average palace vote of us$2 millions, but that on education has been considerable, an average of us$4 millions a year. The official publications of the Ethiopian government and indeed the speeches of Hailé Sellassié have made much of achievements in this field. Yet apparently paradoxically, Lipsky states that 'among the social deterrents to economic development the most tangible is the extremely low level of education'.

THE MINISTRY OF EDUCATION

From the first Hailé Sellassié quite openly endeavoured to develop and use schools to produce a cadre of bureaucrats dependent upon his leadership. In the 1950s he often remarked to young men 'it is Our hope that you, like your fathers, will work hard to serve Us and Our country'. He retained the portfolio of education himself to show his quite genuine concern for its development, and some progress was made, notably in the capital. However, the succession of ministerial reshuffles which occurred in the 1940s and '50s prevented proper and continuous planning despite a quite disproportionate amount of allotted revenue being spent on administration (see Table 9).

A bitter joke common amongst junior officials of the Ministry of Education was that the vice-ministers or assistant ministers responsible for education had time only to give one order before a general *shum-shir* dictated their translation to another ministry or an embassy overseas. The Amharic orders were 'attention', 'quick march', 'slow march', 'halt', 'stand at ease', 'about turn'—and such variants as 'move to the right', 'move to the left' and even 'all fall down'.

The author has discussed elsewhere the fact that secondary and higher education in Ethiopia developed at a rate out of proportion to the growth of primary education.[24] The report on the first Five-Year Plan while recognising educational development as 'remarkable' and 'one of the most solid achievements of the postwar liberation period' nevertheless commented, '. . . not inconsiderable waste could have been avoided with better planning and coordination. This is especially in evidence in the lack of a sufficiently co-ordinated and balanced system. Broadly speaking the higher institutions have been allowed to expand without corresponding expansion of the lower levels. . . . The result is that secondary schools and institutions for higher learning are not working at full capacity. The present student capacity of the upper level is far in excess of the current flow of students from the lower levels qualified for admission to the upper levels. . . .'

Despite the numerous graduates from her own colleges and from universities overseas and despite the award of scholarships to other Africans which has helped fill secondary and university places, United Nations statistics revealed that the Ethiopian educational system, considered overall, lagged way behind the systems developed elsewhere in Africa (see Tables 8 and 9). Since 1960 this has been admitted in Ethiopia but in the 1950s few dared whisper it in the face of intensive government self congratulation over the achievements which had been made. This was probably honest if mistaken, for when UNESCO published comparative statistics for African countries in 1961 Hailé Sellassié refused to believe them and tension developed between him and the Minister of State responsible for education, who shortly afterwards was appointed an ambassador abroad.[25] Most of the educational problems of Ethiopia—the serious imbalance apart—differ from those of the rest of Africa only in degree. There is a high drop-out rate, many students are over-aged, classrooms are grossly overcrowded, the pupil teacher ratio is too high, the enrolment of girls is very low and qualified teachers are few.[26]

In parallel fields the picture was similar. The average newspaper readership per thousand Ethiopians was two compared with eight in Nigeria and Uganda, twenty in the UAR and thirty-two in Ghana. Statistics covering the number of radio receivers, the publication of books, visits to cinemas, etc. reflect the same basic pattern.

COMPARISONS AND CONCLUSIONS

It is not unusual for younger generations to express dissatisfaction at the state of their country's development and at the rate of its change. This is especially true in a developing continent in the throes of political, social and economic revolution. It is not so common, however, for them to make disparaging comparisons with neighbour nations. This, however, is exactly what members of the post-Occupation Ethiopian student generations did and, what is more pertinent, continued to do after the completion of their studies, their return from abroad and their entry into government service. In was significant, therefore, that the new élite in mixing with other Africans, especially in Ethiopia itself, came to identify themselves with the aspirations of the African masses and their leaders, and with those as yet rather emotional and general concepts, such as 'the African Personality', 'African Socialism', 'Pan-Africanism', etc. Most came to suspect and some even to discard the two basic institutional concepts of Ethiopia—the monarchy and the Christian Church—at least as far as they were traditionally interpreted.

The few with opportunity to assess Ethiopia's comparative standing in Africa never doubted her potential but claimed that apparent development of her economy, at least in the 1940s and early 1950s, was very largely the reflection of fluctuations in the world coffee market. Even if they recognised that slow yet definite economic growth had occurred, they nevertheless maintained that a major break-through was needed to overcome basic paralysis at the root of the Ethiopian economy. That this existed was admitted by most economic advisers; and serious writers who have analysed the issue, notably Luther and Lipsky, have stressed that its causes are not to be revealed by economic analysis alone. The experts who compiled Ethiopia's first Five-Year Plan had stated that 'the Ethiopian economy is moving within a closed circle of cause and effect which hampers its evolution'. In a search to find a way of breaking this circle, the minds of certain younger Ethiopians turned towards revolution.

17

Girmamé Neway

The country was stagnating under autocracy. That yoke had to be thrown off to open the way to our renaissance.— PRESIDENT NASSER in his foreword to Colonel Anwar el Sadat's *Revolt on the Nile*, London, 1957

Ethiopia is on the threshold of economic development . . . in the course of this process, fundamental modifications will necessarily occur in the existing social and political order.— G. LIPSKY, *Ethiopia*, New York, 1962

CHILDHOOD

In 1924, not far from St George's Cathedral, Laketch, the wife of Aleka Neway, who was Dean of the Cathedral, gave birth to her second son. She was of the Moja family and she named the child after her illustrious great-grandfather Dejazmatch Girmamé. The Mojas, like the Addisgé family group, come from Menz, the heartland of Shewa and are a mixture of certain *balabat* strains. Like most Shewans they have Galla as well as Amhara blood. They have produced an independent-minded warrior stock, witness Kegnazmatch Mokria, a pre-war commander of the Imperial Guard, Dejazmatch Fikré Mariam and Tademe Zelleka the Patriots, Kegnazmatch Hailé Zelleka, the prisoner on the hill at Debra Zeit (see note, pp. 50–1) and others.

In times of crisis in the history of great nations, individuals have occasionally been born whose ideas and yearnings are not idiosyncratic but the first expression of new ideals and trends of thought. In the beginning such trends are seldom numerically demonstrable except among the really 'sensitive', but they are the stuff of which history is made. Girmamé proved to be such an individual.

Girmamé's brother, Mengistu, was eight years older than he, old enough to be a cadet at Holeta before the Italian war and to travel to Djibouti and Khartoum with the exiles. Girmamé, however, grew up in Ethiopia during the period of the Italian Occupation and he afterwards described those 'five unfortunate years' as 'a bitter pill to swallow'.[1]

Girmamé attended the Tafari Makonnen School and later the Hailé Sellassié I Secondary School. Although not outstanding he was serious and rather intense. He worked fairly hard, he played football and he liked to argue—in fact he enjoyed himself like any other young schoolboy. He did, however, display an early tendency to assert himself and take the lead. Indeed his school career was not without excitement. There were several anti-Jesuit incidents at Tafari Makonnen school and his former school fellows at Hailé Sellassié I Secondary School recall how he and another boy named Seyoum Sabat, were locked up for a day in the Ministry of Education building. Every Christmas Girmamé went with all his school-mates to the palace to greet the Emperor and he also received from his monarch a banana or some other fruit on Hailé Sellassié's customary visit to the school at the end of each strict Lenten fast.

Several photographs taken at Hailé Sellassié I Secondary School survive, for Girmamé's group was significant. One picture has been published several times.[2] It was taken in the early 1940s and the group includes Mikael, the son of Ras Imru; Zewdé, the son of Leul-Ras Seyoum's daughter and the Tigréan Dejazmatch Gabré Sellassié; Endalkatchew, the son of the tall Addisgé noble Ras-Betwoded Makonnen Endalkatchew and in the centre Girmamé Neway with a fierce frown on his young face.

After his secondary education Girmamé was one of five students sponsored by Crown Prince Asfa Wossen to go to the United States for further studies.* He was very excited by this prospect, not least because his adventurous spirit had been stirred by reading the story of the American Revolution and the ideals and sacrifices of its fathers. He took his first degree at the University of Wisconsin, was active in the Ethiopian Students' Association in America (he was its second president) and he contributed to the *Ethiopian Student News* published in New York. The Ethiopian Ambassador in Washington, Ras Imru, knew Girmamé and was

---

* In view of subsequent events it is interesting to note all the names. The others were Seifu Mahtemé Sellassié, Mulatu Debebe, Lemma Frehiwot and Girmamé Wondefrash.

impressed by his seriousness. Girmamé had several close friends both Ethiopian and American and he tended to mix with serious people with whom he could exchange ideas. His writing and conversation reveal some aspects of his developing thought patterns. He soon began to ask himself certain basic questions.

THE MIND OF THE REVOLUTIONARY

After commenting on the differing views of Hobbes and Locke on the relationship between man and his environment and the origin and nature of society, Girmamé, in an article entitled 'Strength in Unity' claimed that an underlying theme was common to both philosophies.[3] He argued that man's 'physical and mental limitations' prevented him both from adequately protecting himself and from satisfying all his wants by 'individual effort'. Moreover, he wrote that 'practically all of man's greatest achievements can be attributed to his collective endeavours for the common good'. An interesting reaction in view of the tradition of individualism in Ethiopia and the intrigues and divisions of the court and countryside. Girmamé did not discount what he called 'the individualistic aspects of man's nature' but he developed a quite dogmatic faith in the masses, in their virtue and collective insight, which was to become a crucial part of his philosophy. He also believed that man possessed a natural 'propensity towards collective endeavour . . . prompted by necessity and by his own social nature'.

Girmamé built on the theory that 'the physical and mental limitations' of individuals made an organised society a necessity and that government developed 'as man's wants and needs for protection progressively changed', and more than that, 'institutional factors not only grew hand in hand with them, but gradually assumed the role of regulating the phases of human life'. He did not, however, subscribe to the view that men are riveted eternally in absolute obedience to the authority which they originally created. The purpose of government, he wrote, was to 'devote itself to the alleviation of the various wants existing among its members and thereby to strengthening the nation.' Else it would 'reap a harvest of perpetual poverty, human misery, discontent and instability in which it will perish'. His later writing suggests that Girmamé's concepts of human needs were not limited to the material. In 1952 Girmamé considered that a government which was not devoted to the common good could not compete and would be very susceptible to the colonial ambitions of others because the false excuse (Girmamé wrote 'trumped-up lie') could be produced that 'imposed rule is purely in the interests of the subjugated nation'. Later this fear lessened as his imagination was fired by the liberation movements and the first tangible successes of African nationalists. Most important, he clearly considered that those who had first delegated power to government had the right to revoke it, for Girmamé's concepts of government were totally opposed to those of Ethiopian tradition.

The roots of the Ethiopian tradition of government are to be found in the *Fetha Negast* (the Law of Kings), translated from the Arabic of Ibn al Assal, a thirteenth-century Copt. It quoted Moses from Deuteronomy 'Thou shalt in any wise set him king over thee, whom the Lord thy God shall choose; one from among thy brethren . . . [and the king] shall write him a copy of this law in a book out of that which is before the priests the Levites'. This king had also to be obeyed because of Christ's requirement that the things of Caesar be rendered unto Caesar. St Paul's Epistle to the Romans was also quoted, 'Let every soul be subject unto the higher powers. For there is no power but of God; the powers that be are ordained by God. Whosoever therefore resisteth the power resisteth the ordinance of God; and they [the peoples] that resist shall receive to themselves damnation. . . . for they [the rulers] are God's ministers'.[4] Girmamé did not subscribe to the view that society originated by a divine act—nor did he describe its purpose as God given. If he had it would have been open to him, though not essential, to accept some form of government in which political power was in the hands of priests or divine kings who were specialists in the will and purpose of God. Also he could have accepted that power should be delegated from above as and where necessary. But he did not subscribe to that view and it was logical for him to postulate some form of government in which the rulers felt responsible to the people and even in which power was delegated upwards from the people to their rulers. Nothing then would be more natural and proper than for men to discuss what laws should govern them and whether the government was good enough to be *allowed* to continue.

The dilemma of the increasing numbers of modern educated Ethiopians is precisely this : although they can no longer accept the role of the Solomonic tradition and the concept of being 'chosen people' as the basis of the state, any more than they can accept that the Ethiopian Christian Church is fit to be the cement of their society, they are uncertain how to effect a change. Many regard the perfecting of techniques of government to mask this dilemma as Machiavellian—and often say so. Rather, they seek an alternative philosophy. Girmamé believed that the new élite had a major role to play and urged them to 'stand united'. At the conclusion of his article 'Strength in Unity', he wrote 'It is imperative that we remember that we are the ones in whom Ethiopia has entrusted her future destiny and role in domestic as well as foreign affairs'. The importance of Girmamé Neway is that faced with the dilemma of the new Ethiopian generations, *he began to think it out*. And more than that, finding it possible, he later chose to act upon his thoughts.

GIRMAMÉ'S GRADUATE STUDIES

Girmamé enjoyed student life in the United States but while he retained his great admiration for the American Revolution he became disillusioned by American society as he saw it. There is no doubt that the greatest shock he received was from his observation of the status of America's negro citizens which he considered a mockery of the high ideals of the United States constitution. His friends all say that it was this which spurred him to read more and more left-wing literature until he sometimes expressed the opinion that the position of the Negro was a function of the American economic system and that talk merely of 'racial prejudice' was superficial. He began also to comprehend the positive aspects of the movement which is becoming known as the African Revolution. He realised that students from other parts of the continent were not only *against* colonialism, they were *for* a New Africa.

Girmamé, who had meantime moved to Columbia University, was led by this awareness and the interest in problems of land tenure natural to any educated young Ethiopian to present in 1954 a 114-page thesis, entitled *The Impact of the White Settlement Policy in Kenya*, in partial fulfilment of the requirements for that university's MA in political science. The writings of several of his generation—the early articles of Endalkatchew Makonnen, son of the *ras-betwoded*, for example—display deep interest in the problems of emergent Africa, but Girmamé was influenced more than most in this direction. His thesis is in many ways quite a remarkable document and among the interesting issues upon which it touches is the Mau-Mau insurrection. It is divided into seven chapters and a bibliography.

The introduction deals with the inspiration which the history of the United States provides to anti-colonial movements particularly in Africa, and with the differing impact of territorial imperialism on the traditional African patterns in the west and east of the continent. The second section is a brief but erudite historical survey of those events of the 'Scramble for Africa' which led up to the 'permanent European settlement policy' in Kenya. The third section, entitled 'The Kenyans and their land' is a detailed and interesting reconstruction of that settlement policy in practice up to the 1930s. It seeks to demonstrate that the land policies of the Kenya government amounted to legalistic theft. It touches on the impact which these land policies had on the tribes of Kenya, in particular the Masai, but it also briefly notes the early political responses of the Kikuyu and other tribes. 'The Kenyans and the fruit of their Labour' is the title of the fourth section. This deals with the establishment of African 'reserves', the miserable living standards therein, the introduction of taxes and the resultant growth of a class of landless and underpaid African labourers on European-owned farms. Section five is entitled 'The Political Tutelage of Kenyans and the March of European Settlers towards Self Government'. It describes the domination of the legislature and the government by forces sympathetic to settler-interests and argues that since these interests alone enjoyed the advanced form of political democratic practice obtaining in Kenya, they and only they were being guided to self government. Government nomination of chiefs on the other hand is seen as a politically retrogressive innovation since tribal elders had previously needed the tacit consent of the tribesmen for their appointment and this, it is argued, was not essentially altered by the Native Authority Ordinance establishing local councils. The sixth section, entitled 'The Kenyans and the Official Educational Policy', points out the great disparity in the educational opportunity made available to the settler community on the one hand and to the Africans on the other, and it examines the role of the missionaries in what is seen as a deliberate policy of restraining the political development of Africans. The conclusion upholds the aspirations of the Kenya Africans and demands a new approach to all issues by both settler and government, failing which it predicts that change will occur outside the framework of democratic practice in the form of a relentless 'people's struggle' of which Mau-Mau constitutes but a beginning.

Girmamé's thesis contained only one reference to Ethiopia and that a very indirect and unimportant one. Nevertheless, he could hardly have considered the weighty topics which he did in a vacuum, or without making frequent mental cross-references to Ethiopia, the only part of Africa which he knew personally, the more so since, as will be argued below, he was a Pan-Africanist.

Of course, Girmamé's thought patterns continued to develop after he left the United States and returned to Ethiopia. For that reason alone it would be dangerous to attempt any full assessment of his mind from the 1954 thesis. Also that document is in parts somewhat general and superficial, but there is no means of telling whether this is not a reflection on the teacher rather than the taught. It must be remembered that the comprehensive American African Studies programs of the 1960s were either not in existence or were merely in their infancy in the early 1950s. Omissions from both the twenty-item bibliography and the footnote references cannot but suggest that the tutorial guidance Girmamé received was somewhat inadequate.*

Girmamé's anger at what, from recollected early conversations in the United States, we know him to have considered the social and economic stagnation of his own country, coupled with his rejection of Ethiopia's traditional national philosophy, eventually led him to inspire a revolution and, on its failure, to choose suicide rather than capture. It is not, therefore, surprising to find a noticeable emotional element in the style of the thesis, particularly in the introduction and conclusion. Whether or not this is a stylistic fault is not relevant to the present argument (or to much else). Suffice it to say that parts of the thesis read like a political manifesto.

Much light is thrown by the thesis on Girmamé's 1954 attitudes to colonialism; to the United States; to the African Revolution and Pan-Africanism; to the social and economic conditions which can stand in the way of a people's advancement; to Marxism-Leninism and to Revolution. It is extensively quoted below not just to illustrate Girmamé's developing thought patterns in areas in which they were later taxed or have been called in question, but also because it has not been read in Ethiopia and to some extent it expresses what the 1960 Revolution was about.

The thesis displays Girmamé's anger at territorial imperialism in general. Possibly this stems from his identification with the cause of the countries of Africa and Asia, whose 'cheap labour and raw materials were needed to meet the insatiable appetite of industries' in the industrialised countries, as well as from his own injured pride and childhood experiences during the Occupation of Ethiopia by the Italians. Also important were his reading and discussions with fellow Africans and Americans. Despite his attraction to left-wing writers, for example S. and K. Aaronovitch,[5] Girmamé does not appear to class the United States as an imperialist power, which a communist would naturally do. Indeed, his writing shows that from the example of the United States he drew hope for the

---

* This is hardly the place to list the deficiencies of his bibliography. Suffice it to point out one of many serious omissions. It appears that Girmamé was not led to read any of Jomo Kenyatta's writings, in particular *Kenya, the Land of Conflict*, London, 1945.

future of Africa—'The United States (a country in which it was said that all animals, and with them the human species, degenerate) has evolved into one of the few most powerful nations in the world, actually eclipsing the traditionally arrogant European states with the brilliance of her prodigious achievements.' Girmamé in fact went further than this when he stated that 'History-making incidents in the Gold Coast [Ghana], Nigeria, Uganda, South Africa and Kenya are more or less the modern counterparts of the agitation preceding the Boston Tea Party incident'. Doubtless in the 1960s some politically conscious young Africans would argue that the last statement is at best a misleading half truth, and would grow suspect of the clarity of Girmamé's thought. However, half truths and even contradictions are as often a measure of immature and inadequate training as they are of really basic confusion.

From recollected conversations we know that Girmamé believed that the material success of the United States could, to a large extent, be attributed to a revolutionary basis which propelled the country. He was inspired by the dedication of that small group of people who first challenged the then mightiest of the world's powers and so laid a foundation for a great nation. In his thesis he wrote of the 'unrivalled technological and no less intellectual advancement' of the Americans and of the assistance they gave to the struggles of other peoples to 'satisfy their national aspirations'. 'Over the years the zeal for freedom has been re-kindled and the flame of hope and determination to be free has been fanned by the example of the American people.'

However, Girmamé did make one interesting distinction '. . . some of these people have received certain assistance from the *government of the United States* and *all* of them have always had the sympathy of *the American people* who are conscious of their colonial origin . . .'* Many observers have noticed a tendency on the part of the Ethiopians to say what is expected of them—a tendency which is not unnatural in any society where advancement depends on patronage more than on ability. But when Girmamé wrote these sentences he probably meant them and was not merely trying to please his American examiners. Girmamé was not only intelligent, he was also a very direct person—perhaps more so than another young African radical of his generation who also died young and in so doing wrote himself into history—Patrice Lumumba.

Girmamé, like Lumumba and like the great majority of students from sub-Saharan Africa, felt almost instinctively anti-

---

* Author's italics.

colonialist and Pan-Africanist. For example, in a footnote Girmamé wrote 'despite the fact that among the various tribes in the past there were important customs which distinguished one tribe from the others, this is no longer true. The impact of the European settlement policy has affected the customs and interests of all the tribes substantially to the same degree. This fact has given them a distinct common ground of concern and destiny. . . .' No student of Kenyan politics before and since independence would so underestimate the continuing significance and reality of tribalism but, nevertheless, Girmamé's words reflect a Pan-African idealism typical of his student generation of young Africans. To speak of the 'Africans of that region' as 'Kenyans', wrote Girmamé, was both 'practical and appropriate' but it was, nevertheless, 'a rather restricted name applying to one of the sub-divisions of the whole'.

At a time when few Ethiopians were disturbed by reading that their battalions serving with the United Nations forces in Korea were involved in 'a struggle against world communism'—or were 'overthrowing the Red beast' as one writer put it[6]—Girmamé indicated his reluctance to take sides on Cold War issues, the typical African nationalist aim of non-alignment. Talking of the newly independent peoples in eastern and southern Europe he stated :

> . . . certain western politicians gravely question the independent status of these countries . . . For our purpose, however, we would assume them to have attained their independence after the disintegration of the Austro-Hungarian empire following the first World War. In the same manner discounting the actual state of affairs in Asia, especially relative to China and North Korea, the great majority of the peoples of Asia after decades of arduous struggle against European colonial powers have at last succeeded in instituting their own national representative forms of government composed of men and women elected from amongst themselves.

Although writing early in the 1950s the young Girmamé was also quite clear about the nature of the African Revolution which has so changed that continent since the second World War. He wrote :

> . . . comparatively, the beginning of a substantial and consciously organised movement dedicated to vindicating the human race in conjunction with the efforts of peoples in other parts of the world has for a long time been overdue in Africa . . . [but] . . . the scattered disturbances of Africa today are

precursors of the tremor which is to follow. The revolution will continue no doubt until Africans re-assert their right to be masters of themselves and of their continent.

Since the failure of the attempted *coup d'état* of December 1960, and to some extent even before it, Girmamé has sometimes been described as a communist. 'Accused' might be a better word, bearing in mind the quarters from which the statements usually originated. But he was not. He was a Pan-Africanist. As a student he followed George Padmore, Norman Leys and others, all of whom were of course to some extent influenced by Marxism-Leninism but all of whom consciously put their Pan-Africanism before their socialism. Colin Legum has pointed out that the early leaders of the Pan-African movement, George Padmore among them, 'unequivocally reject international communism and Moscow leadership . . . the strength of their anti-communism lies rooted in their own experience of it . . . George Padmore by the title [and content] of his most important political work *Pan-Africanism or Communism* defines the nature of the challenge as he saw it'.[7]

But as with his masters, so with Girmamé, the influence of Marxism-Leninism is apparent in his writing. Non-Marxist historians, who tend to regard the imperialist acquisition of Africa as something of an accident, would doubtless carp at Girmamé's description of chartered companies as 'a time honoured spearhead of British policy', and the statement that the Scramble for East Africa (in his indignation Girmamé uses the descriptions 'rape' and 'blitzkrieg dissection') was 'an integral part of the overall plan of the imperialist powers'. They would deny that Kenya's white settlers 'increased their wealth by robbing more of what is *already produced*, thereby causing the general population to grow poorer and poorer'.* Nor would they accept the view Girmamé borrows from Aaronovitch of the role of the Christian Church as a conscious opiate of Kenya's colonial masses.

Girmamé was very critical of the Christian Church. Few historians would accept, as it stands, his remark that 'a very modest reflection would soon disclose that neither Livingstone's . . . objective of spreading Christianity on the continent nor his ardent belief in ameliorating the material circumstances of Africans has even to this day made any appreciable headway'. Most would also qualify Girmamé's conclusion to his section 'The Kenyan and the Official Educational Policy' where he expounds the view that having missionaries as the chief agents for the education of Kenyans ensured (he quotes Aaronovitch) 'that the vast majority

---

* Author's italics.

of them will never be educated; that those who are will learn little and that the greatest pains will be taken to protect them against dangerous ideas'. It can be argued, however, that for long periods of world history the message of the Christian Church was interpreted to sufferers as advice that their lot was natural and that their way out was not an earthly one. Certainly for centuries revolutionaries in Europe had to be heretics. It is interesting to speculate to what extent Girmamé projected into Kenya the typical young educated Ethiopian's view of the Ethiopian Christian Church. But a man who chooses to discuss Kenya settlers, personified by Lord Delamere, in the company of Robert Calhoun of the Southern States, John Hawkins the slave-trader, and 'ex-minister Daniel Malan and Co.' is predominantly resentful of racialism rather than capitalism. Girmamé's aside that Hawkins was 'presumably a Christian missionary', which doubtless refers either to that captain's order to his crew to 'serve God daily and love one another', or to his slave ship, the *Jesus*, throws further light on his attitude to religion which was not necessarily dictated by Marxism.

All this is not to say that Girmamé did not admire the courage of early communists who died for their ideas of social justice, or the great material achievements of the Soviet Union once the Tsars were replaced. We know from recollected conversations that he did—and sometimes with Ethiopia in his thoughts. Also he was suspicious of the economics of capitalism and sometimes tended to argue that western democracy lacked all effectiveness if its ideals were opposed to economic interests. In this he was much influenced, his friends relate, by the speeches and activities of Senator McCarthy and his followers. Girmamé once remarked of their campaigns that 'truth' was ever the casualty, never 'vested interests'. But the very fact that he expressed horror at 'the extent to which the American state was prepared to suffer untruths' at the same time confirms that he did not believe its responses to be entirely conditioned by economic determinism.

Although in his thesis Girmamé emphasised that his arguments demonstrated that 'the interests of the European settlers in Kenya are *directly opposed* to those of the Kenyans especially on the vital issues of land and the fruits of the labour of the Kenyans',* in his conclusion he did not take the Marxist-Leninist view that conflict was *inevitable*. Instead he wrote, 'if there is the necessary will and determination on the part of the European settlers not to make it necessary for the Kenyans to resort to violent methods there is not any insurmountable obstacle in the way of a peaceful

---

* Author's italics.

and gradual approach as a practical method of tackling the problems of Kenya . . . [and] . . . no reason why the basic changes as in land, education, etc. cannot be accomplished within the framework of democratic procedures'.

When he dealt with colonialism and land ownership his main concern was of course for Kenya but both the emphasis he gave and the vocabulary he chose leave no doubt that Ethiopia was never far from his mind. White Kenyan settlers are successively described as 'a landed aristocracy', 'a feudalistic landed aristocracy' and 'part of a feudal system'. He wrote also of 'despotic rule over the rights, interests and lives of the overwhelming majority'. Girmamé dwelt much on improper land deals and appropriations and he criticised court findings on land disputes. It is inconceivable that he considered these issues without making mental comparisons with Ethiopia in the spheres of land appropriation and justice —and such comparisons could hardly have been to the disadvantage even of the Kenyan administration.

It may not have been the dictate of economic dogmatism alone and it could hardly have been the observation of any of his tutors who had visited Kenya, or impressions gained from reading the lives of the farmers themselves, which led him to state that the settler-farmers did not behave 'with the genuine spirit of pioneers seeking to build a new home with their own labour and sweat' but chose rather to be a 'landed aristocracy living in a leisurely fashion made possible by the toil of others—Kenyans'. To the author's knowledge no Kenyan politician castigates the settlers as a body of inefficient farmers or idle absentee landlords : the dispute in Kenya, though not in Ethiopia, was and is quite different. But was Girmamé thinking about Kenya or the *gabar* system and Addis Ababa's absentee landlords? He wrote :

> There were to be no high wages. For one thing a feudalistic landed aristocracy cannot give high wages. Higher wages reduce the income of feudal landlords because it is not part of a feudal system to expand agriculture and other outputs by progressive improvement of the techniques of production as one way of offsetting the high cost of labour and of increasing the income. Feudal lords increase their wealth by robbing more of what is already produced, thereby causing the general population to grow poorer and poorer [then as if to bring himself back to his subject he added] and the European settlers of Kenya are no exception to this rule.

Like—but so unlike—the Ethiopian *rases*, Girmamé felt that 'giving education to such people [the African masses] was tantamount to putting the strongest weapon and the greatest strength in their hands, with which they could fight back and in time cast aside the yoke of despotic oppression and exploitation'. Girmamé believed that in the changing climate of modern Africa no people would long continue to tolerate land systems such as he had described. 'Social conditions [he stated] are responsible for the inflammatory situations prevalent in several parts of Africa', and he also wrote 'a people kept in the shadow of ignorance, superstition, etc., is easier to rule, they can be terrorised, cajoled, divided and so on with less effort and brought into submission'.

Yet despite these statements it is possible that Girmamé, albeit with such famous socialist thinkers as Auguste Blanqui, rather underestimated the importance of the level of political consciousness reached by the masses. He wrote :

> Political maturity is the degree of a people's political consciousness of the past, present and, to a certain extent, the future. This political consciousness is mainly determined by the economic status of the people in the society. Therefore, despite some divergencies of political maturity among the various peoples, wherever the dominant objective social cause is basically similar, the resultant force of their activities will follow, more or less, a parallel line leading up to the point of progressively eliminating the given common cause. . . . The political maturity of Africans will not be found wanting . . . except in the general area of leadership.

And Girmamé had an answer to that, at least as far as Ethiopia was concerned.

But political consciousness is not *found* at all. It is created through years of conscious toil. If Girmamé implied, as he seemed to, that the inert masses wait merely to respond to the call of a leader then he was of course in error. A peasant will follow his baron and the traditions he understands and will fight the man who would give him security of tenure and prosperity, if that man has not previously convinced him that serfdom is not his natural condition and that there is a way out.

Girmamé mentioned that 'in 1920 Harry Thuku began his organisational work among the Kikuyu' and stated that 'within a couple of years he gained wide popularity and his followers grew in number very rapidly. This necessitated the creation of a definite organisation having a set of objectives. His group came to assume the name of the Kikuyu Central Association'. Girmamé did not, however, dwell on the 'gaining of wide popularity' or the 'definite organisation'. He noted that Thuku was arrested and later deported and that this inspired a 'greater fighting spirit in the Kikuyu as well as in some members of other tribes' and allowed new leaders, 'Jomo Kenyatta, Jesse Kariuki and Joseph Kangethe to . . . immensely strengthen the vigour of the association'. Girmamé then commented that the Imperial government at last realised that individual leaders were not so important as the fact that the movement itself had become a political reality.

From his discussion it does seem doubtful whether Girmamé fully realised how much pain and effort went into creating the climate for, and the organisation of, the Mau-Mau insurrection—which is really what his thesis led up to. Had he read more and had it only been possible in the early 1950s for him to have spent an evening with any Kikuyu nationalist leader who had managed to avoid detention in Kenya (such as Mbiu Koinange who had also been a student at Columbia) he would soon have learnt that the awakening of political consciousness and its cultivation to the point of revolutionary fervour was no natural or simple matter, more especially since the colonial government *did* distinguish all along between the basic causes of unrest and the activities of those who brought the politically dormant mass of the people to such a pitch of political awareness that there had to be changes of the people's dictation.

Girmamé listed that the new leaders 'once again launched a mass demonstration . . . [with the result that] the Imperial government appointed a commission . . . to investigate the conditions which precipitated the agitation prevalent at the time . . . [and that] the land problem was found to be the leading factor'. He did *not* mention how Harry Thuku's outlawed East African Association and his Young Kikuyu Association preceded the Kikuyu Central Association. He did not mention the Kavirondo Taxpayers' Welfare Association, the Wakamba march on Nairobi, the arrest of Samuel Muinde, Jomo Kenyatta's championing of the evicted Wataita tribesmen, the Mombasa strike, Mbiu Koinange's independent schools, the establishment of the Kenya African Union, its statements, its colony-wide meetings, its 1947 conference in Nairobi and its membership of more than 100,000. Girmamé seems to have been unaware of the role of the official party newspaper and the seven others whose combined paying circulation, let alone readers, numbered 20,000, or the propaganda songs set to religious tunes, the role of the trade unions and the 1949 general strike, etc.

In Ethiopia neither Patriots nor the many post-war conspirators had spared much thought for the psychology of the masses. The leaders of the Kenyans, however, perhaps because of their own grass roots, never considered how much political con-

sciousness they would *find*; they *knew* how much they had consciously *awakened*. No one dedicated to revolution as a doctrine,
and certainly no communist, would have glossed over the political
awakening of Kenya without really asking *how* it occurred. Despite
this omission, however, Girmamé had a remarkably clear grasp of
the historical relevance of what was happening in Kenya. He
wrote, 'together with peoples of other parts of the world, Kenyans
have become fully aware of the significant implications of the
share of life that is imposed upon them. Equally also they have
become conscious of their strength to resist such an allotment. As
such the age of the passive submission of Kenyans has gone for
ever'. So it had, though many in that country did not realise it.

Girmamé commented that Kenyans would have to 'rely on
actions of their own; actions based on all and any feasible means
which will help in uplifting them from the abyss of poverty, political and educational oppression, and social degradation, and in
restoring to them the right to their country [for] . . . the vindication
of the cause of mankind has to follow the arduous and costly path
of persistent and relentless struggle'. Girmamé saw beyond individual events and immediate struggles to suggest a collective significance and an overall pattern. He referred to Mau-Mau as 'a
prelude of the history of the struggling Kenyans in action', and he
predicted 'in the course of their struggle Kenyans will no doubt
have the active and moral support of millions of Africans as well
as of peoples of other continents and countries'. Then, like a prophet half mindful of the six short years he had then to live, he
concluded his thesis in capitals with the words : 'The current MAU-
MAU MOVEMENT might "successfully" be suppressed . . . but as long
as the cause that created it remains basically intact, there will
emerge other MAU-MAU MOVEMENTS more effectively organised and
embracing the membership of more Kenyans—FOR ONE PHASE OF
THE PEOPLE'S STRUGGLE ENDS ONLY WHERE THE VICTORY OF THEIR
JUST CAUSE BEGINS.'

POLITICAL PARTIES IN EMBRYO

In 1954, Girmamé Neway, the young political scientist, began to
consider where best to study for a doctorate. He would have been
good material. He undoubtedly understood the challenge of emergent Africa and had dedicated himself to the building of a new
Ethiopia and to the alleviation of the poverty of the Ethiopian
masses, even if perhaps he was as yet unsure of the psychology of
those same masses. An idealist, he had shown himself both sensitive
and receptive to all the ideas to which he had been exposed. He

hated colonialism; he had espoused Pan-Africanism; his thought had been influenced by both American Liberalism and Marxism-Leninism, but dominated by neither and in several areas his vigorous mind cried out for greater challenge and guided reading. He knew a little of politics though nothing of revolution and was, above all, an honest man, loved by the many friends he had in America.

But he was recalled to Ethiopia by his government. After the usual period of waiting about, to remind him of the status of young, if educated, men, he was attached to the Ministry of the Interior (then headed by the rich former Patriot Dejazmatch Mesfin Sileshi). From that moment his disillusionment grew.

Girmamé was not at first openly critical of the Emperor Hailé Sellassié. Back in 1952 he had written 'As each of us has been wholeheartedly behind His Majesty—each of us to the extent of his individual capacity—it is a short step to stand united in order to make more effective his unceasing efforts for the peaceful progress of Ethiopia'. However, Girmamé did not remain long under the spell of Hailé Sellassié's considerable personal charm. He recognised the Emperor's political skill and ability to seem all things to all men and therefore he began to explore how best to gather together a pressure group to hustle the Emperor towards reform.

Girmamé's personal tastes were simple. He wore his hair full in traditional style, but in dress he was unorthodox. On a few occasions he wore a red tie in public, but more often he wore plain khaki-drill. This aroused some sympathy, for many Ethiopians have rebelled at the way in which strict court protocol, imported from Sweden, has been reflected at lower class levels thus leading people to think that simple clothes and even their own traditional clothes are in some way inferior to tails, dinner-jackets and smart suits. A son of Blattenguetta Hiroy, the pre-war foreign minister, was once turned away from a palace reception because of his dress. When he was admitted later, wearing a dinner-jacket, he solemnly slopped food all over it saying that it was the garment, not he himself, that was welcome at the Palace. This man was considered something of an eccentric, but unlike him, Girmamé never sought to amuse his companions at the bar of the Itegue Hotel or in the comfortable home of his elder brother, Colonel Mengistu Neway, second in command of the Imperial Guard.

Girmamé Neway soon came to figure in the first attempts to organise the new returning élite. His family and his dress as much as his outspoken nature attracted some attention. He was noticed by the Emperor's security services, by conservatives like Makonnen

Habtewold and Ras Abebe Aragai and by more progressive leaders, among them Blattenguetta Takelé Woldé Hawariat, who soon afterwards was made *Afe-negus* (Lord Chief Justice). Takelé was not very impressed with Girmamé whom he appears to have considered somewhat impetuous. Ras Imru, on the other hand, continued to take an interest in Girmamé.

After the *ras* had spent seven years as ambassador in Washington he was created a prince but again posted abroad for five more years as ambassador in Delhi. Leul-Ras Imru had supported a controversial scheme to modernise the Amharic alphabet—a scheme incidentally opposed by the Ethiopian Christian Church which argued that it was sacrilegious because most Amharic letters were derived from Ge'ez, the language of the Church liturgy and literature.[8] However, Imru was not a political factor of great significance. He was feared by the more conservative of the court circle who reminded the Emperor of the high regard in which the Holeta-trained officers held Leul-Ras Imru, and of the aim of some of the participants in the Betwoded Negash conspiracy to make him president of an Ethiopian republic. In the 1950s, they argued that Imru was by then too out of contact with the country's internal administration to be trusted with ministerial office. Also Hailé Sellassié considered him to be too naïve, particularly with regard to Egypt and Islam, to be trusted with the Foreign Ministry. Thus the ageing prince spent his time waiting for overseas appointments or on leave from them. For his part he did not fear the Emperor or anyone at court. On his return from the United States he caused considerable alarm to the landowning classes and even to some of his own relatives by deciding to divest himself of his land in favour of his servants and their heirs. It is said that by 1960 he had only five *gashas* of land to his name, but this has been difficult to verify. Certainly in Addis Ababa he had only the land where his residence was situated. His status in the imagination of the new élite—or as they described themselves 'enlightened Ethiopians'—rose considerably, for he seemed to acknowledge the national need for land reform. Among the less sophisticated there grew up what will be called 'the Imru myth'—a belief that the appointment of Leul-Ras Imru as prime minister would liberalise the Ethiopian system of government overnight. Foreigners jokingly called him 'the red *ras*'.

In 1954 Leul-Ras Imru left for India. One of his daughters accompanied him and the other was posted elsewhere abroad. Their Addis Ababa residence which had belonged to his father, was, therefore, unused and Imru decided to allow graduates returning from overseas to use it as an informal club. The key was entrusted to one of them—Ketema Yifru (acting foreign minister in

1964). Girmamé attended these meetings and tried hard to give the group some definite organisation—to an extent which some resented. At the weekends outdoor sport was organised and many spent their leisure time reading and debating, but later meetings showed signs of becoming less serious occasions. However, two factors led to the break-up of this group. The first was the development of a serious split between graduates who had returned from Britain and those from the United States, and the second was that a number of Imperial Guard officers began to attend the meetings. At the time they were suspected of spying for Brigadier-general Mulugeta Bulli and, indirectly perhaps, for the Emperor. It was even argued that the group was not yet strong enough to be significant and that, therefore, its existence, which encouraged 'self advertisement' and rivalry in personal struggles for leadership, actually divided progressive Ethiopians to the advantage only of the régime.

An attempt to form a Hailé Sellassié I Secondary School *alumni* association had also failed. It had been sponsored by four young men just down from Oxford University, all from important families. They were Mikael Imru, a radical, Zewdé Gabré Sellassié and Endalkatchew Makonnen, both considered progressives, and Amaha Aberra whose attitudes were conservative. Amaha, son of one of the murdered Patriot-sons of Leul-Ras Kassa Hailu and, through his mother, grandson also of Leul-Ras Seyoum Mangasha, had in his veins the blood of the rulers of Wag, Lasta, Gondar and, in fact, most parts of highland Ethiopia. He had been concerned with a projected aristocrats' club while at Oxford and although ambitious and proud was respected by many for his forthrightness. He quite openly asserted that Ethiopia should be controlled by her leading aristocrats in her own as well as their interests. He argued that the superiority of the progeny of certain families was only too apparent in the history of nations and that, therefore, such as he had not only the God-given sanction, but also the duty to lead and rule.

All associations in Ethiopia have to be registered with the Ministry of the Interior. Amaha's attempt to obtain permission to register a constitution for the association had been unsuccessful. Zewdé and Mikael had also tried in vain. Colonel Kiflé of the Security Department had ruled somewhat typically that if the Emperor agreed, then the group might be formed, but not otherwise. It had, therefore, been decided to invite Hailé Sellassié to be patron of the society and an appointment had been made for the association's officers-elect to do this personally. Only after the Emperor had accepted this position and in the course of their reception, did they mention their difficulty in obtaining registration. Hailé Sellassié smiled, 'It will be dealt with,' he said. But it was not.

Most of the young men correctly concluded that powerful persons in the court circle were afraid that, whoever led it, this group might become Ethiopia's first political party and would be difficult to control. Having put themselves in the position of being refused—in Ethiopia it is seldom polite to actually say 'No' outright—these leaders of the *alumni* felt that they could not openly challenge their government further. They retired into the background for a time, but discussion, nevertheless, continued.

However, towards the end of 1955, Girmamé Neway sent out invitations in a renewed attempt to form the *alumni* association. At a meeting attended by about forty persons it was decided to proceed without registration and Girmamé was elected president for a year. When news of the meeting spread the association rapidly grew in popularity. There was some little indignation on the part of those who had not known of the first meeting—they included Mikael Imru, Zewdé Gabré Sellassié, Endalkatchew Makonnen and Amaha Aberra, and another better attended meeting was held. There was some campaigning on behalf of Amaha Aberra and an intellectual named Seyoum Sabat, who had worked at the State Bank before making his way to Switzerland and the United Kingdom to broaden his ideas and experience, but Girmamé Neway was again elected president.

The group was not completely confined to former students from Girmamé's old school, and for some time he cherished the hope that it might grow into a significant pressure group to support moves towards social and economic changes in Ethiopia. The great majority of the new bureaucracy created by the pattern of government education in Ethiopia were agreed that changes were necessary. But because of that very educational pattern—a column not a pyramid—they were unable to communicate their ideas to the masses of the people, who regarded them almost as foreigners, outside the traditional structure of Ethiopian society which alone conditioned loyalties. Not all the educated élite could accept that their effective status was merely that of a new executive arm of traditional monarchy—albeit skilled in several technical directions. An American sociologist has recorded that one of the new élite exclaimed in private, 'The Emperor will have to learn that our education is not a plaything he can turn on and off as he pleases.'

It is possible that Girmamé underestimated the limitations of their position, but in any case he rejected it. Although he had no cut-and-dried plan for change, he certainly contemplated revolution as a last resort. He continued to read widely on socialism and international affairs and in discussion he put forward socialist views, somewhat akin to those of Harold Laski.

Girmamé spoke to many educated people about land reform and stressed that Ethiopia neared a time of crisis in her long history if only because of her changing African environment. Some were fascinated, some grew frightened, some informed upon him and several urged him to be sure to relate his ideas to political reality. Referring to the masses, one remarked, 'Whether you like it or not this is a feudal country.' Girmamé must have listened to them for he became a founder-member of a new group, the Union of the National Church. At a meeting which was attended by many prominent people, Girmamé took the chair (some say uninvited) and spoke perhaps too much and too long. Abune Teophilos, most progressive of the bishops, was annoyed. 'Am I then to allow the Church to encourage a society merely to provide a platform for the views of Girmamé Neway?' he said as he left the meeting.

But once again internal divisions arose amongst the new élite. They are often said to have been encouraged by the Security Department officers, but they arose accidentally at a social party given in 1956 by the graduates of the growing University College of Addis Ababa. This time tension grew between graduates trained abroad and those from local colleges. They slanged each other in Amharic—'local graduates', 'American manufactures' and 'English BAs failed'—and this greatly damaged the cohesion which was developing.

From the first, Girmamé had held long conversations with his elder brother Mengistu the Guards' colonel. Hailé Sellassié liked Mengistu and approved of the fact that Ras Abebe, Minister of Defence, did not. There was even gossip that Mengistu might be given one of the Emperor's grand-daughters in marriage. Girmamé was quite keen on this suggestion for he thought it would bring them both more influence and the opportunity to bring about the widespread reforms, particularly in land tenure, that he talked over with his brother. 'You are all but engaged,' he said, and turned other women from the house.

On October 3, 1956, Colonel Mengistu was promoted brigadier-general to succeed Mulugeta Bulli as commander of the Imperial Guard. On the same day other colonels were promoted brigadiers-general, including Tsigué Dibou, who became a close friend of Mengistu Neway. Tsigué had been an exile in British Somaliland and Kenya during the war. He had re-entered Ethiopia with the South African and British armed forces and had risen

to the rank of colonel in the army. In Harar and in Addis Ababa
he had acquired some reputation for brutality but he was direct
and efficient and with this promotion was appointed commander
of the police force.

Mengistu was very fond of Girmamé, his brother, and
admired his agile mind. It is traditional in Ethiopia that an elder
brother is tolerant of the untempered enthusiasms of younger
members of the family. Few noticed, therefore, when very slowly
the brigadier-general grew to share the indignations of his younger
brother. Meantime Girmamé became disenchanted with his former
school fellows. He could get them to debate endlessly but they were
undisciplined and nothing tangible was ever achieved. Moreover,
he became very conscious of the way in which all their meetings
were penetrated and watched by the security forces and the spies
of conservative leaders, in particular Makonnen Habtewold. Attendance at meetings began to drop off for the same reasons, but also
because a few of the group felt that Girmamé's efforts to channel
their aspirations and dissatisfactions into directions which might
one day lead to action, were somewhat high handed. As the brother
of Mengistu, he was already accepted as a trusted companion of
the younger service officers of the post-war generation. These young
men, better trained and better educated than the survivors of the
pre-war campaigns or the rewarded Patriots, did not, at all, differ
from their civilian fellows in their objectives, but only in their
possession of arms. They had much in common with Girmamé and
he turned more and more to them.

THE ARMED FORCES

In 1955, after a gap of many centuries, Ethiopia again began to
develop a navy. Based on the Eritrean port of Massawa but with
headquarters in Addis Ababa, its development was guided by
Norwegians, and a flag officer was sent to Ethiopia on attachment.
The deputy commander of the Ethiopian Navy was Commander
Iskander Desta, son of the Emperor's eldest child, Princess Tenagne
Worq, and the Guragé Ras Desta Damtew, who had been murdered during the Italian Occupation. The Ethiopian Navy consisted of a few Yugoslav motor torpedo-boats, American coastal-
patrol boats and a reconditioned United States seaplane tender as
flagship. It was very small compared, for example, with that of the
UAR, whose fleet included destroyers and submarines, but by 1960
it was gaining experience rapidly and had joined in exercises conducted by NATO powers.

Much more important, however, was the air force which

really dated from its reorganisation in 1947 by Swedish advisers. It was equipped with eighteen Saab trainers and two squadrons of Saab 17 light bombers. In 1958 the first jet aircraft were introduced, through a United States military assistance program. This step marked the beginning of the replacement of Swedes by Americans. Helicopters and other planes followed. A transport squadron flew DC3s and C47s. In 1960 a squadron of American supersonic F-86-F Sabre jet fighter-bombers was delivered but in that year the commandant was still a Swede, General von Lindhal. Leul Makonnen and later Leul Sahlé Sellassié, the Emperor's youngest son, were placed in the air force by the Emperor. However, Sahlé did not prove temperamentally adjusted to the high position in the force for which he may have been intended. The second-in-command in 1960 was Brigadier-general Assefa Ayena, a Gondari.

After the war the Ethiopian military had been reorganised under British supervision. Veterans, Patriots and recruits had at first been mixed up together in fifteen regiments, British officers and Ethiopians who had graduated as officers before the war being appointed to the senior posts. Some years later the British moved into advisory positions. The officers of the veteran army had been made NCOs and sent on courses. Their individual qualities had been assessed by 1944 and the Emperor then decided to transfer some 14,157 trained army personnel into the police force. Afterwards military commissions were awarded to those NCOs remaining who had passed through periods of training and grading. Later, following advice from the British military mission, the military was reorganised into eleven brigades. These, with a twelfth formed after the federation of Eritrea with Ethiopia, were grouped into three divisions with their headquarters in Addis Ababa, Dessie and Harar. Auxiliary units were also formed.

Ras Abebe Aragai became Minister of War (later retermed 'Defence') and several influential persons carried high military rank although they were not called upon to perform military duties. These included the Crown Prince, Leul Makonnen, Dejazmatch Mesfin, etc. The list of serving officers included several representatives of the Shewan nobility, for example, Colonel Abiye Abebe, husband of Hailé Sellassié's daughter Princess Tsahai and Merid Mangasha, whose promotion had been more rapid than most. These two were to become important.

In 1951, soon after the British advisers left, a mutual defence treaty was signed between Ethiopia and the United States. Ethiopian forces began to adapt their training methods to suit American patterns and equipment. A United States military assistance and advisory group (MAAG) was attached to the Ministry of Defence under an agreement signed in May 1953.[9] It worked with the army and later, in 1960, the senior American officer in the MAAG team, Brigadier-general Chester de Gavre and another officer, Colonel Campbell, were to be important. The Ethiopian army developed to comprise twenty-three infantry and four artillery battalions, an airborne rifle company and an armoured squadron. This growth was possible through American military assistance on a vast scale.* The United States acquired an important military base at Asmara in Eritrea. The actual agreement has not been published but it is filed in Geneva. It affirms the right of the United States to import equipment without customs or other examination, specifies the lease of the base for twenty-five years and makes provision for extension of the period should it be mutually desired.

The nine battalions of the Imperial Guard, although they also had American equipment and sent several officers to the United States for training, were quite separate from the army. The Corps of Guards was regarded rather as the 'crack' force although its battalions and support units possessed only light armoured vehicles and no tanks. There was considerable jealousy between the guardsmen and other ranks in the army. No action or speech made by either the Emperor Hailé Sellassié or any high government official lessened the tension between the two forces. A third force, the territorial army, was more traditional. It was then ill-equipped and far less trained and disciplined in the modern sense, but, nevertheless, it constituted an important reserve. The police force was smarter and better trained in Addis Ababa (and Asmara) than in the provinces, where it included many poorly trained former Patriots. It numbered over 25,000 and after 1956 was commanded by Brigadier-general Tsigué Dibou.

THE POLITICAL CONSCIOUSNESS OF THE MILITARY

Hostilities between North and South Korea in the early 1950s and the subsequent involvement of United Nations forces also had considerable effect in Ethiopian military circles. The issue was presented as one of collective security and Hailé Sellassié, already a world figure in that context, immediately committed Ethiopian forces. In 1951 Mulugeta Bulli, then a brigadier-general and commander of the Imperial Guard was ordered to select crack

---

* By mid 1963 Ethiopia had received US$73,799,000 in United States military assistance, representing about half the total United States military assistance to Africa. Economic aid 1946–63 was US$122,400,000.

troops for the '*Kagnew*' battalions as they were called. This name was subsequently coined by the Americans for their base at Asmara.

Mulugeta, as has been noted, was of Galla stock from Be'cho in Sidamo province, famous for another soldier, the Patriot leader Geressu Duké. Mulugeta had been chief training-officer at Holeta before the Italian war, had suffered exile in Djibouti and Kenya and had re-entered Ethiopia with the Emperor, from Khartoum. He was an austere man. He did not attend wild parties and drank little. He usually avoided the intrigues and back-biting of the court circle. He was considered honest and it did not pass unobserved that he had not received those large presents of money and land which were thought to mark out those very close to the régime. Mulugeta was a good soldier and liked by his men. He was ambitious but inclined to be hesitant and cautious.

After a brief training spell an Ethiopian expeditionary force under the command of Colonel Kebede Gebré, also to be important, entrained for Djibouti and on April 16, 1951, sailed for Korea in an American troopship. Partly through reflected glory, Mulugeta Bulli himself became very popular in Ethiopia. After July 1952, when General Neguib and Colonel Gamal Abdul Nasser, founder of the secret 'Free Officers' Association', overthrew the Muhammad Ali dynasty and sent King Farouk away from Egypt in his yacht, several of Mulugeta's officers urged him to act likewise, but he hesitated. Mulugeta argued that Egypt and Ethiopia differed greatly in the relative power of the Christian Church and Islam, in provincial tensions and in the personality of the monarch. Some of his officers warned him he could wait too long, but he remained undecided. He visited Korea and noted how fighting beyond their own frontiers rapidly broadened the intellectual horizons of his officers. The United States government invited him to visit America in 1953. Perhaps his moment came and passed. Although he definitely toyed with thoughts of taking over the government of his country and forcing reform through military dictatorship, and, moreover, never discarded such ambitions, he did not act.

The Ethiopian battalions were generally considered amongst the toughest fighters with the UN forces in Korea. Many soldiers and officers distinguished themselves. One name subsequently very important was that of Captain Workneh Gebeyehu, the operations officer of the second *Kagnew* battalion who served in Korea from March 1952 to April 1953. Workneh was from Gondar. His parents were poor and as a boy he had made his own way to Addis Ababa. He was helped by certain Swedes and attended Menelik II School. He first really distinguished himself while on an

Imperial Guard training course. He greatly admired Mengistu Neway, then a colonel and training-officer of the Imperial Guard, and established a close relationship with him, almost that of adopted son.

Workneh was physically very small but his mind was active, subtle and restless. Later Hailé Sellassié asked Mengistu, by then brigadier-general and commander of the Imperial Guard to suggest a discreet and able officer who could be placed in charge of special security and intelligence work. Mengistu suggested Workneh and he soon gained Hailé Sellassié's complete confidence. He was promoted major and in May 1959 was gazetted assistant minister in the department of security of the Ministry of the Interior. His power grew accordingly and was soon resented by the courtiers and ministers, particularly by Makonnen Habtewold. In December 1959 Workneh was promoted lieutenant-colonel and made special vice-chief of staff of the Emperor's private cabinet. His name inspired considerable fear in Ethiopia.

A number of the military officers who, like Mengistu, had been abroad during the Occupation were much influenced by their foreign training and experience. They were the natural leaders of the more informed post-war officers who were drawn from the senior classes (grades) of academic secondary schools but whose promotion in nearly all cases was blocked by older, less able, majors and colonels who were often former Patriot commanders. Doubtless partly as an outlet for their frustration but also as sincere nationalists, these officers often discussed the future which they considered must one day bring them greater political influence.

In 1958 the Emperor established a new military academy at Harar in the south-east of Ethiopia. It was run by Indian officers on lines rather more Sandhurst than Sandhurst. Apart from isolated cases where powerful relatives intervened or where the boys themselves deliberately failed their examinations or ran away and hid, the empire's secondary-school graduates who had gained the best academic results and were fit, were drafted to this academy for a three-year course before being commissioned. This was despite the claims of the University College established in 1950 and the other colleges of higher education in Ethiopia. Ethiopian officers, several of whom had been trained at Sandhurst Military Academy in Britain, were posted to the staff.

Significant discussion of Ethiopia's grave internal problems was developing by 1960 amongst both the cadets and the instructors at the Harar Military Academy. However, it was Girmamé Neway who pioneered such debate amongst serving officers in Ethiopia. Mengistu lent him lorries to organise picnics, but events on such a scale could not pass unnoticed. Ras Abebe Aragai, minister of defence, fearing that influential officers, including Mengistu, were being subverted, urged the Emperor to imprison Girmamé and demote Mengistu. After the meetings of the Hailé Sellassié I Secondary School Former Students' Association, security officers had reported to the Emperor that Girmamé had the confidence and mental ability to be dangerous. Hailé Sellassié had been cautious. Those of Girmamé's former school fellows, who were also from leading families, were given preferment to the rank of junior minister but Girmamé was not. However, the Emperor knew that Brigadier-general Mengistu had served him well in the past and was to a large extent financially dependent upon his favours. He relied upon the Imperial Guard commander to influence his younger brother. It is said that the Emperor also argued that another hothead among the Moja family was nothing unusual and, in fact, every one of them owed much to him in terms of land, money and position and perhaps others were jealous. But he, nevertheless, assigned Lieutenant-colonel Workneh Gebeyehu, trusted head of his own secret service to permanently watch over Girmamé and influence his ideas. If either can be said to have dominated in the ensuing struggle between the two minds, it was not Workneh's —but this he naturally did not report to his master.

GIRMAMÉ AND THE AMERICAN ALLIANCE

Early 1957 was an important period for the Ethio-United States alliance and there were many visitors. The vice commander of the United States Forces in Europe arrived in January and after successive intervals of a few days there followed Lieutenant-general Addleman, Deputy Chief of Staff for military operations, General Van Fleet and then the director of the International Co-operation Administration (Point-4). In March Vice-President Nixon arrived and in April President Eisenhower's special envoy to the Middle East visited the Ethiopian capital. A special joint communiqué explained that the United States government would use armed forces in the Middle East to help any nation subjected to armed attacks by any country under the control of international communism; that the United States did not seek to establish any sphere of influence, to fill any power vacuum or to secure military bases in the area; and that Ethio-American relations were based on four principles:

1. Respect for the sovereignty of all nations under the Charter of the United Nations.

2. Protection of the right of nations to choose their own form of government without interference.

3. Non-intervention and non-interference in the internal affairs of one state by another.

4. Recognition of the independence of nations and the obligation of nations to respect the just rights and interests of other states.

Even so about that time it became apparent that a growing number of younger Ethiopian government officers of the rank of director or director-general were disturbed by their country's increasing dependence on the United States. To some extent this feeling can be attributed to the fiercely independent spirit of Ethiopians and perhaps also to an historically justified xenophobia. Also not all American experts proved, in fact, to be so; their high salaries were resented and the manners and attitudes of some—particularly those from southern and mid-western states—appeared brash and patronising to many Ethiopians.*

Girmamé himself was typical in that he did not welcome too close an involvement between his country and the United States. He was aware of the several tangible advantages which Ethiopia derived from the 1950s period of pro-American policy : quite apart from military aid, she received assistance on an impressive scale from the International Co-operation Administration (Point-4) and later the Agency for International Development (AID). Girmamé, however, feared that foreign aid always tended to strengthen the government in power. This aspect of aid is admitted by several American writers and Girmamé thought it detrimental to Ethiopia's long-term interests.[10] He often spoke in private of the danger of the United States government's equating her best interests with those of the small group of aristocratic landowners who dominated the Ethiopian government but who, nevertheless, opposed agricultural reform and educational and other development. He gained the reputation of being anti-American and there were not wanting those who therefore described him as a communist.

Ever since his return from the United States, Girmamé had openly discussed the problems confronting Ethiopia, especially in the spheres of land tenure and productivity. Facts concerning the real situation in the provinces disturbed him. He knew of the terrace cultivating Konso peoples, for example, who live in the much dissected plateau region south of Lakes Abaya and Shamo and east of the Rift-valley wall; he knew that they had been conquered by

---

* Although the sincerity and hard work of others, particularly in the teaching profession, did much to counteract these impressions.

Menelik's armies only sixty years previously; that the first 'Amhara' had gone to live there quite twenty years later, but that the 'Amhara' governor was, nevertheless, reported as owning some 1,000 *gashas* of land. Girmamé considered that his own studies of land settlement in Kenya were not irrelevant to issues in several parts of Ethiopia. His criticisms of many of the actions and policies of senior officials in the Ministry of the Interior were soon resented.

Reports of his quiet but blunt and informed comments and more particularly the enthusiastic way in which they were repeated by younger bureaucrats and military officers reached most ears, including those of Major-general Mulugeta Bulli. He had not prevented Girmamé from stimulating discussion amongst the younger officers but, on the other hand, he had no wish to be eclipsed himself. Also he had little time for Girmamé's brother Mengistu. He rather despised the libertine behaviour of the commander of the Imperial Guard and of his friend Tsigué Dibou, the police commandant. Encouraged by Ras Abebe Aragai, Makonnen Habtewold, Makonnen's brother Aklilu, and other conservatives, Mulugeta in audience with the Emperor accused Girmamé and others of communism. Possibly he was clearing the field before he made his own move. The particular group of officers around Mulugeta applauded this. They seldom understood Girmamé and considered him pushing. They wanted direct and disciplined military dictatorship to end 'provincial rivalries'. They argued that the intellectual military and civilian group which was drawn to Girmamé would produce debilitating discussions and compromise which might end, with or without the monarchy, in a mere Shewan reshuffle.

Meantime Hailé Sellassié decided that he must act. He sent Girmamé to the south as a governor. Perhaps he thought that Girmamé might learn from experience how difficult it was to grapple with tradition in Ethiopia. But Mulugeta Bulli also lost influence. In April 1958 he was appointed chief-of-staff in the Emperor's private cabinet. It was after General Abboud staged a successful *coup d'état* in the neighbouring Sudanese Republic in November of that same year that the Emperor's attitude to Mulugeta is said to have more noticeably cooled. A year later, in December 1959, he was removed altogether from a position of direct military power and appointed Minister of Community Development, hardly a significant ministry in Ethiopia even in 1964. Mulugeta did not give up his ambitions and his would-be revolutionary caucus continued to meet, but he was preoccupied for some time with the task of getting his ministry transferred from right under his monarch's watchful eye in the palace compound, to a new site in that area of the capital which was still known by its Occupation name of *Casa Inces*.

UNREST AMONGST THE STUDENTS

It was not only in military circles that unrest began to manifest itself in the 1950s. Tension also increased in Ethiopia's colleges of higher education, which have subsequently (December 1961) been grouped together to form the Hailé Sellassié I University.

A University College had been founded in 1950. The Emperor had entrusted its control to the bilingual French-Canadian Jesuits who already ran Tafari Makonnen Secondary School. An attempt to enter into special relationship with London University, never popular with the Jesuits, fell through after the visit of a commission from the Inter-University Council. The college developed independently, awarding degrees after four years of full-time courses. Student entry was at GCE o-level standard, after twelfth Grade of Secondary School. The author has argued that this independence was probably for the best and has traced the development of higher education in Ethiopia, elsewhere.[11]

The Imperial Ethiopian College of Agriculture and Mechanical Arts was founded in 1952 near Harar. This college was assisted by the United States government and there was a contract relationship with Oklahoma State University. It offered a four-year course and a B.SC. in several agricultural fields. Also in 1952 the Imperial College of Engineering was opened in Addis Ababa. It offered four- and later five-year courses leading to a B.SC in Electrical, Civil and Mechanical Engineering. In 1954, assisted by the Swedish government, a college of building technology was opened in Addis Ababa. It developed a complicated timetable of specialised and technical instruction and many of its courses were never designed to be of university standard. Also in 1954 a Public Health College was opened in Gondar with the assistance of the United States government, WHO and UNICEF.

The students of several of these colleges began to confer in an attempt to form a National Union of Students. Several conferences were held between 1957 and 1960 and on December 11, 1960, a few days before the Revolution, a statement resolving to 'bring about the formation of the National Union in the very near future', and an agreed constitution, were circulated. However, prior to this time, the Student Council of the University College acting to some extent on behalf of all Ethiopian students had affiliated to the Co-ordinating Secretariat of the International Student Conference (CO-SEC) whose headquarters are in Leiden, Holland.

University College students were for several years subjected
to strict discipline by the Jesuits—for example, dancing was
forbidden—and they were even referred to as 'boys and girls'.
Student resentment mounted and in 1958 a more liberal Jesuit
replaced the former Dean of Students. Discipline was relaxed a
little but student restlessness still increased.

The national press was strictly controlled. An American
editor who left Ethiopia in 1952, wrote the following :

. . . Time after time nearly the whole paper was blue-
pencilled . . . except for the market reports, shipping news,
etc., and in consequence we could not go to press at all . . .
there was no appeal except to Makonnen Habtewold, Minister
of Finance . . . all copy had to be in the censor's hands at
least four days before publication . . . even when the paper
became a daily . . . one of the officials of the censor's department frankly stated the position, 'what do we want with any
newspapers? They only set people talking about a lot of things
which are not their business. We never used to have any'.[12]

The films *Hamlet* and *Julius Caesar* suffered likewise—the latter
was shown in Addis Ababa without the murder of Caesar ! Films the
YMCA wanted to show were banned. Even the Jesuits, who seldom
took issue with the government, sent a copy of the Bible to the
Security Department official who insisted on censoring a dramatic
version of the trials of Job to be performed by the students.

It was, however, another influence which led to a great increase in student activity. The first Conference of Independent
African States held in Accra in March 1958 was informed that
Emperor Hailé Sellassié proposed to offer 200 scholarships for
English-speaking Africans who would like to attend Ethiopia's
institutions of higher education. In addition to this, many secondary students, including the relatives of some East African political
leaders, were admitted into Ethiopian schools. At the University
College the student news-sheet *News and Views* was more or less
directly controlled by the Dean of Arts in the national pattern.
Moreover, debates as such were not customary but oratorical contests were held at which speeches, checked by college lecturers,
were made. When the contests were public, copies of the speeches
were also previously submitted to the government security department. Pan-African students, excited by the prospect of life in an
independent African country, stood aghast.

In 1959 the leadership of a newly formed debating society
and the Student Council, although it remained Ethiopian, was
much influenced by the views of the Pan-African scholars. A long

pamphlet on the scholarship scheme commissioned by the Ministry of Education and compiled by a Kenyan student—but not published on the advice of an influential member of the University College authorities—contained the following comment :

> For instance in Makerere College, the University College of East Africa, the student guild is purely a student national union independently run by students and having no direct link with the college authorities. Whereas, at the University College of Addis Ababa the student council is by constitution a part of the college authorities and not a national student body. This renders the body almost useless to the students and more than useful to the college authorities. Time has now come, I think, for students in Ethiopia to have a *national* student body that would help tremendously in improving their social life and promoting firm relationships with students outside the country.

This view was quite typical. However, the vociferousness of many of the 'scholarship students', as they came to be called, to some extent masked the slowly growing resolution and solidarity on the part of Ethiopian students, particularly since the latter found it expedient to allow the visitors to associate themselves closely with—and sometimes even to lead—their struggles with the college authorities for greater freedom of expression, more control over their own affairs and agreed and respected written constitutions for their organisations.

It was not so much dissatisfaction itself that Ethiopian students learnt from the 'scholarship' students, as their methods of frontal assault on authority. The Ethiopians saw themselves shackled by their national tradition of blind obedience—to parents, to the Christian Church, to the monarch and thus to authority in general—more particularly since they had already come to despise the national body politic so riven with provincial faction and family rivalry. They deliberately fostered an increasing student 'solidarity' and in this task they felt the college authorities to be their conscious enemies. Certain students were known to report on college affairs to the security police (in return for a small stipend); to the Ethiopian Christian Church; to senior officials in the Ministry of Education and to various Jesuit members of the University Council—in the Dean of Students' office the personal files of Roman Catholic students were known to bear a special mark in red. Student leaders believed the authorities feared any closing of student ranks and that therefore, they sought to divide them.

Eventually, reports of the participation of the college authorities in intrigue aroused wider resentment. Back at the time of the Inter-University Council commission, the content of several of the Jesuit-taught courses had been criticised. In 1959 Paul Vergese, an Indian clergyman, then private chaplain to the Emperor and later to become an officer of the World Council of Churches, and Endalkatchew Makonnen, Vice Minister of Education, complained jointly to the Emperor (who was Minister) that students in the arts faculty of the University College knew that if they failed to reproduce uncritically the philosophical and quasi-theological arguments of the Jesuits, they would be given low marks (grades)—and that this knowledge corrupted their moral integrity. The Emperor, who several students argued was behind all this in order to divide them, in actual fact ordered that several courses be changed forthwith.

A few of the more aware of the Ethiopian students, together with several students from other African countries, judged the time opportune to challege the censorship of the student paper. The Dean of Arts, doubtless feeling harrassed on all sides, accused one of the scholarship students of being a communist. The student promptly affected great indignation and reported this to several members of the government and the word was withdrawn. This and other incidents—the scholarship students delighted in commenting on the attitude of the Roman Catholic Church to Mussolini's invasion of Ethiopia—led the Jesuits, who had little knowledge of other African countries, or the political movements inspiring their youth, to regard all scholarship students with suspicion. They, on their part, soon realised that their presence in Ethiopia was often used by the Ethiopian government as political propaganda and they exploited this fact, and the suspicion of Ethiopian government officials of the Jesuit Order, to their own advantage. A group of college students led by students from East and West Africa decided to publish their own news-sheet which they termed *The Campus Star*. After three issues it was suppressed by the college council on the excuse that its articles and editorial were unsigned. In actual fact its defiant tone and the assertive nature of its political content—broadly Pan-African and anti-colonial, but not communist—gave offence. Knowing the paper was likely to be banned, its editors included a cartoon critical of the papacy which had the desired result of attracting wide sympathy.

Relations between the scholarship students and the Ethiopians were not always harmonious but the Ethiopians admired their spirit and elected several to student office. One became secretary of the University College Student Council when he was only in his second year. He was so outspoken that the authorities felt compelled to arrange a scholarship for him in the United States. In private groups the Pan-African students voiced their shock at what they considered the comparative economic and educational backwardness of Ethiopia. Ethiopian students, who were fast discarding their fathers' prejudices against other Africans—the *Kebra Negast*, chapter 74, declared 'The will of God decreed sovereignty for the seed of Shem and slavery for the seed of Ham'—grew embarrassed and angry. They read Pan-African literature, and the views of the lay members of the faculty who had travelled in Africa were sought with interest. Lectures given by African leaders, particularly Tom Mboya and Julius Nyerere, whose humility amazed them, made a deep and lasting impression. They learnt with horror that political thought in Africa in the late 1950s had moved from admiration of their age-long independence, and the achievement of the battle of Adowa of 1896, to a point of regarding the nature of their government as an embarrassment to the ideals of the African Revolution.[13] In 1958 the Mwanza Conference of PAFMECA asked the first AAPC to discuss 'the democratisation of all independent African States'.* International student opinion was no different. CO-SEC officials admit that they organised their 1960 East-West-Central African Study seminar in Addis Ababa specifically with a view to stimulating Ethiopian students into greater political activity. They succeeded. Before the conference had begun a student leader and a vice-minister reached the point of physical tussle and before the delegates had departed the University College students struck against a somewhat harsh disciplinary decision on the part of the Dean of Women.

For his part, the Jesuit Dean of Students had some understanding of what was happening but the University authorities argued that the strike was the result of a lack of strength on the part of the office of Dean of Students. That office was enlarged, but the Dean was declared to be ill and was replaced by a non-Catholic and lay Dean with an Ethiopian graduate as Assistant Dean. The college President informed them of a message from Emperor Hailé Sellassié : 'You are to teach three things. Discipline and discipline and discipline.'

The year 1960 was marked by several minor trials of strength between the student council and the University authorities, although on a personal level relations were much improved. The students' main complaints remained the same. They quoted the

---

* Pan-African Freedom Movement of East and Central Africa and All African Peoples Conference.

Constitution of Ethiopia, Article 41, 'Freedom of speech and of the press is guaranteed throughout the Empire, in accordance with the law'.[14] The authorities could hardly state that the Ethiopian constitution was not very relevant to the discussions which they were obliged to hold with members of the government, nor could they dwell on the requirements of the government security department, although the students knew these well enough. The authorities interpreted 'in accordance with the law' in the light of the College Charter, itself a legal document. The Charter defined the office and duties of the Dean of Students and stated that in Ethiopian Law he was responsible for student extra-curricular activities and discipline 'both on and off the campus'.[15]

In November 1960 quite a petty incident concerning the allotment of seats on Ethiopian Airlines' inaugural 'trans-Africa' flight presented an opportunity for mounting discontent to manifest itself again. There was some personal jostling between the leaders but after mass meetings the student-body decided to enjoin all its leaders to boycott the flight, as one speaker put it, that 'their West African brothers might learn how they were oppressed'. After a decent interval another Dean of Students resigned under pressure from the authorities who, quite unlike the students, considered him not sufficiently authoritarian. He became adviser to Pan-African students and an amicable agreement was made under which his Ethiopian assistant, who nevertheless agreed with him, consented to take over the post of Dean to try his hand at reconciling what he also privately suspected were irreconcilables. That was Monday, December 12, 1960.

Thus no really serious student unrest—at least in the form of violence—preceded the Revolution. Parallels would suggest that such passivity is extremely rare. Unrest normally begins in the new University Colleges. It would be an interesting project to study the extent to which this resulted from the fact that the attitudes of the University College administration closely reflected those of the imperial government, or Ethiopian parents and of the Ethiopian Christian Church. Nevertheless, at the end of 1960, if the students had never openly criticised their government, as distinct from their college authorities, they were even so in a mood of both anger and frustration, symptomatic of their analysis of the national situation—the same analysis which Girmamé Neway had made some years before.

GIRMAMÉ AS A GOVERNOR

The provincial administration in Ethiopia is technically the responsibility of the Ministry of the Interior, but Girmamé's appointment as governor of Wellamu sub-province in the province of Sidamo, was, like all such appointments, decided by the Emperor. Girmamé was the equivalent elsewhere in Africa of a district commissioner or government agent. He was well received by the people, for his famous forefather, Dejazmatch Girmamé had negotiated with the Wallamu chiefs prior to the re-occupation of the area by Menelik II and had been present at that time also.

Girmamé led the people to build roads and bridges. He set up primary schools and tried to secure books and teachers from the capital. After he had been a governor for just over six months he is said to have produced some Eth. $30,000 (about £4,300 or US$12,000) to be spent on a school. He surprised everyone by announcing that the money did not come from government sources but from bribes, 'which [he said] I have accepted, since it is a tradition—though a bad one—and have put aside for this project'. When he added that more funds were needed the people made efforts to raise them—especially, Girmamé once joked, those who had offered him bribes and who were fearful lest he disclose their names. Such conduct on the part of a powerful official came as a surprise to the people, and made a great impression. As has been pointed out, bribery is an accepted fact in Ethiopia. There is even a popular fable concerning a woman who bribed a judge with a jar and who complained when judgement was given against her. The other party had, however, made a present of a donkey. 'Woman', said the judge, 'a donkey has passed by and kicked your jar to pieces.' Girmamé was patient and just in the law courts and travelled widely talking to and working with the people. 'Trust me', he would often say, 'and I will show you a better life.' He laughed aloud when the landowners and the police warned him that his familiarity was 'lessening the prestige of the Emperor's governor'.

He organised the people into their own watch committees when they complained of the dishonesty and brutality of 'Amhara' police. Of crucial importance, he distributed undeveloped land to the landless, as the African government of Kenya has begun to do. The landowners complained of this and of Girmamé's settling squatters from their land, leaving them with no labour supply. Girmamé bade them hire labour but instead they went to Addis Ababa. Dr Levine states that a wealthy landowner named Desta Fisseha 'managed to arrange Girmamé's transfer through the customary channels of Palace intrigue'.[16] Girmamé was recalled to Addis Ababa and kept waiting for an audience with the Emperor. In conversation Roman Catholic missionaries and the Protestants from Sidamo province spoke openly in Girmamé's praise but at court it was whispered that he was a communist who had tried to subvert the people and unsettle the countryside.

Eventually Hailé Sellassié called Girmamé and asked him why he had interfered with the land-tenure systems. 'Because I was the governor,' Girmamé replied, 'and the people had nothing to eat because they had no land.' He believed the Emperor would support him but he did not.* Instead Hailé Sellassié posted Girmamé to Harar province, as governor of Ji-jigga, the little fort and township built around some wells below the Marda Pass on the track to Hargeisa in the Somali Republic by Bejirond Takla Hawariat when he had been governor there back in 1916. There there were no land-tenure problems for the people were nomadic. Outwardly calm, as 'Amhara' custom dictated, but inwardly furious, Girmamé deliberately neglected the customary court etiquette of kissing hands on appointment. He merely bowed slightly to the monarch and to the horror of many present at court, he turned on his heel and left.

In the difficult desert lands of the south-east the people considered Girmamé Neway a good governor, a view even begrudgingly admitted by his enemies in Addis Ababa. Girmamé had to spend hours presiding over Somali litigation. Often he was in the law courts from early morning until late at night. After its creation in 1960 he had also to deal with security problems on the borders with the hostile Somali Republic. Apart from the obvious need for wells and the greater care of existing waterholes, Girmamé considered improvements in hygiene, through clinics and education, to be of paramount importance. He was appalled to discover eight clinics and hospital buildings empty and deteriorating. Built of West German pre-fabricated material they had been erected by the Ministry of Works, then headed by Dejazmatch Mangasha (Leul-Ras Seyoum's son) for he learnt that they had been promised to the Ethiopian Somalis by the Emperor when he had toured the area in 1956. Girmamé went to Addis Ababa to discover why the Ministry of Public Health was neither staffing nor equipping the buildings. That ministry disclaimed all knowledge of them! Girmamé, who was never philosophical over evidence of lack of co-ordination and proper planning in Ethiopia, was further disappointed to be informed that the ministry had committed its resources elsewhere

---

* With this in mind, the author remarked to Hailé Sellassié in 1962, after Girmamé's death, that Girmamé had been prevented from doing in Wellamu what Hailé Sellassié himself had done in Chercher in the 1930s. The Emperor accepted the comparison, smiled but made no immediate comment.

and, in any case, failed to see why all this provision was necessary for perhaps 500,000 people, while at the same time more populous provinces like Goré, Gemu-Gofa and Arusi were without any hospitals. Girmamé, who would have accepted the latter point at the planning stage, wearily reiterated 'but the buildings are there'.

Girmamé made several such journeys to Addis Ababa to stir officials into action and to get decisions. He sought furniture and provisions for the school buildings in the Ogaden and also asked the Ministry of the Interior for thirty-seven lorries and some tractors. This request was placed before the minister, Ras Andargatchew Messai, who was well acquainted with Harar province. He did not like Girmamé but he was on sound ground when he pointed out that precedent did not exist for the granting of provisions on the scale requested to governors of sub-provinces. Girmamé pressed this and other claims to Emperor Hailé Sellassié, sometimes with success, but Ras Abebe Aragai, Minister of Defence and, since November 1957, chairman of the Council of Ministers, and Makonnen Habtewold, Andargatchew's predecessor at the Ministry of the Interior, then Minister of Commerce and Industry, combined to try to frustrate any development which would add to Girmamé's influence—for both continued to fear him.

For his part, despite intellectual isolation in the desert, the governor of Ji-jigga calmly reconsidered his own role. He saw with increasing clarity that such as he could not hope in 1960 to bring about any fundamental changes through further participation in the existing system. However, he could not admit defeat at the hands of what he considered an anachronistic and immoral tyranny—particularly since through his brother Mengistu he had perhaps the means of change.

It is never possible completely to analyse a man's motives and actions out of the context of the man himself. Girmamé was self-assertive and inclined even to be headstrong. It was this personality as well as his family background and education which gave him the self confidence to consider and actually attempt what within the confines of Ethiopian traditional thought—prior to 1960—must be recognised as almost the unthinkable. He decided to challenge, and if possible overthrow, not just an Emperor, but the whole system of Ethiopian government itself. This is the crux of his importance.

It is probable that Girmamé overestimated the political consciousness of the Ethiopian masses and, therefore, miscalculated the degree of popular support which he might command in such an adventure. But he was by no means certain that he could succeed. There existed a close and vital parallel between his thoughts on Ethiopia and the thesis he had written on Kenya seven years before. He was quite convinced that he had but to initiate an otherwise inevitable process. Whether or not he was personally successful, he would set in motion a pattern of events which would eventually lead to 'victory' for the 'just cause' of the Ethiopian people.

18

A Coup d'État is attempted

In some western circles there is a naïve notion that the régime's extraordinary antiquity gives it stability.—G. SHEPHERD, JR., *The Politics of African Nationalism,* New York, 1962

In most [attempted] coups . . the conspirators were too obsessed with their immediate political problem to give much thought to the theory of the operation they were attempting.—D. GOODSPEED, *The Conspirators—A Study of the Coup d'Etat,* London, 1962

In the case of most African countries at grips with the dilemma of change—variously referred to as the current African 'Renaissance' or 'Revolution'—many special studies exist in the fields of economics, sociology and politics. Further, they are complemented by numerous impressions of observers, biographies both of colonial administrators and of the new architects of change and even by the philosophical and other writings of several of those architects themselves. Not so Ethiopia. It is the author's consciousness of this general deficiency which leads him to attempt within one volume more than an historical narrative which might not permit the discussion of economic background, the conflicting pressures upon the new élite or the thought of individuals such as Girmamé Neway at such length. The author's intention is to assist the understanding of *contemporary* Ethiopia and he writes in 1964. Whatever the final judgement of history (if such there is) with regard to the emphasis to be placed on the events of 1960–1, it will never be denied that they illustrated all the threads of Ethiopian life, the values of young and old, the psychology of the masses, the popular support of Emperor Hailé Sellassié I in Addis Ababa, Asmara and elsewhere, the role of the Christian Church, the aristocracy, the military, etc., the courtesy, the fatalism and the personal courage of individual Ethiopians. And above all, the recognition of the current necessity for a national myth.

THE REVOLUTIONARY GROUP

Aleka Neway died in August 1959 and traditional circles in Addis Ababa rather disapproved when his two sons Girmamé and Mengistu both arranged to marry before the end of that year. The possibility—even probability—that Girmamé would eventually opt for a revolutionary solution to Ethiopia's problems has misled some observers into suggesting that the brothers had long planned their attempted *coup d'état*. It is hardly likely that their double wedding would have taken place had that been the case. It seems more probable that the two brothers did not finally decide that the state of their country's affairs justified their attempting a *coup*, until 1960, the actual year of the Revolution, but this is not known for certain. There was no apparent change in Brigadier-general Mengistu Neway's outward behaviour after the vital decision was made. Often, in the company of his friend Tsigué Dibou, the police commandant, he continued to act as if little mattered to him other than his own enjoyment and, of course, the efficiency of the Imperial Guard. Mengistu who had a reputation as a *bon viveur*, was a strikingly handsome man, slender, immaculate and with an amused and at times almost supercilious smile playing on his lips. He was aware how much he irritated the pompous old nobles at court by toying with his moustache, but he was known, nevertheless, as an Emperor's man and a popular officer.

Full assessment of the place which the brigadier-general holds in the Ethiopian imagination depends upon the understanding of certain fundamental Ethiopian attitudes. In so far as it is possible to ascribe attitudes to a whole people, the Ethiopians generally may be said to display a marked tendency towards fatalism. However, their heroes are, nevertheless, those who do not conform, especially if they act dramatically in their lives or in the manner of their deaths. Courage is more important than achievement and a man who makes a dramatic move, be it heroic or tragic, is remembered and judged on that move alone. Whereas in the United States or Britain, a leading figure, and even his wife and relations, are expected to be successful and to have conformed to approved patterns all their lives, the Ethiopian is more often judged only on the actual occasion which he chooses, or which obliged him, to show his hand. Girmamé Neway's *bon vivant* brother quite merited his reputation and foreign observers held this against him, even after his initiation of the *coup d'état*. However, to the Ethiopian, if Mengistu's earlier life was important it was only so as an illustration of how successfully he hid a mounting feeling for the plight of the common people right up to the time he made his important *dramatic* gesture on their behalf—as it were revealing for the first time his full nature and inviting the judgement of his fellow men.

Before they embarked on the planning phase of their *coup* Mengistu and Girmamé considered whom they should invite to join them. It was agreed to keep those fully in the secret down to a minimum but to sound out others in order to gauge their reactions, to predict who would be in sympathy and to decide whom to arrest. It was agreed that persons of high social or military rank would be best approached discreetly by Mengistu but that the more educated younger officers and civilian intellectuals should be left to Girmamé.

Subsequently it was widely reported in the world press that there had been little attention to detail in the planning of the *coup*, but this is untrue. The two brothers carefully discussed all significant service officers, particularly Major-general Mulugeta Bulli, Brigadier-generals Aman Andom, Nega Hailé Sellassié and Abiye Abebe. There seemed little point in approaching Mulugeta, the popular Minister of Community Development. He was not personally well disposed to the two brothers, it was known that he had ambitions of his own and he was closely watched—in the summer of 1959 the Emperor chose not to leave him behind when he left on a state visit to the Soviet Union. It was decided that he be arrested and perhaps later given the opportunity to join the new government. At the beginning of 1960, Brigadier-general Aman Andom, an Eritrean protestant, was second-in-command in the bureau of the chief of staff of the armed forces. Although he was considered to hold progressive views, and was popular with the troops he was also very close to Mulugeta and loyal to the Emperor. Reluctantly he was considered a danger. Nega Hailé Sellassié was minister of state in the Ministry of Defence. He appeared something of an unknown quantity and it was considered safe and wise to let him remain so. He entered hospital in 1960 and, in fact, played no part in the Revolution.

Brigadier-general Abiye Abebe, the Emperor's son-in-law, was Representative in Eritrea. He was known to feel strong personal loyalty to the Emperor and it was felt that his reaction, if approached, would be to question why he should oppose a government which had given him so much. Nevertheless, his very position in the politically conscious city of Asmara would, it was thought, oblige him to come to terms with a new government if a *coup* was quick and successful. The same reasoning applied to the commanders of the military forces located in the provinces at Debra Markos, Harar, Negellé and Quiha. It was also felt that immediate orders given by a new government to the commander of the territorial camp at Debra Berhan across the Shewan plateau north of the capital and to the tank squadron at Nazret down in the Rift valley, would be obeyed. It was argued that at worst these commanders might only procrastinate a little until certain that the new government was in control. Some other senior officers who were considered eventually posed no problem since by the end of 1960 they were away serving with the United Nations contingent in the Congo.

So far as the remaining senior officers were concerned, the most important proved to be the chief of staff of the armed forces, Major-general Merid Mangasha, a Shewan aristocrat distantly related to the Emperor's family and to that of Leul-Ras Kassa. An ambiguous reply he made early in 1960 to a remark of Mengistu's and the fact that Merid's grandfather, Dejazmatch Mangasha, had been out of favour with Hailé Sellassié, led Mengistu to assume— mistakenly as it turned out—that Merid would support an attempted *coup*.

Mengistu believed that Brigadier-general Makonnen Deneke, the Emperor's ADC would side with successful changes of government, but he was uncertain of Brigadier-general Esayas Gebré Sellassié. Esayas had succeeded Mulugeta Bulli as special chief of staff in the Emperor's private cabinet. The brothers predicted, however, that Esayas, Major-general Kebede Gebré, the commander in chief of the ground forces, and Dejazmatch Kebede Tesemma, a former governor general of Gojjam, who, as a minister of state, was chief of staff of the territorial forces, would all follow Merid Mangasha. Mengistu felt that Brigadier-general Tsigué Dibou of the police would join them and Girmamé agreed but stressed that it might prove necessary to arrest Brigadier-general Assefa Ayena, second in command of the air force.

Underlying assumptions were that military, air force and police officers below the rank of colonel and major would all support the movement; that ordinary soldiers and NCOs would obey orders and need not be informed and that a cadre of committed officers drawn from the Imperial Guard—described in 1960 by a foreign student of Ethiopian affairs as 'a splendid corps of some 5,000 men'[1]—would be all that was necessary to effect the actual arrests. Several of the guards officers were Mojas, descendants of

Dejazmatch Girmamé or his two brothers, or had married into the Moja family. But others who were approached also unhesitatingly joined the conspirators. It was never for a moment doubted that Brigadier-general Chester de Gavre of the United States army and General von Lindahl of the Swedish air force would remain neutral. Girmamé likewise felt that most civilian government officials of the rank of director-general downwards would support the contemplated change of government and it was wise to let only a few into the secret to do the organisational work necessary to appoint a new government and get it away to a clear start. Those trusted included Girmamé's school friend and Moja relative, Girmamé Wondefrash, who had abandoned his early conservative ideas to become a committed radical. Like his namesake he was a governor (of Ulat Awlalo in Tigré). The fact that several Mojas were deeply implicated in the plot is perhaps more important in understanding Hailé Sellassié's subsequent view of the *coup*, rather than the *coup* itself. There were several other civilians, by no means all of them Mojas, whose implication it might not be prudent to discuss. Suffice it to say that the Council of the Revolution included both serving officers and civilians.

The council considered the role of the Security Department and in particular of Lieutenant-colonel Workneh Gebeyehu. The officers of that efficient department were mainly Gondari—a quite deliberate pattern to ensure their loyalty to the colonel in the delicate work which was their lot. There were obvious advantages in securing the colonel's sympathy. As a boy, Workneh had voiced progressive opinions and unconnected with the planned *coup* a group of young people had consciously and on occasions successfully tried to influence him to devote his attention to checking corruption amongst certain high officials rather than to hounding the educated whose exasperation with the régime was continually reported to him. For example, in 1956 the actions of five young men who conspired to Ethiopianise certain posts held by Indian officials of the State Bank had been interpreted by Makonnen Habtewold as opposition to the régime, but Workneh had frustrated his attempt to get them flogged. It is, however, also true that Workneh very much disliked Makonnen. After a visit to India, Hailé Sellassié remarked that he had never met Workneh's equal when it came to analysing the working of both eastern and western trained minds. Workneh's posting to Korea and other travels, including a visit to Japan in 1957 on Hailé Sellassié's behalf to study trade prospects, certainly increased the colonel's realisation of the comparative lack of development in Ethiopia.

Most Ethiopians feel that gratitude and personal loyalty are almost inseparable. The Emperor alone had made Workneh the powerful figure that he was. It has, therefore, been assumed that a violent but concealed struggle occurred in his mind before he decided that a course of action against the Emperor's personal interests was, nevertheless, his duty as an Ethiopian. Contemporary Amharic literature, incidentally, illustrates the absorbing interest which tales of human dilemma have for the Ethiopian. The author has been able to establish that Workneh did discuss the need for internal change with certain members of the new élite. He voiced disillusionment with the ministers, about whose affairs he was, of course, very knowledgeable, and he contended that trained and dedicated young nationalists were so soon corrupted in the Ethiopian government service that there was obvious need for the fresh inspiration which a revolution might provide. When he spoke of the mechanics of *coups d'état*, which he did on a few occasions, he showed himself to be in favour of very careful planning. 'Take time,' he advised, 'make a job of it. Take three years if you wish, I will inform you if information coming through my department indicates any leakage of your plans.' The colonel was also aware of the ambitions of the officers close to Mulugeta.

Both before and after the attempted *coup d'état* of 1960, the significant events of Ethiopian politics were cloaked in great secrecy by the Emperor's government. The fact that discussion, although extensive, to a large extent remained furtive, bred many rumours. Few Ethiopians are aware of the fact that although the Council of the Revolution decided to approach Workneh they did not confide any final detail to him. It was actually Girmamé who spoke to Workneh—but not until November 1960, although by then the colonel already knew about their group.

Workneh once remarked: 'There is a book called *A Man of Three Faces*. That is your Ethiopian!' The depth of the Gondari colonel's own cynicism remains a mystery to this day and he is perhaps the most fascinating character in the drama that followed. Although he associated with members of potentially revolutionary groups and was no doubt to some extent swayed by their arguments and committed suicide on the failure of the attempted *coup*, there is no practical means of telling to what extent he insured his own position with the Emperor. Such is the myth that is growing up around Workneh in the early 1960s that young Ethiopians tend to speak only of the radicals he 'saved' from punishment and forget that in the 1950s little was said of him save that he had blood on his hands. He was the one conspirator of whose involvement Hailé Sellassié later refused to believe and in 1961 in the turmoil following the *coup* on one or two occasions late at night the tired and aged Emperor terrified his servants by calling that Colonel Workneh Gebeyehu should be sent for.

THE PLANNING PHASE

It was recognised by the Council of the Revolution that an operation to secure the persons of the nation's leaders would need to be carefully planned and speedily executed. At first, however, discussion centred on which of these should be arrested. The key figure was the Emperor himself. Three persons were trusted to have access to the Emperor at all times—even to the bedroom. They were Makonnen Habtewold, Workneh and Mengistu. Since the last was in the conspiracy Girmamé urged him to suffocate the Emperor as he slept. He refused. Mengistu felt, in view of the Emperor's services to the nation prior to 1935, that some way might be found to let him live under restriction—perhaps in the small palace opposite the dam at Koka, or abroad. Some of the officers had read Colonel Anwar el Sadat's book *Revolt on the Nile* and studied the Egyptian revolution.[2] The way in which King Farouk had been sent away from Egypt in his yacht much impressed them. But no firm decision was reached on this most vital of all issues.

The Empress Menen had her own court party and it was decided that she would need to be placed under guard. So also would Crown Prince Asfa Wossen who had been the first to sponsor the education abroad of certain of the conspirators. However, it was thought, in view of the tension which had long existed between the Crown Prince and his father, that the former might consent to be used to help secure the support of the people. There was no question of making a previous approach to him, however. The other children of the Emperor were not felt to be so important.

Hailé Sellassié's favourite son, Leul Makonnen, Duke of Harar, had been killed in 1957. A Volkswagen in which he travelled was overturned on the straight murram road south to Sidamo. The author has indicated that he believes Hailé Sellassié to be the son of Ras Makonnen and the Crown Prince to be son of Hailé Sellassié, and discounts the scandalous stories to the contrary to which the Ethiopian feudal system gave rise and which have been used to political advantage by pamphleteers in recent years. In the same way it is necessary to mention that a tale developed and was subsequently similarly used concerning the death of the Duke of Harar. It was whispered that as a result of an *affaire de coeur* concerning a widow who lived just north of Bishaftu, a

young officer shot the Prince, but that all was ruthlessly suppressed
by one of the Prince's companions.*

Princess Tenagne Worq, the wife of Ras Andargatchew, the
Minister of the Interior, was not discussed separately from her husband. Leul Sahlé Sellassié, the Emperor's artistic youngest son
was ignored and this, it transpired, was a mistake. The oldest
grandson, Commander Iskander Desta was distrusted, but only because of his relationship with the Emperor. He was known to be
vigorous and progressive. In 1960, Iskander was sent to attend
the Prince Henry the Navigator celebrations in Lisbon and was
again abroad in Brussels for a royal wedding and then in London
in December.† It was decided that the younger grandchildren, who
were looked after by an English couple, should be placed in custody. There was never any intention of harming any member of
the Imperial family and none, in fact, was harmed.

One courtier was much discussed and it was agreed that he
be arrested. This was Aba Gebré Hanna Jimma who had figured in
the final imprisonment of the deposed Emperor Eyasu (see page
180). Aba Hanna was Palace Chaplain. There are two contrasting
images of this bent old man who looked his seventy-one years. His
mother had been a Gojjami but his Galla father, a *fitwrary* from
Salalé, had served in the Emperor's province of Harar and it was
there that Hanna had been born. He had served Menelik II before
his great chance came, and he was chosen to study at the monastery
of Debra Libanos. Long close to Hailé Sellassié, in 1936 he had even
accompanied him into exile at Bath, England. To the young princes
at court he seemed a kind and holy old man, but beyond its confines he was unpopular. To many of the post-war generation he
seemed another Rasputin. Suspicious townsfolk accused him of
corruption, partly because he always accompanied the Emperor
and was responsible for distributing money. Hailé Sellassié would
name a sum after hearing a petition but Aba Hanna, who was in

---

* The author has found no evidence to support this story. A former head
of the Ethiopian Red Cross informed him that the Prince's injuries,
described at the time by a Swedish doctor who certified death, were consistent with accounts of an automobile accident. Also Makonnen had
enemies who might have invented scandalous stories. There was some
criticism of his commercial activities and jealousy over his alleged
friendship with certain foreign merchants. One of these—a Greek—had
died in a robbery in 1956 and some public resentment had followed the
subsequent hanging of three Ethiopians.
† In 1960, progressive opinion in Addis Ababa, which resented such
actions on the part of the Emperor's government as affronts to African
nationalism, was particularly angered at the raising of diplomatic representation with Portugal to Embassy level.

charge of the Emperor's special treasury, would later award only a fraction of it. Workneh once asserted that this was known to the Emperor. There is no evidence to support the gossip that existed about Aba Hanna but it is, nevertheless, important that he was painted as a symbol of a rich, land-owning Church, dispensing some little paternal charity but having no viable social gospel in the midst of the material poverty of the people. Aba Hanna was a very powerful man. In a feudal court, where access to the monarch is all important, even an Emperor's personal valet can be more powerful than many a minister.

It was further agreed that leading representatives of other important dynastic families would have to be arrested but the time was not thought auspicious to draw up a carefully considered final list. Several nobles, however, were discussed and among the first was Leul-Ras Seyoum Mangasha, the Prince of Tigré.

The son of Ras Mangasha of Tigré, Seyoum was born in his mother's province of Gojjam two years before the death of Emperor Yohannes, who was his grandfather. In 1960 he was seventy-four years old. Most of his early life had been spent in Tigré and his background was traditional. Seyoum was deeply affected by the instruction he received at the hands of the Christian Church and at court where he learnt Amharic. He was a *dejazmatch* at the age of ten, a *ras* at twenty-seven and a prince at forty-three, when Hailé Sellassié was crowned Emperor. He bestowed the title marshal upon Seyoum, who was one of the commanders of the Ethiopian forces at the time of the Italian invasion. After the fall of the Ethiopian government Seyoum was taken to Italy and kept there for two years and two months.

In 1960, Seyoum was governor general of Tigré. Several of the 1960 conspirators considered him personally responsible for the failure of relief measures to prevent starvation during the serious famine of 1958–9. It is true that some supplies of food given by American famine relief organisations were misappropriated and that others were not transported to the stricken areas and deteriorated at the port of Assab. The administration, headed by Leul-Ras Seyoum, was inefficient, but it is inconceivable that he personally acted against the interests of the Tigréan people in such a matter, or was involved in any corrupt practice. Certain of the conspirators also resented the inadequate provision of schools in the provinces and discussed a remark the aged governor general of Tigré is said to have made to those who pressed him for educational advance : 'I have educated two of my sons for you. Be content.' The author considers this remark apocryphal, but that in no way affects the impact made by its repetition. In fact, Seyoum, in his anxiety to support the Christian monasteries of Tigré, which he considered in need of subsidy, chose to divert the only funds seemingly available, some of those earmarked for education—in which field of course, the Tigréan monasteries were in their way significant. Nor did Seyoum have the power of absolute decision over Tigréan affairs for the Emperor always placed high ranking Shewans in the upper levels of the Tigréan administration.

Leul-Ras Seyoum travelled to Harar in 1960 to attend the unveiling there of a memorial to Ras Makonnen, Hailé Sellassié's famous father. In mid December he was still in the capital preparing to leave for Makallé. His progressive and hard working son, Dejazmatch Mangasha, was Minister of Works in 1960. His daughter's son, Dejazmatch Zewdé Gebré Sellassié (see note on page 166), another progressive, was *kantiba* (mayor) of Addis Ababa, but was sent abroad as ambassador to the Somali Republic in 1960.

When members of the powerful northern families were discussed Liquamaquas Tadessa Negash, a minister of state in the Ministry of Justice, but formerly vice minister of the Interior, was also mentioned. Tadessa came from Addigrat. He was very close to the Emperor. Through his father, who died during the Italian invasion, he was a descendant of Sabagadis of Agamé, the famous noble who had been the power in Tigré prior to the times of the Emperors Tewodros and Yohannes. This fact had been recognised by the Italians, who had taken Tadessa to Rome, as well as by Hailé Sellassié. Tadessa was also connected with the Shewan families for his mother came from Menz. Since the Neway brothers were also from Menz and since Tadessa's wife was a near relative of Mengistu's wife (they were both members of the *wagshum's* family) those courtiers who never grasped that the revolutionaries were inspired by wider issues than family ambition have remained puzzled by the decision to arrest Tadessa, more particularly since he was subsequently killed.

There were important representatives of other families also —particularly that of Leul-Ras Kassa Hailu. That conservative and religious old prince had died in 1956 leaving a little book of thoughts entitled *The Light of Wisdom,* which, as its preface announced, was 'squeezed from the Bible'.[3] Only one of his four sons survived the Italian Occupation and he was then the governor general of Gondar. His special position was recognised and he was created a prince. This son, Asrate Kassa, proud head of the powerful Kassa family, was a tall, dark and well-built man who consciously behaved as an aristocrat. In 1960 he was vice president of the Senate and known as a man of action. He was to be a key figure. His nephew Dejazmatch Amaha Aberra, who had opposed

Girmamé's candidature as president of the former students' association of their old school, was away as ambassador in Yugoslavia in
1960.

The head of the Addisgé family, Ras-Betwoded Makonnen
Endalkatchew, another giant of a man, previously prime minister,
was president of the Senate in 1960. When seen with his dogs in his
country house Makonnen seemed almost the prototype English
aristocrat. Among other works he had written about his own
family.[4] His writing was important to him and at the age of sixty-
nine his failing eyesight caused him to fear that he might not
be able to set down all that he wished. In December 1960 he
therefore journeyed to Asmara to seek medical advice and treatment. His son, Lij Endalkatchew Makonnen, another schoolfellow
of Girmamé, was also away. This son's Foreign Office career—he
was a delegate at the Bandoeng Conference in 1955 and the Suez
Canal Conference in 1956—had been interrupted when he became
vice minister in charge of the Ministry of Education in 1958.
However, in early 1960 he was sent out of Ethiopia to Britain as
ambassador.

Leul-Ras Imru, the former Viceroy, returned from his
ambassadorial post in India, but in 1960 was appointed ambassador
to the Soviet Union. However, he did not leave Addis Ababa
immediately and was still making arrangements for his departure
at the end of the year. Because of his popularity and because of
the 'Imru myth', referred to above,* no rebel group could afford
to ignore him. His radical son, Lij Mikael, wore his hair in the style
of the Emperor Tewodros. Yet another former student of Hailé
Sellassié I Secondary School, he was appointed ambassador to the
United States in 1960. These postings of father and son with
regard to both internal affairs and foreign affairs were regarded
as a typical piece of Hailé Sellassié's considered diplomacy. With
Girmamé's posting to Ji-Jigga, nearly all the emerging leaders of
the new élite were removed from the seat of power, i.e., the court
in the capital, at some time during 1960. This fact did not go
unobserved by younger Ethiopians.

Besides the imperial family and nobility, most of whom
would have to be arrested, though some might subsequently join
the movement, the ministers, provincial governors general and
other powerful men were considered. Chief among them was the
chairman of the Council of Ministers, Ras Abebe Aragai : Abebe's
maladministration of the Ministry of Defence had aroused wide
resentment and, moreover, he was a former Patriot leader.[5] Not

---

*See page 353.

only could he order any hesitant general to oppose the movement but he still had great influence over the peasant masses. It was agreed that he would have to be arrested. Ras Andargatchew Messai, the Emperor's son-in-law, who was Minister of the Interior, and other ministers in his ministry, such as the vice minister Afe negus Eshecté Geda, were obviously on the list, as was the Vice Minister of Information, Amdé Mikael Dessalegn, for the radio would need to be controlled. Many others were discussed including Mesfin Sileshi, another former Patriot who had become a rich *ras*; Mesfin's brother, Dejazmatch Bezebeh Sileshi, who was somewhat less important; Yilma Deresse, the Galla Minister of Finance, who incidentally did not like the Mojas for family reasons; Aklilu Habtewold, who was Foreign Minister, Minister of the Pen and Deputy Prime Minister and last, but by no means least, Aklilu's brother Makonnen Habtewold, the Minister of Commerce and Industry. It was decided to attempt to arrest all these men, perhaps even while they were at court.

Any group of conspirators that has decided that a change in their government is a political necessity and that a *coup d'état* is the appropriate means of effecting it must consider wherein lies the strength of the existing régime. Only then can the necessary action be planned to paralyse it. In 1960, the monarchy, or rather the person of the Emperor, dominated the Ethiopian government. For a *coup* to be successful he had, therefore, to be killed or secured. For anyone who knew Hailé Sellassié even to consider that he would have accepted exile abroad and refrained from interference in Ethiopian politics is quite fantastic. Although this matter was taken out of the conspirators' hands by subsequent events, as will be shown, that it should have been the subject of discussion in the preparatory phase was the major weakness of the attempted *coup*.

The Ethiopian government was a court government. It was, therefore, reasonable to believe that the Imperial family, the nobility and the ministers could all be apprehended on some pretext and immobilised by one swift blow struck at this nerve centre. Miscalculation first over the attitudes and then over the support available to certain of the generals proved the second weakness. The conspirators should have ensured that any military leader who was neither committed to supporting them nor to remaining passive was effectively removed from the control of armed forces simultaneously with the first sweep directed at the court.

However, in Ethiopia another institution besides the monarchy was central to the nature of the state—the Ethiopian Christian Church. The conspirators paid the Church far too little attention. If any Ethiopian peasant, or soldier on the highlands had been asked for what he was prepared to fight, he would have replied 'My King, my Church and my Country', in that order. Prolonged negotiations with Alexandria, all concerning a greater measure of autonomy for the Ethiopian Christian Church, had commenced soon after the liberation. A series of concessions made by the Coptic Church in Egypt had led to Abune Basilios becoming the first Ethiopian archbishop, and in June 1959 his status as head of the Ethiopian Christian Church was raised to that of Patriarch. Thereafter the Ethiopian Church was to all intents and purposes autonomous. Although a very old man whose health was not perfect, his personal influence, quite apart from that of his office, was very significant. It should have been obvious that his support, or apparent support, was a vital necessity. Instead he was not arrested and, incredibly, the Crown Prince's subsequent speeches and the other propaganda of the Revolution did not even mention God. This was the third major failing on the part of the conspirators. To some extent these weaknesses may have been the result of haste. The preparation phase of the *coup d'état* had not been completed at the end of 1960, when whispers reaching the ear of Makonnen Habtewold forced the conspirators to act prematurely.

WORKNEH AND MAKONNEN

Makonnen was a small, thin man. He was not ostentatious in his dress—he usually wore a shabby old overcoat—or in his habits. He rode in a Volkswagen not a Mercedes, as was customary for ministers, but he looked crafty and his high pitched voice had no warmth in it. More than anyone else, he seemed to typify the old régime. Some Ethiopians were slightly in awe of his early connections with sorcerers on Mount Zikwala. More feared his spy ring which was said to include several Europeans as well as Ethiopians and to rival that formerly run by Woldé Giorgis Woldé Yohannes. Through the operators he maintained in every ministry he knew most things that were going on and could get things done very quickly when he chose. The Emperor used Makonnen as his check on intelligence supplied by Lieutenant-colonel Workneh Gebeyehu of the Security Department. Makonnen's enemies, and he had many, accused him of nepotism—besides Aklilu, another brother, Akalaworq, was also a minister—but they feared Makonnen's long-standing closeness to the Emperor and his cunning. Makonnen was loyal to his family and his following and was in no way a modern man, but his critics numbered many not basically unlike him except in the measure of their 'success'.

For several years Hailé Sellassié had approved of the continued power of Makonnen Habtewold, which included that of his brother the deputy prime minister. The Emperor knew that Makonnen's presidency of the Ethiopian National Patriotic Association—a potentially subversive group—made it difficult for that body to become in any way a political opposition. Indeed, the association's newspaper *The Voice of Ethiopia,* was as often as not more conservative than the papers more directly controlled by the government. Also in his favour was the fact that Makonnen feared the military—he had not forgotten how the young officer cadets had resolved to hang him back in 1936, and there was little fear of his being involved in any military plot.

Although both understood the monarch's plan always to balance and play off those about him, Workneh and Makonnen were natural rivals. When the latter had been Minister of the Interior he had spoken out more than once against Workneh but the Emperor had not listened. Finally indeed Hailé Sellassié had said irritably, 'Get from my face Makonnen. You do not like to see anyone rise! You speak against everyone for you are a jealous man.' And shortly afterwards Makonnen had been moved from control of the Ministry of the Interior, and therefore its security services, and made Minister of Commerce and Industry. He had retained some reservations but had decided he must trust Workneh. In 1959, while the Emperor was on a state visit to the Soviet Union, Makonnen's spies had reported that a plot existed to assassinate Hailé Sellassié and that a bomb was to be thrown by a former Patriot leader, Fitwrary Hailu Kibret. Makonnen had told Workneh who retorted that he should not worry about it. There had been no developments.

Then in late 1960 Makonnen's agents again picked up and relayed some disturbing news. They reported an accidental slip made in conversation by a young officer, a member of the Council of the Revolution, who was proving a little over zealous in his efforts to bring new members into the Girmamé-Mengistu group. Makonnen, in fact, knew very little. He thought perhaps the army might be planning a revolution. Ethiopians can easily contain dangerous secrets. (Hailé Sellassié had known of the Betwoded Negash conspiracy for three months and had continued to congratulate and decorate its participants right until the last minute.) Makonnen decided not to make any hasty accusations. Instead he asked Hailé Sellassié to take him with him on the state visits to West Africa and South America which were being planned for the end of 1960 but the monarch refused.

In July, Workneh had discussed with the Emperor one of those periodic shuffles, or *shum-shir,* which prevented government officials remaining in any office long enough to gather a powerful group of supporters around them. They discussed the military. Workneh recommended that the popular and able Brigadier-general Aman Andom be posted to Harar in charge of the 3rd Division and the frontier with the new Somali Republic. The conspirators had no part in this but were relieved for Aman was a general to be reckoned with and they had not dared approach him.

Mengistu had, however, made some gentle and oblique references to change in Ethiopia to Lieutenant Dereji, son of the great Patriot Hailé Mariam. Dereji, trained at Sandhurst, had married Immabet Sophia Desta, a daughter of Princess Tenagne Worq, earlier that year. Workneh suggested to Hailé Sellassié that Dereji should be promoted captain and posted to Harar as second-in-command of the Military Academy to understudy the Indian commandant. It seemed a sensible appointment to the Emperor who always tried to use marriage alliances in the accepted feudal manner.* However, Dereji was angry at having to leave Addis Ababa. He warned the Emperor that a plot against the régime was developing amongst the officers of the Imperial Guard. The Emperor appeared to ignore him and may indeed have regarded Dereji's remarks as the result of personal rancour, for he knew Mengistu was not concerned in the posting. But he could hardly have forgotten Dereji's warning.

The Council of the Revolution continued to meet. Sometimes Mengistu would drive from his house at night in a small Volkswagen with a *shemma* done up close around his head. Meantime, especially from September 1960 onwards, Workneh was busy making arrangements for Hailé Sellassié's forthcoming state visits. He did, however, let it be known that he might be prepared to negotiate with the Girmamé-Mengistu revolutionary group through an intermediary. The Council of the Revolution discussed whether to act before the Emperor left on his state visits but decided against this. Girmamé suggested machine-gunning the ministers as they assembled to see the Emperor off to the Sudan but Mengistu and others stated that such an act would bring international disgrace on the country and prejudice any new government. It was thought wiser to wait until the Emperor returned. Workneh, whom Girmamé approached with only partial success at the beginning of November, never attended meetings of the Council of the Revolution until after the *coup* was sprung, but he was known to be

---

* Through his own children, Hailé Sellassié tried at one time or another to consolidate his authority over Eritrea, Wello, Harar and the Air Force—and through the Princess's children, over Tigré, the Navy, the Imperial Guard, the Military Academy and the University.

against any mass shooting. He argued that a semi-military trial of those guilty of putting their own interests before their country's would raise the new government's prestige both at home and abroad.

In the latter part of 1960, some dissatisfaction developed in military circles over the government's neglect of a claim for an increase in pay for the officers of the Imperial Guard. They had argued that they were better soldiers than the officer cadets of the Harar Academy whose pay had been raised. A group of five officers led by the Guard's major, Yohannes Miskir, a member of the Council of the Revolution, wanted to call a strike. They also went to Workneh. Mengistu, perhaps partly because he felt this action might precipitate matters, threatened Yohannes that another major would be ordered to replace him as head of the Logistics department of the Imperial Guard. The actions of Yohannes are rather unclear at this stage, but somehow reports of a split in the officer corps of the Guard reached the Minister of State in the Ministry of the Pen, Gebrewold Engeda Worq—a conservative of humble origins who was a conspicuous property owner in the capital. He had been close to the Emperor since before the Italian war and had fought in his company at Maichew.[6] He spoke to Hailé Sellassié who mentioned the matter to Workneh. It may have been this which led to the recall by telegram of Workneh's deputy, then in Yugoslavia, so that he might accompany the Emperor on the state visits and leave Workneh, who had already packed, free to remain in Ethiopia.

Hailé Sellassié then left Addis Ababa to begin his series of state visits. With him went Princess Aida Desta; Aklilu Habtewold, the Deputy Prime Minister; Ras Mesfin Sileshi, the Minister of the Imperial Court and Dejazmatch Asfaha Woldé Mikael, the Chief Administrator of Eritrea. Others in the party were the Emperor's grandson-in-law Lij Kassa Woldé Mariam, Getachew Mekasha of the Africa department of the Foreign Office, etc. Just before his departure Hailé Sellassié called Workneh and Mengistu to him. He gave them money and remarked : 'I leave the country in your hands.' But Makonnen Habtewold was also left behind.

In the second week of December 1960, on the surface Addis Ababa was calm. Newspapers gave much space to the Emperor's tour—front-page headlines such as 'Liberian President Lauds His Imperial Majesty's Enlightened Leadership' were commonplace.[7] The Crown Prince accepted a gift of books from the British Council, Princess Tenagne Worq opened a conference of African Women, and so on. But the calm was deceptive. Makonnen Habtewold became daily more convinced that the army was about to rebel. He spoke of this to Mengistu and Workneh but both managed to conceal their alarm and attempted to reassure him that his fears were groundless.

A message was also sent to the Emperor in West Africa. Hailé Sellassié discussed it with Aklilu Habtewold and they must have discounted it for the Emperor continued his journey on to South America. It appears probable, however, that he communicated with Mengistu and perhaps also with Workneh. He is said to have telegraphed, among other things, that Girmamé should return to his work in Ji-Jigga. The two brothers discussed developments. It was clear that leakages of their intentions could only increase. Without consulting Workneh, the Council of the Revolution met and decided it had no alternative but to act at once.

THE INITIAL SUCCESSES OF THE ATTACK PHASE

At about 5 pm on the evening of Tuesday December 13, Brigadier-general Mengistu Neway's trusted chauffeur began, on his master's behalf, to assemble a group of young officers at the headquarters of the Imperial Guard. This tall modern building stands opposite and but a stone's throw from the fine wrought-iron main gates which opened into the grounds of the palace called Prince's Paradise. Two hours later Thompson sub-machine guns and pistols were drawn and issued to a group of officers. Not all of them, let alone the Guardsmen, knew what was afoot, but, as one officer put it later at Brigadier-general Mengistu's trial, the motto of the Imperial Guard was : 'Our rule is never to question.'

Meantime, Mengistu left by car for the police headquarters to meet his friend, Tsigué Dibou, the police commandant. In the car on the way back to the Guard's headquarters Mengistu confided to him the full details of the plan, but at that stage the police commandant would not agree to join the conspirators. Thus, when they arrived at the Guard's headquarters, Mengistu demanded Tsigué's pistol and placed him under arrest. Two officers remained to guard him and Mengistu himself assured him that he would be released as soon as the Crown Prince had been effectively abducted.

Then Girmamé Neway, who had come to the Guard's headquarters on the pretext of a farewell dinner with his brother prior to his own anticipated return to his governorship at Ji-Jigga near the Somali border, drove together with Mengistu to the Empress's villa. A small group of armed Guards officers followed in a second car. Mengistu spoke separately to the two guard commanders who were having their meal at the villa. He ordered that one should escort Girmamé and the officers from the second car into the grounds of the villa through a broken gap in the wall, and added that from that time on no one was to be allowed in or out of the compound. He smiled at one of the majors. 'Today you can prove yourself a soldier worthy of trust,' he said. He ordered his officers to conceal themselves in the shrubbery in the northern part of the garden. It was about 9.30 pm.

Dinner was over at the villa of the Empress and a film was being shown when Mengistu was admitted into the hallway. He sent a servant to summon the Palace chaplain, Aba Gebré Hanna Jimma. When the priest entered the reception room Mengistu greeted him and told him that the morale of the army—not the Imperial Guard—was low and there was cause for anxiety over their loyalty. He replied that since the Minister of the Interior was still there, the matter should be discussed in his presence and accordingly Ras Andargatchew Messai was sent for and the news repeated. It was decided to inform the Crown Prince who also joined them. The Crown Prince then asked Andargatchew whether he should not summon other dignitaries. Andargatchew replied that the former Patriot leader, Ras Abebe Aragai, chairman of the Council of Ministers and Minister of Defence and Makonnen Habtewold, should be called. The Crown Prince agreed. Then as the group moved through to a telephone, Andargatchew commented that the army generals Merid and Kebede might be included. Whether Mengistu accidentally made a serious tactical blunder or whether he was quite convinced these generals would support the *coup* is not known for certain, but he must later have bitterly regretted his answer that they need *not* be called. Ras Andargatchew said he would also telephone Afe negus Esheté Geda, who was vice minister at the Ministry of the Interior and he made the calls.

When Ras Abebe Aragai and Makonnen Habtewold arrived they were admitted through the gates on foot, surrounded by armed officers and ordered into Mengistu's car inside the compound. Makonnen had been driving around the city most of the early evening in his Volkswagen, looking in vain for Workneh. He had been warned that matters were coming to a head. In his disturbed state he had chosen to obey Ras Andargatchew's telephone summons, despite the entreaties of one of his spy network. Makonnen had answered the latter that he would now really discover what it was that was happening, but they never met again.

Mengistu was still giving orders when Afe negus Esheté Geda was admitted on foot after a brief argument with the sentries. He was duly escorted by a captain to another car. Aba Hanna, the old priest, then came out of the villa and said he wished to return to the main palace. Mengistu walked along with him and showed him into one of what was by then a line of cars outside the gates. He then ordered a lieutenant to escort Ras Andargatchew into the same car.

As Mengistu re-entered the villa, by a coincidence he met the Crown Prince on his way out and showed him into another car which he waved up—a Japanese vehicle, the property of the Imperial Guard and driven by his brother Girmamé. The remaining empty cars were driven away to the nearby HQ of the Second Shaleka (company) of the Imperial Guard and handed over to the guard commander there. A guard was left on the Empress and the guards on the villa gates were warned to speak to no one about what had happened. Those officers still hidden emerged to join the brigadier-general in a fourth car, which brought up the rear of the procession. The convoy, headed by Girmamé in the company of the Crown Prince, moved off quietly back to the Imperial Guard headquarters.

ADDIS ABABA IS SECURED

During the night and early hours of Wednesday morning many ministers and dignitaries were telephoned and summoned on a variety of pretexts including the false report that the Empress was dying. Some like Workneh and Tsigué Dibou, the police commandant, decided to throw in their lot with the conspirators. Others, like Ras Abebe Aragai and Major-general Mulugeta Bulli, Minister of Community Development, could not bring themselves to the point of opposing the régime in these circumstances, and were kept under guard. Some appeared to be willing to help but were later thought to be contemplating a double game and were then also placed under guard. Still others, like Brigadier-general Makonnen Deneke, vice minister of the Imperial Court, sat around, apparently stunned by it all and for a long time came to no decision.

When he arrived Workneh was angry that he had not been consulted earlier. 'I know the things that should be done,' he said and asked Mengistu what steps had been taken. Contingents of the Imperial Guard were sent to take over the State Bank, the Ministry of Finance, the radio station and the two telecommunication stations. Colonel Gashaw of the Addis Ababa police was given money for police rations and ordered to see that there were no disturbances in the city. Several of the police officers who were called glanced at their commander, Tsigué Dibou, for a sign of his approval before they accepted orders from Mengistu. Officers from Workneh's Security Department made further arrests and were sent to disconnect the telephone system. That step, Workneh remonstrated, should have been taken earlier. By the morning of Wednesday, December 14, armoured cars were stationed at all important crossroads, the troops guarded the approaches to embassies, schools and the University College. Small detachments were stationed on the roofs of key buildings, particularly those near the Hailé Sellassié I Star Square (or Piazza as it was more usually called) at the city centre. The city was effectively taken over.

The dignitaries arrested included Leul-Ras Seyoum Mangasha, Prince of Tigré; Dejazmatch Bezebeh Sileshi; Liquamaquas Tedessa Negash, minister of state in the Ministry of Justice; Amdé Mikael Dessalegn, vice minister of Press and Information; Abdullahai Mumie, vice minister of Finance who was from Harar; Haji Farrar and Kebret Astatkie, the Muslim vice minister and the assistant minister respectively in the Ministry of the Interior, the latter also hailing from Hailé Sellassie's former province of Harar; and the conservative Keeper of the Seal, Gebrewold Engeda Worq, minister of state in the Ministry of the Pen. Others summoned included some who were not thought a danger to the *coup* but who were felt to share responsibility for the nation's backwardness. Lemma Woldé Gabriel was called. Lemma had been brought up in the palace and apart from one misdemeanour in the days of the Regency, which had cost him several lashes, he had remained close to the Emperor. He possessed a long *curriculum-vitae* of ministerial and judicial appointments and in 1960 was vice minister in the Ministry of Mines and State Domains. Two senators, Blatta Ayelé Gebré from Harar and Dejazmatch Letibellu Gebré, a Patriot from Menz who had been involved in the assassination attempt on Marshal Graziani, both arrived and were detained. Having heard second-hand of the supposed critical condition of the Empress, Dejazmatch Letibellu had come of his own accord and to his subsequent complete misfortune, refused to be sent away. Adamew Tesemma, a diplomat with a post in the Ministry of Defence, likewise came but was not called. A few of those telephoned checked with the Imperial doctor, and ignored their summons.

The progressive former Patriot leader Afe negus Takelé Woldé Hawariat was contacted with news of the illness of the Empress. He replied, 'I am not a physician', and stayed away. Hailé Sellassié's cousin, the former Viceroy of Ethiopia, Leul-Ras Imru, was also contacted and came to the headquarters of the Imperial Guard. He described his arrest at Brigadier-general Mengistu's subsequent trial. Since Imru feared no one and had no personal axe to grind, his evidence was possibly the most reliable at that trial. He said : 'I met Mengistu. I asked him what had happened, and he replied,

"Nothing. Everything is all right. The Crown Prince is here, and you may hear about everything" . . . and I went into the Crown Prince's room, greeted him and asked him what had happened. Mengistu stated that the army, the Guard, the police force and the air force had together overthrown the government. I asked him who they were that had done this, and he replied : "There is a Committee." I asked him whether I could go and see them and talk to them, but he said that would not be allowed. I then retorted angrily, "The Congo became a laughing stock. Are you going to make our country a laughing stock?" But then it dawned on me that we were under arrest, and I sat down and remained quiet . . .' Imru was waited upon and accorded every courtesy. He spent most of his time in the company of the Crown Prince, who at times appeared somewhat distraught.

Thus the attack phase of the *coup* successfully secured the capital city and the means of government without a shot being fired. The ministers of the Ministry of the Interior were immobilised. Leading conservatives were detained. Influential figures including the Crown Prince, Imru and Mulugeta Bulli were all controlled. It is true that certain potential counter-revolutionaries had been ignored or had slipped the net and were still at large in Ethiopia, but an obvious priority of the next phase of the *coup*, that of consolidation, should have been their speedy arrest and detention before they could recover from their surprise and organise support. They included in particular the Patriarch, Abune Basilios, head of the Ethiopian Christian Church, that vigorous and proud noble Leul-Dejazmatch Asrate Kassa, son of Leul-Ras Kassa Hailu and vice president of the Senate; certain senior service officers, notably Major-general Merid Mangasha, Major-general Kebede Gebré and Brigadier-general Esayas Gebré Sellassié, all of the army, and Brigadier-general Assefa Ayena of the Imperial Air Force.

THE COUNTER-REVOLUTIONARIES ASSEMBLE

The interruption to the telephone system of the capital was not quite quick enough to prevent several vital calls, in the main made by the wives of those arrested. These calls could serve as an interesting example of the tight family and marriage connections binding the powerful circles in Ethiopia, so typical of feudal society.* As

---

* There is not space between the present covers to deal with the events of December 1960 in any greater detail than is attempted. However, the author hopes to publish at a latter date an annotated translation of the proceedings of Brigadier-general Mengistu Neway's trial.

a result, alarm spread and two small groups gathered. The first, called by Major-general Merid Mangasha, chief of staff of the armed forces, included Major-general Kebede Gebré, chief of staff of the ground forces, Brigadier-general Esayas, chief of staff of the Emperor's private cabinet and other army colonels and majors. The second, formed a little later, was called by the Crown Princess to the Crown Prince's villa. Dejazmatch Kebede Tesemma, chief of staff of the territorial forces, was summoned in the early hours of Wednesday. He later reported that it consisted of the Princess, Leul-Dejazmatch Asrate Kassa, head of the Kassa family who had been with the Crown Prince only a few hours before the arrests, and two other conservatives, Balambaras Mahtemé Sellassié Woldé Maskal and Fitwrary Workneh Woldé Emmanuel. This group believed a *coup* to have been sprung by the Imperial Guard in co-operation with the army. There is record of the conversations that took place.[8]

The Crown Princess said, 'I have called you to inform you that the Crown Prince had his dinner at the Empress's villa with the Empress but when he left the villa he was surrounded and taken by the Imperial Guard. Ras Andargatchew who was with him was also arrested. It is further rumoured that they have arrested Ras Abebe and Ato [Mr] Makonnen Habtewold. What is behind all this and what can be done?' Asrate Kassa then suggested that an attempt to capture the Crown Prince's children should be anticipated and that since the precincts of the foreign embassies were safer than anywhere else, the Princess and the children should be taken to any one of them. Dejazmatch Kebede protested that there must be a reason for what was happening and before taking any step that might add to the confusion they should ascertain whether anything had happened to the Emperor and if so what arrangements had been made to communicate the news. The Crown Princess replied that it was said that the Guard and the army had conspired together against the régime, and the present necessity was to find the best way of discovering the whereabouts of the Crown Prince and the other dignitaries.

Leul-Dejazmatch Asrate Kassa's mind appears to have worked the fastest. He had quite grasped what was happening and was a step ahead of the Princess. The Ethiopian state was, he knew, organised to meet such dangers and he remarked that if the Imperial Guard and the army had made a joint plot then the obvious course was to muster the territorial army. 'Therefore,' he said, 'let Dejazmatch Kebede go at once to their depot at Debra Berhan and gather forces. Let him bring here all the available territorial soldiers and all such other persons who might be of any help.'

Kebede shrank from involving his comparatively undisciplined territorials and more particularly feudal levies. However, he conceded that he was prepared to make the two-and-a-half hour drive to Debra Berhan up on the plateau to the north of the capital, if it was really necessary. He warned that precipitate action could well result in the creation of nationwide chaos and added : 'If we bring in the territorial army at this stage we must consider the consequences to the city!' Ultimately, however, it was agreed that the territorial forces should be mustered. 'While it is hoped that the future state of affairs will render their use unnecessary,' Asrate explained, 'if there is no better news by midday then it will be advisable to call them in and they must be prepared.' Dejazmatch Kebede then returned to his home with the intention of preparing for his trip to Debra Berhan.

It must have been soon after leaving the Crown Princess that Asrate learnt of Major-general Merid's group and realised that a major part of the army might yet be persuaded not to support the actions of the Imperial Guard. According to information subsequently published by a guest then staying at the British Embassy,[9] the British ambassador was aroused in the early hours by the news that Leul-Dejazmatch Asrate Kassa had arrived at the embassy with two companions 'in a humble looking car obviously not his own'. Asrate said that the Imperial Guard and some of the police force had rebelled and the Crown Prince and most of the ministers were under arrest—and that 'he, somehow, had escaped the net'. On behalf of the imperial government he asked the ambassador, Mr—later Sir—Denis Wright to convey this news to the Emperor. The ambassador forthwith contacted the London Foreign Office. Kassa and his companions then moved on to join Major-general Merid Mangasha's group at the headquarters of the 1st Division of the army.

Asrate was not the only one to consider attempting to contact Hailé Sellassié. The ailing Empress Menen managed to send secretly to her youngest son, Leul Sahlé, that he should raise the alarm through his ham radio. At first he declined, saying that he was loyal to his brother the Crown Prince and needed orders specifically from him, but after an argument he was persuaded to try.* His message which referred to the '. . . crucial moment in the life

---

* A few months before his death in 1962, this artistic and talented young Prince recalled this incident. He used the word 'bullied' and added 'and I want no medal for that'. Sahlé, who was very critical of his father and the government, spoke also of the gap between the haves and have-nots in Ethiopia which he knew to have angered Girmamé Neway, whose personal strength he much admired.

of the country . . .' was picked up in several places, notably by
another amateur in Hayes, Middlesex, England who relayed it to
Ethiopian embassy officials in London and to the press.

It was inevitable that news of the *coup* should spread
throughout the world and it was in any case intended that public
announcements should be made on Wednesday morning. Meantime, and for many more hours, it would have been a simple matter
to arrest Asrate Kassa and the army generals even if that meant
storming the 1st Division headquarters. However, confident of their
success, the revolutionaries argued over secondary issues. Their
rebel fervour and effort began to dissipate into channels which
could have little significance until the attempted *coup* could be
completely consolidated. Which, in fact, it never was. Mengistu,
despite the advice of his brother, Girmamé, hesitated to authorise
action which might lead to bloodshed. Revolution, however, is not
for the dilettante. It was Lenin who pointed out that once begun
it must be carried through with absolute ruthlessness to the end.
The initiative began slowly to slip from the hands of the Council
of the Revolution. Meanwhile, from the army headquarters Asrate
Kassa sent for the patriarch.

THE PROPAGANDA OF REVOLUTION

The prisoners were placed under guard in rooms in the headquarters of the Guard and Workneh addressed the twenty-five man
Council of the Revolution and insisted that they appoint a prime
minister and announce a peaceful change of government. There
followed discussion over the functions of such an appointee and the
issue was only shelved when Workneh suggested that Leul-Ras
Imru be appointed prime minister as a temporary appointment. A
Revolutionary Proclamation was drawn up by Girmamé and
Workneh, who actually wrote it down, and the Crown Prince was
asked to record it on tape. The following is a translation from the
Amharic :

A PROCLAMATION!

Ethiopia's history has been renowned for 3,000 years but during that long period the implements of the farmer, the busi-
nesses of the small trader and all other spheres of life have
seen no changes. There have been continued ignorance and low
standards of living. There has been no progress whatsoever.
This is because a few self-centred persons instead of working
for the common interest have chosen to indulge in selfishness
and nepotism. The Ethiopian people hoping one day to be

freed from ignorance, illiteracy and poverty have waited patiently all this time but nothing tangible has materialised from a mountain of promises.

No other nation has manifested such patience. The great strides being taken by the newly independent African states, advancing as they are day by day, have made the people of Ethiopia realise that these new nations are achieving so great a rate of progress that they are leaving Ethiopia far behind in economic development, education and living standards. In the last few years there has been stagnation in Ethiopia! An atmosphere of dissatisfaction and discontent has grown up amongst farmers, merchants and professional people; amongst members of the armed forces and the police and amongst the younger educated Ethiopians—in short amongst the entire Ethiopian population.

There has been an attempt to destroy this kind of new movement. Just as the bee whose hive has been disturbed becomes violent so also have some opponents abandoned all restraint. But despite that they have been unable to hold back a growing awareness amongst the Ethiopian People. Thus has this movement resulted in a new government which has dedicated itself to the welfare of the whole Ethiopian People and to the security of the country. And now it gives me great pleasure to announce the success of this movement to the Ethiopian People.

The few selfish persons who fight merely for their own interests and for personal power, who are obstacles to progress and who, like a cancer, impede the nation's development are now replaced. And I have, as of today, agreed to serve you and Ethiopia as a salaried official under the Constitution.

Know that all decisions and appointments declared by the new Ethiopian government formed by me, and supported by the armed forces, the police, the younger educated Ethiopians and by the whole Ethiopian People, are effective from this moment on!

People of Ethiopia! Let your unity be stronger than iron bonds! Today is the beginning of a new era for Ethiopia in the eyes of the whole world.

Copies of the Proclamation were duplicated for distribution and other policy statements were prepared. On the morning of Wednesday, December 14, government departments, the State Bank and shops were open and functioning. On the orders of the Council of the Revolution, officials of the Ministry of Foreign Affairs sent out notifications to the foreign press and embassies 'taking pleasure in announcing' a change of government. The word 'Imperial' was discussed. A prominent member of the new élite who had been invited to sit with the Council pointed out that the word proved a great embarrassment at the United Nations and it was, therefore, deleted from the notepaper. Goytom Petros, a senior foreign ministry official questioned the validity of these instructions but his minister of state, Blatta Dawit Okbagzy, assured him that the Crown Prince had authorised them to obey all instructions given by Brigadier-general Mengistu Neway. Oral requests for recognition were also made. The prime minister's office, rather than the Guard headquarters, became the centre of activity and notification was sent to the provincial governors informing them of the 'peaceful change' and requiring them to continue to maintain law and order.

At first the citizens of Addis Ababa had no idea that anything so momentous was taking place. Then at about 11 AM a military truck toured the streets announcing that the Crown Prince had taken over the government. 'If the Emperor has given it to him I suppose it is all right,' old folk muttered. At about midday the Addis Ababa radio broke silence. The Crown Prince was introduced by an announcer and the tape of the Proclamation which Girmamé had taken to the broadcasting station was played. The recorded speech was repeated all the afternoon to the accompaniment of stirring military music played by the Imperial Guard band. At the same time as the broadcast began, sheafs of duplicated copies of the Proclamation were dumped in the town and at the colleges and schools. Perhaps it was hoped that the students would explain matters to the townsfolk.

An authority on *coups d'état* has stated that a recognised pattern of the *coup d'état* is that radio propaganda, prepared in advance, 'can gain time for the development of the revolt, can confuse and dishearten government supporters and can even influence, at least temporarily, the international situation [and that] it is of little practical importance whether the news thus disseminated be true or false for it will almost certainly be many hours before the listeners can appreciate the real situation'.[10]

The Amharic of the Proclamation was vigorous and stirring but the content was such that, especially on first hearing, it appealed mainly to those who had been exposed to ideas from the outside world. In short, its language was that of the African revolution and its audience the converted. A paraphrase of parts of it was prepared and broadcast in English and a government policy statement on the part of the new government (reproduced below) was also made. Thus this Amharic speech may be assumed to have been aimed at the Ethiopian masses. As a revolutionary tactic the repetition of a selection of the more scandalous undercurrents of Ethiopian court life might have been more effective in swaying the citizens of Addis Ababa in 1960. For example, a 'discovery' that the monarch had become a Roman Catholic would have seriously affected public opinion—but the revolutionaries, particularly Girmamé, were too idealistic to employ such deceit. Their Proclamation mentioned neither Hailé Sellassié nor the name of God, and as stated, the careless omission of the latter aroused uneasiness amongst the general population in the city.

Mengistu soon realised the confusion of the people and decided to ask the students of the University College and other centres of higher education to demonstrate and help to get the revolutionary message across to the citizens. But winning over the people or at least securing their acquiescence, though important in the long run, was not his major problem. Mobilisation of the people to consolidate the *coup* should have been considered secondary to the pursuit of any surviving supporters of the former government lest through persuasion, propaganda, foreign support or a combination of all of these, they were able to muster forces sufficient to counter-attack. Indeed, Workneh and Girmamé were for forcibly arresting Asrate Kassa and the army generals. But the Council of the Revolution was so confident of the success of the *coup* that they did not press this opinion. Tsigué saw the danger more clearly and urged immediate action, but Mengistu mistakenly considered that the army generals and others who had gone to the headquarters of the 1st Division could be persuaded to co-operate. They may well have encouraged him in this view if only while they strengthened their own hand. Mengistu repeatedly and emotionally declared that he wished to avoid bloodshed. Girmamé also wanted to arrest Brigadier-general Assefa Ayena, deputy commander of the Imperial Air Force, but then it was Workneh's turn to object. Assefa like himself, was a Gondari and, therefore, to be 'trusted' he insisted. And that proved a major miscalculation.

On Thursday, December 15, Radio Addis Ababa repeated that 'as announced yesterday, a Representative People's government has been peacefully established in the Empire under the direction and leadership of the Crown Prince. Peace and calm continues throughout the country, the whole population, including the army and police are wholeheartedly co-operating with the new government'. The radio also announced in Amharic, English and Somali that 'His Highness Ras Imru has been appointed prime minister of Ethiopia . . . the man to whom an appointment has now been made is a man who has identified himself with the people and a man who looks forward to progress'. And later, 'Let us now all unite and stand behind the new government which stands for progress. You have already heard of the appointment of Ras Imru as prime minister. Ras Imru is likeable and a great statesman and needs absolutely no introduction to the Ethiopian people. . . . His loyalty to the country and the Ethiopian people is known to all. His appointment as prime minister of the new representative government of Ethiopia is just reward for his loyalty and devotion. In this appointment Ethiopia can be confident.' Another appointment was claimed to be that of the popular Major-general Mulugeta Bulli as 'Chief of staff of the Ethiopian armed forces'.

The policies of the new government were detailed :

Here is an important proclamation by the new Ethiopian government which outlines its new aims as follows :

1. It is clear that the fantastic progress achieved by the new independent African states has placed Ethiopia in an embarrassing situation. The new government will have as its aim to restore Ethiopia to her ancestral place in the world.

2. The new government will adhere to its international obligations and continue its existing relations with friendly nations.

3. Capital investments made by foreigners in Ethiopia will not be disturbed in any way provided that such investments contribute to the general well-being of Ethiopia and its peoples.

4. New factories and industries will be set up and put into operation to help the people improve their standard of living.

5. As agriculture is the mainstay of the country's economy every assistance will be given to the farmers to raise agricultural production.

6. The Ethiopian trader will likewise be given all assistance to improve his business and so contribute to the improvement of the country's economy.

7. Many young Ethiopians are seen loitering in the streets. As these young people should be in school, the new government aims to educate these young persons and to find employment for those who are now unemployed.

8. One of the problems of Ethiopia's advancement is the lack of technical know-how. The new government will estab-

lish technical schools in the country to deal with this
problem.

9. Members of the armed forces will have more clearly
defined privileges and personal freedom and hereafter the
armed forces will not be known under two separate titles,
namely Imperial Bodyguard and the Imperial Ethiopian
Armed Forces. In future there will only be one name The
Ethiopian Army.

10. ... [This item is not audible on the author's tape recording.]

11. A curfew is now in force in the whole Empire of Ethiopia
from 7 o'clock in the evening until 6 o'clock the next
morning. This will be observed until further notice.

Although no foreign government had time to consider recognising
the new government, the question was raised in the British House
of Commons.

Most Ethiopian diplomatic emissaries abroad kept a discreet silence—the nearby consulate-general in Nairobi was noted by
the Kenya press to boast a notice, 'No office hours today'. There
were, however, exceptions. The London embassy under Lij Endalkatchew Makonnen spoke immediately for Hailé Sellassié; Tafari
Sharew, the ambassador in Sweden and his first secretary Lij Abaté
Getachew were as quickly for the rebels. Lij Abaté was the son of
Ras Getachew who had collaborated with the Italians and whom
Hailé Sellassié had banished to the provinces, and much has been
made of this. Tafari Sharew, a protégé of Ras Mesfin Sileshi, had
been a very successful businessman in Ethiopia. However, he had
been disliked by Woldé Giorgis and by representatives of leading
families. He had refused a ministerial appointment, spent some
time under house arrest and had apparently been discarded by
Hailé Sellassié. Difficulties had also arisen over his lands which he
could hardly settle while away in Stockholm. On these grounds
some subsequently labelled him an opportunist governed only by
personal animosity towards Hailé Sellassié. However, he was not
without personal reasons for disliking Mengistu as well.

Tafari Sharew greeted reporters at a press conference with
uplifted arms and the cry of 'Liberty! Democracy', and denied a
suggestion of communist influence in the *coup*. He is said to have
accused Hailé Sellassié of amassing a fortune in British, Swiss and
American banks.* Several papers reported that he stated:

---

* The *Daily Herald*, London, December 16, 1960 is quoted. Others
besides Tafari Sharew have published similar suggestions. However, the
author is convinced that Hailé Sellassié is not personally much interested
in amassing a fortune for its own sake.

Hailé Sellassié has misused the people's goodwill . . . we are not interested in his future prospects . . . he has much money and could receive more if he agrees to stay away. Freedom of expression has been quite unknown, the people have lived under the oppression of a secret police and people have been condemned without coming before the proper courts . . . The Emperor's speeches are written by an American . . . it is remarkable that a representative of the democratic American people has stood beside a feudal absolute ruler as adviser and counselled him in a direction contrary to everything which could be called democracy.[11]

The United Nations contingent in the Congo included some 1,800 of the Imperial Guard. Several comments in favour of the changes at home were made by Ethiopian officers to foreign correspondents. The *Observer* reported an alleged statement hailing 'an end to centuries of feudal oppression and corruption'.[12] The commander of the Ethiopian contingent subsequently denied that these statements had been made. Similar statements were attributed to the Ethiopian chargé d'affaires in the Congo but he also subsequently denied them and on returning to Addis Ababa published a lengthy attack on the professional ethics of *Time* and *Newsweek* reporters. Editions of these papers were banned in Ethiopia, but one Ethiopian editor, apparently harnessing the *double entendre* of Amharic, published a lengthy editorial which, although it ended 'as an expression of justifiable indignation . . . the pernicious issues . . . have rightly been withheld from public curiosity' also succeeded in advertising the two magazines in bold print in twenty-two places.[13] Broadly speaking the typical initial reaction of the world press was that change was bound to happen in Ethiopia sooner or later but was really expected only on the death of the Emperor Hailé Sellassié.

MENGISTU COURTS THE STUDENTS

At exactly 11 AM on Wednesday morning, December 14, a Guards officer rang the bell at the University College but could not bring the students together. He announced another meeting later in the day and meantime excited groups of students read the mimeographed copies of the Crown Prince's Proclamation. Similar events took place at other colleges and the Council of the Revolution soon realised that it was assured of the support of the vast majority of the Addis Ababa student population. Student leaders from all colleges, none of whom had prior knowledge of the *coup*, were called to the headquarters of the Imperial Guard in the afternoon and met Mengistu and other officers. The meeting lasted an hour and took place in a small office on the second floor.

Throughout the world young students tend towards dissatisfied idealism but for reasons which have been indicated the students of Ethiopia felt particularly frustrated over the state of their country's affairs. It is not surprising that Mengistu made a great impression upon them—that day one student commented to the author, 'His Excellency the General stood before us with his eyes blazing honesty and with the poor people's broken bread on the table behind him!' Mengistu, capless and in light brown gabardine uniform, shook hands with everyone and said in Amharic: 'We have called you not only to inform you of events but to seek your help and co-operation, for our cause is one in which you are equally concerned. The economic and social plight of the majority of our population does not change and in many cases conditions are actually deteriorating. In the capital as well as elsewhere in the country most of the land is owned by a few people and they add daily to their holdings without working at all. There is no equality of opportunity for the majority. Only a very small group enjoys the *de facto* protection of their property by law. The rights of the rest are not respected and worse—they cannot even complain of this! Many true Ethiopian Patriots have been mistreated to suit interests incompatible with the national interest and undeserving folk rewarded in their stead.'

The brigadier-general then made reference to his ministerial hostages by pointing to the bread and saying, 'These pieces of dry bread were served last night to some of those privileged in order to draw their attention to the kind of life led by the average Ethiopian under their administration. Of course, they could not eat it!' There were smiles but he continued in serious vein, 'Now do not misunderstand us. Our actions are in no way self-assertive. You know me for example. As things stand in our country I am one of the privileged. As commander of the Guard I can get anything I want —a car, a villa, furniture and servants. But I must risk this in the wider interests of all. To be frank, we are no longer sure that we will succeed, for at the last minute some have shown reluctance to join us. But this we know for sure. Once we start the fire, it will burn on by itself. And then we will have done our part.' Mengistu also remarked that he had made the Crown Prince read the Proclamation; that he had enquired of the Ethiopian Christian Church whether it would support the new government and on receipt of a non-commital answer had made several pointed remarks about the wealth of the Church and the contrasting poverty of the people. He said a group of young men had worked out the new government appointments and before the meeting broke up, he remarked of the hostages, that if necessary he would destroy them—he used an Amharic expression describing them as 'mere empty bags'—'that Ethiopia should never be the same again'. But not all those present heard the last comment and were not really thinking in terms of violence.

In the University College, the Students' Council met and decided to approach all their fellows. An evening meeting was held in the dining hall with the whole student body present, save the scholarship students from other African countries who met informally and decided that these events were 'the internal affairs of Ethiopia' and that they should take no part. Two representatives from the Guard, but no university staff members, attended the mass meeting of the student body. It was reported in an edition of the college paper *News and Views*.[14] The article quoted one speaker as saying, 'Now is the time to clear your throats and speak, to clear your minds and think'—an order of events indicative of the atmosphere so charged with emotion. Another speaker stated : 'Today marks a new era. The old régime has been overthrown and a new one established on behalf of the people.' There was almost—but not quite—unanimous support for the Revolution and it was decided to organise a public demonstration to this effect on the next morning. Organising sub-committees were formed and student representatives from other colleges were contacted. The whole night was spent drawing up and duplicating a statement for distribution to the public, composing a marching song, and painting large coloured banners.

It would have been impossible for the College authorities to successfully forbid the demonstration, and they did not try. Most of the professors and lecturers, like other foreigners in the city, huddled round radios and listened to the sketchiest reports from the BBC and other foreign stations. They began to discuss the probable reactions of Hailé Sellassié away in Brazil.

HAILÉ SELLASSIÉ LEAVES BRAZIL

Reports transmitted from the Foreign Office in London, from diplomats and pressmen in Brazil and finally from the Brazilian government before it received the Ethiopian Foreign Ministry's telegram concerning the change of government, were all communicated to Hailé Sellassié. After holding private discussions with members of his entourage, Hailé Sellassié apologised to his Brazilian hosts and arranged to fly back to Africa in his own plane. He received foreign ambassadors before he flew to Monrovia, Liberia and thence to Chad where he arrived on Thursday, December 15. He was much encouraged by action taken by Brigadier-general Abiye Abebe, his son-in-law who was Representative in Eritrea. It is not clear how Abiye acquired an accurate picture of the situation in the capital but he soon established some communication with the small but growing group, led by Major-general Merid Mangasha and Leul-Dejazmatch Asrate Kassa in the 1st Division headquarters in Addis Ababa. Abiye then sent a telegram from Asmara to several Ethiopian embassies abroad contradicting the telegrams sent from the Ministry of Foreign Affairs in Addis Ababa which had announced the formation of a new government under the Crown Prince and declared them to be 'without foundation or validity'. Later in a second telegram Abiye stated that 'the Crown Prince and the acting foreign minister are under pressure from certain elements of the Guard and police' and that 'the army, the air force and the country at large are loyal to the Emperor'.[15] He issued similar statements to the press in Asmara.

In Harar the army detachments, with the exception of the artillery, appeared at first to welcome the news of the *coup* in Addis Ababa. The Military Academy was divided. However, the provincial governor general, Colonel Kiflé, promptly ordered the temporary confinement of the few Guards officers at the Academy and declared for Hailé Sellassié. Colonel Kiflé, who held the title of *dejazmatch*, was fifty-two years old. He had trained in Alexandria and St Cyr and before the Italian war had been second-in-command of the Guard. Previously in charge of public security, Kiflé was close to Hailé Sellassié. The commander of the 3rd Division of the army, Brigadier-general Aman Andom, alerted his troops, correctly anticipating an attempt by the Somali Republic to take advantage of the confused situation. Patrols he sent out reported penetration of Ethiopian territory by some fifty to one hundred Somalis. The general dispatched a company under a battalion commander to surround them. When reports indicated a rapid build-up of Somali forces he himself flew to the front. The Ethiopian encircling movement finally contained a push by nearly 5,000 Somalis who were heavily defeated and their invasion repulsed. Meantime Captain Dereji Hailé Mariam, the Emperor's grandson-in-law who was the newly appointed deputy commandant of the Military Academy, rushed away to Addis Ababa only to die in the fighting that was to occur there.

In Jimma, the senior students at the Agricultural School voiced immediate support for the *coup*. The governor general, Colonel Tamrat Yigezu, grandson of the famous Dejazmatch Yigezu, surrounded them with troops 'for the protection of the school'. In Gondar, the governor general, Dejazmatch Kiflé Dadi, a Moja, nevertheless sent out orders to the leaders of the people to maintain calm in the name of Hailé Sellassié. Although the provincial governors declared for the Emperor they might not have done so had they not learnt that Major-general Merid Mangasha and the others remained at liberty. In general, events happened with such speed that everything was over before the country people themselves realised what was taking place. Only students knew because of their access to radios and particularly to foreign news broadcasts.

As soon as possible, Hailé Sellassié established radio contact with his son-in-law in Eritrea. The crew of his plane report that, unlike other dignitaries (some of whom said they would have preferred him to have gone to Switzerland) Hailé Sellassié was calm and cheerful. However, a failure developed in one of the four engines of the DC6 and he grew worried and declared, 'I know there will never be peace in Ethiopia without me—I have got to get back.' After landing at Fort Lamy, Chad, it was found that the shaft of an engine had broken. The crew were undecided what to recommend until Hailé Sellassié enquired, 'Are you worried for your own lives or for mine?' On receiving their embarrassed and somewhat indignant answer, he smiled and said, 'Then we will go— and go now!' Their plane, using only three engines, flew on over the southern Sahara. An Ethiopian officer from Asmara had flown to Khartoum, and greeted Hailé Sellassié who inspected a guard of honour, had a short private conference with the Sudanese president and spoke to Sudanese cabinet officials, diplomats and the press. Then, in the company of this emissary, Hailé Sellassié telephoned his son-in-law. Once in contact he asked that Abiye identify himself by a secret formula previously arranged between them. Hailé Sellassié listened to the latest available account of the situation before deciding to fly on to Asmara, capital of Eritrea. This stop lasted forty-five minutes of Friday, December 16.

THE GO-BETWEENS

Meantime in Addis Ababa on Wednesday, December 14, Girmamé, Workneh and others busied themselves organising the new government, while Mengistu, the Crown Prince and Leul-Ras Imru conducted a series of complex negotiations with the counter-revolutionary group assembled at the 1st Division headquarters. In spite of his briefing by Leul-Dejazmatch Asrate Kassa at their hurried audience with the Crown Princess, Dejazmatch Kebede Tesemma, the commander of the territorials decided not to proceed at once to Debra Berhan but to go instead to the headquarters of the Imperial Guard and see for himself what really was happening. He proved quite willing to be a negotiator—a popular position in Ethiopia and elsewhere when the outcome of events is unclear— and Mengistu sent him to try to arrange a conference between Major-generals Merid and Kebede and himself, in order, he said, to avoid bloodshed. After seeing the Crown Prince, Dejazmatch Kebede left for the army headquarters. There he found the two major-generals, Leul-Dejazmatch Asrate Kassa and the others, together with Brigadier-general Esayas and some other officers. Merid was perturbed that Dejazmatch Kebede had not yet called out the territorials.

The *dejazmatch* explained that he had visited the headquarters of the Guard and he repeated the conversation he had had there with Mengistu, who, he reported, had been eager that there should be mediation and had asked him to say to Merid : 'If we can meet and talk this affair over it will prevent any bloodshed and will straighten matters out.' 'Where am I to meet him?' asked Merid suspiciously. 'At the headquarters of the Guard,' the *dejazmatch* replied. Merid, understandably, shook his head. 'I shall not go to his office. If he wants to meet me let us meet on neutral ground—perhaps even at your house. But I am afraid I still think he has not told you the full facts and I do not believe our meeting will straighten matters out. As for Major-general Kebede and myself, we shall not go to the Guard headquarters,' he declared.

Asrate Kassa seemed disturbed at this trend towards negotiation but Esayas remarked that if a meeting could prevent bloodshed he was prepared to meet Mengistu anywhere. So it was that Dejazmatch Kebede and Brigadier-general Esayas left for the headquarters of the Guard, avoiding the rebel government's roadblock near the Ministry of Finance. Esayas met Mengistu who appears to have tried, unsuccessfully, to persuade him to join issue with the new government. It is not clear how the conversation went because in the first part of his report at the subsequent trial of Brigadier-general Mengistu, Esayas clearly endeavoured to avoid incriminating Mengistu. However, he did add :

While Brigadier-general Mengistu and I were talking, a captain came and called him away. When he returned he finally said : 'I will tell you the people who are working these problems over. These people have decided to change the régime. It has been decided that the Emperor should be confined in safety somewhere. The Crown Prince has agreed to this and he will issue all statements. The whole idea has the support of many people in the army and elsewhere—and I'm sure you can easily meet with these people and talk to them.' At this point he was again called out but again returned to say that the Crown Prince would like to meet Major-generals Merid and Kebede. He asked me to go and bring them. However, I replied that I would not do so unless ordered directly by the Crown Prince. Then I went out and sat outside for some minutes with Brigadier-general Makonnen Deneke before being called into the Crown Prince's room. The Crown Prince asked me to go and bring Major-generals Merid and Kebede so that they might talk things over. I agreed, bowed and left.

Back at the army headquarters I told all I had heard to Major-general Merid and the others but they replied that this was tantamount to being forced to go—and that therefore they would not go. I then said that since it appeared that both sides would be involved in a conflict there ought to be a meeting on neutral ground and that I might bring some bishops to ensure that all was settled without bloodshed. After delivering the news to the other generals, I then went to the Patriarch and asked if he would mediate or send certain bishops and he agreed.

Esayas did bring three bishops to meet with Mengistu as the latter told the students, but they lent little constructive weight to the discussion and nothing was achieved. An afternoon meeting was scheduled to take place at the Patriarch's house on Wednesday but it never occurred. Esayas departed and by the time Dejazmatch Kebede returned, via his own house, to the army camp, all thought of negotiation there at least was over.

The Patriarch was in attendance and the gathering had swelled by the addition of several nobles. Merid said his main concern was that he had insufficient troops but he had called up the tank squadron from Nazret. He had reason to believe that the air force was now with him and for these two reasons he could not lose. He had called for troops from wherever they were available and he raised again with Dejazmatch Kebede the issue of the territorials. Then discussion turned to what the Patriarch should be quoted as saying on an Amharic leaflet to be distributed to the public. The following form was agreed upon :

> To my children the Christians of Ethiopia and to the entire Ethiopian peoples.
> Yesterday, December 13, at about 10 in the evening the Imperial Guard soldiers who were entrusted with the safety

and welfare of the Royal Family committed crimes of treachery against their country. They were led by a handful of officers who undermined their faithfulness and violated their oaths of loyalty. While the Emperor is away making new friends for Ethiopia the traitors summoned and threatened some members of the Royal Family and high officers of the government. They declared that they had formed a new government saying that they had changed the 3,000-year-old stable government. This was announced by radio at 1 PM in the afternoon and in order to confuse the ill-informed they made it appear, again by using the radio station, as if the army, the air force and the police had agreed to their plot.

The entire Ethiopian people will not fail to appreciate the wisdom and courage of the Emperor and above all else the people are fully aware of their indebtedness to their Emperor. The Ethiopian people are ardent believers in their faith and will not be shaken by rumours and by empty words. The Ethiopian people are a faithful and a great people. The army personnel are unquestionably faithful to the Emperor and to their country. I have confirmed my own certainty that this was so while actually amongst them.

The army, the air force and the police force have not participated in this conspiracy. Therefore I admonish you not to waver in your loyalty! To keep your words of promise and to serve only the Emperor! Do not listen to the traitors! I adjure you not to follow them in accordance with the authority given to me.

Abune Basilios,
Patriarch.

Merid Mangasha and Kebede Gebré also worded the first of several leaflets of their own. This denied the involvement of the army and air force, denounced the 'few treacherous officers' of the Guard and reaffirmed their loyalty to their 'great leader, the servant of Ethiopia, His Imperial Majesty Hailé Sellassié'. All the leaflets were actually radioed to and duplicated by the air force authorities at Debra Zeyt. In all this Merid's group showed considerable political acumen. The psychological impact of the Patriarch's pronouncements was in itself quite sufficient to offset the radio propaganda and student demonstration then being instigated by the revolutionaries.

When he spoke of his concern at the small number of troops available to him Merid indirectly admitted that militarily speaking he should not have been able to recover from the success-ful surprise element of the *coup d'état*. On Tuesday night and Wednesday the rebels had superior forces at the points where they were needed in the capital, but they did not use them because of indecision in their high command. Once political strategists have decided to seize a government by force, military tacticians must neutralise every pocket of potential reaction. People, not buildings, constitute a government and the chief of staff of the armed forces is far too vital a figure not to be secured. Major-general Merid Mangasha, like Fitwrary Habta Giorgis before the battle of Sagalé in 1916, recognised that time was on his side if he could procrastinate. Also like Habta Giorgis, he requested and received support from an interested foreign power, in Merid's case, the United States of America.

THE FOREIGN GENERALS

Merid's contention that the support of the air force and the tank squadron from Nazret put him in an invincible position proved cor-rect. But it is clear that for a long period both sides counted on the support of Brigadier-general Assefa Ayena, the senior Ethiopian officer in the Imperial air force. He appears to have tried to remain uncommitted as long as he could, but not unnaturally he emerged on the winning side when this position was no longer possible. In the early hours of Wednesday morning, Merid ordered Assefa, by letter written in Amharic, to place the air force on the alert and await instructions from the army. Assefa merely relayed this to the Swedish general von Lindhal, commander of the Ethiopian air force. At the time Assefa was even uncertain of the stand which Merid was taking.

General von Lindhal called the expatriate officers together. He stated that they were employees of Hailé Sellassié and must not support the apparent change in government. If necessary they would be evacuated to Aden or Nairobi. There were British arrangements he said, but even if they fell through, the United States government, which was co-operating with Britain, would act independently. He at no time stated that he was in direct con-tact with the United States government, although certain Ameri-can officers afterwards claimed that he implied it—and further that they assumed when an 'attack' order eventually came, that it had at the very least the approval of their government.

American interest was natural and inevitable considering their own base in Asmara, their agreements with Hailé Sellassié, their influence at the air force base and the presence of their military mission (not to mention their fear that in Girmamé Neway they had educated a communist).* Their involvement was obvious and unconcealed—an American colonel later rode in an open jeep in front of Hailé Sellassié's vehicle when after subsequent fighting the latter re-entered the stricken capital—and it has been discussed, even criticised, by several American political writers. For example, Vernon Mackay later wrote: 'Many Americans ask whether we have not become too closely identified with the ruling Americo-Liberian oligarchy in Liberia whose policies have been less than progressive. Others were uneasy when our assistance was instrumental in putting down the palace revolt in Ethiopia in December 1960, which was in part a libertarian reaction against a semi-feudal régime. Yet Liberia and Ethiopia have two of our oldest and most extensive aid programs.'[16]

All through Wednesday, acting on Merid's orders, air force transports flew about forty-four trips to airlift nearly a thousand troops from Dira Dawa, Debra Markos and in particular Gondar and Negellé to the air force base at Debra Zeyt, some thirty-five miles south of the capital. On that afternoon a task force of five heavy tanks, several tracked machine-gun carriers, wheeled troop carriers and jeeps called by Merid from Nazret, thirty miles farther south, stood by for some time at Debra Zeyt, where the junior air force officers were demanding to know more of what they were being called upon to do. Later the tanks and troops continued up to Addis Ababa. Light aeroplanes circled the convoy as it approached the headquarters of the 1st Division at the southern limit of the capital and the road was closed to other traffic. Air force planes flew reconnaissance photographic sorties over the city to cover the Guard headquarters and camps, their movement zones and their ammunition centres.

At 10 PM on Wednesday, a 'Prepare for battle' order was received from Merid. Targets listed, according to Assefa's evidence at Mengistu's trial, were:

1. The Guard Headquarters. In order not to injure the arrested dignitaries, the attack should be only on the top floor [sic]
2. The separate headquarters of the 3rd Shaleka [company].
3. The Guard garage.
4. The headquarters of the Guard heavy artillery.

---

* The editorial of *The Times* (London) on Friday, December 16, 1960, included the sentence, 'There is a United States base at Asmara and it is possible that the Americans who are firm supporters of the EMPEROR may find some means of helping him.'

Receipt of this order brought the growing concern amongst the air force officers to a head. Assefa himself left by car towards Addis Ababa but did not reach that city.

Merid Mangasha meantime approached the head of the United States military mission and asked for advice on the planning of an operation to recover control of the capital to be based on aerial photography of the disposition of the rebel forces, and for the loan of telecommunications equipment. The quiet American commander, Brigadier-general Chester de Gavre, was in a spot. He procrastinated until he could seek political advice from Ambassador Richards, who was doubtless already in immediate contact with Washington. The ambassador, the author was informed shortly afterwards by a United States diplomat, told the soldier that he was accredited to the Emperor's government and there seemed little doubt that these generals and in particular Merid, represented the Emperor's government. His duty defined, Brigadier-general de Gavre gave Major-general Merid the benefit of his advice. Moreover, from this time on the ambassador himself began to play a very considerable, though to this day, still somewhat enigmatic part in the whole proceedings. He succeeded Dejazmatch Kebede Tesemma as the chief go-between.

'PEACEFUL CHANGE'—THE LAST BIDS

On Thursday at about 9 AM nearly every student of the University College, both men and women, formed up in a procession extending almost right round the sports field behind a national flag. Some appointed as marshals wore bright armbands and gave out song sheets and bundles of leaflets for distribution to the townsfolk. The banners were unfurled and, with shining eyes revealing a happiness and confidence which observers confessed they had never witnessed, and which the broader pattern of events certainly did not justify, the student procession set off through the gates towards the town centre to meet up with their fellows from the other colleges. They sang loudly and well. In free translation their Amharic song might be rendered :

> My countrymen awake ! Your history calls to you.
> Let slavery depart. Let freedom reign anew.
> Awake ! Awake ! For dignity—her sake.
> My countrymen recall—your value and your due,
> Take courage and stout heart—Great joy shall be with you.
> Awake ! Awake ! For dignity—her sake.*

---

* In literal translation, the student song is as follows: (Line 1) Wake up

The student manifesto which was distributed spoke of the backwardness of Ethiopia and the injustice of the old régime. It affirmed the students' love of their country and their debt to the tax payers. The influence of the African revolution was obvious in the phrase, 'Countries and peoples which have recently become independent are leaving us behind in every respect. Ethiopia has a history and a tradition of over 3,000 years yet still she creeps behind— we say this because we have realised where we stand from our studies and our analysis of the present world.' This manifesto made the Revolution's sole reference to Hailé Sellassié, albeit a veiled one. As an example of 'corruption and maladministration', it said, 'all power is concentrated in the hands of one man'. Besides criticising the exploitation of the peasants, the corruption of the courts and existing disparities of living standards and wages it also voiced the popular student complaint, 'There exists no freedom of speech or of the press'.

The banners bore Amharic slogans—'Ethiopia is peacefully changed for us all!' 'For everyone—a bloodless revolution!' 'You who have suffered under injustice—Wake up!' 'Let us stand peacefully with the New Government of the People', and the largest of all proclaimed, 'Our Goal is Equality, Brotherhood and Freedom'.

Guardsmen mingled with the crowds. Guards officers in a jeep checked with the demonstrators that all was well and that no protection was needed. The reaction of the citizens was at first a somewhat confused curiosity. The reception was mixed near St George's Cathedral but once the procession reached the market area their reception was positive. Many Muslims and Eritreans who were not greatly in sympathy with the régime lived in the market area but acclamation appeared universal. People joined in the song and many attached themselves to the procession. There was heavy demand for the leaflets. Farther along the route employees of the State Bank cheered and a minister looked on from the window of his ministry. It was nearly midday when the procession, after having toured the city, made its way to the southern slopes of the town where the headquarters of the 1st Division of the army is located.

The students had every intention of attempting to persuade the soldiers to lay down their weapons but a platoon commanded by a junior officer blocked the route beyond the railway station. The

---

my compatriot, do not forget yourself for you have a history behind you. (Line 2) Erase your slavery and renew your freedom today. Wake up, wake up. (Line 3) Do not forget yourself. Your dignity will be safe-guarded and you will be rewarded with eternal happiness. Wake up, Wake up, do not forget yourself.

generals refused to discuss matters, he said, and added that he had
to give them ten minutes to turn back or he must order his soldiers
to open fire. A later unconfirmed report stated that the generals
showed themselves directly to their troops fearing the disloyalty of
younger army officers. Some students shouted that they must talk
to the soldiers and explain what the revolution stood for and their
column began cautiously to advance. A clicking of rifle bolts followed, but at this point Ethiopian lecturers rushed on their
students and with physical force hurled back those in the forefront. The demonstration broke up. Then members of the faculty
drove batches of weary students back to the colleges and other
spectators including several secretaries and attachés from foreign
embassies who 'happened' to be around the nearby Ras hotel went
home. No shot was fired, but the radio announced in English and
Amharic : 'A group of bandits under the influence of two traitors
—former generals—Merid Mangasha and Kebede Gebré opened
fire on peaceful civilians demonstrating for the new Representative
People's Government. Several of the civilians were killed in this
inhuman massacre and many were wounded.' An Amharic radio
statement added the words, 'The Crown Prince has ordered that
those who have done this shooting be apprehended.' It is said
that students in Cairo came out on strike in support of their supposedly martyred colleagues.

Another speech recorded by the Crown Prince was broadcast.

We recall our previous Proclamation which we made on
Tahsas 5, 1953 [December 14, 1960] when we announced the
creation of the new Government of the People, since we knew
that such was in the vital interest of the people of Ethiopia.

We also said that this Government of the People should
be given every co-operation, but we learn that Major-general
Merid Mangasha and Major-general Kebede Gebré do not
support the concepts of this newly established Government of
the People. Understanding that this is contrary to the wishes
of the Ethiopian people and in order to give such advice as was
necessary for them to correct their mistake, We, being in Our
palace, called them to Us. But they failed to obey Our command. They chose rather to follow selfish motives of their own.
Because of this unlawful act they are now stripped of all rank
and appointment.

The processes of education reveal to us the degree of
civilisation attained by the developed countries. But it is known
that the people of Ethiopia have been deprived of this very

education. As proof of this look at the low living standards of the people of Ethiopia. And not only those; note the actions that have been taken against the interests of thousands of children who should form the real basis of the nation. We think these are the most important proofs. As you remember, all sorts of excuses have been used to dismiss from school the children who are the very future of your lives. And now, unemployed, they fill the streets of the city. Understanding that these dismissals are a great disservice to backward Ethiopia, We have ordered that from this day onwards all the students who have been so dismissed should return to their former schools.

People, especially those living in Addis Ababa, have been deprived of the right of owning land and building homes. No one can fail to comprehend their frequent sufferings. From this day onward every person will be given land according to his needs and will be able to live in peace. Moreover, those whose land has been taken away have, for a variety of reasons had but a little money cast in their direction. By returning this money they will from now on be entitled to take back their land.

The military is one of the most important arms of the state. Yet the Ethiopian soldier has been given very little money, not even enough for the bare necessities of life, let alone the expenses incurred by families with many children. We all know that the Ethiopian soldier has suffered poverty and hunger. From this day onwards the starting salary of all ranks between private and sergeant (*asir-alika*) will be E$40 a month. From above the rank of sergeant to lieutenant (*meto-alika*) and according to rank up to major (*shaleka*) some E$50 will henceforth be added to the previous salaries.

Merid promptly offered an even larger increment all round (E$60, and caused the air force to scatter leaflets over Addis Ababa, bearing his signature together with that of Major-general Kebede and more particularly that of the Patriarch. The air force also set up a 'loyal' broadcasting station, calling itself the 'Voice of Ethiopia'. 'The Emperor Hailé Sellassié is with us under the protection of the army', it claimed (prematurely) and appealed in Amharic to the peoples of the capital and countryside to remain loyal. The broadcast also denied that the Crown Prince was involved in the Revolution and appealed to the insurgent generals to ask their sovereign's pardon.

On Wednesday, December 14, 1960, Mengistu had transferred the Crown Prince, Imru and the dignitaries across the road from the headquarters of the Guard to the palace called Prince's Paradise. There Leul-Ras Imru, the nominal prime minister, began to assert himself.

Imru, in many respects a liberal and kindly man was, nevertheless, an old man, a prince and a product of the Ethiopian feudal system and had even been the Viceroy years before. After the Restoration he had used his influence on previous occasions to reform that system but, quite unlike Girmamé, he could never have entertained thoughts of overthrowing it. He understood the masses and the political realities of Ethiopia in 1960, and on Thursday he grew hourly more alarmed and said openly that much lay still unresolved. Although not completely informed, he sensed the impending crisis and sought desperately to avert bloodshed. After a brief discussion with one of the official secretaries from the United States embassy who came to visit him, he called Mengistu to him. In front of the Crown Prince he said : 'Why should we allow people to massacre one another? To prevent this I am going to see the Patriarch and ask him to take some action.' Mengistu raised no objection but although Leul-Ras Imru left in the company of some Guards officers he found that the Patriarch was not at home. Because of his fears he sent a major to the 1st Division headquarters with orders to seek out the Patriarch. But Abune Basilios sent back the message that he had already signed leaflets of excommunication against the rebels and, moreover, that the senior army officers with him had no wish for there to be any meetings. This news finally decided Mengistu. 'So the army officers refuse to come,' he said to Imru. 'Then I shall order an attack.' And with that he bowed and left.

But by midday surprise was lost and the balance of power had changed radically in favour of the counter-revolutionaries. By the time the Council of the Revolution finally decided to attack it was far too late and Merid calmly waited for their attack to come. The Guards officers deployed their inadequate forces. Radio Addis Ababa broadcast last bids for support and then just before 2.30 PM on Thursday, December 15, an excited announcer read an 'Urgent Announcement' in Amharic. 'All people,' he said, 'must evacuate themselves as soon as possible from the areas near the railway station, near Mitchell Cotts commercial offices, Menelik Square, Mesfin Harar district and the airport.' Soon afterwards fighting began.

19

Mengistu Neway

Truly, because some people have died on my account I feel a certain sorrow but had God been willing a coup would have come about sooner or later. . . . I did all this for the sake of the Ethiopian people . . . and I am quite unmoved that this Court has sentenced me to death.—MENGISTU NEWAY, replying to sentence, March 28, 1961

In unsuccessful coups, even the execution of the rebels is not always enough to bring the episodes to a close, since the cause for which they died is often later victorious . . .
—D. GOODSPEED, *The Conspirators—A study of the Coup d'Etat,* London, 1962

THE PROTAGONISTS

Although speculation has long persisted in Ethiopia as to when and why Brigadier-general Abiye Abebe, the Representative in Eritrea, and more particularly Major-generals Merid Mangasha and Kebede Gebré first decided to oppose the *coup* leaders with force, all that is certain is that Merid's initiation of counter-measures began early on—in fact, as soon as he reached the 1st Division headquarters. True, no soldier likes to bargain from a position of comparative weakness. True, Mengistu also thought that Merid had tacitly agreed the previous year that the military might one day have to intervene in feudal politics. But that is the probable extent of Merid's involvement and it is rather a different thing from a relative of an Emperor agreeing to support a radical *coup d'état.* Major-general Kebede Gebré was not approached by the group of conspirators who actually precipitated the *coup.* The fact is that both generals, doubtless encouraged by Leul-Dejazmatch Asrate

Kassa, proved loyal to the traditional form of monarchy and to
Hailé Sellassié. Even so, their loyalty may not be of fundamental
significance to the failure of the *coup*. The leaders of the *coup* ran
a grave risk when they overestimated the political awareness of the
people of Ethiopia and left both the head of the state and the
head of the Christian Church at large. Their physical failure was
certain once they diverted their energies into channels which the
theory of the *coup d'état* must define as of low priority and once
they chose to negotiate when time was not on their side and theirs
even a position of increasing military weakness.

Since a large part of the Guard was away in the Congo, the
military forces and police at Brigadier-general Mengistu Neway's
disposal on Thursday, December 15, numbered approximately
4,200. When the leaflets signed by the Patriarch and the army generals fluttered down from the skies some confusion ensued. On the
outskirts of the town considerable popular hostility towards the
Guard developed and although the element of inter-force rivalry,
long encouraged by the government, was important on both sides,
some few Guardsmen, probably those who realised for the first time
that they were not defending their Emperor against the army, abandoned their posts. Some members of the Council of the Revolution
and some Guards officers followed suit, including perhaps those who
believed in a peaceful *coup* but who were not prepared to invoke
civil war, and the realists who did not feel so committed that they
had to die for their cause. The riot police from Kolfé were the first
police detachment to decide to support the army.

It is possible that Mengistu did not know of the troops flown
to the nearby Debra Zeyt air base or of the arrival of the tank
squadron, and was not fully aware of the strength which Merid had
at his disposal by midday Thursday, but at least he knew of the
existence of the leaflet bearing the Patriarch's name and he must
have realised its likely result upon his men's morale. He knew
also that they had only limited ammunition and he had made no
arrangements for sustaining them during even a brief battle period.
Also, Lieutenant-colonel Workneh brought him a copy, secured
by his agents, of the order sent to the air force signed by Major-
general Merid, which listed the targets to be engaged on receipt
of an action order. It is difficult to avoid the conclusion that an
officer of Mengistu's competence and experience must have realised
the military hopelessness of the situation. He probably decided to
risk everything in an attempt to seize Merid and the other leaders
of the counter-revolutionary party who were in the 1st Division
headquarters. His was a cruel dilemma. He believed in the justice
of his cause but also sought to avoid bloodshed. However, the

Council of the Revolution could hardly expect Ethiopians to learn to take them and what they stood for seriously if they refused even to put up a fight.

THE BATTLE OF ADDIS ABABA

It was about 2.40 PM on the afternoon of December 15, 1960, when the firing began. Engagements were sharpest near the army headquarters but a frontal attack by the Guard was successfully resisted. Violent clashes occurred all over the southern areas of the city, especially near the Ministry of Defence and the airport, the main runway of which had been deliberately blocked with planes— and which, by radio announcements, had been closed to all incoming and outgoing traffic. Hundreds of civilians were killed as bullets and shells tore through the mud or *chicka* walls of their homes, and as mortar bombs exploded in the streets. The hospitals were soon choked with dead or dying.* By four o'clock, the rebel radio announced that a cease-fire was imminent and that negotiations between the two sides were to be conducted, but after a lull the fighting continued. It was also erroneously reported that the cadets at the Military Academy at Harar had imprisoned their officers and declared for the Revolution.

Communication between Debra Zeyt air force base and the headquarters of the 1st Division was conducted by radio in 'clear' through Harar, but the attack order, when it came at 3.15 PM on Thursday, was coded. However, it was decoded in thirty minutes and was seen to be signed by Major-general Merid. Orders were passed to the aircrew officers, nearly all of whom refused point blank to obey them. They belonged to the post-war educated age group and sympathised with the revolutionaries. Although taunted by foreign officers they insisted on speaking to the senior Ethiopian officer, Brigadier-general Assefa Ayena. They formed the opinion

---

* Most doctors in Addis Ababa agree privately with the author's own impression that the casualty figures subsequently issued by the Ethiopian government (which had an obvious interest in minimising the whole affair) were far too low.
The official figures were:

	Dead	Wounded
Imperial Guard (and Police?)	174	300
Armed Forces (Army and Police?)	29	43
Civilians	121	442

On December 20 the *East African Standard* published the figure of 2,000 soldiers and civilians dead or wounded in a dispatch from their special correspondents, and sporadic fighting was not then over. *The Times* quoted the same figure on December 22.

that Assefa was most reluctant to authorise an attack on the rebels, whom he referred to as 'your own countrymen' but that he, nevertheless, saw little alternative. He knew that even if Merid were defeated, civil war would result if Abiye's army marched on Addis Ababa from Eritrea, and the eventual involvement of the air force on one side or another was certain.

Major-general Merid subsequently stated that 'at least seventy-five per cent of the battle against the abortive *coup d'état* was won by the air force'. But that remark is true only of the battle of Addis Ababa, which might not have been the only battle even if the air force had held its hand.[1] In the months subsequent to the attempted *coup*, Assefa became very unpopular in progressive circles—so much so that, like Merid, he felt obliged to take an armed guard around with him, and even the air force secondary school students struck against their continued association with the air force. It was soon forgotten how little knowledge Assefa had of what was happening and how he prevaricated even though he had not been trusted by the conspirators. His choice was not that of Merid or Abiye—whether or not the new government should be opposed—but, given the fact of civil war, on which side he should commit himself and von Lindhal's command. Even so, the Ethiopian air force pilots only finally flew their planes when an American captain climbed into a cockpit commenting that they dare not do likewise.

Rumour fast developed that the planes were all piloted by Americans. Girmamé, but not Leul-Ras Imru, thought so at the time and many people in Ethiopia believe so to this day. Their belief was strengthened in 1964 when difficulty was experienced in restraining the personal enthusiasms of American instructors and preventing them from involving themselves in frontier clashes with the Somali Republic. However, the author has discovered no evidence that the machine-gun and cannon strafing and the bombing which occurred on Thursday and Friday was conducted by foreigners. That Ethiopian pilots were sufficiently trained to carry out all the necessary manoeuvres was confirmed by the air force display in January 1961 at which they were repeated.

The F-86-F Sabre jet fighter bombers were the first to take off. Other planes were also used, but much later. The only target attacked on Thursday was the Guard headquarters but the other targets were engaged on Friday. In one run, Tafari Makonnen Secondary School was accidentally badly damaged by bombing but, fortunately, no one was killed and the pilot responsible, who was an old boy of the school, subsequently called to apologise. As well as 'blasting the rebel strongholds', as Brigadier-general Assefa

Ayena put it at a subsequent press interview, the jets encouraged disintegration of the rebel forces by 'shock effect' tactics, which included supersonic explosions.[2]

Students in the University College and elsewhere huddled together in their dormitories and dining halls expecting either to be shot by the military or beaten by the populace. One student was wounded in the chest by a stray bullet. Ignoring the firing Dr Matte, president of the University College, led nearly all his Jesuit staff into the streets to tend the wounded and the dying. Meantime, his students consigned their banners, pamphlets and newspapers to the college kitchen stoves. The scholarship students from other African countries packed their belongings and a delegation asked that for their safety they be evacuated in the college bus to the grounds of the British embassy. There, later, their dancing and singing did much to maintain morale amongst the refugees, who included a few Norwegians, Americans and even French-Canadians. Similarly, the Japanese embassy received several Britons. Many foreigners did not go to the embassies but remained in their houses. Several single women afterwards reported that their Ethiopian landlords arrived with armed retainers to guarantee their safety. Wherever possible, scrupulous regard was shown for the safety of foreigners and there were even instances of local cease-fires being called by officers on either side to allow foreigners to cross roads. Several received slight wounds but only one foreigner was killed and he accidentally.

In his evidence at the trial of Brigadier-general Mengistu, (hereafter referred to as 'the trial') Leul-Ras Imru described how late on Thursday evening Mengistu came to him and asked him whether he thought Hailé Sellassié would return to Ethiopia. Imru repeated radio news that the Emperor had reached Liberia and might even reach Ethiopia by the morrow. 'Yes,' said Mengistu thoughtfully, 'I know him. He has daring.' As night fell, according to Imru, Mengistu showed increasing anxiety at reports reaching him that territorial and military forces had occupied Addis Ababa airport. For his part, Leul-Ras Imru dined with the Crown Prince and both retired to their rooms for the night.

On Thursday evening a strange incident occurred. One of the imperial cars toured the streets to the north of the city, carrying a small figure in the Emperor's uniform. Several Ethiopians who saw it flung themselves flat on the road and cried out. This strange occurrence has never been satisfactorily explained, but the author suspects that Lieutenant-colonel Workneh was responsible for the masquerade.

Many aspects of the attempted *coup d'état* in Addis Ababa

in 1960 are reminiscent of December 14, 1825—the Russian Decembrist revolution. The Russian leaders were also intellectuals whose education had divorced them somewhat from political actualities. They were drawn mainly from the offspring of important families; the revolutionary council was composed of comparatively young officers; they deliberately misled some of their soldiers, etc. Also, the Decembrists were alive to the likelihood of their failure, but Ryleiev, one of the conspirators, had said : 'None the less we ought to make a beginning.' Similarily, in Ethiopia most of the Council of the Revolution soon realised that as a military venture their attempted *coup d'état* was lost and that they had no personal alternative other than to die. However, this possibility, although it had been temporarily lost sight of on Wednesday, December 14, 1960, had been stressed throughout the planning phase—especially by Girmamé Neway. Moreover, the revolutionaries believed that by Thursday night their action would have so shaken the people's faith in the foundations of the régime that its days would be definitely numbered. For this reason, incredible as it must seem to a reader whose only introduction to Ethiopia is this book, that night in the palace called Prince's Paradise the conspirators broke into Hailé Sellassié's cellars and toasted the morrow in the Emperor's own champagne.

Heavy skirmishing with automatic and mortar fire continued throughout the hours of darkness. Many buildings, including the temporary headquarters of the United Nations Economic Commission for Africa, were damaged. The army furiously beseiged Menelik's Great Palace which from a hilltop commands much of Addis Ababa. The city's electricity supply failed. At midnight, police and army forces launched three attacks on the 'piazza' at the town centre from the Gulelé road. There was moderate to heavy automatic firing and bazookas as well as mortars were used, in the face of which the Guard was forced to retire.

In the early hours of Friday morning, the army's heavy artillery fired across the city at the Guard garage, one shell striking the uppermost floor of the Faculty of Arts building of the University College. Tanks, with infantry support, began to clear those pockets and strong points still defended by members of the Guard, who fought, often to the death, to cover the retreat of their main forces back up the slopes from the southern section of the city towards the grounds of the palace called Prince's Paradise, where boxes of ammunition were being distributed in preparation for a siege.

THE FAILURE OF THE LAST NEGOTIATIONS

The afternoon of Friday, December 16, witnessed another lull during which the army forces paused before assaulting the palace where the rebel leaders, the Crown Prince, Leul-Ras Imru and the detained dignitaries were all gathered. Negotiations were renewed between Mengistu, Imru, Girmamé and Workneh for the rebels, and Merid Mangasha for the counter-revolutionaries. The chief intermediaries representing the two sides were Girmamé and Major Assefa Lemma. Assefa Lemma, husband of Major-general Kebede Gebré's sister-in-law, a woman Patriot and parliamentarian named Woizero Sinadu, had long been one of Hailé Sellassié's lieutenants. In 1960 he was a vice minister of the Ministry of the Interior. More important at the time, however, was Arthur Richards, the United States ambassador.

The ambassador later described his part as 'not exactly acting as an intermediary but as someone recognised by both sides to carry messages'. He was quoted in one report as saying that he was 'asked by both sides to help in this way' but in another that he 'had information that trouble was brewing and the embassy offered its services in a humanitarian way as the Red Cross would'.[3] A somewhat garbled report from Italian sources, published in the Calcutta *Statesman* headed 'Key role played by US envoy in Ethiopia' did claim that sections of the army and the air force respectively were 'inactive' and 'contrary to other reports, decided to join the rebels' prior to his 'persuasion'.[4] However, with very few exceptions his role was upheld as purely humanitarian by the world press.

Despite this, his intentions have since been regarded with deep suspicion by most Ethiopian progressives, not primarily because all other ambassadors remained in their embassies but because of the concern of the United States already referred to (see page 412–3) for 'stability' in the Horn of Africa. Bearing in mind the role of Brigadier-general de Gavre they also fail to see how the ambassador could have acted in a disinterested manner. Nevertheless, a subsequent remark made by the ambassador is on record to the effect that the abortive rebellion—and presumably the shooting of the dignitaries—'cleaned the rats out of the henhouse'.[5] All comment on whether Richards' part had any more significance than a humanitarian attempt to alleviate the highly charged situation depends on one's concepts of United States' ends and means in Africa generally. But justified or not, the resentment felt by many Ethiopians over what they see as the role of the United States in the events of December 1960 could one day be a political factor of some importance—especially if a pattern in any way similar were to be permitted to occur again.

Even the order of events themselves is unclear in the evidence given at the trial and the ambassador himself, not unnaturally, wrote exercising his diplomatic right to turn down a request from the defence that he give evidence. It is obvious that there was no agreement between the two sides and that some confusion even arose over what it was that was actually being discussed. The negotiations were, however, interrupted by an attack on the palace mounted by the army tank squadron with strong infantry support.

Mengistu's account of these inconclusive negotiations taken from the trial proceedings is as follows :

Leul-Ras Imru talked to the United States ambassador— Girmamé and Workneh translated for him. The ambassador informed us that the Emperor had reached Khartoum, where he was refuelling, and would go on to Asmara and might even come to Addis Ababa on the morrow. Leul-Ras Imru enquired whether it would be possible to send a messenger to Asmara or for him to write a letter. The ambassador said that it was possible, and added the words, 'I will do whatever Your Highness asks me.' Leul-Ras Imru thanked him and went upstairs. The ambassador left with his followers, the political officer and the military attaché, to visit the headquarters of Major-general Merid. After this the three of them returned and I told Leul-Ras Imru of their arrival. There was another meeting, and the ambassador informed us that a representative from Major-general Merid's side would come to the United States embassy, and he asked that we send a representative from our side to the embassy. Leul-Ras Imru suggested that Workneh be sent, but later he said perhaps Girmamé would be a better choice.

Girmamé went with the American ambassador. When they came back Leul-Ras Imru was asked to go and talk to the ambassador. When he asked what the conversation would be about, Girmamé replied, 'On my part, I did all that I could to prevent bloodshed and explained our position'.

Major Assefa Lemma came from the army side, but frankly I cannot say that he said anything substantial. Then Leul-Ras Imru got some paper and started to write a letter to His Beatitude the Patriarch and to Major-general Merid. Although I was in a position to read what he started to write, I did not attempt to look at it. Leul-Ras Imru asked the ambassador very politely if he would deliver the note to His Beatitude the Patriarch or to Major-general Merid, and the ambassador said this he would gladly do. He left us, and later came back with a letter in reply, but I do not know what this letter said either. Leul-Ras Imru read it, and I think he said :

'This is an answer to a question which I never asked.' He apologised to the ambassador for taxing his energies and they took leave of each other.

Leul-Ras Imru, also describing these negotiations said :

At 10.00 AM I was informed that Girmamé Neway would like to see me, and I went and talked to him. When I asked him why he had sought me out, he said, 'Because the Americans are dropping bombs from the jets. Will you not therefore talk to them?' I replied that I believed they would not do this, and that there was no point in my talking to them, but Girmamé said : 'In order to bring peace and to stop the fighting, please talk to the Secretary of the United States embassy, who has just come here.'

'I did that yesterday,' I retorted. 'However, I will do so again now.' Therefore, I went downstairs and met the Secretary of the United States embassy. In the presence of Brigadier-general Mengistu, Lieutenant-colonel Workneh and Girmamé, I asked the First Secretary whether he could arrange for me to meet the ambassador, especially now that the Emperor was probably in Khartoum, in order that we might send a message to the Emperor. The Secretary replied : 'I will report this to the ambassador, and bring you an answer.' It was suggested that it would be a good thing if Aba Hanna, [the Palace Chaplain] went along also, but while they were discussing this I retired to join the Crown Prince.

At about midday, Girmamé Neway had me informed that the ambassador of the United States, a political officer and their Military Attaché were there looking for me, and I went upstairs to meet them. When I told the ambassador that I had sent a message to him in the morning because I wished to ask him to arrange a meeting, he replied that he did not think the army was willing to meet. He then gave me a letter from the army generals. I read it. It was addressed to Brigadier-general Mengistu and the officers, and was signed by Major-general Merid. It stated in effect that following a message sent to them by myself, they had been ready for a meeting. However, the terms of a message sent by Girmamé Neway and the army major, Assefa Lemma, through the United States ambassador had been found—after they had talked thoroughly with the ambassador—to be unsatisfactory, and accordingly they had no wish to hold a meeting.

I then asked Girmamé whether he had had any talk with the ambassador, and whether he had said anything unacceptable to the army generals. Girmamé replied that he had not really said anything very much at all. So I then asked the ambassador what he thought we should do, and he suggested my writing a letter, which he would have delivered. Up until this point, I had written nothing, everything had been done by word of mouth. I got some paper and addressed a letter to the Patriarch. While I was starting to write to Major-general Merid and Major-general Kebede, the army forces reached the palace, and fighting started outside. Lieutenant-colonel Workneh came in and said that there was no use in writing now, as tanks had entered the palace. I looked out and myself saw tanks smashing through the gates and entering the grounds. The battle raged, and we gave thought to the safe exit of the ambassador and those with him. They were helped to leave. I went up to the Crown Prince.

CARNAGE IN THE GREEN SALON

Several incidents then occurred to which only incomplete reference was made at the trial. Fighting continued north of the town centre and slowly but surely the Guard was forced to retire northwards towards the eucalyptus covered slopes of Mount Entotto. The tank squadron from Nazret and air force strikes proved decisive factors in destroying any real co-ordination but the Guardsmen, many of them unfed since Wednesday, fought a succession of desperate rear-guard actions. Many, left wounded or cornered on their shattered and disorganised forces left the city, were dispatched with sword and hatchet by the people of Gulelé and Entotto—simple folk who lived on the outskirts of the city some of whom had read or heard the words of the leaflet signed by the Patriarch. The Dorzi, a people from Sidamo who work as weavers near the capital were particularly active.

The army forces recovered control of the radio station and broadcast an order that members of the Council of the Revolution be arrested. Meanwhile Captain Dereji Hailé Mariam, the son-in-law of the Emperor who had arrived from Harar, rode in on the first of the tanks as they passed the University College on their way to the palace called Prince's Paradise. A handful of frightened and despairing students waved half-heartedly but dispersed rapidly when a soldier called to his officer : 'Why go farther, sir? Our enemies are here !' 'Coi Tinish !' shouted Dereji over his shoulder at the students, 'wait a little while'. The tanks rumbled on up the hill and smashed through the wrought iron gates of the palace leaving them hanging crazily on their hinges. There were piles of grenades and ammunition every few yards in the palace grounds, but the Guard could do little against the tanks. The leading machine rumbled to a halt just below the portico of the palace. Captain Dereji, courageously but foolhardy like his Patriot father, leapt out of the tank and accompanied by another officer called upon Mengistu to surrender 'in the name of the Emperor Hailé Sellassié'. Mengistu walked out on to the balcony to talk to Dereji, but seeing this, Girmamé, beyond further parley, rushed after him shouting, 'Out of my way woman of a brother', and shot Captain Dereji down as he charged at the palace doors waving his carbine. Another burst of fire from Mengistu's trusted chauffeur followed immediately and the officer with Dereji fell at his captain's side. The army soldiers took cover and raked the palace with bullets.

Lieutenant-colonel Workneh had earlier sent for certain of his files, among them those on several of the imprisoned dignitaries—one witness at the trial implied as a first step towards the preparation of legal indictments. However, the fighting put an end to all such thoughts and the dignitaries were placed under guard in the Green Salon, a sitting room at the northern end of the ground floor, used by the Empress for audiences after breakfast. Many of his staff continued to co-operate with Workneh up until the fighting began and he even called some Israeli advisers of the Security Department, but they played little part in the subsequent events. After he had shown the American party out of the palace—the ambassador, Richards and his aides jumped through a window—Workneh did not further involve himself at the palace but left for Entotto ridge. Mengistu and the others with him returned to the fray.

It was Brigadier-general Tsigué Dibou who led the resistance to the approaching army forces. Traditionally in Ethiopia the *fitwraries*, the leaders of the vanguard, worked themselves into a state almost of frenzy in which they even foamed at the lips before hurling themselves on the enemy. After the battles the *rases* and the *dejazmatch* would ask, 'Who was the hero today?' Brigadier-general Tsigué Dibou, the police commandant was at this pitch. He indignantly refused to retire from the heat of the battle which raged around the front section of the palace and through the smoke and the hail of bullets he called an invitation that all should die with him. He killed many army soldiers as they attempted to rush the portico before he too fell, his body riddled with machine-gun bullets. Major Yohannes Miskir was also killed.

At intervals throughout the day Mengistu had visited the Crown Prince, Leul-Ras Imru, Ras Andargatchew, the Minister of the Interior, and all the dignitaries in the Green Salon and had kept them posted of events. As the battle intensified he went upstairs from the second floor to take his leave of the Crown Prince and Leul-Ras Imru and then, joined by Girmamé and a group of officers and Guardsmen he ran downstairs, along the hallway which runs past the Green Salon to the rear of the palace. An attempt was made to call certain of the detained dignitaries out into the corridor but they refused to be separated. Shouting to the others to do likewise, Girmamé fired his machine-gun into the room and some of those with him, probably including Mengistu, also fired—taking upon themselves the awful responsibility as Mengistu had said, 'that Ethiopia should never be the same again'.

The room was sprayed with bullets. Amdé Mikael Dessalegn, vice minister of Press and Information, seized one of the red leather chairs and rushed forward but was cut down on the threshold. Some dignitaries including Aba Hanna Jimma, the Palace Chaplain, and Makonnen Habtewold being wounded cried out until those who carried out the massacre returned and fired at them again. This happened several times but some lay still feigning death and lived to tell a gruesome tale. Ras Andargatchew Messai, Dejazmatch Bezebeh Sileshi and Brigadier-general Makonnen Deneke, an enormous man, whose thighs were smashed, but whose vast frame protected others, have all since described the shootings. Haji Farrar and Adamew Tesemma were also wounded but survived. The chairman of the Council of Ministers, the former Patriot, Ras Abebe Aragai died of his wounds later in the afternoon. There also died Leul-Ras Seyoum Mangasha, prince and governor general of Tigré; Major-general Mulugeta Bulli, minister of Community Development; Blatta Dawit Okbagzy, minister of state in the Ministry of Foreign Affairs; Liquamaquas Tadessa Negash, minister of state in the Ministry of Justice; Afe negus Esheté Geda, vice minister of the Interior; Abdullahai Mumie, vice minister of Finance; Kebret Astatkie, assistant minister of the Interior; Gebrewold Engeda Worq, minister of state in the Ministry of the Pen; Lemma Woldé Gabriel, vice minister in the Ministry of Mines and State Domains; Dejazmatch Letibellu Gebré and Blatta Ayelé Gebré.

The trial record of Brigadier-general Mengistu Neway's account of the battle reads as follows :

Leul-Ras Imru went out, and while the ambassador was on his way the tanks of the army forces arrived, and the palace was machine-gunned. We took the ambassador, to shelter him, into Ato Ketema Yifru's room [the room of the monarch's private secretary] and he jumped out of the window and left. I then went with other officers to the guests' resting room. . . . I entered the Green Salon once or twice in order to inform the occupants about the negotiations to stop the fighting. Soon, I heard that four tanks were coming closer, and the fighting grew louder and louder. Brigadier-general Tsigué and I went upstairs, and the noise of the fighting was deafening. We did not have a chance. The front of the palace was being machine-gunned, and the tanks crashed through the gates and entered the grounds, and fired towards the palace. Shells from the tanks and machine-gun bullets came through the windows and smashed against the walls. Many furnishings in the room were broken, and fell to the floor. Heavy machine-guns were fired, the chandeliers fell down and plaster fell from the walls. In places, the floorboards caught fire. We started to put out the fire, but since the bullets were flying around us we lost hope. I went upstairs again to another room. There was a plate and a fork there, I recall, and I saw the servant Tefera Hailu sitting with another servant. They were very frightened when I entered, and I said : 'Be calm. When the army comes, say that you are the servants of His Majesty, so that they do not kill you.' I then went into the Crown Prince's room. There were two servants with him, one of them called Adefrise. The Crown Prince was seated, and Leul-Ras Imru was pacing up and down. I told the Crown Prince that I would leave shortly. When I came out of the room I told a servant of the Crown Prince to tell army officers, who would soon be coming, that the Crown Prince was there. 'Guard the door properly,' I said, 'and see that nothing happens to him.' He asked me to give him weapons, but I told him that if the army should see him armed they would kill him. With that I left him and went downstairs, where I noticed that Major Yohannes was dead. We left the palace grounds by the way near the garage gates and reached the river. Leaving Ketchnié Medhané Alem [a district taking the name of its Christian church, Saviour of the World] to one side, we went up Entotto. There we rested for a while before continuing our journey through the night . . .

THE RETURN OF HAILÉ SELLASSIÉ

Soon after 5 PM Leul-Ras Imru and the Crown Prince left their rooms in the Palace called Prince's Paradise. On their way downstairs they met what Imru described as the horrified figure of Dejazmatch Bezebeh Sileshi, one of the survivors from the Green Salon who said he had learned of their safety from 'the servant who looks after the lion'. They sent him out with a white cloth to inform the army that the Guard had left and went to look into the Green Salon. Leul-Ras Imru was reportedly 'very sad'. Then they met Ras Andargatchew and soon afterwards Dejazmatch Kebede. Before leaving by car, Imru to his home and the Crown Prince to his mother the Empress, they ordered Kebede to set the dead to one side and to send the wounded to hospital.

As the army moved off north of the capital into the hills, so students dispersed from the colleges and schools of Addis Ababa. Many were threatened with a beating by their elders. Foreigners drifted home from the embassies. Not a few educated Ethiopians fearing that an action or even a chance remark might be reported to the military authorities, hid or fled the city. Many were arrested and detained. The body of Brigadier-general Tsigué Dibou was hanged up outside the headquarters of the 1st Division of the army. There was considerable but sporadic shooting for many days and a strict curfew continued.

Meantime Hailé Sellassié, who had issued a statement *en route* that the confusion in Addis Ababa was the work of a few 'irresponsible people' and would 'soon pass', landed at Asmara, Eritrea. He added to his previous statement, which had ended, 'We are the ones who initiated the constitutional measures for the maintenance of the rights and privileges of Our people', the view that the Crown Prince could not have been involved in 'such an affair' as the attempted *coup d'état*.[6] He was greeted at the airport by the Representative in Eritrea, his son-in-law, Brigadier-general Abiye Abebe and Ras-Betwoded Makonnen Endalkatchew, the President of the Senate. Several newspapers subsequently published photographs of the chief of the Eritrean Administration, Dejazmatch Asfaha Woldé Mikael kissing the Emperor's feet.[7] The Eritrean people had little knowledge of what had occurred in Addis Ababa for communications were still cut, and they gave the Emperor an enthusiastic welcome. A spokesman at the palace in Asmara claimed that less than 1,000 men had been involved in the revolt. However, figures issued by the government in Addis Ababa six days later stated that 475 members of the Guard had been killed or wounded since the revolt; that 325 were still at large and that there had been 3,100 arrests, after which 400 had been freed, 2,000 released on bail and 700 detained. Final figures were a little higher even than these.

On the evening of Saturday, December 17, Hailé Sellassié flew south to Addis Ababa accompanied by aircraft loads of soldiers from the Eritrean garrison. The Crown Prince, the Patriarch, Major-generals Merid Mangasha and Kebede Gebré, Ras Andargatchew Messai, Dejazmatch Kebede Tesemma and others—not including Leul-Ras Imru—met the planes. Escorted by tanks and armoured cars, the imperial convoy passed through crowded streets to the Jubilee Palace—for the palace called Prince's Paradise was not habitable. On the following day there were state funerals and the Emperor spoke to crowds from a palace balcony. Over the city air force planes wrote his name in smoke across the sky.

Newspapers, not available during the *coup*, were published again—*The Ethiopian Herald* issued a special half-price evening edition on December 19, 1960. The populace read the reported speeches of the Emperor and heard him over the radio. He made repeated reference to the Almighty and identified the achievements of his own reign with divine plan. Typical phrases were : 'ever since that day when Our Lord entrusted to Us the task of leading Our people on the path of progress . . . so have We ever since striven . . . as Almighty God has ordained'. Moreover, the rebels were not only described as men who had no thought for others and as 'a handful of wilful men who, for their own ends, sought to retard and impede the progress which Ethiopia is achieving', but were also condemned in biblical terms : 'Trees that are planted do not always bear the desired fruit.'

Hailé Sellassié sadly developed his political philosophy.

> You all know how much We trusted and how much authority We reposed in those few who have risen against Us. We educated them. We gave them authority. We did this in order that they might improve the education, the health and the standard of living of Our people. We confided to them the implementation of some of the many plans We have formu- lated for the advancement of Our nation. And now Our trust has been betrayed . . .

The Emperor urged an end to violence and said of those who had crushed the rebellion, 'We cannot reward them . . . Almighty God, who elected Us to lead Our people, will reward them'. Of the rebels he stated, 'The judgement of God is upon them; wherever they go, they will never escape it'.[8]

THE SUICIDES

Once clear of the palace grounds, the small group of Guardsmen with the rebel leaders made their way together up the slopes of the Entotto ridge. The silvering radical Girmamé Wondefrash, badly wounded in the leg, limped along as best he could for some way but finding it impossible to go on, bade his friends hurry ahead and crawled into a peasant's hut near the northern extremity of the city. There he killed himself.

On Saturday, Lieutenant-colonel Workneh Gebeyehu was discovered by a military patrol, hiding near a cave not far from a bridge on an Addis Ababa street, which winds up the slopes of Entotto. He killed several soldiers who tried to rush him, but in so doing he emptied the last magazine of his carbine and discarded it. Then the little Gondari colonel made his dramatic gesture well calculated to ensure that his death would not be forgotten by Ethiopians. He pointed a parallel between the Council of the Revolution and the failure of a would-be reformer from history, the Gondar Emperor whom modern Ethiopians regard as a hero. 'Tewodros has taught me something!' Workneh shouted to his assailants. He put his pistol into his mouth and he killed himself. His dead body was hanged outside St George's Cathedral on December 18.

Although some were subsequently released, those arrested as suspected members of the Council of the Revolution included Getachew Bekelé, the acting minister in the Marine Department, Hailé Mariam Kebede, vice minister and manager of the River Awash Valley Authority (a former leader of the Chamber of Deputies and the son of Ras Kebede), Lemma Frehiwot, executive secretary of the Coffee Board, Captain Asrat Deferess, information officer of the Imperial Guard (who like Girmamé was a graduate of a United States university), Captain Kebede Gudetta, an enormous man who was Hailé Sellassié's personal bodyguard, and many other officers and civilians. Ketema Yifru and Goytom Petros of the Foreign Office were detained for questioning but later released. There were many arrests.

A leaflet was issued by the chief of staff of the armed forces with the photographs of Brigadier-general Mengistu Neway and his brother Girmamé Neway. It was a mixture of polemics, fatherly moralising and practical details. Besides offering a reward of E$10,000 and a special prize per head for their capture, it commented : 'People who seek to establish a truth should not run away but that is what they have done and it reveals that the motive behind their treason was self-interest.'

On Sunday, the group, which included the Neway brothers, split up, but Mengistu, Girmamé and Captain Bayé Telahoun of the Guard stayed together. They wandered in the mountains of Addis Ababa until the following Wednesday and were helped to make their way south to the lowlands. On Friday, they journeyed towards the volcano, Mount Ziqwala, on which the Moja family had land. They travelled all night and on into Saturday. At about four in the afternoon, the peasants began to call out the traditional yodelling call of warning, and soon afterwards the weary group found itself surrounded by police. A skirmish ensued. Captain Bayé was either shot or killed himself. Mengistu disarmed a wounded policeman and made his way to another, at the same time calling to Girmamé. But he did not reach him for at that moment Girmamé shot his brother and then killed himself. The infuriated police fired into Girmamé's body smashing a leg, but they found that Mengistu still lived. The Brigadier-general had suffered a severe bullet wound on the lower part of his right cheek, his right eyeball was exposed and blind, his left eye was also damaged but the bullet which had ploughed across his face had not entered the skull. He was taken unconscious to the hospital of the 1st Division of the army.

The news was reported to the Emperor Hailé Sellassié who demanded to see Girmamé's body. It was washed and thrown on the steps of the Jubilee Palace. The monarch ordered that, together with the corpse of Captain Bayé Telahoun, it be hanged and left for a day outside St George's Cathedral for all to see. On the next day, December 25, a great crowd jostled round the gibbets. It is said that one man was pursued by police towards the Abune Petros memorial for crying out, 'Never mind, Girmamé, one day we shall raise you a statue in gold', but if so he was not typical. For the most part, the crowd jeered and was hostile.

THE IMMEDIATE AFTERMATH

The military failure of the *coup* was followed in Addis Ababa by several months of political instability, popular discussion and unrest on a scale greater even than during the period of the overthrow of Eyasu. Prisons and special camps constructed for detainees were soon full to overflowing. Conditions were not good and although women were allowed to bring in food there was much suffering, particularly on the part of relatives of the conspirators. Meanwhile, in press conferences, Hailé Sellassié spoke of pardons, enquiries and trials. But enquiry concentrated only on the involvement or otherwise of personalities and family groups—at no time were the underlying causes of the *coup* examined. The Emperor even hinted to foreign journalists that such were to be found only beyond the Ethiopian frontiers. He announced that there would be no changes in Ethiopia as a result of the Revolution and gently remarked that evidence of the possible involvement of some foreign power in the *coup* was being examined. In East Africa it was assumed that he referred to the UAR; in the United States, to the Soviet

Union. An Egyptian military mission had arrived by air at the beginning of the *coup*, and they and their Ilyushin-14 plane were detained for several days, but their arrival was in no way connected with the revolution which had occurred. Nor, despite speculation in some sections of the British and American press, did the fact that the Russian ambassador was the first diplomat to call on the Emperor have any significance.[9]

Members of both houses of parliament led by Leul-Dejazmatch Asrate Kassa, came to the palace publicly to re-affirm their loyalty and to condemn the revolutionaries. As well as remarking that they had all witnessed that 'Almighty God had taken revenge on the traitors', and predicting 'yet more revenge of God is to come upon them', the Emperor said : 'You have heard the declaration of the traitors—declarations which they issued with regard to the economic development of Ethiopia and the growth of the welfare of the Ethiopian people—and you have realised that there is no purpose or program in them which We have not planned and which We have not started in accordance with Our program for the economic development and welfare of Our people.'[10]

The 1950s had indeed seen endless programs and plans in Ethiopia but the real point is the one Zartman makes of the revolution in the UAR : 'Little has been new in Nasser's [first] decade of domestic policies. There is scarcely a measure—including agrarian reform, the High Dam, and parliamentary elections—that had not been discussed or even tried before the revolution. The junta's contribution up to 1961 . . . was to bring these plans an *élan* and energy that carried them towards fruition.'[11]

For some weeks incoming foreign papers containing any critical comment on Ethiopia were banned or confiscated, but many typed copies and Amharic translations were privately circulated in Addis Ababa, as they have been on several occasions since. Much, though not all, of the world press soon reverted to its pre-revolution position, and other students of Ethiopian affairs have noted that many a *volte face* was involved.[12] This is not the place to consider representative examples but a case in point is the *New York Times*. An editorial on December 17 concluded that 'anyone who knows a little about Ethiopia knows that the Emperor under (*sic*) a new constitution and with a manifest interest in educating his people and giving them a better standard of living has done pretty well. From this distance it is good to see him back'. Two days previously Hailé Sellassié had been described as 'one of the few remaining absolute monarchs in the feudal pattern'. Between those dates it had been reported that the new régime had a 'socialistic and nationalistic touch akin to the neighbouring régimes in the UAR and

Sudan', and that 'in spite of his long service in the United States Mr [Ras] Imru was not considered particularly friendly to the United States'.*

But foreign interest in the attempted *coup* soon subsided. At the same time political discussion increased inside Ethiopia. One manifestation of this was the number of anonymous communications, both revolutionary and counter-revolutionary, and duplicated revolutionary pamphlets which began to circulate almost as soon as the sporadic firing typical of the evenings up until the end of 1960 had died down. The pamphlets represented the reaction of several unconnected and otherwise powerless groups of western-educated Ethiopians (not students) who felt that they had somehow let the revolution down and that they had to help to keep the spirit of the attempted *coup* alive while another was organised—other plots have in fact been uncovered by the government security department in 1961 and again in 1964. The pamphlets were significant in that they persisted for many months on a considerable scale. The Emperor read several of them and was both angered and distressed by their content. There were many arrests.

A typical example—one of many in the author's possession —contains several interesting foreign references. Besides criticising Merid and the army soldiers, it begins : 'People of Ethiopia your unity must have bonds of iron'—a quotation from the revolutionary proclamation read by the Crown Prince—and runs as follows :

The struggle of Tahsas 5-7 will prove the first honourable chapter in Ethiopian history . . . our country became a second Hungary for some time but since this is only the first round and not the last chance, we should not lose hope even for one minute. Rising with sacred ideals we have to be avenged for the blood of our brothers. To get our freedom, to make it possible to govern ourselves, we should fan the fires of the movement and keep it burning like the torch of the marathon. So must our spirits burn till we reach the desired goal.

Our brothers who were living happily, even luxuriously, Mengistu, Girmamé, and Workneh, had everything to lose, but having observed our difficulties and our problems they ignored

---

* As has been mentioned, whilst serving as ambassador in the United States, Leul-Ras Imru had been subjected to indignities on account of the colour of his skin. To note his reactions without their cause is most misleading. Although quite beyond the scope of the present book, there is food here for serious thought on the wider implications of this particular 'colour problem' particularly if government policy is influenced by press comments.

their riches. Because the plans they made for us were not successful, their fate [that of the last two] and their desert was to be hung up and jeered at by the people. But in that very place where they were hanged we shall erect a marble monument, in the near future. The spectacular monuments we see shining today will lose their lustre and will pass away . . . death comes only once; death is nothing. But to die for a worthy cause is sacred martyrdom. Let every old man be strong; let every young man rise up; and soldiers, do not let us down!

Others concentrated on the young . . . 'Do you know what young people with the same level of education do in other countries in similar circumstances? . . . If branches of the forest trees all united they could trap the lion', etc.

The Addis Ababa newspapers contained several examples of the *double entendre,* so typical of Amharic style, supporting the arguments used during the *coup.* These carried over even into English and French, particularly in articles and editorials on customs of the Ethiopian Christian Church, such as pilgrimages, etc. But on the surface the government press worked hard to project the traditional concepts of Ethiopian government. A typical example from *The Ethiopian Herald* read : 'Greater love hath no man than this that he lay down his life for his friend—the scripture particularly applies to those valiant ministers and key civil servants who dared the threats of rebels and lost their lives in the course of defending Ethiopia and her gallant Emperor.' The magazine *Menen,* extolled in Amharic instances of economic advancement in Ethiopia as personally attributable to Hailé Sellassié; claimed that he had personally 'delivered his people from the oppression of the Italians'; praised the machine-gunned dignitaries 'who died to keep word with king and country and who will live from generation to generation until the end of the earth'; scorned the defeated rebels who 'found nowhere to go' and 'dropped in the valleys', and laboured the ingratitude of 'those few traitors whom He [the Emperor] had raised from the dust, taught, appointed and decorated with high orders'. Such themes were maintained in the English editorials of the government-controlled press and developed in the Amharic ones in *Addis Zemen* and elsewhere.[13] As the days passed, the wounded Brigadier-general Mengistu Neway came to be identified more and more with the anti-christ.

Most college authorities in Addis Ababa insisted that all their students sign an abject letter of apology accepting any punishment in advance, addressed to 'The Redeemer of Ethiopia, His Imperial Majesty Hailé Sellassié, Emperor of Ethiopia' as a condition of re-entering college. The letter expressed the students' surprise and horror at the *coup*. It stated that although it was their duty to follow the Crown Prince in the absence of the Emperor, and despite being forced by members of the armed Guard to 'express such opinions' as they did, they acknowledged a 'traitorous act towards a parent who has brought us up, who is our father and our mother' and begged understanding and forgiveness. Not all who signed had read the letter and most were soon ashamed of it.

The Emperor then ordered that students and young people be not regarded as rebels. Soon afterwards he called them to the Jubilee Palace to receive a public pardon but many refused to go stating that they feared they would be machine-gunned. Meantime there were a few arrests and questionings. Threatening letters from the relatives of certain of the dignitaries who had died were received. On the other hand, pamphlets exhorted the students to keep up their struggle. For some time they were thoroughly demoralised, although they did appeal to the Emperor to cancel Leul-Dejazmatch Asrate Kassa's verbal order that Workneh Gebeheyu's brother—who had been held prisoner for three months without any evidence being found against him—be expelled from the University College and banished to the provinces.

Together with most of the population of Addis Ababa, the students awaited the filling of vacant government preferments which in some cases followed a period of mourning. Major-general Merid Mangasha and Kebede Gebré became Minister of Defence and chief of staff of the armed forces respectively. Brigadier-general Assefa Ayena was promoted and took command of the air force. A loyal officer took over as police commissioner and it was announced that the Imperial Guard was to be reconstituted. Ras Andargatchew Messai was relieved of his post as Minister of the Interior. He was appointed governor general of Sidamo province, where his wife had large estates. He was succeeded by the other son-in-law, Brigadier-general Abiye Abebe, who retained for some time his post of Representative in Eritrea. Leul-Ras Seyoum's son, Mangasha, was created *leul-dejazmatch* and succeeded his father as governor general of Tigré. Ras-Betwoded Makonnen Endalkatchew retired as president of the Senate and was succeeded by Leul-Dejazmatch Asrate Kassa. Asrate's nephew, Dejazmatch Amaha Aberra (who tried at this time to form an unofficial conservative party with the aim of ensuring that the leading government posts remained in the hands of members of the traditional families) was appointed governor general of Begemidir. The previous governor, the Moja Dejazmatch Kiflé Dadi was transferred to Kaffa as deputy-governor general. Two younger men, Lij

Endalkatchew Makonnen and Dejazmatch Zewdé Gebré Sellassié,
previously ambassadors, were appointed Minister of Commerce
and Industry and Minister of Justice respectively. Brigadier-
general Makonnen Deneke, who had survived wounds received in
the Green Salon, was appointed minister of state in charge of
security in the Ministry of the Interior. Many younger men were
among those promoted, particularly in the Ministry of Foreign
Affairs. However, the machinery of Ethiopian government was in
no way altered, even if the *coup* had resulted in more than the
customary *shum-shir*. Meantime, the conversation of the citizens of
Addis Ababa came to be dominated by speculation over what fate
held in store for Brigadier-general Mengistu Neway, held captive
in the military hospital.

THE TRIAL

The interest of the outside world in the treatment to be accorded
Brigadier-general Mengistu Neway was recognised in Addis Ababa.
Various conservatives proposed a summary trial somewhat akin to
that which followed the Betwoded Negash conspiracy. Soon after
his return, the Emperor announced an enquiry and the establishment of courts martial. The Minister of Justice urged as fair a trial
as possible. News that there was to be a trial was everywhere well
received. Members of the Ethiopian intelligentsia discussed how
best to obtain legal assistance. A number of their attempts to secure
a foreign lawyer fell through, but the International Jurists were
contacted. As a result, the Jurists asked that they might be permitted to send an observer to the trial. Prime Minister Aklilu
opposed this but the matter went to the Emperor for decision. He
heard a plea that the Jurists were neo-communists but, nevertheless,
ruled that any approval was to be the responsibility of the Minister
of Justice. Zewdé promptly accepted this. Dr Edvard Hambro, a
Norwegian professor of law and a former Registrar of the International Court of Justice, accordingly left Bergen on February 26,
1961, to attend one week of the trial hearings, which were spread
over six weeks, and the Jurists subsequently published his interesting report.[14]

   In the High Court of Addis Ababa, the hearing of the
Crown v. Brigadier-general Mengistu Neway began on February
10, 1961. The charges were read before three judges, Blatta Woldé
Kidan, Colonel Abebe Teferi and Ato Wubué Woldeyes. The fact
that the wife of one of the judges was a relative of Makonnen
Habtewold, one of the assassinated ministers, might have disquali-
fied him in other countries. Three defendants, Brigadier-general

Mengistu Neway, Captain Kiflé Woldé Mariam and Lieutenant Degafé Tedla were charged by the Attorney General on behalf of the Crown with 'aggravated homicide . . . in that they together with persons now dead and others unknown, on Tahsas 7, 1953 EC, at about 4 PM at Ghenet Leul [Prince's Paradise] Palace, Addis Ababa, with deliberate intent to kill, killed in a cruel manner, by shooting, fifteen dignitaries'.

Mengistu was also charged with 'outrages against the constitutional authorities contrary to Article 250 of the Ethiopian Penal Code', in that on the fourth day of Tahsas 1953 EC he attempted to overthrow the government by causing with threats of violence His Imperial Highness the Crown Prince to proclaim by means of a broadcast the creation of a new government, which change of government he intended to maintain with the aid of the Imperial Guard which he was commanding', and 'armed rising contrary to Article 252 of the Ethiopian Penal Code', in that 'on Tahsas 4, 1953 EC, he raised an armed rebellion against the constitutional authorities in that he arrested ministers of the Realm, caused the Imperial Guard to attack the 1st Division of the regular Ethiopian Army and thereby frustrate any armed opposition to the ousting of the duly constituted constitutional authorities'.

The court sat on February 10 and 20 but the main hearings began on February 27. Thereafter press comment was allowed for two weeks, which included the period of the visit of Dr Hambro. Only prosecution evidence was published. Hearings in the month of Megabit (i.e. from March 10 onwards) were not reported. This may be partly because sections of the government press nevertheless endeavoured to build up popular sympathy for Mengistu. For example, the editor responsible for the Amharic and French report from which the following (hopefully but incorrectly marked *à suivre*) is taken, got into serious trouble :

Mengistu had not lost much weight, and still retained his tough physique. His unshaven face looked like that of a warrior of Genghis Kahn. He looked to right and left of him, stroking his moustaches. He could have had no doubt that all the people assembled there were awaiting his doom. But he did not look worried. His uniform was the one he had always worn, but without the insignia of a general. . . . This trial was impressive. There are some who say there has been nothing to compare with it in Ethiopia since the troubles caused by Abawukow and company. One remembers the plot of Betwoded Negash and Hailé Sellassié Gugsa, but there the comparison ends.[15]

Mengistu's own attitude at the trial was most dignified. The proceedings—conducted of course in Amharic—were not really public, seats being reserved mainly for the relatives of those who died during the revolution, but even they praised the bearing of the brigadier-general. Mengistu experienced considerable difficulty in arranging his defence for very few Ethiopians dared help him. This is clear from several of the court documents and the fact that the Ethiopian lawyer assigned to his defence disappeared and made repeated attempts to be relieved of his duties on the grounds that he was unwell, that his client did not want him, etc. At one stage, police had to be ordered to bring the defence advocate to court.*
The question of securing an advocate of his choice was one of four counts on which Mengistu lodged appeal with the Supreme Court. These were :

1. That he was not given enough time to secure a foreign lawyer.
2. That he was tried by civilian judges and therefore ought to be detained in a common jail instead of being held in military custody.
3. That the Chairman of the court be replaced.
4. That he be granted an audience with the President of the Supreme Court.

The *Afe negus* eventually turned down this appeal on all counts but on several occasions Mengistu maintained that his case should not have proceeded meantime. A remark he made on February 20 is typical :

> I will not be hurried. Why, even litigation over a small piece of land can rot in your files for more than ten years, let alone so big an affair as this. Until the 20 Yekatit [February 27] then, I am not even prepared to discuss whether I have advocates. But on the proper day I will inform the Court about this.

---

* One of the relevant court documents in the author's possession contains the following statement signed by one of those whom Mengistu asked to help him. '. . . Far rather than choose an advocate for Mengistu Neway, I would myself like to prosecute him for the following reasons: firstly, Leul-Ras Seyoum Mangasha was my wife's uncle and was to me as a father; secondly, the children of Woizero Kongit Abnet, the wife of His Excellency Ras Abebe Aregai are to me as brothers; thirdly, Lieutenant Dereji Hailé Mariam is to me as a brother for he is the son of my grandfather's uncle; fourthly, Liquamaquas Tadessa Negash was as my brother and the others were to me as fathers and brothers. Further, since I completely condemn Mengistu's attempt to overthrow the régime I would myself seek to prosecute . . '

Professor Hambro seemed satisfied with the fairness of the trial, bearing in mind the 'autocratic nature of the Ethiopian government . . . the absence of an independent judiciary and a strong and well organised bar' and he elaborated on these points. He also noted 'in view of the hundreds in custody' that it was 'strange that only three people were charged' and he revealed his awareness of the general possibility of pressure—both moral and physical—on those who could be witnesses.[16] The most important facts arising from Mengistu's trial are that it was possible for its form to be the subject of discussion, that it was a show trial and that it was far from typical. Even so, it aroused much discussion in private houses and in public bars in Addis Ababa. In the Ras Hotel, 'The Law—Our Law' was toasted in English—in Amharic it would have been 'Mengest, Mengistu' and on more than one late evening the *Marseillaise* was sung in the Itegué Hotel. References were made to the fact that Jomo Kenyatta had been ably defended by a British advocate—and the fact that the comparison was made was even mentioned in the Nairobi press.[17] But comparison with Kenya was hardly reasonable. Ethiopia was an independent country.

The prosecution called twenty-seven witnesses—the defence only eight. Doctors, survivors of the Green Salon shootings, Guards officers, government officials and palace servants were all called, although not all were co-operative. However, the evidence of Dejazmatch Bezebeh Sileshi, Brigadier-general Makonnen Deneke, Ras Andargatchew Messai and the chief of the palace servants was damning enough. Leul-Ras Imru, Dejazmatch Kebede Tesemma and Brigadier-general Esayas Gebré Sellassié were the main defence witnesses. Brigadier-general Assefa Ayena also gave evidence but the Crown Prince, Major-generals Merid Mangasha and Kebede Gebré, Leul-Dejazmatch Asrate Kassa, the Patriarch and the bishops were not called. Mengistu Neway himself took the stand for several hours. Although a defence objection to the tape recording of the proceedings was registered, tapes were made and taken to the Jubilee Palace.

Mengistu described the events of the Revolution and took responsibility for nearly everything himself. He frequently reiterated that he had sought to avoid bloodshed. He spoke of the teaching of Christianity with reference to the dignity of all mankind and the fact that the history of Ethiopia was so often wrongly represented as the story only of a long succession of monarchs. He touched on the backwardness of the country, of its government and even, in some respects, of its armed forces, and he spoke of witnessing the countless grievances presented by the people to Hailé Sellassié on the latter's various provincial tours. He claimed to have served honestly since his first commissioning in the Guards and to have followed the Emperor's own injunction, that 'those that are appointed to office are meant to be servants of the people and not *vice versa*', but he also observed that 'there are but few who are true to the ideal. Most forget and do not follow it'. He spoke of the maldistribution of land, the antiquated provincial administration and the consequent misery of the peasants 'both in summer and in winter'. On March 21, his advocate asked that he be allowed to sign a copy of this speech but permission was refused.

In cross examination, the prosecuting counsel skilfully emphasised the evidence which touched closest on the charges. Mengistu's answers were open and sometimes not devoid of a certain humour and polish. The following were among the exchanges which occurred :

Q : Why did you act as you did?
A : It was necessary to do something to improve the standard of living, not only of the soldiers but of the whole population. That was my aim.
Q : But were you not aware of the Constitution of the Empire?
A : Yes, I know there is a Constitution—why, I have even voted for Woizero Sinadu at the polling station near Janhoy Meda.
Q : Precisely! Did you once consider speaking to your Member of Parliament about the issues?
A : No, I did not think of telling the Member of Parliament about the injustices done to the people.
Q : Instead you chose bloodshed and murder?
A : Those whom I mentioned in my testimony were those who know that I did not wish to see unnecessary bloodshed between the army and the Guard, but rather to complete the matter in a peaceful manner. Nor did I wish to see the death of the soldiers or of those dignitaries who are said to have died.

In emphasing the 'outrages against the Constitution' counsel found himself allowing Mengistu to point out that the rebels' government had a measure of support.

Q : Why did you all go to the Prime Ministry?
A : We went because those there were helping us.
Q : Indeed? How is it then that the army did not attack that building?
A : They would hardly attack an empty building after we had left . . .

Counsel then altered his line of attack to dwell on Mengistu's part in 'changing the... constituted authority'.

Q : When was Leul-Ras Imru appointed Prime Minister?

A : I don't exactly remember the time, but on Thursday.

Q : Who appointed him?

A : I myself appointed Leul-Ras Imru as Prime Minister—and Major-general Mulugeta Bulli as Commander-in-Chief of the Armed Forces.

Q : On whose authority?

A : I did this on my own authority.

Q : Where did the Crown Prince make that proclamation?

A : I made him make the proclamation in a room on the ground floor of the Palace [called] Prince's Paradise.

Q : Who recorded it?

A : It is not my wish to identify the person who tape-recorded it.

Q : When did you attack the army?

A : We started firing heavy guns at about 2.30 PM but the army started shooting and the planes were firing well before we fired.

Q : Did you give no thought to the safety of the ministers you held hostage?

A : I could not give any serious thought to that because the attack gave us very little chance.

Q : What was your intention in arresting them in the first place?

A : I arrested the ministers so that they should not be obstacles to my plans. But I was prepared to give them protection and equality like any other Ethiopian—they were Ethiopians after all! After I had accomplished what I had planned I would have released them. They would not have been victimised or subjected to any unnecessary injustices. Their positions would have been filled by educated Ethiopians and that would have resulted in the lifting of the burden of oppression from the Ethiopian people. In fact they would even have given evidence against themselves. Then they would have been permitted to follow commerce or agriculture. I still firmly believe that it would be to the benefit of the whole population if the educated Ethiopians were to be given responsibility and the direction of the government.

In answer to questions from lawyers defending the other accused, Mengistu stated that they merely obeyed orders and were not previously party to his plans.

THE ARMY PAY CRISIS

The Emperor was well aware of the mounting tension in the city but was taken by surprise when it manifested itself in a demand from the army soldiers for a pay increase. Certain conservatives grew increasingly apprehensive and argued that the troops should be pacified in case they were needed when the Mengistu verdict was announced. In their last attempt to secure the allegiance of the military before the fighting began the Council of the Revolution had announced a wage increment for the armed forces. That had led Merid to promise an even greater increase, but Hailé Sellassié had not subsequently felt that the nation could afford it. The Patriarch intervened in favour of an increase on the grounds that his name was used by the counter-revolutionaries and the honour of his office was, therefore, involved. But the Emperor still refused and his comment that it was no affair of the Church caused the Patriarch to retire to the Monastery of Debra Libanos from which Hailé Sellassié had personally to bring him back. Mounting military pressure did lead to salary increments for police and army personnel up to the rank of colonel, to cost E$4,606,520 (approximately US$1,850,000) effective from March 10, 1961. They were announced by the Emperor to a group of senior military officials at the Jubilee Palace some four days after that date. The Emperor spoke of the Patriots; he urged 'unity of purpose', and added that 'the high cost of living and the consequent hardships' faced by the armed forces, the fact that salary scales were 'not properly balanced', together with 'the faithfulness with which the army and the police forces serve the country', had all led him to order these increments despite the fact that the government was 'facing economic problems'.[18]

However, the troops were not satisfied, especially the non-commissioned officers and soldiers. Moreover, all those stationed in Addis Ababa were subjected to considerable criticism over the part they had played in the December fighting when people began to re-think the issues at leisure and to question the support they had instinctively given to the counter-revolutionaries. The attempted *coup* had been sprung and defeated before most of the common people knew of the issues involved, but the increase in scandalous gossip about the dynasty and the ministers also had some effect. There were renewed whispers of an old tale concerning the sacrificing of children at Bishaftu crater-lakes, at Debra Zeyt, etc., and one macabre coincidence made a great impression. The car carrying the body of one of the machine-gunned dignitaries to be buried, overturned on the road from the capital. The driver was killed and the grisly contents of the coffin were thrown upon the road. Some superstitious folk asked whether this were not a sign that even Heaven rejected those who had been slain by the revolutionaries. Concern over the trial of Brigadier-general Mengistu and the spate of anti-government pamphlets which, despite arrests, found their way even into the court room, further increased disquiet; and in February the anonymous writers of these tracts turned their attention to the army.

A number of communications were sent to the generals, in particular to Merid Mangasha, Kebede Gebré and Assefa Ayena. Typical among these was one sent on February 8, chiding the generals over the alleged oppressive nature of the Ethiopian government and inviting them 'instead of being loyal to one man . . . [to seek] everlasting honour like Brigadier-general Mengistu Neway, Lieutenant-colonel Workneh Gebeyehu and Ato Girmamé Neway' by bringing about changes, since they were in an unequalled position to do so. 'Don't you know of the cry of your country and the sorrow of your people? [it ran] A government established upon spies and a secret police system is like a house built on sand. . . . Are you not an Ethiopian? When the people are oppressed do you not feel it also? . . . It does not befit anyone to co-operate with the present government and perpetuate its tyranny. History outlives personal glory and honour. . . . It is imperative that you release the people who are imprisoned like cattle, without trial, in all the police stations. . . . The people who have been under colonial domination are achieving their independence and freedom, but Ethiopia lives under the tyrannical rule of one man. All this may result in foreign intervention as has been the case in the Congo, or the infiltration of neighbouring enemies. . . . If you believe in a totalitarian police state that is established for the benefit of the rich then know that you are an enemy of the People.' This letter ended : 'Freedom for Ethiopia! Freedom of employment! Freedom of thought! Freedom of speech! Freedom of the press! These are the demands of Ethiopia. [Signed] The People of Ethiopia.'

There were many threatening telephone calls (Major-general Kebede Gebré ordered one to be traced only to find it emanated from his own headquarters) and the conservative leaders, Major-general Merid Mangasha in particular, took strict precautions for their personal safety. Whether or not these communications had any effect is an open question but rumours to the effect that Merid Mangasha was about to arrest Hailé Sellassié and establish a more liberal régime were current in Addis Ababa for several days and the government certainly telephoned the University College authorities to ask whether their library contained a copy of the post-war constitution of the Empire of Japan.

A terse and critical pamphlet was distributed to the Addis Ababa soldiery and may have played some part in sparking off the number of protest meetings which they held, privately at first, and then quite openly on March 20, 1961. It read :

To the Armed Forces,

The medals which you received in recognition of your killing of your brother Ethiopians certainly carry no weight and in fact, in the opinion of the Ethiopian public are quite valueless. Moreover it is high time you understood that this régime which thrives on deceit, lies, injustice and oppression makes use of you to attain its end precisely because it regards you as mere sheep. From now on we would like you to take warning and remember the saying of our fathers : 'It was with his own hand that he ate his other hand.'* Remember this and take care that this saying shall in no way apply to you and to us.

Some senior officers including several generals addressed a mass meeting of angry soldiers at the stadium on that day, but were not given a sympathetic hearing, and a major was beaten up. A wave of apprehension gripped the city. The French and American embassies issued an alert to their nationals and some schools closed in the afternoon—Merid Mangasha was among the first to withdraw his children from St Joseph's school.

Meantime a large body of dissident soldiery marched on the Jubilee Palace and after forcing a side gate gathered under the portico and demanded that the Emperor hear them. Hailé Sellassié appeared and received what the soldiers stated was a forty-eight hour ultimatum demanding a further increase in salary. Some armed groups then left the capital to await a decision.

On March 22, it was clear that Hailé Sellassié was about to give way. The government-directed *Ethiopian Herald*, describing what had happened as the 'presentation of a petition', commented that the Emperor had replied recounting the instances of his great concern for the soldiers' well-being and had added, '. . . this being the case where else would you go but come to Us?' But he had also warned them against becoming 'the instruments for the spread of . . . false ideas' and the victims of 'certain vicious and rumour-mongering people' who were trying to destroy their 'high reputation' at a time when 'enemies of the country' were attempting to

---

* An Amharic proverb, meaning that one can kill one's own brother, possibly in ignorance.

weaken the nation 'through false and malicious propaganda'. He did, however, undertake to 'study and take into consideration' their petition.[19]

Later on the same afternoon, the Emperor broadcast to the nation in a voice lacking its usual steadiness. He announced a further monthly increment in pay and allowances of E$16 a month for all soldiers. Cabinet ministers, government officials, senior officers of the armed forces and a delegation from the dissatisfied soldiers and non-commissioned officers were all in attendance. The Emperor reiterated the difficult economic position of Ethiopia and stated that the money would have to come from cuts in the salaries of civilians—a scarcely popular move, but one which served to divide opposition to the established government into two groups, military and civilian. A fairly accurate report of the crisis carried by the press of Kenya and Uganda caused the Ethiopian Diplomatic Representative in Nairobi to issue a prompt statement which included the comment, '. . . it would not be dangerous if the increases were to be cut from the salaries of younger Ethiopian government officials. In fact they would be pleased to share what they had with the army and police who are in financial difficulties because of the high cost of living'.

And such, indeed, was the general government line. On March 29, 1961, the *Ethiopian Herald* carried an announcement that on the previous day 'a detachment of the Imperial army consisting of privates and non-commissioned officers expressed regret and begged His Imperial Majesty's forgiveness concerning the effects of recent army petitions for an increase in salary which were used as an instrument of false alarm'. They added that the Emperor was 'well known for His traditional paternal interest and solicitude for the welfare of the Ethiopian people', and in particular the armed forces, and that 'not being certain as to how the [announced] increment would affect present salaries individually', they had decided to petition their Emperor for 'clarification of this point . . .' Hailé Sellassié replied again, '. . . to whom else could you go? Your action in avoiding entrance to the palace by way of the main gate but doing so by an unobtrusive one is conclusive proof of the fact that you had no ulterior motive in presenting Us with a petition . . .'[20]

David Nelson, a popular West Indian journalist and correspondent for the London *Daily Mail*, was ordered to leave the country within forty-eight hours for 'giving publicity to certain unfounded and grossly distorted stories', which action was construed as 'political activity detrimental to the safety and security of the state'. The government-controlled press castigated foreign residents for spreading 'false news', keeping their children from certain private schools, thus affecting the state schools, and spreading groundless alarm and despondency. The situation, they claimed, was 'normal' and security 'had not been in the least disturbed'.[21] Most people who saw Nelson's telegram, even if they thought it unwise to send it, admit today to having considered it a very valid comment on the turmoil in Addis Ababa in early 1961.

In the University College, slogans against the army and the proposed cuts in government salaries appeared on the blackboards and disaffection was rife, if devoid of the opportunity of effective expression. One senior government official who had witnessed the award of the second increment remarked to the author : 'When the soldiers threw their hats into the air, self-satisfied and happy, many of us grew hot [angry] and thought—you greedy people, what have you done for your country?' They also knew that it was politically shrewd to buy off any dissident soldiery just when the Mengistu verdict was due to be announced, and their hearts fell in antici-pation of what was to come. The pamphlets also recognised that the motives of the soldiers were not so much political as mercenary —in some ways akin to those of the so-called mutineers in Tan-ganyika, Uganda and Kenya in January 1964—when they turned their attention once again on to the townsfolk. The content of their anonymous tracts began to include more and more dynastic scandal, not because they believed it—often they did not—but because with the uneducated masses it found a readier ear than did the language of social revolution and Pan-Africanism.

SENTENCE

Meantime, one underground group managed to arrange that Brigadier-general Mengistu be abducted from his place of deten-tion but he refused to be freed. There is no doubt that he still believed his dead brother's oft repeated remarks that, successful or not, their *coup* represented the vanguard of inevitable change. This sense of history caused the general to remark that he preferred to die. He phrased this in Amharic with great power saying, 'I go to tell the others the seed we set has taken root'.

The final verdict was given on Megabit 19 (March 28, 1961). It was that Brigadier-general Mengistu Neway be hanged in a public place and that Captain Kiflé Woldé Mariam and Lieutenant Degafé Tedla, be sentenced to fifteen and ten years' imprisonment respectively. It was stated that the second and third defendants had no prior knowledge of the *coup*. All were deprived of their rank and decorations and their property was confiscated.

Mengistu said :

I shall not appeal, and am quite satisfied. I am glad that I
have been given the chance to say even this much. Man may
judge man, but it is for God, who has not left created man
without counsel and help, to examine and objectively judge
by his deeper motives and aspirations. Only when a person is
given the opportunity to speak is his well-being or discontent
expressed—but when the right to speak and write is denied
him, his grievances are neither known nor expressed. . . . Had
these two others been sentenced to death, that would have
grieved me much more. I do not appeal, since it would be
unfair to bring unnecessary strain to the relatives of the
deceased, when they have to come always to these long drawn
out proceedings ! Truly, because some people have died on
my account, I feel a certain sorrow, but had God been willing
a *coup* would have come about sooner or later. . . . I did all
this for the sake of the Ethiopian people and I pray that God
soon gives true judgement to the Ethiopian people [*literally*
that God will hold the judgement in His hand].

As to my death, I have been prepared to die since the
4th Tahsas, 1953 [December 13, 1960], and I am quite unmoved that this Court has sentenced me to death.

Degafé Tedla and Kiflé Woldé Mariam appealed unsuccessfully to the Supreme Court. In fact, sentence on the latter was
increased and he also was subsequently hanged.

Only a handful of relatives and important dignitaries were
informed of the time of the execution which took place very early
in the morning of Megabit 21 (March 30, 1961), some two days
later. Survivors from the Green Salon ventured out from hospital
to see Mengistu Neway brought to a gibbet erected in the Addis
Ababa market area. There was a fine early morning drizzle. Mengistu was a little concerned lest the noose be incorrectly adjusted—
he probably recalled the execution of Belai Zelleka, at which he
had been present, for that rebel leader had lived for many minutes.
Mengistu spoke to the Emperor's ADC, a Brigadier-general who
years before had been in exile with him in Khartoum, and was
reassured. Contrary to several reports the former brigadier-general
gave no funeral oration but shook hands with those about him
before leaping from the back of the waggon as it pulled away.

News of what had been done spread quickly. By the time
the sun had begun to climb, the whole market area of the city was
thronged. Uneasy policemen confiscated cameras but there were no
disturbances. Mengistu's face was so calm that rumour developed

that he had died on the previous day by his own hand. Such was the measure of the political awakening which had occurred in Addis Ababa that the occasion in no way resembled the hanging of the body of Girmamé Neway. There was none of the ribaldry and laughter of the previous December. The old market was filled with silent African citizens. In Ethiopia, when someone dies, mourners come to the house throughout the whole day; they say nothing; they just sit. Then they go. On the day Mengistu Neway was hanged the whole market area of the capital was just like that.

During his long reign, Hailé Sellassié had forgiven many of the challenges to himself. But to challenge Ethiopia's ancient tradition was another matter. Moreover, the vengeful relatives of those who had died in the Green Salon constituted a pressure group he could hardly ignore. But the subtle Emperor did not himself return to the palace called Prince's Paradise (which was presented to the University), but went to live in the Jubilee Palace pending the building of yet another. Many had therefore hoped that he would find some way of avoiding a public execution as too absolute an identification with those who had opposed the revolutionaries, especially since he had been quick to notice that the latter had refrained from mentioning his name in their propaganda. But there was no stay of execution and the ageing Emperor thus failed that day to frustrate the growth of a new and more modern myth.

After Mengistu's execution the tenseness in the capital momentarily relaxed. But a succession of conspiracies and crises— involving not only courtiers but also senior military officers, soldiers, intellectuals and students soon became the political norm in Addis Ababa and Asmara. Prince and pauper alike recognised that something irrevocable in the history of their country had been allowed to happen. A cause had not only been defined within an Ethiopian context but had also acquired its martyrs.

It may be said that in late 1960 and early 1961 Africa's wind of change blew across the High Plateau of Ethiopia bringing a new political awakening. For better or for worse, the timelessness and traditional remoteness of even the heart of Ethiopia is ended once and for all. Only time will tell whether the new myth growing around the Neway brothers and the *mores* of their attempted *coup d'état* can ever quite displace the story of Solomon and Sheba as an inspiration for the Ethiopian nation—as Girmamé and Mengistu intended that it should. However, those who have seen the gloom and despair on the faces of leaders of yet another generation of young Ethiopians slowly changing into resolution, know that it has a chance.

Epilogue

*...Ethiopian delegates now sit at each general conference
board. It need hardly be said that this by itself is insufficient.
Before them and their companions there stretches out under
a leaden sky a wide, grey prospect.*—D. MATHEW, *Ethiopia,
The Study of a Polity,* London, 1947

The years 1961–65 have seen greater change in Ethiopia than any
previous decade and this has been in no small measure due to the
shake-up caused by the events of 1960—but even so changes of a
fundamental nature have yet to occur. No 'Nasser' has so far
emerged from the maturing generation of proud young army
officers. Nor have the intellectuals yet produced a 'Castro'. Doubtless this is in part due to the suspicion of one Ethiopian for another;
to the skill displayed by Hailé Sellassié in calculating and balancing
disunities; to his personal popularity in certain rural areas and to
the abiding strength of Ethiopian tradition. So often the first
question asked by the peasant is 'who is his father?'. The Empress
Menen, Leul Sahlé Sellassié, Ras-Betwoded Makonnen Endalkatchew and others have died and their funerals have been
impressive occasions.

Court intrigue, so typical of the 1940s and 50s has continued
—for example, the summer of 1961 and the autumn of 1964 both
witnessed the uncovering of plots against the régime. In 1961
Dejazmatch Takelé Woldé Hawariat, the *Afe negus* (Lord Chief
Justice) once again disappeared from the political forum. He has
not been charged or tried, as far as is known, and is said to live
under restriction in Goré or Jimma. Another former Patriot, Fitwrary Hailu Kibret and his nephew were secretly hanged in 1962.

In September 1964 the scare led to a reshuffle of the appointments of certain senior officers and Colonel Imru of the Marine Department was arrested. He was neither charged nor released by the end of the year although it is said that Leul-Ras Imru interceded on his behalf. The cabinet met to discuss the measure of unrest in Addis Ababa which involved both military and civilians, and heard a report from Dejazmatch Kiflé of the Security Department.

The rift between the Crown Prince and the Emperor has grown no narrower nor has the former been encouraged to play the more prominent role in public affairs which any consideration for the stability of the throne in Hailé Sellassié's declining years might appear to require. Indeed some prominence has been given to the young Duke of Harar, the eldest son of the late Leul Makonnen. Perhaps Hailé Sellassié still suspects the loyalty of Asfa Wossen—the latter did not know that he would be required to accompany his father to the Belgrade Conference of non-aligned States in 1961 until dinner at the Palace on the night before his departure. In Court circles there have been attempts to dispossess the Moja family of land and a continual struggle between a group of aristocrats led by General Abiye Abebe (appointed President of the Senate in 1964) and Leul-Dejazmatch Asrate Kassa (transferred from that office to be Governor General of Eritrea) on the one hand, and an ambitious group of bureaucrats led by Prime Minister Aklilu Habtewold on the other. Hailé Sellassié is probably closely briefed on these groupings since on his return from attending the funeral of President Kennedy of the United States he remarked to the Prime Minister that he knew of a dinner party the latter had organised at Bishaftu in his absence, at which some guarded concern had been expressed over the state of the body politic. Mounting discussion in this circle over limited changes in the internal structure of the Ethiopian government were postponed in late 1964 on the excuse of work involved in preparing for the state visit of the British queen. This visit, like the first African Summit Conference, led to the further beautification of Addis Ababa. But the new works and structures typified by a huge municipality building, are felt by many Ethiopians to add only to the façade of development and to leave the real needs of the people unsatisfied. Indeed just prior to the state visit some resentment was caused when children were prevented from attending classes if they could not afford a junior or senior school uniform at E$9.30 and E$13.50 respectively.

Some few more factories have been opened and a large-scale cotton scheme has begun operation at Tendaho. Tentative beginnings have been made in the sphere of Trade Unionism.

There is close association between the Ministry of Community Development and the Trade Union federation and the latter is not yet permitted to operate fully in Eritrea (where of course the concepts of political parties and trade unions are not new). There are still no political parties in Ethiopia but since these might operate on a provincial or ethnic basis there is no great clamour for them. Parliament itself has no deep roots, despite councils being traditional in certain areas. In its present form it may not survive any future change of government. On the other hand, there has been some fairly outspoken debate although it is not reported in the press and the educational level of the members is not high. Seyoum Sabat, an intellectual who contested an election in 1961 and held public meetings, was arrested shortly afterwards and detained for some years without charge or trial. In the summer of 1964 some interest was aroused in an outspoken debate after which the Senate rejected a proposed loan of £5,000,000 which the Ministry of Finance had arranged with Italy, on the grounds that its terms compromised Ethiopia's independence. Underlying issues were, however, quite complicated, not least because the Senate contains a considerable proportion of elderly notables and former Patriots who are contemptuous of many officials of the government whom they consider to be former collaborators or to belong to inferior social classes or ethnic groups. Also, on one occasion the Prime Minister was obliged to apologise for an apparent attempt to by-pass Parliament. However, the *Aqebe Saat* (the ministers' weekly individual appointments with the Emperor) remain a much more important part of the government of Ethiopia.

The conservatives openly stated that the new National University, largely financed by the United States, would obviate the necessity for the young to go abroad and develop 'new ideas' out of touch with undefined 'traditional values'. However, the struggle of intellectuals for frank discussion of the nation's problems has continued. In August 1961 new deterrents were decreed including 30 lashes for persons convicted of 'insults, abuses defamations or slanders of the Emperor . . . the publication of inaccurate or distorted information in any form concerning judicial proceedings . . . the defence of a crime, spreading false rumours . . . false charges . . . inciting or provoking others to disobey orders issued by the lawful authorities', etc. In early 1962 it was ordered that students be no longer allowed direct access to library shelves in the University College and in mid-year the cabinet decided that all students' hostels in the capital should be closed. The obvious intention was to frustrate discussion and prevent the students from becoming a political force as has happened in certain Middle Eastern and South American countries. This move on the government's part drew protests from the administration of the University, from Faculty organisations, from the students themselves and from international student bodies and it led to several minor incidents. By the summer of 1962 Dr Bentley, the idealistic American President of the University, had clashed with the government and left the country. Dr Levine, appointed head of the proposed Department of African Studies, had been declared a prohibited immigrant and had returned to the United States. Others who left Ethiopia about this time or shortly afterwards included the Associate to the President and the President of the University College. There followed a lull in student activity, but in February 1965 they again demonstrated through the streets of the capital with banners calling for the abolition of serfdom and for land reform. Students from Girmamé Neway's old school have also demonstrated against alleged 'corruption'.

Several organisations have sprung up amongst the new elite but thus far they have concerned themselves largely with their own sectional and professional problems and not with national issues. But their influence increases.

The military has likewise increased in influence, despite its internal divisions having been emphasised by increased training and provision for the territorial forces. Apart from Merid Mangasha, the Minister of Defence, who is associated with the Court aristocrats, the active generals have tended to refrain from throwing their influence on any side within the Court intrigues and if a challenge is made, although a puppet monarch could perhaps be retained for a period, it might be to the whole system. Several were taken by surprise in early 1965 when Eyasu Mangasha was appointed Chief of Staff of the army and Kebede Gebré and Esayas Gebré Sellassié were posted to govern Harar and Sidamo provinces respectively. Recent mass promotions of Warrant officers and NCOs to junior commissioned rank have been widely interpreted as an attempt by Court circles to weaken the solidarity of the younger service officers. Like other groups within the state the army has used its political influence to secure further increments of pay but has so far made no move on a wider basis. Individual soldiers feel some guilt over their part in the events of 1960–61 but the degree to which the army is an integrated command remains an open question. The influence of tradition on the lower ranks is very strong and it a mute point as to whether the soldiers would remain loyal to the military High Command if its authority were challenged by a senior member of the aristocracy or by the Patriarch.

It is similarly unclear whether attempts to reform the Ethiopian Christian Church—which is losing ground only in the cities—through orders from the throne or the Patriarch's office would be effective owing to the vested interests and the ignorance of the rural clergy and the amorphous nature of church organisation. There is perhaps a need for a ministry of ecclesiastical affairs. There has also been recent evidence of continued ultra-conservatism on the part of the bishops in the sphere of church doctrine.

The neglect over the years of the promotion of a positive program of national unity throughout the empire is beginning to tell in Eritrea, Harar, Bali and Sidamo, although vigorous programs of public works organised in Tigré by the Governor General, Leul-Dejazmatch Mangasha Seyoum, besides maintaining peace in the province, have attracted wide attention even in Addis Ababa. Numerous incidents, such as the suicide of the police commandant a few minutes before his anticipated arrest have followed on the abolition of the federal status of Eritrea. Respect for Hailé Sellassié has declined in Eritrea, *shifta* activity has increased and there have been reports of terrorists being trained by the UAR. The new régime in the Sudanese Republic seems not so friendly to Ethiopia as was that of General Abboud and there have been demonstrations by 'Eritrean separatists' in Khartoum. Similarly there has been some unrest amongst Ethiopian Somalis in the Ogaden area of Harar Province where terrorists infiltrating from the Somali Republic have encouraged disturbances. The situation has closely paralleled that in North-Eastern Kenya and subversive propaganda has found an ear even amongst the Sidamo and Borana peoples.

The ambition of the Somali Republic to expand its frontiers at the expense of Kenya and Ethiopia in order to include all Somali tribesmen has led Kenya and Ethiopia to conclude a treaty of mutual defence. Sizeable military clashes on the Ethio–Somali border have been followed by cease fires arranged in the interests of African unity. It is in this sphere of foreign affairs that the greatest Ethiopian achievements have been made. This is not unconnected with the fact that conservative interests are not so involved and young men whose progressive ideas might threaten the *status quo* at home have deliberately been seconded to the Foreign Office and embassies abroad. Ethiopia's 'African' policy has led to a breach with Portugal, her historic ally, but has so far succeeded in almost isolating the Somali Republic in African circles—largely on the grounds that the re-drawing of African frontiers on tribal considerations is a generally retrogressive measure in the context of a continental struggle for unity. The headquarters of the Organisation of African Unity like the United Nations Economic Commission for Africa, have been permanently established in Addis Ababa. On January 22 and 23, 1965 the *Ethiopian Herald* carried reports of the enthusiasm of the people of Djibouti and the French territory to join 'Mother Ethiopia'. Chiefs and members of the Adal and Issa tribes petitioned a sub-committee of the OAU Liberation Committee for union with Ethiopia. In 1964 Emperor Hailé Sellassié's successful state visit to Kenya, Tanzania and Uganda emphasised the friendship of these countries with Ethiopia. Nevertheless, it is not impossible that the nature of the Ethiopian Government could one day prove an obstacle to the promotion of Ethiopia's best interests in African circles.

The possibilities of power readjustment within Ethiopia are clearly endless, and as the seventy-three-year-old Emperor ages, quite inevitable. The personal rule which he has epitomised will not be possible, let alone desirable, for any succeeding monarch. That fact, coupled with the tension between Ethiopia and her Islamic neighbours, must mark out the Horn of Africa as an area of considerable potential instability. However, the author is not one of those who considers the difficulties facing Ethiopia to be insurmountable, or who predicts that the present state-framework of Ethiopia will not survive. Even so, it appears by no means certain that a synthesis of the historic traditions of Ethiopia and the radical ambitions of her new generations, which is also adequate to release and channel the frustrated or latent idealisms of the 'new elite' can come about painlessly. The future of Ethiopia lies in the hands of the intelligentsia, the bureaucracy and the younger military officers. The current political problem lies in the fact that none of these groups can accept the political role at present allotted them, i.e. that of being a technical arm of a feudal government. Since 1960, several observers have criticised the 'new elite' in Ethiopia as being self-seeking and corrupt and in no way different from their elders. They perhaps forget that a personal motive is only replaced by a national motive and cynicism is only discarded when there is purpose and idealism at the very centre of the national government itself. Indeed there is a proverb in Ethiopia, 'A mother who steals never trusts her children': the children likewise.

THE ETHIOPIAN CALENDAR

The Ethiopian Calendar (EC) corresponds to the Julian not the Gregorian calendar (GC) except that it begins (at the time of writing) in the second week of September.

Thus:

```
1951 EC is 1958 to 1959 GC
1952 EC is 1959 to 1960 GC
1953 EC is 1960 to 1961 GC
1954 EC is 1961 to 1962 GC
1955 EC is 1962 to 1963 GC
1956 EC is 1963 to 1964 GC
1957 EC is 1964 to 1965 GC
1958 EC is 1965 to 1966 GC
```

The Ethiopian year consists of 12 months, each of 30 days, followed by a period *'Pagumien'* of 5 days (6 days in leap year)—hence the *Ethiopian Airlines* advertisement 'thirteen months of sunshine'. The names of the twelve months are:

Meskerem	*Megabit*
Tikimt	*Miazia*
Hidar	*Ginbot*
Tahsas	*Senie*
Tir	*Hamlie*
Yekatit	*Nehasie*

The Amharic names of the days of each week (which begins on Monday) are:

Monday	*Segno*
Tuesday	*Maksegno*
Wednesday	*Rebu*
Thursday	*Hamus*
Friday	*Arb*
Saturday	*Kidamie*
Sunday	*Ihud*

As in Arabic and Kiswahili the hours are counted from 6 AM (approximate sunrise). Seven PM is thus one o'clock at night. Traditionally in the countryside each day begins at sunrise.

Maksegno, Tahsas 4, 1953 (EC) was Tuesday, December 13, 1960 and

Hamus, Megabit 21, 1953 (EC) was Thursday, March 30, 1961.

ETHIOPIAN TITLES AND MODES OF ADDRESS*

Since the Emperor is the fountain of nearly every title, it is worth study-ing the translation of his own dignity from the Amharic. He is 'Negus Neghest' or 'King of the Kings' (of Ethiopia). This title, together with the traditions of imperial lions and ceremonial umbrellas, may be traced to ancient Aksum and is probably derived from early Persia.† Another title, proclaiming the legendary descent of the Ethiopian kings from King Solomon and the Queen of Sheba (identified with Queen Makeda of Aksum) is variously translated 'The Lion of Judah has Prevailed', or 'Conquering Lion of the Tribe of Judah'. Article 2 of the Revised Con-stitution of Ethiopia (1955) is relevant. It reads:

> Article 2: The Imperial Dignity shall remain perpetually attached to the line of Hailé Sellassié I, the descendant of King Sahlé Sellassié, whose line descends without interruption from the dynasty of Menelik I, son of the Queen of Ethiopia, the Queen of Sheba, and King Solomon of Jerusalem. . . .

The Solomonic Line is discussed in the text but the Emperor's divine right to rule is further confirmed in his title 'Elect of God'.

> Article 4: By virtue of his Imperial blood, as well as by the anoint-ing which he has received, the Person of the Emperor is sacred, his dignity is inviolable and his power indisputable. . . .

The nature of the absolute monarchy of Ethiopia is rooted in Ethiopian culture and history. It is undergoing some modification but its traditional basis only became constitutional in the reign of Hailé Sellassié I.

The title of the Empress is *Itegue,* and an ancient Shewan title, *Merid Azmatch,* in 1964, dignified His Imperial Highness Crown Prince Asfa Wossen Hailé Sellassié. *Azmatch* or, literally, 'field commander' approximates to marshal or general. The legitimate sons of the monarch are princes and are addressed as *Leul* (not to be confused with *lul,* mean-ing a coronet), and his daughters are *Leilt* or princess. These titles are carried to the third generation only in the case of the children of the heir and the brothers. Hailé Sellassié has introduced the title Duke into the Imperial family for use when princes are appointed governors of pro-vinces. Menelik only conferred it upon foreigners. However, it gives no status in the hierarchy since that is derived from the duke's existing status as *Leul.* While normally the form of address for the rank of *Mesfin* or

'Prince', the term really only implies 'high', often in social position or power. [*Leul Egziabher* means 'Almighty God'.] Incidentally the Palace *Guenete Leul*, is sometimes translated as 'Prince of Paradise' but is more exactly rendered from the Ge'ez as 'Prince's Paradise' or 'Paradise of the Prince'.

The highest title, *negus* or king, has not been granted or seized since 1928. Lij Eyasu, who was *negus* of Kaffa, created his father Ras Mikael *negus* in 1914, Ras Woldé Giorgis became *negus* in 1917 and Hailé Sellassié himself became Negus Tafari in 1928. The ancient title of *Bahr-Negash* (*negus*), literally 'King of the Sea', once dignified the kings of the northerly areas, roughly present-day Eritrea and northern Tigré. The title implies that this king rules not only these lands but also the seas and even beyond—it has, however, long been in disuse.

Although other titles of feudal origin have tended to run in families in almost every case they are not automatically hereditary. The daughters of royalty, even of an Imperial princess, are *immabet*, the nearest English equivalent of which is 'Lady' but the emperor may create them *leilt* (princess) just as he may create more distant relatives and others *immabet*, or they may marry a prince and thus become princess. A member of a princely house may be created *leul-ras* or *leul-dejazmatch* and is then referred to as his Highness and not his Excellency as is the usual case with a *ras* or a *dejazmatch*, but their children are unaffected. The use of the title *leul* in conjunction with that of *ras* or *dejazmatch* dates only from the Regency period prior to the coronation of Emperor Hailé Sellassié.

Betwoded, 'the beloved' (by implication a courtier beloved and trusted by the Emperor) or *ras-betwoded* is an ancient title which was similar to first councillor and was carried, for example, by the late President of the Senate, Ras-Betwoded Makonnen Endalkatchew. It is given only once in a monarch's reign. In 1964 the Prime Minister, Aklilu Habtewold, was also Minister of the Pen. In former times the latter office was that of Emperor's or a provincial king's historiographer, but it later became roughly Privy Seal and carries the title *tsahafé taezaz*. This title remains with those who have held the office of Minister of the Pen. Another important functionary is the *Afe negus*, literally 'mouth of the King' or more rarely *Afe mesfin*, literally 'mouth of the Prince' (and by implication vehicle for the breath, words and even thoughts of the royal master); on occasions the *Afe negus* reflects the monarch's authority even over princes and is roughly Lord Chancellor and Lord Chief Justice in English equivalent (though he is not President of the Senate). Like *tsahafé taezaz* the title is not relinquished when the post of President of the Supreme Court passes to another as indeed it has in recent years. It is only dropped when a superior title is conferred. Thus Afe negus Takelé Woldé Hawariat remained *Afe negus* when he was displaced and detained in southern Ethiopia but Afe mesfin Andargatchew Messai no longer uses that title but rather the title *ras*.

Ras, literally 'head', is a title conferred often but by no means invariably upon the heads of important houses, provincial governors, ministers and high officials. It is equivalent to a Marshal-Duke. *Dejaz-match*, the 'Marshal of provincial headquarters' is equivalent to a Count. *Fitwrary*, 'commander of the vanguard', is similar to a knight. His right hand is the *kegnazmatch* or 'marshal of the right' and his left the *graz-match*, 'he who leads the left wing' (of that army). Then comes *balam-*

baras, 'commander of the fort', and *basha*, roughly equal to a 'quarter-master sergeant'.

The obvious former military significance of these titles became irrelevant with the establishment of a modern army in this century which replaced the feudal levies who served under these commanders. Western nomenclature of rank is used for commanders above the rank of lieutenant-colonel, but below this, former feudal terms are still used even in the modern military. Beneath the rank of lieutenant-colonel, *shaleka*, literally 'commander of one thousand', is major, *shambel* is captain, *mulu ye meto-alika* is lieutenant and *mikitil ye meto-alika* is second-lieutenant, literally 'commander of one hundred'. *Maga bi amsa-alika* is sergeant-major, *amsa-alika* or 'commander of fifty' is colour or staff sergeant, *mulu asir-alika* is sergeant, *asir-alika*, or 'commander of ten' is corporal and *mikitil asir-alika*, lance-corporal (of course the Amharic alphabet is different from the above).

Military ranks are used in the air force, which is commanded by a general and not an air-marshal, and to some extent in the police where the rank *azaj* is similar to commissioner. The navy is a young force and the highest position, in 1964, was held by the Emperor's grandson Commander Iskander (Alexander) Desta who is often out of courtesy, but not from protocol, referred to as His Highness. There was also a Norwegian flag-officer on attachment.

Each Province, or *auraja* is ruled by a governor general or *taklé agara gazhi*. The provinces are themselves divided into more than seventy sub-provinces or *werada* each ruled by a governor or *agara gazhi*. There are further sub-divisions. The landowning chiefs and traditional leaders are the *balabat* and the *shums* (more properly *seyoums*). In Begemidir, Gojjam and Tigré the balabats have been stripped of their power—though not necessarily their political influence—by the Shewan central hegemony to a rather greater extent than have those in predominantly Galla regions where, incidentally some tend to be rather corrupt. The *shums* have often been used by the central government in executive capacities, for example, as magistrates and tax collectors.

To return to the court, there are certain specific titles of note such as *raise-mesafint*, or first of the nobility, and provincial titles such as *wagshum*, the hereditary ruler of Wag-Lasta, descendant of the Zagwé kings, a line of so-called usurpers of earlier times, who has special privileges. It follows for example that the Shum-Agamé is Governor of Agamé, similarly the Shum-Tembien is Governor of Tembien. The Governor of Ambassel is *Jantirar*.

A special *fitwrary*, the *'turka-basha fitwrary'*, was very senior and Minister of War. *Liquamaquas* is the title of a noble *aide-de-camp*, a position which derived from the two officers who dressed as the Emperor in order to distract attention from him in battle. Englishmen have held this position to Emperor Tewodros in the mid nineteenth century.

Civil titles include *kantiba* or mayor, *negadras* or 'trade commissioner'* and *bejirond* or 'chief accountant'. *Lij* literally 'boy' is used as

---

Such officers were responsible for controlling trade and customs and it is the author's belief that the title derives from the word for trade i.e. the *'ras'* of the trade (or caravan). However, it is also explained as being derived from *'Nagarit'* (a drum), hence 'he who is entitled to drums'. See G. Huntingford, *The Prester John of the Indies*, Appendix V, Vol II, Cambridge, 1961.

an honorific for the sons of noble houses. The late minister of state in the Foreign Ministry, Blatta Dawit Okbagzy, used to tease the present Minister of Commerce and Industry, Lij Endalkatchew Makonnen, son of Ras-Betwoded Makonnen Endalkatchew, when he worked with him. If the *blatta* wanted the messenger whose name was Gebré, he would shout instead, 'Lij!' and then add, 'Not you, Endalkatchew'. Blatta Dawit who had a great sense of humour was killed in the Green Salon in December 1960. *Blatta*, literally 'youth' is a title implying learning and, like *lij*, it can be held at any age. *Blattenguetta* is an even higher title and is literally 'Master of Youths'.

Within the Church the Patriarch is correctly 'His Beatitude', though the Ethiopian press often uses 'His Holiness'. *Abune*, literally 'his paternity', or 'our father', is used for bishops and for the archbishop now made patriarch. *Aba* means 'father' and is the mode of address for a priest.

Colloquial terms are as follows. *'Guetta'* is a term of respect, 'my Master' or 'Sir', and originates from the title of certain wealthy folk who were called upon to judge in disputes between the less fortunate. An important figure may be referred to in the third person as a *'Tillik sau'* or 'great man'. *Ato* once meant a gentleman, rather as did Esquire in England, but is now in general use for Mr. *Woizero* is now similarly in general use for Mrs, and *woizerit* a more recent word for 'Miss'. This term implies virginity. Women keep their own names on marriage. Familiar modes of address include *'Gashé'*, or 'my shield', to an older person and *'Wondemé'*, or 'my brother'. A *shemagalé* is an elder, or an old man.

A Circular Letter sent by the Emperor Menelik II in 1891 to the Heads of State of Britain, France, Germany, Italy and Russia.*

Being desirous to make known to our friends the Powers [Sovereigns] of Europe the boundaries of Ethiopia, we have addressed also to you [your Majesty] the present letter.

These are the boundaries of Ethiopia:

Starting from the Italian boundary of Arafale, which is situated on the sea, the line goes westward over the plain [Meda] of Gegra towards Mahio, Halai, Digsa, and Gura up to Adibaro. From Adibaro to the junction of the Rivers Mareb and Arated.

From this point the line runs southward to the junction of the Atbara and Setit rivers, where is situated the town known as Tomat.

From Tomat the frontier embraces the Province of Gedaref up to Karkoj on the Blue Nile. From Karkoj the line passes to the junction of the Sobat river with the White Nile. From thence the frontier follows the River Sobat, including the country of the Arbore, Gallas, and reaches Lake Samburu.

Towards the east are included within the frontier the country of the Borana Gallas and the Arussi country up to the limits of the Somalis, including also the Province of Ogaden.

To the northward the line of frontier includes the Habr Awaz, the Gadabursi, and the Esa Somalis, and reaches Ambos.

Leaving Ambos the line includes Lake Assal, the province of our ancient vassal Mohamed Anfari, skirts the coast of the sea, and rejoins Arafale.

While tracing today the actual boundaries of my Empire, I shall endeavour, if God gives me life and strength, to re-establish the ancient frontiers [tributaries] of Ethiopia up to Khartoum, and as far as Lake Nyanza with all the Gallas.

Ethiopia has been for fourteen centuries a Christian land in a sea of pagans. If Powers at a distance come forward to partition Africa between them, I do not intend to be an indifferent spectator.

As the Almighty has protected Ethiopia up to this day, I have confidence He will continue to protect her, and increase her borders in the future. I am certain He will not suffer her to be divided among other Powers.

Formerly the boundary of Ethiopia was the sea. Having lacked sufficient strength, and having received no help from Christian powers, our frontier on the sea coast fell into the power of the Mussulman.

---

* From the London Public Records Office, Foreign Office papers 1/32. Rodd to Salisbury, 15 May 4, 1897.

At present we do not intend to regain our sea frontier by force, but we trust that the Christian Power, guided by our Saviour, will restore to us our sea-coast line, at any rate, certain points on the coast.

Written at Addis Ababa, the 14th Mazir, 1883 EC (April 10, 1891).

Translated direct from the Amharic.

STATISTICAL TABLES

Bearing in mind the primitive methods of collecting and processing data, the differing criteria of collection, the susceptibility of published statistics to political sensitivities, etc., the Ethiopian statistics here included should be treated with caution. As stated in Chapter 16 nothing more than a general impression can be safely based upon them.

For ease of comparison, assume

£1 Sterling to equal E$7
E$1 to equal US$0.40

Table I—LEADING ETHIOPIAN EXPORTS
As Shown in Customs Returns
(by value, in thousands of US dollars)

	1960	*1961*
Coffee	37,759	37,550
Cattle hides	3,061	3,325
(compare leather and leather manufactures)	6	20
Sheep skins	2,667	4,400
Goat skins	1,638	1,946
Other skins	368	382
Cereals and pulses	8,993	7,211
Vegetable Oils	6,591	6,020
Ch'at	2,825	4,338

Oilcakes, fruit, vegetables and salt were also exported.

Adapted from *Ethiopian Statistical Abstract*, Addis Ababa, 1963.

Table 2—ETHIOPIAN GOLD PRODUCTION
Approximate figures from published sources
(by value, in thousands of us dollars)

EC	GC	Adola Field	Total
1937	1944–5	?	4,256
1938	1945–6	?	2,694
1939	1946–7	?	2,393
1940	1947–8	?	2,309
1941	1948–9	?	1,569
1942	1949–50	1,388	1,893
1943	1950–1	1,055	1,224
1944	1951–2	868	892
1945	1952–3	758	800
1946	1953–4	711	800
1947	1954–5	661	801
1948	1955–6	709	806
1949	1956–7	581	769
1950	1957–8	868	958
1951	1958–9	1,813	2,111
1952	1959–60	688	973
1953	1960–1	770	1,039

Note: Ethiopian gold production is measured in Maria Theresa ounces (31.1025 grams) and not the customary troy ounces (28 grams). A troy ounce is worth us$35.00.

Adapted from Ethiopian Budget Revenue Actuals EC 1942–53 or production figures to be found in *Economic Progress of Ethiopia*, Addis Ababa, 1955; *Ethiopian Economic Review* No 5, Addis Ababa, 1962; *Ethiopian Statistical Abstract*, Addis Ababa, 1963, and H. Quinn, 'The Mineral Industry of Ethiopia', *Ethiopia Observer*, Vol. VI, No 3, 1962.

Table 3—NEWLY MINED GOLD PLUS GOLD EXPORTS
Selected African Countries
(by weight in kilograms)

	1957	*1958*	*1959*	*1960*
S. Africa	529,716	549,177	624,108	665,105
S. Rhodesia	16,703	17,257	17,632	17,502
Ghana	24,584	26,525	28,401	27,340
Tanganyika	1,975	2,123	3,011	3,319
Ethiopia	605	1,094	1,200	480

Note: Table 2 shows gold production only. In the case of Ethiopia, which in both tables includes Eritrea, there is, nevertheless, some discrepancy from the above figures. United Nations figures appear to be lower than Ethiopian government figures, which in turn are lower than those quoted by the Professor of Geology cited. Equivalents from Table 2 for the fours years beginning September 1956 would read 681, 850, 1873 and 868 kilograms. However, these discrepancies, while pointing to the degree of caution necessary in the reading of statistics in Ethiopia, in no way alter the general picture.
One kilogram of gold is worth US$*1,125.25.*

Source: ECA *African Statistics,* Vol. I, No 2, June 1961.

Table 4—THE TRADE OF SELECTED AFRICAN COUNTRIES IN 1959
(by value in millions of US *dollars)*

	Imports	*Exports*
Ethiopia	84.0	72.9
Sudanese Republic	163.8	191.8
Ghana	316.5	317.4
United Arab Republic (not including Syria)	615.8	443.0
Morocco	335.1	331.7
Kenya, Tanganyika, and Uganda	340.3	360.7
Nigeria	502.4	458.2
The Central African Federation	420.4	523.5
South Africa	1,368.3	1,201.0

Note: The combined populations and areas of the countries in the East African Common Market do not greatly exceed the Ethiopian figures and these statistics ignore trade between them.

Source: Economic Commission for Africa, *African Statistics,* Vol. I, No 2, Addis Ababa, June 1961.

Table 5—EXTERNAL TRADE IN 1961
(*by value, in thousands of* US *dollars*)

	Ethiopian Exports	Ethiopian Imports
USA	29,222	8,031
Japan	1,735	14,344
Western Germany	19,909	9,172
Italy	8,200	4,985
France	2,309	2,054
United Kingdom	4,316	2,516
Holland	1,991	4,599
Yugoslavia	862	1,118
Czecho-Slovakia	644	170
USSR	505	1,115
Red China	4	422
Rest of Africa	5,086	792

Notes

1. Much of the trade scheduled as with Aden and some scheduled as with Djibouti (the latter included in the Rest of Africa figures above) is actually destined for, or is from, the USA, whose real trade with Ethiopia is therefore larger than reflected above i.e., more than 39 per cent and 11 per cent of the export and import trade respectively.

2. Ethiopia's main African trading partners, the Sudanese Republic and the UAR, are not included with the Rest of Africa figures above. Their trade, with the Aden (entrepôt), Saudi Arabia and Iran trade, totalled nearly 16 per cent and 10 per cent of the exports and imports respectively.

3. In 1961 there was also a small amount of trade with Ceylon, India (also sometimes via Aden), Indonesia, Hong Kong and, though in hardly significant quantity, with Hungary, Bulgaria and Poland.

4. Ethiopia has no trade with the island of Taiwan (Formosa). Although there is trade with Red China, Ethiopia had not afforded diplomatic recognition at the time of writing (1964).

Adapted from Statistics derived from Ethiopian customs trade returns and published in *Ethiopian Statistical Abstract*, Addis Ababa, 1963.

Table 6—ETHIOPIAN BUDGET—REVENUE
(*in millions of* US *dollars*)

	Post Restoration Average*	1951 EC 1958–9 GC
Customs	12.3	19.3
Taxes from Land (including land tax, education tax, tithe, cattle tax, etc.)	6.5	7.5
Other Direct Taxes	2.5	4.0
Indirect Taxes	4.5	9.4
TOTAL ORDINARY REVENUE	33.3	58.4
TOTAL ACTUAL REVENUE	39.3	78.7

* Total revenue from September 1941 to July 1960 regarded as a period of 18 years' duration.

Adapted from Budget tables published in *Economic Progress of Ethiopia*, Addis Ababa, 1955, and *Ethiopian Economic Review*, No 5, Addis Ababa, 1962.

Table 7—ETHIOPIAN BUDGET—EXPENDITURE
(*in millions of* US *dollars*)

Ministry or Heading	Some Post Restoration Average*	1951 EC 1958–9 GC
Defence (the Imperial Guard, Army, Air Force and Marine)	8.8	14.5
Interior	5.7	8.8
Public Works and Communications	3.4	5.6
Justice	.9	1.2
Foreign Affairs	1.0	1.9
Press and Information	.2	.6
Civil List and Imperial Palace	2.0	3.9
Ministry of the Pen	.1	.1
Prime Minister's Office	.1	.1
Finance	2.7	1.6
Mines and State Domains		3.0
Commerce and Industry	.2	.4
Agriculture	.4	.9
Posts and Telegraphs	.4	.6
Health	1.1	2.3
Education	4.0	7.8
Economic and Technical Assistance Administration (including contributions to Ethiopian-American Joint Fund Activities)		2.0
Parliament		.7
Community Development		.5
Public Debt		1.8
HIM Hailé Sellassié I Welfare Trust		.3
Planning Office		.1
Pensions, Stores and Supplies		.1
Small amounts to National Library, Ecclesiastical Office, Auditor General's Office, War Reparations Commission, etc.		.4
TOTAL ORDINARY BUDGET EXPENDITURE	34.3	59.3
TOTAL ACTUAL BUDGET EXPENDITURE	37.8	79.1

* Total expenditure from September 1941 to July 1960 regarded as a period of 18 years' duration.

Notes

1. In 1951 (EC) extraordinary expenditure was higher than had previously been customary but because of the 'system' of 'budgetary decision', extraordinary expenditure has often amounted almost to being a second budget.

2. The author has been unable to discover whether the secret 'political purposes' votes—for example, that administered by the Emperor's Representative in Eritrea which by itself was quite large—are included in published figures under the head, 'Ministry of the Interior'.

Adapted from Budget tables published in *Economic Progress of Ethiopia*, Addis Ababa, 1955, and *Ethiopian Economic Review*, No 5, Addis Ababa, 1962.

Table 8—STUDENT ENROLMENT IN SELECTED AFRICAN COUNTRIES

	Year	Popula-tion (millions)	Primary	Secondary	Technical	Teacher Training	Higher
ETHIOPIA	1960	20	176,522	5,624	1,963	943	941
GHANA	1959	7	483,425	170,066	4,563	4,334	1,051
NIGERIA	1959	36	2,775,938	111,868	7,498	26,617	1,978
SUDAN	1961	11	334,300	66,405	2,821	980	3,039
UAR	1961	26	2,829,904	448,360	126,426	28,788	2,339

Notes

1. The Ethiopian population figure is approximate for there has been no census, and birth, death, and infant mortality rates are similarly unknown.

2. Exact inter-country comparison is not possible because of differing systems and criteria. The above figures normally exclude adult education, special schools, apprenticeship courses and correspondence schools.

Adapted from ECA *African Statistics*, Vol. I, No 2, June 1961.

Table 9—THE STRUCTURE OF EDUCATION—SOME COMPARISONS

	Ethiopia 1959	Ghana 1959	Uganda 1959	Kenya 1958	Tanganyika 1958
No of Primary school students	158,005	483,425	501,699	651,758	422,832
No of Secondary school students	8,144	178,581	41,633	20,291	15,315
% of all students to population aged 5–19 years	2.8	48.3	27.6	37.9	17.6
% of Primary students to population aged 5–14 years	3.8	66.7	52.2	52.1	24.1
% of Secondary students to population aged 15–19 years	0.5	29.4	4.4	3.9	2.1
No of teachers	5,500	15,546	19,440	15,229	9,711
Educational expenditure per inhabitant (US dollars per annum)	0.52	4.20	2.80	2.80	1.87
Percentage of illiteracy among adults	95–9	77–81	70–5	85–80	90–5
Percentage of educational funds spent on administration	37.0	14.4	4.4	4.1	6.9

Notes

1. The total population of Kenya, Tanganyika and Uganda may be compared with that of Ethiopia which is probably something over twenty millions. The population of Ghana in 1959 was something under seven millions.

2. NB. In the UNESCO statistics, a student is taken as a child attending school for a total of one to ten years and the average is much nearer one year than ten.

3. The figures above were supplied by the Ethiopian government to UNESCO but considerable uproar followed their publication. The Minister of State in charge of the Ministry of Education was appointed as ambassador and the Ministry later commented that statistics covering attendance at schools run by the Ethiopian Christian Church have been omitted. However, in private conversation Ministry officials took neither the figures supplied by the Church nor the quality of that education very seriously. Later statistics showed an increase in secondary teachers and pupils, but this was apparent rather than real, having been achieved by counting standard (grade) seven and eight as 'secondary', in accordance with UNESCO recommendations that Africa follow a six- and not an eight-year primary education schedule.

Adapted from The Educational Situation in Africa, a UNESCO document prepared for the Education Conference, Addis Ababa, May 15–25, 1961, and published previously by the author in the *Makerere Journal*, Vol 8, Kampala, 1963.

ACKNOWLEDGEMENTS

Hedley Warr, a friend, was the first who said : 'You ought to write a book.' Then many Ethiopians paid me the compliment of urging me to write about their country—and in differing and sometimes (to themselves) even dangerous ways, helped to make it possible. But I would not have left Ethiopia and begun to write without the initial encouragement of Cranford Pratt, then Principal of the University College of Dar-es-Salaam, and others, notably certain East and Central African politicians who doubtless prefer not to be named, but who believed that some book relating Ethiopia to the African revolution was necessary. I have enjoyed the continued encouragement of Sir Alexander Carr Saunders, Canon Selwyn Gummer, and a host of others.

I spent four happy and interesting years in Ethiopia and the writing of the book has taken two and a half years more. They have been rich and varied years and much incidental has happened. I owe a great debt to the many friends who have helped me to find somewhere to lay my head and temporary work, mainly in Africa, during this time. I have drawn greatly from them—one in particular—and there seems little chance of my being able to repay the way they made light of difficulties which to me seemed almost insurmountable and encouraged me to keep writing regardless of the ups and downs of life. Since the text of this work is not without certain implied and direct criticism of the government of the United States it is worth recording that in the writing of it I have received more interest, encouragement and concrete help from individual Americans than from anyone except Ethiopians themselves.

I am especially grateful to members and former members of the faculty of the University College in Salisbury, especially Professor Eric Stokes, and Alison and Desmond Graham, and to Makerere University College in Uganda for hospitality, the arranging of seminars, for helpful discussion and permission to use material previously published in their journal. In Salisbury, I was encouraged and helped by Nathan Shamuyarira, Josiah and Ruth

Chinamano, Davis Magabe, Dick Walker and others; in Nairobi
by Bill Miner, Paul Fordham, Mel McCaw, Dr and Mrs Schwartz
and others—and many more both in Africa and Britain. I have
received wonderful co-operation and help from the archivists of
newspaper offices in Nairobi, Kampala and London, from a member
of the International Commission of Jurists, from the staffs of
university libraries, from the MacMillan Library, Nairobi, the
National Archives, Salisbury, the British Museum Reading Room
and Newspaper Library and from the Royal Geographical Society.

A team of indefatigable ladies have typed my notes and
manuscript with hardly a word of complaint about the intricacies
of Ethiopian names and titles. I am especially grateful to Mrs
Guard, Mrs Walker, Mrs Pybus, Mrs Beale and to my mother.
There is no universally accepted way of spelling Ethiopian names.
I have followed the Imperial Ethiopian Institute of Mapping and
Geography as closely as possible. The maps were drawn from my
sketches by Michael Young and Trevor Allen of the Department of
Geography, University College, London.

Richard Brown, Lecturer in African History in Salisbury,
read a first draft and made valuable criticisms. Colin Legum and
Geoffrey Robinson have between them done very much more than
edit my manuscript and I am grateful to them both. Of course,
many others, nearly all Ethiopians, several with very senior positions have read and commented on parts or all of the manuscript.
Some have sat long hours discussing and translating many more
documents and statements than are used in the present volume, but
mentioning their names would serve no useful purpose. They know
how indebted I am to them. With so much help I must, nevertheless, claim responsibility for any mistakes and for the weaknesses
of the book—some of which I am very conscious of and not all of
which can be attributed to the limited distance between these covers
for so vast a subject. The interpretations of the facts and the
evaluations of the political importance of what may or may not be
facts are, of course, my own.

RICHARD GREENFIELD

London, 1965.

Bibliographical Notes

Detailed bibliographies covering several centuries of the accumulated work of students of Ethiopian history, languages and culture exist and can be consulted, for example, in the British Museum, in the Library of Congress and elsewhere. Useful *Registers of Current Research on Ethiopia and The Horn of Africa* are published by the Institute of Ethiopian Studies (Box 1176, Addis Ababa). A full bibliography would fill several volumes and this short note, which can serve only as a superficial guide, should be supplemented by others—one, for example, that is stronger in the area of linguistic studies is to be found in Edward Ullendorff, *The Ethiopians* (second edition; London and New York, 1965) a useful introduction to Ethiopian traditional patterns.

Several books and papers in Amharic and English by Ethiopian scholars such as Professor Afeworq, Negadras Gabré-Hiwot Baykedagn, Taklé Tsadik Mekuria, Ras-Betwoded Makonnen Endalkatchew and others are referred to in the chapter notes. Several other Ethiopians have kept valuable documents and memoirs which it is hoped will one day be published in Amharic and a European language. It is well to remember that there has long been a tendency in Ethiopia for historians and chroniclers to represent history in the light of the power politics appertaining at the time of their writing. Chronicles 'discovered' at Lake Ziway during the reign of Menelik II could serve as an extreme example, but the standard work on that monarch's reign by Gebré Sellassié (also variously, Gabra Selase, Guèbrè-Sellassié, Gabre Selassie, etc.), *Chronique du règne de Ménélik II* (trans), 2 vols, Paris 1930–1, is a case in point. It is quite superficial to judge this as 'dishonest'. It is merely a traditional courtesy considered due to a monarch—but the modern student needs always to bear it in mind. It has affected recent accounts—such as that of the battle of Maichew—as much as older ones and more recently has also been followed by foreign writers. Hailé Sellassié's biographer, Christine Sandford, for example, is completely uncritical of that monarch. The epilogue of S. Pétrides, *Le Héros d'Adoua Ras Makonnen* (Paris, 1963), another example, concludes of Hailé Sellassié, 'Il n'y a rien de plus haut, sinon Dieu'. Leonard Mosley, *Hailé Sellassié the Conquering Lion* (London, 1964, Englewood Cliffs, N.J., 1965), which concentrates on the period 1892–1935, is, like Gebré Sellassié, an interpretation which might thoroughly delight members of certain limited Shewan circles but, at the same time, would horrify a Tigréan or a Galla. Even so, the comment of Ethiopian and other workers, particularly in the field of agricultural economics, is rapidly becoming less circumscribed by traditional deference and a pattern of modern scholarship fast develops at Ethiopia's national university.

Ethiopian studies have also long attracted the service of scholars of many nations. The seventeenth century tradition of Ludolph has been maintained in the twentieth century by many thorough and authoritative contributions to Ethiopica, including those from Lincoln de Castro, Ignazio Guidi, Carlo Conti Rossini and Enrico Cerulli of Italy; Marcel Cohen and Jean Doresse of France; Friedrich Bieber, Enno Littmann and Eike Haberland of Germany; S. Strelcyn of Poland; Mary Rait of the Soviet Union; Hans Jacob Polotsky of Israel; Wolf Leslau, Frederick J. Simmoons and Donald Levine of the United States; J. Spencer Trimingham, G. W. B. Huntingford, I. M. Lewis and Edward Ullendorff of the United Kingdom; Richard Pankhurst, Sven Rubensen and Stephen Wright of the Ethiopian National University and many others. Their valuable papers and books are far too numerous to list individually.

The most useful journal available is the *Ethiopia Observer* (published in Addis Ababa and London). Particularly since it became a quarterly in 1961 and abandoned an occasional propagandist note it has become quite invaluable to the student of Ethiopia. *The Journal of Ethiopian Studies* (Addis Ababa) is also very sound. *Cahiers d'Etudes Africaines* (especially 5, 11, 1961), *Politique Etrangère, Présence Africaine* and *Annales d'Ethiopie* (all published in Paris) are useful. In the United States *Foreign Affairs, The Middle East Journal, Africa Today, Africa Report,* etc., should be consulted. In Italy *Rassegna di Studi Etiopici* carries many interesting papers. In London recent editions of *African Affairs* have not maintained earlier levels of interest and informed comment and there has been disappointingly little in the *Geographical Journal, Africa,* etc. However, very useful papers are to be found in the *Journal of Semitic Studies* and the *Journal of African History. The Journal of Modern African Studies* also is indispensable to the understanding of trends in modern Africa. Apart from an English translation of the important speech read by Hailé Sellassié at the founding of the Organisation of African Unity, papers on the Somali frontier dispute and some reviews, it has not at the time of writing (1964) yet turned its attention to Ethiopian affairs, but one expects much when it does.

Until recent years Ethiopian studies have been rather dominated by historians, linguists, botanists, geologists and others, but stone-age archaeologists, sociologists and political scientists are at last turning their attention to Ethiopia—Donald Levine's *Wax and Gold—Studies in Amhara Culture,* for example, is eagerly awaited.

Despite errors in the historical section, the most useful comprehensive survey available to date is certainly George A. Lipsky, *Ethiopia: Its People, Its Society, Its Culture* (New Haven, 1962). *Guida dell'Africa Orientale Italiana* (Milan, 1938) and Margery Perham, *The Government of Ethiopia* (London, 1948), though dated, are still valuable.

Several standard works are available in English.

For historical background: Jean Doresse, *Ethiopia* (trans) (London and New York, 1959); Sir E. A. Wallis Budge, *A History of Ethiopia* (2 vols, London, 1928); A. H. M. Jones and Elizabeth Monroe, *A History of Ethiopia* (Oxford and New York, 1955).

There is also a slim but stimulating volume in the Institute of Race

Relations series, Czeslaw Jesman, *The Ethiopian Paradox* (London and New York, 1963), but it is marred by many errors of fact. For economic background see Richard Pankhurst, *Introduction to the Economic History of Ethiopia from Early Times to 1800* (London and New York, 1961); Ernest W. Luther, *Ethiopia Today* (London and Stanford, Calif., 1958); and H. Huffnagel, *Agriculture in Ethiopia* (Rome, 1961).

There is as yet no work on the Ethiopian Christian Church to compare with J. Spencer Trimingham, *Islam in Ethiopia* (London and New York, 1952).

The best travel account, apart perhaps from those of early visitors such as Bruce, remains David Buxton, *Travels in Ethiopia* (London, 1957), but Thomas Pakenham, *The Mountains of Rasselas* (London, 1959) is entertaining.

The author's indebtedness to all the scholars and writers above listed will be obvious to the reader and is freely and gratefully acknowledged. A large selection of articles, papers and official statistical tables published by the United Nations, the Ethiopian government, 'Ethiopian exiles', etc., have also been consulted. So have many papers and books written in Amharic or European languages—particularly by the scholars above listed. Much of this book is the result of primary research but a short selection of books *published in English* which the author found to contain information of interest and relevance to his present task follows below.

Aaronovitch, Sam and K., *Crisis in Kenya* (London, 1947).

Abul-Haggag, Youssef, *A Contribution to the Physiography of Northern Ethiopia* (London and New York, 1961).

Allen, William E. D., *Guerrilla War in Abyssinia* (London and New York, 1943).

Alvares, Francesco, *Narrative of the Portuguese Embassy to Abyssinia, 1520–1527* (London, 1881).

Anwar El Sadat, *Revolt on the Nile* (London, 1957).

Asfa Yilma, Princess, *Hailé Sellassié, Emperor of Ethiopia* (London, 1936).

Atnafu Makonnen, *Ethiopia Today* (Tokyo, 1960).

Badoglio, Pietro, *The War in Abyssinia* (London and New York, 1937); *Italy in the Second World War* (London, 1948).

Baker, Samuel, *The Nile Tributaries of Abyssinia* (London, 1867).

Baratti, Giacomo, *The Late Travels of S. Giacomo Baratti into the remote Countries of the Abissins . . .* (London, 1670).

Bartleet, Eustace J., *In the Land of Sheba* (Birmingham, 1934).

Baum, James E., *Savage Abyssinia* (New York, 1927; London, 1928).

Beckingham, C. F. and Huntingford, G. W. B., *Prester John of the Indies* (London and New York, 1961); *Some Records of Ethiopia, 1593–1646* (London and New York, 1954).

Beke, Charles T., *The British Captives in Abyssinia* (London, 1865).

Bent, James T., *The Sacred City of the Ethiopians* (London, 1893).

Berkeley, George F., *The Campaign of Adowa and the Rise of Menelik* (London, 1902).

Bidder, Irmgard, *Lalibela* (London, 1958).

Birkby, Carel, *It's a Long Way to Addis* (Cape Town, 1942).

Blanc, Sir Henry J., *A Narrative of Captivity in Abyssinia* (London, 1868).

Blundell, Herbert J. Weld, *The Royal Chronicles of Abyssinia, 1769–1840* (Cambridge, 1922).

Bono, Emilio de, *Anno XIIII. The conquest of an empire* (London, 1937).
Boyes, J., *My Abyssinian Journey* (Nairobi, 1941).
Bruce, James, *T.avels to Discover the Sources of the Nile* (Edinburgh, 1790).
Buchholzer, John, *The Land of Burnt Faces* (London, 1955; New York, 1956); *The Horn of Africa* (London, 1959).
Budge, Sir E. A. Wallis, *The Book of the Saints of the Ethiopian Church* (4 vols), (Cambridge, 1928).
Burton, Sir Richard F., *First Steps in East Africa* (London, 1856).
Busk, Douglas, *The Fountain of the Sun* (London and Chester Springs, Pa., 1957).
Butler, J. R. M. (ed.) *History of the Second World War,* vol 2 (London, 1949).
Carter, Boake, *Black Shirts, Black Skins* (London, 1935).
Castanhoso, Miguel de, *The Portuguese Expedition to Abyssinia* (London, 1902).
Cerulli, Enrico, *Folk-Literature of the Galla of Southern Abyssinia* (Harvard African Series) (Cambridge, Mass., 1922).
Cerulli, Ernesta, *Peoples of South-West Ethiopia and Its Borderland* (London, 1956).
Cheeseman, Robert E., *Lake Tana and the Blue Nile* (London, 1936).
Ciano, Galeazzo, *Ciano's Diaries, 1939–43* (London, 1947–52).
Collins, Douglas, *A Tear for Somalia* (London, 1960).
Comyn-Platt, Sir Thomas, *The Abyssinian Storm* (London, 1935).
Cooke, Anthony C., *Routes in Abyssinia* (London, 1867).
Coon, Carleton S., *Measuring Ethiopia and Flight into Arabia* (Boston, 1935; London, 1936).
Cotton, Percy H. G. P., *A Sporting Trip Through Abyssinia* (London, 1902).
Coupland, Sir Reginald, *East Africa and Its Invaders* (London, 1956).
Cox, Richard, *Pan-Africanism in Practice* (London, 1964).
Darley, Henry, *Slaves and Ivory* (London, 1926).
Davidson, Basil, *The Lost Cities of Africa* (Boston, 1959); *Old Africa Rediscovered* (London, 1960).
Davis, Russell and Ashabranner, Brent (eds.), *The Lion's Whiskers* (Boston and London, 1959).
De Cosson, Emilius, *The Cradle of the Blue Nile* (London, 1877).
De Prorok, Brym Khun, Count, *Dead Men Do Tell Tales* (New York, 1942; London, 1943).
Drysdale, John J., *The Somali Dispute* (London and New York, 1964).
Dufton, Henry, *Narrative of a Journey through Abyssinia in 1862–63* (London, **1867**).
Dunckley, Fan. C., *Eight Years in Abyssinia* (London, 1935).
Durand, Mortimer, *Crazy Campaign* (London, 1936).
Dutton, Eric A. T., *Lillibullero or the Golden Road* (Zanzibar, 1944).
Fage, J. D., *An Atlas of African History* (London and New York, 1958).
Fallers, Margaret C., *The Eastern Lacustrine Bantu* (London, 1960).
Farago, Ladislas, *Abyssinia on the Eve* (London and New York, 1935); *Abyssinia Stop Press* (London, 1936).
Ferguson, H. A. L., *Into the Blue* (London, 1955).
Finkelstein, Lawrence L., *Somaliland under Italian Administration* (New York, 1955).
Forbes, J. Rosita, *From Red Sea to Blue Nile* (London, 1927).

Foster, W., *The Red Sea at the close of the Seventeenth Century* (London, 1948).
Gandar, Kenneth Dower, *Askaris at War in Abyssinia* (Nairobi, 1942); *Abyssinian Patchwork: An Anthology* (London, 1949).
Gilmour, Thomas L., *Abyssinia, The Ethiopian Railway and the Powers* (London, 1906).
Gleichen, Lord Edward, *With the Mission to Menelik* (London, 1898).
Gobat, Samuel, *Journal of Three Years Residence in Abyssinia* (London, 1834; New York, 1850).
Goodspeed, D. J., *The Conspirators: A Study of the Coup d'Etat* (London and New York, 1961).
Grabham, George W., and Black, R. P., *Report of the Mission to Lake Tana* (Cairo, 1925).
Griaule, Marcel, *Abyssinian Journey* (London, 1935); *Burners of Men: Modern Ethiopia* (Philadelphia and London, 1935).
Grühl, Max, *The Citadel of Ethiopia* (London, 1932).
Gunther, John, *Inside Africa* (New York and London, 1955).
Hallé, Clifford, *To Menelik in a Motor Car* (London, 1913).
Hamilton, Edward, *The War in Abyssinia* (London, 1937).
Harmsworth, Geoffrey, *Abyssinian Adventure* (London, 1935).
Harris, Sir William Cornwallis, *The Highlands of Æthiopia* (London, 1844).
Hartlmaier, Paul, *Golden Lion: A Journey through Ethiopia* (London, 1956).
Hayes, Arthur J., *The Source of the Blue Nile* (London, 1905).
Henderson, Kenneth (ed.), *The Making of the Modern Sudan: The Life and Letters of Sir Douglas Newbold* (London, 1953).
Henty, George A., *The March to Magdala* (London, 1868).
Hodson, Arthur Wienholt, *Seven Years in Southern Abyssinia* (London, 1927); *Where Lions Reign* (London, 1929).
Holland, Trevenen J., and Hozier, Henry M., *Record of the Expedition to Abyssinia* (London, 1820).
Hollis, Christopher, *Italy in Africa* (London, 1941).
Holt, P. M., *The Mahdist State in the Sudan, 1881–98* (Oxford and New York, 1958); *A Modern History of the Sudan* (London and New York, 1961).
Howard, William E. H., *Public Administration in Ethiopia* (Groningen, 1956).
Huntingford, G. W. B., *The Galla of Ethiopia* (London, 1955).
Hyatt, Harry M., *The Church of Abyssinia* (London, 1928).
Isaac, Charles A., *Modern Ethiopia* (Addis Ababa, 1956).
Isenberg, Karl W. and Krapf, Johann L., *Journals* (London, 1843).
Jacoby, Catherine Murray, *On Special Mission to Abyssinia* (New York and London, 1933).
Jesman, Czeslaw, *The Russians in Ethiopia* (London, 1958).
Johnston, Charles, *Travels in Southern Abyssinia* (2 vols), (London, 1844).
Kebede Mikael, *Ethiopia and Western Civilisation* (Addis Ababa, 1949).
Kenyatta, Jomo, *Facing Mount Kenya* (London, 1938; New York, 1962).
Kenyatta, Jomo, *My People of Kikuyu* (London, 1942); *Kenya, The Land of Conflict* (London, 1945).
Kimble, George H. T., *Tropical Africa* (2 vols), (New York, 1960).
King's African Rifles—War Journal of the Fifth (Kenyan) Battalion (Nairobi, 1942).

Langer, William L., *The Diplomacy of Imperialism* (New York, 1951).

Legum, Colin, *Pan-Africanism* (Revised edition, London and New York, 1965).

Leslau, Wolf (ed.), *Falasha Anthology* (New Haven, 1951).

Lewis, I. M., *Peoples of the Horn of Africa* (London, 1955); *Pastoral Democracy* (London and New York, 1961). *The Modern History of Somaliland* (London and New York, 1965).

Lobo, Jerenymo (Jerome), *A Voyage to Abyssinia* (London, 1735).

Longrigg, Stephen H., *A Short History of Eritrea* (Oxford, 1955).

Ludolphus (Hiob Ludolf), *A New History of Ethiopia* (J. P.'s trans), (London, 1684).

MacCreagh, Gordon, *The Last of Free Africa* (New York and London, 1935).

Macdonald, J. F. *Abyssinian Adventure* (London, 1957).

MacFie, John W. S., *An Ethiopian Diary* (London, 1936).

Makin, William J., *War Over Abyssinia* (London, 1935).

Marein, Nathan, *The Ethiopian Empire—Federation and Laws* (Rotterdam, 1954).

Markham, Sir Clements R., *A History of the Abyssinian Expedition* (London, 1869).

Martelli, George, *Italy Against the World* (London, 1937).

Mathew, David, *Ethiopia: The Study of a Polity 1540–1935* (London, 1947).

Maydon, H. C., *Simien: Its Heights and Abysses* (London, 1925).

McKay, Vernon, *Africa in World Politics* (New York, 1963).

Mitchell, L. H., *Report on the Seizure by the Abyssinians* (of an Egyptian Army scientific expedition) (Cairo, 1878).

Mohr, Paul, *Geology of Ethiopia* (Addis Ababa, 1963).

Moorehead, Alan, *The Blue Nile* (New York, 1961; London, 1962).

Murdock, George P., *Africa: Its People and their Culture History* (New York, 1959).

Nesbit, Lewis M., *Desert and Forest* (London, 1934); *Hell-Hole of Creation* (New York, 1935).

Newman, E. W. Polson, *Ethiopian Realities* (London, 1936); *The New Abyssinia* (London, 1938).

Norden, Hermann, *Africa's Last Empire* (London, 1930).

O'Leary, De Lacy, *The Ethiopian Church* (London, 1936).

Oliver, Roland, and Fage, J. D., *A Short History of Africa* (Harmondsworth, 1962; New York, 1963); and Mathew, Gervase (eds.) *The History of East Africa*, vol 1 (Oxford and New York, 1963).

Padmore, George, *Africa: Britain's Third Empire* (London, 1949); *Pan-Africanism or Communism?* (London and New York, 1956).

Pankhurst, E. Sylvia, *The Ethiopian People* (London, 1946); *Education in Ethiopia* (London, 1946); *Eritrea on the Eve* (London, 1952); *Ethiopia: A Cultural History* (London, 1955); *Ex-Italian Somaliland* London, 1951); and Pankhurst, Richard, *Ethiopia and Eritrea* (London, 1953).

Pankhurst, Richard, *Kenya: The History of Two Nations* (London, 1954).

Parkyns, Mansfield, *Life in Abyssinia* (2 vols) (London, 1853; New York, 1854).

Pearce, Francis B., *Rambles in Lion Land* (London, 1898).

Pearce, Nathaniel, *Life and Adventures in Abyssinia, 1810–19* (2 vols) (London, 1831).

Pirajno, Alberto D. di, *A Cure for Serpents* (London and New York, 1955); *A Grave for a Dolphin* (London, 1956).
Playne, Beatrice, *St. George for Ethiopia* (London, 1954).
Plowden, Walter C., *Travels in Abyssinia and the Galla Country* (London, 1868).
Poncet, Charles J., *A Voyage to Æthiopia* (trans) (London, 1709).
Portal, Sir Gerald H., *My Mission to Abyssinia* (London, 1892).
Potter, Pitman B., *The Wal-Wal Arbitration* (Washington, 1938).
Quaranta, Ferdinando, *Ethiopia: An Empire in the Making* (London, 1939).
Rassam, Hormuzd, *Narrative of the British Mission to Theodore* (London, 1869).
Reusch, Richard, *History of East Africa* (Stuttgart, 1954; New York, 1961).
Rey, Sir Charles F., *Unconquered Abyssinia* (London, 1923); *In the Country of the Blue Nile* (London, 1927); *The Romance of the Portuguese in Abyssinia* (London, 1929); *The Real Abyssinia* (London and Philadelphia, 1935).
Rittlinger, Herbert, *Ethiopian Adventure* (London, 1959).
Robinson, Henry Rowan, *England, Italy and Abyssinia* (London, 1938).
Rennel of Rodd, Lord, *British Military Administration of Occupied Territories in Africa during the years 1941–1947* (London, 1948).
Rosenthal, Eric, *The Fall of Italian East Africa* (London and New York, 1941).
Ross, M., *First Third (King's African Rifles)* (Nairobi, 1944).
Russel, Beatrix, *Living in State* (London, 1961).
Russell, Michael, *Nubia and Abyssinia* (Edinburgh, 1833).
Salt, Henry, *A Voyage to Abyssinia* (London, 1814).
Salvemini, Gaetano, *Prelude to World War II* (London and New York, 1953).
Sandford, Christine, *Ethiopia under Hailé Sellassié* (London, 1946); *The Lion of Judah Hath Prevailed* (London and New York, 1955).
Schaefer, Ludwig F. (ed.), *The Ethiopian Crisis: Touchstone of Appeasement?* (Boston, 1961).
Schoff, Wilfred H. (ed. and tr.), *The Periplus of the Erythraean Sea* (London, 1912).
Segal, Ronald (ed.), *Political Africa* (London and New York, 1961).
Simoons, Frederick J., *Northwest Ethiopia: People and Economy* (Madison, Wisconsin, 1960).
Skinner, Robert P., *Abyssinia of Today* (London and New York, 1906).
Skordiles, Kimon, *Kagnew—The Story of the Ethiopian Fighters in Korea* (Tokyo, 1954).
Smith, Arthur Donaldson, *Through Unknown African Countries* (London and New York, 1897).
Smith, Frederick Harrison, *Through Abyssinia* (London, 1890).
Somali Government, *The Somali Peninsula* (London, 1962).
Starkie, Enid, *Arthur Rimbaud in Abyssinia* (Oxford, 1937).
Stationery Office, His Majesty's, *The Abyssinian Campaign* (London, 1942).
Steer, George L., *Caesar in Abyssinia* (London, 1936); *Sealed and Delivered* (London, 1942).
Stern, Henry A., *Wanderings among the Falasha* (London, 1862); *The Captive Missionary* (London and New York, 1868).

Stigand, Chauncy H., *To Abyssinia through Unknown Land* (London, 1910).

Strandes, Justus, *The Portuguese Period in East Africa* (trans) (Nairobi, 1961).

Swayne, Harald G. C., *Seventeen Trips through Somaliland and a Visit to Abyssinia* (London, 1895).

Sykes, Christopher, *Orde Wingate* (London and Cleveland, 1959).

Talbot, David A., *Contemporary Ethiopia* (New York, 1952); *Hailé Sellassié I: Silver Jubilee* (The Hague, 1955).

Taylor, A. J. P., *The Origins of the Second World War* (London, 1961; New York, 1962).

Thomas, Sir Henry F., and Zuzarte Cortesao, A. F., *The Discovery of Abyssinia by the Portuguese in 1520* (trans) (London, 1938).

Touval, Saadia, *Somali Nationalism* (Cambridge, Mass., 1963).

Trevaskis, G. K. N., *Eritrea: A Colony in Transition* (London and New York, 1960).

Vatikiotis, P. J., *The Egyptian Army in Politics* (Bloomington, Indiana, 1961).

Virgin, Eric, *The Abyssinia I Knew* (London, 1936).

Vivian, Herbert, *Abyssinia; Through the Lion Land . . .* (London, 1901).

Wakefield, T., *Footprints in Eastern Africa* (London, 1866).

Waldmeier, Theophilus, *Autobiography* (London, 1886).

Walker, C. H., *The Abyssinian at Home* (London, 1933).

Waugh, Evelyn, *Waugh in Abyssinia* (London, 1936).

Wellby, Montagu S., *Twixt Sirdar and Menelik* (London, 1901).

Wilkins, Henry S. C., *Reconnoitering in Abyssinia* (London, 1870).

Winstanley, William, *A Visit to Abyssinia* (London, 1881).

Woolf, Leonard, *Empire and Commerce in Africa* (London, 1920); *The League and Abyssinia* (London, 1936).

Work, Ernest, *Ethiopia—A Pawn in European Diplomacy* (London and New Concord, Ohio, 1935).

Wyche, Sir Peter, *A Short Relation of the River Nile* (London, 1673).

Wylde, Augustus B., *Modern Abyssinia* (London, 1901).

Zagiella, Ignacy, *Abyssinia According to the Account of a Polish Traveller in 1864* (Warsaw, 1935).

Zartman, I. William, *Government and Politics in Northern Africa* (New York, 1963; London, 1964).

Maps

The scale of the maps on pages 46 and 114 does not permit the full representation of the peoples and kingdoms of Southern Ethiopia Those particularly interested are further referred to three magnificent German volumes by Ad E. Jensen, Eike Haberland, H. Straube and others.

1. *Altvölker Süd-Äthiopiens*
2. *Galla Süd-Äthiopiens.*
3. *Westkuschitische Völker Süd-Äthiopiens.*
   (Frankfurt am Main, 1959-63).
   Further volumes are in preparation.

NOTES AND REFERENCES

(EC = Ethiopian Calendar)

I. ETHIOPIAN ROOTS

Chapter 1   Earliest Times
1 A. Smith, *Through Unknown African Countries*, New York, 1897
2 See G. Huntingford's chapter in *The History of East Africa*, ed. R Oliver and G. Matthew, Vol. I, Oxford, 1963
3 G. Murdock, *Africa, its People and their Culture History*, New York, 1959
4 See the author's article, 'Afro-Ethiopia', *Makerere Journal*, Vol. VIII, Kampala, 1963
5 See F. Anfray, 'Archaeological Discoveries in Ethiopia', *Illustrated London News*, March 25, 1961, and elsewhere
6 J. Doresse, *Ethiopia* (trans.), London, 1959
7 R. Greenfield, 'Geography Notes', *Ethiopia Observer*, Vol. V, No 3, London, 1961
8 L. Kirwan, in a personal communication to the author, but see his 'Nubia—an African Frontier Zone', *Advancement of Science,* Vol. XIX, No 18, London, 1962
9 W. Vycichl, 'Le titre de Roi des Rois—Etudes historiques et comparatives sur le monarchie en Ethiopie', in *Annales d'Ethiopie*, Paris, 1957
10 E. Littmann, *Deutsche Aksum Expedition*, Berlin, 1913

Chapter 2   Christianity and Myth
1 A. H. M. Jones and E. Monroe, *A History of Ethiopia*, Oxford, 1955
2 S. Pankhurst, *Ethiopia, a Cultural History*, London, 1955
3 *Ethiopia—Illuminated Manuscripts*, UNESCO, New York, 1961
4 For a full discussion see Bishop T. Poladian, 'The Doctrinal position of the Monophysite churches', *Ethiopia Observer*, Vol. VII, No 3, London, 1964
5 See V. Matveyev, 'Northern Boundaries of the Eastern Bantu', *Proceedings of the 25th Orientalist Congress*, Moscow, 1960
6 See *The Somali Peninsula,* Somali Government Publication, London, 1962
7 See A. Curle, 'The Ruined Towns of Somaliland', *Antiquity*, No 43, 1937
8 E. Ullendorff, *The Ethiopians*, Oxford, 2nd ed., 1965.
9 Published in C. F. Rey, *The Real Abyssinia*, London, 1935
10 D. Buxton, *Travels in Ethiopia*, London, 1949
11 I. Bidder, *Lalibela*, London, 1958

12 Ludolphus, *A New History of Ethiopia*, 2nd ed., Germany, 1684, quoted by W. Cornwallis Harris in *The Highlands of Æthiopia*, London, 1844. Harris often quotes Ludolphus without acknowledgement
13 Remarks of Brig.-gen. Mengistu Neway, Wednesday, December 14, 1960
14 J. Doresse, op. cit.

Chapter 3   Diversity and Struggle
1 For a later translation see W. C. Harris, op. cit.
2 See 'The Rebellion Trials in Ethiopia', *Bulletin of the International Commission of Jurists*, No 12, November, 1961
3 See the writings of Taklé Tsadik Makuria, Consul-General in Jerusalem (in 1964)
4 E. Haberland, *Galla Süd-Äthiopiens*, Vol. II, Stuttgart, 1963
5 Aleka Taye, *A Brief History of Ethiopia*, Addis Ababa, 1914 EC
6 D. Buxton, 'The Shewan Plateau and its People', *Geographical Journal*, Vol. CXIV, Nos 4–6, December 6, 1949
7 R. Oliver, *The Dawn of African History*, London, 1959

II.   ETHIOPIA EMERGENT

Chapter 4   Out of Chaos
1 J. Bruce, *Travels to Discover the Source of the Nile*, London, 1790
2 C. J. Poncet, *A Voyage to Æthiopia* (trans.), London, 1709.
3 C. W. Harris, op. cit.
4 Arnauld d'Abbadie, *Douze Ans dans la Haute Ethiopie*, Paris, 1868
5 Ras-Betwoded Makonnen Endalkatchew, *Taitu Bitull*, Addis Ababa, 1950 (EC). A short historical novel in Amharic
6 A. Moorehead, *The Blue Nile*, London, 1962. For the character of Tsar Ivan, see V. Kluchevsky, *History of Russia*, Vol. II, London and New York, 1960, etc., G. F. H. Berkeley, in the January 1930 issue of *The Nineteenth Century and After*, also compares the two Emperors
7 M. Fallers, *The Eastern Lacustrine Bantu*, London, 1960
8 R. Pankhurst, 'Firearms in Ethiopian History', *Ethiopia Observer*, Vol. VI, No 2, 1962
9 Sir Samuel White Baker, *The Nile Tributaries of Abyssinia*, London, 1867

Chapter 5   Tigré versus Shewa
1 But see E. Work, *Ethiopia, a Pawn in European Diplomacy*, New York, 1935, and W. Langer, *The Diplomacy of Imperialism, 1890–1902*, New York, 1951
2 A. Oliver and J. Fage, *A Short History of Africa*, London, 1962
3 R. Pankhurst, 'Firearms in Ethiopian History', op. cit.

Chapter 6   Rebuilding the Empire
1 See H. Marcus, 'Ethio-British Negotiations concerning the Western Border with Sudan', *Journal of African History*, Vol. IV, No 1, 1963, and G. Sanderson, 'The Foreign Policy of the Negus Menelik, 1896–8', *Journal of African History*, Vol. V, No 1, 1964. A useful paper on this issue is S. Rubenson, 'Some Aspects of the Survival of Ethiopian

Independence in the period of the Scramble for Africa', *Proceedings Leverhulme History Conference, September, 1960*, Salisbury, 1962

2 See the *Ethiopia Observer*, special issue on Harar, Vol. II, No 2, March 1958

3 Gebré Sellassié (Gabra Selase), *Chronique du règne de Ménélik II* (trans.), Paris, 1930–2

4 M. Gruhl, *Abyssinia at Bay* (trans.), London, 1935

5 C. Jesman, *The Ethiopian Paradox*, London, 1963

6 This visitor was M. Wellby. See his *'Twixt Sidar and Menelik*, London, 1901—but for a more complete discussion of the conditions in the conquered provinces see Margery Perham, *The Government of Ethiopia*, Oxford, 1948

7 See a translation of one of their records, P. Wyche, *A Short Relation of the River Nile*, London, 1673, etc.

8 R. Skinner, *Abyssinia of Today*, New York, 1906

9 See, for example, 'Sellassié's Message to the Negro', *Ebony*, March 1964 (the first number of the African edition)

10 All the Somali quotations above are taken from *The Somali Peninsula—a New Light on Imperial Motives*, Somali Government Information Services, London, 1962

11 G. Savard, 'The Peoples of Ethiopia', *Ethiopia Observer*, Vol. V, No 3, 1961

Chapter 7   The Scramble Halted

1 S. Rubenson, 'The Protectorate Paragraph of the Wichele Treaty', *Journal of African History*, Vol. V, No 2, London, 1964. Mr Rubenson, like the author, does not seek to be pedantic in his translation of Amharic names. Uccialli, the Italian rendering of Wuchali (Wichale), is often followed by European historians

2 S. P. Petrides, *Le Herós d'Adowa—Ras Makonnen—Prince d'Ethiopie*, Paris, 1963

3 G. Sanderson, 'Contributions from African Sources to the Military and Diplomatic History of European Competition in the upper valley of the Nile', *Proceedings of the Leverhulme History Conference, 1960*, Salisbury, 1962

4 J. T. Bent, *The Sacred City of the Ethiopians*, London, 1893

5 S. Rubenson, 'Some Aspects of the Survival of Ethiopian Independence . . .', op. cit.

6 G. F. H. Berkeley, *The Campaign of Adowa and the Rise of Menelik*, London, 1902

7 G. Gamerra, *Fra Gli Ascari*, Rome, 1899

8 Margery Perham, op. cit.

9 R. Pankhurst, 'The Franco-Ethiopian Railway and its History', *Ethiopia Observer*, Vol. VI, No 4, 1963

III.   TAFARI MAKONNEN

Chapter 8   The Shewan Coup d'Etat

1 Dr Merab, *Impressions d'Ethiopie*, Paris, 1921–9. The detail of Taitu's family and court party is drawn directly from this work

2 See Taklé Tsadik Mekuria, *Behaviour of Human Beings and Methods of Living Together* (Amharic), Addis Ababa, 1941 (EC)

3 See *Documents relatifs au coup d'état a Addis Ababa du 27 September 1916*, Dira Dawa, 1917
4 See B. de Prorok, *Dead Men Do Tell Tales*, London, 1943—and others
5 L. Mosley, *Hailé Sellassié*, London, 1964
6 See de Montfried, *Le Masque d'or ou le dernier Negus*, Paris, 1936

Chapter 9   Ras Tafari's Path to Power
1 See de Montfried, op. cit., and pamphlets in Addis Ababa and Cairo, 1961–2
2 J. Baum, *Savage Abyssinia*, London, 1928
3 A. Hodson, *Seven Years in Abyssinia*, London, 1927
4 C. F. Rey, *Unconquered Abyssinia*, London, 1923
5 See de Montfried, op. cit., but G. Steer, *Caesar in Abyssinia*, London, 1935, denies this
6 R. Pankhurst, 'Misoneism and Innovation in Ethiopian History', *Ethiopia Observer*, Vol. VII, No 4, 1964
7 R. Forbes, *From Red Sea to Blue Nile*, London, 1927
8 C. Jacoby, *On Special Mission to Abyssinia*, London, 1933
9 E. Dutton in *Lillibullero or the Golden Road*, Zanzibar, 1944
10 E. Dutton, op. cit.
11 Christine Sandford, *The Lion of Judah Hath Prevailed*, London, 1955
12 E. Dutton, op. cit.
13 F. Dunckley, *Eight Years in Abyssinia*, London, 1935
14 General E. Virgin, *The Abyssinia I knew* (trans.), London, 1936

Chapter 10   A Radical Paternalism
1 Dr Seyoum Gebré Egziabher in the *Journal of the Society of Public Administration*, Hailé Sellassié I University, Vol. I, Addis Ababa, 1962
2 L. Farago, *Abyssinia on the Eve*, London, 1935
3 General E. Virgin, op. cit.
4 G. Steer, op. cit.
5 *Popolo d'Italia*, Rome, 1931. As quoted in D. Talbot, *Hailé Sellassié I Silver Jubilee*, The Hague, 1955
6 R. Forbes, op. cit.
7 de Montfried, op. cit.
8 D. Buxton, op. cit.
9 de Prorok, op. cit.
10 L. Mosley, op. cit.

IV.   WAR WITH ITALY

Chapter 11   Hailé Sellassié—Conscience of the World
1 For a useful short bibliography and a good summary of the attitudes and, where relevant, the actions of the nations of the world see L. Schaefer, *The Ethiopian Crisis—Touchstone or Appeasement?*, Boston, 1961. It does not include Ethiopian opinion so reference should also be made to Emmanuel Abraham, 'The Case for Ethiopia', *Journal of the Royal Africa Society*, Vol. XXXIV, No 137, London, October 1935, and to the writings of Sylvia Pankhurst and the speeches of Hailé Sellassié
2 J. Baldwin, *The Fire Next Time*, New York, 1963
3 A. Eden (The Earl of Avon), *Facing the Dictators*, London, 1962. The

author is indebted to this work for much of the detail in this chapter.
4 Marshal Graziani, *Il fronte sud*, Milan, 1938
5 P. de Bono, *Anno XIIII—The Conquest of an Empire*, Rome, 1937
6 M. Durand, *Crazy Campaign*, London, 1936
7 C. Birkby, *It's a Long Way to Addis*, Cape Town, 1942
8 L. Farago, op. cit.
9 K. Dower, *Abyssinian Patchwork*, London, 1949. The author mistakes the officer's rank, *Shaleka*, for his name. His Amharic remarks were translated at the time by the consul at Djibouti, Andargatchew Messai.

Chapter 12   Defeat and Departure
1 P. Badoglio, *The War in Abyssinia* (trans.), London, 1937
2 M. Durand, op. cit.
3 The quotations from Colonel Konovaloff's diary which appear in this chapter are taken from G. Steer, *Caesar in Abyssinia*, op. cit.
4 Reproduced by S. Pankhurst in the *Ethiopia Observer*, Vol. III, No 11, December 1959
5 G. Steer, op. cit. The author is indebted to this book for many details in this chapter

Chapter 13   The Patriots
1 This chapter is expanded from an article 'Remembering the Struggle' which the author published in the *Makerere Journal*, Vol. IX, 1964. But see also files of the *New Times and Ethiopia News* for these years which contain the current reports from Djibouti
2 G. Steer, op. cit.
3 P. Badoglio, op. cit.
4 Quoted in E. Rosenthal, *The Fall of Italian East Africa*, London, 1941
5 S. Pankhurst, 'The Ethiopian Patriots as Seen at the Time', *Ethiopia Observer*, Vol. III, Nos 10–12 and Vol. IV, No 1, London, 1959–60
6 Tedessa Metcha, *The Black Lion* (Amharic), Asmara, 1943 (EC). Some of the following detail (supplemented by conversations with survivors) and, in particular, the story of the capture of Ras Imru, is drawn from this work. Other Amharic sources for comment on the Patriot struggle include Taklé Tsadik Mekuria, *History of Ethiopia from Tewodros to Hailé Sellassié*, Addis Ababa, 1946; *Silver Jubilee*—a publication of the Ghenet Military Academy, Addis Ababa, 1952; and Asress Eyeniso, *The House of Aksum*, Addis Ababa, 1951. (The title and part of this work is in Ge'ez.) All the above dates are EC
7 R. Forbes, op. cit.
8 L. Farago, op. cit.
9 Some accounts of the three Patriot sons of Leul-Ras Kassa—Dejazmatch Wondwossen, Dejazmatch Aberra and Dejazmatch Asfa Wossen can be found in Demissé Tolla of Salalé, *Journey from Time to Time—Memories of the Five Years of Patriot Struggle* (Amharic), Addis Ababa, 1947 (EC)
10 J. T. Bent in *Fortnightly Review*, September, 1896 as quoted in A. Smith's *Through Unknown African Countries*, New York, 1897
11 A somewhat garbled version of this incident is included by P. Hartlmaier in his *Golden Lion* (trans.), London, 1956, but see rather *Ethiopia Observer*, Vol. III, No 9, October 1959

12 Taezazu Hailé, *Hailé Mariam Mammo* (Amharic), Addis Ababa, 1947
13 K. Dower, *Abyssinian Patchwork*, London, 1949

Chapter 14   Victory and Restoration
1 E. Rosenthal, *The Fall of Italian East Africa*, London, 1941—a
  quotation from a captured conference report
2 *The Abyssinian Campaigns*, HM Stationery Office, London, 1942 (out
  of print and stocks destroyed in the blitz)
3 Christine Sandford, *Ethiopia under Hailé Selassié*, London, 1945, and
  The Lion of Judah hath Prevailed, op. cit.
4 A. Pirajno, *A Cure for Serpents* (trans.), London, 1955
5 This correspondence is reproduced in Appendices in G. Steer,
  Sealed and Delivered, London, 1942
6 *The Making of the Modern Sudan—The letters of Sir Douglas Newbold*, London, 1962
7 Sir P. Mitchell, *African Afterthoughts*, London, 1954
8 All these communications are published in the appendices to G. Steer,
  op. cit.
9 Quoted by D. Talbot, *Hailé Sellassié I Silver Jubilee*, The Hague,
  1955

V.   REVOLUTION

Chapter 15   Two Decades of Intrigue
1 Lord Rennell of Rodd, *British Military Administration of Occupied
  Territories in Africa*, London, 1948
2 Lord Rennell of Rodd, op. cit.
3 Sir Philip Mitchell, *African Afterthoughts*, London, 1954
4 This may be confirmed from Sir Douglas Newbold's letters and Lord
  Rennell of Rodd's work, both cited
5 S. Longrigg, *A Short History of Eritrea*, Oxford, 1945
6 According to Ethiopian Sources. See S. Pankhurst, *Ethiopia and
  Eritrea 1941–52*, London, 1953
7 C. Jaener, 'The Somali Problem', *African Affairs*, April 1957
8 D. Collins, *A Tear for Somalia*, London, 1960
9 I. Lewis, 'The Somali Conquest of the Horn of Africa', *Journal of
  African History*, Vol. 1, No 2, 1960
10 See S. Touval, *Somali Nationalism*, Harvard, 1963 and J. Drysdale,
   The Somali Dispute, London, 1964
11 See *The Somali Peninsula*, Government of the Somali Republic,
   London, 1962, and *The Somali Republic and African Unity*, (Former)
   Consulate General of the Somali Republic, Nairobi, 1962. Also the
   writings of I. M. Lewis, in particular *A Pastoral Democracy*, London,
   1961 (which to some extent supercedes the earlier *Peoples of the
   Horn of Africa*, London, 1955); *The Modern History of Somaliland*,
   London, 1965; 'Pan-Africanism and Pan-Somaliism', *Journal of
   Modern African Studies*, Vol 1, No 2, June 1963, and 'The Problem
   of the Northern Frontier District of Kenya', *Race*, Vol V, No 1,
   July 1963
12 Mesfin Woldé Mariam, 'The Ethio-Somalia Boundary Dispute',
   Journal of Modern African Studies, Vol 2, No 2, London, 1964, and
   the same writer's Amharic articles in *Addis Zemen* and elsewhere.
   The student seeking to understand the Ethiopian position might con-

sult a file of the *Ethiopia Observer*; the works of S. and R. Pankhurst especially *Ex Italian Somaliland*, London, 1950; *Ethio-Somalia Relations*, Imperial Ministry of Information, Addis Ababa, 1962 and the speech of Prime Minister Aklilu Habtewold at the African Summit Meeting, 1963 in *Ethiopia Observer*, Vol. VII, No 1, 1963

13 Machiavelli, *The Prince*, Florence, 1532 (trans.)
14 D. Levine, 'Hailé Sellassié's Ethiopia—Myth or Reality', *Africa Today*, May 1961
15 L. Farago, *Abyssinia on the Eve*, London, 1935
16 G. Trevaskis, *Eritrea—a Colony in Transition, 1941–52*, London, 1960
17 S. Longrigg, op. cit. and G. Trevaskis, op. cit. It is fortunate that Longrigg, Trevaskis and Lord Rennell of Rodd should have written books on Eritrea. The last chief administrator published a short paper, see Sir Duncan Cumming, 'The Disposal of Eritrea', *African Affairs*, Vol VII, No 1, 1953
18 *Time*, October 13, 1952
19 *Ethiopian Herald*, May 24, 1960
20 G. Krzeczunowicz, 'The Régime of Assembly in Ethiopia', *Journal of Ethiopian Studies*, Vol. I, No 1, Addis Ababa, 1963
21 Press statement by the chairman of publicity of the National Board of Registration. See 'First Ethiopian General Election', *Ethiopia Observer*, Vol. I, No 7, London, 1957
22 G. Lipsky, *Ethiopia, its people, its society, its culture*, New York, 1962

Chapter 16   Three Thousand Years
1 G. Afevork (Afeworq Gabré Yesus), *Guide du Voyageur en Abyssinie*, Rome, 1908
2 L. Farago, op. cit.
3 E. Waugh, *Waugh in Abyssinia*, London, 1936
4 R. Pankhurst, 'The Foundations of Education, Printing, Newspapers, Book production, Libraries and Literacy in Ethiopia', *Ethiopia Observer*, Vol. VI, No 3, 1962
5 L. Farago, op. cit.
6 *United Nations Economic Survey of Africa since 1950*, New York, 1959
7 D. Levine, 'On the Conceptions of Time and Space in the Amhara World View', Accademia Nazionale di Lincei, *Atti del Convegno Internazionale di Studi Etiopici*, Rome, 1960
8 E. Luther, *Ethiopia Today*, New York, 1958
9 For an English translation by Mengesha Gessesse, see 'Ethiopia's Traditional System of Land Tenure and Taxation by the late Gebrewold Engeda Worq', *Ethiopia Observer*, Vol. V, No 4, 1962
10 Tayé Gulilat, 'Coffee in the Ethiopian Economy', Part II, *Journal of Ethiopian Studies*, Vol. I, No 1, Addis Ababa, 1962. (Part I is to be found in the *University College Review*, Vol. I, No 1, Addis Ababa, 1961.)
11 International Bank for Reconstruction and Development, Economic Survey Report, *The Economic Development of Kenya*, Nairobi, 1962
12 See *African Statistics*, Vol. I, No 2, June 1961, published by the ECA and the Statistical Year Books published by the United Nations
13 E. Luther, op. cit.
14 See the United Nations sources, op. cit., and Economic Research Service of US Department of Agriculture, *Indices of Agricultural Production in 28 African Countries*, Washington, 1962

15 H. Quinn, 'The Mineral Industry of Ethiopia in 1961', *Ethiopia Observer*, Vol. VI, No 3, London, 1962

16 T. Murdock, two unpublished manuscripts quoted in G. Lipsky, *Ethiopia*, New York, 1962, but noted as 'not available for distribution'.

17 E. Luther, op. cit.

18 Atnafu Makonnen, *Ethiopia Today*, Tokyo, 1960

19 H. Quinn, op. cit. This article is the source used for statistics specifically on the Adola region

20 'Some Recent Developments in the Mining Industry', *Ethiopian Economic Review*, No 5, Addis Ababa, February 1962

21 The statistics in this section are drawn from tables in the United Nations (ECA) *African Statistics*, Vol. I, No 2, June 1961 and the *Ethiopian Statistical Abstract*, Addis Ababa, 1963

22 See G. Lipsky, op. cit.

23 J. Gunther, *Inside Africa*, New York, 1955

24 R. Greenfield, 'A Note on the Current State of Higher Education and University Research in Ethiopia', *Makerere Journal*, Vol. VIII, Kampala, 1963

25 'The Educational Situation in Africa', a document prepared for the UNESCO Education Conference, Addis Ababa, May 15–25, 1961

26 Tadesse Tereffe, 'Progress, Problems and Prospects in Ethiopian Education', *Ethiopia Observer*, Vol. VIII, No 1, London, 1964

Chapter 17   Girmamé Neway

1 Girmamé Neway, 'Strength in Unity', *Ethiopian Student News*, New York, March 1952

2 See S. Pankhurst, *Education in Ethiopia*, London, 1946; and *Mirror of Addis Ababa*, Addis Ababa, 1950

3 Girmamé Neway, op. cit. All quotations in this section are from this article

4 See a longer discussion on Ethiopian traditional government in R. Pankhurst, *An Introduction to the Economic History of Ethiopia*, London, 1961

5 S. and K. Aaronovitch, *Crisis in Kenya*, London, 1947

6 K. Skordiles, *Kagnew—The Story of the Ethiopian Fighters in Korea*, Tokyo, 1954

7 C. Legum, *Pan-Africanism*, London, 1961

8 S. Messing, 'Changing Ethiopia', *Middle East Journal*, Vol. IX, No 4, London, 1955

9 G. Weeks, 'The Armies of Africa', *Africa Report*, January 1964

10 See V. McKay, *Africa in World Politics*, New York, 1963, etc.

11 R. Greenfield, op. cit.

12 W. Seed, 'Censorship in Ethiopia', *New York Times*, October 7, 1952. See also *News Chronicle*, October 31, 1952

13 See R. Cox, *Pan-Africanism in Practice*, London, 1964

14 *Negarit Gazeta*, Vol. XV, No 2, November 4, 1955

15 ibid., Vol. XIII, No 13, August 26, 1954

16 D. Levine, 'Hailé Sellassié's Ethiopia, Myth or Reality', *Africa Today*, New York, May 1961

Chapter 18   A Coup d'Etat is Attempted

1 E. Ullendorff, op. cit.

2 Colonel Anwar El Sadat, *Revolt on the Nile*, London, 1957. A shortened English version of an Arabic original

3 Leul-Ras Kassa Hailu, *The Light of Wisdom* (Amharic), Addis Ababa, 1962. A posthumous publication arranged by his son, Asrate Kassa

4 Ras-Betwoded Makonnen Endalkatchew, *The Noble Family* (Amharic), Addis Ababa, 1947 (EC) and *The Race of One's Dreams* (Amharic), Addis Ababa, 1949 (EC). This latter title, in which the word 'race' is used in the sense of a steeplechase, is Amharic idiom implying a warning against undue concentration on material things and attempts to attain the unattainable

5 L. Mosley, op. cit.

6 Gebrewold Engeda Worq, *The Battle of Maichew and its History* (Amharic), Addis Ababa, written 1928 but first published in printed form in 1941 EC

7 *The Ethiopian Herald*, December 7, 1960

8 A report dated December 29, 1960 and written by Dejazmatch Kebede Tesemma at the request of Lieutenant-colonel Tamrat Yigezu. This is very similar to the evidence given by the *dejazmatch* later at the trial of Brigadier-general Mengistu Neway. Many of the conversations reported in this and the ensuing chapter are based on evidence given at that trial

9 Sir Harry Luke, 'Witness of Ethiopia Palace Revolt', *The Times*, December 30, 1960

10 D. Goodspeed, *The Conspirators—A Study of the Coup d'Etat*, London, 1962

11 The *East African Standard*, Nairobi, December 17, 1960 is quoted, but these remarks were very widely reported

12 The *Observer*, London, December 18, 1960

13 *The Ethiopian Herald*, Addis Ababa, December 26 and 31, 1960

14 *News and Views*, Vol. IV, No 10 of December 16, 1960. This edition was not distributed and was burnt by the students. Its index number was used again on December 29, 1960. However, fortunately for the historian, five copies had previously been removed from the pile by a Jesuit staff member without the students' knowledge

15 *The Times*, London, December 16, 1960

16 See V. McKay, *Africa in World Politics*, New York, 1963 who is quoted, and J. Montgomery, *Aid to Africa, New Test for American Policy*, Foreign Policy Association (headline series), New York, September–October 1961

Chapter 19   Mengistu Neway

1 *The Ethiopian Herald*, Addis Ababa, December 27, 1960

2 In an interview reported in *The Ethiopian Herald*, op. cit., and referred to also in the trial of Brigadier-general Mengistu Neway

3 *Rand Daily Mail*, Johannesburg, December 21, 1960, and *New York Times*, December 21, 1960

4 *Statesman*, Calcutta, December 23, 1960

5 L. Mosley, op. cit.

6 These statements were widely reported. See, for example, *The Times*, London, December 17 and 19, 1960

7 See, for example, *East African Standard*, Nairobi, December 21, 1960 and *Newsweek*, New York, January 2, 1961

8 *The Ethiopian Herald*, Addis Ababa, December 19. 1960

9 *East African Standard*, Nairobi, December 29, 1960; *New York Herald Tribune*, Paris edition, December 21, 1960; *Daily Express*, London, December 21 and 22, 1960
10 *The Ethiopian Herald*, Addis Ababa, December 27, 1960
11 I. W. Zartman, *Government and Politics in Northern Africa*, London, 1964
12 D. Levine, op. cit.
13 *The Ethiopian Herald*, Addis Ababa, December 20, 1960, *Menen*, Vol. V, Nos 2–3 (single copy), Addis Ababa, November–December 1960
14 See *The Rebellion Trials in Ethiopia*, op. cit.
15 *L'Ethiopié d'Aujourd'hui*, Addis Ababa, March 11, 1961
16 *The Rebellion Trials in Ethiopia*, op. cit.
17 *East African Standard*, Nairobi, March 25, 1961
18 *The Ethiopian Herald*, Addis Ababa, March 14, 1961
19 *The Ethiopian Herald*, Addis Ababa, March 20, 1961
20 *The Ethiopian Herald*, Addis Ababa, March 29, 1961
21 *The Ethiopian Herald*, Addis Ababa, March 25, 1961

Index

The reader will have observed from the text that there are no family or surnames in Ethiopia. An Ethiopian's first name is his own and is therefore the name used in this index. The second is normally, but not invariably, his father's. Titles and ranks are abbreviated and those later superseded are not to be found in this index, nor are persons listed under their titles or ranks. There is no universally accepted style for the transliteration of Ethiopian names. The author has followed the Imperial Ethiopian Institute of Mapping and Geography fairly closely. Where known, the preference of persons mentioned in the text has been followed with regard to the spelling of their names but the author has sometimes used different spellings to avoid confusion between individuals with similar names.

Major references or definitions are indicated in **bold** type face. The initial letters of the particular province in which Ethiopian towns and settlements are located is indicated in parentheses following index entries and the page numbers of maps on which they are marked follows in *italic* figures. Provincial boundaries have not been historically constant and those of 1964 are followed.

The following abbreviations are used:

TITLES
Emp.—Emperor; Dejaz.—Dejazmatch; Bet.—Betwoded; Fit.—Fitwrary; Keg.—Kegnazmatch; Graz.—Grazmatch; Bal.—Balambaras; Neg.—Negadas; Bej.—Bejirond; Liq.—Liquamaquas; T.T.—Tsahafé Taezaz; Gen.—all ranks of General; Col.—Colonel; Woiz.—Woizero.

PROVINCES
(E)—Eritrea; (T)—Tigré; (B)—Begemidir & Simien; (Wo)—Wello; (G)—Gojjam; (W)—Wellegga; (Sh)—Shewa; (I)—Illubabor; (K)—Kaffa; (A)—Arusi; (G.G)—Gemu Gofa; (S)—Sidamo; (B)—Bali; (H)—Harar.

A—Appendix; T—Table.
The appendices are on pages 459-465; the tables on pages 466-472

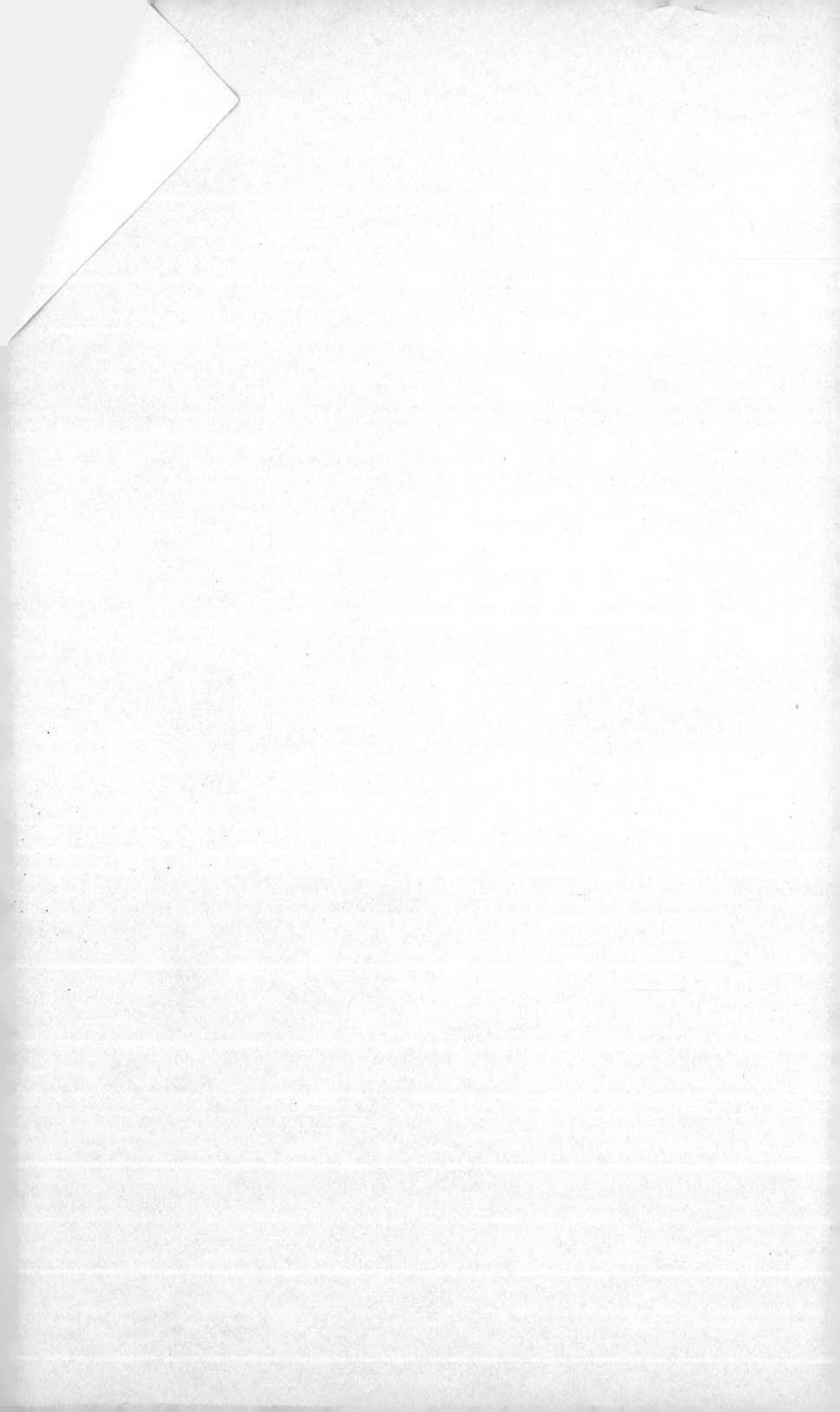